MINNESOTA
Aviation History
1857-1945

NOEL E. ALLARD · GERALD N. SANDVICK

MAHB PUBLISHING, INC.   P.O. BOX 284   CHASKA, MINNESOTA 55318

To the Memory of George Holey 1912-1989

Cover illustration:

The gold and green Benoist Number 43 hydro-aeroplane of Julius H. Barnes is portrayed on an excursion flight around the Duluth, Minnesota, harbor. Pilot, Tony Jannus, is perhaps teaching William D. "Gasoline Bill" Jones, how to fly. Note the harbor's famous aerial bridge in the background features the original transfer coach instead of the present-day lift span.

The Benoist has special significance in aviation history, for it was this very airplane, shipped from Duluth to Tampa, Florida, in the Fall of 1913, modified and refurbished, that was used to conduct the initial flight of the world's first airline, the St. Petersburg-Tampa Airboat Line. On 1 January, 1914, the first scheduled airline carried a single paying passenger on each trip between the two cities, and continued the service several times a day for three months, missing only four days due to weather or mechanical problems.

Painting by Robert J. Lemm of St. Paul, Minnesota.

MINNESOTA AVIATION HISTORY 1857-1945

© Copyright 1993 Minnesota Department
  of Transportation

First Edition
Library of Congress Cataloging in Publication Data
93-091653
   Allard, Noel E.
   Sandvick, Gerald N.
   Minnesota Aviation History 1857-1945
   ISBN 0-9637807-0-0 Hard Cover
   ISBN 0-9637807-1-9 Soft Cover
Printed and Bound in U.S.A.

TABLE OF CONTENTS

Foreword

In what is now being touted as the Space Age, most of the general public takes it for granted that huge aircraft routinely transport several hundred passengers at a time on scheduled flights from Coast to Coast and continent to continent almost at — sometimes faster than — the speed of sound. It is distressing that the feats and raw courage of aviation's pioneers frequently fade into the mists of history.

It is difficult to realize how new aviation really is. Most historians generally consider that the Age of Flight began when the Wright brothers let the genie out of the bottle on the sand dunes of North Carolina in December 1903, only two generations ago. That was contemporaneous with the development of the "horseless carriage" — the automobile.

This account of the growth and development of aviation in Minnesota embraces 88 years of Minnesota aviation history, from the time when Minnesotans flew in balloons, four years before the Civil War began — and 46 years before First Flight.

Minnesota's first powered, controllable, *heavier-than-air* flight took place in 1910, the year from which the authors have chronicled a detailed commentary essentially focused on the feats and failures of the earliest aviators, citing the dates and places of their performances.

From there, every aspect of the slow but gradual growth of Minnesota aviation is set out in these annals, including the names of air show entrepreneurs, pilots and participants, one of whom was a shy Minnesota lad named Charles A. Lindbergh.

Modern aviation did not arrive all at once, full-blown, and from the beginning wasn't all fun and games. The authors detail the financial and political problems involved in the creation and operation of early airfields and airports all over the state, and write about the people who created the support systems on those airfields, a new level of business called "fixed base operations," which provided operational support for airplanes: fuel, repairs and maintenance, aircraft sales, storage, parking; they were, and still are, marinas of the sky.

The who-what-when-where-how-and-why approach has infused the accounts of early aerial thrill-shows, and famous aviators, and the development of the aviation industry in Minnesota, including the feats of air mail pilots and the routes they flew, which later developed into the route structures of the early airlines. There is a listing of Who's Who in Minnesota Aviation from the beginning — all *real* people, who influenced and contributed to the development of the first 90 years of Minnesota's aviation tradition.

What Noel Allard and Gerald Sandvick have produced is a monumental work of historical research, organization and creation, a glowing history of a continuing story of the brave men and women of Minnesota who made it happen. It is valuable, not only for technical or historical research, but because it captures the flavor of aviation's romance and adventure as Minnesota aviation has developed up to 1945, when World War II ended.

One would hope that there will be a sequel covering the following 50 years.

Frank Kingston Smith

Acknowledgements

This book owes its existence to the Minnesota Department of Transportation, specifically to its Aeronautics Office. Without a grant provided by the Department, the research might well have carried on for the next millennium. Our specific thanks are due to the book project committee for their oversight and encouragement to finish the manuscript and get it into print.

The authors would like to honor Mr. Sherman Booen for his leadership in the preparation of this book. A Minnesota aviation history book was his dream for over two decades. It was through his untiring efforts, that the funding was obtained for its research and writing. Through his leadership and drive, this work was completed. No one could ask for a more dedicated project manager, or a better friend.

We would like to thank the other book committee members for their contributions. Specifically we thank Mr. Raymond Rought, Aeronautics Office Director, for his sponsorship; Mr. Duane Haukebo, Aeronautics Office Assistant Director, for his liaison between the Office and the authors; the late Mr. George Holey, who started recording Minnesota aviation history before this book was conceived, and Mr. Vince Doyle, Mr. James Borden and Mr. Johan Larsen.

We would like to acknowledge the most appreciated help of Mr. James Borden and Mr. Joseph Williams. We commend them for their great contribution of time and effort. They are our "right-hand-men." We would like to thank them for their unselfish donation of time. It took over eight years to prepare the manuscript. Both have made an outstanding effort to help us with the legwork, interviews, and general gruntwork to make this book as accurate and complete as possible. This project would not be finished today, if it hadn't been for them.

Many other people have provided an active role in the preparation of this book. They have donated information from their own research without compensation. This allowed us to provide the overall picture of aviation history in Minnesota. We want to recognize Mrs. Anne Holey, Mr. William Ellis, Mr. James Meyer, Doctor William E. Lovelace, Mr. Steve Tangen, Mr. Roland Sorensen, the late Marvin Zack and Mrs. La Verne Zack, Thomas and Loretta O'Connor. We also thank Kenneth D. Ruble for his material on Northwest Airlines.

A special thank you to the many staff people at the Minnesota Historical Society for their constant willingness to assist us. Particularly we thank those in the Archives and Manuscripts Division.

We also thank several persons who were generous enough to put something into the kitty when needed: Mr. Buzz Kaplan, Mr. Wayne Field, Mr. Ken Brommer, the Minnesota 99's, and others.

Finally, our thanks to the hundreds of people who shared their experiences with us through interviews, conversations, scrapbooks, photos, and letters. Their names are too many to mention here, but have been appropriately noted in the text.

By no means can we forget to thank our families. They allowed us to abandon the realities of everyday life to become involved in this mammoth project.

Noel E. Allard
Gerald N. Sandvick

Preface

We, the authors, think it appropriate to start the book with what we believe the reader should expect from the following pages.

Perhaps, unlike most other history books, this book will not claim to represent dogma. It is important to note that the authors have based the text on the best available data, primary sources, and recollections. We regret that we could not have spoken with, or interviewed, all of the hundreds of persons who might have had additional information. We did our best.

We believe that history is never recorded in its absolute or perfect fact. There are always other aspects of a historical event that may be added to the basic story long after it is recorded. There is always another side to the story, another witnessed account. The "final word" is never final!

So we have not attempted to claim that what is written here is the "final word," rather the basic story. This book contains more information on the history of Minnesota aviation than any other previously published work. We hope the reader will find this a useful reference book for years to come.

It has not been our goal to mention the name of every flyer who flew in Minnesota between 1857 and 1945. We have tried to spotlight the individuals who made a significant contribution to Minnesota avia-

tion during that time. We are proud of what we have done in digging out the names of those real pioneers. Remembered are the people who did something to make headlines in the local papers. Also honored are the people who were outstanding in all areas, and those who were most fondly remembered by aviation people. We sincerely apologize if we have left out the name of someone who should have been recognized.

We have provided technical material for the researcher and historian, mixed with the color and spectacle that are fun to read about. In other words, we would like this book to be a reference for serious historians, and a book full of life for the casual reader.

Some subjects are not covered in depth. For example, much has been written about Northwest Airlines, Speed Holman and Charles Lindbergh. Therefore, we offer a concise section on each.

For those who want to do further research, we have provided footnotes and a bibliography of primary source material. We have hundreds of files on the pioneers. You are invited to contact us if you would like further information. If you have any information on aviation history, please share it with us. We hope the files will become part of a library in a Minnesota Museum of Transportation.

Introduction

The idea of taking to the air has been a part of human dreams ever since the human race developed the imagination to define the sky and watch the birds with awe. Records from the earliest civilizations speak to us of the winged gods of Egypt, flying animal deities of Mesopotamia, and magic flying carpets of Arabia. The pantheons of classical Greece and Rome are replete with the mythology of flying gods and people.[1]

The beginnings of such notions among the earliest peoples to inhabit that central part of the North American continent that would become Minnesota are lost in antiquity. The first Europeans to study Native American culture in Minnesota recorded Indian concepts of the sky and of humans traveling through it. Legends and pictographs of such concepts were doubtlessly far more ancient than their first recording by the whites.

In the legends of the major Indian cultures of Minnesota, both Ojibwa and Dakota stories and songs tell of flight. Ojibwa pictographs commonly used established and widely understood symbols to represent the sky and one traditional song, "I am flying halfway up to the sky" referred to the hawk that the Ojibwa believed could attain altitudes that put it halfway to the top of the sky.

Beyond basic ideas of the sky and observations of bird flight, pictographs occasionally showed a human figure in the sky and Ojibwa songs incorporated such lyrics as "the wind is carrying me around the sky" and "I am called white-haired raven flying around the sky."[2]

A careful observer of Ojibwa customs, Frances Densmore, relates that dreams were of the utmost importance to them. Dreams were not random events of the subconscious, but were deliberately sought through periods of fasting, isolation, and meditation. Once achieved, such a dream was central to the consciousness of an Ojibwa, since it was believed that insights had been gained into earlier states of existence. The idea of aviation was frequent in such dreams. In one especially graphic case, Niskigwum, an elderly Ojibwa, relates that in his twelfth year, (ca. 1849) he fasted for ten days until his "real dream" came to him. It was a "wonderful dream in which he imagined himself to be flying through the air.[3]

The Dakota were mortal enemies of the Ojibwa but the two peoples shared the sky in their legends. In Dakota religious ideas the Wakinyan was a central deity. The Reverend Gideon Pond wrote, at Ft. Snelling in 1866, that "the name signified flyer from ki-nyan, to fly. Lightening emanates from this flyer and thunder is the sound of his voice. This is a universal belief."[4]

Obviously the Thunderbird is being described here, an aerial god of the Dakota that was not only powerful, destructive and ruthless, but massive. A Dakota story tells that "a Wakinyan god was killed and fell on the bank of the Blue Earth River which was twenty-five or thirty yards between the tips of the wings."[5]

Humans in flight were not absent from Dakota legend either. One tradition had it that the Wahkendenda or the "mysterious passing of fire," that is, a meteor, passed over a hill where a Dakota was asleep. The man was taken aboard the meteor and an eventful flight followed which ended when the Dakota outsmarted the meteor and persuaded it to land him safely.[6]

In the 1840's a Dakota medicine man named Cloudy Sky told not only of human flight but of a great air battle. Cloudy Sky, it seems, had lived three times and after his first death his spirit "wandered through the air" and travelled with the Thunderbirds. One day, Unktahe, god of the waters, and sixty of his friends, flew up to engage a contingent of Thunderbirds, forty strong, along with whom Cloudy Sky fought. In a fierce engagement that lasted a whole day, the son of Unktahe was killed, the Wakinyan prevailed, and "the water spirits shrank to their home while the Thunderbirds returned to a presumably more peaceful life in the clouds."

ONE

BEFORE 1900

It is, of course, a large step from flights of the imagination to flights of reality. Not until 1783 did humans possess the means to go aloft, for it was in that year that the first balloon flights were made. For the next century and a quarter the balloon remained the only method for flight, and the first people to take to the air over Minnesota did so in balloons.

In France, during the last months of 1783, two different versions of balloons carried men into the air for the first time. These balloons, hot air and gas filled, have for over 200 years remained the only feasible kinds of these vehicles. The notion of capturing the lifting power of hot air seems to have occurred to the Frenchman, Joseph Montgolfier in late 1782, although he mistakenly ascribed the rising force to some mysterious substance in the smoke from a fire and not to the hot air itself. In 1783, Joseph and his brother, Etienne, built a series of ever larger and more successful balloons, until in September of that year, they sent aloft a sheep, a rooster, and a duck to test the effects of flight on living creatures. The hot air balloon and its live cargo reached an estimated 1700 feet, and when it descended on the outskirts of Paris eight minutes later, it was found that the rooster had injured a wing. This fact caused a certain consternation regarding the possibilities of safe human flight even though it was clear that the duck was none the worse for the experience and that the sheep was contentedly grazing nearby. Fears were put to rest when witnesses revealed that the unfortunate bird had been kicked by the sheep and that its injuries were not related to any inherent dangers of going aloft. The next Montgolfier balloon would carry the first human into the air.

When the Montgolfier's announced that they would build a man-carrying balloon, King Louis XVI insisted that the passengers be two criminals who, assuming a safe return to earth, would be pardoned. At this juncture, Pilatre de Rozier, a young nobleman and member of the prestigious Academy of Science in Paris, objected strenuously. Incensed that common criminals should be considered for the honor of being the first to fly, de Rozier offered himself. A certain amount of intrigue ensued during which the services of Marie Antoinette were enlisted to help persuade her Royal husband of the soundness of de Rozier's proposal. Louis, not a strong-willed character, typically gave in and Pilatre de Rozier's place in the history of flight was assured.

After a series of tethered flights to test the balloon and give de Rozier some practice, the Montgolfiers determined that all was ready. On 21 November, he and a fellow nobleman, the Marquis d'Arlandes, made the historic ascension. Once it was filled with hot air over an open fire, the inflated balloon was cut loose and rose to drift over Paris for twenty-five minutes before landing, without mishap, about five miles from the launch site.

At this same time, in Paris, another amateur scientist was well along in the building of a wholly different balloon. Jacques Charles, like many other scientists of the day, realized that the same principles of buoyancy that allowed a cork to float on water applied to a balloon floating in the air. Hydrogen gas had been isolated in 1766 by the English chemist Henry Cavendish and, since it was shown to weigh about one fortieth as much as an equal volume of air, the possibility of a hydrogen inflated balloon was self evident. Indeed, the Montgolfier's had considered hydrogen before turning to the hot air balloon. The problem was to find a fabric that would contain the light gas without letting it diffuse through too rapidly.

In 1783, Charles succeeded in coating silk with a rubber solution that made for a fabric sufficiently impervious to hydrogen diffusion as to be practical for a balloon envelope. In August of the same year, Charles launched a small test balloon that came to earth fifteen miles from Paris. The balloon was attacked by pitchfork-wielding peasants, who believed it to be Satanic in origin.

Charles and his associates now set about the task of building a man-carrying hydrogen balloon and in doing so they invented the basic type of balloon that would be standard for decades to come. The new balloon was a sphere twenty-seven and one-half feet in diameter with an open neck on the bottom (the "south pole") for filling with gas. On the top (the "north pole") a spring loaded valve was sewn in and could be opened simply by pulling a cord. This allowed the pilot to release gas at will in order to control the descent. A net covered the whole of the top hemisphere and was attached to a wooden ring surrounding the balloon at its mid-point, or equator. A wicker basket for people and equipment was suspended from this ring. Ballast was also carried so that when released the aeronaut had control over ascent.

On 1 November, Charles and an associate flew the new balloon and a massive crowd turned out to see the event. So perfect was the entire flight that Charles flew a second time that day completing the first solo flight ever and the next day the balloon was triumphantly brought back to Paris. Along with the Montgolfiers, Jacques Charles became an instant national hero.[7]

The flights set off a ballooning mania that would not long be confined within the political boundaries of France. Popular fascination with the new mode of travel quickly spread through Europe and across the Atlantic to the newly independent United States. The first balloon to go up in the new world was built by a Maryland lawyer, Peter Carnes. Carnes sent up his hot air balloon in tethered ascents in June, 1784. In one of them, a thirteen year old boy rode up and down again and was the first human to see the new world from the air. Carnes, however, failed in his only attempt at a free flight when the wind slammed the balloon's passenger basket into a wall and the balloon caught fire and was destroyed. Carnes was unhurt but, perhaps not surprisingly, gave up ballooning and went back to practicing the law.[8]

The first free flight in America came in January, 1793, when French aeronaut Jean-Pierre Blanchard ascended at Philadelphia. Blanchard was an experienced balloonist who had flown often in Europe. His American ascent would be his forty-fifth. On 9 January, with President Washington and four future Presidents (John Adams, Jefferson, Madison, and Monroe) looking on, he inflated his hydrogen balloon. He had hoped to finance the enterprise by selling tickets at up to $5.00, but the crowd mostly stood outside the enclosure and watched for free. Since Blanchard spoke no English, he carried a note, personally signed by George Washington, asking anyone to render assistance and give safe conduct to the aeronaut when he landed.

The first successful flight by a balloon in America lasted for forty-six minutes and Blanchard came down in New Jersey to be met by highly suspicious farmers. After seeing the President's note, however, they helped Blanchard return to Philadelphia.[9]

Although the flight had been made, no great wave of ballooning mania swept America and it was a quarter century before another ascent was made. By the 1830s, however, interest was quickening and in 1835, John Wise, America's premier balloonist, made his first ascension. By the 1850s many had witnessed balloon ascensions. Balloonists were considered part explorers and part showmen and a scheduled ascent never failed to draw a crowd. Ballooning was becoming an activity of widespread interest.

The first Minnesotan to fly in a balloon was neither a professional showman nor aeronaut but an upstanding businessman. In September 1857, St. Paul resident William Markoe ascended in a balloon of his own construction. He carried one passenger on the hour and one half flight, and a few days later carried two passengers on a second flight. He never flew again and his balloon was destroyed as it was being readied for an ascension in the spring of 1858. Markoe's career as an aeronaut may have been brief but he and his passengers were the first to see Minnesota from the air.

Markoe was born in Philadelphia in 1820 and was clearly a man who marched to his own drummer. He described himself as a "wild harem scarem boy" until he was twenty one at which age he began a seven year study for the Episcopalian ministry. Ordained and married in his late 20s, he served in a church in Delafield, Wisconsin for five years and then moved back East, living for a time in New Jersey and

Philadelphia. He also abandoned the Episcopalian clergy and, in 1855, converted to Roman Catholicism. Since that faith took a jaundiced view of married clergy, he toyed with opening a girl's school in Wisconsin but it came to naught. He came to St. Paul in 1856 hoping to cash in on the booming real estate market of the western frontier. His achievement was enough for him to live well and, perhaps most importantly, fulfill a dream that he had harbored for twenty years.[10]

In 1856 Markoe wrote that despite the many turns his life had taken, his "fondness for aeronautics" was never lost and that he had "never given up the belief that aerial navigation ... was practicable." On another occasion he wrote of his great interest in flight and thought that he would probably never give up his interest "until I have had a fair trial at it some way or another."[11] Attitudes like these were not widely held in the mid-nineteenth century and Markoe's fascination was shaped by two events.

When he was seventeen, Markoe met William Paullin and made an ascent with him at Camden, New Jersey. Paullin was one of that handful of famous aeronauts who had pioneered the art of ballooning in the United States and Markoe never forgot the experience. Nearly twenty years later, he wrote to the still prominent Paullin, "When I remember, friend Paullin, with what delight I used to watch your ballooning operations, with what zeal I used to hold the cords during inflation & with what a gratifying boyish sense of self-importance I used to take part in the management of your ascension & order about the gaping boobies who wanted to help out but were rather afraid of the big thing & when I recollect our ascent together & the wacking bump & the upset we got when we struck I feel quite like a boy again."[12]

The second influence on Minnesota's pioneer balloonist was his association with Rufus Porter. Porter was a blend of the brilliant and the bizarre whose frenetic career credentials include experience as a house painter, writer, artist, publisher, inventor, and religious zealot. In 1845 he founded the venerable *Scientific American* magazine and his inventions include an elevated railway, a steam powered automobile and a rotary barrel rifle which he sold to Samuel Colt. In the mid-1830s Porter designed and was actively raising funds for the construction of a giant airship to carry one hundred passengers from New York to California in three days. Although the airship was wholly impractical and Porter never came close to building a full scale version, he did build small working models to help promote his dream and, not incidentally, to raise money.[13]

In 1849 Porter demonstrated one of his models in New York and the young Markoe, saw it. He said that he was "much pleased with the exhibition," and he picked up a pamphlet describing the airship which he read carefully finding no flaw in the basic principles. Markoe was more than much pleased, he was absolutely smitten, but, as he later said, "my studies at that time did not admit of my pursuing the subject farther."[14]

Three years later, however, Markoe was a working minister in Wisconsin and, on rereading Porter's pamphlet, was unshakably convinced of the practicality of the scheme. He wrote to Porter asking why the airship had not been built and, unsurprisingly, Porter wrote back saying that a lack of funds was the great barrier. He also said that he was actively continuing his efforts. Markoe sent him $500.00 and shortly thereafter $500.00 more while at the same time persuading three of his relatives to invest an additional $1550.00.[15] This made Markoe a principal stockholder in the Aerial Navigation Company and he received a stock certificate and periodic newsletters describing the progress of the project.

No airship was forthcoming from Porter who had become less interested in aerial travel and obsessed with preparing for the Second Coming. By the summer of 1856, Markoe had lost faith in Porter but not in the idea of flight. He rekindled his correspondence with William Paullin to whom he poured out his hopes, dreams, and troubles with Porter. Paullin, in turn, suggested that Markoe should consider getting some practical experience with ballooning. Later in the year he wrote to Paullin saying, "I feel disposed ... to adopt your good advice & make a few ascensions first in an ordinary balloon."[16]

Once he had decided to fly a balloon he wasted little time in getting advice on how to build it. He asked Paullin about the kind of fabric and varnish coating to be used as well as questions on the production of hydrogen, indicating that he had in mind a gas and not a hot air balloon from the first. He also wrote to John Wise, America's most experienced aeronaut. Wise sent a copy of his book *A System of Aeronautics* at Markoe's request and they continued to correspond about their common interest in ballooning.

The balloon's construction occupied nine months in 1857 during which Markoe kept a careful record of his expenses. His first purchase, in January, was for boards and hardware for spring loaded pressure relief valves. The fact that he was building the first balloon in Minnesota did not exempt Markoe from life's nagging minutia. In February a blacksmith named Huttlemier overcharged him a dollar for tempering the valve springs. In April, he bought new curtains for the privy window and in June the delivery of some balloon material include a charge for "miring horse in mud hole." It is unnecessary to speculate why his expenses also included the odd glass of ale from time to time and once a bottle of schnapps and five gallons of whiskey. The lot of a pioneering balloonist was not an easy one.

He decided to name the balloon "Minnesota," and to hire the production of most components while doing the work on the all important envelope himself. The wicker passenger car was made by a local basket maker, and when it was delivered in February, Markoe dressed it up with several yards of red and green calico topped off with green cords and tassels. The load ring, a wood hoop from which the basket was suspended, gave him headaches when the first carpenter kept him waiting six weeks before confessing that he really did not want to make it. Another carpenter was commissioned but it took "all kinds of expostulations, entreaties, and blandishments" to get the job done.[17]

The major task was the assembly of the gas contain-

ing envelope. Silk or linen was most commonly used and the fabric was cut into carefully laid out panels, or gores, which were sewn together to form a spherical envelope. The fabric, of course, had to be made as impervious as possible to gas diffusion by coating it with a type of varnish. This coating was often a jealously guarded secret, but Paullin and Wise had both generously given their advice. Even the counsel of these two experienced aeronauts, however, could not eliminate all of Markoe's problems.

The Minnesota was going to be a large balloon, forty feet in diameter which would require over seven hundred yards of linen. In late April Markoe bought rolls of wallpaper on which to lay out the pattern of the gores. It took a week and a half, working from morning until night, to cut the gores and then the problem of how to handle the forty two foot long sections of linen in the varnishing process had to be faced. To do this he built a machine in which the gores would be passed through a vat of varnish by means of rollers and then stretched out for drying on a specially built rack. In this way he coated six hundred yards in an hour and a half and stretched it all out to dry by day's end. Markoe regarded his labors with "complacent self-satisfaction" and "glowing delight" when he was finished.

His glowing delight, however, was short lived and a major problem arose. The varnish he had used was made of boiled linseed oil to which he had added camphene, litharge, and lead acetate and, he wrote, "the stuff wouldn't dry, although stretched out in my way for a week, except in a few places where the sun got a chance at it through the windows." On 6 June he sent worried letters to both Paullin and Wise saying that he had run into trouble and needed speedy relief. The solution was obvious albeit laborious. He began to take the gores outside, one by one, and dry them in full sunlight by the simple expedient of draping them over his garden fence. By early July he was informing Wise that "I am alright. I dried all my stuff in the sun both coats. My gores are all cut out and ready to put together."[18]

Putting them together, however, was more difficult than anticipated. For several weeks he had been planning to sew the gores by machine and had tested

July, 1908. International Balloon Race contestants fill their balloons with city gas at St. Paul. (Minnesota Historical Society).

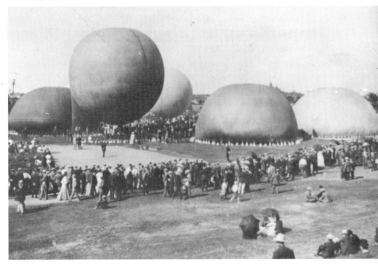

various makes before settling on a Singer. On 4 July he sent a check to the Singer Company. Two weeks later the sewing machine arrived and his troubles began. The varnish coat had left the fabric slightly sticky and the resulting friction prevented its proper feeding through the machine. The result was that the fabric would pucker, random holes would be poked, and the needle would snap. Markoe's account book shows that on the 21st, 23rd, 25th and 27th he had to buy more needles. Finally, he said, "after inflicting manifold merciless & widely scattered wounds upon my linen & breaking all my needles, to say nothing of the danger to my eyes from the fragments of needles. I concluded to abandon further effort." On 1 August he sold the Singer and hired a crew of seamstresses to sew the envelope by hand. On some days as many as fourteen were sewing and it took two weeks. Then several boys were employed to put a final varnish coat on the seams, and around 1 September the Minnesota was complete.[19]

Although he had originally thought of hydrogen, Markoe now intended to inflate the Minnesota with coal gas, a mixture of hydrogen and methane produced by burning coal in a special furnace. It was the first gas to be piped through gas mains for lighting and domestic use in cities. As early as 1821, an English aeronaut had tapped into a London main and flown a coal gas filled balloon. Pure hydrogen has a substantially greater lifting power than coal gas but the latter possessed several advantages for nineteenth century balloonists. Hydrogen was expensive and cumbersome to produce since it required casks of sulphuric acid and iron filings, plus the assorted paraphernalia to cool, dry, and purify it. Coal gas was much cheaper and an Aeronaut could simply hook up to a municipal gas pipe and fill up. The heavier coal gas molecules did not diffuse through the envelope as readily as hydrogen either, so it was less a problem to keep a balloon inflated to capacity once filled. The advantages of coal gas were cost and convenience which often outweighed its inferior lifting power.

Coincidentally for Minnesota's premier aeronaut, the St. Paul Gas and Light Company had been formed in March 1856 and a plant built on 5th and Olive Streets in that city. Gas production began and the first street lights were lit on 19 September, 1857, just three days before Markoe was to inflate his balloon.

By late September Markoe was ready. He had hoped to sell $500 worth of tickets at a dollar each to those desiring to witness the inflation at close range. The Minnesota had cost him over $1,000 and he naturally hoped to recover some of the expense, but, as he wrote to Wise, "Money, though always acceptable, is not my object. I believe I was inspired purely by a love of the glories of the thing itself."[20] It was a good thing he felt that way because ticket sales did not come close to the $500 goal. Still, on the 21st, Markoe had the balloon hauled to the gas works in preparation for inflation. Paying spectators or no, he was ready to go aloft.

The clear calm air of 22 September could not have afforded better weather for the state's first aerial voyage. The huge balloon was a magnificent sight, forty feet in diameter and seventy feet tall from car bottom to envelope top. By mid-morning a crowd of three to four thousand had gathered to see the event,

most of them, unfortunately for Markoe's ticket sales, watching free from the bluffs overlooking the gas works. By about 10:00 a.m., inflation was well along, when it became clear that the output of the gas works would not be sufficient to fill the balloon beyond about half of its capacity. At 11:00 a.m. Markoe decided to go anyway and he and his passengers stepped into the car and cast off. The Minnesota refused to rise. On board were Markoe, William S. Crawford, proprietor of the dry goods store where Markoe had bought much of his material, Samuel S. Eaton, an insurance agent, and H. H. Brown, a young man from Philadelphia. There were also bags of ballast sand, ropes, anchors, overcoats, and a goodly supply of "provisions and necessaries for a long journey."[21]

The problem was remedied by offloading Messrs. Eaton and Brown along with some ballast and provisions. The two men, it was reported, agreed to stay behind only with great reluctance. The order to cast off was given again and this time the Minnesota went up slowly and gracefully amid cheers and applause from the crowd. Markoe had spent $45 to hire a band for the historic event and it now struck up "a stirring air" to send him on his way into the heavens. The balloon became stationary at about 300 feet and to go higher to catch the winds, Markoe and Crawford were forced to dump most of their remaining ballast, a length of rope, "water, some liquor and other refreshment." With this sacrifice the Minnesota rose higher until it caught a breeze and moved out of sight.

Before noon they had drifted over Pine Bend and the two aerial travellers were utterly amazed at this first view of the state territory from the air. They could see as far as the St. Croix Valley and Stillwater to the east and to Shakopee in the west. The area around St. Paul seemed "like one vast marsh... dotted with lakes and ponds." As they continued to drift southward, "as glorious a panorama of plain, field, forest, farm, river, lake, and city burst on their vision as ever was unfolded to any traveler in the heavens." With "delicious sensation" they sailed along suffering no inconvenience from the cold even though they had left their overcoats on the ground. Markoe later estimated their altitude at three miles, no doubt a wild overestimate. Regrettably no barometer was carried so no reliable altitude figure is possible.[22]

The Minnesota had been following a southeasterly course which put it over Hastings at noon when the breeze increased slightly and began to carry the balloon almost straight south. By 1:00 settlements were becoming sparse and Markoe, wanting to land where help was available, began to descend. He pulled the valve rope and, as lifting gas bled off, the Minnesota sank into the more gusty winds at ground level. Markoe threw out both of his grappling hook anchors, one after the other, but neither gained purchase and the balloon skipped along the ground giving the occupants a severe shaking. Crawford, with supremely poor timing, was dishing up a pan of chicken pie for lunch when Markoe began to let down. The landing was a hard one and, as Markoe put it, "the wheels and swings were terrific. For some moments I was bewildered, blinded and stunned." Crawford's Prince Albert suit was doused with the chicken pie.

They had come down on a farm about five miles from Cannon Falls amid a startled group of Norwegian harvesters. Markoe yelled at them to grab the trailing ropes and help make the balloon fast but one of the astonished farmers grabbed for a rifle instead. Fortuitously, the English speaking farm owner appeared and commanded the men to lay hold of the flapping monster. Finally enough gas was lost and the collapsed balloon was folded, loaded on a farm wagon, and hauled to Hastings where the riverboat Frank Steel had just tied up to the wharf. Markoe, Crawford, and the Minnesota, completed their journey on the riverboat, arriving in St. Paul about 3:00 the following morning. In a wonderfully understated summary, the *Daily Minnesotan* said of the historic voyage, "Thus successfully and pleasantly occurred and terminated the first balloon ascension in Minnesota."[23]

The 1857 Territorial Fair, coincidentally enough, was scheduled for October 7, 8, and 9 and the managers of the Fair lost little time in scheduling Minnesota's one and only aeronaut as the newest attraction. In late September the press reported that he had agreed to make an ascension and editorialized that "We are glad of it. Mr. Markoe's last ascension was entirely satisfactory and there are hundreds of persons who would like to witness one." So central an attraction was Markoe that the phrase "The Balloon Fair" gained currency. The event was to be held on the Capitol grounds, a location that created certain difficulties. A part of the area was enclosed by a high board fence but the rest was "fenced" by two watchmen and an unfriendly bulldog. Markoe would, therefore, have relatively little shielding from the wind during the first few seconds of the ascension. Since a gas main did not run to the Capitol grounds, he planned to inflate the Minnesota at the gas works and tow it the several blocks between.[24]

This was accomplished on the morning of 8 October and now, unlike the first flight, the gas supply was sufficient for full inflation. Eaton and Brown who were denied boarding on the first flight could now go along and the usual array of equipment plus "a case of Beaumont and Gordon's best" were loaded on. The Fair was being held in the heat of a political campaign since the election of a Territorial Governor was set for 13 October. Henry H. Sibley and Alexander Ramsey were, respectively, the Democratic and Republican candidates. Sibley was also President of the Agricultural Society which sponsored the Fair and thus, the Fair's chief officer. Seeing the balloon ascension as a piece of Democratic campaign trickery, many Republicans refused to attend.

A good crowd was nonetheless on hand when, at 10:30 a.m. on the 8th, the Minnesota "sailed into ethereal space in grand style." Taken by a brisk wind, the balloon rapidly sailed north. After about one half hour, Markoe decided to land and the real excitement began. He spotted a cleared field and valved off gas but the wind was too sharp and he missed. Faced with being blown into nearby trees, ballast was jettisoned and the balloon shot upward. By this time they were in the vicinity of Forest Lake and their second try at a landing narrowly avoided disaster. As they descended the malevolent wind pushed the Minnesota toward the waiting branches of a large oak tree. With no ballast to toss out, Markoe had to let events run their

course. The balloon crashed through the upper limbs, rebounded, and settled back down, just touching the surface of a pond. Now, essentially out of control, it skipped ashore and seizing what he thought an opportunity, Eaton jumped out with the intention of securing the unruly balloon to a stump. His action, however, lightened the load by 160 pounds and the Minnesota shot upward "almost as rapidly as an arrow from a well strung bow." The anchor rope was stripped from Eaton's hands and he watched helplessly as his two companions "resumed their voyage toward Lake Superior." Astonished and alone, he concluded that they would probably not land again on this side of the "British possessions" and began his trek home.

Markoe and Brown had become "a little alarmed," and, admittedly, their situation was less than promising. All the ballast had been used, both anchors were gone, and the encounter with the oak had severed the gas valve control cord. The cord had broken near the neck of the balloon some fifteen feet above the gondola where the end dangled out of reach. With no way to valve off gas, the Minnesota could not descend and the stiff wind was carrying it north at an alarming speed. It was "a situation in which the strongest heart might quail."

The intrepid Brown, however, saved the day. Taking the severed control cord in his teeth, he climbed the network of ropes to the wood ring from which the gondola was suspended. By standing on this ring he could just reach the other end of the cord and was able to tie them together. Markoe could now valve off gas and the Minnesota began to come down. The landing was, in reality, a semicontrolled crash into the tree tops about four miles from where Eaton had jumped out. Markoe and Brown secured the balloon to a tree and climbed down. They were soon located by Ed Austin, a local farmer who had seen their descent. He arrived with help and by cutting down two or three trees, the Minnesota was freed with only a few tears in the envelope. The hospitable Austin provided the aeronauts with a good dinner, helped them load the deflated balloon on a farm wagon, and transported them back to St. Paul. Markoe's record book for the day lists "Expenses of getting balloon out of woods - $10.00" and a like amount for "fare to St. Paul in Ed Austin's wagon."[25]

In mid October, Markoe put the balloon in storage for the winter with every intention of flying again when the weather warmed in 1858. He still hoped to recoup his expenses. Eaton and Crawford had each paid $50 for their rides, but even with ticket sales and the Fair contract, Markoe had recovered less than half his cost of building the Minnesota. He remained optimistic, though, and in March began repairs and plans for a new season of flying.

In May he received permission from the St. Paul city fathers to put up a fence and charge admission at Seventh and Jackson Streets. By the end of May, the Minnesota had been refurbished and the passenger gondola now sported blue denim with red tassels. Markoe had advertised his first flight of the new season for 1 June, but on that afternoon, with the balloon partly inflated, the wind rose and prohibited the flight. The hundred or so spectators inside the fence were disappointed, but Markoe promised to try again and refunded their admission money.

On the morning of 5 June, a Saturday, he was ready again. Although it had not been advertised, a small crowd assembled to watch. By 11:00 a.m. the Minnesota was fully inflated but the wind had risen again and was so gusty that the men holding the restraining ropes were having trouble. The wind batted the balloon and finally it proved too much. The *Daily Minnesotan* reported that "the leviathan flopped and struggled and swayed down to the ground." At this juncture a "monstrous rent" was torn in the envelope and the folds of linen "fell like a cloud on the spectators." Not surprisingly the release of around thirty three thousand cubic feet of coal gas nearly suffocated close bystanders and the enclosure was quickly evacuated.[26]

After the destruction of the Minnesota, Markoe did not rebuild or repair it and his career as an aeronaut ended. He went on to accumulate substantial land holdings, entered St. Paul politics, was elected alderman, and served as President of the Common Council of that city. He died there in December 1916, sixty years after he had started building Minnesota's first vehicle of the air. William Markoe had risked life, limb and fortune to bring his dream to reality and in achieving that dream he became the first Minnesotan to attain the sky.

In the years between Markoe's flight and the turn of the century, all corners of the state witnessed balloon ascensions. These were most often pure entertainment aimed at drawing a crowd for a local fair or some other celebration and were frequently accompanied by a parachute jump by the balloonist. One ascension, however, was to have historic significance because of the passenger carried aloft. A half dozen years after the Markoe ascensions, a flight took place that was important in planting seeds for the future. The nation was in the Civil War in 1863, and since it was the biggest war of the time, officers of several foreign armies came as observers to see what lessons might be learned. One was a young Prussian Army Lieutenant who, nearly forty years later, would design and build the world's first successful rigid

Charles K. Hamilton flying his hydrogen-filled airship over Minneapolis in August of 1906. The old Minneapolis Exposition Hall is prominent in the background, across St. Anthony Falls. Hamilton used a gasoline engine to drive a propeller at the front of the machine for motive power, and a large moveable cloth panel at the rear for steering. (Gerald Sandvick)

airships.

Ferdinand von Zeppelin spent time as an observer with the Union Army in the early summer of 1863, and then decided to take a trip through the Great Lakes region as he said he wanted "to get as many actual impressions as possible of the cultural history of this part of the world."[27] He took a steamer across the Great Lakes to Superior, Wisconsin, and then a canoe trip down the St. Louis River before arriving in St. Paul. As chance would have it, across the street from his hotel, a well known balloonist was set up to make ascensions. John H. Steiner was a German immigrant who was earning money by taking thrill seekers aloft for $50 each. These were tethered ascensions "so as to prevent bidding complete good-by to *terra firma*."[28] Zeppelin made his acquaintance and, on 19 August, went up in the balloon. It was a simple enough up and down ride but Zeppelin later said "While I was above St. Paul I had my first idea of aerial navigation strongly impressed upon me and it was there that the first idea of my Zeppelins came to me."[29]

A humorous episode in Steiner's St. Paul ballooning was his attempt to take a famous politician aloft. Alexander Ramsey had just gone from being Governor to U.S. Senator in the summer of 1863 and he thought it somehow appropriate to go up in the balloon. The contemporary account of the affair in the St. Paul *Pioneer Press* is unimprovable:

One of the richest incidents of the day was the attempt of Senator Ramsey to pay a visit to the realms of space. He got into the balloon and rose in the air about thirty feet, but the specific gravity of the Senator was so great that all the gas the balloon held was insufficient to elevate him...

But the Ramsey blood was bound to show itself, and Miss Marion Ramsey, a young lady of ten years, made the ascent on her own account, and said, when she came down that...she would go up as long as her "pa" was willing to pay..."[30]

Nationally known aeronaut, Samuel A. King, briefly put Minnesota in the spotlight in 1881 with an attempt at a record long distance balloon flight between Minneapolis and Boston. Upper air currents were imperfectly understood but king believed they were predominantly from west to east and that, therefore, a transatlantic flight was possible. To try his theory he intended a test flight to Boston and came to Minneapolis in the autumn of 1881 with the idea of accruing publicity and money to defray costs. The Great Northwest Exposition was a rival to the State Fair for entertainment at the time and the balloon take-off for an historic flight from the exposition grounds would be a major attraction. The balloon was named the Great Northwest and was 60 feet tall when inflated with its full 100,000 cubic feet of hydrogen. Hydrogen was dangerous and expensive but had much more lift than coal gas and a hot air balloon was out of the question for a flight of that duration.

The Great Northwest would carry the usual ballast but also scientific instruments, rations for two weeks, camping equipment, King himself, an Army Signal Corps representative, and five newspaper reporters from New York, Boston, Chicago, Minneapolis and St. Paul. The *Pioneer Press* reported that with the scientific instruments was "a bottle of brandy for cramps."[31] The Exposition site was in south Minneapolis and liftoff was scheduled for Wednesday, 7 September, but weather delayed the launch until the following Monday. The ascension came in the late afternoon, unfortunately in a dead calm, and the balloon rose, sank, dropped ballast and rose again. The *Pioneer Press* reported they attained 4200 feet but this was probably a rough estimate and certainly exaggerated.

In any event, King had trouble maintaining a stable altitude and the Great Northwest slowly drifted to the southeast. By dusk they had made it just past the city limits of St. Paul and King decided to pack it in for the night. A crowd of onlookers was hailed and they helped lash the giant balloon down in a pasture for the night. King's plans for a better day were dashed when stiff winds arose on Tuesday and increased constantly until, by Wednesday, a gale was battering the balloon to the point that weights and secure lashings were of no avail. As the Great Northwest thrashed about it was torn and by Thursday the hydrogen lifting gas was gone, the balloon a wreck, and the test flight abandoned.[32]

For the last third of the 19th century balloon ascensions were *de rigueur* at state and county fairs across the country and the itinerant aeronauts certainly found admiring crowds in Minnesota. In September 1881 the Rochester grandstand was filled in the afternoon to witness the balloon ascension which took place.... and in 1891 Professor C. J. Eddy made a parachute jump from his balloon at Browns Valley which was a wonderful performance as all present are ready to testify. Even in relatively late 1898 several thousand people showed up in St. Cloud to watch a flight by an unnamed "lady aeronaut" whose performance seems to have pleased them.[33] The prose used in reporting these activities often bordered on the breathless, as evidenced in a Minneapolis Tribune article about a Mrs. T. S. Williams who made a parachute descent from her balloon in 1894. "Up went the balloon until nearly lost to view...the air was stirred by scarce a breeze and the sight of the air navigator was awe-inspiring and beautiful. With the ease and grace of a swallow skimming the air and seeking a foothold on the ground the strange traveller came back to earth..."[34]

As ballooning became more common, a jaded note sometimes crept in as it would with airplane and space flight in later decades. A newspaper story in 1874 for example, tells of a Professor Denniston going up for ten minutes in his giant balloon "Estella" and making $150.00 for his work. The paper also observed that while the flight was safely performed, "once you have seen one ascension you have seen them all. There is a striking similarity in the way the so called Professors do it."[35]

Tragedy and death unfortunately sometimes accompanied these performances. Hastings had a particularly bad year in 1892. In July a certain Mlle. Loretta Montrose and her horse, not curiously named Montgolfier, were scheduled to "make the most sensational and terrific double balloon ascension and parachute jump ever attempted in the history of the country." The balloon, however, caught fire during inflation and the act was spoiled. In August, amateur aeronaut Ferdinand Hobe, making only his second

flight, was to go up and make a parachute jump. He apparently misjudged his altitude and fell too far before opening his parachute. Hitting the river at considerable speed, he sank immediately and, when his body was recovered, efforts to resuscitate him were fruitless. It was reported that the exhibition managers cautioned him against the attempt but that "disappointment in love made Mr. Hobe reckless, and he would have his way."[36]

The lives of the exhibition balloonists depended not only on their own skill but were frequently at the mercy of the weather or ground crews. A tragic example of the latter happened in Walker in early August 1899. Edwin M. East, billed as a "noted aerialist and comedian" was to make a by now routine ascent and jump. His hot air balloon caught fire just before takeoff but the fire was extinguished and the balloon patched and reinflated. On ascent the wind began to carry East out over Leech Lake and it appeared that he could not use a knife he carried to cut himself loose and parachute to shore. As the balloon began to come down well out in the lake, it was discovered that no one had thought to have a boat ready. East was now "begging piteously for a boat" and the Myrtle D. was sent out but had so little steam up that it took twenty minutes to reach him. After a search, the boat towed the balloon ashore but East had vanished and the Walker newspaper admitted that "It was a terrible mistake that no boat was on the lake to look after him when he fell."[37]

Balloon flights over the state continued through the first three decades of the century and are far too numerous to count. Virtually all were exhibition flights and held during one state fair or another or were specially staged balloon races. The goal of these races was nothing more than to put several balloons into the air and see which one could drift the farthest distance from the launch point. These events, however, drew many spectators, and one such race was held in the summer of 1908 at Lexington Park in St. Paul.

Half a dozen large balloons were launched before a reported crowd of 30,000 who "sighed in relief" at the successful ascensions. The winner, an entry from Chicago, was aloft for seventeen hours, but light winds took it only eighty-five miles south to Blooming Prairie.

Minnesota was sometimes on the receiving end of balloon races as well. In October, 1909, a balloon participating in a race commencing in St. Louis, came down at Wahkon, Minnesota, a distance of over five hundred miles. This particular event moved the *Minneapolis Journal* to accurately summarize that, "such balloon races where contestants have so little control over the gas bags and no means of propelling them, are of no utility whatsoever in solving the problems of airlift, nor do they contribute in any way to our knowledge of the laws that govern the earth's atmospheric envelope. So far as any useful end is served, one might as well throw a number of bottles into the sea and award a prize to the one that drifted the greatest distance."[38]

After 1910, balloon racing as a spectator sport was rapidly eclipsed by airplane flying shows which offered sights and sounds that were far more stimulating. A small number of serious scientists throughout the nation, however, saw balloons as practical vehicles to explore and gain information about the upper atmosphere. Several widely reported high-altitude balloon flights were made, particularly during the 1930s, when interest in upper atmospheric research was high and airplanes still could not fly at high altitude for extended periods. Jean Piccard was one such scientist.[39]

Born in Switzerland, Piccard had joined the University of Minnesota faculty in the spring of 1936, holding appointments in both the chemical engineering and aeronautical engineering departments. He was a chemist by academic background, and was convinced that ballooning was the best way to gather data on the upper atmosphere. He had made several widely publicized high-altitude balloon flights with his brother, Auguste, and later, with his wife, Jeanette Ridlon Piccard. By the spring of 1937, he was pursuing a new idea in ballooning.

Piccard's thesis was that the standard balloons, made of rubberized cotton fabric, could not exceed about ten miles of altitude. As the outside air became thinner during ascent, the stress of the gas on the fabric increased to the bursting point, and thickening the fabric only made the balloon heavier, and therefore, less capable of great heights. Rubberized silk would be an improvement in strength and weight, but would be too costly. The solution, he believed, lay in latex rubber balloons which were light and could expand at high altitude while retaining the necessary safety margin against bursting. Because no rubber balloons were made large enough to loft instruments and a crew, Piccard proposed to cluster together several small weather sounding balloons of the type in common use.

In the spring of 1937, he therefore built a unique contraption that he called the *Pleiades*. The arrangement consisted of ninety-two latex balloons, which, when inflated, were about four feet in diameter. They were grouped in two clusters, one above the other, all attached with cords to a central rope. At the bottom dangled an aluminum gondola that would carry Piccard and a few instruments. In a conventional balloon, a rip panel was used to rapidly spill the gas upon landing and thus prevent the balloon from bouncing along the ground in the wind. With multiple small balloons, this was clearly impossible, and Piccard came up with a solution that was innovative, but as it turned out, dangerous.

To lose height in increments, he planned to carry a knife and a pistol with which to deflate lower cluster balloons that were nearest to him. To rapidly release the entire upper cluster, a piece of T.N.T. fuse was installed on the main rope and connected to an electrically fired blasting cap. About half of *Pleiades* lift could thus be instantly jettisoned upon landing.

The purpose of *Pleiades* was to prove that the concept of such a balloon would work, and Piccard hoped to reach a height of about two miles. The Rochester Kiwanis Club had agreed to sponsor the flight and their motivation was both a desire to promote science and to give Rochester a measure of publicity.

On July 18, 1937, all was ready, including a 160-man ground crew directed by Jeanette Piccard, herself a licensed balloonist. Liftoff was from Soldier's Field in Rochester shortly after midnight, and about two hours later, Piccard reached his planned high point of two miles. To stabilize at that altitude, he began to cut individual balloons free, but the newly freed shot up and stuck under the upper cluster, where they annoyingly, continued to supply lift. He now began a laborious process of pulling individual balloons down close enough that he could puncture them with his knife, a situation which did work.

At about 5:00 a.m. in the dawn's light, Piccard decided to land. He stabbed more balloons and established a gradual descent, when he spotted an open field in a valley near Lansing, Iowa, about one hundred miles southeast of Rochester. Needing a more rapid descent now, Piccard pulled his revolver and shot about a dozen balloons, making a smooth landing in the field. On hitting the ground, and wishing to stay there, he detonated the T.N.T., which jettisoned the upper balloon cluster as planned. Unfortunately, the T.N.T. had been packed in excelsior, which immediately caught fire right above Piccard and the gondola. He scrambled out, but the gondola and instruments were totally destroyed in the ensuing conflagration. "It was just one more experience," Piccard said later, "I know now that I must not use excelsior around T.N.T."

A few days later a testimonial dinner was held by the Rochester Kiwanians. Jeanette was given a medal and Jean a wristwatch, while 200 guests heard his account of the flight. He remained convinced that *Pleiades* had proved his concept to be correct and that a larger version could reach the stratosphere. Lack of money, however, prevented Piccard's idea from seeing further practical application. The coming of the war, of course, meant that such experiments took low priority and by war's end, new plastic films were available for high altitude balloon work. Piccard's *Pleiades* was, and remains, unique in the history of ballooning.

1   On the archaeology of aviation see Clive Hart, *The Prehistory of Flight*, University of California, Berkley, 1985, and Charles Harvard Gibbs-Smith, *Aviation: An Historical Survey from its Origins to the end of World War II*, HMSO, London, 1970.

2   Frances Densmore, *Chippewa Music*, Minneapolis, Ross and Haines, 1973. (Reprint of Smithsonian Institution Bureau of American Ethnology Bulletin No. 45, Washington, D.C., USGPO, 1910, and Bulletin No. 53, 1913.)

3   Frances Densmore, *Chippewa Customs*, Smithsonian Institution Bureau of Ethnology Bulletin No. 86, USGPO, Washington, D.C., 1929.

4   Gideon H. Pond, *Dakota Superstitions*, in Collections of the Minnesota Historical Society, St. Paul, 1896, p. 228.

5   Mary Eastman, *Dahcotah: or Life and Legends of the Sioux Around Ft. Snelling*, John Wiley, New York, 1849, p. xxiv.

6   *Ibid.*

7   On these earliest balloon flights see, for example, L.T.C. Rolt, *The Aeronauts*, New York, Walker and Co., 1966, and Donald Jackson, *The Aeronauts*, Alexandria, Va., Time-Life Books, 1980.

8   Tom Crouch, *The Eagle Aloft*, Washington, D.C., Smithsonian Institution Press, 1983, p. 66-67.

9   Jeremiah Milbank, Jr., *The First Century of Flight in America*, Princeton University Press, 1943, p. 23-29.

10 Rhoda Gilman, "Pioneer Aeronaut: William Markoe and His Balloon," *Minnesota History*, Dec. 1962. Markoe Letter Book, 26 September, 1856. The Markoe Letter and Day Books are in the collection of Markoe family papers, Minnesota Historical Society, Manuscripts Division.

11 Markoe Letter Book, 26 September and 13 December, 1856.

12 Markoe Letter Book, 13 December, 1856.

13 Rhoda Gilman, ed., *A Yankee Inventor's Flying Ship*, Minnesota Historical Society, St. Paul, 1969, p. 2.

14 Markoe Letter Book, 26 September, 1856.

15 *Ibid.*

16 Markoe Letter Book, 13 December, 1856.

17 Markoe Day Book, various entries January-June 1856, and *St. Paul Daily Pioneer and Democrat*, 28 August, 1857, p. 3.

18 Markoe Letter Book, 6 June, 1857 and Day Book, 12 February, 1857 and 27 April, 1857. Litharge (Lead Oxide) was probably used to promote drying while Camphene retarded attacks on the fabric by insects and mildew.

19 Markoe Letter Book, 23 April, 1857, Day Book, 1 August, 1857, and *Pioneer & Democrat*, 24 September, 1857, p. 3.

20 Markoe Letter Book, 15 July, 1857 and Virginia Kunz, *St. Paul: Saga of an American City*, Windsor Publications, Woodland Hills, CA. 1977, p. 43.

21 Markoe Letter Book, 15 July, 1857, *Pioneer & Democrat*, 23 September, 1857, p. 3, 28 August, 1857, p. 3, and Jeremiah Donahower, "The First Balloon Ascension in St. Paul," Donahower Papers, Minnesota Historical Society.

22 *Daily Minnesotan*, 24 September, 1857, p. 3.

23 This account of the flight is drawn from Donahower, Markoe Letter Book, 23 April, 1858, and *Daily Minnesotan*, 24 September, 1857, p. 3.

24 *Daily Minnesotan*, 29 September, 1857, p. 3; Darwin Hall and R. I. Holcombe, *History of the Minnesota State Agricultural Society*, St. Paul, 1910, p. 39.

25 *Daily Minnesotan*, 10 October, 1857, p. 2; *Pioneer & Democrat*, 10 October, 1857, p. 3; *St. Paul Daily Globe*, 12 August, 1893.

26 *Daily Minnesotan*, 2 June 1858, p. 3; 7 June, 1858, p. 3.

27 Letter from Zeppelin to his father in Rhoda Gilman, "Zeppelin in Minnesota: The Count's Own Story," *Minnesota History*, summer 1967. For a detailed account of Zeppelin's activities in America see, by the same author, "Zeppelin in Minnesota, A Study in Fact and Fable," Minnesota History, Fall 1965.

28 *St. Paul Pioneer Press*, 12 August, 1863, p. 4.

29 Gilman, *Minnesota History*, Fall 1965. p. 285.

30 *St. Paul Pioneer Press*, 20 August, 1863, p. 4.

31 *St. Paul Pioneer Press*, 12 September, 1881, p. 6.

32 For a detailed account of King's flight see Rhoda Gilman, "The Balloon to Boston: Samuel A. King and the Great Northwest," *Minnesota History*, Spring 1970. Contemporary accounts are in the *St. Paul Pioneer Press*, 13 & 16 September, 1881.

33 *Rochester Post*, 9 September, 1881, p. 2 *Inter-Lake Tribune*, 11 July, 1891; and *St. Cloud Daily Times*, 14 October, 1888.

34 *Minneapolis Tribune*, 16 September, 1894, p. 7.

35 *Minneapolis Tribune*, 13 September, 1874, p. 5.

36 *Hastings Gazette*, 25 June, 9 July, and 6 August, 1894.

37 *Cass County Pioneer*, 4 August, 1899.

38 *Minneapolis Journal*, 12 July, p.1; 20 July, p.7, 1908; and 8 October, 1909, p. 20.

39 Here and six paragraphs below, see: University of Minnesota, Institute of Technology, *Minnesota Technology*, November, 1937, Archives of the University of Minnesota; Interview with Donald Piccard, transcription in possession of authors; Jean Piccard, "The Voyage of the Pleiades," undated, unpublished manuscript, National Air and Space Museum; and *Rochester Post-Bulletin*, 23 July, 1937. Extensive papers and press clippings concerning Piccard's work and the *Pleiades* flight in particular, may also be found in the John D. Akerman papers, University of Minnesota Archives, and in the "Piccard, Balloon Flight" files, Olmstead County Historical Society, Rochester, MN.

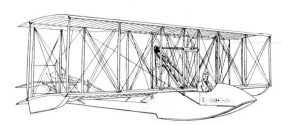

TWO

1920s: THE PIONEERING YEARS

Aviation in Minnesota began in the first decade of this century and was in many ways typical of the early patterns in flying development that were unfolding elsewhere in the nation. Several Minnesotans received publicity for flying machines that, in the end, were more fantasy than fact, some made glides or powered hops and a few at early dates made true powered flights. The public, however, saw flying only when Glenn Curtiss or other renowned aviators came to the state to put on exhibitions. Early flying exhibitions, mostly staged at the State Fairgrounds, were immensely popular since flying, in 1910, was considered more entertainment than it was transportation. From that year on, flying became increasingly more commonplace, but the public never lost its fascination with airplanes and the men and women who flew them.

Aviation can be broadly divided into two areas: aeronautics or heavier-than-air flight, and aerostation or lighter-than-air vehicles such as balloons and dirigibles. Aeronautics, in contrast to aerostation, means heavier-than-air flight and, by definition, powered flight. The first such flights were made in December 1903 by Wilbur and Orville Wright over the wind-swept dunes of Kitty Hawk, North Carolina. Only a handful of witnesses saw these historic first flights and the Wrights proved to be uncommonly shy of publicity and it was not until 1908 that the public really became aware of the Wrights activities.

Public enthusiasm over aeronautics exploded on the scene in 1910. The first air show ever was held at Reims, France, in August 1909, where upwards of 200,000 people paid to see the most celebrated aviators of Europe take to the air. In the next several months dozens of air meets were held at cities in Europe and the United States. January, 1910, saw the first of these in America at Los Angeles. Thereafter, no self-respecting city wished to be without its own demonstration of the science of aviating. Newspaper reporting on these activities naturally inspired people in all parts of the nation to dream up their own flying machines, so both the airshows and local inventors were a part of the aviation scene by 1910. That year in Minnesota was marked by two major developments: airshows where the public saw flying for the first time and the first successful flights by local aviators in their homemade machines.

The birth of aeronautics in the state, however, was preceded by partial successes, failures and flights of fancy. One of the earliest home grown designs for a heavier than air machine proved more whimsical than flyable despite the fact that it was actually

patented. Designed in 1908 by a Minneapolis druggist named Edward LaPenotiere, the device was intended to take off straight up by means of two screw shaped fans which were mounted vertically and powered by a gasoline engine. The wing was to be a series of hinged aluminum blades which would be vertical as the machine ascended. At the desired altitude the engines would be shut down, air pressure would close the blades to form a solid horizontal wing, and the craft would glide to the earth. Mr. LaPenotiere had learned aeronautics by watching the birds fly and was confident of the success of his machine. He did not, however, decide on the type of fans to be used, did not build a model to test his ideas, and did not know when such a machine could be built. He did know that it would be expensive.[1]

Even more imaginative was the hybrid helicopter-balloon envisioned by Oliver K. Chance of Minneapolis. Described as "a scalp specialist and an air-shippist" who had "solved the problems of aerial navigation," Chance designed a craft consisting of a large aluminum saucer under which a gas bag would be placed to provide lift. Hanging ten feet under the balloon was to have been a basket or car which would carry no less than the pilot, the required operating levers, a fifty horsepower engine and room for five passengers. Three propellers and a system of rudders would give maneuvering ability. A long shaft would run from the engine in the control car to the top of the device and turn a large horizontal propeller to control ascent and descent.

Chance was nothing if not confident. The utility of the aluminum saucer, he said, was that if one was up in the air "ever so many miles" and the engine quit, that it would act as "such an admirable parachute that it will require two hours and thirty seven minutes" to regain *terra firma*. A printed advertisement promised that his machine "ascends and descends vertically. It balances. It hovers. It lands lightly like a feather. It is safe. Its lifting power is immense. Its speed is phenomenal."

Chance evidently did build demonstration models, one of which was smashed in an encounter with a wall, but no full scale device was built. He did attempt to sell stock to finance construction of a full scale machine but it came to nothing. It is doubtless of significance that when asked if he had any practical experience at aviating, Chance replied, "Bless my soul no...It wouldn't be safe."[2]

An aircraft design by Minnesotan E. H. Eichenfeldt received a measure of international recognition when it was included in the 1910-1911 edition of the prestigious directory, *Jane's All The World's Aircraft* which was published in London. Eichenfeldt, born in Minneapolis and a resident of Mankato, had received a patent on a unique biplane which had a curved upper wing that arched into the upward angled lower wing. A 25 horsepower motor was intended to be mounted on the front and a rudder in the rear allowed steering. The device would weigh 510 pounds and be constructed of steel tubing covered with sheet aluminum. Eichenfeldt built at least four models of his design and flew them successfully, on occasion in the assembly room at the Minneapolis Courthouse.[3] A full scale version was not built, however, and Eichenfeldt's flying machine vanished into obscurity.

The variety of ideas for a flying machine was nearly endless. In early 1910 B. W. Fall of Minneapolis, invented an "aerocycle" which involved two engines, ten wings and a gyroscope. A contemporary newspaper account said the machine was "still in the blueprint stage" where it seems to have remained.[4] By 1910, however, the first tentative steps off the ground had already been taken by local inventors.

In October 1908 Robert and Henry Robertson, twin brothers from the Lynnhurst area of Minneapolis, made glides that were at least partially successful. The Brothers constructed a kite-like glider of fabric and wood with which they seem to have managed a few short glides. Such was the fervency of interest in flying that the *Minneapolis Journal* called the kite "the first real experiment with flying in Minneapolis" and breathlessly proclaimed that the Robertson brothers "may well rank with Montgolfier, the Wrights, and Zeppelin."[5]

The age of powered flight in Minnesota had something of a false dawn in early 1909 when Ralph Wilcox and A. C. Bennett attempted to get airborne off the ice on Lake Minnetonka. The machine they used was of their own construction but was clearly patterned on the Wright biplane.

Ralph Wilcox was a member of a prominent Minneapolis family which was involved in various manufacturing enterprises including automobiles. Bennett, who seems to have designed the machine, was a business associate. The aircraft was built by the two men in the shops of a family business, the Wilcox Motor Company on Marshall Avenue in Minneapolis, in the autumn of 1908. Resembling the Wright Brothers' machines in both size and general

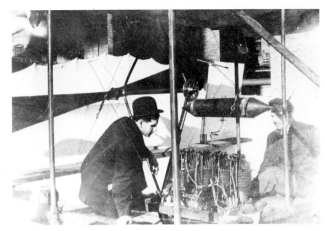

Ashley C. Bennett (left) and Ralph Wilcox are generally credited with building the first heavier-than-air flying machine in Minnesota. The year was 1909. Here, they tinker with their engine in a picture thought to be taken in 1907. (Gerald Sandvick)

layout, the Wilcox-Bennett aircraft was powered by a 25 h.p. four-cylinder air-cooled engine which turned a single pusher propeller. The control system they used is unrecorded.[6]

In late January, 1909, the two men, with Ralph's brother Harry watching, tried to fly near the family's summer home on Lake Minnetonka. The machine was lashed to a tree with a rope, the engine run up and the rope released. The biplane made a short run downhill on an iced runway and hopped into the air. In later years, Harry Wilcox said "The machine barely got into the air... I've seen skiers go higher."[7] At least two attempts a few days earlier had failed because of engine problems, and even the hop that was completed did not bring much newspaper attention at the time.

A year later Wilcox and Bennett tried again with essentially the same aircraft, but using a more powerful eight cylinder engine. They may have accomplished further hops, but more engine and propeller troubles prevented sustained flights.[8] In any event, after their second try at flying, the two men abandoned aviation and went back to the automobile business.

January 1910 saw not only Wilcox and Bennett's

Another view of the Wilcox-Bennett airplane, under construction at the Wilcox Motor Car Company in North Minneapolis. (Minnesota Historical Society)

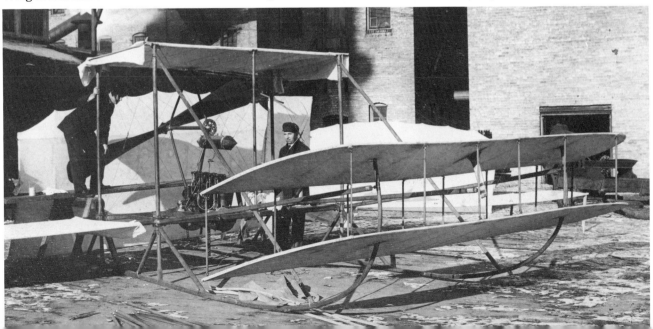

The Wilcox-Bennett airplane landing on the ice of Lake Minnetonka after a brief "hop." Although not able to sustain flight, the machine appears to have been built along the lines of the Wright Brothers airplanes. (Gerald Sandvick)

second try, but across the Twin Cities from Lake Minnetonka, John O. Johnson managed to briefly stagger into the air from the frozen surface of White Bear Lake. Johnson's 600 pound machine was of his own design and construction and was powered by a 20 h.p. engine. The wingspan was 30 feet, but the wings were arranged one behind the other rather than in the common configuration of one above the other.[9] This arrangement had been tried by others, most notably Professor Samuel Langley in Washington in 1903. It failed for Langley and worked no better for Johnson.

On the afternoon of 25 January several bystanders gave Johnson's machine a push as he revved the engine. Although accounts vary slightly, he flew no more than 200 feet and his altitude was probably 20 feet when the engine quit and he made a hard landing on the ice doing major damage to the propeller, rudder and landing skids. Johnson was clearly not a man lacking in self confidence and his evaluation of the affair was to "...feel encouraged by my first success for I did prove that I can fly as well as those fellows who have been winning medals all over the world."[10] A few weeks later Johnson announced plans to build a monoplane which he believed would mark a new era in aerial navigation and put the Wright Brothers to shame. Self-assurance seems to have been all that came of it though, and Johnson faded from the aviation scene after his one powered hop.

The endeavors of Wilcox, Bennett and Johnson mark the first attempts at true airplane flight in Minnesota. In both cases their machines left the ground but in neither case was a true flight accomplished, probably because adequate power and an effective control system were lacking.

When we seek the origins of aviation, it is important to understand just what is meant by a successful flight. By aviation, we mean a heavier than air machine that is powered rather than a motorless glider. In addition to a practical source of power, an effective control system is necessary. An aircraft moves through three axes during flight: pitch, yaw, and roll, and many early builders did not understand the necessity of controlling for this three directional movement.

Perhaps the major criterion for calling a particular flight successful, however, is whether it was sustained and not simply a powered hop off the ground. If an aircraft is launched downhill or uses a mechanical assist such as a catapulting device, a certain distance will likely be covered through the air simply due to

imparted momentum. The noted British aviation historian, Charles Harvard Gibbs-Smith, has suggested, for this earliest period in the history of powered flight, that a sustained flight be defined as one which accomplished a distance of about a quarter mile, or about 1300 feet.[11]

The choice of a quarter mile is, quite obviously, arbitrary, but does represent a sensible standard all the same. If a machine can travel a quarter mile in the air, it has gone a distance well beyond that for which momentum alone could account. The machine's own propulsion system must have been of help. It is also unlikely that a machine could fly such a distance without being under some degree of control. Without reasonably effective control the craft would most probably stall, dive, roll or skid into the ground after a few dozen feet at most.

The quarter mile criterion does, however, represent a realistic distance for a day in which engines were balky and control was a trial and error learning process. Several successful aviators, including the Wrights, did accomplish this distance with relative ease in their early experiments. A successful airplane flight then, as distinguished from a glide or powered hop, should have been made in a machine which incorporated a motor, an effective control system and accomplished a distance of about a quarter mile.

Wilcox and Johnson had made powered hops. The dawn of flight in the State would come only in the summer of 1910, and it would come in spectacular fashion.

The age of powered flight came to Minnesota during four sweltering days in June 1910. Thousands of people flocked to the State Fairgrounds and endured heat, humidity, and heavy rain storms to see Min-

Poster proclaiming the highlights of the first organized Minnesota flying event, the June, 1910, airshow at the State Fairgrounds. The names of famous aviators and auto racers of the times are headlined. Others, participating in the exhibition but not mentioned in the headlines, included Eugene Ely, first person to land on the deck of a ship, and Ray Harroun who would win the very first Indianapolis 500 race in 1911. Of all the participants, only Glenn Curtiss made substantial flights during June's show, due to unpredictable weather. Curtiss, however, was spectacular; at one point pitting his airplane against a race car driven a few circuits of the track by Barney Oldfield. (Gerald Sandvick)

nesota's first air show. They witnessed flights by several prominent aviators, but the star of the show was Glenn Curtiss himself, one of America's greatest pioneers of aviation.

Experience had shown that there was money to be made from the airplane as a new form of entertainment, and promoters were not slow to capitalize on it. The first American air meet had been held in January, 1910, near Los Angeles and for the next many months aerial spectaculars were common through-out the country. There was something in it for everyone. Huge crowds and commensurate gate receipts attracted promoters, and fees plus prize money lured the aviators. It was not impossible for a flyer to earn from $5,000 to $20,000 for making a few flights on an afternoon or two. The paying customers got to see aeroplanes in flight and, since public knowledge of aviation was still simple and unsophisticated, they only wanted to see how fast, how high and for how long an aeroplane could fly. And, of course, whether the aviator could do it all without getting killed.

Minnesota's first airshow began to take shape in February 1910. At that time Minnesota State Fair Secretary, C. N. Cosgrove had entered into serious negotiations with various exhibition flyers including the French aviator Louis Paulhan. Paulhan was the only European pilot making a splash in this country. He was an enormously colorful figure and had appeared at the January, 1910, air meet near Los Angeles where he quickly had become the darling of the crowds. He traveled with his wife, two mechanics, two Farman biplanes, two Bleriot monoplanes and a poodle. He was also a superb pilot and his $19,000 of prize money at Los Angeles topped the winnings of any other aviator there.

Cosgrove tried to get Paulhan to come to Minnesota but was informed that the Frenchman wanted a guarantee of $12,000 plus 75% of the gate receipts.[12] A certain amount of haggling followed but Paulhan's appearance became a moot point when a U. S. Marshal served him with an injunction requiring a $25,000 bond against any exhibition earnings. The Wright brothers had convinced the Court that Paulhan's flying was an infringement on their patents and that royalties were due them. Paulhan was furious and he canceled further exhibition flying in this country, thumbed his nose at the Wright's by flying free for all to see over New York, and went back to France in a huff.[13]

By mid-March Cosgrove was negotiating with the Curtiss exhibition people in the hope of promoting an airshow in June 1910. Cosgrove had competition, however, because the Minneapolis Automobile Show Association was also interested. The Association had been sponsoring auto shows for several years and its officers were prominent Minneapolis businessmen including Harry Pence, Harry Wilcox, and F. E. Murphy, all involved in the auto business. In late March, both Cosgrove and Auto Association Manager Walter Wilmot, had gone to Chicago to try to conclude an agreement for the Curtiss aviators to appear in Minnesota. Wilmot made a verbal agreement with Curtiss representative, L. K. Bernard, which provided that Glenn Curtiss and two other pilots would fly in the Twin Cities from 22 through 25 June. The price

Bud Mars in flight over the infield of the State Fair racetrack during the State Fair in September of 1910. Both Wright and Curtiss aircraft performed for the crowds. (Gerald Sandvick)

would be $20,000 plus a percentage of the gate.

Cosgrove, it seems, conducted separate negotiations with Bernard and was offered a similar deal in the event Wilmot and his Association turned it down. They did not, however, and in a letter of 25 March, Bernard confirmed the agreement in writing.[14] With the airshow now guaranteed, the Fair Board and the Auto Show Association quickly agreed to cooperate, probably because while the latter owned the contract, the former owned the only feasible place to hold such a show. A memorandum, in any case, was signed in mid-May with the two parties agreeing to a division of the gate receipts after the Curtiss team had been paid.[15]

Having assured themselves of the flying, the promoters went on to create not just an airshow but a four day extravaganza. To keep the aerial activity going, dirigibles were hired to fly along with the airplanes. On the ground, automobile and motorcycle races were scheduled, one of the drivers being no less than the legendary Barney Oldfield, and just for good measure a steed named Minor Heir, billed as the fastest horse in the world, was hired to race against the newer mechanical modes of conveyance.

Public interest in flying had been high for months. As far back as February the *Minneapolis Journal* reported that a popular 1910 Valentine's Day card carried the verse:

> Come my dear and fly with me
> You my Valentine will be
> We'll sail up in my aeroplane
> And our hearts will ne'er be
> twain.[16]

Though possibly less than profound poetry, such verse evidently struck a popular chord.

As the airshow neared and it became clear that Minnesotans would finally see airplanes in flight, the newspapers became almost rapturous. One editorialist held that the aeroplane was the most inspiring of all vehicles and would soon be on par with the automobile and motorboat because it would be incomparably superior to travel through "the clean, fresh, dustless roads of the sky." Flying would provide "boundless room on every side with the countryside spread out like a green, alluring map, with no mountains or valleys or rivers or ravines to conquer, save those yet mysterious configurations of the atmosphere."[17]

As June came, excitement about the airshow was intense. The *Minneapolis Journal* altruistically reported that the meet was "intended to promote and stimulate interest in aviation from an educational standpoint rather than to simply furnish sensational spectacles."[18] A few days later, though the paper could hardly contain itself when it said that "the Twin Cities and the Northwest are on the eve of beholding what will doubtless prove the most stupendous spectacle of the kind never seen in this section of the country."[19]

The show was held at the State Fairgrounds from 22 June to 25 June, a Wednesday through Saturday. Auto and motorcycle races, while exciting, were no novelty, and the scheduled dirigible races caused little stir. The time was passing when dirigibles could compete with airplanes and a "race" between dirigibles was really a euphemism for two partially controllable gas bags heading in more or less the same direction at approximately the same time of day. In any case, dirigibles had flown over the Twin Cities before. It was the airplanes that absorbed the public's attention.

By the 21st, fully a half dozen pilots with their aircraft and spares had arrived, which made for one of the largest concentrations of aviators that North America had ever seen. Glenn Curtiss was the center of attention. The first American other than the Wright brothers to fly, he had become a designer and builder of aircraft and the premier exhibition pilot. The team that came with him consisted of Charlie Willard, J. C. "Bud" Mars, and Lincoln Beachey. Willard was the first man Curtiss had taught to fly, and Mars had come aboard at an early date, too. Both were already famous and as experienced as aviators could be in 1910. Lincoln Beachey was the newcomer to the Curtiss team and still considered something of a student during his Minnesota appearance. Within another year, though, he would be known as the most skilled and daring of all the exhibition flyers, and even Orville Wright would later call Beachey "the greatest aviator of all" with whom no other flyer could compare.[20]

For Eugene Ely the Minnesota air meet was the turning point of his career. He owned a Curtiss airplane but was just breaking into the airshow business. This was only his second appearance. Born in Davenport, Iowa, Ely was working in Portland, Oregon, in early 1910, when a local automobile dealer he knew bought one of the first Curtiss airplanes. Having purchased it, however, the man was afraid to fly it, so Ely volunteered and immediately smashed it. Being mechanically inclined, however, Ely repaired the machine and cautiously taught himself to fly, acquiring the feel of flight as he went along. By the spring of 1910 he was flying well and decided to try to make money at exhibition flying. He made two successful flights at a show in Winnipeg and then moved on to the Twin Cities.

He thus met Willard, Mars, and especially, Curtiss who was always looking for new exhibition flyers. Liking Ely and being impressed with his work, Curtiss signed him to the team. For several months Ely flew shows for Curtiss, and in November, 1910, made history when he became the first pilot to fly off a ship

in a demonstration that Curtiss had arranged for the Navy. Like many exhibition pilots, Ely's career was not a long one. He died in the crash of a Curtiss airplane in October, 1911, at Macon, Georgia, two days short of his 25th birthday.[21]

The somewhat obscure figure of Whipple Hall completed the list of flyers. An independent aviator, flying a Curtiss-built machine, Hall's main claim to fame seems to have been his billing as the "world's heaviest aviator."[22] At 210 pounds he would have greatly strained the flying machines of those times, and though he tried mightily indeed, he could not get off the ground in Minnesota's summer heat.

The event opened on 22 June with auto and motorcycle races being run, but it was the airplanes that had attracted the crowd of 18,000. Six machines were ready to fly and were surrounded by curious throngs of spectators who inspected the "monstrous looking machines, great of sweep of wing and frail of support and framework with their motors seemingly hung to a nothingness of silk and bamboo."[23]

Around 4:00 p.m., Curtiss' aircraft was readied for takeoff from the inner racetrack area in front of the grandstand. As his engine crackled and he began to roll, the crowd stood up to catch every move of the first aeroplane flight in the State. A huge cheer went up as Curtiss left the ground. He attained an altitude of 50 feet when strong gusts forced him down to an inelegantly hard landing which damaged the machine. He had flown about one half mile, never leaving the infield. It was hardly an auspicious flight for Glenn Curtiss who had won $10,000 weeks earlier for a 150 mile flight from Albany to New York. Still, it was the first airplane flight in Minnesota, and the crowd loved it. Mars and Ely each tried twice and failed, but by 6:00 Curtiss' machine had been repaired. He again flew about a half mile and not over 50 feet high, but this time his aircraft nosed into the ground and cartwheeled. Curtiss climbed out of the debris unhurt, but his machine was a wreck.[24]

The problem had been the weather. The temperature had reached 96° degrees with winds gusting to 15 m.p.h. and the grandstand at the fairgrounds was compared to the "firebox of an oven with all the drafts open." Curtiss said "This is absolutely the most difficult aviating I ever attempted...conditions were never worse for flying than they are right here today."[25] However modest they may have been, the first flights over Minnesota were now history, and the aviators promised that with improved atmospheric conditions they would really show what flying was all about.

The second day of the meet saw the hot gusty weather continue, but the flying improved greatly. Curtiss led off with a flight that left no doubt about his conquest of the air. A crowd of 12,000 saw him fly for nearly ten minutes at up to 700 feet as he dipped and circled in front of the grandstand, moved out over machinery hill and on toward Lake Johanna. He covered well over six ground miles and left the crowd in such amazement that they could scarcely believe what they were seeing. When he landed "the men and women in the grandstand yelled themselves hoarse, threw their hats into the air and clapped their hands."[26] It was a remarkable flight under the conditions and Curtiss' success was due to his change of aircraft. Having wrecked one machine the previous day, he now switched to the Hudson Flyer, the same aircraft in which he made his historic Albany-New York flight. The Hudson Flyer had a 50 h.p. V8 engine while the other machines present had four-cylinder engines of 25 or 30 h.p. The extra power made all the difference in the blistering weather.

Mars made a short flight of perhaps a mile, but Hall, Ely, and Beachey failed to get off the ground at all. Ely drew more comment on his natty white suit than his attempt to fly, and Beachey was having his troubles with an experimental monoplane. To give the people their money's worth, Curtiss agreed to fly a second time. He made a spectacular flight of about five minutes duration circling the grandstand and flying out to the northwest of the fairgrounds. On his landing, the crowd again went wild. Curtiss was typically modest saying that his flying wasn't really very much and that if there was more moisture in the air he could do much better. He also commented or concluded that "Minnesota has a fine climate to live in, but it is worthless for airship flying."[27]

Friday, 24 June, was the third day of the aerial spectacular. Charlie Willard finally made a successful flight, albeit brief, and again Mars, Hall, and Ely just couldn't arise in the gusty 94 degree heat with their four cylinder engines. Lincoln Beachey continued his disappointing efforts to get his monoplane off the ground and late in the day after the crowd had gone, he wrecked the machine against a fence trying one last takeoff.

Curtiss made up for these disappointing tries by doing the show's best flying. A lightning storm moved through the cities in mid-afternoon which kept the crowd smaller than on the previous days, but Curtiss rambled through the clouds making four flights. He was confident of conquering the air and his machine was described as "majestically proud although scarred with the wounds of past encounters with obstacles." After two perfectly controlled flights of about four minutes each, he flew a third time for an incredible ten minutes. Flying north to Lake Johanna, Curtiss then circled west and south of the Fairgrounds. Coming back he did a bit of "fancy flying" in front of the grandstand and even buzzed a group of newsmen which caused some to dive and the rest to flee. He had covered more than nine miles and made flying look almost routine. Then, considering the poor flying done on the first day of the show, Curtiss made a fourth flight in order to make amends. This time he flew for seven minutes. His day's total was 25 minutes in the air over a distance of twenty five to thirty miles.[28]

Saturday, the last day of the event, brought many flights though none of great duration. Indeed aircraft flights were "as common as raindrops...they got up like Democrats in a party convention."[29] Curtiss made two flights that totaled seven minutes in the air, and Mars and Ely each made flights of about a mile. Except for Curtiss, Willard was the most successful when he made a flight of over two minutes which was also the last of the show. Although the press continued to glorify the aviators, a somewhat jaded note had crept in after four days of flying. When Curtiss sailed around the air with such ease and security, the *Minneapolis Tribune* complained "that some folks fell

to wondering why they separated themselves from their admission money to see such a commonplace stunt."[30]

The first Minnesota airshow was over. For four days the weather had conspired against the aviators prompting Curtiss' complaint that "the conditions here are the worst I have ever encountered."[31] No matter how dangerous and difficult, Mars, Ely, and Willard had flown, and Curtiss had flown brilliantly. Coming to Minnesota as the greatest of aviators, he left with reputation intact. He packed up immediately after the show and headed home to Hammondsport for a few days and then on to another major air meet at Atlantic City on the 4th of July. Ely was now a member of the Curtiss exhibition team and, with Willard and Mars, went on to a flying demonstration at Sioux City.

The flyers had brought aviation to the state, and 50,000 people had seen them cavort through the air. In Minnesota the Age of Flight had begun.

In all respects, the year 1910 marks the birth of powered flight in Minnesota. Following the state's first airshow in June another aerial spectacular took place during the State Fair in September which also featured aviators of national renown. Between those two public exhibitions, Minnesota's first "home grown" airplane took to the air.

The honor of being the first Minnesotan to build an airplane and successfully fly it probably belongs to a St. Paul auto mechanic, Fred Parker. Parker, 22, had a garage in the Hamline area of St. Paul at 665 North Snelling Avenue. He had evidently been smit-

Fred Parker seated in his unique monoplane in the backyard of his family's home in St. Paul. An auto mechanic, he had designed an ingenious "multi-axis" tail for pitch and yaw control while shifting his weight to control roll movement. (Gerald Sandvick)

ten by the desire to fly at an early age, and during his teens built a series of impractical devices to get himself into the air. By early 1910 he was building biplanes and monoplanes based on successful aircraft then flying Europe and America. He usually crashed, however, and a sister commented that he "has broken every other bone in his body except his spine."[32]

The mechanically inclined Parker seems to have been fascinated by various aircraft types that were widely known in 1910 and worked in the Hammondsport, N. Y. shops of Glenn Curtiss for a short time. His first practical airplane designs were biplanes patterned on Wright and Curtiss types, but he seems to have had little success with these. Both types were

Fred Parker in flight, August, 1910. This old photo shows that Parker was successful in getting airborne. Records indicate that he flew for some eight minutes and reached an altitude of 100 feet. (Gerald Sandvick)

relatively complex biplanes and their control systems were not yet easy for backyard inventors to duplicate.

Indeed, Parker was concerned about the controllability of Wright and Curtiss aircraft, saying that they required an expert to handle them. "I have puzzled my head and smashed my bones over biplanes long enough," he pronounced, "the monoplane is the thing." In Curtiss' machine the engine is so powerful that vibration makes his aeroplane almost impossible for a man to handle. It takes a long education in aviation to fly in a Curtiss or even a Wright machine. The biplanes are hard to turn in the air and hard to balance."[33]

Parker could have learned the details of several types of monoplanes with ease. In France, Louis Bleriot had been building monoplanes since 1907, and, in 1909 he made the first flight across the English Channel in one of them. In addition to Bleriot, Alberto Santos-Dumont, and Henri Farman were flying monoplanes in France, and in the United States the first monoplane had been flown in upstate New York late in 1909. These flights and the details of the aircraft involved had been widely publicized.

Parker's first monoplane seems to have been closely based on the Farman. The details are not known, but the wing on Parker's machine had a span of 23 feet and a width of 6 feet, the exact dimension of the Farman wing. In mid-August this machine was smashed when Parker attempted to fly it. It was probably underpowered and did not get far off the ground.[34]

He then turned his attention to completing a second monoplane on which he had also been working. This one was somewhat smaller and substantially lighter than the first, weighing only 132 pounds. The width of the wing remained at 6 feet but Parker shortened the span to 20 feet. The wing was built of six curved ribs covered with lightweight linen. The cruciform tail was also linen covered with a span of slightly over 5 feet while the fuselage was simply an open wood framework.

The engine was mounted in front and was reported to have been an 18 h.p. French engine "of the same type as the one used by Santos-Dumont."[35] In all likelihood, therefore, Parker was using a Duthiel-Chalmers engine. Duthiel-Chalmers was a Paris firm that sold several types of aeronautical engines and

one of them was a two cylinder model which was rated at 18 h.p. The 56 pound engine was aircooled with its cylinders in a horizontally opposed configuration. It turned at 1200 r.p.m. and had a bore and stroke of 125 mm (4.92) and 100 mm (3.94 in.) respectively.[36]

The four and one half foot propeller had wooden blades which appear to have been bolted into a metal sleeve which in turn was slipped over the crankshaft. There was probably no reduction gearing so that the engine directly turned the propeller at about 1200 r.p.m. Given the lightness of Parker's aircraft, this engine and propeller combination would have supplied more than enough power to get it airborne.

Parker's control system was straightforward and at the same time imaginative. An aircraft in flight, it will be recalled, is capable of motion around its vertical, lateral, and longitudinal axes, motions which are respectively termed yaw, pitch, and roll. In yawing the nose of the aircraft moves sideways, in pitch it moves up or down, and in roll the nose maintains direction while the aircraft rolls about an imaginary line drawn from nose to tail. For an aircraft to fly in a safe and practical way the aviator must be able to control the movement of his machine in all three directions in order to accomplish coordinated maneuvers.

Parker solved the problem of control in a simple, direct, and ingenious fashion. To provide control in pitch and yaw he built a cruciform tail unit which was attached to the framework by an automobile universal joint. There was no fixed stabilizing area the whole tail was moveable. Wires connected the tail surfaces to a lever at the pilot's seat which allowed him to move the tail and thus control for pitch, yaw, or a combination thereof.

The basic idea in longitudinal control is to differentially alter the airflow over the wings and thus cause the aircraft to roll to the side with the lesser amount of lift. In 1910 the two most common mechanical methods of doing this were the Wright brothers' "wing warping" in which the wing tips were mechanically twisted and the Curtiss system of ailerons or the attachment to the wings of small hinged surfaces to direct airflow up or down. Parker's monoplane did not incorporate either of these mechanical systems of roll control; but another possibility did exist.

If an aircraft is sufficiently small and light, it can be made to roll by simply shifting the pilot's weight from side to side. Weight shifting is the method of control used in modern hang gliders and was used by

John Schwister, originally from Winona, Minnesota, had lived for many years in Wausau, Wisconsin. He returned to Minneapolis where he built this Curtiss-type aircraft in 1911, calling it "The Minnesota Badger Biplane" to honor his two home States. His adventures included a broken wrist suffered during an exhibition at Fort Snelling later the same year. (Don Hanson)

gliding pioneers as far back as the 1890s. It is a method not as effective as the others, but in Parker's aircraft it would have been good enough to allow him to turn a circle and return to his starting point for a landing. Parker's control system may not have been sophisticated, but clearly it was effective.

Minnesota's first monoplane did incorporate another innovative feature in its variable incidence wing. The angle of incidence is essentially the angle at which the wing is attached to an airplane. This is the angle that Parker could vary and in doing so he also changed the angle of attack. The latter is the angle at which a wing meets the oncoming air and as the angle of attack increases, so does the lift of the wing.[37] Parker, it appears, attached his monoplane's high wing in such a way that it could be tilted up or down to some degree. Two push rods were linked to a lever near the pilot's seat which allowed the operator to change the wing's incidence. In a slow, lightweight aircraft tilting the wing up (increasing the angle of incidence) would have allowed the machine to virtually float in for a landing. The whole idea, as Parker put it, was "to gain ease in alighting," and to make the machine "so easy to handle that the average man can fly it."[38] The landing gear consisted of two bicycle wheels up front and one in the rear.

Parker had built the airplane in his shop, which was located in St. Paul on an otherwise empty block bounded by Snelling and Asbury Avenues on the west and east and Blair and Lafond Streets on the north and south. The empty block was his flying field. On 26 August, 1910, Parker made his first flight in the new monoplane and stayed aloft for eight minutes at a height of over 100 feet. The flight was witnessed by several residents of the area.[39] Parker made several circuits around the field and may have covered a true distance of about 4 miles if an estimate of airspeed is set at about 30 m.p.h. It was clearly a flight that was controlled, sustained, powered and even witnessed. The first flight in Minnesota by an indigenous aircraft had been accomplished.

The St. Paul mechanic-aviator apparently took the aircraft up once more on the 29th or 30th in an even longer flight but came to grief on August 30. A wheel parted company with the aircraft on takeoff and the machine apparently skidded sideways shattering the propeller.[40] The plane was repaired and a new propeller obtained. On September 1, Parker signed a contract to exhibit, and hopefully fly the monoplane at the forthcoming State Fair. The aircraft was displayed at the Fair during the second week of September but, for whatever reason, Parker did not fly it there. After the 1910 State Fair, Fred Parker, like many amateur airplane builders of the period, simply fades into obscurity.

Much of the earliest flying in Minnesota was affiliated with the State Fair, which was natural and, in retrospect, inevitable. Flying was entertainment more than anything else prior to World War I, and the Fair was always on the lookout for new shows to present. Fair officials were expert in promoting events of this sort and it was obvious that exhibition flights drew the crowds that the Fair wanted. Selling tickets and collecting the money was an integral part of Fair activity while the Grandstand provided the necessary seating and viewing for a big event, be it a horse race, auto race or aerial exhibition. The area in front of the grandstand was sufficiently large to pitch a tent or two to keep the flying machines out of the weather and, most important of all, the infield of the racetrack was adequate for taking off and landing.

In the summer of 1910 the Fair Board's Executive Secretary was the same C. N. Cosgrove who had been one of the principals in arranging for Curtiss to fly at the June airshow. For the coming 1910 State Fair, however, Cosgrove contracted with both the Curtiss and the Wright firms to supply aviators. This, it was hoped, would insure that flights would really be made since the Fair Board took a less than charitable view of the aviators who had failed to get up during the June show. Indeed, the contracts required the aviators to fly in order to be paid.[41] In arranging for both Curtiss and Wright machines to fly, Cosgrove had added an element of a contest, too. For about a year competition between the two firms had been growing. There was still camaraderie among aviators so the actual rivalry in the air was somewhat veiled but, beginning in 1909, the Wrights had filed the first of a series of lawsuits against Curtiss. They alleged that the design of the Curtiss machines infringed on patents held by them and that the Wrights were, therefore, owed royalties. The whole episode, unfortunately, became more personal and bitter as time went on, but it also tended to keep the public interested in seeing which type of airplane could fly the best.

The Wrights sent pilot A. L. Welsh to the Minnesota State Fair with one of their machines while the Curtiss aircraft was handled by J. C. Mars. This was the same "Bud" Mars who had accomplished only a couple short flights at the June airshow but aimed to redeem his reputation in Minnesota now. Bringing these exhibition flyers to the public was not an inexpensive proposition. Fair Board records show that after the Fair, Mars was issued two checks totaling $2500.00 and the Wright Company a check for $2400.00.[42]

To add an element of local interest, Fred Parker was hired to exhibit and fly his monoplane. Parker had flown in late August. While it is not known who approached whom, Parker's flights were reported by the Minneapolis and St. Paul newspapers and Fair officials certainly were aware of this local aviator. In

Exhibition pilot, Tom McGoey, poses for a portrait in his exhibition Curtiss D-II aircraft, reportedly somewhere in Minnesota during 1911. (Bob Lemm)

This "headless" Curtiss Pusher aircraft is about to fly an exhibition flight at the Freeborn County Fairgrounds at Albert Lea in 1912. The pilot is thought to be Art Smith. The term "headless" means that the elevator apparatus of the airplane does not project out in front of the ship, but is contained at the rear. (Otis Simonson)

any event, a Memorandum of Agreement between Parker and the Fair Board was concluded on 1 September, 1910, in which Parker agreed to exhibit his machine in a tent, the location of which and any admission charge to be determined by the Fair Board. As to flying demonstrations, Parker agreed to make one flight each day of the Fair between five and six p.m. and he would have one try only unless the Fair Board elected to give him more attempts. He was to take off from in front of the grandstand and circle the one mile racetrack at an average altitude of at least 40 feet.[43]

It appears, however, that Parker never got off the ground during the 1910 State Fair. He was to collect $75.00 a day for each day he flew, but there is no mention in State Fair financial records that he was ever paid and the daily press is also silent about flights by Parker. Minnesota's first home grown aviator was, unfortunately, not able to make a public reputation before the crowds of the State Fair.

The 1910 State Fair lasted for six days, from Labor Day, Monday, 5 September through Saturday the 10th. In addition to the holiday and the opening of the Fair, a National Conservation Congress was being hosted in St. Paul. Several political dignitaries were in town, and, of course, could not resist a speech to a crowd. And so it was on Monday that fairgoers were occupied by speeches from Governor Eberhart, Senator Knute Nelson, and finally President Taft, himself, while on Tuesday a Teddy Roosevelt appearance kept the crowd's attention. It was a good thing. Those who came to see flying saw a fizzle.

On Monday, Bud Mars made a short flight around the infield in front of the grandstand but went no higher than 60 feet. In attempting to show the crowd a Wright biplane in flight, A. L. Welsh got off alright but in negotiating a turn he was flipped by a wind gust (the Weather Bureau reported gusts of 24 m.p.h. that day) and nosed into the ground from a height of about 50 feet. His machine was wrecked, and Welsh's left ankle was severely cut by a bracing wire. It was miraculous that he wasn't hurt worse.[44] He was given hospital treatment and then retired to his quarters

at the Dykman Hotel, his flying finished for the duration of the Fair. The aircraft was so demolished that it could not be repaired despite the fact that the Wright people had brought a large supply of spare parts with them.[45]

This turn of events obviously put the Wright Company's contract in jeopardy, but they acted with alacrity. On receiving Welsh's explanatory telegram, the Wright firm immediately shipped a new aircraft from Dayton, Ohio, and then ordered a change of itinerary for their star pilot, Arch Hoxsey. In a career as short as it was spectacular, Hoxsey had become one of the best known aviators in the country.

Born in Illinois in 1884, he was mechanically inclined and in love with automobiles as were many early aviators. This led him to work as a mechanic and chauffeur for a wealthy financier, a job which landed him in Los Angeles. It was there at America's first great airshow in January, 1910, that he saw his first airplane and resolved to learn to fly.

He went to Dayton, approached the Wright brothers, and was accepted as a student. The Wrights had just gone into the exhibition flying business and had established a training program for their pilots at Montgomery, Alabama, to take advantage of a better climate than Ohio afforded. Hoxsey, along with another new student, A. L. Welsh, arrived there in April and their arrival made a total of five students who Orville Wright then taught to fly. In May, Hoxsey and Walter Brookins made several flights by moonlight which was probably the first night flying in history.

Hoxsey's first exhibition flying came in June, 1910, and for the next six months, he flew at cities and towns from New Jersey to California. He was skilled and fearless and quickly became known as a daredevil and the "King of the Air." Among other feats, he set a new world altitude record by climbing to 11,474 feet over California in December, established a duration flight record (3 hours, 16 minutes), took Teddy Roosevelt up for the first ex-Presidential airplane ride, and escaped numerous crashes with his body more or less intact.

In late December, 1910, Hoxsey flew at an air meet in Los Angeles where, ironically, his flying career had begun. On the last day of the year he was aloft performing a series of maneuvers when a strong gust hit him and evidently snapped major spars on his machine. The aircraft collapsed into an airborne mass of wood and canvas and plummeted straight down from 600 feet. Hoxsey was killed instantly. He was 26 years old and his calling as an aviator had lasted from January to December 1910.[46]

In St. Paul, the State Fair skies stayed clear but the early September winds continued to plague exhibition flights. On Tuesday, Mars got in one brief hop, but had engine trouble. On Wednesday, wind gusts of 35 m.p.h. were recorded, and both Mars and Parker kept their fragile machines on the ground. Thursday was more of the same. Mars was ready to fly, needing only a break in the winds, and the new Wright airplane had arrived from Dayton. Hoxsey, too, had come in from a Nebraska State Fair date at Lincoln. It is doubtless a commentary on the determination of these early aviators that Hoxsey, who had come to replace the injured Welsh, was himself not in top physical form.

Just two days before he came to St. Paul he had a mishap in Lincoln. While taking off from the infield of a small race track, which was surrounded by barns, a grandstand and tall trees, he collided with the side of a barn. His aircraft was wrecked but, of course, a new one was waiting in the Twin Cities. When he arrived, however, the *Minneapolis Journal* reported that Hoxsey "looks like he has a combination toothache and lost a fight with a hornet's nest. His left cheek is puffed, his left eye is closed, and he limps and wobbles."[47] Another source indicates that he "barely escaped death" in the accident.[48]

At least on Friday the bedeviling winds abated and in the light breezes of late afternoon both Hoxsey and Mars made splendid flights. Perhaps 10,000 people jammed the grandstand to finally see some flying, and they were rewarded with a first in Minnesota when they actually witnessed "two modern airships in action," a Curtiss and a Wright in the air at the same time.[49] Hoxsey, after coaxing a balky engine to life, took off from the racetrack and circled the Fairgrounds in a picture perfect flight. He attempted no stunts and kept the aircraft under absolute control, went up nearly 1200 feet, and landed back near the racetrack an impressive twenty-one minutes later.

Hoxsey had been up for five minutes when Mars cranked up his more powerful 8 cylinder Curtiss. His flight was shorter than Hoxsey's and he went no higher than 300 feet, but he also did a series of crowd pleasing low altitude dives and glides. He landed, slightly damaging his machine, and a few minutes later Hoxsey set down next to him.

Everybody loved it. The crowd waved hats, handkerchiefs, and canes and cheered themselves hoarse. Fair Board President, J. M. Underwood, ebulliently shook the pilots' hands saying "Boys, those were bully flights."[50] The *St. Paul Pioneer Press* sniffed that the flying at the June airshow had been "mere child's play in comparison," and then rhapsodized of Mars' "whenever the nervy aviator went by the grandstand, he appeared to be riding on a billow of air that would put the pink blush of shame on a deep blue wave of the sea."[51]

Comparing the performance of the two machines was an irresistible temptation. Clearly, the Wright aircraft had flown longer and gone much higher but the Curtiss was thought to be better behaved. The

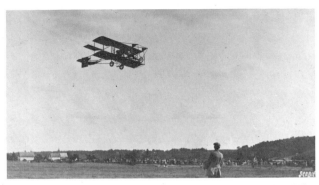

Aviator, Floyd E. Barlow, flies a Curtiss biplane at New Ulm in August of 1912, before a sizeable crowd. (Phil Vogt)

Minneapolis Journal judged that Mars' aircraft "did not look as stable and durable as did that of Hoxsey's, appearing in comparison more like a little bird. He moved faster and turned quicker than did that of the Wright make."[52]

On Saturday afternoon, the final day of the 1910 Fair, both aviators flew once more. Although it was a clear day in the low 70's, the wind was a nuisance again, coming from the southwest at 9 m.p.h. but with sharp gusts of up to 25 m.p.h. Hoxsey's first attempt, at 5 p.m., saw him unable to lift off, but Mars did make it. He circled the one mile race track in a flight of about 3 minutes. By then the two big propellers of Hoxsey's Wright were turning again and this time he got off into the sharp wind. Flying to the west end of the Fairgrounds he turned back to the east doing a few circles and figure 8's along the way. Over Machinery Hill he hung nearly motionless in the air for almost five minutes and landed after a flight of 16 minutes.[53]

Although the first four days of the Fair had been disappointing, Mars and Hoxsey had thrilled the public on the last two days. Both of these "menbirds" had held the crowd spellbound as they made their sensational flights. What seemed most impressive was the control they kept over their machines even as they had to fight the wind. Their flying was described as having the "ease and grace of a bird" and the "operators handled their machines with such ability that they were able to fly at will over any of the aerial courses despite the fact that the wind was rough and choppy at intervals."[54]

The two pilots, of course, did not linger to enjoy their new found Minnesota fame. There were contracts to be fulfilled in other places. Mars crated his Curtiss and headed for Rock Island, Illinois, where he began a five day fair date on Monday, 12 September. In later September he was in Helena, Montana, to fly at a Fair, when he decided to try to win a prize that had been offered for a flight over the Rocky Mountains. He crashed into a 7500 foot high summit but was found by a search party, uninjured beside his smashed aircraft. Back at Helena, the Governor of Montana gave him a gold watch with a fob containing a gold nugget and sent him on his way to Seattle where he flew a five day engagement in early October.

Hoxsey's next date was in Milwaukee at the Wisconsin State Fair. He left Minnesota on Saturday, arrived in Milwaukee on Sunday, and flew there from Monday through Friday. Although handicapped by poor grounds from which to fly, he performed well until the last day when his aircraft swerved on landing

This often-seen photo shows Alex Heine flying around the Minneapolis courthouse in 1913; the first recorded flight over the Loop area in a heavier-than-air machine. (Gerald Sandvick)

and ran into the crowd, hurting eight people. Hoxsey escaped injury.[55]

By mid-September, 1910, Minnesota had taken to the air. There would be more flying to thrill the crowds at future State Fairs and numerous home grown machines and the self taught builders and pilots would soon appear. Wilcox, Bennett, Johnson and Parker had pointed the way for the amateur inventors. It had, however, been some of the most illustrious names in early aviation that had riveted public interest on the new art of aviating. After the feats of Curtiss, Ely, Hoxsey, and the rest, neither entertainment nor transportation in Minnesota would ever be quite the same.

With the historic tenth year of the decade past, aviation activity began to spread to non-metropolitan communities but the State Fair would remain an annual focus for the latest in aviation's capability. The years between the 1910 airshow and the end of World War I saw little decrease in public enthusiasm to see the aviators perform their deeds. Notes of caution began to creep in as when, in 1911, the *Minneapolis Tribune* editorialized that people "probably have to discover more about flying."[56] The two national exhibition firms of Wright and Curtiss were in competition for the lucrative airshow contracts which sometimes led them to promise flight schedules that the pilots could not meet. There were also individual free-lance aviators, almost too numerous to count, who were eager to fly at county fairs. The aircraft of the time were not able to make long flights because of frequent engine troubles and generally frail construction. Crashes and forced landings were common and weather, too, was always a factor. The airplanes were, therefore, crated and shipped from town to town by train and time was necessary to rig the aircraft for flight once they arrived. Any adverse weather or mechanical problems resulted in delayed flights and missed train schedules and the real wonder is that these early exhibition pilots flew as often as they did.

Citizens of Fairmont and New Ulm experienced disappointments for just these reasons. In August, 1911, Curtiss pilot, William St. Henry, missed train connections in St. Paul and thus disappointed about 3000 spectators who had come from "as far away as Algona and Ft. Dodge, St. James, Lakefield and other towns" to see the first flight in Fairmont. St. Henry

arrived several hours late and the Commercial Club, having lost about $250.00 promoting the non-event, attached his airplane, and the local sheriff took possession and locked it up in a storeroom. Matters were worked out the next day, however, and St. Henry made one afternoon flight which ended in a forced landing due to a broken fuel line. He packed up and left for Marshalltown, Iowa, on the 5:12 train. The local paper told Farimont that the whole thing was the "enterprise of the Curtiss Exhibition Company and any disappointment must be laid to them alone." Apparently few people saw the delayed flight and the event was unprofitable as well as disappointing.[57]

In August, 1912, New Ulm was holding a celebration billed as "a homecoming and 50th anniversary of the Indian Massacre." Floyd Barlow, a Curtiss aviator and Iowa resident, made three successful flights on Wednesday, 21 August. He went on to Yankton, South Dakota, on the 23rd and 24th, and was to return to New Ulm for more flights on Sunday, the 25th. Wind delayed the Yankton flights and the newspaper account gives some idea of the complexities of scheduling and planning involved in the exhibition business. "In order to reach New Ulm for the flights on Sunday the 25th, it was necessary for him to leave Yankton at 7:40 p.m. on Saturday the 24th, reaching Minneapolis at 7:18 a.m. the next morning. Arrangements had been made...with the Minneapolis and St. Louis Railroad Company to attach a 50-foot baggage car to the first excursion train running in here on Sunday and to convey Mr. Barlow and his airship in that car." Since it took four hours to take down and set up the aircraft, and Barlow had missed all his train connections anyhow, he simply sent a telegram saying "Can't possibly fly New Ulm twenty-fifth. Could not catch train here."[58]

Thomas McGoey was a free-lance pilot from Grand Forks who was typical of the era. From August to October, 1911, he arranged appearances at fairs and celebrations at Hibbing, Sauk Center, Little Falls, Rochester, and Duluth. In early September, he flew for six minutes at Sauk Center but ran out of fuel and smashed through a fence when he force-landed. The same month he gave Rochester its first view of aviation at the Olmstead County Fair when he climbed to 3000 feet over the southern part of the city. On descent his engine quit and he force landed on railroad tracks, luckily sustaining no damage to himself or his ship. The newspaper accounts indicate the awe with which these early birdmen were watched because McGoey apparently "defied gravity...heedless of the great gap between himself and *terra firma*...in flights declaring the supremacy of man's mind over the forces of nature." The crowds were described as open mouthed and enthusiastic and McGoey as "but 32 years of age, young in years but old in skill and judgement."[59]

Flying in these pioneering years took other paths than local fairs and there was a great interest in establishing speed, altitude, and distance records. Minnesota was the starting point for one such distance record attempt, a flight from Minneapolis to New Orleans. The two cities are slightly over 1900 miles apart and when the flight was proposed, no aircraft had ever come close to flying that far. The idea originated with a group of businessmen who had formed the St. Louis Aero Club and in August, 1911, Spearman Lewis, representing that group, came to Minneapolis. His purpose was to present a proposal to H. A. Tuttle, the President of the Minneapolis Commercial Club. A prize of between $15,000 and $20,000 would be raised to pay an aviator to make a flight down the Mississippi. Cities along the way would contribute to the fund, and it was expected that business would prosper as thousands of people came to see the flyer land and takeoff as, town by town, he worked his way south. To add an element of practicality to the enterprise, a few pounds of mail would be carried.

As the northernmost major city on the great river, Minneapolis was the logical starting point and Tuttle agreed that the Commercial Club would raise $3000 by the second week in September. In mid-September it was announced that a total of $15,000 had been pledged by businessmen in Minneapolis; St. Louis; Lansing, Iowa; and Quincy and Cairo, Illinois.[60]

The aviator hired to make the flight was Hugh A. Robinson and there would seem to be several reasons for his selection. There were relatively few people who could fly in 1911 and Robinson was a prominent member of the Glenn Curtiss exhibition team. During 1910 he was one of the Curtiss pilots who had done pioneering work in building and flying "hydro-aeroplanes" as pontoon equipped aircraft were then known. The fact that the 30-year-old flyer was a Missouri native probably did not hurt his selection either.

The start of the flight was set for mid-October, a fact dictated by Robinson's heavy exhibition flying schedule which was typical of the showman flyers of the age. From mid-September to mid-October he made flights at McAlaster, Oklahoma; Williston, North Dakota; Chanute, Kansas; Dubuque, Iowa; Houghton Lake, Michigan; Evansville, Indiana; Sedalia, Missouri; Muskogee, Oklahoma; and St. Louis, Missouri.[61]

Soon after the whole plan was made public, a disagreement arose. Since he would fly a Curtiss "Hydro" aircraft, Robinson wanted to takeoff from the river. The Hydro was a standard Curtiss biplane of the period on which the wheels had been replaced by pontoons and it would not, therefore, alight on land. The promoters wanted a departure from lake Calhoun so that more of Minneapolis would be overflown with a commensurate increase in publicity. Robinson was darkly suspicious of getting too far from water but was finally convinced that so many lakes dotted the area that his safety margin would be preserved. He relented, but still planned to take a train ride along the river to inspect the route. "I have no idea how long a flight to New Orleans will take," Robinson observed, "I'll fly at around 1000 feet and can maintain 60 miles per hour."

The start was now set for October 13, a Friday. On the 8th, his aircraft was test flown at St. Louis and then dismantled, crated, and shipped by rail to Minneapolis. The aviator, himself, arrived at the Radisson Hotel on 10 October and announced that since his machine would carry 18 gallons of gasoline, which was good for about 200 miles, he hoped to make it to Prairie du Chien on the first day. A disturbing note was sounded when he said that New Orleans was slow

Tony Jannus does a low altitude turn for the camera with a paying passenger during sight-seeing hops from the Duluth Harbor in the summer of 1913. (Aero & Hydro Magazine, 9 August, 1913)

in coming up with their share of the money, but he declared himself ready to go as soon as he got the $3000 from Minneapolis.

On 11 October Robinson made a test flight of his reassembled airplane and an estimated 25,000 people ringed Lake Calhoun to see him go aloft for 13 minutes. The aircraft, emblazoned with the number 13 and the name "Minneapolis Makes Good," functioned perfectly.

The morning of Friday the 13th saw stiff winds; however at 9:00 a.m. Robinson lifted from the Lake. He circled for eight minutes, but it was terribly hard going and the winds forced him back down to the immense disappointment of the 35,000 citizens who had turned out to see the historic departure. At 1:00 p.m. Robinson, tired of waiting for the wind to abate, caught a taxi back to the Radisson. Near Summit and Hennepin the taxi collided with a streetcar and sustained substantial damage. The uninjured Robinson, whose day it had just not been, scrambled from the taxi and opined that the automobile was a terribly dangerous form of transportation.

After the bad luck of Friday the 13th, the weekend weather turned to fog and rain which persisted to Monday. Robinson busied himself fine tuning his aircraft. He made another brief test hop, strengthened the pontoons, installed a slightly larger gas tank, and waited for the weather to cooperate.

At last, on 17 October, the sun rose in a clear sky, a quick preflight check showed that all was ready. As the eight cylinder engine ticked flawlessly, Robinson shoved a roll of tape into his pocket and lifted from Lake Calhoun's surface at 9:02 a.m. Climbing to 1000 feet, he flew over St. Paul and set a course for Hastings. He passed over Red Wing at 10:05 and made Wabasha at 10:30. Shortly before 11:00 he ran out of fuel and landed on the River a few miles north of Winona. He had covered 110 miles in 89 minutes but the landing had damaged a pontoon. The rest of the day and all the next was spent making repairs in Winona.

The most spectacular day in Robinson's odyssey was Thursday, 19 October. Five thousand residents of the Winona area came to watch him takeoff shortly after

8:00 a.m. The crowd was treated to an unplanned bit of daring when, after avoiding a sightseeing boat, Robinson could not gain altitude and the Chicago and Northwestern Railroad bridge was looming in his path. His only choice was to fly under it, which took a bit of skill since the height from the water to the bridge deck was but 25 feet.

Robinson reached LaCrosse in 25 minutes and stopped long enough to drop off a small packet of mail and have coffee and rolls at a local cafe. The weather was clear with light breezes as he winged his way from LaCrosse toward Prairie du Chien. Although a bolt fell out of his steering system, the aircraft remained controllable and at Prairie du Chien he "dropped in as gracefully as a bird on the wing," had lunch, and proceeded with the business of flying down the Mississippi. Swirling air currents near Guttenburg, Iowa, created a momentary problem but by mid-afternoon he had landed at Dubuque, where he spent the night. He had flown an astonishing 160 miles in a single day.

The technical side of the flight was now going smoothly but disaster was looming on the financial side. After landing at Rock Island, Illinois, Robinson got word that the St. Louis promoters had not raised their promised $2000 and that several other cities seemed to be dragging their feet, too. Brief and bitter negotiations by telegraph led nowhere and on Saturday, five days and 380 miles from Minneapolis, Robinson flatly refused to fly another mile without pay and canceled the flight.

Minneapolis promoter, Tuttle, demanded a flight to New Orleans or a refund of his city's $3000. The St. Louis Aero Club professed shock at the aviator's "arbitrary action." For his part, Robinson refused to negotiate any further and ordered his airplane crated and shipped to Oklahoma, saying "my time can be more profitably spent in exhibition work than in a flight merely for glory."

The first attempt to fly the length of America's greatest of rivers thus ended abruptly and on a sour note. The problem had been that merchants along the way were mainly interested in the money spent by out of town folks coming in to see the airplane pass through. Businessmen, quite naturally, wanted Robinson to adhere to a set schedule. From the pilot's point of view, however, this was an impossible demand. Delays due to weather and mechanical problems were absolutely unavoidable. The delay in departing Minneapolis and further schedule slippage en route had rendered promises of arrival times meaningless. To Robinson, the businessmen in their respective cities had not kept their part of the agreement and to the businessmen, Robinson was not doing what he had promised to do. No one was happy.

In the end, though, bitterness between Robinson and at least the Minneapolis businessmen vanished. W. G. Nye of the Minneapolis Commercial Club said "we do not blame Robinson but we do blame A. B. Lambert (St. Louis Aero Club President) and Spearman Lewis, his representative, who told us all towns had been lined up."

On 23 October, the aviator released a statement explaining that the withdrawal of financial guarantees had made it impossible for him to pay expenses much less make a profit. In a personal telegram to Tuttle,

he praised Minneapolis' generosity saying "I didn't expect much but I expected to be able to pay my expenses. I want to thank Minneapolis for their kindness and I will carry Minneapolis' name on my ship indefinitely to show my appreciation."

The flight had fallen far short of its ambitious goal but, still, it had put Minnesota on the aviation map because of the national publicity given the flight. It had also been the first time that an airplane had been used to carry mail from town to town in the midwest. Perhaps more than anything, though, 1911 was still a tentative time for aviation, and the fact that such a feat was even tried was audacious. Getting as far as Rock Island wasn't bad.

In later years, Robinson said he regretted not finishing the flight and added that "as far as records were concerned, getting there alive was a record in itself. I was lucky to get through."[62]

Alex T. Heine was a Minneapolitan who became obsessed with learning to fly and became one of the earliest licensed aviators in the state. He worked as a machinist to earn money to attend a flight school in Chicago and, when it went bankrupt, a school in California. By 1913 he was building his own airplanes at a shop on Lake Street and 36th Avenue and in that year became the first homegrown pilot to make a large public splash.

In late 1913, Heine was using the parade grounds at Ft. Snelling as his landing field and was making so many flights that it was almost becoming routine, even to the point of making eight hops on 11 December and carrying a passenger on five of them. On the 12th he made the flight for which he will always be remembered when he circled the Minneapolis Courthouse Tower three times. Given the frequency of mechanical problems in that age, it was a courageous feat. As Heine said, "As long as you were over an open field you didn't mind so much but it wouldn't have been pleasant to have the plane tip over the buildings...I flew from the Fort to the Courthouse, around the Courthouse Tower three times and back again. It took me 18 minutes. The pigeons on the tower were scared to death. They flew out in fright. The roofs of all the buildings in town were crowded. It was quite an event."[63]

It was also 19 degrees below zero and the pilot sat in front of the engine in a completely exposed seat. The windchill Heine experienced is better left to the imagination.

Only two days later, Heine again made history when he took Mrs. Ida Vernon up for a ride. Probably the first woman in Minnesota to ride in an airplane, she and her husband were acquainted with Heine. She apparently said she would like a ride, at which her husband scoffingly bet that she would be afraid. With her two young sons in tow, she showed up at Ft. Snelling on a Saturday afternoon and told the surprised Heine that she wanted to go up. After failing to talk her out of it, Heine supplied Vernon with a stocking cap and set of goggles and made a brief circling flight to about 300 feet. Vernon was reported as being excited about it and her husband as "terror stricken."[64]

Although the various individual flights around the state received their share of attention and helped create an aviation conscious public, it was at the State

Fairs in St. Paul that the biggest names in aviation performed and the largest numbers of people saw and read about them. Because the 1910 flying at the fairgrounds had drawn such crowds, the Fair board continued to stage aviation events missing only 1913.

The contract for 1911 went to the Wright Company which agreed to supply "two Wright fliers fully equipped and in charge of two competent aviators, one of whom, having made a reputation during the past season."[65] It was a no fly, no pay contract in that the bottom line was payment to the Wright firm of a maximum of $4800.00 which would accrue at $200.00 per flight. A flight was defined as putting the machine in the air for at least 10 minutes and 200 feet altitude. The first three days were sodden and muddy and saw only two flights. The last three days were better and 12 flights were made. The two aviators were the well-known Howard Gill and Frank Coffyn, the latter by now a veteran who had gotten flying lessons from Orville Wright himself.

Neither of their first attempts was auspicious. Coffyn encountered gusty winds and a balky engine and crashed. With thousands watching from Machinery Hill, Coffyn stood up and yanked the control levers in a desperate effort to regain control before his crash. He was unhurt and when asked, "Were you fairly close to death?" he replied, "We always are."[66]

Gill needed helpers to push his machine through the mud on takeoff. He made a brief ascent and needed four men to push him out of the mud on landing. Both men flew again the next day and both experienced engine failures but no crashes. The attitude of these aviators was summed up by Gill, who said of his engine failure, "we have to get used to little thrills... Those who stick in this game have to become accustomed to nerve-wracking experiences."[67] The last three days of the Fair saw enthusiastic crowds, several good flights of up to 14 minutes, a photographer being taken for a ride, both planes in the air at the same time, and comments by Governor Adolph O. Eberhart. The Governor allowed that he was greatly interested in aviation "for I believe some day it will be practical."[68]

The contract for the 1912 Fair shows the interesting trend of Curtiss and the Wrights no longer having the field to themselves and a corresponding drop in the

Although poor quality, this Jackson County Fair photo shows a Bleriot-type aircraft performing an exhibition in 1915. (Bob Johnson)

aviators fees. The National Aeroplane Company got the contract, agreed to furnish three aircraft (a Curtiss, a Wright, and a French Nieuport) for $2800.00. Since they made a total of 17 flights, the pay was $164.70 per ascent. The pilots that were sent had a distinctly international air about them; American W. C. Robinson, Marcell Tournier from France, and Paul Studenski, born of Polish parents in St. Petersburg, the then capital of Russia. The latter had learned to fly in 1910 at French pioneer Louis Bleriot's school and had come to the United States in 1911. The exhibition pilots continued to keep hectic schedules and in late August and early September, Studenski flew at Owatonna, spent a week at the Iowa State Fair, did five days in St. Paul, and went on to South Dakota. Several days were bedeviled by strong winds but the pilots made flights of up to 6000 feet and 15 minutes. Studenski crashed on the first and fifth days of the Fair. On the latter, he had a near mid-air collision with Robinson, ran out of gas, and flipped over on landing. Tournier startled the crowd on one landing by simply flying directly into the large canvas hangar that had been erected to shelter the airplanes, "as if it were an auto entering a garage."[69]

Possibly concerned with the spectre of a jaded audience, the Fair board made a one-day contract for 12 September, 1914, with arguably the most famous pilot currently working. Lincoln Beachey had been trained by the Curtiss team in 1910, but by 1914 he had his own exhibition business and was a veteran of the circuit. His specialty was looping and he was the first aviator to accomplish the maneuver. The contract called for three flights worth $1000.00. "On the loop-the-loop flight he is to loop-the-loop at least three times. On the fancy flying flight he is to race an automobile..."[70] He seems to have more than entertained the crowd as it was reported that he "performed his looping-the-loop feat" and that he also "shut off his engine at a great height and dropped through space upside down" until he flipped upright and made a "graceful landing" before the spellbound crowd.[71]

When Lincoln Beachey left Minnesota he had only five more months to live. In February, 1915, he was performing at the Panama-pacific Exposition in San Francisco and, of course, doing his trade mark loops and a new vertical S maneuver. He was flying a newly built experimental monoplane which went into an uncontrollable dive. When he tried to pull back to level out, loud cracking noises were heard and the crowd saw both wings collapse just before the aircraft hit the bay at high speed. The wreckage was quickly recovered by divers from the battleship *Oregon* and "thousands of people watched in silence from the

Lincoln Beachey poses with two of his mechanics in this photo from 1914. Beachey was in Minnesota to perform at the Minnesota State Fair. (Gerald Sandvick)

shore and many removed their hats when Beachey's body was lifted up."[72]

In September, 1915, Europe had been at war for a year and the airplane as a weapon had been demonstrated in France. Reflecting public curiosity, the State Fair contracted with Patterson Aviators of Detroit to stage the "War of the Nations" in which mock dogfights, bombing and ground attacks were performed. These were replete with much smoke, fire, and assorted explosions, all of which, it was hoped in the company brochure, would cause the spectators to shudder and gasp, "their hearts almost stop beating."

For flying of a more pacific nature, the Fair board hired Art Smith who was 19 but already famous, and a 28 year old native of Pennsylvania, DeLloyd Thompson. Smith was to be paid $3000.00 for an extremely detailed program that included "10 loop-the-loops, fancy turns, vertical drops, rollover loops, wing slides, tail slides, flying upside down with hands off the steering wheel and arms outstretched." He was also to make night flights with fireworks attached to his air-

The first airplane to fly in Jackson County. For 1915, this home-built tractor biplane looks almost modern compared to its contemporaries. Flown by Frank Kastory of Chicago, who was paid $675 for the exhibition flight. (Bob Johnson)

craft. Art Smith would clearly be a busy and endangered young man.[73]

He did, however, live up to expectations. Although one day of flying was lost to rain, Smith made several spectacular flights including one where he did 17 loops. One headline, suggesting that the principle of *sic transit gloria* was still alive, read "Beachey Outdone by Young Flyer," and indicated that Smith had "tossed, turned, and tumbled with abandon in what is conceded to be the most daring flights ever witnessed at the Fair." DeLloyd Thompson arrived for the last day of the Fair and had a bad time of it. His first landing ended with failed brakes and encounter with a fence, while the second flight was highlighted by a stopped engine and forced landing north of the fairgrounds. On his third flight, he did win a race with an automobile.[74]

The last two State Fair flying shows before the end of the war were relatively tame affairs. DeLloyd Thompson came back as the lone aviator in 1916 and acquitted himself for the previous year with a series of looping and diving flights, both in the day and at night. The 1917 Fair was a disappointment when pilot Lawrence Brown, identified as a former flyer with the Carranza Army in Mexico, had his aircraft damaged in shipment. It was not until the last day of the events that he was able to make two modest flights.[75] More on the 1917 State Fair in Chapter Three.

In the years between Minnesota's first flying and the end of the war, the assorted exhibition pilots had brought aviation to the direct view of hundreds of thousands of people. Advances in aviation technology would allow the barnstormers and thrill show flyers of the 1920s and 1930s to greatly eclipse what the aviators of the pioneering years could do. Except that they had done it first and paved the way for what would follow.

For the Shell Prairie Fair at Park Rapids in the 1910s, this early aviator posed with a troup of colorfully-dressed carnival performers. (The Murphy Museum of Photographica, St. Cloud.)

MINNESOTA AVIATION ACTIVITY DURING THE GREAT WAR

In 1914, at the beginning of the Great War, though America professed a policy of isolationism, preferring to stay out of a foreign conflict, events began forcing the U. S. Government to accelerate the program of arming itself and building its military strength.

In Minnesota, the entire Army National Guard was federalized early in 1917 and sent to training bases in other states to prepare for overseas duty. Governor Joseph A. Burnquist authorized the establishment of the Minnesota Home Guard as a replacement to protect iron ore mines, docks, and other strategic facilities within the State, as well as to be available for local emergencies. Like every other state, Minnesota began to mobilize and train manpower. One of the more aggressive training grounds was the Dunwoody Institute of Minneapolis.

Dunwoody Institute was founded in February of 1914 with an endowment from the estate of William Hood Dunwoody, who had been vice president of the Washburn-Crosby Milling Company, Chairman of the Board of Northwestern National Bank and a Director of the Great Northern Railroad. It had been Dunwoody's life dream to build an industrial institute in the Minneapolis area patterned after the Stout School at Menomonie, Wisconsin. He did not live to see his dream mature, but the school did open in the Fall of 1915 in temporary quarters at the old Central High School in Minneapolis while a suitable building was being erected in the downtown area.

In the Fall of 1916, classes began in a new building located across the road from the Minneapolis Parade Grounds (known simply as The Parade). During that school year, classes were given in telephone technology, auto mechanics, and the printing trades. Baking courses were offered for men of draft eligibility who were then encouraged to enlist in the Army as fully-qualified bakers. Dunwoody was listed as an official induction station.

In April of 1917, Dunwoody officials, under the leadership of Charles A. Prosser, offered the Navy Department a plan for the duplication of classes similar to those being taught at the Annapolis Naval Academy. The Navy Department gratefully accepted this offer, and by June, no less than 1,000 enlisted Naval cadets from the Great Lakes Station in Chicago were undergoing training in an expanded curriculum of courses for electricians, shipfitters and shipwrights, carpenters, coppersmiths, boilermakers, blacksmiths, machinists, radio operators, painters, printers, and clerks.

In June, Admiral Robert Peary visited the Twin Cities to select a Naval Aviation training site. Among those areas under consideration were the State Fairgrounds, Speedway Field, and a site near Lake Minnetonka where access to water would provide a realistic training scenario. Walter Bullock was hired to "bomb" the city with leaflets announcing the admiral's luncheon with city officials.

A Naval Aviation section was not officially set up at any of the Minneapolis sites, but the training of Naval Aviation technicians was begun at Dunwoody under the sponsorship of the Minneapolis Aero Club's Aerial Coast Patrol, (a citizen's group of pilots who drew their funding from the American Power Boat Association's annual powerboat regatta on the Mississippi River through the Twin Cities). Naval technician training was able to progress through the Navy's donation of a Wright-Martin torpedo bomber for classroom work.

An interesting sidelight is that one of the original Curtiss exhibition aircraft, an experimental monoplane, flown briefly by Lincoln Beachey at the June 1910 Minnesota airshow, was also part of the Dunwoody classroom teaching aids. The Aero Club had acquired it following Beachey's death in February, 1915, and turned it over to Dunwoody.

In February, 1918, when the Naval unit was designated part of the Naval Reserve Flying Corps, a more senior officer was needed, and Commander Warren J. Terhune replaced Ensign Colby Dodge. Terhune's career would take a turn for the worse following the war, when as the Governor of American Samoa in the Pacific, he would be charged with scandal, leading to his suicide in November, 1920. A Naval Board of Inquiry later exonerated him of all wrongdoing.

While the Naval training was going on, Dunwoody was also training Army technicians. From the original baker's courses, the school had branched into aviation technical trades. The first group of 1200 Army men filled the school's halls and classrooms. Resident trainees overflowed hastily erected barracks next door and men had to be quartered at posh downtown Minneapolis hotels.

In December, the U. S. Army allocated two Curtiss Jennys to provide demonstration flights for the trainees, basing the planes at the Parade. On 23 December, 1917, the *Minneapolis Tribune* noted that pilot, Captain A. W. Farrow, went aloft over the city, demonstrating dives and rolls, and at one point, "swerved sharply around the machine of Walter Bullock who was also in the air."

AIR SERVICE MECHANICS SCHOOL

As America entered The Great War in 1917, the country was pitifully prepared to aid the international conflict with qualified aviators or aircraft. The U. S. could muster only 52 officers in the Aviation Section of the Signal Corps, (of which only 35 could qualify as Military Aviator,) and 1,100 enlisted men as support personnel. The Army was operating only four flying fields, and less than 1,000 military aircraft had been built in the preceding eight years, those mostly under contract to British and French firms.

Military planners in America and in the governments of its allies envisioned fleets of aircraft darkening the skies of Europe to turn the tide of battle in their favor. Before that dream could come true, planes would have to be designed, manufactured and shipped; thousands of pilots and tens of thousands of mechanics would have to be recruited and trained. Camps, depots, schools, and flying fields would have to be built.

With an initial allocation by the War Department of $55 million dollars, to be spent on military aviation, preparations were made to undertake the necessary manufacturing and training. It was soon apparent that this money was but a drop in the bucket compared to the real need. A bill was finally passed by Congress that granted $640 million to the War Department. The plan was to have 5,000 pilots and 50,000 mechanics in France by the spring of 1918. The plans called for 25 flying fields and the immediate establishment of two large mechanics schools, one at Kelly Field in San Antonio, Texas; and the other in St. Paul, Minnesota. Each school was to be capable of graduating 5,000 men a month!

The school in St. Paul came as a direct outgrowth of the work done previously by the Dunwoody Institute in Minneapolis, where a few Naval aircraft mechanics had been training since February, 1917. As the numbers increased at the Federal government's urging, Dunwoody itself would be too small, so a new and larger facility was sought. The huge automobile warehouse of the Willys-Overland Company on University Avenue in St. Paul was selected. On 12 February, 1918, Dunwoody was authorized to begin training two thousand men per month at the St. Paul location. By the time the building was remodeled to accommodate the training, the government had assumed control of the entire operation.

The school was originally called the Aviation Mechanics Training School, then changed to United States Army Air Service Mechanics School. Major Walter R. Weaver, formerly of Wilbur Wright Field in Dayton, Ohio, took over as commandant. The four story building was large enough for eighteen acres of classrooms, drill halls and shops. Outside the building, twenty-three acres of land were developed to include barracks, motor test shed, and welding shop. Other enterprises such as barber shops, confectioneries, pool hall, and laundry were soon erected or moved into adjacent buildings in the neighborhood.

In the Overland Building shops, students were assigned to one of three repair squadrons and were required to study up to fourteen separate courses. The three units included the 864th, 871st, and 872nd Depot Repair Squadrons. The 864th curriculum included carpentry, vulcanizing, electrical, cop-

persmithing, welding, instrument repair, machine shop, and sheet metal; the other two squadrons were dedicated as aero engine mechanics. Drill, physical training, and general military knowledge also were required subjects. A huge cafeteria and hospital quarters occupied portions of the main building.

Across the street, the huge Illinois Steel Warehouse was leased, to be used for further classrooms. An advance flying field was established on the Earle Brown Farm between Osseo and Camden, north of the city of Minneapolis. Mechanics would be sent there for final field training on flying aircraft and given familiarization flights in Jenny aircraft. At the Overland Building, Liberty, Hisso, and Le Rhone rotary aero engines were used for engine class instruction, while LWF aircraft fuselages were brought in for practical construction and repair applications. In

Propeller repair class showing students working at repair and carving new propellers. (The Propeller)

The Aero Exhibit Building on Machinery Hill at the Minnesota State Fairgrounds, 1918. (The Propeller)

One of the engine mechanics classroom bays in the Overland Building. Note the students working on Hisso and Le Rhone engines. (The Propeller)

The Overland Building, University Avenue, St. Paul, at the height of usage by the Air Service Mechanics School. The building today houses FBS Mortgage Company. (The Propeller Volume 1, Number 28)

September of 1918, the school staged a massive display in the Aero Exhibition Building at the Minnesota State Fairgrounds, with elaborate sets portraying each of the trades learned by the students.

By the end of 1918, 3,000 student mechanics were in training at any one given time. Men were arriving from all over the country. Instructors had been recruited from civilian occupations, many from Dunwoody Institute. The school was efficient and well-managed. Its cadre produced a series of seventeen training manuals for the various subjects, the most advanced texts of their day, and still considered definitive on their subject matter. Copies of any of these are collectors items today.

On 11 November, 1919, the Armistice between Germany and the Allied forces was signed. The construction of work at the Mechanics School was immediately halted, all new recruiting was cancelled, and those students still ungraduated were sent to Kelly Field to finish out their training or given immediate discharge. The Overland Building and other adjacent facilities were quickly returned to their civilian owners. One hundred thirty-six aero engines were crated and sold to civilian operators such as Marvin Northrop and Clarence Hinck.

Information for the above material was obtained from the following sources:

The Propeller booklet, Volume 1, Number 28, 1919, final issue of the weekly newspaper by the same name, printed at the Air Service Mechanics School, St. Paul, MN.

Jerold E. Brown, *From The Ground Up, Air Planning in the Office of the Chief Signal Officer 1917-1918*, Aerospace Historian, Air Force Historical Society, Fall, 1986.

Holbrook and Appel, *Minnesota in the War With Germany*, "The Air Service Mechanics School," Minnesota Historical Society, Volume One, Chapter IX, pp. 219-234, 1928.

MINNESOTANS IN THE GREAT WAR IN THE AIR

Many men from Minnesota offered their services to the Allied cause during the years before America's involvement in the war through the British Royal Flying Corps, the Royal Canadian Flying Corps and the French Lafayette Escadrille and later Lafayette Flying Corps. They also volunteered in later years with the U. S. Naval Air Service and the Army Air Service, seeing duty as pursuit or bomber pilots, and observers.

Only three Minnesotans are listed in the official records of the Lafayette Flying Corps as having become Aces. Lt. Murray Guthrie of Minneapolis was credited with six aerial victories; Lt. Martinus Stenseth of Twin Valley, Minnesota, credited with six; and Lt. George Furlow of Rochester with five.

Second Lt. Lawrence T. Wyley of Duluth, is recognized as having shot down four enemy aircraft, as is David Haskins Backus of St. Paul. Backus enlisted through the Norton-Harjes Ambulance

Corps, and from there, found his way into the French Aviation Service, eventually to the 94th Aero Squadron, (American Air Service unit commanded by Captain Eddie Rickenbacker). Backus earned the Croix de Guerre and the Distinguished Flying Cross (DSC).

Lt. Douglas Kennedy of Minneapolis, one of three members of the *Minneapolis Journal* newspaper staff to enlist, claimed three aerial victories as a member of the British Royal Flying Corps. He was once wounded by anti-aircraft fire five miles behind German lines, but managed to glide back across to safety, breaking several bones in the resulting crash-landing. His mates from the newspaper, who enlisted with him, included Lt. Ralph Gracie of Bemidji, who was credited with two victories prior to being shot down over the North Sea in July, 1918; and Lt. Warren Chreiman, who was shot down, taken prisoner, and later escaped back to his own lines.

Lt. Raymond O. Seevers was credited with three aerial victories, and his unit claimed 25 additional, behind German lines. He led the US 139th Aero Squadron as unit Commander.

In the Great War, more so than any conflict to follow, it was often impossible to confirm a victory. In the fighting behind German lines, very little information would be announced and records of the German squadrons were not available until much later. Aerial victories were further obscured by the fact that a number of squadron mates often fired at the same enemy aircraft during a single engagement, all making claims for the victory.

Lt. Winston E. Hitt of St. Paul claimed to have shot down fifteen German aircraft as a member of the Royal Canadian Flying Corps. The records for this accomplishment has not come to light, but among the more unusual aspects of Hitt's service, was the claim that he had been shot down once each by German Aces, Oswald Boelcke, and Max Immelmann.

Other Minnesotans credited with one or more aerial victories include: 2nd Lt. Irving P. Corse of Minneapolis, one aircraft shot down and one German balloon; Lt. Lloyd A. Ruth of Minneapolis, single victory as an observer from the 91st U. S. Aero Squadron on the day before the Armistice.

Many other Minnesotans fought in the air war, but with different luck. The first Minnesotan killed in aerial combat is listed as Navy Ensign Thomas N. McKinnon, lost in a seaplane accident near Dunkirk. Lieutenants Wold and Chamberlain, for whom the Minneapolis airport would later be named, were both killed in action near Chateau-Thierry. Ernest Groves Wold, from Minneapolis, was killed while flying a reconnaissance mission when his ship was struck by anti-aircraft fire. He was reportedly the holder of a world time-to-climb altitude record, having ascended to 20,000 feet in 35 minutes during his training in the Lafayette Flying Corps. Cyrus Foss Chamberlain was killed by bullets from a German aircraft in 1918, while on patrol as a pursuit pilot.

Lt. Charles K. Johnson was killed during a bombing raid in August, 1918, while a member of the British Royal Flying Corps. When his squadron was attacked, Johnson went back to the aid of a comrade whose plane was under siege by the enemy. Both aircraft were shot down.

The air war took a toll on the observers in reconnaissance aircraft. Observer James Higgins of Rochester was wounded during a bombing mission over Ostende-Zeebrugge, Belgium. His pilot managed to crash-land in Allied territory, but died in the attempt. Higgins was hospitalized through the end of the war. Edward B. Cutter of Anoka was a casualty while acting as an observer, as was Lt. Richard Moody, who was later posthumously awarded the French Croix de Guerre. Lt. Irving Roth of Minneapolis was killed during an aerial combat near Etain, France, and Lt. Aaron M. Rosenbleet was shot down, captured, and interned in a German prison camp. He escaped to make his way back to Allied lines.

Pilot Manderson Lehr's death in July, 1918 was recounted in a letter to his parents by his observer who lived through the mission, "It was 10:00 morning. We were told the Boche were coming and were ordered to make a flight between Chateau-Thierry and Dormans. The weather was bad. Rain was falling in torrents. The clouds were at 2,000 feet. There was only one thought in our minds, however, to get the Boche, so we set out. Three airplanes, the Commander of the squadron at the head, we at the right. Your son was my pilot.

"They first attacked us from the rear and the left, I released a torrent of shot at them and caught one of the machines on the wing. I hit a second off the rear, and in another second the plane was nose diving. During this time, a third had placed itself beneath our tail about 50 feet,and it gave us terrific shell fire. I released to look at him (your son). His hands were off the controls and his head was bowed. By this time, the artillery fire against us was unbearable and the airplane was burning. I was wounded too, but managed to steer to the edge of the forest where American soldiers released me." (*Minneapolis Journal* 15 December, 1918)

One of the more publicized local figures to achieve fame for his aerial exploits during the Great War was Rufus Randall Rand, Jr., son of the vice president of the Minneapolis Gas Company. Rand was mechanically inclined and is rumored to have begun driving the family auto at age 10. As a teenager, he became interested in railroading and aviation. He studied at Yale University, and later Williams College in Massachusetts where he helped organize an Aero Club. In 1916, he earned a flying diploma at the U. S. Army's aviation school at Mineola, Long Island,

New York, becoming the first licensed pilot from Minnesota.

In April of 1917, with U. S. having declared war on Germany, Rand joined the Norton-Harjes Ambulance Service, a branch of the American Field Service. From this organization, like many other Americans, he joined the French Army and transferred into the French Flying Corps. He progressed rapidly through the training and with 26 logged hours, was given his flying certificate. He then went through further training and was assigned to squadron N.153 of the Lafayette Flying Corps, a front-line squadron. His first combats were flown in the newest French aircraft, the Morane-Saulnier AI, a monoplane. In the first 22 hours of flying, he had been involved in six combat engagements, during which his guns had jammed on three occasions. Following a bombing raid on his airdrome by a German raider, he and two others took off and strafed German troops on the front lines in revenge.

When the Morane fighter was withdrawn from service following structural problems, the unit received the Spad 7, unexcelled in combat and able to absorb an enormous amount of punishment. In the following three months, Rand was shot down three times, but the strength of the Spad saved him each time. During this period, he managed to claim two probable victories. When Rand's patrol shot down a German reconnaissance aircraft, each member of the squadron was given partial credit. Thus with only a single partial victory, and seven more unconfirmed claims, Rand was mustered out in November, 1918, holding the rank of adjutant, and owning the French Croix de Guerre with Palm and Star. He returned home with a new wife, a nurse he had met during his tour of duty.

Following the war, Rand was active in the Minneapolis business community, helping to start the Greyhound Bus Company, and constructing the Rand Tower office building in Minneapolis. When World War II broke out, Rand returned to the air as a major in the U. S. Army Air Force to participate in the landings in North Africa and later served as executive officer at a bomber base in England. When World War II was over, he again joined the business community and became president of the Minneapolis Gas Company. He was elected state commander of the American Legion and served as a regent of the University of Minnesota.

WALTER BULLOCK

*W*ALTER R. BULLOCK was born 5 August, 1899 in Buffalo, New York. As a young boy, Walter moved around the country following the needs of his father's stockbrokerage business. In 1908, the family lived in Dallas, Texas, then moved to Macon, Missouri where Walt and his older brother, Robert, attended Blees Military School. The next move was to South Bend, Indiana, and in 1911, the family ended up in Minneapolis. Walter was the youngest of three brothers, but the family was well-disposed and Walt had the luxury of a more-than-modest weekly allowance.

During that first year in Minneapolis, young Bullock learned of the exhibition flight of Hugh Robinson, the Curtiss exhibition pilot, who was to take mail from Minneapolis downriver to New Orleans, starting from Lake Calhoun. Probably because of the publicity, Walter started building model airplanes at the tender age of twelve. He concentrated very hard on detailing his models with an inherent sense of precision. This craftsmanship was to show itself in later full-sized creations.

The event that forged Bullock's future occurred on 12 January, 1913. As he was leaving the Emerson

Schoolhouse in Minneapolis, on his way to the Maryland Hotel, where the family was living, young Bullock was stunned by the sight of an aeroplane buzzing over the city. The aeroplane was a home-built, Curtiss-type machine being flown by Minneapolis native, Alex T. Heine, a railroadman turned aeronautist. That day, as Heine circled the Minneapolis Courthouse, the first person to ever fly over that city's loop district, it made a deep impression.

Bullock soon began to make pilgrimages to Heine's shop near Lake Street in South Minneapolis, to watch aeroplane building and tinkering in progress. At intervals, when a certain amount of tinkering was completed, Heine would take his flying machine to a large field south of the administration building at Fort Snelling, where he would assemble it and take it up for short flights. Bullock soon considered himself the official "watchman" for the project, helping where he could, and keeping the sightseers from trampling the pieces and helping themselves to souvenirs. As a reward for his dedication and help, Heine would often allow Bullock to stand behind him on the framework of the machine as he hopped it into the air. When Heine sold his first airplane to Art Bourns and began to build another at his shop, Bullock continued to hang around. In later years, Bullock remembered that Heine loved building airplanes even more than flying them.[76]

Bullock continued his model-building career in 1914, building a beautiful model Curtiss seaplane and in 1915 he had begun putting his weekly allowance and his building skill to work producing a full-sized Curtiss-type aeroplane in the backyard on Aldrich Avenue, where his family had recently moved. His interest had shifted to real airplanes and his aeroplane project took shape slowly but surely as he spent many hours in careful craftsmanship. Later that year, when the family moved to Pillsbury Avenue in Minneapolis, he brought the project with him and continued with the woodworking.

On Labor Day weekend that year, the Twin City Motor Speedway and the American Automobile Association promoted the first big race at the brand-new high-banked concrete speedway near Fort Snelling. Part of the grand-opening ceremonies included the appearance of aviatrix, Ruth Law, with her Curtiss Pusher airplane. While interested in the in-

augural racing event, Bullock was even more interested in Law's biplane, and Ruth Law became his instant idol. He spent the race weekend sitting by the flying machine and watching Ruth. He made friends with her and her mechanic, Joe Westover (who was to become a Minnesota Air Guard pilot several years later).

Following the race weekend, Bullock returned to his backyard project, which by now was beginning to cause some concern to his parents. Indeed, it was getting far enough along that they could see it would be finished soon. This situation required Bullock's father to make a serious decision. Either he must send Bullock to a bonafide flying school where he could get the benefit of learning to fly under proper conditions, or the lad might just try to teach himself how to fly with unknown consequences.

Thus it was that during the summer of 1916, without having graduated from high school, Bullock enrolled in the Curtiss Flying School at Newport News, Virginia, with his father's blessing (and probably some of his father's funding). He arrived there 16 October, 1916, and after 8 hours and 6 minutes of instruction, was ready for his solo flight test. He made three flights and brought his machine to a stop within 150 feet of a designated spot, which was the standard Curtiss test requirement. He also drove the plane to a height of a mile and a quarter, (the school requirement was 329 feet). His records indicate that he flew at the rate of $1 per minute and his time at that point had cost $686. Being licensed at age 17 made him the youngest pilot in the United States. Art Smith, another early Minnesota pilot was 19 when he was licensed.[77]

At the Curtiss School, Bullock's instructor was James (Jimmy) Johnson, but he took instruction also from Bert Acosta, Stewart Cogswell, Victor Vernon and Walter Lees. His test was flown in a 90 h.p. OX-5 Jenny on 29 November, 1916. He was issued FAI license number 630. (Federation Aeronautique International; the world licensing body at that time, based in France). Bullock's CAA license was issued in 1925 with the number 605.

Bullock was later issued Minnesota Aviator's license #9 by Minnesota Aeronautics Commissioner, Ray Miller.

On his return to the Minneapolis area, Bullock

Walter Bullock's interest in flying began at an early age. When most teenagers were busy with bicycles and scooters, Bullock began constructing a full sized airplane in his family's backyard. This photo dates from 1915. (Walter Bullock family via John Hankinson)

Bullock at the controls of his first Curtiss Pusher airplane, purchased in Pawtucket, Rhode Island, and rebuilt at the Curtiss School at Newport News, Virginia. In this 1916 view, Bullock, only 17 years old, is already flying exhibitions in the East. (Bullock family)

Bullock's Curtiss Pusher, returned to Minnesota for the winter of 1916-1917, here being operated from the ice of Lake Calhoun in Minneapolis. (Bullock family)

advertised for an OX-5 engine for his yet-to-be-finished home built Pusher. He had also heard about an airplane at Pawtucket, Rhode Island, that was for sale, and he talked his father into buying it. The plane was supposed to be complete and ready to fly, but when he went to pick it up, Bullock found the wings needing complete rebuilding. He brought this Curtiss plane back to the Curtiss school and shops at Newport News where the work was done.[78]

Following the rebuilding, Bullock had the plane shipped back to Minneapolis. In the winter of 1916-1917, he reassembled it and brought it to Lake Calhoun, in the heart of the city, where he began flying it from the frozen surface. One of his first riders was Charles "Speed" Holman.

To rig the Curtiss for balanced operation, Bullock wired an iron weight behind the front wheel. In later life, Bullock revealed that it came loose one day and crashed through the roof of a nearby home. It did no personal damage but Bullock's father had to pay for the roof repairs. The incident also led to the first aviation legislation in Minnesota with the residents of the neighborhood demanding that Senator Wm. F. Brooks, then President of the Aero Club of Minneapolis, introduce a bill to furnish protection to property owners by "regulating the methods of flyers."[79]

The Minneapolis Park Board also looked askance at this operation from a city lake for reasons of safety and persuaded Bullock to cease activities. Before

Walter Bullock sweeps in for a landing on Lake Calhoun over the Lake Street bridge spanning the channel to Lake of the Isles. (Bullock family)

the winter ended, Bullock had left; but not before making a dead-stick landing on the ice and breaking up the airplane. He had already decided to purchase a J-1 Standard, so he brought the Pusher's fuselage home, but left the wings, which eventually slipped into the water as the ice thawed in the spring. Perhaps somewhere at the bottom of Lake Calhoun, the remnants of the Pusher's wings still exist.

1917 was an active year for the young aviator. With the coming of spring, Bullock decided to go into the exhibition flying business. It was being done by others across the country with profitable results. He opted for a tour of the Northeast, beginning in Massachusetts in March. His early exploits included an exhibition at Framingham, where he nearly lost control of his ship in a wind gust; then an episode at Cambridge, near Boston, where he had contracted to make a flight over Fenway Park, where the Boston Braves Baseball team was playing. Bullock landed his Standard biplane, on a local beach; planning to leave it there for the night prior to the exhibition. Local citizens who knew nothing of the deal, discovered it, and called the police. Fortunately for Bullock, they did this instead of stripping it to the bones. When Bullock arrived the next morning, the police were dutifully standing guard waiting for the culprit to show up. Everything was settled, if not forgiven, when Bullock produced his contract with the local Chamber of Commerce.[80]

In June of 1917, Bullock returned to Minnesota. That month, the State Fairgrounds was the site of a large aviation show. Walt Bullock's idol, Ruth Law, would be there to stage an exhibition. On the 23rd, after dropping U. S. Savings Bond literature over the cities, Bullock landed at the fairgrounds. His landing was a bouncer. A few minutes later, when he met Ruth Law, who had witnessed the landing, she put her arm around his shoulder and admonished him, "that's all right, sonny, you'll learn." Because he admired her so much, he remembered this incident for the rest of his life, and enjoyed retelling the story.

The fourth of July saw Bullock flying an exhibition at Stillwater, Minnesota. Since Stillwater had no flying field or place to land, he fulfilled his contract by taking off and landing from a bluff on the Wisconsin side of the St. Croix River. Another exhibition was flown at the County Fair at Canby, Minnesota, with the following results: The flyer's contract called for him to be paid a fee of $500 for the exhibit. After he'd been paid, the Fair Board discovered that other fliers had been giving the same performance in other communities for nothing more than the money they picked up hauling passengers after the exhibition. They demanded that Bullock turn over the proceeds from his passenger rides, but he refused and came away with his pockets stuffed with money. Bullock knew the Fair Board was pretty annoyed about it, and claimed that was the reason they didn't ask him back for 50 years.[81]

In late July, Bullock again shipped his Standard to the East Coast. This time he began a barnstorming trip through New Hampshire, starting at Manchester where he had a contract with the Red Cross. Luck was not with him on this trip. Climbing out of the

In the spring of 1917, Bullock lined up exhibition flights across the country. This view shows the aircraft crated for shipping to the next exhibition site. Flying between shows was impractical in those days. (Bullock family)

fairgrounds in a strong wind, he had to make a low-level turn, and was caught by a gust of wind that slammed him back onto the ground, wiping out his landing gear. This repaired, his tour continued in August at Hamilton, Ohio, then at Ionia, Michigan for a County Fair the 15th through 18th. There he dropped an itinerant parachutist from his Standard. The chutist landed on some telephone wires and had to cut himself from the hanging chute straps. The chute belonged to Bullock and he hurried over after a hasty landing. The man offered to sell Bullock eight parachutes and a balloon which he claimed to have, for $85. He was to ship them to the next show location. Bullock never saw the man or the eight parachutes or balloon.[82]

The tour took Bullock to Lewiston, Maine for the Somerset Central Fair, September 3rd through the 6th, then on to Skowhegan, Maine, where on 23 September, bad luck struck again. It was reported in the Boston Globe 13 April, 1917, that the "boy aviator" had a crackup which injured his ribs and head and did $800 worth of damage to his plane. Bullock had made one exhibition flight, then half an hour later, went up again and "dipped and volplaned through space, sweeping down close to the crowds and then spiralling up to dizzying heights. But on

landing, he crashed through a fence. Women fainted and men put their hands in front of their eyes fearing to see the daring aviator mangled to a pulp."

Bullock freed himself and in a short time repaired the airplane. He returned to Minneapolis in October and advertised to sell his plane's Curtiss Model O engine, radiator, and prop. In December, he advertised his "factory-built" Curtiss Pusher biplane for sale. He didn't sell it then, however. On Christmas Day, 1917, Bullock flew it over the Twin Cities, dropping War Savings Stamp literature on behalf of the Aero Club of Minneapolis.

In February, 1918, Mr. Earle Brown, a Director of the Aero Club, had placed his 580 acre farm in northwest Minneapolis at the disposal of the Club to be offered to the Army Air Service as a training field. That was turned down, but the field was used by students of Dunwoody Institute and the St. Paul Air Service Mechanics School for their required flight familiarizations. In July, the Brown farm became the first Twin Cities flying field, housing six airplanes in individual hangars. The Ashley Aeroplane Company opened for business there, with Walter Bullock as chief pilot and general manager and partner, Enos Ashley, offering flying instruction and aircraft sales.[83]

A group of Naval Cadets, also being trained at Dunwoody, received some familiarization flights at the Brown Farm Field. Among them was Clarence Hinck, who received his first air ride from Bullock.

Postmaster E. A. Purdy, a director of the Minneapolis Aero Club, had been advocating an airmail service between Minneapolis and Chicago. J. P. Ernster, an officer of the *People's Savings Bank* offered his private plane for this purpose if Bullock would pilot it. Purdy's request fell on deaf ears in Washington and the plan was turned down.

In the fall of the year, Bullock, imbued with patriotism, enlisted in the Army Air Service. Ironically, he was not qualified to become a pilot due to color-blindness, but could serve as a mechanic. In the spring, the Armistice ended the war with Bullock having been in uniform for less than 90 days.

Though the Earle Brown Field was advertised as having the best equipment and best flying field conditions in the Northwest, Bullock left when winter set in because it was isolated and the roads were closed by snow. There were no snowplows in the area.

That winter, Bullock finally sold his Curtiss Pusher to early flyer, Fred Parker.

Bullock's bounce at the Minnesota State Fairgrounds, June 23, 1917. (Bullock family)

On June 23, 1917, the famous lady flyer, Ruth Law, came to the Minnesota State Fairgrounds for an exhibition. It was a very big thrill for Walter Bullock to meet her and for him to demonstrate his airplane in her presence. She was many years his senior, and when Bullock bounced a landing, she gave him motherly encouragement. (Bullock family)

Generally considered to be the first airport in the Twin Cities, the field at the Earle Brown farm in Brooklyn Center offered Bullock a spot to build a hangar and a home base between his exhibition trips. Here, in 1919, he sold airplanes with Enos Ashley and gave some air rides and instruction. (James Borden)

In February, 1919, Lieutenant Bullock and Major W. C. Garis, (later Assistant Minnesota Adjutant General), teamed up to fly from the Twin Cities to Duluth, on behalf of the Minnesota Motor Corps, a branch of the Home Guard. The pair became the first persons to make an aerial trip between the cities. On February 22, despite the intense cold, they landed on the frozen bay to the delight of a large crowd. They had departed from Lake Calhoun, stopped at Moose Lake for fuel, where a team of horses was employed to haul the gas onto the lake and brought with them mail to be exchanged between Minneapolis Mayor, J. E. Meyers and Civic and Commerce Association VP and general manager, H. M. Gardner, and their counterparts, Duluth Mayor, C. R. Magney and Duluth Commerce Association's, W. I. Prince. This unofficial airmail flight made its return to Minneapolis in three hours.

In 1920, Bullock, phased out the Brown Farm operation, settling on a new location in Robbinsdale. There, he and Ashley took up where they had left off. Bullock bought a cracked-up Jenny from C. H. Forrester of Fort Arthur, Ontario. In April, Bullock had a chance to sell a J-1 Standard in Brainerd and departed for an extended stay to give flying instructions to the owner in his new airplane. Cyril Stodolka needed ex-

In 1922, Walter Bullock was flying this OXX-6 Curtiss MF Seagull at Breezy Point, near Brainerd, for Captain Billy Fawcett, magazine publisher. (Bullock family)

actly 256 minutes to solo, whereupon he launched his own barnstorming career.[84]

Robbinsdale became one of the few early airports, along with a field in Fridley where Clarence Hinck had set up operations and was running a Flying Circus; the Twin Cities Airport (Speedway Field), where Wilbur and Weldon Larrabee had started the Security Aircraft Company, and launched fixed-base operations; and Curtiss-Northwest Airport in St. Paul, where Bill Kidder was offering aerial services of all kinds.

A colorful character named "Captain Billy" Fawcett took his first airplane ride at Robbinsdale from Bullock and that started a friendship that would last for many years. Captain Billy was a writer and a knowledgeable magazine publisher, whose very popular, "Captain Billy's Whiz-Bang" humor magazine, was a best-seller. Fawcett's office was across the street from the Golden Valley Golf Course and he would often hire Bullock to take him for a round-trip to a resort at Breezy Point. They would return to land on the golf course and go across the street to the office for a drink or two. Occasionally, Fawcett, who loved to fly, would talk Bullock into going aloft again in the afternoon after some imbibing and on more than one occasion turned out to be a wild ride.[85]

In 1922, a gentleman in Duluth purchased an OXX-6 engined Curtiss Seagull flying boat from Bill Kidder. It had only marginal value in the Twin Cities because there were no lakes from which flying was legal. In Duluth, however, owning a seaplane was a natural, because of the nearness of the Bay. "Chick" Keyes and Morrie Salisbury were assigned to deliver the plane. A problem developed soon after takeoff and the two had to make an emergency landing at Moose Lake. After they fixed the problem, they took a leisurely lunch, and quite suddenly the weather closed in. For three days, pilots and flying boat were marooned, mostly because there wasn't any wind after the weather cleared and the boat couldn't get out of the small lake. The flying boat never did make it to Duluth. Captain Billy heard about the orphan and bought it for the purchase price of $12,000. Walt Bullock flew it to Brainerd and went to work for Fawcett.[86]

Bullock also fell in love that year. Lillian Larson became his wife, and tells the story: "My sister and I had gone to a dance, planning to meet our dates there. When we got there, her date had two of his friends there, Walter Bullock and Jimmy Piersal. I was told later that when Bullock spotted me, he said, 'there's my gal.' We were introduced. Actually, I already had a date and a whole string of dances ahead of me, so Bullock had to wait."

Then Bullock began coming to my school every day when I was a senior. Somehow he got me up to Breezy Point and talked me into marrying him. I dropped out of school and we spent the summer of 1922 at Breezy Point while Bullock worked for Fawcett."[87]

(Lillian Larson was one of three sisters to marry men who became Northwest Airlines pilots. Her sister Jean married Bob Johnston; sister Lenora married Homer Cole; and a niece, Beatrice, married pilot Dick Pears.) Walt and Lillian came back to Minneapolis that fall and he went to work at Robbinsdale again. Future star, "Speed" Holman, hired Bullock to install an OX-5 engine in a Thomas-Morse airplane during this period. Bullock and Homer Cole partnered in selling airplanes and flight instruction. In 1923, Bullock worked for Marvin Northrop. Northrop sold airplanes, and aircraft parts and supplies from a downtown Minneapolis warehouse, located at 5th Street and Washington Avenue North. Many an early aircraft builder or rebuilder made a weekly trek to the Northrop store to buy engines, wheels, spruce lumber, cotton fabric, nuts, bolts, instruments, etc. Bullock handled aircraft sales from Robbinsdale Airport. That year, Walter and Lillian had their only child, a daughter, Marilyn.

During 1924, Bullock bought back the Standard airplane he sold Cyril Stodolka, because Bullock cracked it up for him. Bullock had borrowed it and was flying near Brainerd when the engine stopped and Bullock parked it in the woods. There is no mention as to what happened to it after that. Bullock taught early aviator, Gene Shank, to fly in the Fawcett Seagull during 1924.

During the late spring and early summer, a man named Ralph Samuelson, invented and pioneered the first use of water skis in the Lake Pepin area. He thrilled the people of Lake City during its annual Water Sports Carnival, when he got Walter Bullock to pull him across the lake at the unbelievable speed of 80 miles per hour behind the Fawcett seaplane. In recent years, a plaque was dedicated and mounted in Lake City commemorating the man and the event. The original skis and a boat prop of the period are hanging in the Lake City Bank.[88]

In 1925, Bullock was back barnstorming again. This year he joined the Del Snyder Flying Circus. Another Minnesotan, Noel Wien, later to become one of Alaska's most famous airmen and owner of Wien Airlines, was the other half of the aerial portion of the circus. The troupe took along a wing-walking ace by the name of George Babcock. At the Illinois State Fair at Springfield, they were executing an aerial change-of-planes with Babcock. Wien had taken Babcock up in one Jenny from which acrobat had climbed out and walked all over the wings and hung by his toes over the edge of a wing and other amazing feats. During the finale, Bullock was to come down in another Jenny dangling a rope ladder with gas pipe rungs to pickup the performer. A gusty wind was

blowing; Babcock was perched precariously atop the Wien Jenny's wing and Bullock's ladder was swinging back and forth...when it caught under the "masts" on Wien's wing. (The "masts" were a pair of the upright ends of wing struts that protruded through the top of a Jenny's wing panels, and were supported by bracing wire.) The ladder became tightly stuck in this structure!

A puff of wind hit Bullock's Jenny and the ladder tightened, crushing the leading edge of his wing. It was being jerked taut and limp by the movement of the airplanes. Thirty seconds seemed like an eternity with the planes locked together. Babcock worked furiously and perilously between the two moving wings, and finally got the ladder unhooked. He climbed into Bullock's plane, exhausted, but having saved the day.[89]

1926 was also memorable for Bullock because that year he suffered a bad crackup at Upper Sandusky, Ohio, while with the Snyder Air Circus tour. Flying in the show and advertising for the Crescentyne Radio Receiver Company on his Standard's tail, he had been hopping passengers for some time. One man had taken several rides with him during the preceeding few days and once more approached. "This time I want a $25 stunt ride" he demanded. In part because the man was so demanding, and also because he had spent a good deal of money with Bullock, Bullock obliged, but against his better judgement. Bullock had just filled the center section fuel tank with 50 gallons of gas, planning to take simple hops, and had never done aerobatics with a full tank. In the first maneuver, a loop, the plane stalled and went into a flat spin. There was nothing that Bullock could do but ride it down, angling his wing so that it hit the ground before the nose and absorbed some of the shock. The passenger sustained a broken wrist, arm, and nose. He also received a gash on his hip, extensive bruises and went into shock. Bullock was also in shock, though uninjured otherwise. He staggered to his hotel room, only later being persuaded to visit a doctor for treatment of cuts and bruises. The Standard was destroyed and the pieces carted off as souvenirs by the spectators, as was the habit in those times.

Lillian Bullock used to follow the circus and was lagging behind because she had a premonition. She stopped at the newspaper in Sandusky and encountered George Babcock. She knew something was wrong when George asked her to go back for some

Not all of Bullock's barnstorming was accident-free. Here, at Upper Sandusky, Ohio, in 1926, he wiped out a Jenny while hopping rides. Both Bullock and his passenger were slightly injured. As noted in the photo, the spectators rushed to collect souvenirs. (Bullock family)

tools that Bullock needed. She went instead to the hospital and found Bullock impatiently waiting to leave. What did they do next? They hurried to Warren, Ohio, where Bullock bought another airplane! After all, he did have contracts to fulfill.[90]

An interesting footnote. In 1977, the same man, Mr. William Olpp, Jr. returned to Bullock the pair of goggles that he had borrowed for that fateful flight, having forgotten them after the crash.

Bullock and Speed Holman had become close friends, and for Bullock, that had its advantages. Holman, who had hired on with Colonel Brittin in 1926 as one of the first pilots for the fledgling Northwest Airways, was an irrepressible daredevil who insisted on following his own schedule of aerobatic displays and cross-country racing in addition to his airline duties. In 1927 he felt the compelling need to enter the National Air Derby from New York to Spokane. He simply went to his boss, Colonel Brittin, and told him he was going to take a leave of absence. Brittin was agreeable only if Holman hired a replacement for himself while he was gone. At Bullock's, suggestion, Holman hired him on the spot, with no fanfare, examinations, apprenticeship time or whatever, as a temporary replacement. Thus Bullock became the sixth pilot hired by Northwest Airways. On 1 September, 1927, Bullock went to work for what was to be a 30-day period.

The flights that Northwest flew between Minneapolis-St. Paul and Chicago were mostly mail flights in 1927, though the Stinson Detroiters could carry as many as three passengers (one had to sit in the right front seat). The truth was that there just weren't that many folks willing to fly from town to town in those days.

The airline made five round trips a week between the two terminals, each pilot making two trips one week and a single one the next week. A flight went east the first day, laid over that night, and returned the next day. Stops were made at LaCrosse, Madison, and Milwaukee, and what portion was flown after dark in the winter months had to be made from the pilot's memory of every streetlight and lighted billboard along the route.

Bullock remembered two passengers among the first few that chanced a flight after Lindbergh's voyage made headlines: "The two most interesting passengers I had were two beautiful gals, who got on one afternoon. They were sisters. Lindbergh had just flown the ocean, so it was 'Lindbergh this and Lindbergh that.' These gals got on, and they had a suitcase with them. They sat in the back seat and opened the suitcase. They had a pint of whiskey, I guess, and they had a picnic lunch. It was a beautiful day, and we flew down the River. In those days we flew at 500 to 1,000 feet right down the Mississippi River, and it was beautiful. Oh they were so enthused! We stopped at LaCrosse. We didn't stop at Madison that time, but, about there, it started to rain, and it got rough and we had a head wind. We had left at 2:30 in the afternoon, remember, and now we were running late and they got sick. We got into Chicago about ten o'clock that night. It was black and it was raining, and they were both so sick that they never wanted to see an airplane again. And they were so enthusiastic when we started out."[91]

On the 6th of October, Charles Holman, returned to the Cities, a hero, having won the New York to Spokane National Air Derby. Bullock was invited to ride with Holman and Mayor Leach in the victory parade through the streets of Minneapolis.

In between flights for Northwest, Bullock continued his own pursuits. He checked out the future president of the Mohawk Aeroplane Company, Leon Dahlem, in a Canuck (Canadian Jenny). Working for a real estate Company, he flew prospective land buyers around Lake Minnetonka, past the shorelines where they could get a bird's eye view of potential property. Cottages sold in those days for $245 to $795, and there was much interest. These flights were made in a large Curtiss HS-2L seaplane with an enclosed front passenger compartment. When Lindbergh made his triumphant tour of the United States following the successful trans-Atlantic flight, his stop in Minneapolis attracted thousands to Wold-Chamberlain Field. Bullock was there and borrowed a Waco 10 from Gus Imm to make a trip around the patch to enjoy the view. (Gus was a barnstormer from the Fergus Falls area who had flown in for the event.)

One of Speed Holman's regular exploits that received considerable attention was a periodic flight under the St. Paul High Bridge in his Laird biplane. Bullock admitted to flying a Northwest Stinson Detroiter under the High Bridge once without fanfare, just to satisfy himself that he could do that too.[92]

Holman and Bullock were such good friends that they used to spend a good deal of their non-working hours together with their wives and others from the airline. Bullock remembered that Holman always drove his car with the gas pedal pressed flat to the floorboards, and when they often raced from the airport to their homes in South Minneapolis, Holman usually won. Once he almost did not, however, as he was stopped by the police. Bullock motored slowly past him, but stopped a little farther up the road to wait for him. When Holman roared up alongside, he announced that he had managed to talk the police officer out of writing a ticket, and promptly zoomed off ahead of Bullock.

In 1928, Northwest began carrying passengers with regularity and Bullock was still flying. His 30-day arrangement had become a full-time job. Bullock continued to build scale models. In the early spring of 1929, he exhibited perfectly scaled models of the three aircraft being flown by Northwest Airways at the Detroit All-American Aircraft Exposition. The Stinson Detroiter, Ford Tri-motor and Hamilton Metalplane were so beautiful and attractive that, when Henry Ford, visited the exhibit, he was quite taken with them. As a result of Ford's interest, Colonel Brittin was prompted to announce shortly afterward that Northwest would undertake producing the models in quantity. There is no evidence that Bullock ever built additional copies, or that Northwest followed through with the plan.[93]

Bullock did continue to build other models. He wrote a series of articles during the 1930's for Popular Mechanics Magazine which detailed his techniques for building the Ford Tri-motor. He also served as Chief Judge in 1932, 1933, and 1934 for the Statewide model airplane building contests, sponsored by the Northwestern National Bank of Minneapolis.

During the months of June and July, 1929, a refueled endurance record was being attempted over Wold-Chamberlain Field, with a new record being the goal of Thorwald "Thunder" Johnson, Owen Haugland,and Preston Crichton, among others. Several attempts had been made, each one seeming to bring them closer to their goal. Walter Bullock was among the ground and refueling crew. On the fifth attempt, with seven days and nights having passed in the air, the pair of Haugland and Crichton, flew over low and slow to drop a message to the ground crew from their Cessna AW "Miss Minneapolis." For some inexplicable reason, the ship stalled and plunged to the ground from 150 feet. Crichton was killed immediately and Haugland was mortally injured. Walt Bullock, who had just finished reading the dropped note, was called on to rush Haugland to the hospital. Unfortunately Haugland died the next day.[94]

In 1930, Speed Holman won the Thompson Trophy Race at Curtiss-Reynolds Airport in Chicago. Bullock flew Holman's personal Laird there for him to have available for aerobatic performances. That was one of the few times that anyone other than Holman ever flew Speed's Laird. Both Bullock and Holman were sworn in as honorary Deputy Sheriffs that year in Minneapolis. Supposedly, when the Sheriff's Department needed someone for an aerial search or chase, these pilots would be called upon. No records indicate whether any such duties were performed.

A most tragic event occurred on 17 May, 1931. Charles "Speed" Holman was killed during an aerobatic exhibition in Omaha, Nebraska. Bullock and Lillian were on a fishing trip at the time and returned to hear the sad news. Bullock sadly eulogized his friend, "he was a perfect pilot, absolutely thorough in everything he did."[95]

Bullock was one of the pallbearers chosen by Holman's widow, Dee, to bear the casket from the Scottish Rite Temple in Minneapolis to the hearse, and from the hearse to the gravesite at Acacia Park near Mendota, Minnesota. Lillian could not attend the funeral as she was hospitalized with an appendicitis attack. Four months later, appendicitis would be the cause of Bullock's promotion to the position of Operations Manager of Northwest Airways. Chad Smith, who became Operations Manager following Holman's death, died on the operating table during an appendix operation. Bullock took over the Operations post on 1 October, 1931.

Since joining the airline in 1927, Bullock had earned much less than he had in his earlier years as a barnstormer. Salary hikes were few and far between, and the hours long and the work tedious and draining. When former Northwest pilot, Dave Behncke, organized the Airline Pilot's Association in July of 1931, Bullock was one of the 24 early pilots from various airlines who figured as "key men," charter organizers.[96]

Bullock had confrontations with the President of Northwest at that time, Richard Lilly, and was eager to join the ALPA and see it succeed. Despite his eagerness to join, he had never gotten along with Behncke, nor had his predecessor, Holman. Holman had engaged in yelling matches with Behncke, even fisticuffs, and eventually was instrumental in getting Behncke fired from Northwest. Bullock admitted that, "Behncke...was a hot-aired kind of a guy, but he had a lot of guts and he knew every politician in the country. Hell, we'd have been dead without Behncke." ALPA, in its dealings with the nation's airlines would take much deserved credit for the well-being and lifestyle of all future airline pilots.[97]

In February of 1932, the pressure of Holman's death, Chad Smith's death, the ALPA struggle, and the daily burden of the Operations office he held was almost too much for Bullock. He wrote to Colonel Brittin, then working as a lobbyist in Washington on Northwest's behalf. Bullock shared his intentions to quit the airlines with Brittin. In a long, rambling letter, Brittin told him to keep the faith, told him that, "...as operating manager, you have responsibilities far beyond those that you have as an individual. If you left your present position for any reason, the man who would take your place would crucify every man that had been loyal to you and revered the memory of Charlie and Chad." His message apparently did its job, because Bullock never turned in his resignation.[98]

Instead, things took a different turn causing Bullock to leave Northwest. Bullock related in later years that in 1932 he was framed by the new Traffic Manager in Milwaukee, Croil Hunter, in a way that got him fired. Bullock explained, "Hunter had been having dinner and asked a friend where he could get drinking alcohol. (This was during the period of Prohibition when the purchase of liquor was illegal.) The friend said he could get all that Hunter wanted. To get it, another fellow and myself would have to haul it. To be a good guy, I said sure, I'd do it. We had five one-gallon cans of it wrapped in brown paper with my name on it and it went up in the airplane to Milwaukee. They had witnesses there to see it come off. I was fired. I got a desk job for the next sixteen months. I never had a high regard for Hunter after that. At the same time I was never convinced that Richard Lilly hadn't put Hunter up to it." There might have been some friction between Bullock and Lilly, dating from the formation of ALPA, as Bullock had been a strong advocate of the union.[99]

Bullock then went to work as a line pilot for Hanford Airlines. Hanford operated from Wold-Chamberlain Field, flying mail and passengers between Minneapolis, North and South Dakota, Omaha and Kansas City. He flew their fleet of Fokker and Ford Trimotors, Lockheed Vegas, and Lockheed 10A's, and a Boeing 40B. Minneapolis early-bird pilot, Eddie Croft, recalls Bullock coming in from a trip in a Trimotor, wringing wet and angry as a hornet. The Trimotor windshield leaked. Ed was working in the Hanford hangar on his own Travel Air biplane at the time. "Bullock raised hell about the leaking windshield. He sure was wet... and mad."[100]

Bullock remembered the Boeing 40B with little reverence. "I remember one day we went out in the 40B, the old open-cockpit Boeing, it was wintertime and it was miserable; a face mask would have helped but we didn't have them. It was more than twenty below this day...and I was supposed to go out in a Ford...Minneapolis-St. Paul to Omaha. So I had gone

Bullock flew a war-surplus P-38 in the Bendix National Air Race in 1946, finishing ninth. The plane was sponsored by Shorty De Ponti, FBO at Wold-Chamberlain Field, Minneapolis. (Minnesota Historical Society)

to the airport in just my uniform. Well, we picked up enough clothes around the airport, and I made the trip. Fortunately, when I got up to three or four thousand feet, we had an inversion, there the temperature wasn't too bad.[101]

The job at Hanford lasted a year and a half, during which time Bullock's most memorable moment was making a wheels-up landing in a Lockheed 10A on a foamed runway at Kansas City.

As if it were a soap opera, in 1937 Northwest bought the airmail routes from Hanford and got Walter Bullock back in the deal. Bullock always wondered if Hunter, in accepting him back, was not apologizing for the frame job in 1932. At any rate, he went back to the bottom of the seniority list, so his new NWA seniority dated from 11 February, 1937, instead of 1927.

During 1938, Northwest took delivery of Lockheed 14H "Sky Zephyr's." The plane was later found to have structural design problems. In January, one of the new ships crashed 12 miles northeast of Bozeman, Montana, taking the life of another Minnesota pioneer aviator, Nick Mamer. Rudder flutter was determined to have been the culprit. Next, Fred Whittemore, early-bird pilot and Air Guard officer, was killed when his "Zephyr" hit a canyon wall on a ferry flight from California to Minneapolis. Other 14H incidents occurred as well, and Bullock suffered his only airplane accident in one of them, an event that would cost the life of a passenger. On 8 July, 1938, taking off from Billings, Montana, the plane refused to gain altitude and returned to the ground 1100 feet beyond the end of the runway, bouncing from the top of a knoll and sliding 350 feet down a grass-covered slope. It came to rest at the edge of a 40 foot cliff. No one might have been injured had the airliner not hit an outcropping of rocks along the way, which spun it around and cracked it open, throwing a female passenger from the fuselage. She suffered a fractured skull and died at the scene. Ironically, she had been insistent about sitting in just that seat on that flight, to the annoyance of the crew and other passengers.[102]

Because he had switched off the ignition moments before the plane struck, there was no fire, but what had been the cause? Bullock claimed that he could not get enough power out of the engines even though he had pushed the propeller pitch levers to the maximum. A CAA investigation followed with Northwest

company pilot, Gene Shank, taking a similar ship up, to try to duplicate the crash conditions. He made several flights before it was discovered that on both the crash ship and the test ship, a limiting stop had been installed by Northwest mechanics in the control quadrant that prevented maximum low propeller pitch from being obtained. The reason had been well-enough intentioned, that of saving the engines from damage by overrevving. Needless to say, the limiting stop was removed from all 14H's and Bullock was exonerated.[103]

Unfortunately that was not the end of the 14H's troubles. In January, 1939, "Cash" Chamberlain was killed along with four others in a 14H at Miles City, Montana. Even Mel Swanson bellied one in on the Hohag farm at the end of the Wold-Chamberlain runway. It was to everyone's great relief when the reliable DC-3 was introduced soon afterward and the 14H's put out to pasture.

With the declaration of war following Pearl Harbor in December, 1941, Northwest was contracted by the Air Transport Command to haul troops and material to remote air bases in Alaska and to the islands in the Aleutian chain. Northwest, under the Air Transport Command, NACA,(the National Advisory Council for Aeronautics), and the Air Material Command, set up a cold weather flight test laboratory at Wold-Chamberlain Field. One of the greatest obstacles to flying was then, (and still is), icing. In June, 1942, under Major A. F. Olson, of the Army Air Force, Northwest Captains W. R. Bullock, A. E. Walker, A. F. Becker, and co-pilots Richard Barton, Spencer Marsh and David Brenner began a program of confidential research, looking for both the causes and the prevention of aircraft icing on wings, propellers, windshields, and tail surfaces.

In flights that took them all over the North American continent, Walter Bullock and the others sought out icing conditions that most pilots would have avoided by any means.

Perhaps the most famous aircraft of the test fleet was a B-24 bomber rigged with a spray bar in front of the inboard engines that would spray water onto the propellers, engines, and wings. Nicknamed "Squirtin' Gertie," it helped scientists study the impact and buildup of ice. Another of the memorable fleet was a B-25 nicknamed "Flamin' Mamie." This ship's exhausts were fitted with collectors which would route large amounts of hot air into "boots" along the aircraft's leading edges. The tests resulted in the creation of hot air boots and alcohol spray units on the propellers.

Bullock recalled his experiences in this program, including one flight to Edmonton, Alberta, Canada, in the worst winter icing conditions just to test the systems. The program gave Bullock the chance to fly a great number of military aircraft types, including all of the most modern fighter aircraft, the P-61 "Black Widow," and the P-82 Twin Mustang. He flew all the bombers too, including a captured German Junkers JU-88A-4, which is now in the Air Force Museum.

Flying anything and everything had its problems. Keith McCarthy, who flew as a crewman for Bullock, remembers one incident with humor. He relates that

Closeup portrait of Bullock with the P-38, 1946. At this time, he was a Captain for Northwest Airlines. (Bullock family)

Bullock with his homebuilt Bleriot II replica in 1965. Powered by a Continental engine, Bullock flew this aircraft for many years in exhibitions around Minnesota. The airplane is now on display at the San Diego Air & Space Museum. (Bullock family)

they often would have to simply board the aircraft, take a few minutes to familiarize themselves with the switches, fire up and take off! Once they brought a C-54 from Minneapolis into Squantum Naval Base outside of Boston, at night. After landing, they were told that the Navy didn't allow the big R5D's to land there. (The R5D was the Navy's designation of the C-54, or DC-4 in civilian terminology.) "They asked me who landed it and I pointed to Bullock. Then I told them, 'till we climbed into it this morning, we'd never been in one'. 'My gawd', they said. Then they invited us to the officer's club and treated us royally. We stopped there often after that."[104]

Another program which involved Bullock was a mass flight to India in C-46's. Fifteen Northwest pilots, ten from Trans World Airlines and five from Air Transport Command, teamed up to make the four and a half day, 15,000 mile journey. Though all arrived safely, within sixty days of their delivery there were only nine aircraft left. The route had taken them from Wilmington, Delaware; through Natal, Brazil; across to the Ascension Islands; to Acra, Aden, Arabia, Karachi and finally to India. Bullock recalled a takeoff incident: "I think Wilmington had a lot of sabotage on those airplanes. We had no more than gotten nicely off the ground at Wilmington, when the right engine stopped. And having a tremendous load on board, it wasn't funny. So I reached down and pulled the booster pump back on to see if it was something in the gasoline system. A mechanic came rushing to the front...'Turn that off!" he hollered, 'the gasoline is coming out of the nacelle and running back around the exhaust pipe.' What had happened was that the gas line had backed off the carburetor and the booster pump is back there, and it was just shooting raw gas at the carburetor, spraying it all over the inside of the nacelle and it was coming out and running all over the exhaust pipe. That would have made a beautiful torch, you know. We had to shut it off. We went into Baltimore, got it fixed and went on our way. Each plane was loaded with over 51,000 pounds of gear and we flew at 16,000 feet going over. The plane had an Air Force crew, I was the only civilian among them."[105]

It is a strange situation that those same Northwest pilots find themselves in today. They worked for the Air Transport Command, they actually flew Air Force

missions, in Air Force uniform, yet today they have no G.I. benefits. They are not eligible to be members of the VFW, they cannot get G.I. loans, and they cannot be buried in a National Cemetery. On the balance side of the sheet, they did maintain their seniority with Northwest and the benefits from that have been good to them.

EPILOGUE: WALTER BULLOCK

Following the war, like so many other men of that time, Bullock decided to go into air racing. Shorty DePonti, Wold-Chamberlain FBO would sponsor him, and thus a war-surplus P-38 nicknamed "Golden Gopher" was purchased and made ready for a season of racing. An unfortunate ground loop damaged the landing gear, making the ship unusable, and with plenty of the breed around, another was soon found. This one, an F-5G model, registered NX 70006, and nicknamed "Golden Gopher II," was polished and tuned for the 1946 races. Bullock's only race was the Bendix Trophy Race, a trek of 2048 miles from Van Nuys, California to Cleveland, Ohio. He did this at an

Bullock flying high over the Twin Cities in his replica Curtiss Pusher sometime in the 1950's. After his retirement from Northwest Airlines in 1960, he was continuously busy in his shop at Lakeville, Minnesota, turning out home-built aircraft one after another. (Bullock family)

38

Bullock in his workshop at Lakeville, Minnesota, in the early 1970's. (Lillian Bullock)

average speed of 355.9 m.p.h., significantly off the 435.5 m.p.h. of the winner, Paul Mantz in a P-51C. Bullock's time was good enough for ninth place, however, several places ahead of fellow Minnesotan, Lee Fairbrother, who finished 16th in a P-38J.[106]

In 1947, Bullock built a replica of the Curtiss Pusher he had owned many years before. He added balloon tires and a reliable Continental engine and flew it for a number of years, giving exhibitions around the State. In August of 1947, he flew on C. W. Hinck's "Famous Flyers" program at Rosemount, Minnesota, and at the State Fair.

In 1951 and 1952, Bullock served as vice president of ALPA. By 1952, he had accumulated 21,940 hours in the air (the equivalent of 2 years), and topped the list of high-time pilots at Northwest. Second was Captain Russ McNown with 21,500 and four other Captains had more than 20,000 hours each.

In this replica of Lincoln Beachey's modified Curtiss Pusher, known as the "Little Looper," Bullock flew exhibitions during 1969 and for a couple of years afterward. The aircraft is now owned by Vern Dallman of California, who continues to fly exhibitions in it at the time of this writing. (James LaVake via Curt Erickson)

In 1954, Bullock was the target of anti-aircraft while piloting a DC-4 near Taipei, Formosa, enroute to Tokyo. Although the plane wasn't struck, the State Department was most vexed when the Chinese Nationalists claimed it was a target-practice mixup.[107]

The following year, Bullock set a speed record flying from Okinawa to Tokyo in a Lockheed Super G Constellation. Though the scheduled time was three hours, 35 minutes, Bullock and co-pilot Gene Markham brought the Connie to earth in two hours and 29 minutes.

One incident aboard a Constellation was a source of tension. "Coming out of Shemya Island, enroute from Tokyo to Anchorage, one time. It was dark at the time and there was fog right down on the deck. If you could get a plane off safely, everybody was happy, regardless of what the rule book said. We were no sooner off the ground than there was this strong smell of gasoline. And that's dangerous. So we shut off all the electrical, told nobody to throw a switch or anything. We didn't even want to use the radio because we didn't want any sparks. We couldn't figure out how gasoline could be stinking in the cabin like that. The Constellation carried no fuel in the fuselage at all, the gas lines didn't even run through the fuselage. We had the stewardess ask every passenger if they had a cigarette lighter or any such thing that could be leaking gas. Nobody had such a thing. So here we were sitting waiting for this thing to blow up any minute. I thought we might as well blow up at twenty thousand feet as three, so we just kept climbing and going. Finally, a Japanese woman who had been sleeping and didn't hear the stewardess ask the questions, woke up and the stewardess questioned her. 'Oh yes', she replied. At Shemya, her baby boy had been sick, so they took him to the passenger agent who cleaned his little coat with gasoline and it seems she had laid this coat right down where the heat comes on in the Constellation. That heat had spread the fumes and we were all sitting up front waiting for doomsday."[108]

1960 was an important year for Bullock. He was 60. The FAA decision to retire airline Captains at age 60 was made while Bullock was out on a trip. He actually got the news while he was flying a DC-7 from Tokyo to Seattle. When he stepped off the plane, he was done! He was emotionally crushed at the manner in which he was informed. His official retirement ceremony took place 15 March, 1961.

Although Bullock never got the opportunity to fly a jet-powered airliner, he enjoyed flying the DC-7's and Constellations, but he loved the Boeing Stratocruiser most of all.

Bullock loved to build airplanes in his home workshop in Lakeville, Minnesota. In 1958, he built up a Wittman Tailwind airplane with an 85 h.p. Continental engine. After his retirement, he produced a replica Bleriot 11 and flew it in airshows across Minnesota during the next few years. Almost every Minnesota aviation buff can recall seeing him perform in the Bleriot. He was even invited back to Canby, Minnesota, where he'd had bad ink almost 50 years previously.

Bullock next undertook the restoration of a Canuck Jenny, and a Standard J-1 belonging to Johan Larsen.

In 1977, Bullock was still rebuilding old aircraft. Here he wraps a turnbuckle connection before soldering it on a Curtiss Canuck Jenny at the Aircraft Museum operated by Johan Larsen at Flying Cloud Airport in Eden Prairie. (Noel Allard)

He also built a replica of the 1910 Lincoln Beachey "Little Looper." The Beachey flew for the first time in 1969, equipped with a LeRhone rotary engine. It's test flight ended beyond the edge of the runway when the brake, an oak board, pressed against the nosewheel tire by one's foot, failed to slow the airplane.

The J-1 Standard was finished and rented to Frank Tallman, Hollywood stunt pilot, who flew it in the movie, *Ace Eli and Roger of the Skies.* Tallman cracked it up unintentionally, and Bullock got to rebuild it a second time. Johan Larsen's Jenny and Standard were rebuilt, and Larsen purchased the Bleriot, all of which were displayed at Larsen's Aircraft Museum at Flying Cloud Airport in Eden Prairie, Minnesota, during the period 1975 through 1977. The planes were subsequently sold to the San Diego Aerospace Museum, where they can be seen as of the writing of this book.

In 1971 Bullock also finished building a friend's Volkswagen-engined Curry-Watt biplane.

Bullock flew his last solo flight in a J-2 Cub belonging to Johan Larsen early one day in 1977, from his farm in Lakeville to Flying Cloud Airport and back. At that time, Bullock was 78 years old and had logged better than 31,000 flight hours during his 61 years of flying. He was member of the National OX-5 Hall of Fame; a candidate for membership in the National Aviation Hall of Fame; a QB, (Quiet Birdman); a member of the Early Birds, (those persons who flew prior to December, 1916), a member of the Hump Pilot's Association, and in 1988 was one of the first six pioneers to be enshrined in the Minnesota Aviation Hall of Fame.

Bullock listed some 102 aircraft types in his logbooks, and was proud to say that he was never a co-pilot. He had been hired as a pilot by Northwest and never relinquished the Captain's seat.

On 4 April, 1986, Walter R. Bullock died of Cancer at his retirement home in Venice, Florida, at age 86.

1900s The Pioneering Years   Documentation

1 *Minneapolis Journal*, 11 August, 1907, Sect. 1, p. 6. A version of part of this chapter first appeared in *Minnesota History*, 48/2, summer, 1982.

2 *Minneapolis Sunday Journal,* 19 November, 1908, Sect. 1, p. 7 Another description of Chance's airship is to be found in the *Minneapolis Journal,* 24 June, 1908.

3 *Minneapolis Journal*, 29 April, 1909, p. 7.

4 *Minneapolis Tribune*, 21 February, 1910, p. 2.

5 *Minneaoplis Journal*, 20 October, 1908, p. 3.

6 *Minneapolis Journal*, 17 October, 1908, p. 2

7 *Minneapolis Star*, 17 March, 1953.

8 *Minneapolis Journal*, 27 February, 1910, part 2, p. 1.

9 *White Bear Life*, 28 January, 1910, p. 1.

10 *St. Paul Dispatch*, 27 January, 1910, p. 5.

11 The definitive statement of what flight is and who first accomplished it is to be found in Charles Gibbs-Smith, *Aviation: An Historical Survey*, London; HMSO, 1970, and the smaller pamphlet *The Worlds First Aeroplane Flights*, London: HMSO, 1965.

12 *Minneapolis Journal*, 28 February, 1910, p. 11.

13 Curtis Prendergast, *The First Aviators*, Alexandria, Va: Time-Life Books, 1980, p. 91.

14 Letters, L.K. Bernard to Walter Wilmot and C.N. Cosgrove, both dated 25 March, 1910, Minnesota State Fair Board Records, St. Paul, Minnesota, contracts for 1910. Among the more interesting contractual details was the Curtiss insistence that only aircraft approved by them could be exhibited, an obvious effort to exclude any Wright brothers' machines. In return, they promised the Minneapolis men that no other flights would be made within 100 miles of the Twin Cities prior to 1 July, 1910.

15 Memorandum of Agreement between the Minnesota State Agricultural Society and F.C. Murphy, 17 May, 1910, Minnesota State Fair Board Records, St. Paul, Minnesota, Contract for 1910.

16 *Minneapolis Sunday Journal*, 13 February, 1910, Sect. 2, p. 2.

17 *Minneapolis Journal*, 14 June, 1910, p. 4.

18 *Minneapolis Journal*, 29 May, 1910.

19 *Minneapolis Sunday Journal*, 19 June, 1910.

20 Sherwood Harris, *The First to Fly*, New York: Simon & Schuster, 1970, p. 282.

21 Harold E. Morehouse, "Flying Pioneers Biographies," Unpublished manuscript, National Air and Space Museum, Washington, D.C., no date.

22 *Minneapolis Journal*, 20 June, 1910.

23 *Minneapolis Journal*, 22 June, 1910, p. 1.

24 *Minneapolis Tribune*, 23 June, 1910.

25 *Ibid.*

26 *St. Paul Pioneer Press*, 24 June, 1910, p. 1.

27 *Ibid.*

28 *St. Paul Pioneer Press*, 25 June, 1910, p. 1.

29 *Minneapolis Sunday Tribune*, 26 June, 1910, p. 1.

30 *Ibid.*

31 *Ibid.*

32 *St. Paul Dispatch*, 27 August, 1910, p. 1.

33 *Minneapolis Journal*, 27 August, 1910, p. 6.

34 *St. Paul Dispatch*, 27 August, 1910, p. 1.

35 *Ibid.*

36 Robert W. A. Brewer, *The Art of Aviation*, London: Crosby Lockwood and Son, 1910, p. 83.

37 There is, of course, a definite limit to this relationship of angle of attack and greater lift. If the angle of attack becomes too great airflow over the top of a wing is sufficiently disturbed so that all lift is lost. The aircraft then "stalls" and the loses altitude until recovery can be made by increasing speed and decreasing angle of attack., i.e., diving. A stall at low altitude is not a happy event for an aviator.

38 *St. Paul Dispatch*, 27 August, 1910, p. 1.

39 *St. Paul Pioneer Press*, 27 August, 1910, p. 10. *The Pioneer Press* reported that "many" residents witnessed the flight. The *St. Paul Dispatch* and *Minneapolis Journal* both reported the number of witnesses as eight.

40 *St. Paul Daily News*, 1 September, 1910, p. 1.

41 *St. Paul Dispatch*, 27 August, 1910, p. 2.

42 Minnesota State Agricultural Society (Fair Board), Disbursements Ledger: Dec. 1908 - Sept. 1910, p. 185. The payment was made by check no. 7737 for $2,000.00 and no. 7738 for $500.00 to J.C. Mars and check no 7750 for $2400.00 to the Wright Company, all dated 10 September 1910.

43 Memorandum of Agreement between Fred Parker and the Minnesota State Agricultural Society, 1 September, 1910, Minnesota State Fair Board Records, St. Paul, Minnesota, Contracts for 1910.

44 *Minneapolis Tribune*, 6 September, 1910, p. 3.

45 *St. Paul Dispatch*, 6 September, 1910, p. 16.

46 Harold E. Morehouse, "Arch Hoxsey - Early Wright Exhibition Pilot," from *Flying Pioneers Biographies*, unpublished manuscript, National Air and Space Museum Library, Washington D.C., no date. An excellent published account of the activities of many early aviators, including Hoxsey, is to be found in Sherwood Harris, *The First to Fly*, New York: Simon and Schuster, 1970.

47 *Minneapolis Journal*, 8 September, 1910.

48 Ray P. Speer, "History Notes 1854-1912," unpublished history of the State Fairs, no date, Minnesota State Fair Archives, St. Paul, Minnesota.

49 *Minneapolis Journal*, 10 September, 1910, p. 14.

50 *St. Paul Pioneer Press*, 10 September, 1910, p. 7.

51 *Ibid.*

52 *Minneapolis Journal*, 10 September, 1910, p. 14.

53 *Minneapolis Journal*, 11 September, 1910, p. 8. An airplane's ground speed is its airspeed coupled with any wind factor. If, for example, an aircraft flies at 35 m.p.h. and the wind is 20 m.p.h., the airplane's groundspeed would be 15 m.p.h. into the wind or 55 m.p.h. with the wind. Hoxsey's groundspeed was obviously so low that he appeared nearly motionless.

54 *St. Paul Pioneer Press*, 10 September, 1910, p. 7 and *Minneapolis Journal*, 11 September, 1910, p. 8.

55 Morehouse, "Flying Pioneers Biographies."

56 *Minneapolis Tribune*, 3 September, 1911.

57 *Martin County Sentinel*, 4 August, 1911.

58 *Brown County Journal*, 31 August, 1912.

59 *Minneapolis Journal*, 3 September, 1911, p. 7 and *Olmstead County Democrat*, 29 September, 1911.

60 *Minneapolis Journal*, 11 September, 1911, p. 12.

61 Morehouse, "Flying Pioneers Biographies."

62 The contemporary press accounts of the flight are best told in the 1911 *Minneapolis Journals* of 22 September; 10, 13, 19,22, 23 October and the *Minneapolis Sunday Tribune*, 8 October, 1911.

63 *Minneapolis Journal*, 19 August, 1927, p. 35.

64 *Minneapolis Journal*, 14 December, 1913, p. 1.

65 State Fair Board Contract Files, Contracts for 1911.

66 *Minneapolis Journal*, 5 September, 1911, p. 5 and *St. Paul Dispatch*, 5 September, 1911, p. 1.

67 *St. Paul Pioneer Press*, 6 September, 1911, p. 1.

68 *St. Paul Pioneer Press*, 9 September, 1911, p. 10, and 10 September, 1911, p. 7.

69 *Minneapolis Journal*, 6 September, 1912, p. 1 and *Minneapolis Tribune*, 7 September, 1912, and Morehouse, "Flying Pioneers Biographies."

70 State Fair Board Contract Files, Contracts for 1914.

71 *St. Paul Pioneer Press*, 13 September, 1914, p. 2.

72 Harris, *The First to Fly*, p. 294.

73 State Fair Board Contract Files, Contracts for 1915. The Paterson Aviators Brochure is also in this file, copy in possession of the authors.

74 *St. Paul Pioneer Press*, 10 September, 1915, p. 8; 12 September, 1915, p. 1; and *Minneapolis Journal*, 7 September, 1915, p. 12.

75 *St. Paul Pioneer Press*, 5 September, 1916, p. 5; 7 September 1916, p. 6; and *Minneapolis Journal*, 8 September, 1917, p. 2.

Walter Bullock biography   Documentation

76 Interview with Walt Bullock by George Holey, Air Museum of Minnesota, 27 October, 1965.

77 *Minneapolis Journal*, 11 December, 1916.

78 Interview with Walter Bullock by Geo. Holey 27 October, 1965.

79 Undated newspaper clipping, scrapbook of Holman Field miscellany, John Lammertz collection.

80 *Boston Globe*, 13 April, 1917.

81 *St. Paul Pioneer Press*, Magazine Section, St. Paul, 24 December, 1939.

82 Interview with Walt Bullock by Lance Belville, 13 January, 1986.

83 Theodore Wirth, *Minneapolis Park System*, 1944.

84 Interview with Cyril Stodolka by Noel Allard, 20 September, 1986.

85 Interview with Walter Bullock by Noel Allard, 19 May, 1973.

86 *Minneapolis Journal*, 11 December, 1916.

87 Interview with Lillian Bullock by Noel Allard, 15 July, 1987.

88 Sandra Zanish, *Credit Union Insight,* Spring-Summer 1980.

89 Interview with Walter Bullock by Lance Belville, 13 January, 1986.

90 Interview with Lillian Bullock by Noel Allard, 15 July, 1987.

91 Interview with Walter Bullock by George Holey, 27 October, 1965.

92 Interview with Walter Bullock by Noel Allard, 20 September, 1974.

93 Ruby Clark, *Air Travel News*, June 1929.

94 *Minneapolis Tribune*, 18 June, 1929; *Minneapolis Journal*, several successive days beginning 27 May,1929.

95 Interview with Walter Bullock by Lance Belville, 13 January, 1986.

96 George Hopkins, *Flying the Line*, ALPA International, 1982.

97 Ibid.

98 Letter from Colonel Brittin to Walt Bullock, 24 February, 1932.

99 Interview with Walter Bullock by Noel Allard, 19 May, 1973.

100 Ed Croft correspondence with the author, 8 November, 1987.

101 Interview with Walter Bullock by George Holey, 27 October, 1965.

102 Interview with Lillian Bullock by Noel Allard, 15 July, 1987.

103 *Air Commerce Bulletin*, US Dept. of Commerce, 15 August, 1938.

104 Keith McCarthy correspondence with the author, 26 July, 1986.

105 Interview with Walter Bullock by George Holey, 27 October, 1965.

106 *Racing Planes and Air Races*, Reed Kinert, Aero Publishers, 1967.

107 *Minneapolis Star*, 22 December, 1954.

108 Interview with Walter Bullock by George Holey, 27 October, 1965.

THREE

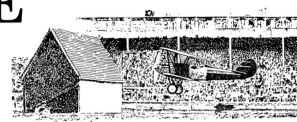

BOB LEMM

1920s — 1930s: SHOW BUSINESS AND ENTREPRENEURS

THRILL SHOWS

As mentioned in Chapter Two, the very first flying done for public demonstration was done as a grandstand event at the Minnesota State Fair. The Fair was sponsored by the Minnesota State Agricultural Association, during the early 1910s. It was only natural that the spectacle of aviation was harnessed as a means of entertainment.

In 1917, the world's attention had been focused on Europe where the Great War raged. Newspaper headlines across America spotlighted the aerial warfare and the exploits of Aces such as Amercia's Eddie Rickenbacker. This added to the public interest in aviation. Therefore, that year, the State Agricultural Association's Board of Directors, (the State Fair Board), were more than willing to listen to presentations by promoters of various aviation entertainment acts.

Agent William H. Pickens represented DeLloyd Thompson and Katherine Stinson. Stinson was a woman pilot, making headlines across the country, not only as the first major woman flyer, but an exhibition pilot of great skill, and a member of a family that would figure prominently in the future of American aviation. Picken's fee for either Stinson or Thompson was $500 per day for exhibition flight. Pickens also represented Lawrence Brown, whose specialty was a difficult night aerial demonstration with fireworks attached to his airplane.[1]

In addition to Pickens, an agent representing the Howard Aeroplane Company, offered the services of local youth flier, Walter Bullock. Another agent, George Slagle, made a presentation that promoted flyer, Harry Wagner, and various aerial acts, for a grandstand show.

The result of these presentations was that the Fair Board secretary was sent to Chicago in August to witness a night performance of Lawrence Brown's act. The Fair contracted with Brown for two daytime and one nighttime aerial show for each of the six days of the Fair. Brown's total fee was $3,000. A newspaper account indicates, however, that Brown flew only a single daytime flight and Katherine Stinson was brought in to fill the remainder of the contract.[2]

There is no evidence that Bullock flew during Fair Week, though he had been seen there in June during the appearance of Ruth Law's exhibition visit. Besides Katherine Stinson, Law was the only other outstanding woman aviator in the country at that time. A special art exhibit on the Fairgrounds featured 140 wartime aviation paintings of the Frenchman, Henry Faure, whose works were touring the country.

In 1918, agent Walter Raub proposed a balloon flight for the grandstand show that would feature the dropping of several parachutists. (The parachute had only recently been perfected and was a great curiosity.) No evidence indicates that Raub received a contract. It is more likely that a flyover of military "Jennies" from the Earle Brown Farm field were the Fair highlight. They were flown by instructor pilots of the St. Paul Aviation Mechanics School. Curiously, the school's aviation mechanics also staged a wild-west show as a grandstand feature.[3]

It appears that 1919 was the first year that a wing-walking acrobat was booked at the Fair. The star was Ormer Locklear, the country's premiere aerial attraction. The Fair Board made an attempt to engage the Ace, Eddie Rickenbacker, but he was overbooked for appearances following his return from European combat and the Minnesota State Fair did not fit into his schedule. In fact, his reply to the Fair Boards solicitation was that he was "giving up flying unless forced to it."[4]

C. W. Hinck, representing the Federated Fliers, offered the services of his stunt pilot, Dick Grace, indicating that he could perform "like Locklear."[5]

Locklear, whose busy schedule prevented him from appearing more than a single day was to be paid $1,000 for his act. To fill in the other six days of the Fair, the Board contracted with Lieutenant Walter Pack of the Army Air Service to follow with five days and five nights of exhibition flights. His total fee was $2,500.

Locklear didn't disappoint the crowds in his single performance. In practice, while he was climbing from one plane to another, the two ships locked wings. When the pilots landed to inspect the damage, Locklear was interviewed. He was asked if he were risking his life? "Why," he replied, "there's nothing dangerous in that work. I do absolutely nothing that could be called a risk of life...my idea of danger is driving a racing automobile." (He was known to have done that too.)

Locklear then launched into his standard speech about how safe flying was and indicated that he thought it a simple matter to land an airplane on Nicollet Avenue if the need arose.[6]

For his wing-walking performance, Locklear dressed in white coveralls for better visibility to the crowds. A record one-day Fair attendance of over 200,000 persons turned their eyes skyward to witness his antics on the wings of biplane Jennies. So spectacular a performance was Locklear's, that he was presented a wrist-watch at a banquet that evening, by Fair Board President, Frank W. Murphy. Locklear promised to wear the watch "until I am gone."[7]

Not all factions appreciated the aerial act, however. Minneapolis newspaper editorials bode ill. One indicated that while the transfer from one plane to another in the air was thrilling to watch, it could be fatal to the performer if he fell. The impact would be instantaneous to him, but would linger forever in the minds of those who were watching, and therefore, should be banned.

Local merchants were not as outspoken as the newspapers. Many garnered advertising revenue during Fair Week with tie-in advertising. The local Pure Oil distributor offered an ad in local papers featuring a testimonial by Locklear regarding their products. William Kidder ran an ad that explained how Locklear and his partners were flying the Curtiss Jenny, which was available through Kidder's St. Paul dealership.

Locklear did, indeed, lose his life years later, in Hollywood. Performing a stunt in front of movie cameras, the glare of fireworks on his airplane at night blinded him and he lost control, crashing to his death.

Co-incidentally, Federated Flier, Dick Grace, followed Locklear to Hollywood for movie stunt work and become an associate of his.

The Fair Board turned down C. W. Hinck's grandstand show proposal, but he had also proposed a stunt-flying contest to occur during Fair Week, and that offer was accepted. Nick Mamer, one of Hinck's pilots, won the stunt flying contest, Marvin Northrop from the Kidder organization came in second, and Vern Omlie, another of Kidder's pilots, from Grafton, North Dakota, was third. Prizes were $250, $125, and $75 respectively. A maximum altitude contest was won by Charles Keyes, one of Kidders pilots, with Mamer finishing second and Ray Miller, still another of Kidder's pilots, third.

Ray Miller won a forty-mile air race, with Mamer second and Federated Flier pilot, Walter Hallgren, third.

Following this week of aerial activity, the Fair Board made improvements to the landing area between the back straightaways of the one-mile and half-mile racetracks, so that planes could takeoff and land more easily.[8]

In 1920, exhibition pilot, Ruth Law, returned. She appeared before the Board to propose an "aeroplane circus" with herself and Al Wilson doing a seven day, seven night stint that would include fireworks during the evening show and races against an automobile during the daytime shows. Her fee for the total week's work was to be $9,000! Her agent, Charles Oliver, signed a contract with the Fair Board. A clause stated that she would not be paid for events canceled due to weather, but she still carried off $8750 for her weeks work. During the week, she made the first auto-to-airplane transfer seen in the Midwest. She also raced her airplane around the Fairgrounds one mile track above Louis Disbrow in his racing car, beating him twice in three lap races.

Though C. W. Hinck proposed carrying sight-seeing passengers out of the Fairgrounds improved racetrack airstrip, granting the Fair one-fourth of the proceeds, his offer was declined. His offer to stage a triple parachute jump was also declined. The major grandstand event of Fair Week, occurred on Friday, when two railroad locomotives on a single makeshift track in front of the grandstands, were crashed head-on. That event netted its promoter $12,500. Between this and Ruth Law's fee, some big money was being spent!

In 1921, Ruth Law contracted with the Fair Board for a performance similar to that of the previous year. She, along with her pilot, Vern Treat, gave the fireworks-on-airplane show after dark each evening.

A woman parachute jumper named Gladys Roy, offered to attempt a world-record parachute jump from 16,000 feet. This was impossible to work into the schedule. Roy was from Minneapolis, the sister of future Northwest Airways pilots, Chad, Lee and Les Smith. She would, however, be on a future Fair program.

The first aircraft exhibit on the Fairgrounds opened in the Steel Machinery Building on Machinery Hill. It featured nine airplanes, including a Curtiss Oriole used by the newly chartered 109th Observation Squadron of the Air National Guard. A Martin bomber, representing the Air Mail Service, was obtained from the State of Virginia at a cost of $750 in expenses. Other planes were exhibited by Mark Hurd and Curtiss-Northwest. Again, the big thrill week spectacular was a head-on locomotive collision.

Interestingly, William Kidder of Curtiss-Northwest, proposed to the Fair Board that a bridge be built across Snelling Avenue from the Fairgrounds to his airport so that Fairgoers might walk across the road and take a sight-seeing ride. The Fair Board quickly squashed this idea, seeing the drain of customers and revenue to such an enterprise. It is interesting to imagine what the future might have been had the Fairgrounds expanded across Snelling Avenue.

In 1922, Ruth Law made a proposal to the Fair Board for her services, but later in the year decided to retire. In her place, to keep up the tradition of having a woman acrobat as the headline attraction, the Fair Board hired aerial acrobat, Lillian Boyer. Charles Hardin, acting as agent for his wife, Katherine Hardin, proposed an act in which she would make a parachute jump each day of Fair week

Lillian Boyer performed wing-walking at the 1922 Minnesota State Fair. Woman performers appeared at various State Fairs in this era. (Minnesota State Fair via Gale Frost)

for a total of $5,000. There is no indication that she was issued a contract. Boyer, on the other hand, performed brilliantly. For the seven-day fee of $7,000 she made a daily auto-to-airplane change, did some wing-walking, and hung from a pendulum suspended beneath the plane of William Brock, first by one hand, then one foot, then by her teeth! Brock followed with aerobatics and nighttime fireworks. At age eighteen, Boyer was the youngest woman to headline a flying circus in the entire country.

She brought her Aerial Circus to the Fair again in 1923 for a similar week-long run. In 1924, the Fair Board heard several proposals. One was from Walter Bullock, another from Gladys Roy. Other proposals came from J. Runser of Illinois and William Kidder. Kidder's proposal featured little-known local performer, Charles "Speed" Holman and Al Blackstone, who was billed as "Diavolo, the Human Fly." Their act consisted of wing-walking and parachute jumping. The fee was a modest $1,000 for the week. Apparently, their names were not considered a big-enough draw for Kidder did not get a contract. Fairgoers cast their eyes skyward during the week, however, to watch skywriting by Fred Wallace.[9] The grandstand show included auto push-ball, auto polo, motorcycle and auto racing.

In June 1925, Speed Holman and Al Backstone, demonstrated to Fair officials, a motorcycle-to-plane change with Holman flying, Art Peterson driving the motorcycle and Blackstone making the change by climbing up a rope ladder to the plane. Though the demonstration was successful, the act was not booked for Fair Week. The big event was the arrival of the great airship, the U. S. Navy dirigible, *Shenandoah.*

Demonstrating a rope ladder change from motorcycle to airplane at the Minnesota State Fair, June 1925. Speed Holman flying, Art Peterson driving, Al Blackstone grabbing at the ladder. (Al Blackstone via Sid Croy)

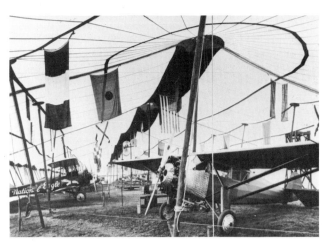

Minnesota State Fair aircraft tent display, 1927. The National Lead Battery Company's Laird LC-B flown by Speed Holman is at left and the Ryan B-1 Brougham flown in by Frank Hawks is at right. The Ryan was a sister-ship to the "Spirit of St. Louis" flown to Paris by Charles Lindbergh. (Noel Allard)

Shenandoah was to be making a five-day excursion from Lakehurst, New Jersey, to the Midwest, visiting many cities. (Another Navy airship, the *Los Angeles,* had planned a visit to the cities in June of that year, but engine trouble had forced a cancellation.) The Fair Board considered spending $50,000 to $75,000 to have a mooring mast built on the Fairgrounds for the Shenandoah visit, but the idea was dropped when the Navy announced the flight would be merely a flyover and not a stop. The day of the flyover was to be on 5 September 1925. The flight never occurred.

Tragedy happened first. Only two days before arriving at the Fair, the airship broke up in a storm over Ohio and crashed. The dirigible was destroyed and several lives were lost. There was no aviation event at the 1925 Minnesota State Fair.

Gladys Roy did get a contract in 1926 that included a parachute jump each day of Fair Week. She had set a woman's parachute altitude record the year before in California and was now quite well-known. Her fee of $1,000 for seven performances was accepted and she would perform wing-walking and blindfolded aerial stunts. Joe Westover, 109th Air Guard member, was her pilot.

In her first jump on 6 September 1926, Roy dislocated her hip on landing, and was out for the week. Joe Westover sent in jumper Harry O. Proctor and Nona Malloy, another woman parachute jumper, to take her place. Public sentiment against letting a woman jump again, in view of what had just happened to Roy, cancelled Malloy's performances. Proctor did the jumps alone for the rest of the week, with Westover providing stunt-flying.

Also on the 1926 program were the St. Claire sisters of Michigan, who piloted a balloon over the Fairgrounds during the week. Whippet dog races on the half-mile track, and John Phillip Sousa's band headlined the grandstand shows.

By State Fair time in 1927, the world had been astounded by the flight of Charles Lindbergh from New York to Paris in *The Spirit of St. Louis.* An attempt was made early in 1927 to bring Lindbergh to appear at the Fair. The Guggenheim Foundation of New York, which was sponsoring Lindbergh's 48-state tour could not fit the Minnesota State Fair time slot into their schedule. The Fair Board had authorized $15,000 for an appearance and expended considerable effort to change the Guggenheim plans.[10]

A plea was made to Lindbergh's mother to speak directly to her son to have him change his routing. Thomas Canfield, Fair Board Secretary, even made a trip to New York to plead the case before the Guggenheim Foundation. Lindbergh remained unavailable.

An aviation exhibit at the Fair was a major attraction, and an 80' x 400' tent was set up and filled with exhibit aircraft. Among the displays was a Ryan B-1 Brougham monoplane similar to *The Spirit of St. Louis.* It was flown there by well-known exhibition pilot and cross-country racer, Frank Hawks. Alongside it was a Waco 10 belonging to Gus Imm of Fergus Falls, Minnesota; a brand-new Air Guard Douglas O-3H biplane; a military DeHavilland DH-4; the National Lead Battery Company's "National Eagle" Laird LC-B flown by Speed Holman; a Buhl Pup; a Mohawk Pinto; and a Hess Bluebird.

Holman flew the Laird in acrobatic displays on Monday and Wednesday afternoons. Navy fliers from Wold-Chamberlin did fly-bys during the week. Frank Hawks, who was a graduate of Minneapolis West High School, did stunt flying during the week.

Again, in 1928, money was budgeted for the aircraft tent display and Ray Miller was appointed Superintendent of the exhibit. Highlighted aircraft that year was the Lockheed Vega of Sir Hubert Wilkins and Carl Ben Eilson, which had been used by the pair for a Polar expedition in 1927 to fly from Point Barrow, Alaska, to Spitzbergen, Norway, a distance of twenty-two hundred miles. The $5,000 fee paid them for the appearance included lectures about the feat, given several times during the week. The two flew the plane daily before the grandstand.

Another exhibition plane was the Breese monoplane "Aloha," piloted by Martin Jensen in the previous year's Dole race from California to Hawaii. The Texaco-sponsored Ford Trimotor that had won second place in the 1927 Ford Reliability Tour was brought in by Frank Hawks, and a Stinson Detroiter aircraft of Northwest Airways was also shown. A Fairchild mail plane belonging to Captain B. D. Collyer, who had flown it around the world in some 23 days, was there, as was the St. Cloud manufactured "Liberty Bell" aircraft, a Travel Air and Monocoupe of Roth-Downs Airways of Minneapolis, an Avro "Avian" of Northern Airlines, a 109th Air Guard Curtiss 0-11 and Consolidated 0-17, plus a Kari-Keen, an American Eagle, and a glider shown by Marvin Northrop. Quite a line-up!

If the display wasn't enough, the aerial activity was monumental. Army Captain, R. J. Walters, contracted to bring in a captive "sausage" balloon to hop passengers in the balloon basket, whisking them up and down while the balloon was safely tethered to the ground. This activity was to last the entire week. Walter's fee was $800, not including the advertising revenue he enjoyed from selling space on the balloons ample sides. On the final day of the Fair, thrill show workers "blew up" the balloon.[11]

A St. Paul couple, June Landis and Archie Phillips, planned to be married in the balloon basket. The couple, minister, and witnesses were to ascend to a height above the Fairgrounds, where the ceremony would take place, broadcast by KSTP radio. There was a stiff wind on the day of the wedding, but the balloon rose and the vows were reportedly spoken on high...or were they?

It was revealed years later that due to strong winds, and the fear someone would be hurt, dummies were loaded into the balloon, while the actual ceremony took place on the ground, out of view of the spectators. When the balloon landed far out in the racetrack infield, the dummies were removed and the wedding couple jumped in. The balloon was then dragged over in front of the stands. At that point the wedding couple jumped out again to a round of applause, nobody the wiser. It was all in good fun and the Fair Board gave the blushing bride $50 in gold pieces as a wedding present.

During the week, Captain Walters took the parachutist, George Babcock, up each day to make a parachute jump from the balloon basket. Each day, many of the exhibit aircraft, such as the Laird, were taken out of the tent, engines fired up and taxied across the backstretch of the mile racetrack to takeoff from the airstrip and thrill the crowds. More than 200,000 persons were reported to have gone through the aircraft display tent in 1928, according to display superintendent, Ray Miller.[12] The first model aircraft show sponsored by the Fair was also held in 1928, drawing 38 entries. In 1929, the crescendo of aerial activity rose still higher. Speed Holman gave four outstanding performances in his Laird during the week. His contract between the Fair and Northwest Airways was signed by Colonel Brittin himself, acting as agent.[13]

A beauty contest was held during the week, and the "Goddess of the Skies" was crowned on the last day. Holman was a judge. The tent display featured, among other aircraft, a brand-new Northwest Airways Hamilton Metalplane, a Universal Air Lines Curtiss Robin, and a Great Northern Aviation Eaglerock Bullet.

In 1929, both George Babcock and Nona Malloy performed. On one jump, however, Babcock snagged power lines and his parachute burst into flames just as he was landing. He escaped unhurt. Nona Malloy, who had been injured in a jump the proceeding week, fulfilled her contract in true-grit fashion, by making a jump each day despite increasingly painful conditions.

C. W. Hinck provided grandstand entertainment consisting of motorcycle races, dog races, rollover cars, auto polo and auto push-ball. He got a contract in 1930 for similar ground activities.

The flying portion of the 1930 entertainment was contracted to William H. Pickens and to Dale "Red" Jackson from Faribault, Minnesota. Jackson was fresh from a record-breaking endurance flight in which he and partner, Forrest O'Brine, spent 647 and a half hours in the air over Lambert Field, St. Louis, in a Curtiss Robin aircraft. Jackson's act at the Fair included a simulated aerial refueling such as was used at intervals during the St. Louis flight. It was during Jackson's act on the final Fair day that Speed Holman interrupted the performance, buzzing the grandstand on his return from Chicago where he had just won the famous Thompson Trophy Race. Speed's

1935. Parachute rigger, W. E. Winterringer shows jumper, Billy Hamilton, some of the nuances of the early parachute harness at Wold-Chamberlain Field. (Vern Georgia)

impromptu series of maneuvers was an expression of exuberance and a salute to Minnesotans.

Picken's contract was cut short earlier in the week as his troupe had suffered a series of both ground and air accidents that left them unable to fulfill their contract. Thus, Jackson, along-with Leo Allen and Leroy Grady, billing themselves as the "Three Flying Sons of Guns," picked up the slack and provided daily airshows with their three aircraft tied to each other by ropes.

In 1931, with the Great Depression on the land, activity at the Fair, as everywhere, took a lower key. Charles Gatchet, of Des Moines, demonstrated the Des Moines Register newspaper's autogiro. Captain W. E. "Pop" Winterringer, of Sioux City, Iowa, did a parachute jump. George Babcock, the parachutist who had performed two years earlier, had unfortunately been killed recently in a jump at the Excelsior Amusement Park on Lake Minnetonka. His widow, Almeda Babcock, jumped at the 1931 State Fair in his place. Her jump almost ended in disaster, as well, when she landed against a building on the University of Minnesota's Farm Campus, next door to the Fairgrounds. Her chute tangled in the roof edging, but held her long enough for fire department ladders to be erected, and, she was rescued. Of some consolation was the $700 fee paid her for the spectacular event.

In 1932, C. W. Hinck's proposal to the Fair Board for the grandstand show was one of three nearly identical plans. Competition from Charles M. Marsh and B. Ward Beam, each offered motorcycle racing, auto polo, auto push-ball, ash-can derby (demolition derby) and trick car-riding. Hinck, the lowest bidder, received the contract, being paid $1200 for the week.[14]

Sixteen aircraft filled the 1932 tent show. Again, a balloon ascension was a daily attraction of the aerial features, with parachutist, Ruth York, jumping from the balloon. Making a jump from low altitude was surely dangerous, and Ruth was injured when she had

to cut loose from the balloon at a mere 300 feet above the ground, her chute barely opening in time.

The year 1933 would prove to be a most spectacular year for the Thrill Show. That year, C. W. Hinck provided a parachutist named Bill Ash, who was to jump from a plane piloted by Elmer Hinck. Promoter, pilot, and grandstand crowd, had to watch helplessly as Ash plunged to the ground, his chutes unopened. Ash's body struck on Machinery Hill and bounced back into the air in full view of grandstand spectators. The 34 year-old native of St. Paul had been attempting to make a delayed jump, holding off pulling his ripcord until it was too late. Because his ripcords had not been pulled, there was some talk that he committed suicide, but that was never proven. He was a student at both Hamline University and the University of Minnesota.

In other events, Barney Oldfield, by this time too old to drive a racing car, drew a crowd when he demonstrated a new farm tractor, taking it for a leisurely spin around the racetrack. Future thrill show promoter, Frank Winkley, was a contestant in the motorcycle races. Future house-crasher, Don Voge, participated in the auto races. In one event, Voge's career nearly ended when he crashed his car through the board fence and was nearly impaled by a timber that slammed through the car's cockpit.

The headline event for 1933 was a locomotive collision similar to the 1921 spectacle. Just as many local Aero Clubs had protested aviation stunts as bad publicity for aviation, the Great Northern Railroad protested the locomotive collision as bad publicity to the traveling public. Never-the-less, two railroads offered engines and cars for the event, with the Soo Line selling the Fair Board two locomotives at the scrap value of $300 each, and some cars for $200 apiece to make up the trains.

The locomotive head-on collision was widely publicized and touted as a cataclysmic crash! Actual-

Captain Frank Frakes, premiere house-crasher, 1935. He is standing in front of a Challenger Robin in this publicity photo. (Vern Georgia)

Frakes house-crash at the Minnesota State Fair in 1935. Waco 9 is about to impact. Note the infield side of the "house" is open to make it easier to extricate the pilot after the crash. (Noel Allard)

The house comes a tumbling down with the plane underneath. Great spectacle, no one hurt. (Noel Allard)

ly the two locomotives hit each other at relatively low speeds. Neither were running more than 20 miles per hour at the point of impact, due to the short length of railroad track laid in the racetrack infield. As they hit, however, small dynamite charges packed in flour bags were detonated to fill the air with noise and "smoke," making the action look impressive. The engines, while thrown off the tracks, barely bent their cowcatchers. After the event, they were hoisted back onto the tracks and continued their course to the scrapyard, paying back the Fair Board the same value as they would have the Soo Line.

In 1934, C. W. Hinck got the Thrill Day show contract. His acts consisted of three motorcycle races, an auto board wall crash and a parachute jump. His fee was $1200. In addition, the Fair Board contracted with 68-year old Pop Winterringer for a parachute jump from a tethered balloon. The Board also arranged for another locomotive collision.

In 1935, a local promoter, Walter Klausler, proposed an airplane "house-crash" as a feature event. Klausler's proposal called for $600 to $1,000 for the crash, "depending on casualties to pilot and equipment."[15]

The Fair Board wanted to know more about this interesting and spectacular event and got hold of a report from a similar event staged at Anderson, Indiana, in the early part of July. At that time, the "crasher," Captain Frank Frakes of Columbia, Tennessee, fought a sputtering engine and side-slipped into a parked car, getting knocked unconscious in the process. The Fair Board decided, that despite the problems, the act drew fabulous crowds and decided to book such an act. They contracted, not with Klausler, but with the Barnes-Carruthers booking association to bring Frakes in for a house-crash on Thrill Day. They hoped to take advantage of the national publicity resulting from his act and the Indiana incident.

A simulated house was constructed in the racetrack infield with two stout telephone poles planted deep in the ground, and a square clapboard frame structure built around them. A flat plywood roof with painted-on shingles and a fake chimney added to the illusion. The telephone poles were there to make sure the wings tore off the airplane, bringing it to a halt. Should the plane emerge from the opposite side of the house, the wingless fuselage would add to the drama.

Frakes flew the plane in from high over the grandstands, dropped into a power-off approach and hit the house at stalling speed. As it hit, the house collapsed

around it. At the same time, dynamite-flour charges were set off with the usual bang and smoke for extra realism. Frakes was helped out of the broken boards and walked away without a scratch. A photo story appeared in the *Minneapolis Star and Tribune* 7 September, 1935.

The event touched off a controversy between the Minnesota Aeronautics Commission and the Department of Commerce on the one side, and the State Fair Board on the other, which was to go on for years. Both governmental agencies concurred that such an event was too dangerous and the perpetrators should be constrained from committing such acts again, or face a lawsuit. They said nothing about the act of parachute jumping that had proven so injurious and even fatal over the years. Clem Sohn, parachute jumper from Lansing, Michigan, was on the same Fair program as Frakes. Sohn, who jumped with "bat-wings," was killed in a jump in France later that year.

The whole subject of house-crashing was controversial. Frakes, in making his statement to the Fair Board for the Barnes-Carruthers group prior to the event, assured them that he had Department of Commerce approval for the crackup. He could point to a string of house-crashes with successful conclusions to prove his point. The fact was, however, that he did not have department approval, a fact that Ray Miller, then chairman of the Minnesota Aeronautics Commission, found out only later. Miller felt forced to write an apology for his ignorance to the Department of Commerce, Chicago office district supervisor. "This office regrets that the violation occurred in Minnesota, and I can only say that I was careless in taking his word at face value instead of checking back through your office."[16]

A view of a house demolished by an airplane. The plane is under the boards, the pilot, Chuck Doyle, is long gone. Note the two telephone poles, erected to tear the plane's wings off, still standing tall. (Chuck Doyle)

The Department of Commerce had notified Frakes back in 1934 that his intentional crashing into a house would be penalized. Thus, following his performance at the Minnesota State Fair, he was contacted by the CAA. Part of the Department's letter read, "...your violations of Air Commerce Regulations have been continued. In connection with this matter, this Department has statements from various sources in which you are reported as saying that you 'have a secret agreement with the Washington Office whereby it is permissible for you to put on crashes of aircraft' and that inspectors were instructed 'to disappear or look the other way when this stunt was performed.'

"Such a statement is a direct misrepresentation of facts and you are hereby given until October 23, 1935 to submit evidence of the correctness of these statements, before this matter is referred to the Department of Justice for further investigation.

"You are further notified that no transfer of title to any aircraft will be made in your name and all Inspectors are being instructed to be on the lookout at all air shows, races, demonstrations, etc. and to prevent such performances on your part in the future."[17]

The letter indicates that, were Frakes to purchase an aircraft to be used in his act, they would refuse to license it. If he were caught in the act of flying an unlicensed aircraft, that alone would be violation of Department rules. Frakes was subsequently fined $500 by the Department, which could only charge him with performing an acrobatic maneuver at less than 500 feet above a crowd, and for not wearing a parachute while performing it. A slap on the wrist...the cost of doing business.

There were lots of ways of getting around the Department. When confronted by the Inspectors in following years, Frakes would claim that his acrobatic maneuver was done out in front of the crowd, not over it. He would even carry a parachute, though not wear it. Since his promoters were purchasing the airplanes, he never had to be involved in the transfer or licensing. This give-and-take with the CAA would continue for years.

In addition to the Frakes house-crash in 1935, there was other activity. C. W. Hinck provided a five-person group parachute jump. His jumpers were Jerry Johnson, who had performed the previous year at the Fair; Irving "Ripcord" Brown; local flyer and smoke writer, Chuck Doyle; Betty Goltz; and Bud Quist. They were all coached by the senior parachute instructor, Lyman "Stub" Chrissinger, who choreographed their jump from a Ford Trimotor flown by Mel Swanson.

In 1936, as in 1929, Captain R. J. Walters brought in a surplus military sausage balloon for passenger carrying and to allow the 109th Air Guard to shoot it down on the final day of the Fair. He collected $1,500, besides income from the revenue flights and an advertising banner that he affixed to the side of the balloon. In addition, Walters asked for, and received, payment for filling the balloon with City gas, at a cost of $557.

C. W. Hinck provided a nine-person group parachute jump, with Mel Swanson again piloting the jump plane, the Freeman Ford Trimotor from Wold-Chamberlain. Jumpers this year were Al Kammholtz,

Parachute riggers and jumpers, Betty Goltz and Stella Kindem pose for a portrait in June 1935 at Wold-Chamberlain. (Vern Georgia)

Rudy Hard, Walt Miller, Earl Barrus, Chuck Doyle, Fred McClocklin, Irving Brown, Betty Goltz and Jerry Johnson.

Ground thrills were provided by Captain Bob Ward and his Hollywood Daredevils, one of which was Chuck Doyle. Irving Brown thrilled the crowd when he jumped alone from a plane from two thousand feet wearing "bat-wings." The wings didn't work very well and Brown plunged toward the ground, with the chute opening virtually the same instant he hit the earth. Brown was shaken up, but not seriously injured. Woman parachute jumper, Betty Goltz, from Minneapolis, furnished further chills. She was substituted for Chuck Doyle in jumping from the sausage balloon by Stub Chrissinger, the event manager. He figured that the excitement of a woman leaping from the balloon would draw a larger crowd. On the final day of the Fair, when the balloon was to be shot down, it would be sent aloft with Betty in it. The 109th Guard planes would make several passes at it, firing blank ammunition from their guns. At a certain point, Goltz was to light a fuse setting off a firebomb that would ignite the gas in the balloon to end the event in spectacular fashion. She would touch off the fuse as she leaped over the side and

1936 group parachute jump performers at the Minnesota State Fair. They are taking a bow before going up for the Thrill Day jump. Standing left to right: Al Kammholz, Rudy Hard, Walter Miller, Earl Barrus, Fred McClocklin, Irving Brown, Betty Goltz, Chuck Doyle, Jerry Johnson. Kneeling: Stub Chrissinger and pilot, Mel Swanson. (Earl Barrus)

48

Here's Danny Fowlie hitting the house at the 1937 Minnesota State Fair. (Photo from a sequence appearing in the Minneapolis Star newspaper, 10 September, 1937)

A view of Fowlie's house-crash from the infield side, showing the open construction of the house. (Jim LaVake)

parachuted safely to the ground.

To do this, Hinck handed Goltz his cigar on liftoff. When the time was right, she held the cigar to the fuse and bailed out. She had trouble pulling her ripcord when the D-ring handle caught in her coverall sleeve. Frantically, she lunged for it again and again, finally getting the chute to open just as she hit the ground. Shaken and pale, she was pulled away just as the balloon, a roaring inferno, struck the ground, igniting part of the grandstand fencing. The whole event was a near-disaster, but fortunately, nobody was seriously injured.[18]

In 1937, the Barnes-Carruthers agency again offered a house-crash by Captain Frank Frakes. His activities had been continuing, (and would through 1939). His act would cost the Fair $2750, according to the proposal, with other backup aviation acts to fill in. The show would be billed as "Captain F. F. Frakes Death Fighters."

Bob Ward proposed a general thrill program that included a "Modern Bronco Buster" a man riding on the hood of a car as it jumped over a truck; the "Human Battering Ram," a man strapped to the hood of a car as it crashed through a flaming board wall, two men on motorcycles crashing double burning board walls, a car driving over several sticks of exploding dynamite, a 60-foot tunnel of flame to be driven through by a motorcyclist, a car crashing a brick wall, a motorcycle leaping two autos, a rollover car act, and a plane with fifteen parachutists making a group jump. The show would end with a plane

Bob Ward's Hollywood Daredevils at the Minnesota State Fair, 1937. Left to right: Bob Ward, George Dockstatter, Bob Nielson, Danny Fowlie and Chuck Doyle. Nielson's airplane was used in the act. (Jim LaVake)

crashing into a barn in the infield. Ward asked for $3,200 to $4,700 for the weeks program, depending on the number of events the Fair Board agreed to.

The Fair Board agreed to contract with Ward and not Barnes-Carruthers. In the deal, they got Ward's man, Danny Fowlie, a local stunt flier, for the house-crash. They also contracted with Pop Winterringer for his annual balloon ascension and parachute jump. The show was so big that events were staged over two Thrill Days.

On Friday, the original Thrill Day, grandstands were packed to standing room only. The program went off seemingly without a hitch, or at least as far as the spectators were concerned. Ward's performers were Bob "Junior" Maas, Chuck Doyle, George Dockstatter, Earl Barrus, Birdie Draper and Danny Fowlie. Maas strapped himself to the hood of Ward's automobile for a ramp jump over a truck, then, laying face down on the hood as the "Human Battering Ram," slammed through a burning board wall. Doyle and Dockstatter drove their motorcycles through three burning board walls, suffering no ill effects. When Dockstatter drove his car into the brick wall later in the program, however, he was knocked unconscious for ten minutes and got brick splinters in his eyes. The brick wall had been quickly constructed with minimal mortar between the bricks to allow it to crumble easily.

Chuck Doyle stood on the top wing of a biplane while it was flown through aerobatic maneuvers. This was called a "center-section act," and Doyle seemingly had "suction cups on his shoes," according to one newspaper article. Though it looked simple, Doyle suffered the only injury in a career of daredevilment. To secure him to the upper wing of the plane being flown by Danny Fowlie, a belt was strapped around his waist. It was fastened to the wing of the plane by wires, and, when tightly cinched and with Doyle pushing against the wing with his legs, held him rigidly to the airplane. The belt had to be tight so it wouldn't slip down around his waist as he pushed upward.

Doyle and Fowlie carefully planned the event for split second-timing. After takeoff, Doyle would crawl out of the front cockpit and atop the wing, slip into the belt and the aerobatics would proceed. But, on this occasion, Doyle had trouble with the belt latch...and it was in front of him, where Fowlie couldn't see it. Knowing there was only so much time until he was

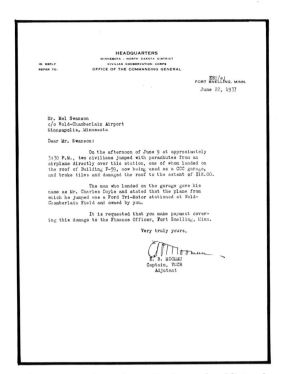

Interesting communique shows the hazards of Saturday air-shows at Wold-Chamberlain, 1937. (Chuck Doyle)

1937. Danny Fowlie with an American Eagle on display at Topeka, Kansas. The plane is set on its nose to advertise the fact that it will be crashed into a house at the Kansas State Fair in a few days. (Chuck Doyle)

upside down, Doyle jerked on the latch and frantically slammed it shut...on his thumb!

He couldn't very well go through the performance with one hand wedged in his belt latch, so he jerked his hand loose, tearing off his thumbnail. Only when he was on the ground later, did he find himself covered with blood, and the audience cheering, having been given the extra thrill of seeing the hero performer wounded in the course of the stunt.[19]

Earl Barrus and Birdie Draper jumped from an airplane holding hands as the announcer called out a "brother-sister parachute jump." Doyle and Dockstatter each drove their motorcycles through a 60-foot tunnel of flame. The tunnel was built of 2 x 2 boards covered with chicken wire. The wire was festooned with excelsior wood shavings, doused with gasoline, then set afire.

The show finale was the house-crash. Danny Fowlie did the honors in a Swallow TP aircraft. Although he was supposed to crash through the house as dynamite was set off, the building was constructed too well. Fowlie's plane merely came to a stop with its tail sticking out of the house and the dynamite was not triggered. Fowlie was extracted unhurt, however, and jumped down to a tremendous round of applause.

Fowlie was quite a character. He knew no fear and was the absolute master of a stunt airplane. His contemporaries, as well as the older pilots of today who can remember his performances, agree that he was the best acrobatic performer they ever saw. He was perhaps Minnesota's best, able to stunt as well, if not better, than other stunt pilots around the country.

Starting as a parachute jumper at age fifteen, Fowlie was a Wold-Chamberlain regular through the 1930's. He learned to skywrite, or "smoke write," as the skywriters themselves call it. He worked for Robert "Red" McManus as a smoke writer. McManus was one of the owners of the St. Paul Bottling Company which held the local Seven-Up franchise.

McManus' fleet of white Laird and Waco airplanes was used by himself and Fowlie for posting the name of Seven-Up across the sky.

By 1939, Danny Fowlie and Don Berent had perfected an act whereby a Piper Cub would land on the top wing of a Waco biplane in flight. The Waco was fitted with ramps that funneled together at the front to pinch the wheels of the Cub, allowing the planes to make shallow turns hooked together. The planes would circle and maneuver in front of spectators at Wold-Chamberlain, or the grandstands at local Fairs, then separate, and make individual landings. In 1940, the act was done with a pair of Cubs, and nicknamed the "Pick-a-back Cub Act." These two planes would take off from the ground hooked together, then separate in the air to do formation aerobatics or separate stunts, including the popular "Crazy-Cub" act of side slips, sashays, and flying between trees. The planes would then come together once more with Fowlie atop Berent, and land hooked up. A further modification for grandstand audiences was to takeoff and land a Cub on ramps built atop an automobile that would circle a Fair racetrack. Again, Fowlie was the pilot for that, with Jack Greiner filling in, occasionally, as car driver.

Fowlie's most spectacular show was in Texas, at the Texas Air Fair of 1941. He helped stage a riotous event at the Arlington Downs Racetrack, between Dallas and Fort Worth. It was supposed to run for

Chuck Doyle races through the Tunnel of Flame on his motorcycle at the Minnesota State Fair Thrill Day in 1937. (Chuck Doyle)

50

Danny Fowlie settles into the ramps atop Don Berent's Waco, practising their airshow routine. He is flying one of Tom North's CPT program Cubs while another hovers alongside. (Budd Stahel)

Closeup of Fowlie and Berent's Cubs prior to a 1940 performance. (Jim LaVake)

nine days, with matinees and evening shows. It was to include a staging of the Battle of Britain with flashing lights, dynamite, exploding gasoline bombs, collapsible buildings, and hair-raising sound-effects, enough "to spook horses as far away as Jacksboro and Mineral Wells."[20]

The first show on 6 December, 1941, was a super spectacular, with a ten-acre mockup of a British village being flattened by bombs from simulated German bombers, while fighters representing both Allied and Axis forces buzzed around overhead. (The fighters were actually Travel Airs, Wacos and Lairds with a few "modern" Culver Cadets thrown in.) An announcer brought the huge show to a conclusion with the admonishment, "...wake up America, this could happen to you." Of course the reader knows what happened...the next day the Japanese attacked Pearl Harbor.

Even while the news of the Japanese attack was being broadcast on Sunday, the second airshow performance was taking place. When it was over, marshalls informed the troupe that all civilian planes would be grounded immediately. The Great Texas Air Fair was over.

At the 1937 Minnesota State Fair, the Fowlie house-crash had seemed to come off without a hitch, but there was much that had been going on behind the scenes. The Federal Government was still on Frank Frakes tail. Ray Miller, chairman of the Minnesota Aeronautics Commission, who had been miffed by the fact that Frakes had committed an illegal act right under his nose in 1935, got the word that Frakes had proposed to do again in 1937. Miller wrote to the Department of Commerce to find out what steps they were prepared to take should it happen again, and what he should do about it.[21]

The Government answer apparently mollified Miller, for he took no action later against Fowlie, even though the event was well advertised and he would have had ample opportunity to prevent it. Croil Hunter, another member of the Minnesota Aeronautics Commission, also wrote to Washington in June when the Frakes proposal became known, and expressed his concern. The return letter to Hunter is quite interesting:

"Mr. Frakes has given this department considerable trouble in the past and as he crashes unlicensed aircraft, so far we have been unable to do anything with the matter. My suggestion is that this is a matter that the local authorities can handle best. We do not have

any trouble from Frakes in the States that require Department of Commerce licensed aircraft and airmen, to enforce it, but usually our opposition to his act merely assists him, in that he is not only defying death, but the Department of Commerce as well."[22]

As of 1939, Frakes was still at it. By his own recollections, he had, up to that time, crashed some 35 aircraft into houses. He even added that he had been praised for his actions, destroying airplanes that were not airworthy.[23]

At many Fairs around the country, the house-crash was being prevented. In 1937, the state Attorney General's Office got a judge to issue a restraining order to stop Clarence Hinck from staging a crash at the Steele County Fair at Owatonna.

If the pace seemed to slacken a bit in 1938, it was understandable. There would never be another house-crash at the Minnesota State Fair, though it was proposed again. Instead, the Fair booked Danny Fowlie to do his airplane takeoff and landing from a ramp car. Thrill Day, however, was a rainy, muddy day. Fowlie's ramp car could make only slow headway on the muddy track, and while he could takeoff from the car, he had a very hard time making the landing. Four attempts were required to complete the act. Other acts were canceled.

The weather was affecting other events as well. C. W. Hinck was contracted to provide a multiple parachute jump. He had signed ten jumpers and pilot, Mel Swanson, and had them standing by, waiting for the weather to lift so that they could make the short flight from Wold-Chamberlin to the Fairgrounds. The act had to be canceled. Hinck appeared before the Fair Board in November to request compensation anyway, stating that his crew had been ready to perform. The

Danny Fowlie preparing to do the "World's Smallest Airport" routine, taking off and landing his Cub on ramps built atop an automobile. (Jim LaVake)

Bob "Red" McManus and a Laird Speedwing aircraft, about to go up for a skywriting job. The plane is white with green and orange Seven-Up symbols. (Vern Georgia)

The famous Laird "Solution" in which Speed Holman won the Thompson Trophy Race in 1930; modified and painted with Seven-Up colors of white, with green and orange trim. It was used as a skywriter by Bob McManus. Photo taken at Wold-Chamberlain in the Spring of 1940. (Vern Georgia)

Board agreed to compensate him $200.[24]

Captain Walters and his sausage balloon were again hired, and the Air Guard once more shot down the device, using blank ammunition from the guns of their 0-38 aircraft. Walters received a $2,500 fee for his efforts.[25]

Local stars headlined the 1939 thrill show. Danny Fowlie, again took off and landed a Cub from ramps on a speeding car. Chuck Doyle changed from one of his motorcycles to a Cub flown by Lyle Thro, via a rope ladder. A comedy Cub act featured Dick Granere, the audience roaring with laughter to his "Admiral of the Swiss Navy" routine, where he pretended that he was a sea admiral and got into the airplane not knowing how to fly.

A multiple balloon ascension was the climactic event. In this act, daredevil, Earl Barrus, was to strap into a sling suspended by ropes beneath fifty meteorological balloons. The idea was for him to ascend and parachute back to the ground from a height of 2,000 feet, landing inside the racetrack. This event was set up and supervised by John Piccard, son of well-known balloonist and University of Minnesota Professor, Jean Piccard. John had purchased the balloons from the U. S. Department of Commerce, who used them to measure cloud ceilings and winds aloft for air navigation purposes. Curiously, the government was buying the balloons from night-club strip-tease artist, Sally Rand. Rand had financed balloon molds and used the balloons in her night-club act before the government ever had a need for them. When the need did arise, the government determined that it would be cheaper to buy the balloons than to have their own molds made.[26]

The balloons were to be inflated from tanks of hydrogen, one tank for each of the fifty balloons; each tank manned by one or two volunteer workers. The balloons were arranged in a circle around Barrus in his sling seat, and attached to the heavy tanks with one cord and to the sling with another. When the balloons were filled, on a hand signal, the workers were to cut the rope attaching the balloon to the tank. The balloon would then lift the sling and Barrus into the air with the second rope. One or two of the balloons burst immediately, and some of the volunteers cut the wrong ropes, leaving only 37 balloons to lift Barrus.

When the contraption reached a height of only twelve hundred feet, it could go no further and started

to drift toward Machinery Hill. Barrus decided to jump anyway, and was fortunate that his chute opened before he hit the ground. He landed near Snelling and Larpenteur, a couple of blocks from the grandstands...and outside the gates of the Fairgrounds. Dragging his parachute, Barrus was picked up by a motorist on his way to the Fair. Without wallet or any other identification, Barrus was unable to convince the gate attendant that he was a performer and should be allowed back in. Thanks to the generosity of the motorist, Barrus' re-admission was paid for. The hapless jumper then had to beg Clarence Hinck to reimburse the helpful motorist.[27]

Earl Barrus had performed the same act at the

Barrus going aloft under the balloons at the Minnesota State Fair. (Jim LaVake)

Earl Barrus poses for a publicity shot in his stocking feet and "bat-man" wings. Circa 1937. (Earl Barrus)

Wisconsin State Fair, at Chippewa Falls, the previous year. That time, on takeoff, his balloon cluster headed right for some high-tension power lines. Not knowing whether the power had been shut off for this event, he bailed out soon after the liftoff, dropping to the ground from what he estimated as 45 feet. His many parachute landings provided enough experience for him to land in a way that avoided serious injury.

Barrus' career had been a trail of similar death-defying episodes. He received his pilot's license in 1936, worked around Wold-Chamberlain airport selling tickets for weekend air rides and did some parachute jumping. His very first leap had been in the group jump at the Fairgrounds in 1936. That day, he landed in a hoglot on the neighboring University of Minnesota Farm Campus. He was to make a hundred parachute jumps around the country after that.

Barrus performed a Crazy Cub act at airshows around the country too. In this act, he would dress up like an old lady who wanted to go for an air ride. When the pilot got out to start the engine, there would be a buzzing smoke bomb set off under the engine cowling. Then, one of the show workmen would pull a pin out of the fuselage structure and the airplane would seemingly break in half. With its belly dragging on the ground, Barrus would taxi it around in circles until it was discreetly repinned for the next part of the act.

The "old lady" would somehow get the plane airborne and commence a show of dips and bounces, side-slips and yo-yo's. Variations of this act are still being performed around the country to the delight of great crowds.

Barrus also did a few house-crashes in his time. He crashed one at Wausau, Wisconsin, in 1939, flying a Waco GXE airplane. He had flown the machine from Mayer, Minnesota, where Clarence Hinck had secreted it from the eyes of the CAA. Barrus's experience with several forced landings from there to Wausau should have dissuaded him from going through with the crash, but it did not. Joe Williams, of Coon Rapids, Minnesota, who helped Earl get started from a small field by the Fairgrounds, tells

the story this way:

"C. W. Hinck had arranged for me to be interviewed on a 'man-in-the-street' radio program. I played the part of Captain Larry Stevens, a WWI ace who was to do the crash. I did the program because C. W. was afraid that the CAA might serve the real pilot with an injunction, and also...Earl hadn't shown up in Wausau yet.

"We bought some heavy wire net to put around the cockpit outside the fuselage to keep debris from the house out of the cockpit; a pillow and a blanket to use for padding the cockpit and instrument panel; and some wire to convert the front seat belt into a shoulder harness.

"When we had the engine running, and the airplane headed into the wind and Earl all set, I said, 'Earl, I've never seen a house-crash and I don't want to miss this one, so will you wait five minutes before you takeoff so I can get back to the Fairgrounds and see it?' Earl agreed, so I headed out. I had just reached the racetrack oval when the Waco circled the Fairgrounds and Earl started his approach. About a hundred yards from the house, the Waco slowed too much and Earl thought it might land before it hit, so he gave it the throttle just as a gust of wind threw him up about 75 feet. There was no possibility of climbing over the trees for another go-around, so Earl just dived into the house at a 30 degree angle. This made a real spectacular crash because at that speed and angle, the airplane just splintered the house along with the telephone poles inside, nosed over and landed upide down with the house wreckage on top of it!

"We had a few very anxious moments clearing away the debris to get Earl out, but there was no fire and Earl seemed okay. He even ran over in front of the grandstand and took some bows."[28]

Earl complained of a stiff and very painful neck the next day. At Wold-Chamberlain, Shorty De Ponti drove him to a chiropractor who manipulated his back, but to no avail. Barrus would find out years later, when x-rayed for another incident, that he had actually broken his neck that day.

Bad weather in 1940 caused the Minnesota State Fair Thrill Show to be shortened considerably. Clarence Hinck had booked "Art Davis and the

Chuck Doyle at the Minnesota State Fairgrounds, 1937. He is sitting on his reliable, boardwall-busting Indian motorcycle. Danny Fowlie's son, Dede, looks on admiringly. (Chuck Doyle)

Don Voge, Circa 1938. (Hinck family)

Wolverine Aces" for a precision acrobatic performance, and as it turned out, that was the only aviation event to occur. Danny Fowlie and Don Berent were two of the Aces, along with Jess Bristow, and Art Davis, nationally recognized stunt pilots. Their performance took place despite cloud ceilings that dipped occasionally to within 100 feet of the ground.

In 1941, Fair Week took place while America was still at peace. Danny Fowlie again performed stunts in a program billed "Blitzkrieg, Battle of the Skies." Jess Bristow showed visitors what dive-bombing looked like, diving repeatedly at the ground in his biplane. The Naval Reserve unit from Wold-Chamberlain, gave a demonstration of bombing and aerial combat. A glider demonstration was given by Everett Welsch and Al Falk. Woman parachutist, Verna Turner, made a leap by herself and C. W. Hinck provided a group parachute jump with four jumpers. Danny Fowlie closed the show with an inverted ribbon-pickup using the fin of his Cub!

With the war on, flying activity at the 1942 Minnesota State Fair was relegated to a glider demonstration by noted glider construction specialist and soaring record-holder, Ted Bellak. (More on Bellak in the chapter on World War II activities.) In 1943, a large display of captured German and Japanese weapons and war materials was shown to the public, but flying was curtailed.

In 1944, a simulated dogfight between a Japanese Zero and an American warplane was the feature attraction. There were no Minnesota State Fairs during 1945 and 1946.

Other promoters who booked Thrill Shows around the Midwest were Jack O. Engel, Frank Winkley, and Walter Klausler, all native Minnesotans. Jack Engel, originally a carnival magician, promoted airshows around Minnesota in the 1920s and 1930s. With the help of W. C. McRae, he promoted a show at Grove City, Minnesota, on 15 and 16 October, 1927 that featured the first All-Minnesota Air Derby. The "derby" was a pair of 65 mile races, one held each day. Gene Shank of Robbinsdale, and Gus Imm of Maynard, Minnesota, took first and second respectively, on both days. Other competitors were Art Sampson of Wahpeton, North Dakota; Jimmy Zarth of Maynard, Minnesota; and Fred Whittemore of Minneapolis. Saturday brought 5,000 spectators and Sunday brought out no less than 20,000.

Whittemore did stunts both days and was scheduled to test-fly a local home-built constructed by McRae and a group of helpers, including Ted Gruenhagen of Minneapolis. In the crush of spectators, the builders didn't notice until the show was over on Saturday, that the crowd had helped themselves to enough souvenir pieces of the airplane to render it unflyable.

Engel also promoted airshows at Alexandria, Montevideo and St. Cloud during 1929. Eventually, he was hired by Clarence Hinck to make Hinck's proposals to the State Fair Board in the 1930s. Engel was a close friend of Del Snyder, who operated a flying circus in the 1930s. Jack Engel's wife owned a restaurant in Grove City and visiting aviators in the late 1920s could count on a good, homecooked meal at the lunch counter. If they were down on their luck, the lunch was often free.

Frank Winkley started his career as a motorcycle racer for Clarence Hinck's Congress of Thrillers. Frank was seriously injured in a 1934 motorcycle race at the Fair and thereafter began a new career as booking agent for Hinck. He eventually went off on his own, gathering a group of fellow stunters to form the "Suicide Club." Winkley booked mostly automobile events with head-on crashes, rollovers, and demolition derbies. Winkley then worked his way into big-time circuit racing and managed the Minnesota State Fair auto racing programs as well as Don Voge's Crystal Speedway auto racing programs.

Walter Klausler was a contemporary of Clarence Hinck. Although Klausler made several proposals to the State Fair Board, he was never granted a contract. His specialty was promoting shows at the local County Fairs, where he had a virtual monopoly.

A 1938 promotional booklet that Klausler prepared to make his case to various Fair Boards, lists among other events: aviation stunts, parachute jumps, motorcycle board wall crashes, auto races, and airplane crashes. Several statements in his booklet highlight the thrill phase of aviation and its use for business purposes. For example, he states; "The outdoor entertainment field is strictly a business and business methods must be used. We have purchased airplanes at the season when owners are willing to sacrifice at next to nothing. We have a complete stock on hand at present for sale or to be used for crashing."[29]

Voge splinters a house at the Ascot Speedway in Los Angeles, circa 1937. (Walt Klausler)

Klausler had two premium aviation acts. The first was an airplane landing on a ramp built onto an automobile. For this attraction, Klausler took his own 1934 Plymouth and built a platform across the top consisting of two planks with wells cut out at the forward end. The idea was for a pilot to land a Cub or Taylorcraft on the ramps, roll forward and drop his wheels into the wells. He solicited Cedar Airport flying instructor, Wally Neuman, to make the first landing attempt in the summer of 1938. The landing was carried off with relative ease and became a staple of Klauslers repertoire. Though Danny Fowlie had little trouble with his ramp act at the Minnesota State Fair, it must be remembered that he did it on the mile racetrack backstretch. Most Country Fairs had merely a half mile racetrack, which allowed less time for the plane and car to get together on the straightaway. Wally Neuman mastered the short track.

Klausler's most spectacular stunt was the house-crash. His featured crasher was Don Voge. While Voge crashed a few houses for Hinck, he did most of his work for Klausler. Voge crashed houses for Walt at Superior and Chippewa Falls, Wisconsin; twice in New Ulm, Hibbing, and Albert Lea, Minnesota; once each at Faribault, Slayton, Spring Green and Sadelia, Minnesota; Sioux Falls, South Dakota; Des Moines, Bedford, and Center City in Iowa; Billings, Montana; and Gilmore Stadium in Los Angeles, altogether some 35 crashes during the late 1930s.

The CAA was after Klausler, like the others, to stop the house crashes. The Department of Commerce was concerned that only licensed pilots should be flying licensed aircraft. In Billings, Montana, they actually had handcuffs on Voge before he got out of the airplane following a crash. Spectators put up such a ruckus that CAA officials hurriedly made out their report and released him.

Once, in Faribault, Klausler's men couldn't get the engine of their old airplane to run smoothly so Voge could do a crash. The worn-out engine just wouldn't develop oil pressure. According to Klausler, during the lull, some little kid in the audience called out "Fake" and the audience got restless. "We quickly poured...some oil into the plane and he took off and hit the house and got out with a cut on his forehead. The local nurse fainted, everything...so the crowd got its money's worth."[30]

A description of one of Voge's Hibbing crashes sums up the event succinctly; "A half hour after the conclusion of the auto races, the restless audience at last caught sight of the Captain's plane coming from the south, barely 200 feet above the ground. It wobbled and wavered through the air, but headed directly for the specially constructed building in front of the stands. It crashed through like a bullet, landing 100 feet beyond the structure. Wings were ripped off, the fuselage ripped and the motor smashed. Not a stick of the building was left standing. The Captain was unhurt.

"Even as Voge was climbing down from the plane, resting on its nose, hundreds of souvenir hunters raced across the track and began stripping the plane."[31]

Klausler indicated that he used to buy the old airplane, contract for the house-crash with the Fair Board, build the house, and do the crash for $500, and make money. In fact, Klausler never paid more than $150 for an airplane and his fee was $500 "and up." The "and up" was for bigger Fairs where more security and publicity was needed.[32]

"House-crashing was not considered especially dangerous. In fact, it was more dangerous hitting a board wall with a motorcycle. One thing we never thought of in those days was fire. Never dawned on us. We'd put up a couple of telephone poles, the plane would come in at about 40 miles per hour, hit the house and slide through. We'd sometimes cut off part of a stick of dynamite and put a cap in it. We'd bury it in a sack of flour or a coffee can full of flour. It would make noise and throw up a lot of dust."[33]

Though it is not common knowledge, Klausler did at least one house-crash himself when he inadvertantly booked two at the same time. Voge did one, and he did the other, but even his family never was the wiser. As to being wiser, Klausler admits that once, when his old airplanes engine just wouldn't start, he went to Marvin Northrop, the aircraft parts dealer in Minneapolis, and convinced Northrup's secretary to loan him an engine. When the house-crash was over, Klausler simply returned the engine, never mentioning what he had done with it.[34]

Beginning in 1929, Klausler also taught auto shop classes at old North High School. He and his students began building racing car chassis. The chassis were sold to racers within the Minnesota Dirt Track Association of which Klausler was, at one time, President. Some of the students, themselves, purchased the cars and began racing careers. At times, North High School-built cars filled the fields of races around the country.

Oops! Lyle Thro taxies into hydrogen tanks at the 1939 Minnesota State Fair. The tanks were to inflate weather balloons for Earl Barrus' balloon parachute jump. (Hinck family)

Don Voge was quite a unique person. He was a large man with a high-pitched squeaky voice. Don had grown up on the family farm, next door to the Robbinsdale Airport near the city of Crystal, Minnesota. He watched with enjoyment the coming and going of the flyers and decided he'd like to fly. How Voge learned to fly is a widely-known story. It seems the airport, run by Gene Shank, was bordered by a certain tree at the edge of the Voge family property. It stood in the way of approach to the main runway. Pleas to the elder Voge, Don's father, to remove the tree, fell on deaf ears. He liked the tree. "It served a purpose for his farming...and that was the end of that!" according to Marvin Sievert, an airport kid in those days, and later, a flyer himself. "Don Voge heard about this and made a deal with Shank, where Shank would give him a couple of flying lessons if the tree disappeared some night. So Donald and some of his buddies went and cut that tree down. I don't remember what Mr. Voge's reaction was, but he couldn't sue the airport or Shank because his own son had cut it down."[35]

Voge never had many flying lessons. As soon as he could solo, he never took another. He apparently never got a pilot's license of any kind. In fact, it was Don's way to flaunt the law, often not paying his bills and living only a step ahead of his creditors.

Voge continued to operate from Robbinsdale during World War II in deference to the ban on civilian flying. He would taxi from his farm to the airport runway, takeoff and go flying. Then, by simply landing at the airport and taxiing onto his farm property, concealing the airplane among outbuildings and trees, he could deny that he had been flying. Other than his house-crashes in the 1930s, Voge's aviation career is unrecorded.

During the same period, he was also racing automobiles across the Midwest. Voge eventually built a racetrack on the family property. Crystal Speedway, or sometimes called Bearcat Speedway was sold by Voge around 1950 to finance Twin City Speedway, a bigger track located in New Brighton. That track operated during the 1960s.

It was at Crystal Speedway that Voge performed Minnesota's last recorded house-crash in 1948 as an added attraction to afternoon auto races. That act also put an end to Voge's flying career. Inspector, George Holey had warned Voge that if he carried out the well-advertised spectacle, Holey would permanently ground him. The irrepressible Voge, carried out his plan, as did Holey!

The Crystal property was later converted to *Glen Haven Cemetery*. Voge, who died in 1969, is buried there.

Chuck Doyle typified the total daredevil! Not only did he perform the aerial stunts such as parachute jumping, wing-walking, motorcycle to plane changes, smoke writing, and banner towing, but risked his life at ground level as well. His repertoire included board wall crashes, tunnel of flame drives, cycling in the revolving "barrel," stepping off a car at 60 miles an hour, leaping over cars and trucks on his motorcycle, head-on crashes, etc. In the act where he "stepped off a car" at 60 miles an hour, he would stand on the rear bumper of a speeding automobile holding onto a rope looped through the cars side windows. As the car raced over a pool of blazing gasoline on a Fair's racetrack straightaway, he would lower himself until he dragged on the ground and through the flames. How did Doyle become interested in such a life, and more amazingly...how did he live through it?

Born in 1916 in South Minneapolis, Doyle never graduated from High School. His concentration was not on schoolwork, but on motorcycles and airplanes. He often sneaked out on his lunch hour, raced to Wold-Chamberlain Field on his "sickle" (as he called it), and hung around there, usually returning late to classes. He found odd jobs at the airport on weekends, selling tickets for local barnstormers such as Bill Shaw and Florence Klingensmith, or sweeping floors at Hanford Airlines. Doyle got his private license in 1933 and immediately bought his own airplane, an OX-5 Travel Air, from Shorty De Ponti.

1939 Minnesota State Fair. Danny Fowlie does a short-field takeoff in front of the grandstand. (Jim LaVake)

Chuck Doyle had the help of a loan from Interstate Finance Company, whose offices were on the field. He modified the Travel Air in the following year by adding a Wright J-5 engine in place of the OX-5.

Doyle made his first parachute jumps in 1935, including his first group jump at the State Fairgrounds. He had to use his emergency chest parachute once in 1936 when his main chute failed to open, saving his life and making him a member of the exclusive Caterpillar Club. That Club was an organization of persons whose lives had been saved by the use of the "silk," as it was called, thus the association with the Caterpillar.

In 1935, Doyle and Stella Kindem did several tandem brother-sister jumps from the Freeman Ford Trimotor during weekend airshows at Wold-Chamberlain, leaping hand in hand. On one occasion, Doyle bounced off the roof of an Army barracks on the Fort Snelling military reservation. Unhurt, he thought his troubles were over until he received a bill from the Government for $18 to cover damages to the roof.[36]

Doyle owned several motorcycles. One, a 4-cylinder Indian, was used for board wall crashes. A 1933 Harley-Davidson was used for ramp jumping over cars. For the board wall crashes, Doyle fastened a U-shaped iron bar to the front motorcycle fork, behind which he could lower his head before impact. Thus single, double and even triple burning board walls were "busted." He added extra springs to the driver's seat, modified the fork to make it stronger, and mounted automobile tires to the rims, all for greater cushioning on his jump landings.

The sturdy Harley was also used for cycle-to-plane transfers. Doyle would drive the Harley at a speed matching that of the airplane overhead, then simply grab a rope ladder suspended from the plane, and climb off his bike. The bike would go careening down the track, usually getting bent up. No matter, it was a sturdy machine and could be hammered back into shape afterward.

In 1937, Doyle signed on with Bob Ward's Hollywood Daredevils. The group performed from Canada, through Minnesota during State Fair time, and finally down into the South, ending the year at Biloxi, Mississippi. Along the way, Doyle did a couple of house-crashes. In Mississippi, the troupe fell on hard times, or so Ward claimed. He had no cash to carry the group over, but instead made some extravagant personal purchases and claimed insolvency. One morning, Doyle, Danny Fowlie, and Bob

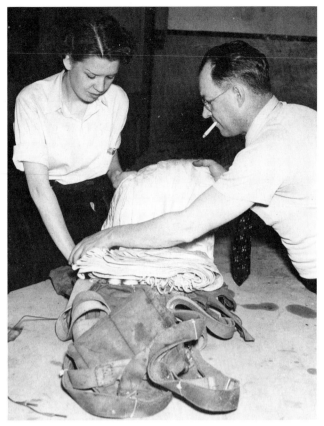

Woman parachute rigger and jumper, Birdie Draper, watches Lyman "Stub" Chrissinger demonstrate some of the fine points of repacking a parachute. Chrissinger was instructor, licensed repacker, coach, advisor, and thrill event choreographer to the local Ripcord Club members. (Vern Georgia)

Maas, who comprised the troupe, woke to find that Ward had disappeared. At Ward's rented home, they found his personal belongings had also vanished. The men were on their own.

Left without any work, they spent their last savings gambling in hopes of gaining enough to get back home. No luck...it turned out to be "tap city" as Doyle puts it. He had to sell his favorite Harley to raise funds. Maas took the bus home, leaving Doyle and Fowlie to ride back on the Indian motorcycle. Running into snow as far south as Joplin, Missouri, the pair put the Indian in storage and took a bus back to the Twin Cities.

Later, Doyle and Fowlie tried to start their own thrill show group, but things didn't work out. Fowlie left to go on his own and, in 1942, Doyle took a job with Northwest Airlines. Northwest gave him an alternative; either quit his stunting or forget about an airline career. He decided on the former, but kept his fingers in crop-spraying, smoke-writing, and banner towing.

The parachutists on the Thrill Show circuit had the roughest time of all the performers. Indeed, parachute jumping in the 1930s was a hazardous occupation. Parachutes of the day were made of silk and weighed from 15 to 18 pounds. Canopies were from 22 to 28 feet in diameter; most were marginally steerable, if at all. Since the $275 to $325 cost of a parachute was high, many of the jumpers rented certified parachutes from a licensed "rigger" such as Stub Chrissinger of Minneapolis. In the late 1930 period, Chrissinger was one of only 19 such licensed riggers

in the country and President of the local Ripcord Club, a social organization of exhibition jumpers.

Chrissinger arranged jumps for promoters such as Hinck and Klausler. He was the local parachute expert, the source of equipment, instruction, and general advice on the subject. His wry sense of humor, stocky build and ever-present cigarette were characteristic of the man. After a promising young acrobatic pilot, Channing Seabury, was killed in a low-level jump from his disabled GeeBee airplane over Wold-Chamberlain, Chrissinger recovered the bloody parachute. Though he laundered it and repacked it, local jumpers would not wear it because of the memory, and maybe a little superstition. Chuck Doyle refused it and Chrissinger accused him of being a prima donna. Doyle later used the chute, but only as a reserve pack.

The Ripcord Club included a veteran jumper named Jerry Johnson, a printer by trade. Johnson set a record on 8 June, 1935, by making fifteen parachute jumps in a single day over Wold-Chamberlain. The event took twelve hours, with the last jump occurring after dark. With each jump, the shock to Johnsons legs would leave him hobbling in pain, but he continued for the record. While he was going up and down, two of his companions from the Club were kept busy repacking the chutes.

Earl Barrus, Bud Quist, Al Kammholz and Walter Miller were members of the Ripcord Club. So too were women jumpers, Betty Goltz, Stella Kindem, Marcella Marcoulier and Birdie "the Rock" Draper. Jumping for exhibition purposes was worth from $50 to $75 per drop and in the 1930s, a lot of money for a few minutes work, even if the job did have its hazards.

Jumping in a strong wind in September, 1937, Birdie Draper was dragged across the ground, getting severly bruised. She landed on a tent on the Fairgrounds on another occasion, and slid off onto the ground, injuring herself again. Eventually, she teamed up with Frank Frakes and toured the country with him.

Marcoulier had her share of close calls as well. In October of 1937, she landed on the concrete ramp in front of the Navy hangar at Wold-Chamberlain, struck her head and was rushed to Northwestern Hospital. Upon her release days later, she indicated she would like to continue the line of work.

Betty Goltz had her problems at the 1936 State Fair as mentioned previously, when her parachute ripcord caught in the sleeve of her coveralls. She went on to earn her rigger's license with instruction from Chrissinger. She became only the 10th licensed woman rigger in the United States. She embarked on a career of jumping at shows across the country.

Chrissinger grabbed local headlines when he recruited six women to become airshow parachutists. One was Birdie Draper, the others were Dorothy Stevens, Eleanor Van De Mark, Dorothy "Jeep" Collins, Alene Vizenor, and Ruth LaFayollette. Other women in the local parachute sorority were Florence Rogish and Delia Parker. Rogish went on to an even-more-dangerous career, that of Roller Derby participant; Delia Parker, to prove parachuting was not the most stressful occupation, agreed on one occasion, to sit in a darkened movie theater alone, to watch both Frankenstein and Dracula movies. This scheme was cooked up by popular newspaper columnist, Cedric Adams. The paper paid Parker $10 for being a good sport, and the University of Minnesota Medical School wired her to an electrocardiograph to measure her "fright level."

Unfortunately, there was real tragedy mixed with mishap for the parachutists. Bat-man chutist, Clem Sohn, of Lansing, Michigan, who had performed so spectacularly at the 1935 State Fair, died in France in 1937. His two parachutes failed to open and he lost his life before a crowd of 30,000 persons. Bill Ash was killed at the 1933 State Fair as mentioned previously, but others followed.

"Ace" Von Korb was another local casualty. On 20 July, 1940, while practicing his routine for the first Aquatennial airshow, Von Korb plunged straight into the Minnesota River bottoms south of the cities. In leaping from a plane piloted by George Holey, Von Korb never pulled either of his ripcords.

His bat-man costume may have been the culprit. It was constructed so that there were "wings" sewn between his arms and sides, and also between his legs. The arrangement was intended to provide a glider-like soaring capability, but was his undoing. A post-mortem examination of his body showed that his shoulders appeared to have been broken when he spread his wings, preventing him from reaching his ripcords. It also appeared that the chest buckle of his parachute harness had slid up to his neck, possibly choking him.[37]

One thing is certain. The thrill show act of parachute jumping was very much more dangerous than house-crashing, yet the one act was approved; the other was condemned.

While the thrill show associated with County and State Fairs were a business for some folks, they were certainly entertainment for the masses. In the decade of the 1930s the airplane was to bring laughs and thrills to the public like no other attraction in America.

BARNSTORMERS

A"Barnstormer," according to Funk & Wagnalls,

is a person who tours the country giving flying exhibitions. In common use, the term refers to persons who not only exhibited, but made a living carrying passengers for sight-seeing purposes. Barnstormers operated from local airstrips or farm fields they might have dropped into. They may have posted advertising handbills ahead of time, or simply buzzed the main street of the nearby town to attract attention; then waited at the nearest farm field for paying customers to arrive. It is a fact that virtually any pilot who owned his own aircraft in the period of the 1920s and early 1930s could be considered a "barnstormer" because that was a part of their life, without any doubt.

The most compelling reason that those early flyers spent weekends, and often the whole week, barnstorming, was the motivation to eke out a living engaged in what they loved to do...fly. For this privilege, they often endured cold nights, sleeping on the ground under the wing of their airplane. They made field repairs to their ships for any number of reasons, mostly due to the unreliability of aircraft engines of that period and the rough farm field landing places. Added to this was the specter of having to leave a damaged airplane in a field to go find a telephone; only to return and find the fabric cut off, the seat cushions, instruments, and any other loose articles in the airplane, gone...thanks to the public's eagerness to take "souvenirs."

Extracting from the curious, whatever fares were possible, from 50 cents to a five-dollar bill; the barnstormers either managed to survive hard times to enter the fledgling airlines or military...or cracked-up their ships, killing themselves. Others, who were less aggressive, were put out of business by the Great Depression, and went into other lines of work.

Because every flyer of the period who owned an airplane was really a barnstormer, it would be impractical and virtually impossible to mention all of the Minnesota barnstormers in this narrative. We would like to profile the backgrounds of a few who were representative of the genre, beginning with the larger organized teams.

THE FEDERATED FLIERS AND CLARENCE HINCK

Clarence Walter Hinck was born in Litchfield, Minnesota, on 15 September, 1889. Of Scandinavian stock, his mother, Clara, was from Sweden; and father, Jens Frederick Hinck, from Denmark. Clarence was the fourth of six children. Lillian, the fifth child, would marry parachute jumper, Harry Proctor. Of the five boys, the oldest was Fred, then came Harry, Arthur, Clarence, and baby brother, Elmer.

Clarence, along with two brothers, Fred and Harry, left Minnesota for North Dakota before he had finished his schooling. Fred became a barber, Harry went on with school, and Clarence became the manager of a tavern-pool hall near Devil's Lake. He homesteaded some property there while still in his twenties, then sold it and returned to Minneapolis, where be bought into one or two seedy hotels along Washington

Avenue. He found the landlord business still a meager living, and had to deliver mail and packages for the Dayton's Dry Goods Company to supplement his income.

Earliest records of Clarence's aviation life begin in 1917, when, at age 27, he enlisted as a Naval Aviation Machinist's Mate and became a student at the Dunwoody Institute Naval Training School, one of a group of 700 cadets. He became close friends with the Commandant of the School, Lieutenant Commander Colby Dodge, and became Dodge's personal driver. Both Dodge and Hinck lived at the Minneapolis Radisson Hotel where they were afforded fine accommodations and excellent food. The hotel was often the scene of grand parties, at which the cadets were invited guests. They ate and drank and had a racous

58

time. Hinck was also in charge of the School's mascot, a bear cub named Evelyn, or "Evie" for short. Clarence led the animal around on a leash, and the pair were familiar sights in downtown Minneapolis.

In 1917, America joined in the Great War, but by the time Clarence and the other students had finished their training, the war was winding down and Clarence was never sent to active duty with a military unit.

Lt. Commander Colby Dodge recruited Clarence Hinck into the newly organized Minneapolis Aero Club. With the war over, the two men looked forward to a business career that, most logically, would involve aviation.

In 1919, Hinck and Dodge joined with a recently returned military aviator named Dick Grace, to incorporate a barnstorming association in Minneapolis, called the Federated Fliers, Inc. Grace's background is interesting. He was born in Minnesota in 1898 and hooked up with a barnstormer in North Dakota as a teenager. He learned to fly, and volunteered for the Navy, earning his wings at Pensacola where he flew the earliest flying boats. Grace then shipped overseas and was assigned to a bomber group in France, flying DH-9 aircraft, then was temporarily attached to a pursuit group in which he flew SPAD's. He was shot down in conbat, but landed safely inside Allied lines. Rehabilitated and transferred to the Italian front, Grace flew Macchi flying boats from Laga di Bolsana.[1]

Upon discharge, Grace joined Colby Dodge and Clarence Hinck as a partner in the Federated Fliers Corporation. He was the pilot and flew the exhibitions, and passenger-hops during the Fliers' 1919 tour

Clarence Hinck and the Dunwoody bear mascot, "Evie," on a streetcorner in downtown Minneapolis, 1918. (Hinck family)

The Commandant's driver, Clarence Hinck at the wheel. In the back seat, Lt. Commander Colby Dodge of the Dunwoody Naval Training Detachment, sits with his wife and a cadet photographer, riding in style! 1918. (Hinck family)

of the Upper Midwest. In 1920, he moved to Hollywood to commence a career as stunt man with Fox Movie Studios. Considered a general stunt man, he wrestled alligators, performed high-dives, auto crashes, speedboat transfers, and wing walking, and starred in a new event, house-crashing. His association with western star, Tom Mix, got him movie serial work as both stunt man and house-crasher. Mix gave Grace a Thomas-Morse airplane that was flown in several movies.

Grace's most famous movie crash was done in the Academy Award winning 1927 movie, "Wings," where he crashed a SPAD airplane into a house. The most popular aviation films of the 1930s include Grace's name in the credits. He was also a writer, penning four books, that dramatized his career, and wrote the script for the movie, "Lost Squadron" for RKO Pictures in 1932.

On the 4th of July 1927, Grace attempted to fly from Barking Sands Airfield on the island of Kauai, Hawaii, to California. He was forced by mechanical problems to return, groundlooped the airplane, thus ending the endeavor.

During World War II, Grace embarked on a second career as a test pilot in the Army Air Force, and was stationed at Yuma, Arizona. He also flew as ferry pilot, from a base at Memphis, Tennessee. He was assigned overseas and completed 20 bombing missions over Germany while Assistant Group Operations Officer of his unit. Dick Grace finally succumbed to emphysema in 1965 after surviving 47 movie stunt crashes and suffering over 80 broken bones.

Grace, Hinck, and Dodge, as partners in the Federated Fliers, sought a base of operations and entered into a 5-year lease for a quarter section of land near what is now the City of Fridley, Minnesota. The lease price for the first year was $100, the total for the five years, $600. This airfield was one of the first in the State. The other original fields were the Earle Brown Farm where Walter Bullock operated, and the Curtiss-Northwest Field on Snelling and Larpenteur Avenues in St. Paul, where an active business was being conducted by William Kidder. Soon, Speedway Field at the present site of Wold-Chamberlain Airport (Minneapolis-St. Paul International) would acquire an operator and join the ranks. Brown Field closed before 1920.

Federated Fliers hangar at Fridley Field, 1921. That's Clarence waving the flag. (Hinck family)

The Federated Fliers corporation was officially chartered by the State on 8 July, 1919. A stock issue was arranged with shares going to the Corporate officers. The business office was located in Minneapolis, but the flying took place at Fridley.[2]

Looking for aircraft to use in their barnstorming operation, and using the influence of Dodge, the Federated Fliers acquired 18 aircraft that had become war-surplus, from the Aero Mechanics School in St. Paul. These aircraft had been used in the school's training program and had been flown from the Brown Farm field, and then stored in the Roanoke Building in downtown Minneapolis. The partners brought the planes to Fridley where they were reassembled. Fifteen JN-4 "Jennies" and three LWF trainers were thus available for exhibition work or for sale. A hangar was built at Fridley in 1919.

Hinck made his first exhibition proposal to the Minnesota State Fair Board that year, offering the services of Dick Grace as a stunt flyer, claiming that he was "like Locklear." The Fair Board turned down the proposal and, in fact, hired Ormer Locklear for the main thrill performance that year. Locklear had become very well known for his wing-walking and stunting.[3]

Clarence Hinck took over the chores of promotion and publicity for the Federated Fliers; Dodge managed the operations; and Grace handling the flying. Hinck grabbed every chance available to promote the group and gain newspaper headlines. One such promotion exploited an "air mail" flight made by Dick Grace from Minneapolis to Eau Claire, Wisconsin. Grace carried letters of greeting written by the Mayor of Minneapolis, the secretary of the Civic and Commerce Association, and William F. Brooks, president of the Minneapolis Aero Club. The mail also included a compilation of the nation's bonded attorneys to be published in the Lane Publishing Company of Eau Claire's annual "Blue Book." The event was recognized as the first local instance of business being conducted by aeroplane.[4]

Hinck directed Grace to fly over the Minneapolis loop with Star newspaper photographer, Drew Blymer, snapping photos that could be used on the front page of the newspaper, and crediting the Federated Fliers, of course. Hinck also accepted the position of Minnesota State Constable, bringing his name further into the limelight.

Circulating promotional material to all civic and commerce associations around the State, brought a deluge of requests for appearances of an airman and an airplane. Most local and county officials were excited about the possibility of having an airplane perform or simply fly over their local summer Fair festivities. It was a time of strong emotion following the heroic return of troops from the European war; and every community was honoring their soldiers with a parade or Fair appearance.

In June, the Federated Fliers provided a plane for an exhibition at Eau Claire, in July at Grand Rapids, and in August, several other places. In September, Hinck's plane was exhibited at the Dakota County Fair where his contract called for him to be paid $750 for two flights by Dick Grace on each of two days - one flight in the afternoon, one flight in the evening.[5] In most cases, Clarence would quote a high figure, perhaps as much as $2,000 for a three or four day exhibition, that included perhaps two flights per day with stunts. When the prospect of losing the date due to too high a price, he would back down and settle on a lower figure.

A typical contract, as with the City of Grand Rapids, Minnesota, called for stunt flying that included: loops, "vrilles," stalls, zooms, tail-spins, side-slips, chandelles, Immelman turns and spirals. Hinck agreed to use competent flyers for the aerial stunts and to employ security personnel to keep the spectators from getting hurt. For this event, his fee was $800. If weather would cancel the performance, he was still to get half the fee.[6]

Hinck asked the Rice County Fair Board for a fee of $1750.00, but settled for $600.00. Even at that, it was a tremendous figure considering what the average working man was earning.

In 1919, in addition to the joy of seeing soldiers

Paul Hamilton with his camera, Elmer Hinck and Walter Hallgren in typical period cloting in this slightly tattered 1921 photo. (Hinck family)

return from the war, and listening to tales of flying over the front lines, the world was excited about a successful flight across the Atlantic by Englishmen, Sir Arthur Whitten Brown and Sir John Alcock. They flew from the U. S. to the coast of Ireland in a little over 16 hours, in a British Vickers Vimy airplane. This feat thrilled the world, and the Twin Cities. When Brown appeared in November at a lecture in St. Paul, he drew a huge crowd.[7] Hinck, who attended the lecture, immediately drew up plans for an expanded 1920 season which would include a larger troupe of pilots and performers.

First additional member to be signed in January, was Lt. Harold Peterson. Equally as colorful as Dick Grace, Peterson was also an ex-military pilot. He had served with the Border Patrol of the Army Air Service at Marfa, Texas, during 1919. That period had been one of high tension along the southwest border, with Mexican raiding parties crossing into the U. S., stealing cattle, pillaging property, and killing American citizens. A particularly vexsome bandit named Pancho Villa, and his henchmen, were the culprits and the U. S. Army was charged with interdicting their raids. Flying DH-4's, the Army service pilots flew daylight patrols back and forth along the border.

Peterson, and a companion pilot, Art Davis, were forced down on their patrol of 10 August, 1919, and a tremendous air search for them ensued. The Army received a ransom note the next day from a Villa henchman, named Jesus Renteria, who demanded $15,000.00 for their release. After two days of negotiations, rough-and-ready Cavalry Commander, Captain Leonard F. Matlack, crossed the border with his U. S. troops at midnight on August 19 from his outpost at Candelaria, Texas. He paid only half the ransom and rescued the flyers. The next day, a force of 300 Cavalry troops again crossed the border in pursuit of Renteria. Lieutenants Frank Estill and Russell H. Cooper, flying patrol in advance of the troop column, spotted Renteria on his white horse with two henchmen, and gunned them down from the air.[8]

The story of Peterson's adventures was front-page news and in January of 1920, Clarence Hinck was fortunate to corral the recently discharged Peterson for a position with the Federated Fliers.

Clarence Hinck, second from left; Elmer Hinck on wing; and Lyle Thro at right; with some show performers, on the barnstorming tour. Circa 1923. (Hinck family)

Like Grace and Peterson, Nick Mamer came as an ex-military pilot. He had started flying with the Signal Corps in 1916, was stationed in the Canal Zone, and later in Europe. During his time with Hinck, he won a trick flying contest at the Minnesota State Fairgrounds, and with Hinck as a passenger, set a speed record in flying from Minneapolis to Duluth in one hour and 35 minutes.

By 1920, the youngest Hinck brother, Elmer, had learned to fly. He was an ex-Army man, having been in the Infantry, seeing action at St. Mihiel and the Argonne in France. Elmer had taken lessons from Peterson and Grace enroute to the exhibitions and did some wing-walking and parachute jumping as his role in the show. He once hung by his knees from the landing gear of a Jenny, to drape a flag advertising the annual Freshman-Sophomore Games at the University of Minnesota Farm School, over the St. Paul campus' heating plant smokestack.

He laughed about a time in rough weather when he was bounced off the top wing of a plane. He said he was "entirely surrounded by exceedingly thin, if somewhat boisterous air." He managed, on that occasion, to break his fist through the top wing's fabric and grab a handhold on a wing rib, saving his life.[9]

In February of 1928, Elmer qualified as a Transport Pilot and joined Universal Aviation School at Wold-Chamberlain Field to spend the rest of his career as an instructor. To most of Minnesota's aviation community, he was "Mr. Instructor," perhaps the best the state ever produced. He was very professional, but had a subtle humor, once telling a student, "airplanes are like women... you never get to understand 'em, you just learn to live with 'em."[10]

From 1934 to 1938, Hinck instructed for Shorty DePonti at Wold, then opened his own flight school. With the coming of the Civilian Pilot Training Program (CPT) in 1939, he and brother, Clarence, contracted with the Government to train student pilots. The School's name was Elmer Hinck Flying Service. Money was borrowed by Clarence and Elmer from Interstate Finance, a loan agency specializing in aircraft related loans. Hinck's office was at Wold-Chamberlain, with most of the training planes located at nearby Nicollet Airfield. (92nd Street and Nicollet Avenue in South Minneapolis).

On 25 August, 1942, tragedy struck the Hinck family, as well as the whole flying community, when Elmer and another instructor, Fred "Fritz" Kraemer, on their way from Nicollet Field to Monticello, were killed. Their Cub Coupe spun in while Fritz was performing impromptu aerobatics. Hitting first power lines, the plane burst into flame upon contact with the ground. The two pilots were trapped and burned to death.[11]

Jack Malone, from Woodstock, Minnesota, was another pilot joining Hinck's group. He had been through the Dunwoody Mechanics School, enlisted in the Signal Corps as an aviation cadet, but never saw oversees duty. He worked as an instructor for the Larrabee brothers, Wilbur and Weldon, at the Security Aircraft Company at Speedway Field. He then joined with Clarence Hinck and worked the barnstorming tour from 1920 until 1924, when he went full time

The purple Jenny, decked out for advertising the Chippewa Falls, Wisconsin, Mardi Gras, 1921. Clarence Hinck stands at far left with members of the Chippewa Falls Chamber of Commerce. In the airplane's front seat is Elmer Hinck, in the rear, Walter Hallgren. (Hinck family)

with the newly formed 109th Air Guard Squadron. In 1928, Malone became a pilot for Northwest Airways and close friends with Speed Holman. He was one of the pallbearers at Holman's funeral in 1931.

In 1933, Malone flew a bucket of Lake Itasca water to the Chicago World's Fair where it was poured into a relief map of Minnesota in the State's exhibit there. Malone was one of the first four Air Guard pilots in the United States to be called to active duty for World War II.

Walter Hallgren was another of Hinck's ex-military pilots. He had joined the Royal Flying Corps in 1917, was trained in Canada, and assigned to a pursuit squadron in France. He spent three weeks in a hospital after being shot down on 4 May, 1918. When returned to active duty, he was shot down again; this time requiring six weeks of hospitalization. Hallgren returned once more to active duty and was discharged in March of 1919. He came to the Twin Cities, barnstormed with Hinck and later took an instructor's job with Universal Flying Schools at Wold-Chamberlain.[12]

Other pilots who began barnstorming for Hinck were; Peter S. Rask, also ex-military; Al Opsahl; Glen Soden; and a Lt. Tattersfield. Horace Inman, an enthusiastic aviator from Minneapolis, was one of several there wasn't room for. He wrote to Hinck, soliciting a job, stating that he was able to, "walk wings, do trap work from the landing gear, make parachute leaps, [and had his] own rope ladder ready to go at a moment's notice."[13] Though he was not hired by Hinck, he did go on to become a well-known barnstormer.

Pumping out advertising material to supply the eager performers with work, Hinck never missed a chance to get something in the newspapers. The story got around, as told by Walt Hallgren, of how the group trailed ducks in the air, tickling them and putting salt on their tails, finally plucking them out of the air and packing them into a bag. This was done, according to Hallgren, because *shooting* ducks from an airplane was illegal.[14]

From Clarence Hinck's 1920 ledger excerpts, the summer barnstorming tour included:

May 30, St. Cloud: featuring Glen Soden, Walter Hallgren, John Malone, Pete Rask, Elmer Hinck and parachute jumper, Harry O. Proctor. Lots of pilots, and lots of planes to carry passengers, the

staple of the barnstorming business.
June 3, Aitkin: Total receipts $332.55
June 4, Brainerd.
June 5, Wadena.
June 6, Detroit Lakes.
June 10, Alexandria.
June 12, Detroit Lakes.
June 13, Fargo.
June 14, Glyndon and White Earth, Minnesota.
June 18, Crookston.

During June, Clarence paid $190.00 to motorcycle riders each two-week pay period, $250.00 to each of the auto polo performers. This was the first mention in Hinck's papers that he employed either attraction. It was done to draw the crowds into the grandstand, that normally would "rubberneck" outside to watch the aerial performances and not buy a ticket.

Motorcycle riders were Del Snyder, Art Spavin and Art Peterson. The same crew did the Auto Polo event in which stripped down Model T chassis with rollover bars were used. A match pitted two such cars against each other, each manned by a driver and a mallet-man. The mallet-man's job was to hit a basketball-sized ball across a line at either end of the racetrack in front of grandstands at a local fairgrounds.

The event sounds pretty dull by today's standards, but it was enlivened by antics such as one car riding up on the back of another and being carried the full length of the track, or when Clarence Hinck was referee, the team would make a close pass at him, forcing him to jump out of the way and lose his hat. Immediately, the cars would run over his hat again and again, to the laughter of the crowd. Clarence's straw hats were purchased in quantity for this reason. In the event of an occasional rollover, the two passengers would generally jump clear, right the car, and the match would continue.

Some additional notes from the Flier's 1920 ledger:
June 20-21-22, Devil's Lake, North Dakota: Total receipts $1,438.07.
June 28, Waverly: Vernon Omlie carried 26 passengers.
July 3, Valley City, North Dakota.
July 6, Wahpeton, North Dakota: Receipts $700.00.

Hinck's Motor derby owned this red transport trailer, circa 1935. Auto Polo/Push-Ball cars and motorcycles are loaded aboard. (Hinck family)

July 23, Fairmont, Minnesota: Receipts $700.00.
July 30, Mankato, Minnesota: Receipts $672.10.

Apparently Harold Peterson and Pete Rask were considered "staff" as they were paid a weekly salary of $300.00 and $250.00 respectively through the summer.

Hinck supplied the *Minneapolis Journal* with regular advertising. An ad offered flight instruction indicating the staff consisted of Lieutenants: Mamer, Peterson, Tattersfield and Rask, "all former commissioned army instructors."[15]

During 1920, news photos were flown to Chicago by Rask and Hinck in the amazing time of seven hours and twenty minutes, including a fuel stop at Barraboo.[16] During the summer of 1920, a fire destroyed the hangar at Fridley Field, causing $15,000 damage; burning up Glen Soden's airplane and a new car belonging to Hinck.[17] Staging for a few weeks at Speedway Field, Hinck soon opened a new office at Robbinsdale Airport, then only a farm field. The fire and related moves scaled down the barnstorming effort apparently, for nothing further appears in the Hinck ledger for that season.

The year 1921 brought the busiest season yet for Hinck. Perhaps one of his most headline-grabbing events happened early in the year. Chippewa Falls, Wisconsin, celebrated its annual Mardi-Gras and Historical Pageant from June 28 to the 4th of July. In March, however, Hinck had been contacted about

A smiling Clarence Hinck stands in front of a wrecked OX-5 Swallow airplane, just house-crashed at Green Bay, Wisconsin, 1938. He is smiling because, (a) nobody had been killed, (b) the crowd was thrilled and satisfied, and, (c) he had successfully completed his contract and would certainly be paid. (Hinck family)

painting an airplane with the dates and touring the Midwest to advertise the event, visiting hundreds of towns. A Jenny was then painted a garish purple with white lettering announcing the activities. Flying was done by Walter Hallgren and encompassed some three months prior to the Mardi Gras. In the course of its tour, the Jenny set a speed record from Minneapolis to Chippewa Falls, a distance of 90 miles in 55 minutes. Not at all bad for a Jenny.[18]

Hinck's 1921 ledger shows the summer tour lasting from the 4th of July until the beginning of October. Some excerpts follow:

July 4, Waseca, Minnesota: Paid $31.17 for fireworks, $50.00 to chute jumper, netted $704.13.
July 8, Heron Lake, Minnesota: Three planes, with Jack Anderson, Lyle Thro and Walter Hallgren carrying passengers. Anderson earned $7.74, Thro $7.74, Hallgren, $15.74, Waldron, the manager, was paid a commission of $12.75.
July 14, Jasper, Minnesota: Carried 47 passengers in three planes.
July 23, Litchfield, Minnesota: Jack Anderson carried 2 passengers and earned $10. He used $11.00 in gas and oil, paid his "shill," (the barker who stirs up business from a crowd), $4.00, and ended up owing Hinck $7.20! Hinck, himself this day earned $8.04.
July 24, Litchfield, Minnesota: Second day, big day! The crews carried some 75 passengers, with Anderson earning $23.00, Jack Malone $102.50, Hallgren $157.50, and Waldron's commission was $30.03. Hinck kept $166.82.

The tour continued through Minnesota during August, spilling into North Dakota toward the end of August and beginning of September, and finally back to western Minnesota in October. The final entry was dated 2 October, 1921.

Several testimonial letters praised the fine performances staged by the Federated Fliers. For example; from Dr. E. W. Arnold, Commander of Legion Post -23-32 of Adrian, Minnesota, "...the wing walking, parachute jumps, sham battles and trick flying, brought cheers from the crowd, and all felt that they had received more than their money's worth."[19]

Charles H. March of Litchfield, stated, "Everything was done with promptness, and your flyers all being so gentlemanly, and everything done with such grace, that it added doubly to the pleasure of the entertainment. It so often happens that performances of this kind do not come up to the advertisement. While your advertisement was good, and called a large crowd, your performance was better than you promised."[20] Mr. W. G. Wright, Chairman of the Publicity Committee of the Jasper, Minnesota, Harvest Festival, wrote in August, "The wing walking, aerobatic stunts, etc., were accomplished so close to the ground that every move of the performer (Elmer Hinck in this case) was visible to the crowd, and the parachute drop was the greatest exhibition of this kind ever witnessed in this section."[21]

So glowing were the testimonials that it almost seems as if Hinck, himself, had written them. That he solicited them from the individuals is undoubtedly true, and had they not been written from different typewriters and hands, on separate letterheads, they would be truly suspect!

Appearing on the 1922 summer tour with Hinck's group were Lyle Thro and Jack Anderson once more. Thro was a stunt pilot and carried passengers. He flew on the barnstorming trail for many years, tried to catch on with a Mexican airline in 1928, and helped to form Bowen Airlines in Oklahoma in 1934. Thro returned to Minneapolis and flew for Hinck again in the late 1930s.

Jack Anderson did not do stunt flying, but carried passengers, the real stock-in-trade of the traveling troupes in those years. Jack flew 1600 hours for the Federated Fliers from 1920 through 1923, according to his logbook.[22] He continued to carry passengers after his time with Hinck, trying very hard to get on with any airline, pleading his case with Robertson, Rapid Airlines of South Dakota, China Federal, Inc. and Northwest Airways. Receiving no offers, he went to work for Universal Aviation Schools at Rochester, Minnesota, until the company closed in the hard times of 1929. Anderson flew his own Eaglerock airplane through the early 1930s, lasting out the depression as best he could, finally entering politics as Big Stone County Registrar of Deeds. There, through wise land investments, he finally succeeded in acquiring some reasonable financial success.[23]

In 1922, Hinck hired others, including parachutist, Harry O. Proctor, who was destined to become his brother-in-law. Vernon Omlie was a stunt pilot for the group, cyclist Roy Bouchard signed on as well as aerial photographer, Paul Hamilton. A Secretary, Lucille Kuhn, and an advance man, J. O. Engel, became permanent staff. Other salaried members were cyclists, Art Peterson, Art Spavin and Delmar Snyder, who were paid $35.00 per week. Elmer Hinck received a weekly $35.00 salary; Jack Malone, a weekly $50.00; Hallgren $50.00; Lucille Kuhn $.35 per hour; Proctor $25.00 to $50.00 per jump; with Charles Hardin and Vern Omlie commissioned for passenger hops.[24]

The summer tour included Aitkin, Crookston, Devil's Lake, St. Cloud, Sandstone, Alexandria, White Earth, Lacota, Valley City, Wahpeton, Brainerd, Superior, Mankato and Fairmont. Details in Hinck's ledger indicate he paid for expenses such as dope paint, linen, bolts, OX-5 cylinders, horse shoes, tail skids, spark plugs, freight on polo cars, guards, fence repair, and advertising.

Clarence Hinck also made a proposal to the Minnesota State Fair that year, but was apparently turned down. His proposed exhibition rate was $1,000 per day.[25]

In 1923, the Federated Fliers went West. Before the tour, Hinck had contacted the Minnesota State Fair Board again, this time regarding the staging of auto races sponsored by the American Legion, on the Fair's auto track on Memorial Day. The Fair Board approved the plan, but there is no record of the races having been held.[26]

For the swing west, Hinck took his wife, Elizabeth, and their son, Irving. He also took along Noel Wien as stunt pilot, parachutist George Babcock, and the motorcycle gang of Art Spavin, Del Snyder, Barney Mattson, and Roy Bouchard. The group played their way through western Minnesota, North Dakota, Montana, Idaho, Utah, Nevada, and finally, California.

Each show profited the company from $500.00 to $1,000.00, big money in those days. But following shows at Chowchilla and Bakersfield, California, things tapered off. California barnstormers had already skimmed the cream of profits from the enterprise. Even though Hinck used his influence with local American Legion officials to circulate his advertising, things had definitely turned down. When, in December, a show at Redlands, California, netted only $159.20, Hinck missed a payroll. He came to Noel Wien and the others with an offer. They could fly for the Mexican revolutionaries. Hinck had sold their planes and the men were to wait for the response from Mexico as to when to start. The response never came.[27] Troupe members were left to find their own work, or their own way home.

The year 1924 saw the Federated Fliers back in business, now operating from a field in Robbinsdale, and restricting their operations to Minnesota and the Dakotas. Beginning in May, they appeared at Hutchinson, Jackson, St. James, Mankato, Wells and Pipestone. At Pipestone, Speed Holman, working for Hinck, performed one of his first stunt exhibits outside the metropolitan Minneapolis-St. Paul area.

In September, at Milwaukee, Wisconsin, overcrowded spectator stands collapsed during a Hinck performance, resulting in the death of a viewer and injury to a number of others. October saw the group closing the season at Ashland, Wisconsin. In 1924, performers included Lyle Thro; Noel Wien, who was salaried in August and September; Joe Westover, a 109th Air Guard pilot; Glen Soden; and pickup performers at various shows. The motorcycle and auto polo teams filled in between aerial acts and included regulars: Art Peterson, Art Spavin, Del Snyder, Tom Matthews, Barney Mattson and Roy Bouchard. Many were on salary. When the motorcycle acts were booked, if there was no local competition, the regulars were given fictitious names and embellished titles. Art Peterson, for instance, who was of Danish heritage, was titled "The Danish Flash" and listed as having been from Copenhagen. Newcomer, Derby Weston, was listed as the Canadian National Dirt Track Champion.[28] This year, George Babcock was the regular parachute jumper.

In 1925, Hinck dropped the name Federated Fliers, and renamed the troupe *Hinck's Motor Derby*, more in keeping with the variety of acts provided. In their seventh season, a new brochure proclaimed "two and a half hours of diversified entertainment."[29] The brochure was aimed at Fair thrill show promoters. The 1925 program would include motorcycle races, auto push-ball and auto polo, aerial acrobats, parachute jumps, and stunt flying. Featured performers were Al "Daredevil" Blackstone as aerial acrobat - walking wings and jumping from a plane piloted by Elmer Hinck- and Speed Holman doing the stunts. Holman was well known after winning the 1924 stunt flying competition at St. Louis, and the National Air Race from Minot to Dayton, Ohio, that same year.

Blackstone's act was characterized as "The oldest aerial acrobat in the profession doing standing loop, walking from wing to wing, standing on head on outer panel of top wing, rope ladder acrobatics in which he hangs by his teeth, one hand, toes, and slides back to ride the tail of the airplane — a hazardous feat that few try.

On 8 May, 1925, Blackstone, Holman, and Art Peterson demonstrated an act to officials of the Minnesota State Fair Board. Blackstone would climb from Peterson's fast moving motorcycle to Holman's J-1 Standard airplane. The Fair Board did not buy the act, but the newspapers eagerly covered the demonstration.

Hinck's detailed journals end at this point, but other sources continue the story. In 1926, Hinck utilized parachutist, Leroy "Stubby" Govin as performer. Among fascinating reports of that year is one in the *Owatonna People's Daily* of 12 September, 1926, that tells of Speed Holman doing knife-edged flight and a spectacular tail-slide that thrilled Fair crowds.

In 1927, the group exhibited in the Midwest again, playing Fond du Lac, Wisconsin, on the 4th of July, and Traverse City, Michigan, on August 1, where 5,000 turned out for the show. Members on this tour were the same as in 1926.

In 1927, Hinck's pilot, Del Snyder, set off on his own to operate a separate flying circus, bringing along brothers Al and Clarence "Nippy" Opsahl. Parachute jumper, George Babcock, split with the larger troupe and went on his own. Both groups bought auto-polo cars, motorcycles, and trailer rigs for between-show transportation.

When 1928 rolled around, Clarence was looking for a new act. He decided on dogs! Dog racing had been drawing good crowds in other States, so Clarence purchased six trained Whippet dogs from Bon Air Farms of Grove City, Ohio. The dogs were named, "Big Bob," "Hodnan," "Lass O'Laughter," "Little Flower," "Girl Shy," and "Zippet." Instructions from Bon Air Farms indicated Hinck should "...feed only once a day, three fourths of a pound of hamburg per dog, mixed with a little ground dry bread, or a tiny helping of Bran, or if you prefer, just a pound of hamburg straight." The letter warned, "By the way, never buy hamburg on the Fairgrounds!"[30]

The Hinck Motor Derby act called Auto Push-Ball required a large leather covered rubber balloon, bumped back and forth in front of the grandstands at a Fair by the same cars used for the Auto Polo events. Pushing the ball past a mark at either end signalled a "goal," and of course, the most goals for a side gave them the win. Hinck inquired of the Helium Company of Louisville, Kentucky, regarding filling the balloon ball with helium instead of air. Was it practical or would it damage the balloon? The Helium Company replied that it was indeed practical, not injurious to health or the balloon, which in fact, it would tend to preserve. Furthermore, the weight of the balloon would be reduced by some seventeen pounds.[31] It is unlikely that Hinck was worried about the ball floating away, as it weighed well over one hundred pounds even then, but he apparently decided not to buy the helium.

Exhibitions that year included those at Menomonie, Wisconsin, on May 20 and Sault St. Marie, Michigan, on July 22.

By 1929, Hinck had long since acquired the title of "C. W." He co-advertised his Motor Derby with the California-based *World Congress of Thrillers*, owned by Charles W. Marsh. Offering a diversified bag of entertainment, thrill shows could provide boxing, head-on auto crashes, ash-can derbies (demolition derbies), as well as dog-racing. The aerial circus still climaxed the show. Typical of 1929 shows was one on the 4th of July at Aurora, Illinois. That show featured Miss Jean DuRand, women's altitude parachute jump record-holder, who had made a leap from 18,700 feet earlier that year. Leroy Govin, aerial acrobat; motorcyclists Derby Weston, Rosaire Truedell, Frank Winkley, and Art Peterson; air work by Robert Hohag and Chad Smith, both of Northwest Airways. Towns played that year included Rockford, Peoria, Carlysle, and El Paso, Illinois. Again, Hinck's proposal to the Minnesota State Fair Board was turned down.

For 1930, Hinck's shows concentrated on dog racing, auto polo, and push-ball and did not include aerial events. Cyclists, Earl Duerr and Weston Farmer were added to the roster. Some locations played were Peoria and Carlysle, Illinois; Fort Dodge, Iowa; the Steele County Fair at Owatonna; and LaCrosse, Wisconsin. Hinck proposed a head-on auto collision, along with somersaulting autos, push-ball, and auto polo to the Minnesota State Fair Board, but records do not indicate whether he got the contract.

In 1931, Hinck finally did get on the Minnesota State Fair program with his motorcycle show. He asked for 50% of the gate and was granted that figure. His motor derby played to audiences at Aurora, Illinois; Chippewa Falls, Wisconsin, for the Northern Wisconsin State Fair; and Des Moines, Iowa. At Chippewa Falls, the program included famous lady flyer, Florence Klingensmith, who held the women's looping record with 1078 "flip-flops." At the same time, publicity indicated that Elmer Hinck was preparing for a U. S. to Tokyo flight.[32] Irving Hinck remembers mention of a Minneapolis to Moscow flight in a Lockheed Sirius aircraft with Clarence as navigator!

Clarence Hinck bought the Tourist Hotel, at Ninth and Hennepin Avenues in Minneapolis. He and his wife, Beth, moved in. It was here that C. W. showed his prankish side. He wired the lobby radio so that he could broadcast through it from a hidden microphone and make "announcements" that would startle his friends and registered guests.[33] The hotel would stay in Hinck's hands until World War II.

The Motor Derby of 1932 held to the same routine for their 14th season. They played the Iowa State Fair at Des Moines, where they shared the program with the charismatic preacher, Billy Sunday.[34] In August, Hinck again proposed motorcycle races, auto polo, auto push-ball, trick riding and an ash-can derby for the Minnesota State Fair and received the contract. There were no aviation events in his repertoire.

In 1933 the Motor Derby again played County Fairs, as well as the Minnesota State Fair. It was at the State Fair where the first fatality to Hinck's troupe occurred during a show, when parachute jumper, Bill Ash, was killed. Hinck later settled with the Ash estate, paying the $50.00 called for in the deceased's contract.[35]

Hinck's total contract for that Thrill Day show had been proposed at $1,000. He settled, however, for $650, providing motorcycle races, an auto board-wall crash and the parachute jump. The major attraction that year, was a head-on locomotive collision in the infield, furnished by another promoter.

Motor Derby activity in 1934 included stops at the Gogebic County Fair at Ironwood, Michigan; Merrill, Wisconsin's Lincoln County 4-H Roundup; the Milwaukee Wisconsin State Fair; and the Chippewa Falls' Northern Wisconsin District Fair.

The Minnesota State Fair featured Hinck's motorcycle racers. Clarence Hinck had been in the habit of paying the racers $35.00 to $50.00 per race date whether they won an event or finished somewhere in the pack. Occasionally a higher purse would be publicized in the pre-event advertising to draw a larger crowd, but seldom was the payoff more than $50.00 per rider. Whether there were any local speed demons to challenge Hinck's clan or not, the boys usually put on a good show because this was their job, and besides...they were having fun.

Once in a while, Hinck would notice the riders dogging it, however, and taking no chances on a poor performance at the Minnesota State Fair, decided to offer an award of $100 to the winner of the feature race. The story goes that with their thirst for this plum, they went at it with renewed vigor, resulting in an accident that severely injured Frank Winkley. Wink's career on the track was ended, but he stayed on as Hinck's program manager for some years afterward.[36]

A parachute jump in 1934 was made by Jerry Johnson, following a motorcycle board-wall crash and the cycle races. Hinck was paid $1,200 for promoting the show.

In 1935, Hinck furnished performers for the LaCrosse Inter-State Fair, and over Labor Day, again was contracted with the Minnesota State Fair. His contract was for motorcycle races only. The major thrill event this year was a house-crash by Frank Frakes.

Hinck attempted to promote a house-crash at Chicago in 1936, but was warned by the Department of Commerce, Chicago District Office, that it was against the law. When Hinck professed that the CAA had allowed it in Minnesota the year before, therefore it should be okay in Chicago, the Department informed him that, not only was it against the law, but that Frakes crash of 1935 was being investigated by themselves and the Justice Department as well as "other agencies." They closed the letter to Hinck stating that they would "use every legitimate means at [their] disposal to stop house crashes."[37]

As with the Minnesota State Fair, most major fair organizations had made deals with the Barnes-Carruthers Fair Booking Association of Chicago to handle the overall contracting with promoters of fair events. Hinck joined the group of promoters who made themselves available to B-C. At one point, Hinck wrote to M. H. Barnes of the Association informing him that "...in regard to the date at Ionia, Michigan.

We can fill the date without trouble and would like to add that it is safe to book us whenever possible as we have the equipment to handle anything that you can get for us at any location. You sign the contracts and we will fill them with pleasure."[38] Hinck was still offering dog racing along with the auto, motorcycle and aviation acts.

Clarence Hinck's son, Irving, became the official driver of a customized red trailer that carried the auto-polo/push-ball cars and motorcycles from show to show. After World War II, Hinck sold the trailer to his friend, Frank Winkley, who used it for several more years.

Motor Derby performances continued in 1936 with shows at Lawrenceburg, Indiana; the Illinois State Fair at Springfield; the Owatonna Steel County Fair and Ionia, Michigan, where Hinck received a total of $747.96, including a guarantee of $350 and 50% of the gate. Winkley was paid $75.00 per show as manager, the head-on auto crashers got $30.00 each and the Barnes-Carruthers agency got a commission of $130.70.[39]

At the Minnesota State Fair, Hinck provided a five-person group parachute jump. His booking there, through Barnes-Carruthers, was worth $1,825.00. The Hinck *Congress of Thrillers*, also played Topeka, Kansas; Minot, North Dakota; and Barraboo, Wisconsin. To explain a foul-up there, Winkley, writing on Hinck's behalf, told Mr. Barnes that they had arrived too late at Barraboo, from Minot, to put on the parachute jump while the spectators were still in the stands, but made the jump over the grounds anyway. Hinck had done the best he could to square things with the management, including putting on a free night show. He mentioned that the Barraboo and Minot dates were not very profitable, and that they grossed only $456 at Barraboo.[40]

In 1937, with Winkley having left the group to make his own bookings, Hinck staged shows at Eau Claire, Wisconsin; and Owatonna, Minnesota; where an intended airplane house-crash was prevented by threat of lawsuit by the State Aeronautics Commission.[41] Over at the Minnesota State Fair, the Barnes-Carruthers organization had received a similar restraining order preventing them from booking Frakes for a second house-crash there. The show did go on, however, with local stunter, Danny Fowlie, crashing the house to the delight of a large crowd. It appears that the Department of Commerce just couldn't keep up with the house-crashing situation in those years, for Hinck and other promotors booked several during 1936 and 1937.

Hinck promoted a house-crash at Green Bay, Wisconsin, in 1938. The flyer who performed the feat was local daredevil, Don Voge. In 1939, Hinck again used Voge for a house-crash at Chippewa Falls. On that same program was a new event, a multiple-balloon ascension in which, Earl Barrus. narrowly avoided injury when the lifting balloons drifted toward power lines and he was forced to leap almost 45 feet to the ground.

Despite the threat of war, some air shows were still being staged. For the 1940 Minnesota State Fair, Hinck again promoted the multiple balloon ascension,

66

but bad weather prevented that part of the show from going on.

Meanwhile, Elmer Hinck, with the backing of C. W., had opened a flight training business at Wold-Chamberlain Field where he and Clarence had procured Civilian Pilot Training contracts. Clarence wished to take advantage of this Government sponsored program to the maximum possible, and thus, on 20 June, 1940, the Articles of Incorporation were drawn up for *Hinck Flying Service, Inc.*, to replace the *Elmer Hinck Flying Service*. A week later, at the first meeting of the Corporation, Elmer was elected President, C. W. the Vice-President, and Harry Hinck's son, Robert, the Secretary-Treasurer. Elmer's salary was fixed at $150/month.[42]

When Hinck Flying Service was incorporated, the Board proposed to buy all the training contracts from Elmer. The CAA would not allow this, however, and on 21 November, 1940, Elmer wrote to the CAA to inform them he would be selling his "facility" to HFS instead. The CAA accepted this and on 16 December, Elmer signed everything over including a summer cross country ground course, and a summer flight instructor's course, among others.[43]

Elmer was keeping a Stinson Junior and a Stinson 10A at Wold-Chamberlain for the cross country training, and a Cub Coupe, three WACO UPF-7's, and several Piper Cubs at Nicollet Field in Bloomington. Ground instructors were Arden Kelton and Everett H. Welch; mechanics were Richard Wolfe, Robert Ferguson, Emil Krumweide, and Jerry Stebbins; flight instructors were Everett Welch, Ben Christian,

The Hinck Flying Service office at Stanton Airport, 1943. It's a cold winter day, "have we got all the students and instructors in the air?" Clarence Hinck might be saying. (Hinck family)

Erling Johnson, E. E. Falk, Frank "Bubs" Christian, Jr., Glen Slack, George Wanchena, and Stafford Palmer. When he needed additional pilots, Hinck hired George Holey and Vern Georgia. The Hinck's CPT contracts were administered by the University of Minnesota.

In 1941, C. W. Hinck became President of the Minneapolis Chapter of the National Aeronautics Association, and also treasurer of the National NAA. He was an officer of the American Legion, and spoke often on aviation matters around the State. He spoke to Legion groups regarding the importance of air commerce in the U. S. and the need for military strength. Hinck also went on record favoring a new Aeronautical Engineering Building on the University of Minnesota campus. The facilities then in use were a part of the Mechanical Engineering Building and were crowded and inadequate.[44]

December 7, 1941! America was at war. Many civilian flying fields were closed and civilian flying came to a halt. The only civilian flying to continue was student training under the CPT program. (More on this program can be found in the chapters dealing with the Second World War.)

In December, Hinck was appointed Chief Warden for Hennepin County's Aircraft Warning Service by the State Adjutant General. In this role, Hinck would oversee all activity relating to watching the skies for enemy aircraft. With the great mobilization taking place, C. W. and Elmer flew to Washington to solicit a major flight training contract the Government intended to issue to Minnesota.

The contract they received was a military glider pilot training contract. It was, then, necessary for them to begin an immediate search for a piece of land on which they could build a large-scale school. C. W. and Ev Welch selected a site near the City of Monticello, Minnesota. On its 300 acres, Hinck proceeded to build a complete air base in virtually no time at all. The nearby estate of Minneapolis banker, Rufus Rand, was also leased to provide a headquarters and later, an officer's club.[45] Rand had been a principal in the Mohawk Aircraft Corporation and was well-known to Hinck and the entire aviation community.

Within a few months, the facilities at Monticello became ready, and by June 1942, the school received its first students. C. W. and his wife, Beth, met the first 200 at the train station. Hinck, always one to enjoy good food, had insisted that first-class food service be available and talked the Monticello American Legion Women's Auxiliary into providing the cooks. The plan worked out well and, even today, the students look back on their stay in Monticello with fond memories of the food.[46]

The trainees also became fond of the townspeople who went out of their way to stage parties and get them together with the town's own young people. A few marriages took placed between women from town and the student pilots. The Hinck family boosted local business through the purchase of materials and groceries, and employed many civilians on the base, making many friends.

A staff of 35 instructors was gathered from around

the country. It included airline pilots taking leaves of absence and instructors from civilian schools. The glider program was part of a nationwide plan geared to provide 10,000 pilots for the eventual invasion of France. There were two other glider pilot training schools in Minnesota, one at Northport Airport near White Bear Lake, and one at Rochester.

In addition to the main field between Monticello and Big Lake, the Hincks also purchased land for three satellite fields. Training was carried out in Taylor-craft L-2 aircraft with the students flying from the main field to a satellite, where they would shut down the engines and practice dead-stick landings. On the ground, they were met by men from the main base, who would hand-prop the engines back to life and send the ships into the air for another circuit. Surprisingly, there was only one fatal accident during the two years of the school's existence.[47]

Two major disasters did hit the program in rapid succession during 1942. The first was Elmer's death in August, as mentioned earlier. A month later, a major windstorm slammed across the base, pulled loose all the tie-down ropes, and blasted the Taylorcrafts into a huge pile. From a fleet of 42 airplanes, only five could be salvaged and rebuilt.[48] The military went out immediately and requisitioned a new fleet from civilian owners who were not able to fly them during this time, and from other training schools. Within a week, Hinck's school was back at full schedule.

In October, the Navy, who supervised the operation of Nicollet Airfield as a satellite training field for its Wold-Chamberlain-based squadron, decided to close it. They considered Nicollet too close to Wold, with the result that traffic patterns were interfering with one another. Clarence Hinck was told to move his flight operations from both Wold and Nicollet. As he still had Government contracts besides the Monticello glider program, he needed a new field for operations. Hinck had also signed a contract to train flight students for the Carlton College WTS (War Training Service) program at Northfield, Minnesota. He decided to move his entire non-glider WTS operation to a small field near Carlton, in the community of Stanton, Minnesota.

There, he took on Jack Kipp as a partner, with Elmer Hinck's widow, Alta, as a company officer. James Willis was named Operations Manager and Chief of Ground School Instruction. In December, E. E. Falk was listed as Chief Pilot and coordinator of the military end of the flight training. Hinck's son, Irving, was a frequent visitor to the field; keeping an eagle eye on the operation, reporting back to Clarence, who had to divide his time between Stanton and Monticello. Jerry Stebbins was Chief of Maintenance and Assistant Airport Manager. Clair Morrill was listed as an instructor.

Nick Flynn, who had been one of Hinck's lead mechanics at Monticello, went to Stanton when the glider program wound down in 1943. He worked there for a year before returning to Monticello. For many years after the war, Flynn worked for Hinck, training veterans to fly on the G. I. Bill. Flynn spent a couple of years as a mechanic for Northwest Airlines; then, in 1960, bought a portion of the Monticello Field

Monticello Army Airfield, used for glider training 1942-1943. View shows the city of Monticello in the foreground. The bridge spans the Mississippi River. (Hinck family)

from Hinck and operated an FBO (Fixed Base Operation) until his retirement in 1978.

Clarence Hinck was never known for wasting a dollar, or for wasting good income-producing flying time. He pushed his instructors to get students trained and out the door. Perhaps he had his eye on the next Government contract; perhaps he wanted to get the flyers graduated and off to help with the war effort. The story is told, that at Stanton, when the temperature outside went down to zero degrees, flying would be stopped. It was too difficult for both students and instructors in open-cockpit Howard DGA-18P's or N3N trainers to function, and not very comfortable for ground handlers either. More than one student remembers that Clarence would step outside the door of the operations building, look at the thermometer, and curse the elements. On at least one occassion, he was seen to hold his ever-present cigar under the thermometer's mercury bulb, thereby raising the temperature reading. He then stepped inside and announced, "It's above zero, get out there and get to work!"[49]

Two groups of 300 glider pilots were trained at Monticello, and by 1944, the Government had enough trainees, bringing its contract to a halt. The WTS program at Carlton College was likewise brought to an end with the training airplanes being shipped to Monticello. Jack Kipp sold his part of Hinck Flying Service to C. W. for $14,000, including his assets of two WACO airplanes and a Travel Air.[50]

In 1943 there had been no flying activity at the Minnesota State Fair, but in 1944, Hinck promoted a glider demonstration by Ted Bellak. Bellak had made a name for himself in 1939, by setting a glider distance record of 56 miles in a flight from Sturgeon Bay, Wisconsin, to Frankfort, Michigan, soaring over Lake Michigan in the process.[51]

C. W. Hinck also had a flight school in his hometown of Litchfield, Minnesota. In May of 1945, he sold that, along with one of the training planes, a J-3 Cub, to Carl Uhlrich.[52]

EPILOGUE: HINCK

In 1946, C. W. again opened a school at Wold-Chamberlain, contracting with Arden A. Kelton to work as Ground School instructor for $700 a month.[53] With G.I.'s returning from the war, and government-financed schooling available, Hinck was able to keep both the school at Wold, and the school at Monticello, going full tilt with a total fleet of 32 airplanes. Most of those G.I.'s planned to go into the airlines.

The Wold-Chamberlain facility offered instruction in the Luscombe airplane for $8.50 per solo hour, but also offered training in Cubs, WACO UPF-7's, and a Piper Super Cruiser. A pilot could earn a Private, Instrument, Commercial, or Multi-engine rating. Hinck also secured the Seabee aircraft distributorship from the Republic Aircraft Company, and sold the planes from both Monticello and Wold-Chamberlain locations. At Monticello, Nick Flynn helped install modifications to the Seabee that raised its performance. The popular modifications included wingtip plates, wing fences, and metal props.

In 1947, the Monticello Airport was the site of the National Model Airplane Meet, (The NATS), sponsored by the Academy of Model Aeronautics. The large airfield was ideal for the event, with Twin City hobby dealer, Paul Ring, as Contest Chairman, and St. Cloud hobby dealer, Joe Williams, as Associate Director.

Hinck continued to promote air shows. In 1949, for example, he booked a show at Hayward, Wisconsin. To cover himself for the expected liabilities, he incorporated *The Famous Flyers, Inc.* Its President was Walter Bullock, with C. W. as Secretary/Treasurer, and "Shorty" DePonti and Jack Kipp as the other incorporators.[54]

At Hayward, the 17 July, 1949, program included a glider demonstration by Malcolm Manuel from the Stanton Airport, stunting by Jack Kipp and Chuck Doyle, a comedy Cub act, a parachute jump by Earl Barrus, and a flight by Walter Bullock in his homebuilt Curtiss Pusher. Bullock needed written approval from his employer, Northwest Airlines, for the performance as well as the standard FAA waiver.[55]

Clarence Hinck, on the right, introducing guest speaker, Roscoe Turner, at some function about 1960. This is a typical C. W. Hinck pose; cigar in hand, and the center of attention. (Hinck family)

In August, virtually the same group performed at Rosemount, Minnesota. In September, at the Minnesota State Fair, Walter Bullock again demonstrated his pusher.

C. W. Hinck purchased the entire assets of the Hinck Flying Service for himself in 1949. Then he and his son, Irving, voted that all property and land become payment to C. W. for the debt of $22,197.60 owed him for services.[56] Hinck moved his offices to Crystal Airport in the early 1950s and continued to sell flight training and Seabee aircraft.

Clarence Hinck died on 25 July, 1966, at age 76. He had been Past Commander of the American Legion, Calhoun Post #231; Past Commander and founder of Aviation Post #511; and Past Chef DeGare of Voiture 45 of the organization 40 Hommes et 8 Chevaux. He was a member of the National Defense Commission of the American Legion, the Fort Snelling National Cemetery Committee, the Showman's League of America, Past President of the National Aeronautics Association, and member of the Elks Club, the Last Man Club, the Minnesota Aviation Trades Association, and was founder and first President of the Minnesota Chapter of the OX-5 Aviation Pioneers of America. Truly, it can be said of Clarence Hinck, that show business and service were his life.

Hinck biography   Documentation

1 James H. Farmer, *Broken Wings,* Pictorial Histories Publishing Co., Missoula, MT, 1984.
2 Incorporation papers, C. W. Hinck collection, Minnesota Historical Society.
3 Minutes, Minnesota Agricultural Society, (Minnesota State Fair Board), 28 August, 1919, Minnesota Historical Society.
4 Contract in C. W. Hinck collection.
5 Contract, 13 July, 1919, C. W. Hinck collection.
6 Contract, 24 July, 1919, C. W. Hinck collection.
7 Brochure for the speech by Brown. C. W. Hinck collection.
8 Stacy Hinkle, "The Ordeal of Lieutenants Peterson & Davis," *American Aviation Historical Society Journal*, Fall 1972. p.190.
9 *St. Paul Pioneer Press*, "The Sock" column by A. E. Vogt, 2 June, 1929.
10 Interview with Joseph Williams by Noel Allard, 28 June, 1936.
11 Undated newspaper clipping, C. W. Hinck collection.
12 *St. Paul Pioneer Press*, "The Sock", 31 March, 1929, p. 6.
13 Letter to Federated Fliers from Horace Inman, 6 October, 1919, C. W. Hinck collection.
14 *Minneapolis Argus*, 26 November, 1964.
15 Newspaper ad, date unknown, C. W. Hinck collection.
16 Newspaper clipping, 9 June, 1920, paper unknown, C. W. Hinck collection.
17 Interview with Elizabeth Hinck by Noel Allard, 1 March, 1987.
18 *Chippewa Herald*, Chippewa Falls, Wis., 24 March, 1921.
19 Testimonial letter, 13 July, 1921, C. W. Hinck collection.
20 Testimonial letter, 8 August, 1921, C. W. Hinck collection.
21 Testimonial letter, 16 August, 1921, C. W. Hinck collection.
22 Logbook of Jack Anderson, in the possession of son Allen Anderson, interview by Noel Allard, 30 May, 1986.
23 Ibid.
24 Ledger, C. W. Hinck collection. Minnesota Historical Society.
25 Minutes, State Fair Board, 17 January, 1922, MHS.
26 Minutes, State Fair Board, 2 March, 1923,
27 Ira Harkey, *Pioneer Bush Pilot*, University of Washington Press, 1974, page 60.
28 Newspaper clipping, undated, C. W. Hinck collection.
29 Brochure, C. W. Hinck collection.
30 Letter to Clarence Hinck from Peter Martin, Bon Air Farms, 12 May, 1928, C. W. Hinck collection.
31 Letter to Clarence Hinck from The Helium Company, Louisville, KY, 16 April, 1928, C. W. Hinck collection.
32 *Chippewa Herald-Telegram*, Chippewa Falls, Wis., 15 September, 1931.
33 Interview with Allen Anderson by Noel Allard, 30 May, 1986.

[34] *Des Moines Register*, 3 September, 1932.
[35] Receipt, C. W. Hinck collection.
[36] Interview with Elizabeth Hinck by Noel Allard, 21 October, 1975.
[37] Letter to Clarence Hinck from Inspector George West, Chicago Office of CAA, 2 December, 1935, C. W. Hinck collection.
[38] Copy of letter from Frank Winkley to Barnes Agency, 30 December, 1935, C. W. Hinck collection.
[39] Ledger, C. W. Hinck collection.
[40] Copy of letter from Frank Winkley to Barnes Agency, 8 July, 1936, C. W. Hinck collection.
[41] Restraining order, 18 August, 1937, C. W. Hinck collection.
[42] Documents, C. W. Hinck collection.
[43] Documents, C. W. Hinck collection.
[44] *Minnesota Legionnaire*, 12 March, 1941.
[45] *Minneapolis Star-Journal*, 26 June, 1942.
[46] *Monticello Times*, 10 December, 1987.
[47] Interview with Nick Flynn by Noel Allard, 23 May, 1988.
[48] Ibid.
[49] Interview with Glen Slack by Noel Allard, 26 October, 1987.
[50] Hinck Flying Service Board Meeting minutes, undated, C. W. Hinck collection.
[51] Who's Who in American Aviation, 1945, Ted Bellak collection.
[52] Letter dated 12 May, 1945, C. W. Hinck collection.
[53] Letter dated 26 June, 1946, C. W. Hinck collection.
[54] Document, 7 June, 1949, C. W. Hinck collection.
[55] Waiver from CAA, 14 July, 1949, C. W. Hinck collection.
[56] Hinck Flying Service Board Meeting minutes, 29 June, 1949, C. W. Hinck collection.

Continuation of Barnstormers section

Contemporary to Hinck's group were a pair of "Flying Circuses" organized about 1920 and based at Speedway Field in Minneapolis. They operated from the Larrabee Brothers' Security Aircraft Company.

The *Minneapolis Daily News* was quick to see the advantages of a new form of advertising. They sponsored a flying circus, and had their name painted on Larrabee's Jennys. F. H. Carlton was the director of the air circus and the featured performers were: Eugene Burke, Wilbur Larrabee, (billed as the Flying Squirrel because of his nimble aerial antics), Bill Butters, Art Williams, Ed Ballough, and wingwalker, Charles Holman, who had not been tagged yet with the nickname "Speed." The *Daily News* continued to sponsor weekend airshows at Wold into 1923, with the main purpose of taking paying passengers up for their first "hops," and publicizing the newspaper.

The *St. Paul Dispatch* was also in the act, sponsoring a similar flying circus based at the Security Company, and using the same performers. Thus, the weekend exhibitions and barnstorming trips across the State and into border cities in the Dakotas, Iowa, and Wisconsin, were carried out under either sponsorship, depending on who was paying the bill.

When Charles Holman learned to fly during this period, he became the number one pilot, and the Dispatch Circus picked up Al Blackstone as the wingwalker and parachute jumper to replace him. Benjamin Foster and J. B. T. Martin took over the operation of the St. Paul Dispatch circus, and with other performers such as: Jack Bohn, Clarence "Dusty" Rhodes, Mel Haarstead, and Eddie Middagh, continued to stage weekend airshows until 1923. At that time, the Security Company sold its assets to Rhodes. Wilbur Larrabee, joined the 109th Observation Squadron of the Minnesota Air Guard, and went into the securities trading business. His brother, Weldon, who was a popular local musician aviation businessman, moved to California to take up a full-time career in the music industry.

Rhodes sponsored the air circus in 1923 and 1924, at which time Blackstone and Holman took it over. Billed as either the Holman-Blackstone Flying Circus, or the Blackstone-Holman Flying Circus, they continued exhibiting and selling rides even after Holman began working as Operations Manager of the new Northwest Airways in 1926.

Blackstone was also performing marathon automobile drives from 1928 to 1930, spending from 100 to a towering 1088 continuous hours behind the wheel of a new car. These endurance events were undertaken to publicize one or another auto agency in Minnesota or one of the neighboring states. When Speed Holman died in 1931, Blackstone carried on with the aerial circus under his own name for another year.

During the period of the organized flying circuses, there was a good deal of exchanging of performers and managers, the participants often moving from one sponsor to another as they made contracts to their advantage. Clarence Hinck's Federated Fliers picked up some of the performers and conversely, he often functioned as the promoter of the Dispatch Flying Circus. The system kept everybody working.

In most areas of Minnesota, outside of the Twin Cities, there were no organized flying circuses. Barnstorming there was an individual effort.

In Big Stone County, on the far western edge of Minnesota, the first barnstormers were Ted Swank, Herb Wilson and Pat Kapaun. The Graceville Airport is named after the later. Swank took his first lessons in 1928 and quit farming to make his fortune in aviation. Ted bought a Travel Air biplane, and with his wife, Pearl, traveled to county Fairs in surrounding

Larrabee's Security Aircraft Company owned this Jenny, leasing it on occasion to the St. Paul Dispatch Flying Circus, the Pure Oil Company, or the Minneapolis Journal for exhibitions and passenger-carrying. Pilot is unidentified, but the man on the rope ladder is thought to be Wilbur Larrabee. (Mrs. Worth Sherrill)

70

Al Blackstone sits dejectedly atop the St. Paul Dispatch Jenny at Waterville, Minnesota in this 1923 view. He is keeping the souvenir hunters at bay while Speed Holman has gone for a phone. Their Jenny has made a hard landing in this wheatfield and collapsed the landing gear and broken the prop. (Bob Lemm)

Al Blackstone sleeping in a store window display following one of his marathon automobile drives. (Al Blackstone via Sid Croy)

communities. Pearl sold air ride tickets for $1.00 a head, and Ted carried the passengers.

Once, they landed on a farm with no money in their pockets, and asked the farmer if they could swap a sight-seeing ride for a place to stay overnight. The deal was struck, and the farmer's family and the Swanks became friends over dinner. The farmer asked the Swanks if they would stay and help on the farm, which they agreed to. Pearl helped cook the meals, and Ted labored with the other hired hands bringing in the harvest. Ted later lost a leg as the result of an airplane accident, and was fitted with a wooden replacement. He returned to flying and barnstorming, never-the-less.

A very interesting flyer from the Ortonville area was John A. "Jack" Anderson. He became a flyer at the ripe old age of 30, worked three years for Hinck's Federated Fliers, accumulating some sixteen hundred hours of logged time before he decided to become an airline pilot. Anderson struggled for years, sending application after application to every fledgling airline he heard of, but failed to secure a position. He turned back to barnstorming in his own Curtiss Robin from 1931 to 1935 to make ends meet, and finally left aviation completely to enter politics.

Lawrence J. Sohler of Eagle Lake in Blue Earth County was an enterprising barnstormer. He began the trade in the mid-1920s and also advertised flying lessons. One of his students was Gustav Imm, who, himself, went on to become an itinerant barnstormer. Sohler owned a Canuck (Canadian Jenny) in which he taught Imm how to fly, and then sold him the airplane. During the period of instruction, the two did the usual passenger hopping, stopping at every small town in southern Minnesota to carry sight-seers. Sohler and Imm then each went his separate way. Sohler bought two curtiss Robins in the early 1930s for barnstorming and an OXX-6 Eaglerock in which to give lessons. By 1929, Sohler had acquired a fine Travel Air 10D cabin monoplane in which he offered charter flights from his base at the new Mankato Airport.

Gustav Imm had immigrated from Poland in 1922, under the sponsorship of his cousin, Minnesota State Senator, Val Imm. Gus Imm took an interest in flying and soloed in 1925. With his Canuck airplane, he came to Jordan, Minnesota, where he kept the plane at the farm of Jimmy Zarth, another barnstormer. In the Fall of 1926, Imm established what he called the

Northern Airport on a farm at Maynard, Minnesota, and purchased a Waco 9. He raced this airplane locally, placing second in the first Minnesota Air Derby at Grove City. Zarth, who had moved with Imm to Maynard, also raced in the Derby. Both men competed in races at Fairs and airport dedications around the state.

By 1927, Imm moved his base of operations to Fergus Falls, where he took over the airport from Len Johnson, Art Kantrud and Roy Aune. Gus Imm built a hangar to keep his plane inside. In the summer, he and Zarth barnstormed; in the winter, he flew powerline patrol for the Ottertail Power Company. Imm tried to get the city council to designate the airfield as the city's municipal airport, but they declined.

Calling the barnstorming troupe the "Northwest Air Tour," Imm and Zarth, along with Ob Seim and Mentor Tekse, flew three airplanes from town to town in northwestern Minnesota, putting on shows to attract paying fares. The shows consisted of balloon-busting, toilet paper streamer cutting, a parachute jump and a dead-stick landing. When things got tough during the depression, they couldn't afford a parachutist and would toss out a dummy wearing the parachute.

"In balloon busting, you have to hit them right on the prop...anywhere else and they bounce away. We were having a whoop-de-doo, taking up passengers, busting balloons and dropping our parachutist with the door off, (the airplane was a Ryan B-1 cabin monoplane and the door was easily removed). We were going full blast. Here comes this guy out...he says...'my name is Inspector so-and-so...can I see your license?' I thought, 'my gosh, it's over there in my baggage somewhere'. The inspector said, when it was convenient, to go and get it. We were doing so many things wrong, carrying passengers with the door off,

Jack Anderson poses in front of his barnstorming OX-5 Curtiss Robin sometime between 1931 and 1935. (Allen Anderson)

Gus Imm has a couple of young ladies as passengers in the front cockpit of his Waco 10. (Gus Imm)

The curious have arrived, the sight-seeing hops are about to begin. Gus Imm's Curtiss Robin. (Gus Imm)

Waco 10 and Waco 9 sit in front of Imm's hangar at Maynard, Minnesota. (Gus Imm)

dropping parachutists...he said...'you know you're not in compliance'. I said I was only going to haul a few more passengers and then shut down. I told my ticket guy not to sell tickets."[38]

Imm relates the business arrangements with his men on the barnstorming tour: "When we were barnstorming, it was strictly business. I paid the ticket man a commission, the other pilot 20 percent. I provided the tents and stuff. When we'd go out, we'd pick two or three towns. One plane would go out with the handbills. He'd land, pull up to a haystack or by the fence and go see the farmer. We'd tell him that next Tuesday we'd like to use his field for flying and we'd give his family four rides free. We had our own tents and would bed down by the haystack. We'd walk the field to look for rocks.

"During the week, we'd do one town a day. We'd put up twenty to thirty handbills in town...we'd ask the merchants if we could put them in their stores. I had the 'bills' printed in red and blue. We'd 'bill' the towns on two days, a week, several days ahead of our hop day. We'd follow the harvest, sometimes we'd land by the threshing team. The farmers were always good about it. In bad weather, we'd find someone to buy us drinks."[39]

Imm's logbook showed that he was out from the 1st of August until the middle of October. In 1935, his group stayed out until November 5. The flying would be so continuous that the airplanes would literally wear out at the end of the season. In the fall, Imm would fly directly to Wahpeton, North Dakota, to drop the plane off with Art Sampson, head of the aviation department at the Wahpeton School of Science. There, the engine would be overhauled, or the fabric replaced for the coming year. By February, it was time to pick up the ship and go back on powerline patrol.

Art Sampson of the Wahpeton School was a native of Belview, Minnesota. He began his career as a pilot back in 1919, learning to fly from Lt. Harold Peter-

son of the Federated Fliers. In 1924, Sampson went to Alaska with James Rodebaugh, and Rochester, Minnesota, native, William Yunker. All three were to fly as charter pilots for the Alaska Aerial Transport Company. After a year of severe "mosquito-bite-anxiety," Art returned home and took up barnstorming. Flying low from town to town, with his cousin, Edward Oie, standing on top of the wings of Art's Lincoln Standard airplane, they attracted much attention.

In 1928, Art became associated with the North Dakota School of Sciences as the first pilot hired by the institution for their new aviation program. He purchased a Canuck, which the students assembled. Through the years, the students overhauled customer engines and rebuilt airframes under Art's careful guidance. The North Dakota School was a mecca for many Minnesotans, all needing quality work. Wally Neuman, Shorty De Ponti, Sven Peterson, B. G. Vandre, and Marvin Heinzel, as well as Gus Imm, regularly used such services.

Surely, one of Minnesota's most colorful barnstormers was Irwin A. Stellmacher. Stellmacher learned to fly from Art Sampson at Wahpeton and returned in a Jenny to the Marshall area of Minnesota, to make a living any which way he could. His first inclination was to go out and fly some passengers. He had posters printed and hung them around mid-Minnesota towns in the early 1920s.

"I remember Balaton, Minnesota, one Sunday," he relates. "I kept flying until it was pitch dark. You couldn't see the ground, but people kept paying $2.50 to go up and see the lights of Marshall and other towns.

"...you couldn't see the ground, so I'd land by car lights. First, you had to look for the telegraph wires, which you couldn't see until they'd catch a glint off the car lights. Then I'd know it was okay to start setting 'er down'. When I could look off to the side and see that I was level with the lights, it was time to touch 'er down'."[40]

Carver County could boast of barnstormer, Elmer Sell. He got interested in flying during World War I and joined the 109th Observation Squadron at its inception in 1921. He also established Carver County's first landing strip on a farm at Mayer, Minnesota, west of the Twin Cities. The strip became known as Sell's Field. Graduating from a Canuck to a Great Lakes biplane, he hopped passengers until his log book showed 9,000 riders in 6,000 air hours.[41] In the off-season, Sell became a teacher, instructing classes

Cyril Stodolka has a pair of pretty passengers posing by his J-1 Standard. Note his attire; dress shirt, tie and coat were the uniform of the day for the barnstormer. (Niels Sorensen)

in auto mechanics, first at North High School in Minneapolis, then out of his own home garage. During the World War II, Sell's airport was officially "closed" and he opened a Desoto-Plymouth auto agency in Mayer.

Eugene Burke from Minneapolis flew a Hall-Scott engined Standard airplane. He recalled part of the barnstorming mystique of the period, "...in South Dakota I landed at an Indian reservation...the pasture was full of rocks. Now if the Indians liked you, they'd do anything for you. They must have taken a liking to me because they never charged me a thing for using their fields. I took several thousand dollars out of the reservation that week.[42]

"Also, if you set down by a threshing crew, you didn't have to put up a sign or anything, because in about ten minutes, you'd have the whole crew around the airplane, digging into their pockets for money. The only person who didn't care for that was usually the farmer whose land they were harvesting. Sometimes I would have to give the farmer's wife a ride. The farmer was usually the last person who would want a ride. The wives had more courage than the men.

"We lived in fleabag hotels most of the summer. They had bedbugs. We would carry straight pins and because bedbugs would run when the lights were turned on, you'd have someone turn on the light and you'd try to stab the bedbugs. If you succeeded, you'd turn in your pin at the desk and the room didn't cost you a thing."[43]

Another pioneer barnstormer was William L. Morse of Grand Rapids. Morse started an aviation career in 1927 as a mechanic, graduated to wing-walking and parachute jumping, working with Clarence Hinck's circuses, and barnstorming the northern portion of Minnesota. He later became one of Minnesota's premiere bush pilots.

One of Minnesota's earliest barnstormers was Cyril Stodolka of Little Falls. Growing up on a farm, machines had always fascinated him. As a youth, he would often sit atop the windmill tower and watch birds circling above the farm. His mechanical ability enabled him to build a crude "whirligig" helicopter model using tin paddles soldered to a wire shaft. Rubber bands turned pulleys that operated from an alarm clock spring. The helicopter's only flight drove it to the ceiling of the farmhouse where it struck hard

Marcus Zum Brunnen in the Eagle Flying Service American Eagle, circa 1932. (Marcus Zum Brunnen)

enough to break.

When Stodolka peeked at an airplane in a tent display at a local Fair, he was filled with enthusiasm and decided to build his own airplane. His plane was so awkward-looking that neither Cyril, nor his brother, Ed, who was also interested in flying, had the courage to try to fly it. Instead, they built a second airplane which appeared more airworthy, and Cyril flew it in 1914. The plane flew only in "hops," rather than sustained flight, and was eventually destroyed in a windstorm. At this point, Stodolka was conscripted into the Army, but found his way to the Lafayette Flying Corps where he started pilot training. The armistice was signed before he ever got into the air.

After the war, Stodolka came to the Twin Cities and took his first flying lessons with Walter Bullock in a J-1 Standard at the Earle Brown farm airport. Stodolka bought the training airplane and flew it back home to Royalton, Minnesota.

His barnstorming career began when he enlisted the help of a friend, Tony Kalis, as wing-walker. The pair put on demonstrations in the area and hopped

Poster handbill from Marcus Zum Brunnen, 1932.

FLY
SUNDAY · NOVEMBER 13
At the
ZUM BRUNNEN FARM
Two Miles South of Hasty
See the Beautiful Lake Region
From the Air
LICENSED PLANES AND PILOTS

Delroy George, Florence Klingensmith and Jack Kipp set a formal pose in front of the mens' Challenger Robin in 1931, at St. Cloud. (Delroy George via Joe Williams)

Elsworth "Spide" Jones and his OX-5 Robin. Note the automobile tires. (Juanita Jones)

passengers following their aerial stunt displays. Charles Lindbergh was from Little Falls, not far from Royalton, and Cyril got to know him. Lindbergh was just another local pilot and was engaged in helping his father campaign for the Minnesota House of Representatives by flying from town to town, where the elder Lindbergh would make speeches.

Stodolka relates one experience on the barnstorming trail, "We stayed over July 5th near Brainerd because of a storm. The next morning, it was hot and muggy and very turbulent. Up higher, the turbulence was less, but the winds were so strong that we weren't moving in relation to the ground, so we had to come down and fly in the turbulence. Over Gull Lake, the plane actually got turned around and was pointed back the way we'd come, at one point. It took us two hours and ten minutes to go just 80 miles. A couple fellows had to come out and grab the wings to keep us from being blown away when we got to the ground. Tony Kalis got out, shook my hand and said, 'that's it'. He quit flying that day and never went up with me again."[44]

The barnstorming continued for four years. Walt Bullock borrowed back the Standard one day for reasons Stodolka couldn't recall, and accidentally cracked it up. Bullock was obliged to buy back the airplane from Stodolka. Without an airplane, Stodolka then sought another line of work, taking a job with the local power company and ending his flying career.

Barnstorming was not without its hazards. Eddie

Croft, from St. Paul, an active barnstormer who earned a living with his Travel Air, remembers one nearly fatal day when he was working for "Mac" McInnis out of Wold-Chamberlain Field. He was sent to fly passenger hops at a Catholic church bouya festival near Centerville, Minnesota, on a beautiful Sunday afternoon. His second hop was with teenage brothers. Just after takeoff, Eddie thought he heard his trusty J-5 engine "sneeze" a couple of times. He couldn't figure out what had happened. One of the boys in the front cockpit held up his arm, Eddie was shocked to see it covered with blood!

Thinking that a bolt or something had snapped in the front cockpit and injured his passenger, Eddie immediately brought the ship back and landed. The ticket seller came running over and started gesturing wildly, pointing at the rear fuselage. Croft looked and saw the turtledeck behind him was ripped open and pellet holes filled the rear portion of the plane. They had been shot at!

An ambulance was called and the young man who had been struck in the arm by shotgun pellets was

After a day of barnstorming in Wisconsin, Eddie Croft and his ticket-seller had their Travel Air engine quit over St. Paul, The resulting crash-landing left Eddie with broken ribs. He sold the plane the next day to Shorty De Ponti for $10. (Ed Croft)

Sven Peterson with his American Eagle at Minneapolis in 1929. (Sven Peterson)

Eldon Sorenson strikes a pose while the engine warms on his Waco 10; Worthington, Minnesota, circa 1929. (Eldon Sorenson)

Jack Blatchely standing in front of Sven Peterson's Challenger Robin. (Sven Peterson)

rushed to the local hospital. Croft found that the plane had been hit by two shots, the first near the front cockpit, the second behind the rear cockpit where he had been sitting. A slight difference in where the shots struck could have done him in!

The sheriff put up a roadblock and caught a duck hunter and his wife who admitted that they had taken the shots because Croft's airplane had scared away the ducks. The man was fined and had to pay for the repair of the airplane. Croft was lucky, the only commercial pilot in Minnesota to have been shot down.[45]

Making a living after the 1929 stock market crash, during the period known as the Great Depression was difficult, indeed. The barnstormer had to hustle. His ticket seller-loader was a vital cog in the money-making routine. Croft remembers, "Generally, you would have a ticket seller who would go along with you. Someone from your home base who would be glad to go along, sell tickets for you, help fuel the airplane, arrange for getting the fuel if you were running low. They usually worked for 10% of the gross. They did a lot of work. They would have to bring you lunch if you were busy. Sometimes you'd fly right through the whole day from 9:00 in the morning until sundown. You'd work as long as business was there."[46]

Bob Baker from Minneapolis was a ticket seller. "For the shilling, the huckstering, I received a commission. Never was so much money made by so few in so short a time," he says, "did I have a microphone? Not in those days...it was simply voice power." Baker shilled for Minneapolis barnstormers, Jack Kipp and Florence Klingensmith. "I'd just say, 'hi...look here, look here, come over, come over, come over.' They'd come over and want to know what this crazy man was hollering about. I'd tell them they could ride in either the open cockpit Waco of Florence's or the closed cabin Robin of Kipp's. They could ride with one of the country's greatest women flyers of all time for only $1.00. The line forms on the right."[47]

It was easy for Baker. Florence Klingensmith was quite a figure with her shiny black, Warner-powered Waco RNF biplane, with silver wings. She was good looking and flamboyant in green riding breeches; and the prospect of accompanying her was irresistible to the young men standing by the fence. Baker states, "I was probably the richest kid on the block. I'd often bring home over $100 a day. I turned some over to my folks for board and room. I got at least $25 every

single day."[48] Quite a salary during hard times!

Baker claims that his share was 10% from the first $100 taken in, 15% on the second $100, and if the take were over $500, he would get a flat $100. Often a paying rider would want some aerobatics...a loop, or a spin, and would be charged up to $15 for that kind of ride. Otherwise, the rides sold for $1.00 for five minutes, and if a fellow was trying to impress his girl, the barnstormer would give them both a good long ride for $25.

Florence Klingensmith was a Moorhead, Minnesota native who had a most colorful career and spent a good deal of her time in Minnesota. Besides the barnstorming, she entered women's air races. She lost her life in 1933, during an air race in Chicago, when the fabric peeled off one wing of her GeeBee racing plane, causing it to crash.

Her traveling companion, Jack Kipp, barnstormed weekends during the mid-1930s while he was a student at St. Thomas College in St. Paul, and a Marine Corps Reserve Officer at Wold-Chamberlain. He and Delroy George owned a Challenger-engined Curtiss Robin.

The ticket seller also functioned as the loader. This was a job with many important responsibilities. First, was to make sure the passengers were loaded quickly into the airplane without stepping through the fabric of a wing. Seatbelts had to be fastened and the passengers fitted with a helmet and goggles for an open cockpit ride. Making sure the door was closed and latched was the next chore, followed by a signal to the pilot that all was ready for takeoff. This was to be accomplished in the shortest time possible so that the profit margin would be as large as possible. Too much time and people waiting would loose interest and wander off, or worst of all, be left with money to spend at the end of the day...not having been able to get a ride.

Most rides included a quick takeoff, a circuit and a landing...often a mere four to five minutes in length. When the hop ship returned to the pickup area, the loader's job began again. He had to make a sprint to the airplane, open the door and unbuckle the passengers' seatbelt, (singular...usually there was only one belt for all passengers of the front cockpit). Making sure the excited passenger didn't step through the wing, or jump off the front of the wing into the still-turning propeller, was part of the loader's task.

Between flights, the loader again became the ticket seller, cajoling the crowds, and doing his best public relations job...and stuffing the "take" into his pockets. Often the days receipts weren't counted until the sun had set, and the barnstormers either lay under their plane's wings, or hiked to town for a hotel room.

In Rice County, young barnstormers, Leon "Deke" DeLong and Lawrence "Abe" Merrill, got their start. DeLong's career began when he made the decision during World War I that the life of a doughboy was not as advantageous to a long life as that of an aviator. After World War I, he stayed in the military, learning to fly at Fort Sill, Oklahoma, then headed for Minnesota when his service time was finished. Here, he took up barnstorming to make a living from 1920 to 1928. While working little towns, hopping rides during the summer, he worked as an auto painter in the winter. DeLong got his first regularly-paid flying job with Universal Air Lines, out of their Chicago station. Speed Holman hired DeLong in 1928 to come to the young Northwest Airways. There DeLong spent the remainder of his career.

Abe Merrill barnstormed through the southern states of Mississippi, Missouri, Alabama, and Florida, before turning northward, ending up in Minnesota. His OX-5 Eaglerock provided 600 hours of sight-seeing profit for him before World War II loomed on the horizon. He took a job as a CPT (Civilian Pilot Training) instructor just prior to the war, and later started the first airport at Faribault, Minnesota.

St. Cloud provided a number of barnstormers. Sven Peterson was one of Minnesota's most active during the late 1920s. Sven, Chet and Marvin Heinzel, Phil Chaffin, Cliff Trossen, Al Luckemeyer, Jack Blatcheley, Millar Wittag, Marcus Zum Brunnen and Elsworth "Spide" Jones, performed weekend exhibitions and carried riders. Accumulating a couple hundred hours, Sven went to Northwest Airways, hoping for a job flying with the airline. "They wanted someone who had 3,000 hours and was 19 years old. That person got $125 a month and had to be dressed up with a collar and fine shoes. I had a job as a tool and die maker, and on weekends could do my barnstorming. The best day I had, I hauled 118 paying passengers, two at a time, and gave two free rides for use of a field. I figure I flew for 12 hours that day."[49] Barnstorming was more profitable than a position with the airline. The future was hard to predict!

Sven continues, "I laid it out so I didn't have to taxi. I'd land and roll up to where the people were and my brother, Frank, would unload and I'd just takeoff from there. When I got laid off (from the tool and die job), I wasn't working for eight months and I'd fly for airport dedications."[50] Sven established St. Cloud's very first airport in 1928, which got the nickname "Northside Airport."

Marvin Heinzel barnstormed the area around St. Cloud too. In 1936, he took a job as an aerial photographer for a Tulsa, Oklahoma, company. He returned to Hibbing as a CPT instructor in 1939. His younger brother, Clayton, followed both brother Marvin and cousin, Chet Heinzel, acting as ticket seller and mechanic.

Phil Chaffin's logbook showed many days of eight to fourteen flights with paying passengers. He flew

Pilot Rudy Billberg is hopping passengers in the Rosseau, Minnesota area, circa 1935. (Rudy Billberg from Shadow of Eagles, *Alaska Northwest Books, 1992)*

a J-1 Standard in 1928 and 1929 on his barnstorming activities. Millar Wittag, a pilot originally from the Minneapolis area, came to St. Cloud to fly a Kinner-powered American Eagle for Al Luckemeyer. Al offered weekend sight-seeing flights and flight instruction. Wittag later migrated to Hibbing, where he became a successful FBO and gained a number of CPT/WTS contracts during the World War II period.

Marcus Zum Brunnen's family owned a farm south of St. Cloud, near the settlement of Hasty, Minnesota. He did Sunday-only flying from the farm in the early 1930s. (Sunday-only, because the farm kept him busy the other six days of the week). Marcus owned an American Eagle 201 which had made the rounds of owners in the area. A companion barnstormer on Sundays was his former instructor from Wold-Chamberlain Field, in Minneapolis, Lee "Skelly" Wright.

Almost all of the early barnstormers flew ships equipped with the famous Curtiss OX-5 motor. The OX-5 was a truly marvelous machine. It's open valve gear fixed the attention of any bystander or potential passenger, both from the outside of the airplane and from the front cockpit where its syncopated jiggling was a most fascinating sight. The motor's sound was melodious; loud, rhythmical and spell-binding. The smell of hot oil, mixed with the exhaust and hot radiator odors combined to provide an ambience only akin to the OX motor.

It developed 90 solid horsepower in its pristine condition...less if a plug was fouled, or the valves worn. It swung a huge prop that one could almost see turning at 1400 rpms. The OX-5 was a heavy engine, weighing in at 390 pounds with its various pumps, pipes, and single magneto. An eight-cylinder, water-cooled engine, rating one horsepower for each 4.33 pounds.

The beauty of the OX-5 engine lay not in the fact that it was exactly handsome, nor had astounding performance, nor reliability, but it was the fact that it was readily available from World War I surplus in a cheap, unending supply. Prone as it was to carburetor ice, plug fouling, magneto shorting, valve gear problems, and cooling system leaks, it nevertheless, became the training ground for a generation of pilot-mechanics, who learned to repair and rebuild it in the field. Many flyers of the period recalled with mixed love and hate how they experienced a forced landing for one of the above reasons every few hours of flying time!

When healthy, however, the brute power of the engine, combined with the rugged construction of biplanes of the period, allowed incredible feats. In 1929, for example, the Brunner-Winkle Aircraft Corporation advertised their OX-5 powered, Bird aircraft, with the slogan, "No field too small, no tree too tall."[51]

Two major modifications were available for the OX-5 to improve its reliability. One was the replacement of the old tappet system with a Miller Overhead valve action, consisting of rollers at the ends of the rocker arms where they were in contact with the valves. This smoothed out the action and did away with the need to hand-lubricate the valves every few hours. Such an engine was "Millerized." The other major modification was the replacement of the cast iron water jacketed cylinders with finned cylinders to convert it to an air-cooled engine. This was known as the Tank conversion.

The OX-5 engine was primarily associated with the Curtiss JN-4 Jenny, and the J-1 Standard after World War I, but through the 1920s, almost every aircraft manufacturer offered at least one model powered with the OX. Suffice it to say, that the barnstormers of the 1920s all cut their teeth flying behind the ubiquitous Curtiss OX-5 engine.

The barnstormers got their first rides in open-cockpit Jennys and Standards. When they had soloed, they could immediately hop passengers, and they, themselves, then became instructors. Following the Jenny and Standard came the Travel Airs, the Lairds, the Wacos, American Eagles, Eaglerocks, and other similar single-engined, open ships. Comfort appeared with the name, "Robin."

The Curtiss Robin aircraft of 1928 was a three-place "Cabin" monoplane. The pilot sat alone in the front seat with two passengers riding on a bench seat behind him. The plane became immensely popular through the 1930s and found widespread use by barnstormers.

The Robin was the barnstorming airplane of choice for such Minnesota notables as Rudy Rydholm, who used his during the decade of the 1930s to make a dollar or two. When Rudy was shopping for his first Robin, he was offered one by Paul Miller, a Clinton, Minnesota, pilot, who wrote, "I'm sure you will be pleased after flying it a while. As far as stability and speed are concerned, they are the best of the OX-5's. Also [they are a] year around money-maker because of comfort and better visibility. There is a favorable growing tendency toward the closed ship, same as cars a few years back. Their trade-in value and sale-ability are slightly better than open ships and dual instruction is more easily given. Besides, one can fly without the bulksome clothes and bothersome and expensive goggles.

"I have taken a Robin off without the stick and flown it entirely with rudder and stabilizer. Without the use of the stick they will recover from a perfect stall."

He went on to offer this advice to Rydholm, "...knock them (other people trying to sell Rydholm a Robin) down on price, boy, that's where you make your profit and don't pay over $600 by any means."[52]

The Curtiss Robin was also the favorite of Howard Deichen of Waseca. He used one during the 1929 to 1930 period to hop rides. Deichen was one of the first four pilots to be licensed by State Aeronautics Commissioner, Ray Miller, on 23 September, 1925. (The other three pilots licensed that day were Joseph Westover, Marvin Northrop, and Speed Holman).

Deichen was the pilot who flew Dale "Red" Jackson's parents to St. Louis in a Robin to make an aerial encounter with their son, who was in the process of setting an endurance record in his own Robin. (The full story of that flight can be found in the next segment of this chapter.)

Sven Peterson, mentioned earlier, remembers his Curtiss Robin. "The only damage I ever had happen was the first week after I got the Robin. They had stirrup pedals and they were made of tubing. The engine on this one cranked from the inside and the crank tube went across the rudder tubing in such a way that it laid right on it. It vibrated, and, of course, it rotated and wore a groove in the rudder tubing. (This Robin had a Curtiss Challenger engine which was well-known for its vibration.)

"We had just gotten that airplane, and, you know, we just had to fly it. It was a drizzly day with about a 300 or 400 foot ceiling and I was coming in for a landing. Our field was short and pretty near every landing we made, we had to slip or slide the airplane in. We also had to land underneath the highline and had to watch the posts.

"Just as I was setting down, I kicked the rudder to straighten out and the tubing of the rudder pedal bent. The left pedal got hooked on a bolt on the fire wall and wouldn't come back. I pounded on the opposite pedal but groundlooped anyway. It didn't really hurt anything too much, but the crank went out.. that day!"[53]

Well-known Iowa barnstormer, Clarence O. Kvale, spent his summers traveling through northern Iowa, western Minnesota, the Dakotas and Montana, hopping passengers from 1933 until 1939. He received his private license in 1930, whereafter, it took him only a year to accumulate enough hours to get his transport pilot's license (200 hours). He then bought a Curtiss Robin with the Tank modifications.

In 1933, Kvale and a ticket-seller-mechanic, Paul Nalewaja, from Browerville, Minnesota, embarked on a season-long tour though the Dakotas and Montana. Kvale duplicated this tour in 1934, bringing along lady parachute jumper, Betty Goltz. By 1939, having made a summer-long barnstorming tour every year, he had logged 2144 air hours hopping passengers, a stint that included 7689 separate flights, hauling an enormous total of 10,252 paying riders.[54]

In Koochiching County, near International Falls, Forrest Rising is credited with being the county's first barnstormer. On a saturday or sunday, a sight-seer might have taken a ride with him in a Curtiss Robin, viewing the scenery of lakes and woods, or searching for coyotes, fox, or a good deer hunting area.

Howard Sevdy of Worthington, Minnesota, was another of the barnstormers who survived the depression by earning money carrying sight-seers. Born in Iowa, Sevdy got his first ride in a Jenny from Lou Donaldson at Lake Okoboji. Sevdy never took any sort of instruction, but flew from town to town with other barnstormers, flying the plane occasionally, and working as loader and ticket-seller at various one-day

Max Conrad's Ford Trimotor in better days with a crowd of customers standing by on his Winona Airport. (Ken Brommer)

Burned out fuselage of Conrad's Trimotor portrays the folly of overpriming an engine. (Ken Brommer)

stands. Eventually, he soloed, and took off on his own. He traveled with Gus Imm, Jimmy Zarth, Obb Seim, and Pete LaFrance in the Worthington/Fairmont area. His first airplane was a long-nosed American Eagle, but he too, soon bought a Robin, paying $365 for it. In 1936, he finally got a legal license. He went to California during World War II, as an instructor at the *29 Palms Air Academy*. Sevdy returned to Minnesota after the war to become the Worthington Airport operator and was quite popular as an airshow pilot.

Sevdy's partner at Worthington, Eldon Sorenson, had a similar background. He also began barnstorming in the middle 1930s with a Waco 10 and a Travel Air 2000. He and companions, Ham Eltgroth of Fairmont; Cecil Shupe of Brookings, South Dakota; Walter H. "Rocker Arm" Krause, of Ormsby, Minnesota and others, traveled southern Minnesota, northern Iowa, and eastern South Dakota, offering rides. In addition to the sight-seeing, Sorenson worked another angle. He and his wife, Verda, flew a 40-horsepower Taylorcraft, with the side doors removed, over the rolling farmland of the area, taking aerial photos of farms. The husband and wife team would then process the pictures in their own home darkroom, drive back to the farms and sell the farmers either an aerial 8x10 picture of their homestead for $2.50, a postcard for a nickel, or Christmas cards for ten cents each.

"I'd take pictures only of farms that looked cared for, or looked prosperous, because I knew the owners could afford the pictures. I'd avoid the farms that looked run-down," says Sorenson. "I made my living in that manner during those years."[55]

Even in the late 1930s, there was still a smattering of barnstorming. Flying an old Travel Air, Waco, or Curtiss Robin, an air minded and footloose lad could still stir up enough paying passengers after landing in a rural wheat field, to make a living.

Many an aviator, who would become a businessman later on, tested his youth in this way. Helmer Bjerkebek of Fergus Falls, was such a person. He and his father had been contract-cattle-transporters and had cash flow through that business, but when aviation called Helmer, the business was put aside. Purchasing an old OX-5 American Eagle in 1939, Helmer rebuilt it during the next year and taught himself to fly it. In 1940, he purchased a Curtiss Robin and

modified it so that the front seat was big enough for two persons. In this fashion he was able to carry three paying fares. He continued to carry weekend passengers until World War II started, pocketing the profits to supplement his trucking income.

Besides the small two and three seat biplanes and cabin monoplanes, larger aircraft also plied the barnstorming circuit. Four-place Stinson SM-8A's were popular, as were six-place Travel Air 6000's. A very colorful, Foster Hannaford, Jr., appeared on the scene with a monster Boeing Model 80 trimotored biplane. He hopped passengers, basing the ship for a time at Robbinsdale Airport, west of the Twin Cities. Of the larger airplanes, however, the Ford Trimotor was the classic.

From the mid 1930s, shoe dealer, Benny Freeman, of Minneapolis, owned a Ford Trimotor that was kept at Wold-Chamberlain. It was hangared and serviced by Shorty De Ponti and flown by Mel Swanson on many a barnstorming weekend.

A legendary Minnesotan, who barnstormed a Ford, was Max Conrad of Winona. His trimotor was purchased from TWA Airlines in 1937 and it was Max's intention to fly round trips from Minneapolis to California. This plan didn't work out; instead Max used the ship mostly for barnstorming in 1937 and 1938. He also used it for stunting at county fairs, carrying parachutists and giving multi-engine training. Foster Hannaford, Jr. was one of his multi-engined students, and one time crunched the big bird onto a muddy field, breaking up the landing gear. The ship was repaired and flown again, but burned on the ground from an engine fire in 1939.

Clyde Ice of Spearfish, South Dakota, was a legend. Clyde's career touched Minnesotan's during the 1930s. Ice's *Rapid Airlines*, employed a Ford Trimotor, flying trips from Rapid City to Rochester, Minnesota. When the airline went flat, Clyde earned a barnstormer's income with the big plane, basing it at Rochester.

Ice's mechanic/ticket seller was Bernard "Bud" Frye, of South Dakota. He migrated to Minnesota after the barnstorming period to operate a CPT program at Marshall, then another at Madison, Minnesota. Frye and his wife ran the Madison airport and provided crop-spraying services for many years.

Hotel owner, Jess Kenyon, of Morris, Minnesota, was another entrepreneur who bought a Ford Trimotor for the purpose of cashing in on the sight-seeing trade. Kenyon, and his partner, Jack O'Brien,

78

promoted weekend airshows in the communities of west central Minnesota. They gathered other barnstormer pilots and their airplanes to go along with the Ford on interstate forays. Though Kenyon was not a flyer, he always rode along, never missing a trip, and often bringing his wife, children, and relatives with him. Harold George, L. P. Quinn, and Thunder Johnson, were pilots of his big trimotor at various times.

In the fall of 1929, Kenyon persuaded Olof "Ole" Anderson, of Fargo, North Dakota, (later a Northwest Airlines pilot), to join the group going west for an extended trip. Ole was flying a Curtiss Robin. One of the others on the tour was Pete Klimek of Baudette, Minnesota, who flew his American Eagle. "Rocker Arm" Krause went along as mechanic.

Though Ole wanted to hop from small town to small town, Kenyon wanted to leapfrog between the bigger cities, leaving the less lucrative smaller towns alone. Ole split with Kenyon, taking Kenyon's partner, O'Brien along with him. Kenyon, never-the-less, barnstormed the Ford through 33 states and Mexico over the four year period he owned it.

In 1933, O'Brien bought out Kenyon's portion of the partnership. Tragedy followed the sale. On 31 March, 1933, the big plane crashed at Neodesha, Kansas, carrying the *Winnipeg Toilers* amateur basketball team home from a Tulsa, Oklahoma, tournament. Several of the players, pilot Alvie Hakes, and O'Brien were killed.

In 1938, L. P. Quinn gathered a group together to make a several-state barnstorming tour, purchasing a Ford Trimotor and nicknaming it the *Rocky Mountain Clipper*. He headed southwest, barnstorming through Arizona, New Mexico, and Texas. One of the pilots who accompanied Quinn on this tour was Ignatius Nalewaja. He had been a carefree mechanic, ticket-seller, and all-around extra hand during the early 1930s. Along with his brother, Paul, a parachute jumper, the pair had barnstormed the countryside with C. O. Kvale and Andrew Buhl, from Browerville. When Ignatius finally got his solo license in 1938, he had already accumulated over 200 hours of cross-country stick time, mostly with Buhl in a Travel Air.

Following the successful tour with Quinn, Nalewa-

Londor Ekloff with his clipped wing J-1 Standard at Wold-Chamberlain, circa 1937. Plane was destined for a house crash. (Vern Georgia)

ja returned to help organize the *Sky Rider's Air Show*. This was a grouping of itinerant pilots and airplanes that went from one local activity to the next. That organization broke up following a serious accident in which Paul Nalewaja was killed. While descending in his parachute, Nalewaja was struck by one of the passenger-carrying planes. Besides Paul, five persons aboard the plane were killed. Ignatius then joined the Air Corps, and eventually flew 35 bombing missions over Germany as a flight engineer aboard B-17's.

One of the better-known group circuses was that of Clarence Siehl and Ed Hammann, both of Mankato, Minnesota. They organized the *Hell Divers Flying Circus* in the mid-1930s. It was a pick-up group similar to other groups already mentioned. There were no salaried or permanent members, but rather a gathering of local flyers and recognized personalities available when an exhibit, performance, or tour, was put together.

Many Minnesotans flew along on Siehl and Hammann's trips through the southern counties of Minnesota in the late 1930's. In 1935, for example, the group included Tom Hennessy, from Winona, Minnesotan Jack Robinson, and Sylvan Hugelin, of Iowa. They took their act through the Midwest and down to Texas over the winter of 1935-1936. During this period, they had three airplanes, including Hennessy's J-5 Laird and Hugelin's autogiro.

At other times, Siehl's group was composed of; Iowan Marcellus King; Ob Seim of Jackson, Minnesota; Leon "Babe" Alsworth of Sherburne; Archie Geiser of Dickenson, North Dakota; Ernie Wille of Hollywood; Paul Mlinar of Minneapolis; and Johnny Osterhouse of Bismarck. Parachute jumpers, Red Lancott and Billy Morgan were on the program at various times during 1935-1937, and Grant Hopperstad was Siehl's regular announcer. During that period, passengers were carried in a Travel Air 6000 and a Taylor Cub. The group toured South Dakota, Iowa, and southern Minnesota putting on a show consisting of balloon busting, ribbon cutting, bombing, "crazy" flying, aerial acrobatics, dead-stick landings and parachute jumping.

Marcellus King was one of the group's most flamboyant aviators of the period. With his colorful round-engined Monocoupe 110, he was a master stunter, and racing pilot, competing around the country in air

Gassing up. This nostalgic scene shows the ofttimes necessary method of refueling from five gallon cans brought to a remote field by horse-drawn wagon. Clarence Kvale atop engine, Andrew Buhl and Paul Nalewaja stand by with the farmer. (Ignatious Nalewaja)

races. He once held a record for flying upside down from New York to Chicago!

A unique and spectacular part of the traveling exhibition was the appearance of a novel autogiro. The first "giro" was exhibited in Minnesota at the 1931 State Fair. It was the Pitcairn PAA-1 belonging to the *Des Moines Register*. It appeared as a feature at fairs and airshows in the upper midwest for two seasons and was purchased in October of 1933 by Harry K. Webb, owner of the Webb Oil Company of Tracy, Minnesota. Webb's pilot was Jack E. Robinson, who employed the machine to tow banners and attend airshows, making demonstration flights as a member of the *Hell Divers* group. With Webb's advertising painted on the side, the oil company enjoyed the benefits of the public's interest. It was seen at Minneapolis, Mankato, Trimont, Sherburne and Tracy, among other stops.

When the autogiro was inadvertently nosed over in landing at Trimont in 1934, it was sold to fellow *Hell Diver*, Sylvan Hugelin. He was a licensed mechanic and rebuilt the giro, recovering and refinishing it. Once repaired, Hugelin had Frank Faulkner, a former Pitcairn Company pilot, checked him out in it. After he had been checked out, Hugelin commenced to exhibit the plane and carry passengers. Logs show that Hugelin flew the autogiro through the 1934 and 1935 seasons, making appearances at Jackson, Willmar, Mankato, Austin, Winona, Hibbing and Bemidji. For the 1936 season, Hugelin installed a larger engine and performed across Minnesota once more, mostly with the *Hell Divers*. The exhibitions were variously billed as "Captain Hugelin's Spectacular Autogiro Exhibition" or "The Amazing Windmill Plane." This machine met its demise when a rotor blade failed in October, 1936. Hugelin bailed out safely before the crash, but the machine was destroyed.

A second autogiro was owned and exhibited by Minnesotans, Mary G. Bryce and W. Hale Ainsworth. It was originally brought to the area by Wisconsinite, Leslie G. Mulzer, ("Major Mulzer"), in 1932, to take part in a big Minneapolis Aquatennial Airshow. Mulzer had been allowed to carry passengers at the 1932 Minnesota State Fair, but was not contracted to fly an exhibition there, the program being too full. In September, 1933, Ainsworth purchased the Pitcairn PCA-2 from Mulzer and hired Millar Wittag and Frank Faulkner to fly it on various outings, using it for banner towing and other aerial advertising. On 2 July, 1934, during a banner towing job, the autogiro crashed at Wold-Chamberlain Field when the banner release mechanism failed, and the banner caught on the ground, slamming the plane to earth. Faulkner scrambled out of the burning ship unhurt, but the plane was totalled.[56]

In the Twin City area, there were many, many, weekend barnstormers who filled Wold-Chamberlain Field, St. Paul Airport, (Holman Field), and the smaller fields around the cities, offering rides. At Wold, some of the barnstormers not previously mentioned were: Londor Ekloff with his clipped-wing J-1 Standard; Chuck Wheelock; Budd Stahel; Warren Hemple; and Alfred "Pete" Lohmar. They had plenty of ticket-selling help from the gang of would-be pilots such as Sig Gudmundson, Jack Greiner, Shorty Hall, and Ellis "Slim" Hallin. Those ticket sellers

Sylvan Hugelin in the Pitcairn PA-24 autogiro at Grand Rapids, Minnesota. (Hugelin family collection of the Winnebago Historical Society via James Meyer)

would also go on to become barnstormers, pilots and aviation businessmen.

One local barnstormer, John Witt, had a marvelous act in the 1930s. Witt would poster a town with advertising a few days ahead of his arrival, as was the custom, boasting of the wonderful and thrilling acts to be offered. One of his famous acts was advertised "See Daring Davis Jump Without a Parachute."

Whether this single promotional item inflated the size of the crowd is up to speculation, but we can assume that many folks turned out to see what kind of a fool would leap from an airplane without a parachute. Imagine their surprise when "Daring Davis" turned out to be a rooster! Witt would simply carry the chicken into the air with him, and when over the crowd at the appropriate time, would toss the bird out of the airplane. "Daring Davis" would do his thing and obediently flutter down, usually landing on a fencepost somewhere in front of the crowd. Witt's promised act would be fulfilled, and the crowd would get a good laugh.

The act ended one fall when the airworn rooster finally lost his last feathers and plummeted to his death. At that point, animal lovers in attendance called upon the local Humane Society to put a stop to such cruelty to animals.

In retrospect, flying at a big city airport like Wold Chamberlain, afforded a youngster interested in aviation, a remarkable opportunity unavailable to outstate youth. At Wold, a young person could hang around and watch lots of flying take place through the week from the middle 1920s on. When the time was ripe, the lad could finagle his way into some kind of work; cleaning, ticket-selling, minor repair, wing walking...but at least being able to meet the airmen and airwomen and listen to their stories. Interested enough, the youth could eventually get a paying job

J-1 Standard Minnehaha in a field at Morgan, Minnesota, 1919, ready to take up passengers. (Phil Vogt)

Bill Shaw's Waco YPF-6, 1938. Carrying sight-seers. Shorty Hall, the ticket-seller, is standing by the cockpit counting the money. (Joseph Williams)

with one of the barnstormers or operators. Thus careers were made.

In the outstate areas, where flying was only a weekend event, an interested young man was bound to his farm duties, and hard pressed to work his way into the company of flyers. He would often have to go to the city, at great expense to himself or his family, to take schooling or flying lessons without the benefit of the "basic training" experienced by his city cousin.

Not only the opportunity, but the availability of the airplane was also a factor. At the big airport, there were always planes for sale. New planes came in and old ones were traded. Prices were reasonable, financing was available, surplus airplanes were literally a dime a dozen in the earliest days. A quick lesson could be had from any of a number of operators or barnstormers. Outstate, the situation was totally different. A plane was harder to find. No lessons were available within a modest distance, none on a regular basis. If a young person wanted to fly, he often had to build his own airplane and teach himself how to fly it.

Some self-taught pilots longed for the opportunity to join exhibition companies to build their flying time, or to join airlines such as Northwest, Hanford, or Universal. Those organizations had their pick from dozens of candidates who were at their doors everyday, some even working part time without pay, waiting for their chance to be hired.

Sad, but true, the traveling barnstormer whetted

C. A. Lindbergh, Sr. (left in straw hat), and Charles (center), assess the damage to their Jenny after a crackup at Glencoe in 1923, while on the elder Lindbergh's campaign tour for Congressman of the Minnesota Sixth District. (Minnesota Lindbergh Associates)

a lot of appetites for flying across the United States, but the opportunity was not available for all who wanted it.

RECORD SETTERS

The most famous record in aviation history was set 21 May, 1927. It was set by Charles Augustus Lindbergh, Jr. when he landed his Ryan monoplane, *The Spirit of St. Louis*, at Le Bourget Aerodrome in Paris, France, after having made the first solo, non-stop flight from the USA to the European continent.

Lindbergh's humble reception in France; his return aboard the USS Memphis, a Navy Cruiser sent by President Calvin Coolidge to escort him home to America; his triumphal ticker-tape parades in Washington, DC, and New York City; and his 48-state tour in the fall of 1927, generated more coverage in the world's newspapers than any other single event throughout the remaining twentieth century.

Much has been written about the flight, not only in Lindbergh's own hand, such as his Pulitzer-Prize-winning, "Spirit of St. Louis," and his followup book, "We," but also in historical publications. One of those publications is the Winter, 1970, edition of the Minnesota Historical Society's quarterly, *Minnesota History*. In an article written by Bruce L. Larson, Assistant Professor of History at Mankato State University, the details of Lindbergh's stops in Minnesota on the 48-state tour are portrayed in great depth. From that article, the following information is derived.

Though almost every state claims Lindbergh as their own for various reasons, Minnesota's claim to Lindbergh's being a native son, has special significance. Lindbergh's father, Charles Augustus, Sr., settled in Little Falls where he bought farmland and built a house on the banks of the Mississippi River and raised his family. When the baby, Charles, Jr. was about to be born, "C. A.," as the elder Lindbergh was known, brought his wife to Detroit to stay with her family, and where she could have the care of the family doctor. It is there that Charles was born. Brought back to Little Falls, the lad grew up on the family farm, taking care of it with his mother while C. A. established a law practise in town.

At age sixteen, young Charles managed the farm. His skill with animals and machinery grew keen. During this period, he would often spend an off-hour lying in a grassy field, gazing at the sky, watching hawks or clouds drift overhead. He dreamed of having his own wings and zooming among those clouds. His interest in science drew him from the farm to enter the University of Wisconsin, but that too, was short-lived as he became fixed on the idea of flying. Lessons followed, and he soon joined a barnstorming troupe as a parachute jumper and wing-walker, a means of earning enough money to continue flying. By April of 1923, he had saved enough to purchase a surplus JN-4D Jenny in Georgia, and make his first solo flight in it.

Lindbergh began barnstorming on his own and returned to Minnesota. He had his share of crackups, including one near Savage, where his Jenny went over on its nose, cracking the propeller. (That propeller is now at the Lindbergh Museum at Little Falls.) In the fall of 1923, Lindbergh, Sr. was campaigning for the U. S. Senate and Charles, the aviator, flew the candidate over the district, dropping political pamphlets. A crackup near Glencoe, surprised, but did not injure, either Lindbergh. The airplane was repaired in the field, but not in time to finish the campaign tour.

In 1924, Lindbergh entered the U. S. Army Air Corps, taking flight training at Brooks Field, then Kelly Field in San Antonio, Texas. From his class of 104 students, he finished at the top of the list of 18 who graduated. Lindbergh was commissioned a Second Lieutenant in the Air Corps Reserve. By 1926, he was flying air mail for the Robertson Aircraft Corporation from St. Louis, to Chicago. It was during this time that Lindbergh became interested in the Ortieg Prize, a $25,000 award to be given to the first person to fly solo across the Atlantic. He felt eminently qualified, and successfully talked St. Louis businessmen into helping him finance the construction of the Ryan Monoplane in which he would attempt the Atlantic flight. The preparations and flight are well-known, but Lindbergh's return to Minnesota bears a closer study.

The cross-country tour was sponsored by the Washington-based, Daniel Guggenheim Foundation, as part of their program for the promotion of aeronautics. The flight was set up to give Lindbergh something to do to keep commercial interests away from him, as every organization and community would be begging for his services as a speaker, or to endorse their products. The tour was a benevolent idea from which no profit was derived, but was intended to publicize aviation and open the country's mind to providing airfields, flight services, pilot training, and the production of private aircraft.

Invitations from every corner of America poured in to the Guggenheim offices, and hard decisions had to be made to limit the flight to a workable schedule. Many cities in Minnesota vied for the honor of being the stopping points within the State. Governor, Theodore Christianson, named a committee to invite Lindbergh to stop at Little Falls, before the cross-country tour even began. Other delegations represented the state American Legion, the 109th Air Guard, and the Minnesota State Fair Board. The Fair Board tried every means at their disposal to connect with Lindbergh, to plead for his appearance at the Minnesota State Fair.

The Guggenheim Foundation, with Lindbergh's advice, based their selection of landing sites on the importance of the city, the interest and cooperation of local officials, personal background relationships of Lindbergh's, and landing facilities. The Foundation was keenly aware that the landing sites would have to be special, because they knew that at each stop, Lindbergh and the airplane would be mobbed. In Minnesota, Wold-Chamberlain Field, and Little Falls, were chosen. In addition to these stops, flyovers were scheduled at various communities.

On 23 August, 1927, Lindbergh's plane arrived from Madison, Wisconsin; making the first flyover at Winona, where it dropped a message of greetings from

The Spirit of St. Louis *has landed at Little Falls, Minnesota, and is parked in a fenced-off area for display. Lindbergh is on his nationwide tour in August, 1927. (Edith Lawrence)*

the Guggenheim Fund that included regrets that a stop couldn't be made. This message drop was to be the standard salute at all flyover spots throughout the country. On the ground, eager citizens created a pile up as dozens dived for the prize. Shortly after this flyover, Red Wing received the same honor. The arrival over that city was heralded by ringing fire bells and shrieking industrial whistles. Lindbergh then swung the Ryan over downtown St. Paul and downtown Minneapolis before heading for the airport.

On arrival at Wold-Chamberlain Field, accompanied by a Department of Commerce support plane, things did not go as smoothly as planned. It was intended that Lindbergh taxi the *Spirit* to the 109th Air Guard hangars for secure overnight storage, but when the crowd got beyond the security troops ringing the landing point, they formed a human wall between the plane and the 109th area. Lindbergh turned quickly and taxied to the Air Mail hangar in the middle of the field, where his plane was securely locked inside.

The arrival was nearly on time, though the last-minute change of plans caused a short delay. Lindbergh was to parade from the airport, through the streets of Minneapolis and St. Paul, to a dinner and speaking engagement at the St. Paul Hotel. In the rush, Lindbergh's entourage tried to make up for the delay by speeding along the route, with the result that Twin-Citizens barraged the newspapers in the next few days with angry letters of how their hero had been whisked past them without due time for the public to enjoy their greeting. Anywhere from 250,000 to 500,000 persons along the route were somewhat disappointed. Lindbergh, himself, later indicated that all across the country, such delays had been cause for officials driving the cars in which he rode, at excessive speeds. He considered the hazards of this to be greater than flying his airplane.

Though 24 August was to be a day of rest for Lindbergh, he hardly had a moment to himself, what with visiting dignitaries and newsmen, but he was able to spend some time with his mother and other family members. On Thursday, Lindbergh took off for Little Falls, flying first over the City of Savage where he had special memories from his barnstorming days, then to St. Cloud, where he zoomed over at low altitude and waved to the crowds gathered below, dropping the usual message of salutation and regrets. Sauk Center was the next community overflown and saluted, then he landed at Little Falls.

No doubt the most memorable day ever in Little Falls history was 25 August, 1927. Warmly greeted at the airport, Lindbergh was paraded through the streets of his hometown, recognizing many personal friends along the route. The parade was elaborate, and included a float with the 1916 Lindbergh family automobile, recently rescued from the junkpile, perched on it. Bands, tractors, a float with a replica of the Eiffel Tower, the Statue of Liberty, etc., and some 50,000 citizens, greeted the hero in a respectful manner, not with the usual big city mob clamor.

Lindbergh spoke at an outdoor reception, making his standard statement about the need for improved flying fields, outlining problems that existed and probable solutions. He spoke of the wonders of flight and its efficiency, compared to other forms of transportation. He even predicted that air routes would soon become more extensive than rail routes, and that travel between continents would become matter-of-fact in the future.

The following morning, Lindbergh visited his boyhood home, and promptly at 11:30 am, right on schedule, took off for his next stop, Fargo, North Dakota.

What impact did the cross-country tour have on Americans, and on Minnesotans in particular? The *St. Paul Pioneer Press* of 23 August, 1927 noted that "for once the world stopped its quarreling and united for a moment to applaud a young man who had accomplished a feat of extraordinary heroism."

Twin Cities newspapers featured front-page stories about Lindbergh, during the entire four-day visit. Minnesotans, like the world, were struck by the humble and earnest manner which endeared Lindbergh to the people. His refusal to commercialize on his achievements, his sportsmanship, courage, and charm, left Minnesotans proud to call him their own native son.

Lindbergh's record flight was the door opening to a host of additional record-attempts over the next few years during the remarkable celebration of flight, brought on by a young Minnesotan's deed.

In the period following Lindbergh's 1927 flight, there were several record-breaking flights by Minnesotans, and other attempts at records that proved unsuccessful.

As aviation fever gripped the nation's pilots and would-be pilots, the frontiers of aerial endeavor presented themselves as fat plums ready for the plucking. Records of speed, time, distance, altitude, aerobatic maneuver, and destination-to-destination were open to whoever had the courage to make a try for them.

In 1928, locals in the Twin City area were thinking about how they could get into the record book just like everyone else. In the crisp air of January, barnstormer, Gene Shank, cranked up his airplane and rattled off 515 loops.[57] He captured local newspaper coverage and the adulation of the Minneapolis Wold-Chamberlain gang enough to pique the appetite of daredevil, Speed Holman, who had recently gained a reputation for himself as a cross-country flier and aerobat. Holman, and fellow barnstormer, Lyle Thro, decided to break Shank's record. On 13 February, 1928, the two of them sprang into the air, fuel tanks

Fine portrait of Speed Holman taken just after his loop record in 1928. (Northwest Airlines)

filled, ready for a friendly competition to see who could fly more loops, hopefully beating Shank's mark.

Thro, in his Eaglerock, began diving and zooming in monotonous manner. Speed, in the National Lead Battery Company's Laird, was doing the same. After 543 loops, the Eaglerock's OX-5 engine began to experience trouble and Thro was forced to retire, leaving the sky to Holman, who continued the dizzying routine. Topping 1,000 loops, Holman still felt like going on, and added another 93 for a total of 1,093 before he, too, retired.

Holman went about his business with Northwest Airways for the next few days. In France, however, a flyer named Alfred Fronval, quickly smashed Holman's record, performing 1,111 loops. The stage was set for Holman to try again.

On St. Patrick's Day, 17 March, 1928, after a night of revelry and psyching himself for the event, Holman, unshaven and suit rumpled, strapped into his trusty Laird. He warmed the engine and made a couple of test hops between St. Paul and Minneapolis, then had the fuel tanks topped off while he ate a brief lunch.

He then took off in the Laird, climbed to 3,000 feet over the St. Paul Airport, put his ship into a shallow dive, and commenced looping. After a few loops, Speed let the ship drift over the City of St. Paul. The noise overhead quickly brought crowds into the streets. Radios broadcast the activity over several stations, and word spread swiftly about what was going on. Huge throngs, attracted by the thought of a new record, poured from closed businesses and abandoned household duties. Persons lined the hilltops on the east side of the river or sat on their front porches, gazing skyward.

Holman, starting with one hundred gallons of fuel, could make four loops per minute, but as his fuel burned off and the ship got lighter, was able to turn six loops a minute. A tally crew at the airport, led by Northwest Airways chief clerk, George O. Miles, climbed to a hangar roof and put out large white fabric panels where Holman could see them, one for each one hundred loops. A great cheer went up from the crowd when the record-breaking 1,112th loop was announced.

A short while before the record was set, the *Min-neapolis Star* came off the press, announcing "Holman Nearing New Mark, Loops 1,005 Times."[58] At 5:16 p.m., Holman became tired of the game and slipped the plane down for a landing at St. Paul, but not before he put on an impromptu aerobatic display for the crowd. He landed, and exhaustedly shuffled into a circle of well-wishers, having turned 1,433 loops, a record that would stand for 21 years. On his departure from the field for supper, he was heard to remark, "Anyone who wants to beat that record, can have it. No more of it for me."[59]

CHARLES W. "SPEED" HOLMAN

Born 27 December, 1898, in South Minneapolis, so close to Christmas, had its drawbacks. The father, W. Judson Holman, was of Scotch-Irish stock, and known to be pennywise. Young Charlie's birthday celebrations were destined to be rather small. After all, "one could not expect to get much of a birthday present when the family had hardly picked the bones of the Christmas goose" as one writer put it.[60]

The life style of the Holman family was ample, however. Judson Holman was a contract cattleman, feeding neighbors' cattle, and marching them to auction at South St. Paul. Charlie helped with the cattle drives from their home in Bloomington. It was good healthy exercise and the boy grew strong and tall, towering over his school chums.

Charlie hung around with older children and picked up their tricks. Once, when his and a chum's father were negotiating a cattle deal, to prove what a daredevil he was, he climbed the farm's windmill tower. His chum, Vern Georgia, kept quiet when asked where Charlie was, fearing reprisals if he tattled. When the cover-up was discovered, Vern was the one who got the licking. Charlie had a habit of blocking Vern's path to the schoolhouse, causing both boys to be late for class. Each got the usual punishment, a slap across the back of the hand with a ruler.

Charlie Holman became interested in motorcycles as a teenager, rebuilding an older machine that he used to zoom around Minneapolis and St. Paul. He took a job at as a repairman at a motorcycle shop in Minneapolis, and occasionally stopped at Speedway Field to watch airplanes at the Security Aircraft Company on the way home.

At the age of twenty, Holman heard that an aviator, Walter Bullock, was operating an airplane from the ice of Lake Calhoun in Minneapolis, and decided that he wanted to take a ride. Bullock obliged, taking Holman up for a trip around the lake, and Holman caught the flying bug. Holman enlisted in the Army, hoping to get into the Signal Corps where he could become a pilot, but he was turned down, due to deafness in one ear. He then joined the 109th Air Guard to be near the airplanes he couldn't fly.

Holman made up his mind that he would become a pilot and begged a job with the Security Aircraft Company. There he did whatever mechanical jobs he could, from painting wings, to working on engines. When the opportunity presented itself, the young daredevil volunteered to make a parachute jump from a Security airplane during a weekend air show. Such shows were staged to bring paying customers to the airport for sight-seeing hops and perhaps flight training or airplane sales.

Charlie's skill at parachute jumping soon earned him the confidence to attempt wing-walking. With his daredevil motorcycling and wing-walking, he was soon nicknamed "Jack Speed." Somehow, Judson Holman was coerced into attending a Sunday air show and was stunned when Jack Speed landed nearly in his lap, revealing himself to be his own son. This revelation convinced the elder Holman to buy his son an airplane so that he could take up flying and set aside the more dangerous line of work.

The winter of 1921 found Holman's first plane, a J-1 Standard, damaged in a freak accident on Bush Lake in Bloomington. When he, and buddy, Vern Georgia, combined to taxi the plane into tree stumps on the shoreline. The winter was spent rebuilding the wing and landing gear.

Skilled Security Aircraft Company instructor, Ed Ballough, gave Holman enough lessons to make him a full-fledged pilot. By 1922, Holman and another daredevil, Al Blackstone, had taken over the Security Company's weekend flying circus, sponsored at that time by the *St. Paul Dispatch*. Holman bought himself a Thomas-Morse S-4C Scout airplane, and with the help of Walter Bullock, and one of Security's mechanics, Guy Carroll, installed a water-cooled OX-5 engine, replacing the original rotary powerplant.

Holman solicited sponsorship from the Washburn-Crosby Flour Company, exchanging expenses for advertising Gold Medal Flour by painting their logo on the sides of his plane. Occasionally, he dropped small bags of the flour, on tiny parachutes, over the city. With this powerful little plane, he also entered the national Pulitzer Races, winning a stunt-flying contest in St. Louis in 1923. The nickname "Slim" was given to Holman by the media during this period, but was soon be changed to "Speed," that nickname following him through the rest of his life.

In 1924, Speed made newspaper headlines when, he and a passenger from Chicago, got lost in a snowstorm on the way to the Twin Cities. Making a forced landing in a field near Hammond, Indiana, the two were uninjured but unable to communicate their plight to the outside world for a full day, causing Twin Cities media to raise fears that they had crashed.

Holman entered the On-To-Dayton cross-country

Mechanic Fred Fischer and Speed Holman load mail sacks into a Stinson Detroiter. The Detroiter was one of the first three airplanes purchased by newly-organized, Northwest Airways, in 1926. (Jim Borden)

race that year, planning to fly from Minot, North Dakota, to Dayton, Ohio. The event was a speed contest with racers starting from various points around the country, and converging on Dayton. The winner would be the flyer with the least time spent enroute. Holman departed Minot with no trouble and zoomed into Minneapolis for fuel. There, it was discovered that he had cracked his propeller on take-off from Minot. After a quick inspection, it was decided simply to wrap tape around the prop and send Holman on his way. He rode a tail wind into Dayton, taking second place in this national event.

Holman continued making headlines as the local hero through 1925 and operating the weekend flying circus. He met Dee Swanson and was married that same year. It was while barnstorming that he cracked up on a take-off, injuring a paying passenger. A damage suit was brought against Holman, but it was dismissed in court when the judge ruled that the woman passenger "rode in the aircraft at her own risk."[61]

In 1926, Holman eagerly accepted a job as first pilot for a fledgling airline called Northwest Airways. The line had just organized, and been granted Contract Air Mail Route Number Nine by the government. Holman's position as Chief Pilot and Operations Manager put him in charge of hiring and daily operations from Wold-Chamberlain Field. He continued his barnstorming and cross-country racing.

Speed Holman is upside down in his Laird over the Twin Cities in this 1929 photo. Speed used the same airplane in earlier configurations without the "speedwing" to set a loop record of 1433 loops in 1928. (Jim Borden)

The National Lead Battery Company "Eagle" with racing number 4 on the side, and Wright J-4 engine up front. Lieutenant Thomas Lane of the 109th Observation Squadron and Speed Holman stand in front of the plane after finishing the 1927 New York to Spokane Air Derby. Plane is registered C-240. (Jim Borden)

In 1927, following Lindbergh's famous flight, Holman won the New York to Spokane cross-country race, one of the featured events of the National Air Races, with a victory margin of nineteen seconds over his former teacher, Ed Ballough. Both were flying Laird airplanes. Holman had brought the Laird he was flying to the Twin Cities the previous year for Lytton Shields, president of the National Lead Battery Company of St. Paul, and a director of Northwest Airways. Holman became Shield's personal pilot, and had exclusive use of the Laird.

Winning the cross-country race was the occasion for a grand parade through the streets of Minneapolis, honoring Holman. The parade nearly didn't pull off, however, because the engine in Holman's Laird broke its camshaft over the mountains of Montana, necessitating him to make a forced landing in a mountain cow pasture. Repairs took two days before Holman could successfully fly out of the pasture and make his way back to the Twin Cities. The local news media reported every aspect of Holman's life on a daily basis.

In February and March of 1928, Holman set his loop records as mentioned previously. Holman again entered the cross-country race, this time from New York to Los Angeles. He took off from New York, but suffered a forced landing in Pennsylvania when fog prevented him from continuing. He broke a propeller in landing and had to have another shipped from Chicago. Underway again, though out of the race, he made it to Los Angeles before other events were finished and entered a cross-country race back to Cincinnati. This, he won handily.

Holman was to set several other records, though none of them quite so spectacular as his loop record. For example, in April, following the loop record, in his role as Northwest Airways pilot, he carried passenger, John P. Greer, from Chicago, Illinois, through Boise, Idaho, Salt Lake City, Utah, St. Louis, Missouri, and on to New York, making stop after stop along the way. The journey covered 5,558 air miles, the longest air taxi journey made by a recognized passenger carrying company to that time.

Holman also perfected the dangerous outside loop, a maneuver few aerobatic pilots were willing to attempt. He entered and won a 1928 cross-country race

Holman in the cockpit of the Laird Solution prior to winning the Thompson Trophy Race, 1 September, 1930. Note the whitewashed race number and the plexigas cockpit enclosures. (Noel Allard)

from St. Louis to Indianapolis, and figured in a spectacular test flight of the Mohawk Pinto airplane at Wold-Chamberlain Field.

The Mohawk was a unique airplane, but had certain spin characteristics that made it unsafe and needing redesign. Holman was asked to give the plane a test flight, the opportunity he eagerly accepted. During a test spin, Holman, like others before him, could not get the plane to stop spinning. Equipped with his parachute, Holman stepped out on the wing to jump. With the change of balance, however, the plane stopped spinning. Holman climbed back in. The plane rolled into the spin once more, and again Holman stepped out. The results were the same, the spin stopped. Holman cautiously climbed back in, but again, the spin started. This time Holman bailed out, and none too soon. Pilot and airplane hit the ground at the same time. For this jump, Holman earned membership in the "Caterpillar Club."

Holman's most productive year was 1930. He gained national prominence for winning the famous Thompson Trophy Race and a total of $100,000. Each year, the cream of the air racing fraternity competed in this event with the fastest, specially-designed racing airplanes available. The unlimited race event was part of the National Air Races, being held in Chicago.

The Laird Airplane Company had produced a special racer for Lee Schoenhair, the Chief Pilot of the B. F. Goodrich Rubber Company. Finished only

The smashed Laird of Speed Holman is being dragged off the infield of the Omaha Airport after crashing in front of the grandstands, killing Holman on 17 May, 1931. (Jim Borden)

a few hours prior to the races, this tiny black and gold biplane featured a new Pratt & Whitney Wasp Jr. engine and had not even been test flown. Speed Holman was at the factory, and at that moment, he had more experience in racing Laird's than anyone else, and was asked to make a quick test hop. In a ten minute flight, Holman pronounced it ready to compete. Schoenhair, Matty Laird, and Holman, agreed that Holman was the only logical person to fly it in the big race.

Arriving at the race site with only minutes to spare before the start, a race number was hastily slapped on the fuselage side in whitewash paint and the race was flagged off. Many planes dropped out, until only five remained. Navy Captain, Arthur Page, was the odds-on favorite to win, flying a specially rigged Curtiss Hawk military pursuit plane. The Hawk had been modified from a biplane to a parasol-winged racer by removal of the whole lower wing. Page gunned the Hawk around the racecourse with great speed, pulling away from everyone. Holman and Jimmy Haizlip were in hot pursuit. With only three laps to go, Page was overcome by carbon monoxide, his plane leaving the racecourse and crashing. Holman assumed the lead and won the race, though drugged in his Laird by the same fumes. Page died the next day of his injuries.

In May of 1931, Holman followed the air racing clan to Omaha, Nebraska, where a weekend of air races were being held. Though not scheduled on the program, Holman volunteered an impromptu performance in his faithful Laird.

Putting on a spectacular, if unsanctioned, low-level performance, Holman closed with his specialty, a series of outside loops. The first of these loops went flawlessly, but on the third, while upside down and fifty feet above the ground, as he pushed forward on the stick to complete the bottom half of the maneuver, a seat-belt bracket failed, and Holman was seen to fall partially out of the cockpit. The plane hit the ground and was destroyed; Holman's body was crushed.

After his remains arrived back in Minneapolis, some 8,000 persons filed past it at the funeral parlor, and 2,000 more attended funeral services at the Masonic Scottish Rite Temple in downtown Minneapolis. A funeral cortege from there to Acacia Park Cemetery, across the Minnesota River from Wold-Chamberlain Field, drew an estimated 100,000

mourners along the route, with 50,000 alone, at the graveside. Rose petals were dropped from Navy and commercial airplanes flying overhead. Governor, Floyd B. Olson, spoke the eulogy, "Charles W. Holman will live in the hearts of his comrades. He was a man of flaming courage, whose modesty and comradeship endeared him to all who knew him. Nature sometimes gives us a man of destiny, and in aviation, Charles Holman was a man of destiny. He lived for the greatest thrill. From his boyhood he sought it. Nature gave him the qualifications and the intent of a bird."[62]

After his death in 1931, it was discovered that Holman had planned a truly remarkable long-distance, aerial-refueled flight, that would surely have been record-setting, if it had occurred. Holman, with Tom Lane, of the 109th Air Guard Squadron, Chad Smith of Northwest Airways, mechanic George Weiss of the 109th squadron, and C. D. Johnstone, writer for the *St. Paul Dispatch*, planned to modify a Ford Trimotor and fly around the world. To that end, Holman had planned to set up aerial refueling at such romantic places as London, Moscow, Omsk, Nome, Edmonton, and Winnipeg.

The Greater St. Louis Curtiss Robin is being readied for an assault on the refueled endurance record in the Curtiss dealership at St. Louis' Lambert Field. Left to right: "Shorty" Chaffee, refueling crew; Forest O'Brine and Dale "Red" Jackson of the endurance crew; and Bill Brewster of the refueling crew. Photo taken sometime in June, 1929. (Vern Georgia)

Like the loop-record craze, the endurance flight fad began in 1928. It would spark the attention of media audiences across the country, and every able-bodied aviator wanted to get in on it. Eugene Shank was no exception. On 21 March, 1928, after his loop record had been thoroughly shattered, he took his OX-5 Waco 10 nicknamed "Willoco," aloft to try for an unrefueled endurance record. Over the St. Paul airport, he circled for twelve hours and 33 minutes until his fuel tank ran dry, claiming a record for OX-5 powered aircraft. (This was only four days after Speed Holman had held St. Paul residents' attention with his loop record.)

Less than a month later, Shank tried again. This time, in the same airplane, he managed fourteen hours and 28 minutes, for another record. This was but a beginning for Minnesota aviators, and their participation in the endurance craze.

It was in 1929 that endurance flights were at their most numerous. In fact, there seemed to be at least one endurance flight in the air somewhere over the U. S. at all times. Across the country, Bellancas, Curtisses, Stinsons, and Cessnas were taking off and literally wearing themselves out in the air. Men, too, were pushing their bodies to unheard of tests of will.

In January, a plane nicknamed *Angelino*, flying over Culver City, California, set a new refueled endurance record of 246 hours. On 13 July, 1929, a young Faribault, Minnesota, native, named Dale

"Red" Jackson, and a flying buddy, Forest O'Brine, set out to best the record. The flight was sponsored by the Curtiss-Robertson Airplane Manufacturing Company of St. Louis, Missouri, under the auspices of Major William B. Robertson, himself. Though employed by the Robertson Company at the time, Jackson was promised additional prize money for bettering the standing record.

A Curtiss Robin with the name, *Greater St. Louis* was prepared for the attempt at the St. Louis airport. Its 170 horsepower Challenger engine was overhauled, and a narrow catwalk welded onto the engine mounts to provide a working platform, so that one of the pilots could make an extra-vehicular-activity to perform minor maintenance on the engine while in flight. A one hundred gallon fuel tank was installed, along the top of which was spread an air mattress so that the off-duty pilot could catch a few hours of sleep.

The record attempt got underway in perfect weather. Jackson and O'Brine spent the next few days leisurely cruising over the Lambert Field airport in St. Louis. A second Robin was to be used as a refueling ship, dropping a hose to the record-setting airplane, which the off-duty pilot would grab and insert into the neck of the fuel tank, replenishing the gasoline supply. The scenario worked flawlessly with food, clean clothes, mail and other amenities being lowered to the crew. Jackson and O'Brine occasionally sent back wise-crack notes to relieve the boredom.

This continued for seventeen and a half days with Jackson's mother and father flown in from Faribault to greet their son in the air. The two planes flew briefly in formation, the folks waving a cheery hello to Dale on the 13th day. Meanwhile, the two flyers' wives kept busy preparing lunches to be passed skyward. In all, some 3,500 gallons of fuel were consumed, along with 158 gallons of oil, all passed during forty-eight mid-air hookups.[63]

Stepping out on the catwalk at 3,000 feet, Jackson had inspected the engine twice a day, occasionally changing spark plugs, and once opening a magneto to clean it. When they landed, Jackson and O'Brine had set a new record of 420 hours in the air, and claimed a bonus of $31,529 from their company and other sponsors. They also received the Curtiss Robin as a gift, though the endurance engine was removed for study and a new one substituted.

The endurance pilots could easily have extended the flight, for the engine was found to be in perfect shape despite the long period of operation. About the 400th hour, Major Robertson had called the boys to come down, stating that there was nothing more to be proven by a longer flight. Still, Jackson and O'Brine continued for another twenty hours, finally landing when it was learned that a close friend, and son of the airfield's founder, George Lea Lambert, had been killed in a flight-training accident.[64]

Before they landed, the pair found time to wash and shave, and change their shirts, much to the amazement of the news media and crowds of spectators. The food-stuffs sent up had apparently been nourishing enough, for Jackson stepped from the Robin upon landing and weighed in at exactly the same as he had at takeoff. O'Brine had gained nearly two pounds!

Before long, the Jackson-O'Brine record was broken, but that did not end the story. Jackson and O'Brine took off again in another Robin on 17 August, 1930. This ship, nicknamed the *St. Louis Robin #1*, took to the air with the boys vowing to fly it until it broke. It finally did break, hatching itself and spitting off two cylinders; forcing the pair to land with no less than 647 hours, 28 minutes, and 30 seconds logged, still another record in the book.

Jackson went on to fly aerobatic performances and remain in the public spotlight until 6 January, 1932, when he was killed while stunting a prototype Curtiss CW-3 Duckling at the Miami American Air Derby. The plane was a seaplane modification of the popular Curtiss-Wright Junior. Faribault, as well as the entire nation, mourned his death.[65]

Not all endurance flights came to such success or heralded endings as Jacksons and O'Brine's. Some, indeed, ended in tragedy. Strange as it may seem, while Jackson and O'Brine were in the air setting their first record, another similar flight was under way over Wold-Chamberlain Field in Minneapolis.

Minneapolis flyers, Gene Shank, Owen Haugland, and Thorwald "Thunder" Johnson were also among those who hoped to get their names in the record book. Haugland was to try no less than five times for the refueled record.

Shank and Haugland's first attempt was planned to start from Wichita, Kansas, home of the Cessna airplane, on 20 May, 1929. Haugland owned two Cessna Model AF's. One would be modified as the record plane, the other serve as the refueler. The record plane was named *Miss Minnesota*, and was to fly from Wichita, to Robbinsdale Airport near Minneapolis, then to the Canadian border, and back, making round trips until it could fly no longer.[66]

The refueling plan, as in the St. Louis flight, was

A refueling hookup about to be made with the Greater St. Louis over the St. Louis countryside in July, 1929. (Vern Georgia)

to drop a 42 foot hose to the record plane. By reaching out of an open hatch above the cockpit and snaring the fuel hose with a hook, the pilots of the record plane could hookup and transfer fuel. Oil, food, newspapers and goodies could be lowered in a bucket or tied to the end of the refueling hose.

The endurance airplane, a dark red Cessna AF with a seven cylinder, 150 horsepower Axelson engine, was the first of only three Model AF's produced by the Cessna Company. It could carry one hundred gallons of gas in its tanks with a bed arranged on top just as in the Curtiss Robin of Jackson and O'Brine. The refueling crew and ground crew consisted of Verne Nelson of St. Paul; Earl Rowland, a test pilot from the Cessna plant in Wichita; O. P. Harrah, pilot of the refueling plane; Andy Kramer, Les Smith of Northwest Airways, and Doug Christianson. The record to shoot at when they took off was slightly over 246 hours in the air, a bit more than ten days!

On the 19th of May, Shank had flown Miss Jean DuRand, a parachute jumper, to an altitude of 19,200 feet for a record-breaking, high-altitude parachute jump, over the Robbinsdale Airport. He then hopped into a Yellow Cab Airliner and headed for Wichita. Because another record flight was in progress, however, Shank and Haugland decided to wait it out and get the results, before departing themselves. That other flight by Robins and Kelly in the Stinson *Miss Fort Worth*, was in flight over Texas, bumping the record by several hours before it was over.

At 8:58 a.m. on 25 May, 1929, Shank and Haugland took off, making their way to Minneapolis with no incidents. In Minneapolis, a mishap occurred, however, that almost did them in. During a regular refueling over Wold-Chamberlain, the hose became caught

Cessna AF endurance plane, Miss Minneapolis to be flown by Thunder Johnson and Owen Haugland. Picture is dated 20 January, 1929. (Slim Cady via Bob Lemm)

Thorwald "Thunder" Johnson and Owen Haugland in front of the endurance Cessna AF, Miss Minneapolis, in June, 1929. (Slim Cady via Bob Lemm)

under the record plane's navigation light. Shank, who was piloting, managed to loosen the hose by wiggling the controls, but the hose then jammed in the supply plane and could not be reeled in, forcing pilot, Harrah, to land with it dragging behind.[67]

The record attempt came to an abrupt halt after only 51 hours, A faulty fuel gauge indicated plenty of fuel remaining, but a sudden quiet from the front of the airplane, and a view of the propeller windmilling lazily proved the tanks were empty. This was followed by a dead-stick landing west of Robbinsdale.

Disappointment soon gave over to plans for the next try at the record. A take off on Wednesday, June 19th, in the same aircraft, renamed *Miss Minneapolis*, brought only thirteen hours of flight time. While cruising over the Minneapolis area, it was discovered that a siphon, accidently left in the reserve oil tank spout had sucked the entire oil supply out into the night air. Things just weren't right. Besides battling a thunderstorm and its turbulence, there was no way to signal to the ground for more oil, the only thing to do was land.[68]

Replenishing the oil supply and checking things over, Shank and Haugland again took off on the 21st, but bad luck dogged them once more. This time an engine failure put them back on the ground the same day, ending the third attempt. There was no report on just what caused the engine to quit, but it must have been minor, for at 5 a.m. on Sunday, 23 June, the next attempt took to the air. Gene Shank was not aboard, however, he had enough of wrestling with disappointment and decided to fly the supply plane instead, his place as co-pilot, was taken over by Thunder Johnson.

This time, everything seemed to go right. The route to be flown was in the form of a triangle, from Minneapolis to Rochester, to Hastings, then back to Minneapolis. Round trips were being counted in an effort to record a mark for the longest distance flown, a mark not well recorded in the big record book. Timers and scorers included: Preston L. Crichton; an official of the National Aeronautics Association, who had installed a barograph aboard the Cessna; and Larry Hammond, Wold-Chamberlain airport manager.

The first night was again filled with thunderstorms, causing Johnson to become slightly ill, and Haugland's hands to become blistered and raw from fighting the turbulence. With the dawn, Johnson felt better, and when a message was dropped to the ground crew, the report was, "...everything is fine, thanks for sending up the horseshoe for luck, and could we get some chewing gum?" Though still in rain and fog, Haugland crawled out of the cockpit and greased the engine rocker arms.

Hundreds of people gathered at Wold-Chamberlain as a 2nd and 3rd day passed, then a 4th and a 5th. Nearly every night was filled with storms, and during the day of 27 June, Haugland was forced to fly within 100 feet of the ground to keep his bearings. A fuel transfer, (one of three daily occurrences), was even accomplished at that altitude. A claim for the greatest distance flown, was lodged when the ship passed the 6,000-mile mark.[69]

When the fog lifted on the 27th of June, Haugland flew out to Buffalo, Minnesota, to give his family and the folks in his hometown, a view of the record plane.

More side trips were made to White Bear and Faribault. Things were going so well now that WCCO radio was to send a plane with short-wave radio aloft to broadcast reports from along the route as the record was about to be broken. Little things like a last-minute fuel transfer, with five minutes of fuel remaining, did not daunt the aviators. Unfortunately, on 29 June, a sticking valve brought to an end the fourth attempt. Only 23 hours remained to break the record set by *Miss Fort Worth*.[70]

In July, Haugland attempted the flight once more. Due to a contractual squabble with sponsor, WCCO Radio, Thunder Johnson decided not to fly as co-pilot, and Preston Crichton took his place. Pilots of the refueling plane were Walter Bullock and Chad Smith of Northwest Airways. With a new engine, *Miss Minneapolis* took to the air at 6:40 p.m. on 22 July, 1929, the crew knowing that Dale Jackson and Forest O'Brine had been in the air for several days over St. Louis.

Seven days passed with the usual storms and side trips. Communities visited were Litchfield, Montevideo, Appleton, Mason City, Albert Lea and Winona. Then, the unexpected happened. While slow-flying, to drop a note to ground crews at Wold-Chamberlain, pilot Crichton stalled the airplane, and it spun in. Bullock and the ground crew had just finished reading the note when they heard the ship crash. Crichton had been killed instantly and Haugland, whom Bullock rushed to the Fort Snelling hospital, died the next day. The flight had logged 11,000 miles, flying 154 hours, 45 minutes, and making 18 refuelings.[71]

To what avail was all this? One might say - none. It was the *Greater St. Louis* flown by Red Jackson, the Faribault native, that got into the record book.

Yet another record long-distance refueled flight occurred during August of 1929. It involved a native of Hastings, Minnesota, Nicholas B. Mamer. "Nick" Mamer had spent his early career barnstorming for Clarence Hinck's Federated Fliers, after a stint with the Air Service in Panama. Mamer eventually migrated to the Washington State area, where he continued to fly with the Washington Air National Guard. He took on contracts with the U. S. Forest Service to photograph large tracts of fire-burned timberland.

Mamer was granted a Buhl aircraft franchise and opened an airline flying between cities in Washington State. His intentions were to build a larger airline, and claim passenger routes from Washington to the Twin Cities. (His airline is covered in another chapter of this book.) To promote the line, he made several survey flights between Seattle, Spokane, and the Twin Cities, and calculated that he could use the current endurance flight craze to his advantage, making a spectacular cross-county flight to publicize his idea for long-distance passenger carrying.

By carrying a heavy load of fuel on his cross-country trip, and being refueled in mid-air, as few times as possible, he could demonstrate the airplane's ability at long-haul passenger and freight transportation. As Mamer put it, "we will be going someplace constantly, which is the only ability the airplane has."[72]

Accordingly, the Buhl Aircraft Company modified one of their new CA-6 sesquiplanes, (having two wings like a biplane, but much shorter lower wings, which help to provide structural strength and some lift, without producing the drag of a full biplane). Buhl installed extra large wing tanks and a special 200-gallon fuel tank in the fuselage. The Wright J-6 engine of 300 horsepower was a reliable workhorse, born of the line from which Lindbergh's sturdy J-5 Whirlwind arose.

The Blackfoot Indian tribe, residing near Spokane, had "adopted" Mamer some time before, and in their honor, he nicknamed the aircraft after one of their spiritual beings, the "Spokane Sun God."

Mamer, and the National Air Derby Association's original planning committee, drew up a schedule for the various refuelings that would be necessary between the West and East coasts. For refueling planes, Mamer decided to use two aircraft that his airline already owned, a Ryan B-5 Brougham, and a Buhl J-5 Airsedan that he had been flying for some time. The two would hopscotch to refueling points in the West as needed.

His co-pilot on the marathon would be trusty *Mamer Air Transport* mechanic pilot, Art Walker. The Texaco Oil Company, under the direction of avid cross-country and racing record-seeker, Frank Hawks, would provide the gas and oil. They would also provide the refueling planes in Chicago and New York. Spokane businesses added $10,000 in financial support.

To get the flight started, a Blackfoot Indian prayer service was held and their Medicine Man spoke to tribesmen and the assembled crowd, "My children of the sun, call on the sun god to bring them back safe and happy."[72] A National Aeronautics Association official stepped up and installed a sealed barograph in the "Sun God." The instrument would confirm the fact that the ship made no landing between its take off from Spokane and its return.

Takeoff got underway at 6 p.m. on 15 August, 1929. Mamer made his way down the West Coast through Oregon, making his first aerial refueling over San Francisco. He then turned east and after encountering headwinds over the mountains, called for his next refueling at Rock Spring, Wyoming. There, turbulent air and the high altitude combined to make this refueling a nightmare.

In a thermal, the Sun God's propeller sliced through the refueling hose, splashing gasoline over the entire airplane, but thankfully, it did not ignite. With the hose shortened to a mere twenty feet, the two aircraft had to snuggle up very close in the turbulent air. Art Walker related that he had to reach up and push away on the belly of the refueling ship at one point during the transfer.[74]

The route next took the aircraft over Cheyenne, Omaha, Chicago, Cleveland, and finally to New York. The flight into New York became a spectacular parade, as nearly a hundred private aircraft came up to provide an escort. Frank Hawks observed the aerial refueling and escorted the Sun God back as far as Pennsylvania, flying alongside in a Lockheed Vega.

Between Cleveland and Chicago, the weather went sour. The Buhl flew through the worst electrical storm that Mamer had ever experienced. At St. Paul, Minnesota, the crew took on 250 gallons of gas, 10 gallons of oil and a welcomed pair of chicken dinners.

The route then continued on to Aberdeen South Dakota, and Miles City, Montana. Arriving over Miles City after midnight and almost out of gas, Mamer circled the field, dropping a note attached to a flashlight. (The Sun God had no radio for communications.) A pleading message asked for fuel. An earlier refueling had been missed due to heavy forest-fire smoke in the area. Now a crew on the ground with no special equipment would have to come to the rescue.

While Mamer circled waiting for the dawn's first light, a plan was devised. At 3 a.m., with the first rays of light breaking the crest of the hills, a J-5 Eaglerock was sent aloft, carrying three 5-gallon milk cans filled with gas. By lowering them one at a time with a rope, each was snagged by Walker, and its contents poured into the tank. Refueler, Frank Wiley, remembered that when Walker popped up out of the manhole in the top of the Sun God to grab the cans, he looked much like a prairie dog in helmet and goggles.[75]

Next, the route continued over Billings, Butte, Missoula, and finally to Spokane. Further refuelings went like clockwork and the crew arrived over Spokane not really sure they wanted to end the record flight. They had momentary thoughts of going for the endurance record, which at that moment was 420 hours, (set by Jackson and O'Brine). An attempt to surpass that record would have enabled them to fly back east and make an appearance at the opening of the National Air Races at Cleveland...a tempting thought.

They did circle around for nearly four hours, while one of Mamer's company pilots carried load after load of passengers aloft in his Ford Trimotor, making a good profit at $5 a head, flying each load briefly alongside the record plane.

The crew of Mamer and Walker finally landed at 6 p.m., after having been firmly told to end the flight. They could go home to bed satisfied that they had set the record for the first non-stop round trip from coast to coast, recorded the longest distance flown non-stop, and having performed the first recorded nighttime aerial refueling.

Mamer did go on to open *Mamer Air Transport*, an air route between Seattle and the Twin Cities. Later he went to work for Northwest Airlines, flying the same routes through his beloved northwest. Mamer lost his life on 10 January, 1938, when his Northwest Lockheed 14 Zephyr shed its vertical stabilizers over the mountains near Bozeman, Montana. The crash killed him and nine others. At that time, he had flown over a million miles in the air, most of them nowhere near as exhausting as his 120 hours from Spokane to New York and return.

The story of Minnesota record-setters would not be complete without mention of an attempted record by Adrian "A. C." or "Mac" McInnis. The date was 9 January, 1939; the plane, a 40-horsepower Taylor J-2 Cub fitted with an experimental, single-bladed propeller and a strapped-on belly fuel tank, holding 37 extra gallons of gas. The departure was from Wold-Chamberlain Field by McInnis and passenger, Harley Jobe, an aeronautical engineering student from the University of Minnesota. The destination: Miami, Florida...non-stop!

The McInnis Cub rests ignominiously in a haystack, a record flight from Minneapolis to Florida aborted in January of 1939. (Vern Georgia)

Federal Inspector, Forrest Longeway, had given the pair a flight permit, and the official record attempt was supervised by University Aero Engineering head, John Akerman, who set a barograph aboard the plane to record its flight for the National Aeronautics Association's record sanction.

At 7 p.m. on a chilly January evening, flares were lit to outline the north-south runway at Wold. The flyers donned their cold-weather leather flight suits and waved a cheery goodbye. The cub rolled down the runway, and lifted sluggishly, clearing the airport boundary fence by a mere 60 feet, and disappeared into the night.

The plane refused to climb, however, and it sank lower and lower into the river bottoms as downdrafts kept it from clearing the surrounding hills. With the aid of a flashlight held by Jobe in the back seat, McInnis steered the plane through ravines and gullies. He tried to jettison the belly fuel tank, but it was either frozen or jammed and would not drop free.

Almost comically, the ship nosed into a haystack on the crest of a hill. It stopped abruptly, knocking both occupants temporarily unconscious, and splitting the fuel tank so that gasoline ran down into the hay. Fortunately there was no fire, and when the pair recovered their senses, they made their way to a nearby farmhouse to report their fate. They had been in the air a scant fifteen minutes. The flight was not attempted again.

MAX A. CONRAD, JR.

Max Conrad was born in Winona, Minnesota in 1903. He developed an ability with machinery at an early age, fiddling with speedboats, oil-burning furnaces, and cars. He enjoyed high school sports, such as swimming, tumbling, track, and baseball. He was also musically minded, and played harmonica, guitar, mandolin, banjo, violin, saxophone and clarinet. He composed his own music and wrote his own lyrics.

Conrad enrolled at the University of Colorado in 1922, but lacked the ambition to settle down to the routine, moving to Detroit to work briefly for the Cadillac and Plymouth companies. He set up a dance band there, and considered that an airplane might make a good method of traveling from job to job. His wanderings took him to the University of California at Berkeley, then to the University of Minnesota, where he joined the track team. It was during a track meet that the P.A. announcer gave a running account of a certain Charles Lindbergh who was then winging his way to Paris in a small single-engined airplane. On an impulse, Max changed his study major to Aeronautical Engineering.

The thought of flying, however, soon erased his enthusiasm for bookwork and he traveled to Chicago to take flying lessons. From there, he traveled to Denver, where he got his private license and bought his first airplane, a Laird Swallow.

In 1928, armed with his new license and airplane, Conrad returned to Winona, Minnesota, and started Conrad Aviation, flying from the farm field of a family neighbor, Charles Biesanz, (whose daughter he would eventually marry). He began offering charter flights and afternoon air rides, and managed to crack up his airplane that same year. Though injured, Max could only think about getting another airplane. He bought not one, but two Spartan 3-place biplanes.

Conrad earned his Transport Pilot's license and began improving the runways on the farm strip. The government added lights and a rotating beacon when the field was designated an Airways emergency landing field. Northwest Airways began making a nighttime airmail stop. Before long, Max owned seven planes and his flight school was bringing in droves of students. Many of them had no money, but Max gave them instruction free of charge. Some continued to fly for Max, working their way along to pay for lessons. Students Tom Hennessy, Elmer Schubert, and Robert Lindrud, among others, would all go on to become well-known Minnesota airline pilots or military flyers.

In the summer of 1929, an accident changed Max Conrad's life. When a woman passenger stepped off the front of the Spartan's wing, Max saw her slipping toward the propeller. He leaped to save her and both were struck by it. The woman was killed; Max's skull was broken and a portion of his brain injured.

For years, he drifted, not able to control his speech, his thought process, his reading and writing, or some of his body functions. A deep depression took him away from aviation as he struggled to re-learn everything. One night, almost in a trance from the despair, he drove to the airport, climbed into his Spartan, and took off, uncertain as to whether he could even control the plane. After flying around to regain his senses, he landed with difficulty. The nagging depression still refused to leave him. Max became deeply religious, finding solace in the church, already a strong influence in his young life.

By 1931, with the help of the clergy, he began to come out of his lethargy. He married Betty Biesanz and got back into the swing of business at the airfield. He increased his fleet of airplanes, taught his brother, Art, how to fly, and then helped him set up a flight training operation at Rochester. That business didn't last long with the depression setting in, and it was soon shut down.

Then, tragedy struck a second time. Art was killed on a charter flight, when the engine of Conrad's Ryan Brougham shed part of its propeller. The broken blade sliced through a main wing spar and the damaged wing folded up, the plane crashing near Cass Lake, killing Art and four passengers.

It was Max, himself, who investigated the accident, proving that the airplane and its pilot were not at fault. An improperly secured propeller was to blame. Ironically, work done by an outside source, and not Max's shop, was responsible. His reputation tarnished, however, Max resolutely continued flight instruction, and charter flying. He purchased a Ford Trimotor with the intention of setting up a yearly round trip from Minneapolis to the Rose Bowl, in Pasadena. This he did from 1922 until 1937. Long distance charter business failed to materialize, and Max used the Ford for instruction, barnstorming, and parachute dropping on weekends.

One day, when the balky center engine wouldn't start, Max overprimed it. The selector valve suddenly broke, and gasoline ran down the firewall behind the instrument panel, flowing outside onto the exhaust pipe. At that inopportune moment, the engine backfired and the gasoline flared up. No passengers were aboard and Max jumped out, leaving the two outboard engines still running. He was powerless to put out the fire before the entire fuselage of the Ford melted to an ingot.

In 1939, Max set up several CPT (Civilian Pilot Training), programs at colleges. Two were in Winona, (one at St. Mary's and one at the State Teacher's College), one at Eau Claire; one at Green Bay; one at St. Thomas College at St. Paul, one at St. Norberts College, near Green Bay, Wisconsin, and a program at Notre Dame University in Indiana.

On 11 November, 1940, there occurred an event that would go down in Minnesota history. The notorious Armistice Day Blizzard stranded motorists, duck hunters, and travelers. Starting as a fairly mild morning, the wind suddenly shifted, the temperature plummeted, and snow began to fall. It accumulated and was driven by the wind until it drifted into huge mountains against every corner of Minnesota.

The following day, the wind still raged. Emergency calls began to pour in to Conrad Aviation for help. Hunters were stranded and would he be able to fly over the river valley and countryside to locate some of them?

Max Conrad prepares to depart the Twin Cities on the start of his round-the-world flight, 1969. (Minnesota Flyer Magazine)

Against everybody's better judgment, Max bundled himself into a Piper Cub, and was literally flung aloft with no takeoff run, tacking back and forth like a sailboat to make forward progress. He searched the frozen river bottoms near Winona. When he'd spot a hunting party, he would often turn into the wind, slow the plane to a standstill, and shout to the mired hunters to follow him through the blinding snow to where a rescue vehicle was waiting. He noted the locations of other parties and passed on their whereabouts to authorities when he landed.

Landing, between flights that went on all day, was a chore. Conrad would maneuver the plane close to the ground and his crew would have to manhandle the airplane, literally pulling it from the air and holding it down while Conrad refueled. He took to the air again and again, flying his mercy missions. Dozens of persons later claimed they owed their lives to his heroic actions.

In 1942, Max suffered yet another tragedy. With the CPT programs now closed, he had consolidated his aircraft at Winona, cramming almost all of his fleet of thirty planes into small hangars there. A mechanic, working on a plane inside a hangar, dropped a pan of gasoline used to clean parts, and the gas ignited. It was January, and the closed hangar doors were fast frozen in their tracks, making evacuation of the aircraft impossible. The entire facility burned to the ground before a bucket brigade could wage an effective battle.

Having lost everything, except a single airplane, Max was at least fortunate in that there was no loss of life. But it meant a new start. In 1943, Max went to work for the Minneapolis Honeywell Regulator Company, flying as their corporate and test pilot. He made many research flights for Honeywell's military projects. Conrad often flew an old Northrop Delta airplane, powered by an enormous 1,000-horsepower Pratt and Whitney engine. During his time at Honeywell, Max bought a grand home in Edina, and was also giving flying lessons at Wold-Chamberlain.

EPILOGUE

After the war, when Honeywell bought a new DC-3, offering its executives more luxurious travel accommodations, Conrad found he was working many more hours than he ever had. He was forced to give up his "hobby" of flight instruction. He sent Betty and his nine children to live in Switzerland, while he kept his work pace at Honeywell.

After two years of isolation from his family, he hatched a plan to fly to Europe. To Max, it was simply a plan to visit his family at the least possible expense, but the press media saw it as a unique record flight. Conrad had written to William Piper, Jr., president of the Piper Aircraft Company of Lockhaven, Pennsylvania, suggesting a flight to Europe by way of Labrador, Greenland, Iceland, and Britain...in a new single-engined Piper Pacer! This would be a feat rivalling Lindbergh's epic journey.

Mr. Piper agreed to give Conrad a Pacer at one-fourth the cost of a new airplane if he successfully made the round trip. Thus, in 1950, Max took the vacation he had coming from Honeywell. He had additional radios and fuel tanks installed in the Pacer, then took off on a new chapter of his life.

Conrad's zeal had been so focused on the trip that he departed before he had secured clearance to land in Greenland, though certain that the approval would be available by the time he arrived. Unexpectedly, he picked up a B-17 escort over Greenland, and when the weather closed in, the bomber crew insisted that he land at Bluie West One airfield. Though he still wasn't cleared to land there, the military had, by their demand, provided the clearance.

In Europe, Betty was convinced to return to the States with the family, but Conrad was still faced with the return flight against headwinds and worsening weather. The flight went well. To his surprise, Max was informed that he had no less than five landing clearances waiting for him in Greenland. He picked up a strong tailwind upon leaving Greenland and things went smoothly for a while. Icing conditions caught up with him a few hours from Labrador, and he had to spiral down through the clouds for thousands of feet to allow the ice to break up and fall off the airplane wings and prop hub. Max finally landed at Labrador, five hours behind schedule, but happy to be alive.

In the following years, Conrad flew the same Pacer on other long trips. He flew from Mexico City to Washington, D. C., and again, crossed the Atlantic, this time to Scandinavia, as part of a Minneapolis Centennial celebration.

Conrad left Honeywell to start up a major CAA project in Winona, aimed at providing young people with flying instruction to build the nation's air transport system. The program was to be funded by the government, but the funding lagged behind Conrad's enthusiasm. He began ferrying Piper aircraft around the world to supplement his income. He made a flying tour of all 48 state capitals to celebrate the 50th anniversary of powered flight in 1953. He gave flying lessons and even did some barnstorming. The Government project failed, plane kits that students were to build went unbuilt and planned hangars were never constructed.

Max was asked to ferry a new Piper Apache across the Atlantic. He jumped at the chance. This time he was to go directly to Paris, and this time, he would

have the luxury of two engines. On the flight, he lost his gyro compass, his trailing antenna for the high frequency radio, and ran into icing conditions. At one point, when he added carburetor heat, the engines stopped. He discovered that he had to hold the carburetor heat controls in position by hand for the remainder of the flight, and leaned the engines to make them run hotter. Conrad successfully landed at a small field outside Paris, having made the trip in ten hours less than Lindbergh's 1927 time.

By the time Conrad's tenth child was born, he had completed his tenth trans-Atlantic flight. By 1958, Max had flown the ocean 39 times. His fortieth trip was in a new Comanche. In 1959, he made his fiftieth trip. That year, Conrad decided to go for some records. It had never before been his intention to break records or garner publicity, rather to earn a salary and keep the bills paid. This time, however, he planned to break two different weight category distance records with a stock Piper Comanche. For these flights, he trained like an athlete, driving himself to miss one night's sleep a week for a month before the flight, making practice trips across the country. He adjusted his rest, eating, and exercise periods between trips, and practiced structuring his time for taking position reports, making notes, radio checks, eating, writing postcards, and monitoring fuel.

He took off from Denver for Paris at the start of the trip, attempting to break the first record, for Class IV aircraft of 3,858 to 6,614 pounds, a record then held by Bill Odom, of approximately 5,000 miles. His trip would be 6,000 miles, nonstop. Headwinds forced Conrad to turn back. A second attempt didn't work out either. Max was forced to fly around large thunderstorms, having to abandon Paris as a destination, opting for Casablanca. There the challenge ended, but not Conrad's drive. Still wanting the record, he departed Casablanca and flew steadily for some fifty-eight hours, 38 minutes, arriving in Los Angeles after flying 7,668 miles.

In 1960, Max Conrad set another record for Class III airplanes, flying closed circuit laps between Chicago, Des Moines and Minneapolis with 180-horsepower engines in the Comanche. With the same airplane, he flew from Casablanca to El Paso, Texas, in sixty-one hours. Closely-allied with Piper aircraft, Conrad had by this time taken up residence near the Piper factory at Lockhaven, Pennsylvania, and by 1963, had made over 150 Atlantic crossings, and 43 Pacific crossings.

In 1964, Max made an emergency landing on a glacier in Greenland, but luckily, was rescued the same day. That year, he modified one of Piper's Twin Comanches for a record flight attempt from Capetown, South Africa, to the U. S. West Coast. After one aborted attempt, he departed a second time, but had to cut this flight short as well, landing at St. Petersburg, Florida.

In 1966, Max planned a flight around the world by way of the poles. If successful he could break three records; equator to equator, pole to pole, and around the world via the poles. Flying an Aztec, nicknamed *St. Louis Woman*, after a daughter who lived in St. Louis, Max finally got the project in the air in 1969.

Weather, poor aircraft performance, and a good deal of soul-searching about his own ability caused him to abandon the flight without crossing the South Pole. During 1970, he screwed up his courage and decided to try again. That flight was to be the last for him. The airplane was wrecked on takeoff from Murdo Sound at the South Pole. There it sits today, perhaps covered by two decades of snow, forever a silent marker of man's endurance.

Max was a quiet, unassuming gentleman. He walked to church every Sunday morning to keep faith with his God, and slept at the various YMCA when he was in a city other than his hometown. His favorite phrase was "let's fly," and it was always included in autographs and on his airplanes. Often separated by thousands of miles from his large family—he loved them sincerely, yet needed to be on his own. He embodied the indomitable spirit of mankind. This man, whose entire life was swept by tragedy and failure, punishing his body and his emotions, was driven, he knew not why, to push on against unbelievable odds. Max Conrad died peacefully in his sleep on 2 April, 1979.

WOMEN IN MINNESOTA AVIATION

Many of Minnesota's women aviators and showpersons are mentioned elsewhere in the text of this book. The wing-walkers and parachute jumpers, for example; the barnstormers and record-setters; the women instructors and students in the Civilian Pilot Training Program; and the early women pilots in the Twin City area. We can spotlight a few others of the more prominent who lent color to Minnesota's history.

Perhaps the two women most familiar to Minnesota aviation fans, are Florence Klingensmith, and Phoebe Fairgrave Omlie.

Florence Klingensmith was a tomboy from North Dakota; a lady who did the things that were done mostly by men in her day. At thirteen years of age, she was driving a car; and at sixteen, was a delivery person for a mercantile store in Fargo, North Dakota. She had been using a motorcycle for this work, but was given a truck when she passed her driver's license test. She proceeded to accumulate several traffic violations, and the store was forced to terminate her employment. Then, she found a job at a ranch, using a horse for motive power.

After that, she came to Minnesota, where she went to work at a logging camp and took courses in electronics, the only woman in a class of four hundred men. In 1929, Klingensmith took up flying and parachute jumping to pay for her flying time. She convinced a group of Fargo businessmen to loan her $3,000 to buy her own airplane, and was able to purchase a snappy, new Monocoupe. By July of that year, she had earned her Commercial license and begun barnstorming and carrying passengers. She also entered air races with the speedy Monocoupe, competing against men flyers.

Klingensmith was nicknamed "Treetops" by her contemporaries for her skills at low-level flying and spent a period as operations manager of the Fargo Airport. She came to Minneapolis, where she worked briefly for Northwest Airways as an airport hostess at Wold-Chamberlain Field. She was a weekend barnstorming regular at the airport, hopping rides in a black and silver Waco biplane.

She was well known for her looping abilities, and set a record of 143 loops over the Fargo Airport. In June of 1931, she performed 1078 loops over the same airport, keeping up this dizzying maneuver for 5 hours and 12 minutes. This women's record stood for decades. In 1931 Klingensmith participated in the National Air Races, entering ten events. She won one race, took first in three dead-stick landing contests, and placed high in all the other events.

In 1932, she won the Amelia Earhart Trophy, a women's event at the National Air Races in Cleveland, Ohio, flying a Cessna racing monoplane. There, she had shrugged off the chauvenistic talk of male competitors, who implied that, perhaps the stresses of air racing were more than a woman could handle. The men had even inferred that perhaps a woman's menstrual cycle had an effect on her performance.

In 1933, barely five years since learning to fly, and only twenty-seven years of age, Klingensmith was again competing at the Chicago National Air Races. She got a chance to fly in a women's race in a J-6-engined GeeBee Y. It was her birthday, and she celebrated by placing second in that race, which was won by Mae Haizlip. The following day, she was

This photo portrays the cold weather flight dress of the well-attired lady pilot of the early 1920s. (C. W. Hinck family)

Florence Klingensmith poses alongside her Waco RNF just prior to her participation in an air race during the 1930s. (Jack Butz)

Phoebe Omlie is pictured at St. Paul in 1928. Phoebe, along with Florence Klingensmith, are the two women aviators most remembered by Minnesotans. (Noel Allard)

allowed to compete in the $10,000 Free-for-all Phillips Trophy Race, generally an all-male race. Until this time, there had been an unwritten rule that women were not allowed to compete; that they lacked the reflexes and strength to handle the speed and "G" forces of such a strenuous event. Klingensmith had proved her skills, however, and was allowed to enter.

At the start of the race, her mechanics had to lace a balky cockpit canopy in position from the outside to keep it from coming unlatched during the race. Once the race was flagged off, Jimmy Wedell and Roscoe Turner jumped into the lead in sophisticated racing planes, leaving Klingensmith in a tight race with others, for third position. On the eighth lap, in front of 40,000 persons, fabric was seen to tear away from the left wing of her tiny ship. Struggling for control, she managed to pull the plane out of the line of racers, and flew off, in an attempt to bring the ship down, away from the crowd. Somehow she lost control of the plane and it slammed into a ditch, throwing her through the canopy.[76]

There were those who claimed to have seen her fighting to get out of the ship. (The canopy was fastened from the outside.) There were some who whispered that she had panicked. Mae Haizlip claimed that the GeeBee had a large amount of nose-down trim built into it for racing, and that Klingensmith, in reducing power for an attempted landing, without rolling in nose-up trim, plunged the barely-controllable plane into a dive. She had made a mental error.[77]

A local sheriff even suggested that she had fainted from panic, and fell against the stick. The funeral was held in Moorhead, Minnesota, where Klingensmith's parents were living.

Florence Klingensmith was one of the original members of the Ninety-Nines, and the National Aeronautical Association by virtue of her loop record. She was a very vocal and visible herald of women's abilities as aviators, writing several newspaper articles on the subject. She competed with men, and lost her life proving that women were equals in air-racing.

Phoebe Fairgrave Omlie was as well known as Florence Klingensmith, though perhaps not as glamorous, or flamboyant. She was also a skilled and competent pilot.

Phoebe Fairgrave is revered by Minnesotans as one of our own, and like Klingensmith, was not a Min-

nesotan by birth, nor did she spend much of her career in the State. She was born in Des Moines, Iowa, and migrated to St. Paul as a teenager, graduating from Mechanic Arts High School. She took up parachute jumping and wing-walking while in High School, setting at least one women's altitude record in 1921, when she leaped from a plane at 19,000 feet.

Aviator, Ray Miller, recalled her first appearance at Curtiss-Northwest airfield.

"Phoebe Fairgrave, a tiny girl, showed up on Saturday or Sunday, when 20,000 or more would line the field to watch the flying. She was just barely able to lug a big parachute into the hangar. She had on a uniform, where she got it to fit her, I'll never know. But she wanted to make a parachute jump. She had made no arrangements for the ride, and I questioned her to find out what experience she had. I discovered she had none, whatever, had never been in a plane before. But she had more guts in that tiny body than it would have seemed to hold.

"I told her she would have to strengthen her body, arms and hands so that she could climb out onto the wing to make the leap. The prop wash would toss her off the wing before she even got both feet on the bottom panel. So she agreed to do this. I told her we wouldn't take her up until she had done this. I offered her some rides during the week, when not much was doing, so she could find out if she still wanted to do it. I assigned Vern Omlie to fly her and teach her what it was all about. That was when she met the man she was to marry.

"She made her first "pull-off" with Omlie flying the plane. (A pull-off is a parachute jump in which the parachute is bundled on the airplane wing, and when the jumper leaps, the chute is pulled out of its bag container, which stays with the airplane.) Omlie spotted her so she would land on the airfield. She came down very gently and easy, but being so light, and not having enough strength in her arms, she was unable to spill the wind out of the chute and was dragged ignominiously across the field for about 300 feet until some of the ground crew could race to her aid and grab the ratlines."[78]

Vern Omlie was a pilot for the Federated Fliers fly-

Almeda Babcock, at right, poses for the Minnesota State Fair photographer in this 1931 print. Uniform of the day for this gutsy parachute jumper: white riding breeches, tie, new boots and gloves and her purse tucked under her arm. Almeda carried on after her husband, George, also a parachute jumper, was killed in a jump into Lake Minnetonka in 1930. (Minnesota State Fair)

Marcella Marcouiller poses on the wing of a Kinner Eaglerock at Minneapolis. Elmer Hinck is in the cockpit. (Minnesota Historical Society)

ing circus. He and Phoebe were married in 1922, and shortly thereafter, moved to Memphis, Tennessee, where Phoebe began taking flying lessons in earnest and accumulated hours to the point that she qualified for and received, the first Transport Pilot's license issued to a woman, #199, issued 30 June, 1927. She and Omlie, opened a flight school at the Memphis Airport and she began participating in exhibitions and air races.

Her record of achievements is as follows:

1928—1st woman participant in the Ford National Air Tour. Finished with no penalty points in her Velie Monocoupe.
1929—Again participated in the National Air Tour in her Monocoupe. Won the 500 cc. engine class of the Women's National Air Derby, from Santa Monica to Cleveland.
Set a women's altitude record for a parachute jump at 25,400 feet.
1930—In the National Air Races, won the Eastern "Dixie" Derby, from Washington, D. C. to Chicago, after flying through most of the eastern States.
Won the 500cc and 800cc closed cabin races for women and came in 5th in the free-for-all race at the National Air Races.
Became an officer of Mid-South Airways at Memphis, Tennessee.
Became publicity person for the Mono Aircraft Corporation.
1931—Won the Santa Monica to Cleveland division of the National Air Races, again in her Monocoupe, as well as the 510cc and 650 cc engine class races.
1932—Flew a 20,000-mile campaign tour as chauffeur for Franklin Delano Roosevelt during his campaign for the Presidency. For her effort, he appointed her Special Advisor for Air Intelligence to NACA. (National Advisory Council for Aeronautics).
1934—Instigated, planned and directed the National Air Marking Program.
1936—Again flew President Roosevelt on his nationwide campaign tour.

1937—Finished 5th in the free-for-all women's race at the National Air Races.
When her husband, Vern, was killed in an airline accident, while riding as a passenger, she resigned from government office to devote her time to research on air safety and flight training.
Authored the Tennessee Aviation Act that provided aviation education and training through public schools.
1938—Directed the first CPT (Civilian Pilot Training) class in Memphis.
1941—Became the Senior Flying Specialist for the CAA. Her duties were to fly around the country selecting and licensing CPT training schools.

Several of the more prominent woman wingwalkers and parachute jumpers have been mentioned in the chapter dealing with the Thrill Shows. Those mentioned were Betty Goltz, Stella Kindem, Birdie Draper, Dorothy Stevens, Eleanor Van De Mark, Dorothy Collins, Alene Vizenor, Ruth La Fayollette, Dorothy Faltico, Florence Rogish, Marcella Marcoullier, Nona Malloy, Almeda Babcock, Gladys Roy, and Katherine Hardin.

Most of the parachute jumping "femmes fatal" went into other lines of work following their jumping adventures. Some, like Florence Rogish, took up other active sports. In her case, the Roller Derby. After making 36 jumps, Rogish decided to take her lumps in a less dangerous, but equally as spectacular, manner. Marcella Marcoullier, who had been taking flying lessons with the money she made jumping, continued, and eventually received her Limited Commercial license. Along the way, she suffered an ironic accident. In 1934, she fell from her bicycle, postponing her flight exam for several days, while nursing a broken leg.

Jean Barnhill came from California, to become an Aeronautical Engineering student at the University of Minnesota. In 1933, Barnhill received her Commercial license as a student at Northland Aviation at Wold-Chamberlain. She was mentioned in the *Airport News* of 29 July, 1933, as one of the best acrobatic flyers in the Northwest, while on her way to gaining

Alice Cross and Frances Pryzymus pose in their flight suits in this circa 1929 photo. (Minnesota Historical Society)

a Transport license.

Barnhill was a member of the University of Minnesota Flying Club. The club was organized to provide a means for licensed, or solo-qualified, University students to fly cheaply. Along the way they participated in national intercollegiate flying competitions. Jean Barnhill was a member of the University's team from 1932 through 1936. With her help, the team won the first-place Grover Loening Trophy in 1934 and 1935. In 1935, the team participated in the annual competition at Purdue University and came away the overall winners.

The national organization, the "Ninety-Nines" was organized in 1929 at the request of Phoebe Omlie. Phoebe suggested that, maybe the 117 licensed women pilots in the country ought to get together as

Charter members of the Minnesota Ninety-Nines at the time of their organizing in 1937. Left to right kneeling: Ella Stene, Audrey Peterson; standing: Ruth Kunz, Vida Shaffer, June Haas, Edie Campbell, Francis Pryzymus Lennon. (Minnesota Historical Society)

an organization. Ninety-nine women took part in the first meeting at Long Island, New York on 2 November, 1929, and became charter members. The association took its name from the number of attendees. The group's first President was Amelia Earhart.

Several States applied for "Ninety-Nines" charters, Minnesota being one of them. The Minnesota chapter organized in the fall of 1937, and its charter members were Rose Dale, who was elected Chairperson; Virginia Marten, Vice Chairperson; and Janet Wakefield, Secretary/Treasurer. Edith Campbell was another of the first five licensed women pilots necessary to start a chapter. Frances Pryzymus Lennon, Ruth Kunz, Ella Stene, Jayne Haas, Vida Shaffer, Audrey Peterson, and Mary Jane Leasman were to follow very soon.

The national organization believed that women's roles in aviation should be recognized, and set a goal of civic visibility and public service. Their first major project was the nationwide air marking program. By 1939, some 19,000 cities were marked, with their names painted on the roofs of prominent buildings, clearly visible from the air. In addition to the town name, a painted arrow pointed in the direction of the nearest airport. Minnesota 99ers got involved in the program in 1938, and completed it by 1939.

One novel and colorful deed the 99ers took part in was the 1940 Aquatennial parade. They built a float shaped like a Monocoupe airplane, covering a wire sculpture with colorful tissue, advertising their presence to all Minnesotans.

Unfortunately, World War II intervened in the women's lives. The Ninety-Nines disbanded, many of the women helping the war effort in one way or another. Following World War II, the group reorganized, but most of the original women did not reappear.

Frances Pryzymus Lennon was born in Ivanhoe, Minnesota, and started flying at an early age. She earned her Private, Limited Commercial, Commercial, and Transport Pilots licenses during the 1930s. When her first husband, Jack Lennon, died, she married entrepreneur, Wally Dale, who ran the Cedar Avenue Airport. When Dale joined the FAA in 1942, the couple moved from Minnesota. Frances quit flying soon after. In her training notebook, Frances wrote of her first introduction to the airplane, "I felt a natural desire to fly when I saw my first airplane. It was high overhead at twilight one fall evening about twelve years ago. The probability of flying was just a dream bubble, my life had no connection with aviation. I was a farm girl..." [79]

Edna Gardner Whyte was the flyingest of Minnesota's women aviators over the years. Though she was born in Minnesota, Edna Gardner did not pursue her flying career here. This outspoken and crusty woman started flying in 1927, at Madison, Wisconsin, then began barnstorming the country. She joined the Navy to become a nurse, and served from 1929 to 1935 in Luzon in the Phillipines. After returning to the U. S. she traveled to New Orleans, where she established the New Orleans Air College, giving flight training until World War II broke out in 1941. During this time, she had flown just about every type of aircraft produced, and participated in women's air

Edna Gardner Whyte (Whyte)

Camille "Rosie" Stein, Northwest Airways Office Manager and General Secretary under Colonel Brittin, started her career at Northwest's inception and retired in the 1950s (Northwest Airlines via Vince Doyle)

races.

When the government bought her strip to make it into a satellite Navy training field, she went to work as an instructor in the WTS program at Meacham Field, Fort Worth Texas. At the end of the war training service program in 1944, she joined the Army's nurse corps.

EPILOGUE: EDNA GARDNER WHYTE

Following the war, Edna Gardner Whyte flew as a corporate pilot, and married George Whyte, who owned Aero Enterprises at Meacham Field. George Whyte died in 1973 and Edna bought land in nearby Roanoke, Texas, establishing Aero Valley Airport, which is now a large reliever airport.

Edna Whyte acquired 129 trophies for her participation in air racing events, having flown the International Air Race 30 times and won it four times, while placing in the money some fourteen times. Her dream of flying for an airline over the years, had been stymied because of a general resistance to accept women as airline pilots. She was once told that a woman in the cockpit would be bad public relations for an airline. Edna was never in the spotlight, like Amelia Earhart, or air racer, Jaquelin Cochran. She was stung, time after time, by the resistance to a woman breaking into a man's world.

Born in 1902, Edna Gardner Whyte was still an active flight instructor in 1991. Her daily schedule included nearly six hours of instruction. In 1990, she calculated that over her 57 years of teaching flying, she had graduated 4600 men and women pilots. Gardner-Whyte died in 1992.

Thelma Burleigh was a housekeeper in South Minneapolis in 1927, watching planes fly over her place of employment on their way to and from Wold-Chamberlain Field. When she read about airmail planes flying between Chicago and the Twin Cities, she was excited. She called the Post Office to inquire as to whether they would be hiring airmail pilots. The Post Office referred her to flying schools at the airport for lessons, and she signed up at Universal Flying School.

It was three years before she could take her flight test for the Private license, because of her work

schedule. She worked during the day, and arranged to take her lessons very early in the mornings. On the days she was to fly, she would awake at 3:30 a.m., catch a streetcar that would take her to within a mile of the airport, then walk the remainder of the distance to the hangar. Following the lesson, she would run to the car line and return to her place of work, to begin promptly at 6:45 a.m.

She had her troubles completing the solo test. Being but five foot, three inches, she had a difficult time reaching the rudder bar, and seeing out of the cockpit at the same time. Her first attempt at a landing without using the rudder brought bounces and swerves, so she slid down in the cockpit and, barely peeking over the instrument panel, managed to make two fairly successful landings, to receive her solo license.

When she completed her Private license, she became the first woman to finish both a ground school and a flying course in Minneapolis. Though resigned to the fact that she would never become an airmail pilot, she planned to continue flying until she acquired her Limited Commercial license, at which time she could teach flying herself. Asked what her aspirations might be, she replied, "Just one thing, I want to become as good a flyer as any man. Then I'll get a job as an instructress with a good flying school and teach girls how to become pilots." When pressed that maybe she ought to give up flying and teach dancing, she said, "Dancing, I love it. But I like flying better." [80]

Claire Leavitt of Tyler, Minnesota, received her Private license on 27 June, 1932, from inspector, Forrest Longeway. She purchased a Waco biplane, and with Elmer Hinck, barnstormed the Twin City area through September of that year. She also took up parachute jumping, and doing odd flying jobs for Hinck's flight school. On the occassion of at least one parachute jump, she was billed as the "Mystery Girl." As such, she made a jump in 1932, into Lake Minnetonka at Excelsior for Sunday entertainment. For a weekend airshow jump at Wold-Chamberlain, the "Mystery Girl" showed up wearing a face mask to conceal her identity and the news media hyped this

Agnes Nohava at the steps of an American Airways Ford Trimotor in 1933. One of the airlines first stewardesses, she got the job because of her training as a nurse. (Agnes Nohava)

event with pictures of "other participants in the air circus attempting to find out [who she was]."[81]

Mention should be made of some of the very earliest aviatrixes. In Martin County, Cora May Fuller received her Private Pilot's license in April of 1931 from CAA inspector, Forrest Longeway. Flying out of the Fairmont Airport, she got her license in a Stinson Detroiter aircraft that she and her husband, Boon Fuller, had purchased. She was the first licensed woman flyer in the county.

In Lyon County, the first lady flyer was Fran Runholt, of Marshall, Minnesota. Nothing of her career has come to light.

Some women who were interested in flying became cabin attendants, later to be known as stewardesses.

Claire Leavitt with fur sleeves on her dress coat and parachute in hand, smiles for the camera prior to going up for another flying lesson. We can presume she changed into more standard flight togs for the lesson. (Richfield Historical Society)

Agnes Nohava was such a person. From Lonsdale, Minnesota, she studied nursing. When American Airways announced that they were looking for registered nurses to work as the first "stewardesses" aboard Curtiss Condor biplane transports and Ford Trimotors, she applied, and was one of the first four women hired for this new position. Her career ended as the DC-3's were going into service. When she got married, as was the custom, a stewardess was required to quit flying.

She had worked for five years and remembers the period as truly an exciting era.

"We were a novelty. We had more fun than girls have today, because we got to know our passengers much better, and we gave them a lot of personal attention. Because no liquor was served, some passengers smuggled liquor on board the aircraft in cough syrup bottles to spike their coffee or milk. We had to watch for this."[82]

"Once, when the plane was readying to land, and it was time for all passengers to return to their seats and fasten seat belts, I found an elderly man trapped in the bathroom. He wouldn't come out because he couldn't get his pants zipped. After I helped him get zipped up, he handed me a ten dollar bill. When I told the Captain of my deed, he laughed and said that he wouldn't pull up any man's zipper for less than ten dollars. I just smiled, and pulled the bill out of my pocket."[83]

In late 1936, Agnes Nohava's plane, a Curtiss Condor biplane transport, met the German dirigible, Hindenburg, at Lakehurst, New Jersey following one of its several transatlantic passenger flights. The Condor was providing a connecting flight to Newark, New Jersey. Twenty three of the dirigible's passengers from Europe transferred from the big airship to her plane. Each had been given a commemorative pin from the Germans for traveling on the dirigible, and one of them asked Nohava if she would like it. She accepted the gift, and in May of 1937, was stunned to hear the news that the Hindenburg had exploded at Lakehurst, claiming the lives of many passengers and crew. Seeing the pin always brought back thoughts of that dramatic event.

Another Minnesotan who became a stewardess was Jean Wahlberg. Jean was a University of Minnesota graduate nurse who was hired in 1941 by Continental Airlines President, Robert Six, to set up a stewardess qualifications profile, and develop a selection and training course. She soon delivered a Hostess Manual which listed among other requirements, that an applicant have two years of accredited college and at least one year of business experience. Married applicants were to be considered only if their spouse was serving in the armed forces overseas.

Some women chose to enter the business end of aviation. Such was the course for Camille "Rosie" Stein of Northwest Airways. Her consistent support of Colonel Brittin through the early years is legendary.

As Colonel Brittin's right-hand person at the St. Paul Association of Commerce, Rosie Stein came to Northwest along with him, and set up her office in the tiny office building tacked onto the former airmail hangar. She fed the wood stove, answered phones, sold tickets, and kept the place in order during the first years. She was eventually elected assistant secretary and director of the company, serving in this position from 1934 through 1941.

Stein assumed the role of director of passenger service in 1939. In that role, she managed the cabin attendants. With the aircraft then in service, such as the DC-3, she had to hire only attendants whose height was less than 5'4". That changed with the inauguration of DC-4 service, and Stein was able to hire taller women. She acquired her nickname in response to the eternal question, "How are things?" to which she would answer, "Everything's rosy." Rosie died in 1954 after retiring from the airline service.

Another dedicated front office secretary and manager was Dorothy Schaeffer. She was the longtime woman-Friday to the first Wold-Chamberlain airport director, Larry Hammond, and four other directors who followed him.

Dorothy was born in Iowa, but as a teenager, moved to a homestead on land that the family had been using as hunting grounds north of Cambridge, Minnesota. From a large family, it was evident Dorothy and her brothers and sisters would have to go out on their own, earning their way through college or business school. Dorothy came to the Twin Cities. When her sister's husband, a military pilot, offered her a ride in one of his squadron's airplanes, she went up for her first air ride. Two sisters were Park Board "banquet girls" (caterers), and in 1937, they went to work in the restaurant at the Wold-Chamberlain terminal building.

As Ms. Schaeffer was spending some time at the airport visiting her sisters, and taking an occasional airplane ride. It was natural that, when Larry Hammond needed an office assistant, the sisters told him about Dorothy. She began working part-time in 1941 at the airport office, while attending business school in Minneapolis.

With the war underway, the airport was undergoing changes, and Dorothy was called upon to become familiar with many facets of airport business. She occasionally filled in as restaurant waitress, waiting on tables filled with junior military officers who were taking their training on the new Honeywell autopilot just down the road. She had some knowledge of mechanical drawings and reading blueprints, and Larry Hammond let her deal with the contractors who were busy creating the wartime facilities at the airport. She had to become familiar with all the utilities, including the outdated electrical system. She recalls an incident that almost led to her demise:

When a line of lights or some apparatus blew a fuse, Hammond would have Dorothy climb down into the electrical vault in the basement of the terminal. He, himself, would go out into the electrical cable tunnel under the ramp with a bullhorn to find the proper cables and connections. He would shout over the bullhorn to Dorothy as to which fuse to pull and replace. "There was this big awful panel and I was just scared to death to go down into that room. I hated it. They had those old-fashioned fuses, big and round, different sizes. They hummed and it was buzzing down there and I just hated it. One day, I was down there and I had protested, but Larry called me 'chicken'. One of these big fuses popped out of its holder, went right by my face, and made a big hole

Dorothy Schaeffer (Metropolitan Airports Commission)

in the wall behind me. I screamed and when Larry came, I showed him the damage and told him that I was never going down there again. I'm quitting unless you get an electrician. He got an electrician."[84]

Hammond's office also drew up the air traffic patterns, as well as setting the taxiing rules and ground procedures. Schaeffer, with some basic knowledge of mechanical drawing, got the call again. She handled the mundane jobs that nobody wanted, like purchasing Hammond's Christmas cards, addressing them, making reservations for every politician and visiting celebrity, begging a seat for them on an already filled airliner. She worked seven days a week until the Metropolitan Airports Commission took over in 1945...then her work week decreased to only six days. She was at the office early to make the coffee, and was the last to leave each night.

She came to be the acknowledged master of every aspect of airport operations, the one to see when one needed something done. As of this writing, though retired, she is still serving as advisor to the Airport Director's office. She can still be found meeting with various airport groups, advising committees on such subjects as beautification, banquets, and, generally, being first-lady of airport activities.

Many other women worked side-by-side with their male counterparts in the aviation business without spotlight or public attention. One that spent nearly 37 years in this role was Helen M. Gamm. She started as a mechanic in the Northwest Airlines overhaul shop at Holman Field in the 1940s. She went to North Aviation at Northport Airport in White Bear to keep books as well as to work as a mechanic. When North Aviation was disbanded, she and Ken Maxwell took

Claire Leavitt by an American Eagle training plane at Wold-Chamberlain Field, 10 June, 1933. (Richfield Historical Society)

over the shop and began to concentrate on propeller work. She later became part owner of Maxwell Aircraft Service, Inc. at Crystal Airport, where she presided as office manager.

One of the more unusual associations with aviation was that undertaken by Jeannette Piccard. Her husband, Jean Piccard, had been intensely interested in scientific research done with high-altitude balloons. She followed his interest by becoming a very skilled balloonist and setting several altitude records. She became a licensed pilot, while husband, Jean, remained the scientist and observer on various flights.

She began her flight training in May of 1934 with Ed Hill, former winner of the Gordon Bennett Balloon Race, as her instructor. Piccard soon soloed, but when the time came for finding sponsorship for the Piccards' research flights, she was turned down because she was a woman. Even the prestigious National Geographic Society, worried about their image, refusing to back her as pilot, preferring not to send a woman...a mother...in a balloon into danger.[85]

Unfortunately, the story of women in aviation in Minnesota is touched by the realm of male chauvenism...as it was throughout the country during the 1930s, 1940s, and even into the 1950s. Women's contribution was lessened to a certain degree by the inaccessibility to the prestigious positions of military, corporate pilot, or instructor. Whenever they were allowed to perform to their full potential, however, they proved to be equally as skilled and proficient as their male counterparts.

In Minnesota, we are proud of our women pilots of the past and at least two, Phoebe Omlie, and Rosie Stein are currently enshrined in the Minnesota Aviation Hall of Fame.

MINNESOTA FLYERS IN ALASKA

Call to mind a land where the sky and horizon blend in ice fog whiteness; where a screaming banshee of wind slams constantly against persons, buildings, and airplanes, with wind-chill temperatures reaching one hundred degrees below zero; where deep shifting snowdrifts change the face of the landscape daily; where no person is recognizable by his features, only by the cut and color of his parka, mitts or mukluks. This is Alaska.

Even in the summer, short as it is, the sun never ranges high in the sky, but only glimmers weakly in a perpetual twilight. On a muddy trail, the mosquitoes swarm with smothering relentlessness. There is never "time-off" to be lazy, the land demands a never-ending toil to wrench a living from the wilderness, to put up supplies of food and firewood, to make mechanical repairs, to overhaul vehicles. This is Alaska.

For some strange reason, Minnesotans had always been attracted to this harsh, forbidding land. It seems almost as if the vagaries of Minnesota's climate were not hardship enough. Although Alaska of the early 1920s, not yet a recognized State in the Union, was sparsely populated by Eskimos and gritty gold-miners whose lust for wealth overpowered their personal discomforts, this did not dissuade the early aviators.

Perhaps it was just those things, the frigid weather

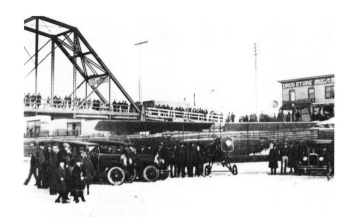

1924. Art Sampson, Bill Yunker and Jimmy Rodebaugh unload the equipment of the Alaska Aerial Transportation Company at Fairbanks, Alaska, amidst much public interest. (Ed Sampson)

with its fog, its winds, its deep snows, set in the picturesque background of rivers, mountains, glaciers and seacoast that compelled the first aviators to go there. To pioneer a new means of travel and commerce such as flying, where a month's dogsled or snowshoe journey could be compressed into but a few hours by airplane. What an opportunity!

Few flyers had ventured into the icy wilderness before North Dakota's, Carl Ben Eielson. Though an experienced pilot, he had ventured northwest in 1922, to teach school in Fairbanks. He convinced local businessmen to purchase an airplane, and he began flying for them in 1923, putting on exhibitions in small towns, stunting and hopping rides to pay expenses. Business was great, but there could be more. Eielson tried to organize an airmail schedule, but Post Office Department red-tape caused him to become discouraged. He returned to the "Outside" as the natives called the United States, seeking to convince the Army that Alaska should be a stop on the international aerial system. Eielson would return to Alaska and become part of its aviation legend.

In 1924, Jimmy Rodebaugh, a railroad conductor-turned-entrepreneur, ventured to start an air service at Fairbanks. It was called the *Alaska Aerial Transportation Company*. He envisioned a transportation system that would haul miners to and from their grubstakes in just hours, instead of the days and weeks, and they would be glad to pay well for the service.

Rodebaugh hired a Rochester, Minnesota, native, William Yunker, as his mechanic. In the search for suitable airplanes, Yunker advised Rodebaugh that the Minneapolis dealer, Marvin A. Northrop, had some Hisso-Standards for sale. Two of those were quickly purchased. Looking for pilots, Rodebaugh found a pair in Minnesota. The first was Arthur Sampson, a fledgeling from Belview, Minnesota, with less than 500 hours in his logbook; and the second was Noel Wien, from Cook, Minnesota, who had only slightly more. Wien would become the most famous of the Minnesota-Alaskans.

Sampson was quickly recruited for the promise of $300 a month in salary, plus his fare to Fairbanks. He had been flying around the area of northwestern Minnesota since 1919. His forte was taking up sightseeing passengers, but he shied away from cross-country hops. Little did he know what lay in store. He and Rodebaugh began operating in Fairbanks with modest success.

Noel Wien was hired shortly after Sampson. (Wien's early years are recounted in the Clarence Hinck biography, earlier in this chapter.) Wien and Yunker arrived at Anchorage in June of 1924 and began to assemble one of the Standards with the intention of flying it to Fairbanks. The trip to Fairbanks was Wien's initiation to the baffling weather conditions he would fly in for the rest of his career. Halfway to Fairbanks, the two men ran into a solid layer of forest-fire smoke that blinded and confused them. The pair had been following railroad tracks and had to drop down to one hundred feet to see anything. They began to worry about running into railroad tunnels.

Narrowly avoiding a factory smokestack near Fairbanks, Wien and Yunker eventually succeeded in finding the rough airstrip, cut earlier for the Eielson airmail flights. Art Sampson and Jim Rodebaugh were there to meet the flyers, along with a horde of townspeople. Sampson invited Wien to stay at his house that night, where the two spent some time talking. "This is bad country, boy," Sampson warned Wien. "Those old Hissos in Rodebaugh's planes have never been overhauled. You're going to go down one of these days, if you fly cross-country, sooner than you think. And when you do, how're you going to walk out? This is just not walking country. Wait till you see it. I've been over it, and I know. It's just not aviation country.

"I learned to fly in Dakota where there's fields everywhere. Here there's nothing but swamp, brush, spruce timber, and mountains. Rodebaugh's got a flight all set for you to Brooks, a mining place, north about sixty miles. Wait till you see what's between here and there. You couldn't make a good landing anywhere...[86]

Sampson wasn't a coward. He was intelligent, but being honest. And he wasn't the first one who had measured the hardships and dangers of the Alaskan way of life against the more comfortable way in the lower States. Sampson stayed to hop sight-seers for a few more days, then departed Alaska for good.

Wien, himself, would gain a reputation for being overly cautious in his flying. Both pilots had been cut from the same cloth. Wien was extremely wary of the unpredictable weather and often refused to fly when it didn't suit his expectations. Despite this, the business thrived. Regular flights were made between Fairbanks and Anchorage, with daily charter flights to nearby towns. Before long, *The Aerial Transportation Company* was expanded and re-organized as the *Fairbanks Airplane Company*, with several merchants from the town purchasing shares. Rodebaugh was the largest stockholder.

It was apparent that the larger business needed larger equipment than the J-1 Standards. During the winter of 1924, flying was curtailed as it had been the previous winter. Rodebaugh sent Wien on a mission to the "outside" to find new airplanes that would be more useful in the tundra. The quest was disappointing. In 1924, no aircraft were being manufactured that suited the purpose of hauling multiple passengers and heavy supplies in and out of miniscule airstrips, river bars, or snowfields. Reluctantly, Wien purchased the only large aircraft available in the States, a huge, single-engined Fokker F. III. Rodebaugh wired the $9,500 purchase price and Wien made a test flight. The plane was a devil to fly, with fluttering rudder and strange new dimensions. The pilot's open cockpit was ahead of the huge wing, and alongside the engine, quite the opposite of the well-appointed, closed-parlor cabin, in which four passengers were able to bask in relative comfort. Wien eventually mastered the plane's peculiarities, and became the only pilot in the company willing to fly it.

When he returned to Fairbanks, Noel Wien brought his brother, Ralph, with him to replace Yunker, who had departed for the lower 48. Ralph was an excellent mechanic, and kept the planes in top mechanical condition. Ralph also turned a part of his own cabin into an auto repair shop, and soon had substantial business from the town, to go along with his airplane mechanical work. It wasn't until 1926, that mechanics had to be licensed and it was Ben Eielson that issued mechanics licenses to both Ralph and Noel.

On 7 June, 1925, Noel Wien flew the giant Fokker 570 miles from Fairbanks to Nome, on the far west coast of Alaska. Expecting to find some type of a landing field at the halfway point, where he could stop and gas up, Wien found only a poor sandbar, and decided to turn back and land at the small town of

Noel Wien's J-1 Standard at Fairbanks, Alaska in 1924. Noel was flying for the Alaska Aerial Transportation Company. (Sherm Booen)

Noel Wien in the monster Fokker F. III in 1925. Local dignitaries mark the occasion of the first commercial flight between Fairbanks and Nome. (Noel Allard)

Ruby. In landing on the town's baseball field, the Fokker nosed over, but nobody was hurt. Noel, and Ralph, who was a passenger, immediately got to work repairing the plane, while three other passengers went into town to recover their wits. A day later, Noel lifted the plane out of the 600 foot baseball park and flew on to Nome with no other incident.

In the winter of 1925, the Wiens left the company as the really cold weather set in. Ralph retired to his home in town to make a living at the auto repair business. Noel returned to Minnesota and during the spring, barnstormed with Delmar Snyder's Air Circus. He received an inquiry about making a trip to the North Pole, but nothing came of it. Few flying jobs were available. Noel Wien grew restless in the next few months and made plans to return to Alaska in March of 1927.

When he arrived in Fairbanks this time, he brought along brother, Fritz. In Anchorage, the three brothers reunited and it was learned that Rodebaugh had also left the *Fairbanks Airplane Company* and started another business. Noel met with Captain Hubert Wilkins, who was planning an expedition to the North Pole and was looking for another pilot. After test flying one of Wilkins planes, however, it was apparent that Noel's services were not really needed. The other pilots hired before him would be doing all the flying, and Noel would likely remain a grease-monkey mechanic.

Noel and Ralph then approached their former employer, the *Fairbanks Airplane Company*, which was now under new ownership, and asked if Noel could buy the old monster Fokker that was not being flown. The price of $5,000 was out of the question, but one of the J-1 Standards that had been stored outside during the entire preceeding year, was available, and the price, while steep, was attainable. The company would sell the beat-up old plane to the Wiens on one condition: that they operate from Nome and not compete with the Fairbanks company.

The deal was struck, and the brothers moved west to begin operating as *Wien Alaska Airways*, flying a route between Nome, Deering, Candle, and Kotzebue on a regular schedule. They usually had passengers waiting to go from one town to the next. In the summer of 1927, Noel purchased a Stinson Detroiter biplane from Captain Hubert Wilkins. This plane was everything that the Standard was not. It had a nine hour range, closed-cabin comfort, com-

passes and better instruments, an adjustable stabilizer, and a reliable, air-cooled, Wright J-4 motor. It even had brakes! With this ship, Noel was able to fly a regular schedule between Fairbanks and Nome.

In 1928, Noel bought a Waco 9 from Rodebaugh's company and began teaching Ralph to fly. Fritz was working elsewhere in Fairbanks, but during the year, he too, began taking lessons from Noel.

The young airline received a contract to fly a Fox Movie Studio documentary film crew to Point Barrow, the northernmost point in Alaska. Noel hired another seasoned Alaskan flyer, Russ Merrill, to help out. Flying his own Travel Air, Merrill would make the flight northward, alongside Wien in the Stinson Detroiter. They departed together, but were forced down in very bad weather, landing on a small lake in deep snow. Wien, with fatter tires on his airplane, could take off again, but Merrill, and two movie crewmen, could not. They were forced to stay on the lake while Wien continued to Point Barrow to drop off the cameras and equipment. Wien planned to return and pick up the stranded flyers.

On his return to the area, Noel realized that every one of the thousands of small lakes that dotted this unfamiliar territory, looked alike. He was simply unable to locate his friend Merrill. The search continued for days. Matt Nieminen, another Minnesotan who was flying for *Anchorage Air Transport*, then a competitor of Wien's, also joined the search. The search for the downed airplane went on for sixteen days before it was located, but the three occupants had walked away from it.

The two pilots took different routes back to Point Barrow, searching along the way for the missing men, and it was Nieminen who spotted the two movie crewmen trudging along a trail. Nieminen landed and picked up two half-frozen, starved, and delirious men, bringing them back to safety at Point Barrow. A full eighteen days from the time of his landing, Merrill was picked up on a dogsled trail by a musher from a small village, one hundred miles from Point Barrow. Merrill was half-conscious, and dehydrated, having trudged eighty miles from his plane. He would survive the ordeal.

Meanwhile, the Wien brothers had other contracts to fulfill, and Noel was not in Nome to make the necessary flights. One of the contracts called for a mail flight from Fairbanks to Nome and Kotzebue. The distance was 570 miles to Nome and another 200 to Kotzebue. Ralph, as a student pilot with only eight hours of dual and two hours of solo, was the only hope of fulfilling the contract. Though suffering from a severe cold, and no one still aware of what had happened to Noel or Russ Merrill, Ralph took off in the Waco and managed to complete the trip. Most astoundingly, he had no trouble, despite his inexperience and the usual bad weather.

In March of 1929, Noel Wien made a historic flight across the Bering Straits to pick up a load of furs from a Russian ship marooned in polar ice off North Cape, Siberia. The trip required Wien to fly 600 miles to reach the ship. He loaded $600,000 in furs into a recently-purchased Hamilton Metalplane, and fueled it with what poor-quality gasoline the Russians could provide. He took off and struggled back to civilation, his engine misfiring all the way. (In the same Hamilton airplane, Ben Eielson later crashed and died as a result of injuries.)

In May 1929, Ralph made a forced landing in a rebuilt Stearman biplane and spent four days lost, before walking out of the bush to the village of Bettles, dragging a sack of mail that had been entrusted to him. The search for Ralph almost delayed Noel Wien's wedding. Ralph had been scheduled to be the best man, but his recovery prevented his taking part. Brother, Fritz, stood in for him when Noel finally wed Ada Bering Arthurs.

In the May 1932 issue of *Aero Digest*, Cy Caldwell, writer of the monthly column, "Person-air-lities," wrote the following humorous quip about the marriage; "Noel has escaped every danger but one. Tourists from the States, mistaking him for a bear, have fired at him and missed. But in May 1929, Miss Ada Bering, daughter of the postmaster of Nome, became interested in him because at first glance, he resembled a bearskin rug they had at home. Imagine her confusion when she found that he was inside, and when he explained, gently, yet firmly, that if she wanted the outfit for a rug, she'd have to take him along with it, which she did. However, as it turned out, she never did get that suit for a rug, because on 4 April 1930, they discovered that they'd have to cut the thing up into rompers for Noel Merrill Wien, who arrived that very day, without baggage."

At the end of 1929, Noel and Ralph decided to sell the company to the fast expanding *Aviation Corporation of America*, (AVCO). Noel Wien returned to the States, expecting to look for other flying opportunities. There, he was a hero, and the press followed him everywhere. He applied for a position with Northwest Airways, at the reccommendation of his friend, Operations Manager, Speed Holman. No jobs were available, however, and 1930 dragged by. Noel decided to return "home" to Fairbanks, once more.

Before Noel and Ada departed Minnesota, a telegram brought dreaded news. Ralph had been killed in a crash in Kotzebue. The news hastened the Wiens' plans to return. Noel had purchased a Stinson Jr., and in December 1930, arrived again in Fairbanks with his wife, baby Noel Merrill, and the youngest Wien brother, Sigurd. Ironically, when he arrived in Fairbanks, a telegram from *Northwest Airways* was waiting, offering him the job he had waited for so long. It was too late, Noel turned it down, and

took a job with *Alaskan Airways*, selling them the Stinson. Many years later, the airport at Kotzebue would be named *Ralph Wien Memorial Airport*.

Sig Wien had learned aviation mechanics while attending Dunwoody Institute in Minneapolis. He served his apprenticeship with *Alaskan Airways* and learned to fly. He was a natural-born pilot. Sig lived with Noel's family. Noel had stopped flying over the winter of 1931-1932, but in the spring, he was at it again. This time he formed *Wien Airways of Alaska* with financial support from his wife and her parents. He bought a Bellanca Pacemaker aircraft. Brother, Sig, became a pilot for the new company.

Things were very fluid in Alaska during the 1930s with airlines being created and going broke overnight. No sooner would a company hire a pilot and get him oriented to the country, than he would quit, buy an airplane and start his own company. Pilots flew contracts for other companies, cut one-another's prices, and watched business thin out for each of them. In 1936, there were 34 air transport companies, whose 79 aircraft had flown nearly 17,000 passengers that year and hauled more than two million pounds of freight.

In 1935, Wiley Post and Will Rogers crashed on takeoff near Point Barrow, in a float equipped Lockheed Orion-Explorer. Both were killed. The two had been headline news because of Post's flights around the world and Rogers' popularity as a humorist. The public clamored for the details of their accident. Those tragic headlines of 15 August overshadowed other news. *Wien Airways of Alaska*, and *Northern Air Tranport* of Nome had merged. The company received its first job assignment. Get photos of the Post-Rogers crash and deliver them to Seattle for the *International News Service*, one of several news services vying for a scoop on the disaster.

The flight became a race with the *Associated Press* pitted against the INS. Wien eventually got to Seattle first, after a hair-raising flight south which consumed twenty hours.

In Seattle, Noel fell in love again. His attention was focused on an ex-*Northwest Airways* Ford Trimotor which was up for sale. He convinced management of the new company to buy it, and he flew it back to Fairbanks.

Noel Wien tries to unstick his J-1 Hisso Standard from the mud at Circle Hot Springs, Alaska, in May of 1929. Ship had landed in soft ground and nosed over, breaking the propeller. (Noel Allard)

Wien Alaska Airlines, Inc. Ford Trimotor under the ice on Harding Lake 27 April, 1939. "Rotten" ice was the culprit, with the plane simply sinking through it after landing. The winching gear worked and the plane was soon back in service. (Robert Ausley)

For Noel Wien, life never did slow to a normal pace. From the merger with NAT, came *Wien Alaska Airways, Inc.* In time, Noel sold out to his brother Sig, but continued to fly for the airline. In 1938, Noel was doing some repair work on his water well, when a sliver of steel flew up and penetrated one eye. Though injured, Noel continued to fly, but the injury got worse. In three months, he was operated on, but the operation was bungled and Noel eventually lost his eye. Still he kept on flying, adapting to his handicap and adjusting his landings and takeoffs to compensate for his lack of depth of field. As if this tragedy weren't enough, he contracted Polio as well, but struggled through that with no permanent damage.

Sig bought out Noel Wien's portion of *Wien Air Alaska* in 1940, becoming President and General Manager. Despite the fact that "Sigwien," as the natives called him, was an executive, his mind was on the airline's operations. His own feats of daring during daily operations were eulogized by writer Jean Potter, "No airline route in Alaska has been more difficult to pioneer. Dimness is Sig's routine. Sometimes the coastal villages are almost buried, with only a few chimneys sticking up from the snow. In this part of the North, where so many flyers have lost their way, Sig never misses. He makes his way from point to point like the engineer of a shuttle train, with never a sign of confusion. He knows the coast so well that he uses small mounds and twists in the shore for checkpoints as another Alaska pilot would use a large mountain or a wide river. He flies the Arctic as precisely as a woman threads a needle."[87]

Sig Wien's contribution during World War II provided rugged charter flying for the Navy's Arctic oil-drilling program. Sig was said to have speeded the Navy's work by many months.

EPILOGUE: WIEN STORY

In 1968, *Wien Air Alaska* merged again, this time with *Northern Consolidated Airlines* to form *Wien Consolidated Airlines*, with Sig Wien as chairman,

and Noel and Fritz among the board members. In 1973, the name was changed back to *Wien Air Alaska* and the company survived until the early 1980s when it was caught in the deregulation-induced profit squeeze and closed down.

Herman Lerdahl, arrived in Alaska in 1935, having been struck by the flying bug back home in Virginia, Minnesota. Ironically, it was a chance meeting with Noel Wien in 1930 that got the flying juices circulating in Lerdahl's system. That meeting had occurred as Wien was making a fuel stop in Virginia, on his way across the states, returning to Alaska. At the time, Lerdahl had talked his way into a joy ride around the patch in Wien's beautiful Stinson. Afterward, casual conversation about flying led Wien to encourage Lerdahl to take up the profession.

Lerdahl's brother, Ed, a pilot and mechanic, had moved to Fairbanks that same year and opened an auto repair shop. He wrote to Herm suggesting that he come up and try to do some flying there. Herm liked the idea, and booked passage. When Herm arrived, Ed proudly announced that they could fix up one of two wrecked airplanes that Ed had purchased, and make some money with it. The rebuilding job looked impossible, but was accomplished, and by May, 1935, Herm had scrounged up his first charter flight. Work came at a regular rate for *Lerdahl Flying Service* in the year that followed.

On 5 January, 1936, Lerdahl took the Stinson to Dawson's tiny airport, near the Klondike River, with a load of supplies for the town merchants. When he landed, the temperature was 63 degrees below zero. Mounties suggested that Lerdahl stay in town until the weather was more comfortable, but that was not in his plan. When he went to start the engine of the plane, the mercury had dropped below the lowest reading on the thermometer taped to the wing strut. One of the Mounties scratched a mark where the mercury had stopped. The U. S. Weather Bureau later calculated that at this point, the temperature had dropped to nearly 87 below!

A plumber's blowtorch was used to heat the cylinders, and hot oil off the wood stove at a local farmouse brought the airplane's engine to life and Lerdahl was on his way. Although he babied it during climbout, the engine soon lost power, and Herm had to return and spend the night anyway. The following morning, the temperature had risen to a balmy eight below and things returned to "normal."[88]

At these extremely cold stops, the oil was immediately drained from the airplane's engine and brought to the nearest cabin or home. A heavy canvas was draped over the engine and hung to the ground. When the engine was to be started for the next flight, a fire pot would be suspended under the canvas, beneath the engine. Its heat would warm the cylinders. At the same time, the engine oil would be warmed over a stove inside the home. After about an hour of engine heating, the warm oil would be poured back into the engine and oil tank, and the engine would usually start.

In the Fall of 1936, Ed Lerdahl was forced to sell the Stinson for hard cash, to build up his auto business. Herm Lerdahl went to work for Noel Wien. Herm's first flight was to Nome ,and beyond, in

Wien's Stinson Detroiter. After making that flight without incident, Lerdahl became a permanent member of the *Wien Airways* staff, and became a shareholder of the company in 1938. In August of 1941, Lerdahl went to work for the *Morrison-Knudsen Construction Company.*

Morrison-Knudsen was fulfilling military contracts, building airfields and other defense facilities at a frantic pace, under the threat of Japanese invasion. The company continued to support the war effort after Pearl Harbor was attacked and Lerdahl remained with them. In 1942, the company sent him to Dallas for instrument training, and when he returned, he continued to fly construction crews and supplies to widely separated airstrips out along the Alaskan Peninsula.

In December of 1942, Lerdahl began working for *Northwest Airlines*, civilian contractor to the Army's Air Transport Command. Lerdahl spent the rest of the wartime period flying DC-3's.

Minnesotans, Johnny Walatka and Rudolph Billberg, had been flying for various operators in this area performing the same tasks as Lerdahl. Rudolf Billberg, from Roseau, Minnesota, flew for Sig Wien. He had gone to Nome, Alaska, in 1937 with his private license, but no experience. In 1939, Wien offered him a job flying out of Nome. Billberg rapidly accumulated time and eventually got all of his ratings, including his Air Transport Pilot certificate. He returned to Duluth prior to World War II, and instructed in the CPT program there. He flew for *Northwest Airlines* in the Air Transport Command during the war, and then went back to commercial flying in Alaska.

Billberg, in forty years of flying in Alaska, was at times, employed by *Northern Consolidated, Wien Alaska,* and *Munz Northern Airlines.* He flew fire-retardant missions with B-25 bombers after the war, and dropped fire-fighters from DC-3's. He often told the story of flying loads of tar, used in the building of runways, in a Hornet-engined Pilgrim aircraft, an ungainly workhorse of a ship. The heavy load required a takeoff run that seemed like miles.

Billberg often noticed a huge grizzly bear sitting on top of a ridge by the runway, watching the airplane on almost every takeoff. After a few trips, he thought he'd have some fun with the bear, so he dove at the bear and chased him off. But on the next trip, the bear was back, and again Rudy dove at him. This went on for days as Billberg flew repeated trips. The bear eventually became used to this diversion, refusing to be chased off, rather sitting on the ridge and waving its paws in the air. One day, Billberg lost a cylinder on the Pilgrim's engine and had to turn around to make a forced landing on a nearby sandbar. He had just touched the airplane's wheels on the ground, when the bear ambled down the hill onto the sand ahead. A bear that big could surely wreck an airplane in a collision, but at the last moment, the bear sidestepped enough to escape. Billberg was stuck with the bear for some time until searchers spotted the airplane and brought help. The load of tar never did make it to its destination.[89]

Robert Ausley, now a retired *Northwest Airlines* Captain, moved to Alaska with his family, in 1919, at the age of one year. He got his first ride in Noel Wien's Hisso-Standard at age nine, and was hooked on flying from then on. He became an airport kid, washing and refueling planes for *Pollack Flying Service.* The owner made an offer to the young lad that was made good five years later. He told Ausley that if he were to get his Commercial license, he would hire him as a pilot. This was a big offer, considering that Ausley did not have a single hour of flight time.

Ausley began his flight instruction in 1936, fifteen minutes or a half hour at a time, as he had the funds. It took a year and a half to solo. Not until 1940, did Ausley get that Commercial license, and the next day, he started flying for Pollack.

During the next year, Ausley flew to the far points of Alaska, out to the Bering Straits, to Point Barrow, and into Canada. He worked briefly for Noel Wien and for *Lavery Airways*, flying a Model A Stinson trimotor and cabin Waco's between Anchorage and Fairbanks.

Ausley recalls that there wasn't really a glamour to flying in Alaska in the 1930s. Rather, it was a means of getting from one place to another, simply transportation. Along with him, on a flight, he regularly took extra equipment, such as: sleeping bags, rifles, axes, snowshoes, and emergency rations. There were no radios or navigational aids until 1940. There were, in fact, only two paved airports in Alaska prior to World War II, those being at Fairbanks and Anchorage. The rest were either sod, like Nome, or just gravel.

"We had a lot of low level operation...visibility was the prime requirement and a lot of our flights were at 500 feet. We'd go up the rivers and down the valleys, and if you couldn't get through one pass, you'd turn around and try another one, or come back. I learned a lot about flying. Like, to fly a valley by staying on the right side because other pilots might be coming back along the other side.

"Like, one old fellow told me; when you get lost, always go downstream. I asked him how I could tell which way was downstream in the winter time, because you can't see the water flowing. He said, you'd see the trees that have fallen down and they will be lodged on a sandbar, and the stump is always upstream. The branches always point downstream."[90]

In June of 1942, while flying the Waco, Ausley heard that the Japanese were invading the Aleutian Islands. The information available was that they were sending a fleet up into the Bering Sea, to Nome, where they intended to make a landing. The U. S. wanted to get as many troops there as possible, and Bob Ausley was assigned to carry four G.I.'s with their full field gear to Nome in the Waco cabin plane.

With all the weight, he couldn't carry a full fuel load and planned to stop at McGrath. As he talked to the soldiers, he discovered that they didn't know where they were going, and had no idea of what was happening. The stop was made at McGrath as planned, but there were no radio communications from Nome to explain what the situation was. Ausley had to circle the Nome airport to identify himself, and believes that he was fired on by friendly troops, but sustained no damage. The tension of the situation was obvious when he was met by an officer with a sub-machine gun upon landing.[91]

In the fall of 1942, Bob Ausley was hired by *Northwest Airlines* to help fly the busy contract schedule with Air Transport Command. Ausley retired from Northwest in 1978.

John Walatka, from the Fairmont area of southern Minnesota, found his way to Alaska in 1937. Walatka helped found and became president of *Northern Consolidated Airlines*. An Alaskan mountain is named after him.

Two Sherburne, Minnesota, brothers, Leon and Lloyd Alsworth, had been taught to fly by Walatka. They also found their way to Alaska. Leon was the first to visit the territory in 1939. He decided to stay there as a pilot. The following year, he returned to the U. S. and bought a Stinson Junior-SR, a four-place cabin monoplane, ideally suited for duty in Alaska. He picked up his brother, Lloyd; and, after a long and arduous journey, landed at Fairbanks on the shortest day of the year. That night, according to Lloyd, at least three different gentlemen beat on the door of their hotel room, each wanting to buy the airplane.

Though Lloyd returned to Minnesota the following year, Leon, whose nickname was "Babe," stayed on. He spent his entire career flying in Alaska. The city where Babe settled, is today named Port Alsworth.

Not so surprisingly, the Stinson Junior SR is still flying, as of this writing. Many of the airplanes flown to Alaska in the 1930s are still flying there. Some have even returned to the lower 48 states, and are in the hands of antiquers. In Alaska, aircraft were so valuable, that unless they were totally destroyed in some incident, they were carefully repaired and returned to service.

Thrill Shows   Documentation

1. *Minutes*, Board Meeting of the Minnesota Agricultural Association, (Minnesota State Fair Board), 4 May, 1917, Volume 11, Roll 3, page 77. Minnesota Historical Society.
2. Ray Speer and Harry Frost, *Minnesota State Fair, The History and Heritage of 100 Years*, Argus Publishing Company, 1964, page 277.
3. Minutes, State Fair Board, 2 August, 1918, Volume 12, Roll 4, page 84. MHS.
4. *Minutes*, State Fair Board, 2 May, 1919, Volume 13, Roll 4, page 48. MHS.
5. *Minutes*, State Fair Board, 2 June, 1919, Volume 13, Roll 4, page 60. MHS.
6. Art Ronnie, *Locklear*, The Man Who Walked on Wings, A.S. Barnes & Co., Inc., pages 154-157.
7. Ibid.
8. *Minutes*, State Fair Board, 3 October, 1919, Volume 13, Roll 4, page 144. MHS.
9. *Minutes*, State Fair Board, 29 August, 1924, Volume 18, Roll 5, page 105. MHS.
10. *Minutes*, State Fair Board, 9 June, 1927, Volume 21, Roll 5, page 88. MHS.
11. *Minutes*, State Fair Board, 5 April, 1928, Volume 22, Roll 5, page 70. MHS.
12. *Aviation*, "Minnesota Show High Attendance," September 22, 1928, page 941.
13. Contract between Fair Board and Northwest Airways, 31 August, 1929. State Fair Main Office, Contract File, State Fairgrounds, St. Paul, MN.
14. *Minutes*, State Fair Board, 16 February, 1932, Volume 26, Roll 6, page 14. MHS.
15. *Minutes*, State Fair Board, 8 April, 1935, Volume 28, Roll 6, page 25. MHS.
16. Letter to George Vest, District Supervisor, Chicago Region of Civil Aeronautics Administration, from Ray Miller, 5 November, 1935, copy in possession of author.
17. Letter to Frank Frakes from Department of Commerce, 8 October, 1935, signed by J. Carroll Cone, Assistant Director (Regulations) and Joseph T. Shumate, Jr., Chief, General Inspection Service, copy in possession of author.
18. *Minneapolis Tribune*, "Fair Stunters Escape Death," 12 September, 1936, page 1.
19. Interview with Chuck Doyle by Noel Allard, 10 April, 1987.
20. *Dallas Times-Herald*, "The Great Texas Air Fair," Al Hartung, Westward section, Picture magazine, 6 December, 1981, pages 28-36.
21. Letter from Ray Miller, Chairman of the Minnesota Department of Aeronautics, to George Vest, Chicago Regional Department of Commerce Inspector, 22 June, 1937, copy in possession of author.
22. Letter from R. S. Boutelle, Chief Inspector, Bureau of Air Commerce, Washington D. C. to Croil Hunter, 2 June, 1937, copy in possession of author.
23. Ann Pelegrino, *Iowa Takes to the Air*, Volume Two, Aerodome Press, Story City, Iowa, 1986, page 276.
24. *Minutes*, State Fair Board, 29 November, 1938, Volume 29, Roll 6, page 168. MHS.
25. *Minutes*, State Fair Board, 15 July, 1938, Volume 29, Roll 6, page 137. MHS.
26. Interview with Don Piccard by Minnesota Aviation History Project, 14 March, 1988.
27. Interview with Earl Barrus by Noel Allard, 17 July, 1987.
28. Resume of incident written by Joseph Williams, March 1988, copy in possession of author.
29. Walter Klausler, *Klausler, Speed, Action, Thrills, promotional booklet*, copy in possession of author.
30. Interview with Walter Klausler by Noel Allard 17 May, 1988.
31. *Duluth Herald News Service*, circa August 1930, 1937.
32. Ibid.
33. Ibid.
34. Ibid.
35. Interview with Marvin Sievert by Noel Allard, 30 December, 1987.
36. Letter to Mel Swanson from Captain E.B. Moomau, Marine Corps Adjutant representing Civilian Conservation Corps, 22 June, 1937, copy in possession of author.
37. Interview with George Holey by Noel Allard, 3 June, 1988.

Barnstormers   Documentation

38. Interview with Gustav Imm by Noel Allard and Joseph Williams, 9 September, 1986.
39. Ibid.
40. Jim Peterson, "Irwin Stellmacher, Flier, Mechanic, Inventor in Cottonwood," *Minneapolis Sunday Tribune Picture Magazine*, 3 July, 1977.
41. *Minneapolis Star*, June, 1959.
42. Interview with Eugene Burke by Lance Belville, Great North American History Theatre, January, 1986.
43. Ibid.
44. Interview with Cyril Stodolka by Noel Allard, 20 September, 1986.
45. Interview with Ed Croft by George and Anne Holey, Minnesota Air Museum, 10 August, 1965, Minnesota Historical Society.
46. Ibid.
47. Interview with Robert Baker by Lance Belville and Val Cunningham, Great North American History Theatre. 10 March, 1986.
48. Ibid.
49. Interview with Sven Peterson by Noel Allard and Joseph Williams, 9 April, 1987.
50. Ibid.
51. Bird Aircraft ad, circa 1929.
52. Letter from Paul Miller to Rueben Rydholm, 10 January, 1933. From Rydholm Papers, Minnesota Historical Society, A-R754/A5396, (AR992) Research Center.
53. Interview with Sven Peterson by Noel Allard and Joseph Williams, 9 April, 1987.
54. Clarence O. Kvale, *Memoirs of the Thirties*, self-published book, circa 1974.
55. Interview with Eldon Sorenson by Noel Allard, 13 June, 1988.
56. James Meyer, *Rotating Wings Above Minnesota, the Autogiros*, unpublished manuscript, Elgin, Iowa, 1989.

Record-setters   Documentation

[57] Earl L. Vogt, *St. Paul Pioneer Press*, "The Sock," p.8, second section, 23 June, 1929.
[58] *St. Paul Pioneer Press*, 18 March, 1928, page 1.
[59] Ibid.
[60] C.D. Johnston, "Speed, The Life Story of Charles W. Holman," *St. Paul Dispatch*, 2 June, 1931.
[61] Results of trial, 1 November, 1928, Hennepin County District Court #316560, Archives, Minnesota Historical Society.
[62] *Minneapolis Journal*, 21 May, 1931.
[63] *Faribault Daily News*, 31 July, 1929, page 1.
[64] *Faribault Journal*, 1 August, 1929, page 1.
[65] *Faribault Journal*, 7 January, 1932, page 1.
[66] *Minneapolis Journal*, 19 May, 1929, page 1.
[67] *Minneapolis Journal*, 26 May, 1929, page 1.
[68] *Minneapolis Tribune*, 21 June, 1929, page 8
[69] *Minneapolis Journal*, 27 June, 1929.
[70] *Minneapolis Journal*, 29 June, 1929.
[71] *Minneapolis Journal*, 29 July, 1929.
[72] Ted Huetter, "Mamer's Sun God," *Air Classics*, Vol. 16, No. 6, June, 1980.
[73] Ibid.
[74] Ibid.
[75] Frank W. Wiley, *Montana and the Sky*, Montana Aeronautics Commission, p.159, p.270.

Women in Minnesota Aviation   Documentation

[76] Steve Tangen, "Tree Tops," unpublished biography of Florence Klingensmith, Farmington, MN, 1986, copy in possession of author.
[77] Robert Hull, *September Champions*, remarks by Mae Haizlip, P.138.
[78] Interview with Ray Miller, Minnesota Air National Guard Historical Foundation records, 2 June, 1956, page 6.
[79] Frances Pryzymus, recipe book/ground school notebook, 3 January, 1930.
[80] *Minneapolis Journal*, 12 May, 1929, page 12.
[81] *Minneapolis Journal*, 5 July, 1932.
[82] Helen E. McLaughlin, *Walking On Air*, 1986, State of the Art, Ltd., Denver, Colorado.
[83] Letter from Agnes Nohava Hincks to the author, 10 June, 1987.
[84] Interview with Dorothy Schaeffer by Noel Allard, 15 December, 1989.
[85] Claudia M. Oaks, *Smithsonian Studies in Air & Space*, U. S. Women in Aviation 1930-1939, Volume 6, page 54.

Minnesotans in Alaska   Documentation

[86] Ira Harkey, *Pioneer Bush Pilot, The Story of Noel Wien*, Ira Harkey, Jr. and Noel Wien Trust, University of Washington Press, page 84.
[87] Jean Potter, *The Flying North*, Curtis Publishing Company, New York, 1945, Bantam Book edition, 1983, page 177.
[88] Cliff Cernick, *Skystruck*, Alaska Northwest Books, Anchorage, Alaska, 1989.
[89] Interview with Rudy Billberg, copies from Hal Bakke, Warroad, Minnesota, 1988.
[90] Interview with Robert Ausley by Noel Allard, 23 October, 1987.
[91] Ibid.

FOUR

1920s — 1930s: DESIGNERS AND BUILDERS

Outside of the thousand or so Waco CG-4A gliders, produced for the U. S. Army by *Northwestern Aeronautical Company* during World War II, Minnesota had no history of mass-producing airplanes prior to 1945. In fact, only a single aircraft designed and built in Minnesota ever received a government Approved Type Certificate, (ATC, the approval needed for manufacturing a line of aircraft). Only a single Minnesota aircraft company produced more than three or four aircraft of a single type of its own design.

THE MOHAWK AIRCRAFT CORPORATION

The *Mohawk Aero Corporation* was formed in 1927, by four forward-looking individuals who hoped to cash in on the popularity of the flying machine, following the Atlantic crossing of Charles Lindbergh. The four were: Leon Dahlem, who became president, Wallace C. "Chet" Cummings, vice president and head of design, George A. MacDonald, vice president and chief pilot, and Sumner E. Whitney, secretary-treasurer.

Dahlem had been a Naval aviation cadet at the University of Minnesota, receiving his Navy wings in 1924. He was on inactive status when he and the others formed the Mohawk Company. Cummings had engineering credentials. He had worked for J. Don Alexander, at the *Alexander Aircraft Company* in Colorado, on the design of the Air King and Eaglerock airplanes.

The Mohawk Company opened for business in the former Rap-In-Wax plant at 2600 Delaware Street in Southeast Minneapolis, near Prospect Park and the Midway area. In the Fall of 1927, the Company incorporated as the *Mohawk Aircraft Corporation*.

Mohawk's first aircraft was designed by Cummings. It was a stubby, low-winged, two seat monoplane that sat up pertly on sturdy landing gear. Though the

1928 Mohawk Pinto MLV. Note the shock struts outboard of the wheels. This photo was taken at St. Paul and shows Charles Lindbergh in the cockpit preparing to go up for a test flight. (John Underwood)

seating was side-by-side, it was also staggered, so that the passenger was slightly behind the pilot, giving both more shoulder room, yet allowing them to remain close enough to yell back and forth in flight. The aircraft was powered by a 60-hp. Detroit "Aircat" engine. A large round emblem with a Mohawk Indian head image was emblazoned on both sides of the fuselage. Just why the name Mohawk was selected as the company name is unclear, but the first airplane's nickname "Pinto" seems a logical follow-on.

Receiving ATC #95 from the government in December of 1928, the Model MLV "Pinto" was the result of a great amount of engineering and stress testing. Production ships began to roll off the assembly line, most powered by a 55 hp. Velie engine. Other Mohawks came to be powered by the Szekely, the Anzani, LeBlond 60, Cirrus Mk. III, Warner, and Kinner engines.

Company literature indicated that the plane's design followed the German Junkers, probably the J-1 series of low-winged, open-cockpit utility aircraft. The 1927 *Aero Digest Magazine* described it as; "advanced design, easy to fly, yet from nose to tailskid, having the constant adherence to the highest level of excellence in structure, beauty, and simplicity." Beautiful it was, in its cream-colored paint job with either black or wine-colored scalloped leading edges and nose. The color scheme was designed by Douglas Rolfe, well-known aviation artist of the time.

Was it easy to fly? Almost every local, and some nationally-known pilots, had a chance to test-fly the aircraft. The list included Charles Lindbergh, Cowboy McMahon, Hiram W. Sheridan, Elmore Wall, "Doc" Ellis, Thunder Johnson, as well as company test pilot MacDonald. Many experienced dramatic handling problems. Speed Holman was hired to do a spin test. The well-worn tale of Speed's near disastrous test flight was related earlier. Speed could not get the plane to come out of a flat spin. George MacDonald had the same experience only a few weeks later, bailing out of a spinning Pinto.

Easy to fly? Doctor Joseph A. Nowicki flew a Pinto in the 1928 National Air Tour and noted it was "like having a tiger by the tail, but sheer fun!"[1]

The Pinto was in need of redesign, and former Stout aircraft engineer, and at that time, University of Minnesota engineering professor, John Akerman, was hired to do the job. He changed the airfoil to provide additional stability and lengthened the fuselage, putting the second cockpit behind the first in full tandem arrangement. The landing gear were also re-arranged so that the oleo struts, which had been outboard of the wheels, were placed inboard. This not only gave the aircraft a wider stance for more directional stabili-

Side view of Mohawk MLV shows the clean lines and Mohawk insignia. Photo taken at the 1929 Minnesota State Fair. (Minnesota State Fair)

1929 Mohawk Pinto M-1-CW Spurwing. The redesigned model with true tandem cockpit arrangement, redesigned landing gear, and stretched fuselage, is a graceful aircraft. (John Underwood)

ty in landing, but facilitated changing tires, lubricating wheel bearings, and other wheel maintenance. Akerman also increased the dimensions of the control surfaces. He even planned to install "Frieze-type" ailerons and slots in the wings of a test model, to give it more low speed performance.

The initial model of the redesign was called the "Spurwing," but company literature continued to use the name Pinto, even when the new ship was granted a different ATC number, #263. The plane, in its new form, was very much more docile. It is clear that the company knew their business, as all advertising brochures of the period 1928 through 1930, were very informative regarding the flight characteristics and design principles of the Mohawk line.

The new Pinto was an innovative design as well, with its original "triplex" safety glass windshields, cockpit-controlled horizontal stabilizer trim, push-pull rods to operate the control surfaces, dual controls, cantilever wing, all-welded fuselage construction and a pair of fuel tanks, one in each wing. The plane was even available with an electric starter.

The redesigned version was officially the M-1-CK with Kinner K-5 motor of 100 hp. , or the M-1-CW with a Warner engine. In 1930, the Army tested one of these at Wright Field, calling it XPT-7. Tests were successful, but no contract was given to Mohawk.

Les Johnson on the Mohawk Company's Model T pickup truck with which he has moved a set of wings and fuselage of a production Mohawk to Wold-Chamberlain for assembly. (Les Johnson)

The year 1930 saw another version introduced. The "Redskin" was a classy-looking M-1-CW, (Warner 110 engine), with a canopy covered, three-place cockpit. It was issued a third ATC #297. That same year, an experimental twin-engined version called the "Chieftain" appeared at Wold-Chamberlain. It was designated M-2-C by the factory, and was to come with two Michigan-Rover engines of 55-60 hp. each. There is some doubt as to how much it flew, if at all. A "Super Pinto" was on the drawing boards in 1931, to be powered by a Wright J-6 engine.

Mohawk's plans had been grandiose. They announced in the *Minneapolis Tribune* of 22 October, 1928, that they had an order for 100 aircraft from the *George Craig Company* of California. Many Pintos were shipped to California, but somewhere along the line, the order either was reduced or cancelled altogether. Mohawk expected the 1929 output to total 300 aircraft with a value of over $832,000. The Velie-engined Pinto was selling for $2775. They also boasted of having dealers in Portland, Los Angeles, Detroit, and New York. The production area of the plant then encompassed the entire 30,000 square feet of the Delaware Street building's third floor and employment was up to 25 persons.

In 1929, the annual *Aircraft Yearbook* lists Stanley Partridge as president, Cummings and Whitney still on board, and Norman Warsinski as general manager. Warsinski was, however, replaced by Colonel G. P. Murphy in that position during the summer of 1928, when the Mohawk Company subsidiary, *Air Service, Inc.* was formed. The new subsidiary was a flight school aimed at training college age students

Inside the Mohawk factory in Prospect Park, Minneapolis, showings a Mohawk Pinto, Model M-1-C under construction. A three-cylinder Szekely engine is mounted on it. Judging from the squared-off tail fin, it could be an experimental model. (Les Johnson)

Mohawk Redskin. Nothing more than a Pinto with an enclosed cockpit. (Noel Allard)

to fly, in the hopes that they would become purchasers of new Pinto airplanes.

As planes were built at the Delaware Street plant, the fuselages were hitched to a Model-T pickup truck, the wings and other components tied in the truck bed, and the airplane towed to Wold-Chamberlain. Retired Northwest Airlines mechanic, Les Johnson, worked for Mohawk. It was his job to drive the truck from plant to airport, where the wings were attached and the ship rigged. Those were 15 hour days for Johnson. The trek took him across the Mississippi River on Franklin Avenue, then out 34th Avenue to the airport. Johnson took every Mohawk produced by the factory along that route, and claims that the total was between 30 and 40 aircraft, a figure that closely agrees with Joseph Juptner's estimates in his books on the approved type certificates.[2]

The Mohawk saga includes some interesting "events." A Mohawk owned by *Northland Aviation* was flying a cameraman over Powderhorn Park in 1931, when the plane ran out of fuel, and dropped unexpectedly into a house at 43rd Street and 17th Avenue, in South Minneapolis, slightly injuring both occupants of the plane, but no one in the home.

Former Northwest Airlines Captain, Bert Ritchie, recalls that prior to his joining NWA, he worked as a chauffer for Mrs. Rufus Rand. He, and friend Joe Kimm, wanted jobs with Northwest as co-pilots and heard that it was possible if each had a pilot's license. They decided to buy a Pinto from Rand and learn to fly. Recalling how big-hearted Mr. Rand was, Ritchie

Northstar Aircraft Corporation's Liberty Bell aircraft. This one is christened the "Spirit of St. Cloud." 1928. (John Underwood)

remembered Rufus asking him how much money he had to buy it with. When Ritchie answered, "not a cent," Rufus suggested that Ritchie see what he could borrow. Ritchie managed to come up with $300 and told Rand all he could get was $275, figuring that he might want to buy some gas for the plane after purchasing it. Rand sold him the airplane, which the two young pilots put 49 hours on and sold for the same $275.[3]

As the depression deepened, A. S. Koch became a vice-president. Akerman, who had been working for Mohawk on a part-time basis while associate-professor of aeronautics at the University of Minnesota, took on the full-time position as head of Aeronautical Engineering. Wealthy businessman, Rufus R. Rand, who, in his philanthropy, kept purchasing aircraft from Mohawk to keep them solvent, finally becoming receiver of the company. By 1931, the company had folded with the deepening Depression.

Businessman, Mark Hurd, was authorized by Rand to dispose of the Mohawk assets, but apparently was never successful in finding buyers for three aircraft in Rand's name, two experimental ships, and the parts inventory. One of Hurd's proposals was to J. Don Alexander of the *Alexander Aircraft Company* of Colorado. Hurd suggested that Alexander buy the rights to the Mohawk and add it to the Alexander line of aircraft. Nothing came of this proposal.

Two Mohawks were listed in the Minnesota state aircraft register in Rand's name in 1930; four were registered to him in 1931; but in 1932, only a single ship. Mark Hurd ended up buying one of the planes from Rand, M-1-CK, 67N. It crashed and was rebuilt, staying on the Minnesota register in Hurd's name until 1936, when it was sold to Ethan Burlingame. The last year that the plane was registered in the state was 1938. Of all the Mohawks built, none are flying today. In fact, only rumors remain of the ghosts of those 30 to 40 aircraft manufactured in Minnesota.

THE NORTH STAR AIRCRAFT CORPORATION

During the late 1920s and through the Depression that followed, many colorful characters, businessmen, entrepreneurs, and charltons, walked the stage of aviation history.

In March of 1928, Captain W. Hoseas Mohlar blew into St. Cloud, Minnesota. He claimed to be a representative of the *American Eagle Company* of Kansas City. He also claimed to have been flying since the days of the Wright Brothers, to have been in the Lafayette Escadrille, and to have designed aircraft for, and been the superintendent of production at American Eagle. Little wonder that St. Cloudites were impressed.

Mohlar announced that he was investigating production facilities for a company called the *Midwest Aircraft Corporation*. They, supposedly, would be general contractors for a tri-motored plane capable of regular trans-Atlantic service. Mohlar would be both designer and test pilot. The eight-passenger ship would have a special wing shaped like the wing of a bird, which Mohlar would call the Hoseas Wing.

It was a rocky start. By the end of April, the plans

were scrapped and Mohlar had severed his connection with the project. He was then rumored ready to organize his own company with the intention of building a smaller biplane for business and personal use. His new company, *North Star Aircraft Corporation*, was duly incorporated and construction began on what was to be a series of planes known as the Liberty Bell. Liberty Bells were to be powered by 180 hp. Hispano-Suiza, (Hisso), engines. The new design bore more than a passing similarity to the American Eagle.

The corporation included, along with Mohlar; M. E. Jones as vice-president; A. D. Merrill Firebaugh, secretary; and Aloys H. Zierten, treasurer. Other St. Cloud area businessmen on the board of directors included Marlin Barker, Frederick Heinzel, and Benjamin J. Korte. The company claimed to have raised $50,000 in capital, and had rented the Firebaugh garage as a factory site. Soon after, it was reported in the *St. Cloud Times* that, because Mohlar had five aircraft orders, production was shifted to the larger area of the Schoener Building near Lake George.

Mohlar advertised for students, offering flight training and ground school, that he would teach. Students would receive enough instruction to get their solo license, free of charge, in return for which they would work in the Liberty Bell factory. Thirty students signed up, and were immediately put to work. In return for a weeks work in the factory, Mohlar provided ground school instruction, two nights a week. His offer was almost too good to be true. One student, Hyacinth Ravely, signed a contract, the last paragraph of which read, "Captain W. H. Mohlar guarantees to aid me in every way possible, that after I have become a Limited Pilot, to aid me in obtaining recognition among the aviation world. Captain Mohlar is contemplating to fly across the Atlantic some time the end of this year and promises that if I prove satisfactory he will give me the first opportunity to travel across with him and share the profits pro-rata."[4]

By June 21, the first Liberty Bell airplane was reported to be almost ready for flight, and a *St. Cloud Times* reporter said he had personally seen orders for dozens of machines. It was predicted that the corporation would become the largest plane building firm in the Northwest. Captain Mohlar, it was noted, had designed several engineering features that would be without parallel in airplane construction. And according to the Times, "several aviation experts" had visited the plant, and were of the opinion that the features would "aid the airplane in flight to such an extent that it will make it as perfect in construction as any plane that can be built."[5]

The plane was actually of standard construction for the times, with welded steel tube fuselage, wooden spar wings, and linen covering. Mohlar claimed it would have a cruising speed of 130 mph. and a seven hour endurance. (It is doubtful that Mohlar contemplated relief facilities, so this last feature seems ludicrous.) Two passengers would sit side-by-side in an enclosed front cockpit; the pilot alone in the traditional open rear cockpit.

Newspaper reports indicated that the plane would be exhibited at the State Fairgrounds in September of 1928, and that the factory was working day and night to reach the deadline. During August, new officers and board members were coming and going on an almost weekly basis. Then on 16 August, came the first hint that all was not well at North Star Aircraft. The company announced that it had decided to move its production out of St. Cloud unless the city would guarantee a loan for $10,000.

In August, airplane production was moved to the Pandolfo Motor Co. building, and on 20 August, Mohlar told the news media that he wanted to buy the building. He stated that he was seeking a responsible St. Cloud man to be made business manager. He also announced that he had plans to build a cabin monoplane as his next project. The fact that plans and reality didn't correspond, seemed to have no bearing on Mohlar's activity.

Finally, on 25 August, the "Spirit of St. Cloud," as the first Liberty Bell ship had been named, was ready for test flight. It did not fly before, or during the State Fair exhibit, but was seen there by thousands of persons over Fair week. Mohlar stood by the plane for eight days, telling fairgoers about the merits of his design and future plans.

Funds had definitely run out, however. Following the Fair exhibit, it was announced that the factory would close in a few days if no new funding were forthcoming. Mohlar had even sent his test pilot, Lester Coyle, out to solicit businessmen for support. Mohlar warned the St. Cloud community that his plant employed local people on its work force, hoping he could coerce the city into providing more funds. But St. Cloud had had enough. One night, a four-foot cross of old automobile tires was burned in front of Mohlar's apartment. A note tacked to his door, read: "Take this notice. Mohlar leave town. Minnesota Chapter No. 7, K.K.K."[6] Some folks speculated that Mohlar, himself, had burned the cross as an excuse for leaving. Mohlar did pack up, and leave the next day. The corporation was served notice of foreclosure on both the plane and the shop.

The plane was repossessed by the creditors, and stored in the garage of Ben Korte, one of the directors of the corporation. A new corporation was to be formed without Mohlar. When the company safe was opened during a final board of directors meeting, it was found empty. There were no plans, no blueprints, no corporate records.

Meanwhile, assuming that a new corporation would be formed, employees who had an interest in seeing the airplane fly went ahead with ground tests and engine run-ups. Chief pilot and mechanic, Les Coyle, was finally able to make the test flight from a field near St. Rosa, (close to St. Cloud). The *Melrose Beacon* of 20 October, 1928, described the first flight five days earlier: "Pointing her silvery nose westward, the tank full, and engine purring contentedly, the "Spirit of St. Cloud" glided across the beautiful St. Rosa flying field. Pilot, Lester Coyle, gave her the gun, and the craft rose. She left the ground, 10 feet, 20 feet, 30 feet, 40 feet. . . she was taking it nicely, and then it happened." As Coyle started to climb, the plane stalled, slid backward, fell on its tail, and plopped over on its back.

Coyle suffered a broken leg, but the plane was a write-off. With the machine unsalvageable, the design suspect, the factory and its equipment repossessed,

The Cloquet Trainer. Somewhat retouched photo shows the second production ship emblazoned with Arco Coffee advertising in 1931. (Jim Borden)

the employees had to walk away. The *North Star Aircraft Corporation* became extinct.

EPILOGUE: NORTH STAR AIRCRAFT

What became of Mohlar? On 12 October, 1928, the *St. Cloud Times* reported on its investigation of the good Captain. He had posed as pilot, mechanic, and chief designer for the *American Eagle Company*. The facts became known; from Washington, D. C. came the astounding news that Mohlar had never obtained either a pilot's, or mechanic's license. He couldn't fly. Inquiries at American Eagle disclosed that he was not a designer at all, but had worked there as a draftsman for only three weeks. In fact, it was very likely that Mohlar had absconded with proprietary plans and drawings from the American Eagle Company, since the Liberty Bell aircraft was such a close copy of the Eagle.

Mohlar surfaced next in Chicago, in November, 1928. A Chicago newspaper informed its readers that Mohlar had been an "Ace" in the Lafayette Escadrille during World War I, was a former design engineer for the American and French governments, and now was the manager of a company called *Chicago Aeronautical Service*. There he was to have charge of student training, passenger flying, and air transportation to all parts of the country. Investigation show that Mohlar's name never appeared on the roster of the Lafayette Escadrille, or the Lafayette Flying Corps.

Much of the information on the North Star Aircraft Company was provided by Dr. William E. Lovelace, University professor and historian from St. Cloud.

THE CLOQUET TRAINER

In 1931, a lesser-known corporate venture occurred in Cloquet, Minnesota. Three men hoped to get into volume aircraft production. The three were: Norman Nelson Sr., Claude J. Phillips, and "Rosie" Rosenthal, who incorporated as *Trainer Aircraft Company*. The company started with a $10,000 investment by brothers, Cavour and Guilford Hartley, of Duluth.

A prototype model was produced, and legendary Duluth pilot, Jake Pfaender, went to Cloquet to test the ship, pronouncing it airworthy. The company made plans to mass-produce the airplane, but adequate financing was very hard to come by during the Depression, and soon the operation was in financial crisis. Phillips, who had designed the nifty looking airplane, pleaded for help. Nelson successfully talked the *Reliable Investment Company* of Cloquet, into allowing the group to work rent-free in a downtown office building. The corporation came up with a stock offering and sold shares for one dollar each until they had enough working capital to begin producing additional aircraft.

The first plane was built with a welded chrome-moly steel tube fuselage structure, a high-lift wing, and a 55 hp. Velie engine. It had side-by-side seats, and a 30 gallon fuel tank. Norm Nelson flew the airplane after its test flight and noted that it flew very well, with excellent short field landing and takeoff characteristics.

A second ship was constructed, with help being solicited from any and every source. A $75 gift from the local Commercial Club was a godsend. When the second plane flew, the group solicited advertising revenue, selling the *Arco Coffee Company* an aerial ad for $25 and painted the name on the side of the aircraft. The ship was flown at local airshows and displayed wherever possible. It had a single seat and featured a more powerful 90 hp. Kinner engine.

When it was obvious that there was no future in the aircraft manufacturing business without adequate capitalization, the group decided to pay off all their debtors by staging a large airshow from the farm field where they had been doing their flying. The grand finale of the airshow was the bombing of the second ship, parked on the ground, by the first, flying overhead. Thus the second plane met its end. The first plane was stored in the factory loft of the *Cloquet Manufacturing Company* for several years, its final disposition is unknown. Most of the creditors were paid off, with the exception of Norm Nelson, but no matter, the fun of flying the airplane more than made up for the expense.[7]

WALDRON AIRCRAFT AND MANUFACTURING COMPANY

Though most often thought of as a Minnesota Corporation, the *Waldron Aircraft and Manufacturing Company* was actually registered as a South Dakota Corporation, probably due to the fact that several

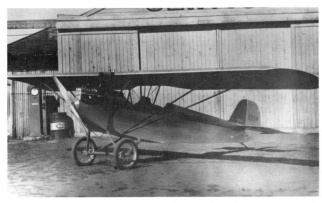

Hickman's H-20/21 about to land at Robbinsdale Airport. (Bruce Sifford Studio via John Underwood)

Orville Hickman's H-20/21 in front of the hangars at Robbinsdale Airport, circa 1932. Note the similarity to both the Pietenpol and the Georgia Special. Hickman played a role in the design of the Georgia Special. (Bruce Sifford Studio via John Underwood)

members of the Board of Directors were from there. The Waldron Company was headquartered at 224 1st Street in Minneapolis, and opened for business in February of 1928. Lawrence D. "Baldy" Waldron was the president; Orville Hickman, secretary/treasurer and chief designer; Chester W. Johnson, an attorney from Minneapolis, was listed as the Minneapolis agent; Gene Shank was named test pilot.

The company seems to have been formed specifically to finance the manufacture of aircraft designed by Hickman. Hickman's background was quite remarkable prior to his joining the company. He had, indeed, paid his dues in the aircraft design business. Having graduated from Ottawa University in 1920 with an Aeronautical Engineering degree, Hickman had worked for the *Swallow Company* in Wichita under Matty Laird, and alongside Lloyd Stearman and Walter Beech. He then had been part of the engineering team that produced the Air King biplane at Lomax, Illinois. His next job was chief designer of the Pheasant biplane in Memphis, Missouri. As many as eleven Pheasants were produced and the aircraft received government ATC #36 in 1928. The design finished, the company had no need for a designer, and Hickman was on the road again.

What happened to the *Waldron Company* is unclear because in May of 1928, only three months after incorporation, the *Starling Aircraft Manufacturing Company* was incorporated in Minneapolis for apparently the same thing. Orville Hickman was listed as president, and Lawrence Waldron as vice-president, with Eugene A. Puffer, secretary/treasurer. They floated a $50,000 stock offering and immediately began building airplanes.

The first Starling aircraft, designated H-11, identification number X5316 was a three-place biplane of standard features for the day. It was powered by an OX-5 engine and incorporated the very latest of design ideas, as its advertising would proclaim: "Inaugurating new principles of design. Although technique is very important in the flying qualities of the airplane, the fundamental principles of design have not been departed from, but those things have been incorporated that have been neglected in the present day plane."[8] It is quite obvious that the Starling was a continuation of the line of biplanes designed by Hickman in the past.[9]

The first Starling was sold and the new owner land-

ed it in a tree. Hickman and Eugene Roggeman bought the airplane back and rebuilt it at Robbinsdale airport, selling it a second time.

As soon as the first aircraft had been completed, Hickman announced plans to build a float version. A second Starling aircraft was started in 1929, this one a larger, closed-cabin monoplane with the designation of H-12 and called the Starling Imperial Monoplane. It was to seat four in addition to the pilot, and was to be powered with a Wright J-5 engine. There is some evidence that this plane was built, used for promotional photos, and then test flown by Gene Shank. It was said to have been wrecked when the engine quit during its test flight, though some claim it was damaged when it hit a snowbank while taxiing.

Unable to find a ready market for either airplane, Starling's financial backing ran out. Thus, with two airplanes built, and no approved type certificate received, the company went bankrupt. Hickman did not slow his own efforts, however. In 1931 he constructed a parasol monoplane with a Ford "A" engine. It was registered with the state as the H-20, but photos clearly show it painted with the designation H-21. Its identification was 593W. Hickman's numbering system is not clear, for, in 1932, he registered an H-16, OX-5 powered biplane, identified as 371 on the Minnesota register.

In 1932, Hickman also opened a flight school at Wold-Chamberlain. He then commenced to construct a racing plane with a Cirrus engine, built to specifications for a category of racing planes, all powered by Cirrus engines, popular in that day. Unfortunately, this plane, too, was wrecked on the way to participate in its first race in Kentucky.

Hickman stayed in Minnesota long enough to become involved with the CPT program, then, following the war, moved back to his hometown in Kansas.

Thorwald "Thunder" Johnson stands alongside the Orville Hickman-designed H-22 Cirrus racer at Robbinsdale Airport in 1934. (Ed Croft)

114

The Akerman T-1 tailless aircraft. Good photo shows the wingtip rudders at the time of its flight test in 1937. (Minnesota Historical Society)

AERONAUTICAL ENGINEERS

Mention should be made of Professor John D. Akerman, the head of the Aeronautical Engineering Department of the University of Minnesota.

While working for the Mohawk Company in 1928, Akerman was invited by University engineering school Dean, Ora M. Leland, to lecture to engineering students on aircraft design. A few such aircraft design classes had previously been taught at the school by Charles Boehnlein. At that time, there were very few universities across the nation that listed aviation courses in the curricula. In 1930, Akerman became the head of a new division of the engineering school, the Aeronautical Engineering Department. His head was full of remarkable ideas.

Akerman taught the theory of aerodynamics, leaving structures, engines, propeller design, airship theory, meteorology, and navigation to other instructors. In 1932, Howard W. Barlow joined the staff, which consisted of Boehnlein, B. J. Robertson, and Joe E. Wise. The balloonist, Dr. Jean Piccard, became a member of the faculty a few years later.

Akerman promoted a flying club within the Department; took part in the research on cellophane balloons with Piccard; assigned the construction of two airplanes as classwork; and with Barlow, designed a raceplane for nationally-known air-racer, Colonel Roscoe Turner. Turner not only set the American landplane speed record with the plane, but won two Thompson Trophy races as well.

Akerman designed a tailless airplane in the year

The lab of the University of Minnesota Aeronautical Engineering School, 1935. Projects are sandwiched tightly together. Note the "Buzzy" is under construction at center. (University of Minnesota)

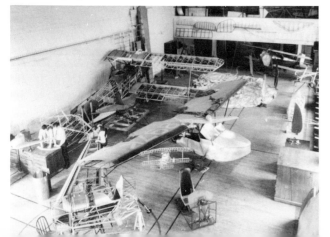

Professor John Akerman's JA-8 "Buzzy" of 1935. Professor Ackerman and his wife are in the cockpit. "Buzzy" was her nickname also. (Roy Pagel)

1934, and it was built over the course of the next few years by aero engineering students and flown in 1937. It was registered in the state as the Akerman T-1, with a Jacobs L-3 three-cylinder 55 hp. motor. It weighed 675 lb. and had a short wingspan of 22 feet, with a length of only 9 feet. Rudders were placed at the wingtips, and the wing featured slots and flaps, quite novel for its day. It was claimed to have cost only $95 in materials, less the engine.

Only a single test flight was made by Akerman himself. Like so many other things, the university figured the liability involved with flying it was too great, and it became a permanent ground fixture until being donated to the Smithsonian Institution. It is today in storage at the Smithsonian's Silver Hill Storage Facility.

Akerman also designed a high-wing, pusher-type airplane in 1935. It was not entirely different from the Curtiss Pusher, Jr. which had been around for several years. Nicknamed the "Buzzy" (also Akerman's wife's nickname), it was registered as the JA-8 and issued experimental license X-89K. A Szekely engine was mounted for power. The aircraft was constructed and perhaps even flew, but many details of this airplane are yet to be uncovered.

Along with Akerman, another aeronautical engineer should be mentioned. William B. Stout was a native of Illinois, but as a youth in the 1920s, came to Mankato. He moved to St. Paul, where he attended Mechanic Arts High School. He became adept at wood carving with a whittling knife and other tools, and built many of his own toys. After graduation, he built a cabin at White Bear Lake, and constructed some of the furniture for it, himself. During the middle 1920s, he attended the University of Minnesota, where he studied aeronautical engineering. Stout started building "screwball machines," as he put it, and applying for patents. He taught two years at Winona State Teacher's College, and began writing "how-to" articles, about building toys, for various magazines.

He also began writing a column for the *St. Paul Dispatch* about whittling toys, using the pen name Jack Kneiff. The column was so successful that Stout earned enough money to travel abroad, and visited Europe where he got the idea to write about aviation. Returning to the U. S., he went to work in the design department of a Detroit auto manufacturer, but soon left, and during the next year or so, moved from company to company, all the time studying the technicalities of aircraft design. He came to champion the cause of single-winged airplanes, or monoplanes, and advocated the use of the cantilever wing with no outside struts or wires. Stout was involved in the design of the first corrugated aluminum passenger plane, and, working with Henry Ford, helped produce the famed Ford Trimotor.

Stout didn't look like an engineer, rather the stereotypical inventor with his tiny moustache and wire-rimmed glasses. He was a skillful writer, with the ability to clarify the most complex thoughts regarding technical intricacies of his inventions. He was also a gifted illustrator, which added to his ability to put an idea across. In addition to these skills, Stout was also an accomplished speaker.

Minnesotans can call Stout one of their own when recalling his Jack Kneiff columns, and the fact that he took all of his schooling in Minnesota, graduating from the University of Minnesota before starting his professional career as a design engineer.

HOMEBUILDERS AND INVENTORS

It would be unlikely that, in any sized book, one could cover the activities of all of Minnesota's homebuilders, even if it were possible to find records indicating who they all were! A few excerpts are appropriate regarding some of the better-known individuals.

Generally regarded as Minnesota's most important designer and homebuilder, is Bernard H. Pietenpol. Perhaps the most loved, most often quoted, most prolific, and self-taught engineer, Pietenpol was, and remains, the inspiration of generations of Minnesota homebuilders. His career in building airplanes spanned the period 1923 until the 1980s.

Born in Spring Valley, Minnesota, Pietenpol moved with his family, first to North Dakota at age ten, then, four years later, to Hutchinson, Minnesota, where he found a job as an auto mechanic. At age nineteen, he moved to Cherry Grove, which would become his home for life. There, he built a hangar, created his airplane designs, and maintained his own airfield. Although he had only a ninth grade education, Pietenpol had a high degree of mechanical savvy, and a keen, observing eye.

Pietenpol's aircraft-building career began in 1923, when he designed his first small biplane. Because aircraft engines of the day were expensive, and Ford Model T engines were rather plentiful, and reasonable in cost, the plane got a Model T engine.

A Model A Ford-powered Pietenpol. This example, built in 1936 by Allen Rudolph of Wisconsin, was made from a Pietenpol-supplied kit. (Gary Hanson)

1931. Nineteen year old Orrin Hoopman stands with the original Pietenpol Sky Scout. He bought the plane from Bernard Pietenpol following a Modern Mechanics magazine article. (Orrin Hoopman)

He then set about teaching himself to fly it.

Pietenpol taught himself to fly by trial and error, during which time, he continually banged up, and rebuilt the airplane. He finally washed it out completely, on a cross-windy day. He simply did not know how to flare for a landing. Years later, his brother-in-law described Pietenpol's first flights to interested homebuilders, by indicating that Bernard would go up 50 feet and come back down 75. Pietenpol realized he needed help, and took several hours of dual instruction in a Jenny, from a local pilot.

Pietenpol's second airplane, built in 1926, was a Gnome-engined biplane which didn't fly very well. A third airplane was designed and built in 1928. It was a parasol-winged airplane, powered by an "Ace" engine. The Ace had four cylinders, sixteen-valves, and an aluminum block. About this time, the Ford Model A car and engine arrived on the scene. Pietenpol decided he would build an airplane to use the Model A engine.

Pietenpol bought all of a local Ford dealer's sample parts and assembled an engine, reworking the former, Ace-powered airplane into a two-seater that would become known as the "Air Camper."

The first Air Camper flew in 1929, and many more would follow. In 1930, Pietenpol read an editorial in a magazine stating that the use of automobile engines in aircraft was impractical and would never work. The magazine, *Modern Mechanics and Inventions*, was a prestigious monthly, that catered to do-it-yourself inventors, mechanics, builders, and science-minded readers of all ages. Pietenpol immediately got in contact with the editor, E. L. Weston Farmer, and told him that the idea was wrong. Farmer challenged him to put-up or shut-up. So Pietenpol and another builder-flyer, Donald Finke, flew two Air Campers from Cherry Grove to Minneapolis' Robbinsdale Airport under marginal weather conditions to prove the efficacy of the auto engined airplane.

Farmer was delighted, realizing that he had uncovered new material for the magazine, and publicized the feat in the next issue of Modern Mechanics. Pietenpol and his friends were deluged with calls and letters requesting plans. Pietenpol had not expected the need for plans when he originally sketched out the wing's airfoil shape on his shop floor, or when he laid out the Air Camper's first fuselage. With the help of neighbor, Orrin Hoopman, a simple set of plans were drawn up, copies made, and sent as requested. The price was $7. 50 per set. Modern Mechanics

116

Wally Hanson stands in front of his Model A Pietenpol in 1935. (Ken Muxlow)

magazine then decided to run the plans in the 1932 edition of their popular, *Flying and Glider Manual*, and with Pietenpol's permission, drew up a more detailed set of plans, which were published in the Manual. By mutual agreement, Pietenpol and Hoopman agreed not to sell any more of the original plans.

The original plans offered some basic directions: "Go to lumber yard and buy materials for the Air Camper and then watch the papers for a yard-goods sale and purchase several bed sheets." Other information included: "Find a new 55 gallon oil drum, cut out the top and bottom for making fittings. This is 1020 steel." Pietenpol designed the plane to be easy to build, safe for the cow-pasture pilot, and inexpensive. In fact, every part of the plane was readily available from hardware store, lumber yard, or auto junkyard. The airplane became so popular that, in following years, Pietenpol began offering kits to homebuilders, so that they could make up their own components, one at a time, then assemble them into an airplane. Or they could purchase already built-up components from Pietenpol and build their own airplane a little quicker.

From Pietenpol's brochure, (exact date unknown, but circa l937), a few packages are listed:
Kit No. 1. All material for building complete set of ribs...$8.50
Kit No. 2. All material for building complete tail unit, less metal fittings ....$9.00.
Kit No. 3. All spruce, plywood, nails, glue, white ash, etc. All materials marked or cut to size for building complete fuselage, less metal fittings...........$28.00.

The Georgia Special in 1930. At this time, it was registered to Herb Hecker and the Lawrence engine is running. (Vern Georgia)

Kit No. 4. All leading and trailing edges, aileron beams, wing tips, compression struts, for building wing, less ribs and wing beams $14.00
Complete set of ribs.......................................$14.00
Built up tail unit $12.50
Built up fuselage..$45.00
Set wing beams (spars)...................................$20.00
Landing gear, complete with fittings............$28.00

Along with the interest in the Air Camper, the magazine received inquiries as to whether the more plentiful Model T Ford engine could be used in the Air Camper. When Pietenpol answered these inquiries, he indicated that the engine was not powerful enough for a two-place aircraft. That answer brought up the obvious request: why not design a single-place airplane for the Model T engine? Thus was born the Pietenpol "Sky Scout," plans for which appeared in the 1933 edition of *Flying and Glider Manual*. The Sky Scout was a scaled-down version of the Air Camper. Both had all-wooden, parasol wings and fuselage structures, with glued and nailed joints. The wing was one piece, from tip to tip, the Sky Scout version being somewhat lighter, and fitted with a hinged flap at the trailing edge, which flipped up, allowing the pilot easier entrance and exit of the cockpit.

Pietenpol died in 1984, but not before spreading his gospel of hard work and genius, across the country. His career was summarized quite well by author, Bob Whittier, writing about Bernard Pietenpol in the April, 1969, issue of *Sport Aviation*: "As to the Man, after seeing where he lived and what he had accomplished, working largely alone and isolated from the rush and bustle of commercial aviation, I could not help but reflect on what an impressive object lesson he is to those who explain away the emptiness of their lives, by the the excuse, 'I never had a chance.'"[10]

Pietenpol's airplanes have retained a popularity to this day; almost every airshow or exhibition witnesses the attendance of one or two examples. In 1987, the original hangar from Pietenpol Field at Cherry Grove, was moved to Oshkosh, Wisconsin, where it was re-erected at Pioneer Airfield, on the grounds of the EAA Museum. It stands in tribute to one of Minnesota's, and the country's, leading home builders. Pietenpol is also a member of the Minnesota Aviation Hall of Fame.

Another local designer whose work appeared in the pages of *Modern Mechanics Magazine*, was Vern

Another view of the Georgia Special. Vern Georgia is in the cockpit. (Vern Georgia)

Georgia. Georgia was a Bloomington youth, who got the flying bug from Speed Holman. As school chums, they took an interest in similar things, mostly mechanical. When Speed started to fly, so did Vern. Though Georgia's career didn't take off in the same direction as Speed's, Georgia kept his interest in flying by building his own airplane in 1929.

He and a neighbor, Herb Hecker, whose sister, Adeline, would eventually become Georgia's wife, borrowed the use of the Hecker farm shed and began constructing a parasol-winged flying machine. For power, Georgia found a Lawrence motorcycle engine, and decided to "soup it up" before installing it in the airplane. The search for a more efficient carburetor and crankshaft was never successful, and the plane did not fly while Georgia owned it. Weston Farmer, of *Modern Mechanics Magazine* took an interest in the design, despite the fact that the airplane had not flown up to that time, and asked Georgia if the publishing company could draw up plans for it, and publish them. Georgia agreed. Unfortunately, when the plans were published in the 1931 edition of the *Flying and Glider Manual*, no credit was given to Vern Georgia. Instead, Orville Hickman, who had originally welded up the fuselage for Georgia, was comissioned to draw up the plans and write the story. The story was written as if Hickman had designed and built the airplane entirely by himself. Never-the-less, the name "Georgia's Special" stayed with the design.

The plane, itself, was a single seater, and, as drawn by Hickman, the plans called for a Clark Y-15 airfoil. The original plane was in Herb Hecker's name in 1930, and photos of it indicate that the Lawrence engine did run at that time. Hickman later called the engine a Lawrence-Hickman and the plans indicated that it had been fitted with a double-throw crankshaft, which apparently balanced the engine better than the original, and offered smoother operation.

When Hecker wanted to sell the plane without Georgia's approval, Georgia removed the wheels so it couldn't be moved. Hecker disposed of it anyway, in 1931, selling it to the Robbins brothers of Paynesville.[11]

A third Minnesota designer to have his aircraft featured in the pages of the *Modern Mechanics Magazine*, was George "Bud" Gere, Jr., (pronounced Gear). Published in October and November of 1932, plans for the Gere Sport Biplane featured rugged strength with low weight. It omitted curved wingtips because they were time-consuming for the amateur to build. Fitted with a Ford Model A engine similar to Pietenpol's airplanes, Gere allowed for the radiator's water tank reservoir to be installed in the center section of the wing. Modern Mechanics article writer, Douglas Rolfe, advocated installing the fuel tank alongside it for better balance. The plane was designed to fit the Chevrolet or Ford automobile engines of the day and the prototype ship flew with a 40-hp. Chevrolet four-cylinder, water-cooled engine.

Gere had other sport hobbies as well, one of which was ice boating. During the Fall of 1932, he had a Le Rhone-engined ice boat, nicknamed "Icicle," that he used to zip around on White Bear Lake. He kept the iceboat tied down on shore between excursions,

and generally propped its skis off the ice on 2x4's to keep them from freezing in. With his aircraft well under construction, and articles appearing in *Modern Mechanics Magazine*, Gere stepped out one afternoon to spend a few hours racing around the lake in the ice boat.

He hand-propped the engine to start it, and let it idle for a few minutes, then reached down to lift the runners off the planks. When he couldn't move them with a slight tug, he applied more effort and lost his balance, falling into the propeller. He was killed instantly.

The Gere sport airplane was finished by Gere's father and some of his friends, and test flown by Elmore Wall, a local pilot from Wold-Chamberlain. Shortly afterward, the aircraft was donated to the University of Minnesota to be used by the students of the aeronautical engineering department for training purposes. The design is rumored to have become the basis for the EAA Biplane, introduced by Paul Poberezny, many years later.

Pietenpol, Georgia, and Gere, were not the first Minnesotans to build their own airplanes, of course. The very first pilots to fly in the state; A. C. Bennett and Ralph Wilcox, Fred Parker, Alex Heine, Otto Timm, etc. , had all built their own aircraft. Each early homebuilder did have his day in the spotlight, and generally a feature story appeared in the newspaper.

For example, the *Minneapolis Sunday Tribune* of 14 May, 1922, portrays a "June-Bug Aerial Flivver" built by H. J. Smith of Minneapolis, as it is about to be tested by Ray Miller at the State Fairgrounds. (Editor's note. The location is more likely Curtiss-Northwest Airport.) The plane looked much like a bathtub with a pole sticking out behind it, on which flimsy-looking tail surfaces were mounted. For power, it was fitted with a two cylinder engine of 30 hp. and featured such novel equipment as a child's tricycle wheel for a tailwheel, and an auto innertube tied to the wheel axle with string for a shock absorber. It is not known if it ever flew, for tests were postponed until the day after the article, due to the engine not working properly and the tailwheel breaking.

Often, well-known, (and very self-confident), pilots were asked to make test flights in these new creations. In 1927, Speed Holman tested a homebuilt

Elmer Bowman poses in front of his unfinished homebuilt. Note the high position of the canard wing atop the nose. Circa 1940. (R. W. Kaplan)

14 May, 1932. Ray Miller aboard the "June Bug Aerial Flivver" of H. J. Smith, a 23-year old engineering student at the University of Minnesota. (Air Guard/Ray Miller collection)

The MacRae homebuilt at Grove City, Minnesota in 1927. Note the Jenny tail and wheels. The Le Rhone rotary engine hardly seems big enough to power the plane, but it was flown many times. (Ted Gruenhagen)

specimen constructed by twenty-three year old Frederick Trump, a student of engineering at the University of Minnesota. The plane featured a wingspan of 19 feet, and was powered by a 28 hp. Lawrence motorcycle engine. At 300 pounds, the machine hardly weighed more than the test pilot. Holman took the single-seater aircraft up for a successful test flight and told Trump that it was a good flying machine, but needed more power and a little more rudder area. Having enjoyed himself, Holman, Mr. Trump, and the tiny machine, were photographed in front of a "big" Northwest Airways Stinson Detroiter aircraft for a contrast in sizes.

"Unique" was the word for the Flying Bathtub designed by W. H. Ramsey of Minneapolis. In 1931, Ramsey came up with the idea for a side-by-side, two-seater tub, suspended beneath parasol wings and a cantilevered steel tube empennage which held the tail surfaces. The plane had an Aeronca, two-cylinder, 30 hp. engine that was perched on a pedestal atop the nose, just in front of the occupants. The ship did fly from Wold-Chamberlain Field, though the test pilot's name and the disposition of the airplane is not known.

Al Schauss has gained the title of Minnesota's Homebuilder Emeritus. His career sparkles with aircraft after aircraft produced at home, using his personal craftsmanship.

Schauss was another mechanically minded, inventive young man. As a youth on the farm, he devised a clever corn-sheller as an easier way to do his daily labor. He came to the big city of Minneapolis and studied everything he could find on airplanes. He taught himself the art of welding, and began designing and building his first airplane. Schauss carved and built his first propeller for that airplane. He comments, "In 1929, I was building my first plane from scratch, a high wing monoplane with a 9-cylinder radial Salmson engine. I started with a few drawings, didn't know what a weight and balance was, never had it on a scale. I figured my moments (center of gravity) with a pencil and paper, no calculator. It flew hands-off the first time. My pastor often asked me if I couldn't figure a better way to commit suicide."[12]

Though Schauss didn't know how to fly at that point, he enlisted the aid of Wally Neuman to test-fly the airplane, and then, because the plane flew so well, had Neuman teach him to fly. Schauss moved the plane to Oxboro airport, where he flew many hours in his creation before it burned in a hangar fire. Schauss started on his next project, immediately. This time he designed a single place biplane. It's motor was to be a three-cylinder Anzani engine of 35 hp., but it was soon replaced with a Szekely engine. The plane flew well and was sold to an itinerant pilot. The new owner was involved in a fatal accident with it, on his initial flight.

By 1935, Schauss was already building his third airplane; this one a two-place closed-cabin biplane which he called the "Schauss Sport." He installed an 85 hp. Ford V-8 engine with a gearbox that reduced the rpms. to propeller speed. He carved another homemade propeller for it. This ship had all the earmarks of being a best-seller, so Schauss had Professor John Akerman of the University make a stress analysis of the airframe and wings. With help from Ed Lampman, Schauss made presentations to various businessmen seeking the financing needed to put the plane into production. Unfortunately, Lampman died at a crucial point in the proceedings, and no financing source developed. Quantity production plans were dropped.

Schauss then rebuilt the "Sport" as a three-place airplane, and hung a 7-cylinder, 85 hp. Le Blond radial engine on it. This improved the looks of the plane, and the performance as well. The Schauss Sport ended its days, set afire by vandals.

Schauss built a Volmer amphibian in 1965, and, though he no longer owns it, still flies the plane on occasion, as of this writing. He continues to carve propellers for homebuilders and ice boats.[13]

Elmer Bowman, of Owatonna, designed and constructed three homebuilt airplanes over the years. His first was a Curtiss-Robin replica, built from his own plans about 1930. He had gone to Minneapolis many

The Paschke homebuilt with OX-5 engine. It's similarity to a Pietenpol is only coincidental, since in 1928, Pietenpol's planes had yet to make their appearance. (Ed Sampson)

Al Schauss' first homebuilt, shown in 1931. Schauss is at the controls, running up the 120 hp. Salmson engine at Wold-Chamberlain Field. (Al Schauss)

times and carefully studied the airplanes at Wold-Chamberlain and other fields around the Twin Cities. He then drew his own plans and produced his airplane. To power the plane, he purchased an OX-5 engine from Marvin Northrop.

Not satisfied with his first effort, Bowman built a second airplane similar to the first, but including improvements. This plane was highly successful and Bowman took up barnstorming. He calculated that he carried between thirty five hundred and four thousand passengers from 1931 to 1935.[14]

Bowman's last creation was a tailless airplane with a canard forward wing and tricycle gear. This airplane, developed and constructed just before the war, was never flown. The beginning of the war had put an end to civilian flying as well as the supply of engines.

Paul and Ted Paschke were farm youths from an area west of Hancock, Minnesota. In 1928, they built their own aircraft, which looked a lot like an oversized Pietenpol. Like so many others, it was powered by an OX-5 engine, and accumulated fifteen trouble-free hours of flying, when it met a strange fate. Paul had it up for a flight one day, and when coming in for a routine landing, encountered one of the farm's large pigs that had wandered out onto the runway. The plane was smashed, and, though Paul did not get hurt, the airplane was a washout.

The brothers then began building a Pietenpol, but before they were finished, Paul purchased a Waco 9. They gave up the building and concentrated afterward on flying.

In Grove City, Minnesota, Walter C. McRae had studied aircraft plans from the magazines of 1925 and 1926, such as *Popular Aviation*. McRae was an auto mechanic of some reputation and gathered friends who were enthusiastic about flying, promising them that, if they would help him construct an airplane - when it was finished - they would all get a chance to fly it. The young men jumped at the opportunity, making several trips to the Twin Cities for parts from Marvin Northrop's company.

To speed things up, McRae purchased the tail and landing gear from a Jenny, and blended them into the final airplane. After close scrutiny of the shapes of airfoils of other aircraft wings, he sketched out his wing's airfoil on a piece of wallboard in his garage.

Since McRae's and his friends had no flying ex-

Al Schauss second homebuilt, a 1932 biplane, powered by a 3-cylinder Szekely engine. (Al Schauss)

perience, they asked Fred Whittemore, of Northwest Airways, to test-fly the airplane. The test flight proved the airplane airworthy, though a bit tail-heavy with the Jenny tail. Some adjustments were made and a brand-new Le Rhone engine purchased from Northrop. The plane was flown again and again. It was shown to the public in 1927 during a weekend air show at Grove City, often called the *First All-Minnesota Air Derby*. After the plane was demonstrated by Whittemore, it was left unattended for the duration of the show. Newspaper accounts state that it was picked to pieces by spectators.[15]

One of the eager young workers on the McRae airplane was Ted Gruenhagen of Minneapolis. McRae was going through a divorce at the time, and for his hard work and friendship with McRae, the airplane was eventually given to Gruenhagen. He patched it up, and had it re-test-flown by the Mohawk company test pilot, George A. MacDonald. Over the next few months, the plane was flown by many persons, including Art Sampson and Gus Imm. Sampson liked it. His comment on its performance was, "Man, can you haul coal with this."[16]

In the late summer of 1928, MacDonald was going to ferry the plane from Grove City to Robbinsdale Airport, but had to wait out a storm. He, Gruenhagen, and several others who had driven up, tied the airplane to a fencepost and retired until the blow was over. Upon their return following the storm, they found the aircraft had been torn loose from its moorings and rolled, end over end, across the field. The

The Ford V-8 powered Schauss-Lampman Special of 1935, with enclosed cabin and Schauss' custom-built propeller. Schauss later replaced the V-8 with a 7-cylinder, 85 hp., LeBlond engine. The plane, planned for quantity production, never made it, but provided plenty of flying for Schauss and others until 1941. (Al Schauss)

A Mead Primary Glider on the Don Braun family dairy farm near St. Cloud in l932. Don is at the controls. (Don Braun)

adventure was over.

Andrew Anderson of Rollag, Minnesota, started building an airplane in 1931, after having studied books and magazines for several years. His airplane had a look similar to that of an American Eagle, and was powered by the same, available, OX-5 engine. In 1932, the plane was test flown by Roy Boggs, from the Wahpeton School of Sciences in North Dakota. He stated that it behaved beautifully. This airplane survived, and was acquired by the Antique Airplane Association's *Airpower Museum* in 1977, and is displayed at Blakesburg, Iowa.

Mention should be made of Burton Nieman. Nieman was a colorful character, a radiator repairman whose avocations were professional wrestling and building airplanes. Nieman built a low-winged, tricycle-geared airplane, which he registered as the "Bertster," but most of the airport crowd nicknamed the "Gooney Bird." Though a clever inventive person, Nieman was not a fine craftsman. Stories of his workmanship indicate that his welding was crude, and the finish of his work, rough and make-do.

Though the work was suspect, Nieman, himself, had no qualms about flying his airplane. To make his first flights, he borrowed a propeller from Ray Haberman, who had spent many hours hand carving it. Not long after, Nieman cracked up the plane, escaping with only slight injuries, but totally demolishing Haberman's beautiful prop.

Undaunted by a record of questionable

Burt Nieman and his ram-jet helicopter in 1958. Though this photo is from a period later than this book portrays, the photo is significant of Nieman's creations. Note the auto engine drive shaft to the rear wheels and the complete rotor blade mechanism overhead. (Ken Muxlow)

The 1931 Mead glider of Al and Matt Slettedahl hangs in the Hawley Falls Clay County Historical Society Museum. (Matt Slettedahl)

achievements, Nieman built himself a ram-jet powered helicopter with the jet units on the ends of the rotor blades. He designed the vehicle to be roadable, as well as flyable, using an Oldsmobile automobile engine to drive the rear wheels and spin up the rotor. The strange car-helicopter could be seen driving the city streets in home movie footage taken by friends. When he tried to run the ram-jets, Nieman discovered that they did not work at the slow blade speeds used for flight. It is rumored that Nieman hopped the machine off the ground on its only flight and landed on a neighbor's garage.

Another of the local flyers whose inventive mind sought out improvements to the equipment of the 1930s, was John Hallman. Hallman felt that the performance of the standard Pietenpol powerplant, the Model A Ford engine, was marginal. True, it provided ample power to carry two persons, but like the Piper Cub, the plane owed much of its performance to a high-lift wing. Hallman decided to cast an aluminum engine block and heads to make a lighter engine. Along with that, he created cast iron cylinders that were finned to provide air-cooling. Not only lighter in weight than the Ford, the air-cooled cylinders enabled Hallman to do away with the heavy and cumbersome radiator and water-cooling system of the Ford.

A wooden mold model was built at the *Serley Manufacturing Company*, with an aluminum master model then cast from it. The master was then cleaned up and used as a pattern for casting each final unit by the *Midwest Foundry* in St. Paul. Cylinder heads followed the same routine. Cylinder barrels were cast by the *Pure Foundry*. The several parts of the engine were assembled using long bolts to anchor the heads, cylinders, and block together. The rocker arm system was taken from a 4-cylinder Chevrolet engine.

Unfortunately, Hallman had not allowed enough space between the cylinders, and the proximity of one to the next, provided insufficient air circulation. The increase in performance was less than expected. Bernard Pietenpol flew with this engine several times and claimed he never landed while it was still running.

Gordon Kindlein admired the Hallman modifications, and decided that he could perfect the system even more. He borrowed the Hallman mold, and cast his own aluminum block, machined his own cast iron cylinders, and went a step farther. He designed and machined an overhead valve mechanism that he felt would further increase the performance. Kindlein, too, was stymied by the closeness of the cylinders, and eventually abandoned his experiments. His eventual solution to the performance problem was to install a more powerful, five-cylinder, Le Blond air-cooled engine in his airplane.

Hallman built several other engines from the same castings. He built one example with the original Ford engine block simply cut across under the cylinders and water jackets, adding his finned cylinders and heads. Both Kindlein and Hallman had used the original Ford crankshaft, camshaft, and pistons in their modifications. One of Hallman's engines was shipped to Johannesburg, South Africa, and two others, still extant, belong to the EAA Museum at Oshkosh, Wisconsin, and Forrest Lovley of Jordan, Minnesota.[17]

Hallman's inventive talents also were demonstrated in his development and manufacture of a variable-pitch aluminum propeller. Small airfoil sections mounted on the top surfaces of the blades, worked to change blade pitch as engine speed was increased or decreased, providing either takeoff or cruise performance automatically.

Several builders constructed homemade gliders. One pair of St. Cloud residents, Ray Russell and Chet Heinzel, built a primary glider from plans purchased from the *Mead Company* of Chicago. The glider was flown many times in 1931, and so enthused Don Braun, another St. Cloudite, that he built a second copy from the same plans. Braun taught himself to fly his glider, having it launched into the air by a rope tied to a speeding car.

Braun's experiences in the glider led him to become an avid aviation enthusiast. He went to work for the *Alexander Aircraft Company* in Colorado, then the *Stinson Company* in Detroit. He went on to join the Canadian Air Force, flew as a ferry pilot and later became a bush pilot in Canada. One of his proudest moments was to land at the North Pole in 1967.

Another Mead Glider was constructed in 1931 by Alvin and Matt Slettedahl of Granite Falls. They answered a printed advertisement for the glider that offered, "$15 starts you. The regular knock-down kit, $89.50, complete, can now be purchased in installments of six convenient self-sufficient groups.... there is no guesswork: You know in advance that your ship will give you gliding at its best."[18] The Slettedahl glider is still around, and is displayed in the Clay County Historical Society Museum at Hawley Falls, Minnesota.

Mention has been made of other inventors and builders elsewhere in this book. Those portrayed in

The Burkholdt homebuilt aircraft at the Minneapolis Aeronautical Show at the Minneapolis Armory in 1927. Details on this aircraft are sketchy, but the plane was built by brothers, Fred and Sanford Burkholdt and appears to have Model A Ford engine. (James LaVake)

this chapter have made outstanding contributions to the historical record of aviation in Minnesota. Our salute to the hundreds of unheralded builders who also developed their own aircraft, and gave of their genius for the advancement of flight.

Homegrown Aircraft   Documentation

[1] Joseph P. Juptner, *US Civil Aircraft*, Aero Publishers, Los Angeles, CA, 1962, Volume One, ATC #95, page 234.
[2] Ibid. Volume One, ATC #95, page 234; Volume Three, ATC #263, page 182; Volume Three, ATC #297, page 276.
[3] Interview with Bertram Ritchie by Noel Allard, 18 September, 1975.
[4] Contract between Captain Hoseas Mohlar and Hyacinth Ravely, 4 May, 1928, copy in possession of author.
[5] William E. Lovelace, unpublished manuscript, History of the Northstar Aircraft Company, St. Cloud, MN, 1988.
[6] Ibid.
[7] Telephone interview with Norman Nelson Sr. by Noel Allard, 30 September, 1987.
[8] Starling Aircraft ad, *Aero Digest*, circa 1929.
[9] Al Kelch, "Orville Hickman, Aircraft Designer," *Vintage Airplane*, EAA publication, December, 1977.
[10] Bob Whittier, "A Visit To B. H. Pietenpol," *Sport Aviation*, EAA publication, April 1969.
[11] Interview with Vern Georgia by Noel Allard, 18 October, 1974.
[12] Al Schauss, speech before the Minnesota Seaplane Pilot's Safety Seminar, Gull Lake, 10 May, 1986.
[13] Norm Peterson, "Homebuilder Emeritus, 'Al' Schauss," *Sport Aviation*, EAA publication, March, 1986.
[14] Interview with Elmer Bowman by Noel Allard, 21 August, 1987.
[15] Undated newspaper clipping from Ted Gruenhagen collection, circa 1927.
[16] Interview with Ted Gruenhagen by Noel Allard, 27 March, 1986.
[17] Interview with Ray Haberman by Noel Allard, 16 October, 1989.
[18] Mead Glider ad, *National Power Glider Magazine*, December, 1930, page 12.

FIVE

1920s — 1930s: AIRPORTS AND AIRMEN

WOLD-CHAMBERLAIN FIELD,
Background and Evolution

One would hardly think of crediting today's booming activity at Minneapolis-St. Paul International Airport, to the Indianapolis racetrack. Far-fetched; hard to draw a relationship? But, in fact, that is just the case!

In 1911, the auto racing world was justifiably thrilled when the great "Brickyard," the *Indianapolis Motor Speedway*, opened for business. The two-and-a-half-mile, brick-surfaced track, became the mecca for racing buffs during Memorial Day weekend. Seeing the great money being made, and the attention being drawn to Indianapolis, created the idea in the minds of certain Indianapolis and Twin City businessmen that the same could apply to this area. A large track built between Minneapolis and St. Paul, with competition at the other end of the summer calendar, a 500-mile auto race on Labor Day in September, would be highly profitable.

Accordingly, funds were subscribed in the next few years. President of the track association was F. H. Wheeler of Indianapolis, and general manager was J. F. Sperry of St. Paul. *The Twin City Motor Speedway* came into being near the military reservation of

Speedway Field, Minneapolis, circa 1920. The only indication of flying activity at the abandoned auto racetrack is the Security Aircraft Company's hangar, built on the concrete of the west straightaway, 34th Avenue runs across the bottom of the picture and 66th Street runs vertically at right. Note the three Air Guard hangars and the airmail hangar in the middle of the field. (Minnesota Historical Society)

Fort Snelling, at the confluence of the Minnesota and Mississippi rivers. The land designated, was located between 60th and 66th Streets on the southern edge of Minneapolis, and between 34th and 46th Avenues. Here, a gleaming concrete oval racetrack was built, two miles around, 87 feet wide, with banked turns steeper than those at Indianapolis. Grandstands were erected to hold 30,000 spectators, with bleachers for another 30,000, along with nineteen garages, (numbered from one to twenty, unlucky thirteen was omitted), a timing building, a huge scoreboard, pit area, and three reinforced underpass tunnels to the infield.[1]

The first event was set for Labor Day, 4 September, 1915. It was billed as a showdown between American-manufactured Stutz and Dusenberg automobiles, and the European Mercedes and Peugeots. Fourteen cars qualified for the race, piloted by the leading drivers of the day. Ralph DePalma, driving the same Mercedes in which he had won the Indianapolis race just a few months before, headlined the field. He was followed by Dario Resta, driving a Peugeot, who placed second in the same event. Resta would win the 1916 Indianapolis. Stutzes were driven by Gil Anderson and Earl Cooper. The great Barney Oldfield started in a Delage. He had a young co-driver, yet unknown, by the name of Eddie Rickenbacker. Within three years, Eddie would become America's aerial Ace of Aces in the Great War. It was Rickenbacker who set the track record, in practice, of 114 miles per hour, quite respectable for 1915. Rickenbacker's time was the fastest ever recorded on the track.

Cooper won the event in a Stutz, one of only six cars

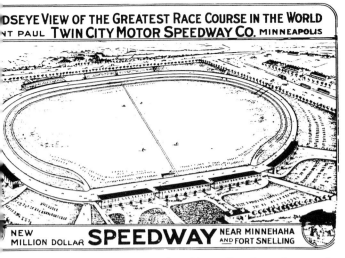

Drawing of original Twin City Motor Speedway from early publicity material (Gale Frost, Thunder In The North, 1980).

A racing car on the track of the Twin City Motor Speedway, 1915. In less than two years, the track would be abandoned and aircraft would take over the field. (Bob Adelman)

to finish, in the time of five hours and 47 minutes. The track, rough to begin with, had beaten the cars to pieces. The third place car finished with the riding mechanic having held up a broken suspension member with his bare hands for over 100 miles.

However exciting the opening race, it was doomed to be the only major speed event held at the track. The concrete, in some areas not steel-reinforced, and subject to the vagaries of Minnesota's climate, began to heave and break up. It was even charged that substandard materials and construction methods had been used by the contractors. The following year, one minor race was held on Memorial Day, another on the 4th of July, and there was no Labor Day event. The final race on the track was the American Red Cross Auto Derby on the 4th of July 1917.

Already, in 1916, bankruptcy proceedings had been started against the Speedway Corporation. In 1917, the grandstands and other structures were taken down, and the lumber sold to pay bills. At a sheriff's sale on 19 November, 1918, Mr. Guy Thomas bought the defunct facility, selling it three days later for $100,000 to the *Snelling Field Corporation*, of which he would become an officer.[2] The name was soon changed to *Snelling Field, Incorporated*.

At the same time that these proceedings were being carried out, a group of Twin Cities aviation enthusiasts, under the leadership of businessman Rufus J. Rand, had formed the *Aero Club of Minneapolis*. In 1917, the creation of such clubs was common across the United States, with progressive, forward-looking individuals thinking about future travel and business opportunities in aviation. This group would soon become involved with the Snelling Field.

By 1919, there were already some local airfields in operation, including the Earle Brown farm where Enos Ashley and Walter Bullock were operating; the Curtiss-Northwest airfield in St. Paul, operated by William Kidder; and the field in Fridley, north of Minneapolis, operated by Clarence Hinck. It was at that time that Wilbur and Weldon Larrabee constructed a hangar, right on the concrete straightaway of the abandoned Twin City Speedway. What better place, with literally miles of ready-made concrete floor available! They commenced to offer flight instruction, sight-seeing flights, and weekend airshows, along with sales of Canadian Curtiss Jenny's.

As poor a racetrack as the Twin City Motor Speedway had been, the area had all the makings of an excellent landing field. The 160 acres encircled by the track was, after all, quite level, its location near both cities...convenient, and the huge white oval, easily seen on a clear day, beckoned to pilots from as far off as forty miles. The Aero Club, by this time, had pinpointed Snelling Field--or Speedway Field as their choice for a proposed airport site.

In April of 1920, Aero Club members, and others, incorporated as the *Twin City Aero Corporation* with State senator, William F. Brooks, as president; J. G. Ordway of St. Paul as vice-president; John Mitchell, St. Paul banker, treasurer; and H. M. Gardner, then vice-president of the *Minneapolis Civic and Commerce Association*, as secretary. The corporation made arrangements to lease the speedway property from Snelling Field, Incorporated.[3]

Also, in April of 1920, the U. S. Congress sanctioned the establishment of an airmail line between the Twin Cities and Chicago, and appointed as Superintendent of Air Mail, C. F. Egge, who was stationed in Minneapolis. By May, both Minneapolis and St. Paul had subscribed a total of $30,000, pledged to the Twin City Aero Corporation to assure the completion of a government-required hangar. It was built and ready for the first airmail flight on 10 August, 1920.

The hangar was 80 x 90 feet in size, and located in the northeast quarter of the racetrack's infield. A military Martin MB-2 bomber, piloted by Walter Smith, flew in the first load of 30,000 letters from Chicago. It was accompanied from Hastings by a Curtiss Oriole, piloted by Lieutenant Ray Miller of the Minnesota National Guard, and an Avro trainer flown by Wilbur Larrabee. An airshow marked the event. It was at this show that a young apprentice mechanic from Larrabee's *Security Aircraft Company*, Charles Holman, made one of his first parachute jumps.[4]

Though the airmail was officially suspended within a few months, the airfield had received its first major public attention.

Also in August, 1920, the U. S. Militia Bureau agreed to establish an Air National Guard unit at the field, contingent upon facilities being available. Thus, in early 1921, the State provided $45,000 for the construction of three hangars for the Guard, each 60x110 feet in size, constructed of wood, and built within the northern circle of the racetrack oval. The hangars were immediately put to use by the newly-formed

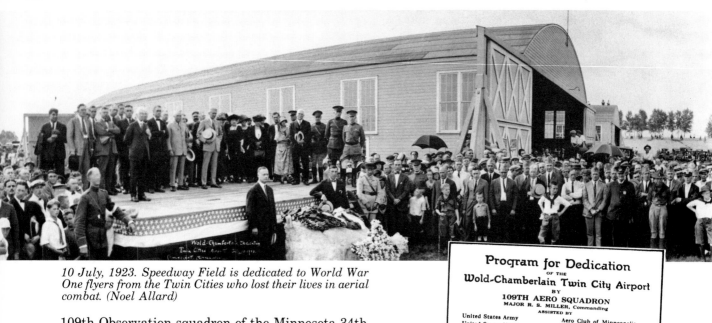

10 July, 1923. Speedway Field is dedicated to World War One flyers from the Twin Cities who lost their lives in aerial combat. (Noel Allard)

109th Observation squadron of the Minnesota 34th Infantry Division. (The Air Guard story appears in Chapter Seven of this book.)

The airfield itself was comprised of at least 100 acres of good landing area, with a useable length of 2700 feet along a northwest-southeast line, and 2300 feet available in the east-west direction.[5] The field came to be known as Speedway Field or Twin Cities Airport.

On 10 July, 1923, the airfield was dedicated to honor Ernest Groves Wold and Cyrus Foss Chamberlain, local pilots who had been killed in France during World War I. Wold was a 1st Lieutenant in the First Aero Squadron, killed in action 1 August, 1918 at Chateau Thierry, and Chamberlain, a Sergeant-Pilot in the Lafayette Flying Corps, was killed in aerial combat at the same place on 13 June, 1918.[6]

It was noted by the *Minneapolis Morning Tribune* of 11 July, 1923, that some 7,000 persons attended the dedication, with Eddie Rickenbacker among the distinguished guests. He was making his second appearance on the site, this time as an honored hero. He had arrived by rail, but the new 109th Air Guard did the flying salute overhead. Speaker, Dr. Marion D. Shutter, eulogized: "We stand uncovered today at the memory of those men, who, with broken wings, went down to disaster and death, like Wold and Chamberlain, and their comrades." A bronze tablet, affixed to a great boulder, was unveiled. It was intended to remain as a memorial near the Air Guard hangars. The boulder was moved to different locations on the airfield over time, resting in its final years in front of the Lindbergh Terminal. During 1991 reconstruction of the rampways between the terminal and parking ramp, the boulder was broken up and carried away. The bronze tablet was saved.

Since the airmail experiment of 1920 had ended so quickly, the public need for speedy airmail service resulted in increased pressure on the U. S. Department of Commerce to reopen the routes. An entrepreneur in Chicago, named Charles Dickenson, received the first federal rights to the airmail route between Chicago and the Twin Cities. His aircraft fleet was a collection of different models, his pilots, local flyers. When accidents and problems followed, one after the other, he petitioned the government to drop the route, and Twin City businessman, Colonel Lewis H. Brittin, took over. Brittin's company was called *The Northwest Airways, Inc.*, and it was granted the rights to take over Contract Airmail Route #9, (CAM 9).

Northwest Airways leased the old airmail hangar from Twin City Aero Corporation for $200 per month and set about a regular schedule of flights. Wold-Chamberlain was the westerly terminus, with stops at LaCrosse, Madison, Milwaukee, and Chicago at the east end.

Though the airport was to service both Minneapolis and St. Paul, cooperation between those two cities came to an end in 1926, when St. Paul undertook to develop an airport within its city limits, and near their Post Office, (one of the airmail requirements). This left Wold-Chamberlain as the municipal facility for Minneapolis alone. For the city formally to acquire the field, an agency with the legal power to acquire land would have to make the move. The only agency so empowered was the Minneapolis Park Board. President Brooks of the Aero Corporation was inclined simply to turn over the Corporation's options on the property to the Board, but things got complicated, and legal proceedings lagged.

The State Legislature passed an enabling act that

allowed city governments to acquire land for airports themselves, but limited the issuance of bonds for that purpose. Anxious to get on with the establishment of a field, the Park Board demanded the City Council to state whether it intended to exercise the option or not. When the Council said, "no," they also indicated that the Park Board should go ahead themselves.[7]

While these proceedings were taking place, Charles Lindbergh made his epic flight across the Atlantic to Paris and the public was imbued with an immediate sense of airmindedness. The *Minneapolis Civic and Commerce Association* appointed a committee of 100 members whose goal was to provide a sound municipal airport. Along with the *Twin City Aero Corporation*, and a newly formed chapter of the *National Aeronautics Association*, the committee of 100's urging of the Park Board to move ahead finally brought action. The Board initiated a development survey of the airport situation. On 1 August, 1927, the Twin City Aero Corp. defaulted on its lease and the property reverted to Snelling Field, Inc. Anticipating takeover of the land, the Park Board paid off the Snelling Field Corporation to the tune of $165,000. They also paid two other landowners a total of $24,000 before the end of the year, and finally got title to the property on 1 July, 1928.[8]

Under Theodore Wirth, the Park Board took action to issue $150,000 in development bonds, and urged that the concrete speedway be removed as soon as possible to make way for runway improvements and land leases.

At this time, the U.S. Naval Reserve petitioned the Park Board to provide facilities on the airfield to handle a Reserve squadron there. Squadron VN-11RD-9 came into being with the Civic and Commerce Association's Committee of 100, implementing construction of a hangar and leasing it to the Navy for $1.00 a year. The hangar, 80 feet wide by 90 feet long,

was constructed to the west of the three Air Guard hangars, and was ready during 1928. A Marine Reserve Squadron, VO-7MR, was assigned to share the facilities with the Navy in 1931.

One of the first businesses to take up residence at the airport was *Mid-Plane Sales and Transit Company*, owned by Mark Hurd and several associates. They set up a hangar inside the racetrack's northwest corner and became the authorized Fairchild and Travel Air distributors for the region. Shortly thereafter, the Park Board approved construction by *Universal Airlines, Inc.* of two hangars along the same row, although outside the racetrack (refer to diagram). Both Mid-Plane and Universal would soon merge into *Universal Aviation Corporation* as documented later in this chapter. This grouped early business activity along 34th Avenue on the airport's west side.

The plan for removal of the racetrack itself, provided that the concrete be buried in three deep pits on the field so that it would not interfere with future runway construction. The removal of 900,000 cubic yards of material and construction of a proper drainage system cost $200,000.[9]

During the summer of 1928, the first lighting was installed, with five floodlights being placed along the south side of the field. The first rotary snowplow was purchased, and the first airport director named. Larry Hammond was selected for the director's job, a position he didn't relinquish until 1957. His first office was in a Park Board warming house set up along 34th Avenue. Hammond worked seven days a week, usually twenty hours a day, often driving the airport ambulance or snowplow.

27 August, 1927. A great crowd eagerly awaits the arrival of Charles Lindbergh in the "Spirit of St. Louis." Lindbergh stopped at Wold-Chamberlain on his goodwill tour of the United States following the famous flight. (Olive Bidon)

126

1928. A good view of the Universal hangars in relation to the racetrack. 34th Avenue has traffic at left. All the aircraft on the ramp are Universal's and the scene is probably a weekend with sight-seers lined up for rides. Note the former racetrack garage footings at lower left. (Roger Poore)

On 3 April, 1929, a request was made to the City of Minneapolis to extend the 34th Avenue streetcar line as far south as 63rd Street, where it would bring passengers right to the airport. Plans were also made to construct a two-story terminal building.

The terminal building was opened in August of 1930. On the first floor, Larry Hammond got a decent private office and another office for operations. He was allowed a secretary, and hired Dorothy Schaeffer. She would become his right-hand, and maintain a knowledge of airport operations better than any file system until her retirement. Roy Johnson was soon hired as Hammond's assistant.

Northwest Airways got a ticket counter and waiting room, since they were, by this time, heavily involved with passenger traffic, along with airmail. The terminal also housed a dining room and lunch counter/soda fountain. In the lobby was a newsstand and cigar counter. There were three additional offices on the main floor for future tenants. The second floor held a Department of Commerce Inspector's office, an office set aside for airways radio service, a pilot's lounge, plus a dormitory with rooms for visiting pilots. The basement held public restrooms; the roof, weather instruments; a nearby garage housed the fire cart, ambulance, and utility vehicle.[10]

The Skelly Oil Company was allowed to put up a gasoline filling station near the Universal hangars to service both airplanes and automobiles.

In 1929, the field recorded 9427 air flights, with 37,563 passengers being carried on 1186 commercial

A view of the racetrack backstretch in 1929. Cars on the track show its giant proportions. Air Guard hangar is in the foreground and airmail hangar at center. (James Borden)

The Universal Air Lines hangars along 34th Avenue, 1929. Note the Skelly Oil station just beyond the second hangar, and the Park Board refreshment stand in the foreground. (Dick Palen via Angelo De Ponti)

flights, 474 transient operations, and 950 sight-seeing flights. In all, some 893,263 persons used the field.[11]

Soon to follow were the airways beacons. An eight million candlepower light, revolving at two r.p.m., was placed atop the Foshay Tower in downtown Minneapolis. Below it, a secondary beacon focused its beam toward the airfield some seven-and-a-half miles away. Another eight million candlepower revolving beacon, with automatic bulb-changer, and turning at six r.p.m., was installed atop a fifty foot tower in front of the terminal building.[12] Construction in the Fall of 1929 included the pouring of a concrete ramp in front of the hangars and terminal.

In 1930 Northwest Airways moved out of the airmail hangar to locate its maintenance base at St. Paul's new airport. At Minneapolis, it bought the northmost of Universal's hangars, (Universal had moved to Chicago). The airmail hangar was then leased by Shorty De Ponti. He, in turn, sub-leased portions to various other local operators and businesses. The Park Board, at this time, had the hangar moved from the center of the field to a position near the racetrack's banked northeast curve.

During the 1930s, people were drawn from the cities to the airport for weekend airshows. The shows featured air races, aerobatic performances, displays, and plenty of sight-seeing rides. Often prominent aviation personalities were brought in to entertain. An example of one such fondly-remembered show, was the air race weekend of 24-25 June, 1933. Local pilot and writer, Jimmy LaVake, wrote in the *Minneapolis Sunday Tribune*, 25 June, that: "Saturday was a perfect day for the races. The wind was a little skittish, but in general, remained from the southwest. Signaled by a flash bomb from the center of the airport, Bennett Griffin, who comes from Oklahoma, and last year rode with Jimmy Mattern on a record trip across the Atlantic, poured it to his plane at two thousand feet and came roaring down on the field in a wide spiral.

"The fun didn't start, however, until Art Davis released three small balloons from his red [Waco] Taperwing and then turned around in his tracks and broke them with his propeller. Art showed his remarkable prowess in the next event by flying high during the whole race and diving on the final lap ahead of traffic...and Harold Neuman."

On the same program, George Gurell, Jr. of Chicago, put a Ford Trimotor through loops, stalls, and even a slow roll. He did a half-loop and flew the giant plane on its back. Johnny Livingston was there

19 September, 1930. Frenchmen, Captain Dieudonne Coste and Maurice Bellonte, arrive in the Atlantic-spanning Breguet 19 "Question mark" for the dedication of the terminal building. (Clarence Opsahl)

1930. The new terminal is under construction on the West side. Parts of the racetrack still exist. (Metropolitan Airports Commission)

to fly in the races and parachute jumper Clem Sohn, performed a delayed jump from 10,000 feet, not opening the parachute until he had come within 600 feet of the ground.

On Sunday, a Navy acrobatic group called the "Helldivers," flying Curtiss O2C-1 aircraft, put on a show of formation aerobatics. An autogiro, flown by Frank Faulkner, and a comedy Curtiss Pusher, Jr. act, were included. In the races, Bennett Griffin beat Harold Neuman and Art Davis in the first race, then Johnny Livingston and Davis beat Neuman in a second event.

In January of 1932, Wold-Chamberlain was designated a Class A-1-A airport by the Department of Commerce, Aeronautics Branch, making it one of the country's major airports. The field continued to grow, gain public support, and generate enthusiasm for air travel.

A giant Works Progress Administration (WPA) project in 1936 resulted in the construction of three major concrete runways. A north-south runway parallel to 34th Avenue was the first to be finished, with two diagonal runways forming a triangle, completed in the Fall.

The Minneapolis Aquatennial Association sponsored a yearly open house and airshow beginning in 1932. Thousands attended this popular event.

During the weekends, local aviators and flight schools got into the act, taking eager Minneapolitans up for air rides. The Brown-Morgan school, Roth-Downs Airways, and individuals like Elmer Hinck,

Billy Parker, Florence Klingensmith, Jack Kipp, Mel Swanson, Bill Shaw, Millar Wittag, Del Snyder, Ken Nisun, Lee Wright, Lyle Thro, Fred Whittemore, Red Fowler, Lyle Strong, and Chuck Wheelock, were prominent among those carrying weekend passengers. Ticket hawkers, Shorty Hall, Bob Baker, and Chuck Doyle helped out. Skywriter, Bob McManus, often added his specialty, an advertising message in the sky.

Wold-Chamberlain became well-known in the late 1930s for its winter treatment of runways. It was one of the only major airports in the country to roll the snow after each snowfall. The airport persevered in this method of "compaction" rather than plowing or blowing for the winters of 1935 through 1939. A spring-toothed harrow was dragged along to break up and level clumps, followed by a series of corrugated pipe rollers towed behind a tractor to do the compacting. The only problems came in the spring when the snow melted; the ground remained soft for an extended period, causing some airliners to get mired down. The compaction method was dropped after 1939.[13]

Wold-Chamberlain Field saw some important visitors stopping in over the years. On August, 1927, Charles Lindbergh arrived in the "Spirit of St. Louis," making a stop on his nationwide tour following the marvelous flight to Paris. Huge crowds attended his appearance, with Lindbergh stashing the Spirit in the

An early 1930s airshow has brought a large crowd to the field. Note the Air-O-Inn at lower right and the Airmail Hangar moved near the old Air Guard hangars — now Navy Reserve. (Metropolitan Airports Commission)

22 August, 1935. A solemn tribute honoring Wiley Post and Will Rogers. The Naval Reserve Helldiver aircraft are in the front row and the Freeman Ford Trimotor is in the back. Note the terminal building, the windsock tower, and the refreshment stands. (Minneapolis Journal via Noel Allard)

1930 view of Wold's new terminal building with a Northwest Airways Ford Trimotor waiting to load. (Don Erickson)

airmail hangar to avoid souvenir-hunting fans. On 19 September, 1930, frenchmen, Captain Dieudonne Coste and Maurice Bellonte, flying a Breguet 19 named the "Question mark," paid a visit as part of a ceremony dedicating the new terminal building. Two weeks earlier that they had made the first east to west crossing of the Atlantic in the same airplane, accomplishing the feat in 37 hours and 18 minutes.[14]

21 August, 1933 saw a visit from Frank Hawks in his Northrop Gamma "Sky Chief," having arrived from New York in five-and-a-quarter hours. He was flying cross-country on a whirlwind trip, and refueled at the Navy base. He left the next morning, commenting that he was expected for lunch in Seattle and would be playing golf there that afternoon.[15]

19 July, 1934 saw the arrival of a flight of Martin B-10 bombers on their way from Washington, D. C., to Alaska, Minneapolis being a stop along the way. A Commanding officer by the name of H. H. "Hap" Arnold was leading the group and spoke at an evening ceremony. He would later become Commander-in-Chief of the Army Air Forces in World War II.[16]

A solemn ceremony took place on 22 August, 1935, when the Naval Reserve, Northwest Airlines, and various civilian operators on the airport, observed a silent tribute to Wiley Post and Will Rogers. The well-loved pair had been killed a week earlier when their plane crashed in Alaska. The memorial ceremony in-

1936. The Works Progress Administration (WPA) has three runways under construction. (Noel Allard)

cluded military and civilian planes which were arranged in a semi-circle in front of the terminal building. Officers and civilians lined up in formal rank for a moment of silence.

On 14 July, 1938, the airport was the scene of incredible exhilaration, when Howard Hughes made his only U. S. stop on an around-the-world flight. Having heard a rumor that Hughes might drop in for fuel, several hundred people were at the airport to watch him touch down. His gleaming, Lockheed Model 14 made a perfect landing and rolled up to the administration building ramp. Hughes came out of the airplane long enough to use the facilities, wash his face, and tell the lineboys to fill only his wingtanks with gas. His unshaven appearance, baggy eyes and mussed hair, told the story of a long flight from Floyd Bennett Field in New York, around the world via Paris, Moscow, Fairbanks, and then to Minneapolis. The ship was gassed with 493 gallons of fuel and was on its way in only 14 minutes, a tribute to the smooth servicing operations of the airport staff, who handled the stop as routine.

By the time Hughes' plane was off the ground, thousands of motorists, on their way to Wold, having heard the news over the radio, jammed highways leading to the airport, and caught only a fleeting glimpse of the silver airplane on its way east.[17]

When he again arrived in New York, Hughes' elapsed time was a record three days, 19 hours, and 27 minutes, beating the former Wiley Post record of seven days and 19 hours.

On 29 August, 1938, the appearance of a B-17 flying into Wold, sent the news media scurrying out for a scoop. The largest plane ever to visit the airport was welcomed on the Navy ramp for refueling during an "intercept" training mission. It was, according to the *Minneapolis Star* of that date, the YB-17, a prototype of thousands of fortresses to be built for World War II. It was on a trip from Langley Field in Virginia, flown by Captain R. B. Williams of the 2nd Bomb Group. Its flight was a chance to give the crew vital training for long-distance bombing missions. The plane's size amazed most reporters.[18]

If they were awed by the size of the YB-17, they were totally stunned by the proportions of the XB-15, which paid a call at Wold on 19 July, 1939. The largest airplane in the U. S. inventory at the time, the XB-15 was also a prototype that was never put into production. It had come from Langley Field, as had the YB-17 the year before, and also stopped at the Navy base to refuel on its way to Seattle.[19]

The Park Board added a third floor to the terminal building in 1937, with several additional rooms for travelers, and dormitory rooms for pilots. It also added a glass room to be used as a control tower. Within a few days of the control tower's completion on 1 July, 1938, Stan Ketcham became tower operator. Ketcham had been the only applicant for the position the first two times it was advertised. The job was advertised a third time by the Minneapolis Civil Service Commission, in hopes that a few additional candidates would apply. This time, a graduate electrical engineer was selected for the job, only to be found unqualified a few days later, with Stan finally getting hired.

Ketcham worked for the Park Board, and in 1942,

when the FAA took over administration of the tower, he continued on, retiring in 1973.

Ketcham got so good at judging the weather that when Larry Hammond, mentioned one night that he was going on a picnic, Ketcham recommended that he bring his umbrella, even though the weather bureau downstairs had assured Larry that it would not rain. The rain came down, and just at the time that Ketcham had predicted. The next day, Hammond asked the weather bureau how a tower operator could do a better job of predicting weather than they could, and they dismissed it as "dumb luck." When Hammond revealed their statement to Ketcham later, Stan agreed; dumb luck and having watched the weather from the glass house for many years.[20]

The tower started controlling aircraft with a 50-candlepower light gun, which could be aimed at an approaching airliner's cockpit to signal landing clearances with a beam of red or green light. When both Northwest and Hanford/Mid-Continent Airlines put pressure on Hammond for better communications; to provide wind direction, velocity, and barometric pressure, Hammond found a 10-watt transmitter at Chicago's Midway Airport. It had been used as a runway marker by United Airlines and had a 278 kilocycle crystal with a fifteen-mile range. Ketcham put a power booster on it and promptly got reprimanded by the FCC for unauthorized tampering of a signal. In the evenings, 6210 kc was used to communicate from tower to aircraft, as this frequency had better wave propogation. VHF radio was introduced during World War Two.

Besides the early light gun, tower instruments included: a wind gauge, with direction and velocity indicator, a telephone, and a Kollsman altimeter that gave the barometric pressure. When the tower closed at 10:00 p.m., the night watchman would respond to an airliner's call by switching on the field floodlights, then dutifully turning them off again when the airliner had taxied to the ramp.

When the tower staff was enlarged, the City hired Dave Buckman and Harry Johnson to relieve Ketcham. It was Johnson's sense of humor that brightened their days. Once, when a Northwest airliner was approaching from Fargo, with the wind from the northwest, the pilot called for a straight-in approach from the west. When ordered to land to the northwest, and therefore to make a big circle around the field before landing, the pilot complained, "I'm out here over Lake

A beautiful photo showing the hangar row on 34th Avenue in 1940. Note the "dirigible" wind indicator on the control tower. McInnis Aviation Service is the tenant of the old public service hangar in the foreground. (Norton & Peel photo via Minnesota Historical Society)

Calhoun and I can see from the waves that the wind is out of the southeast, so I want to land straight in." Johnson told him, "Okay, if you are landing on Lake Calhoun, you are cleared to land to the southeast, if you are landing at Wold-Chamberlain, we're landing to the northwest."[21]

Often the visiting pilots, staying in dorm rooms on the third floor of the terminal, and having extra time on their hands, would come up to the tower to chat with the controllers. Ketcham says this made the job fun. Hubert Humphrey, Mayor of Minneapolis during the 1940s, enjoyed stopping up for a view of the field, whenever he had a few minutes before a flight.

The Air Force became a permanent resident of the field during World War II. A large hangar was built for them in 1944, west of 34th Avenue. The Air Guard had moved to St. Paul in 1931 when new facilities were built for them at that location. They would not return to Wold until 1951, when they were called to active duty for the Korean War. During World War II, Wold-Chamberlain was virtually taken-over by military operations, with only the airlines able to stay. Most civilian flying had been curtailed, and

The Goodman Shows carnival has set up on the section of land to the south of the airport in this 1939 or 1940 photo. The location is just on the other side of 66th Street from the airport and across 34th Avenue from the Air-O-Inn. (James LaVake)

1942. A bird's-eye view of 34th Avenue from a Northwest Lockheed 10A. (Vince Doyle)

civilian operators moved from the field or shut down altogether.

Wold-Chamberlain was the scene of one of the war's most unique military achievements, the hasty modifications of the Tokyo-raiding B-25 bombers of Jimmy Doolittle. A more complete story of the modifications is included in Chapter Seven.

Another major wartime activity located at Wold-Chamberlain was the assembly of Waco CG-4A gliders for the Army. Further information on this program is also included in Chapter Seven.

The period of the late 1930s saw a rivalry between Minneapolis and St. Paul as each laid claim to having the major airport. Each vied for the tenancy of the Northwest Airlines main base. The public sensed that a duplication of airport facilities was an expensive form of competition and called for some sort of consolidation. Intercity relations were less than harmonious on this subject when the 1943 Minnesota State Legislature convened.

To solve these differences, the Metropolitan Airports Commission was created on 6 July, 1943, to settle the question. More on this development in Chapter Eight.

The MAC was granted sweeping powers to promote air navigation, insure Minnesota's participation in national and international air commerce, to develop the Twin Cities as a major transportation center, and to cooperate with Federal and State agencies. MAC was given complete power over all aspects of airport development within a 25-mile radius of the two city halls. The prime result was that Wold-Chamberlain was designated as the official airport for both cities.[22]

The Wold-Chamberlain airport continued with airline and military training during the wartime period without much further change, through the end of 1945.

Wold-Chamberlain Field Structures and Tenants 1919 - 1945

(Refer to diagram below)

1. *Security Aircraft Company* hangar. 1919. Larrabee Brothers. Flight school, aircraft service and repair, and sight-seeing flights. Home of both the *Minneapolis Daily News Flying Circus* and the *St. Paul Dispatch Flying Circus*. Company used the concrete of the racetrack straightaway for the hangar floor and the racetrack garages along 34th Avenue for storage. Security employees were; Wilbur and Weldon Larrabee, owners; Jack Malone, William Butters, and Ed Ballough, instructors; Guy Carroll, chief mechanic; Charles Hardin, parachute rigger and jumper; Ben Foster, promoter of the Dispatch Flying Circus; Charles Holman, Vern Georgia and C. R. "Dusty" Rhodes, students and working employees.

Ownership passed to George Heinrich, Ogden

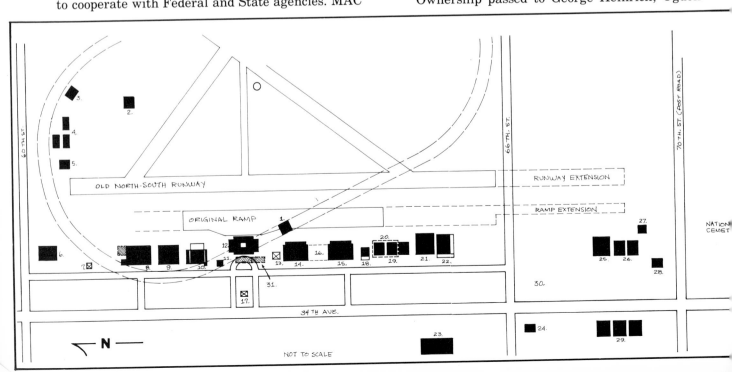

Confer, and Horace Libby, then to C. R. Rhodes in 1923. Rhodes ran the outfit until 1924. The hangar was on the racetrack until 1928, after the two Universal Air Lines hangars were built.[23]

2. Airmail hangar. 1920. Built for the U. S. Airmail with funds from Minneapolis and St. Paul, donated to the *Twin City Aero Corporation* who was the lessee of the field. The first airmail flew in during August, 1920, and used the hangar as a terminal and service facility. Airmail ceased within three months. Not all of the tenants between 1920 and 1926 are known, except *Minnesota Aircraft Company*, Eaglerock distributors, known to have been a tenant. Lyle Thro was a principal of the company. In 1926, *Northwest Airways* picked up the lease on the hangar, having received government airmail contract route #9. Their rent was $200 per month. They vacated at the end of 1929 with Shorty De Ponti and the *Mohawk Aircraft Company* leasing space after that. Mohawk went bankrupt in late 1931 and De Ponti and his partner, Anton Jacobson, operating as *Minnesota Aviation sales and Service Company*, leased the entire building. The Minneapolis Park Board moved the hangar back against the racetrack oval in 1931.[24]

3. Airmail hangar. Second position, 1931. Moved here when the removal of the racetrack had begun. De Ponti held the lease until 1941, subleasing to Hanford and Mid-Continent Airlines from 1936 through 1940. In 1942, the hangar was sold to Tom North, cut down the middle and then into six sections, each being transported on double-flatbed trucks to Northport Airport near White Bear Lake. The hangar was reassembled and used in North's War Training Service (WTS) pilot training program. A small control tower was built on its roof. The hangar, minus tower, still stands, though its fate is uncertain as the airfield is no longer used.[25]

4. Air Guard hangars. Three hangars erected in 1921 by the State of Minnesota for the new 109th Observation Squadron, Minnesota Air National Guard. Size of each was 60 x 120 feet. Wooden construction. Cost to State, $45,000. Rent of $2500 per year paid by the State to *Twin City Aero Corporation*. A control tower was built atop the northmost hangar. During the airport dedication to Wold and Chamberlain in 1923, a memorial stone with bronze tablet was placed between two of these hangars. Two of the original hangars now stand in front of the old terminal building on 34th Avenue, joined end-to-end and used as offices. The third original hangar was scrapped in 1941.[26]

5. Naval Reserve hangar. 1928. Built by the Committee of 100 of the Minneapolis Civic and Commerce Association and turned over to the Park Board, which in turn, leased it to the Navy for $1.00 a year to house the Naval Reserve Squadron, VN-11RD9. The hangar was added onto several times over the years, and is reported

to be incorporated into what stands today, though it is hardly recognizable. In 1934, the Marine Reserve Squadron, VO-7MR, was assigned to co-use the facility.[27]

6. Ice Research hangar. 1943. Erected by the Navy Department. Popular theory was that it was built to house the C-99 Constitution aircraft, though that was never done. Used by Northwest Airlines and NSP, under contract to the navy to conduct static electricity tests. Aircraft were suspended in the hangar's huge bay and lightning bolts fired at them. With the University of Minnesota's help, the small static discharge "wicks" that private, airline, and military aircraft use today, were developed.

The hangar picked up its nickname, "Ice Research hangar" from its use by Northwest Airlines on another military contract. It housed aircraft used in hunting for, and flying through, icing conditions around the country. The purpose of that project was to find ways to combat deadly icing conditions that could befoul an airplane's wings and propellers, causing it to fall out of control.

The hangar was 80 feet high, 300 feet long, and 330 feet wide. It had laminated wooden rafters spanning some 250 feet, supported on concrete piers. The doors stood 65 feet high, with each of their eight panels having its own electric motor to move it. The building was leased to De Ponti in the post-war period, and finally razed in 1977 to open the approach to runway 11L.[28]

7. Park Board warming house. Erected in the 1930s to provide refreshments for weekend airshow visitors and casual travelers. A second stand was erected in position #13.

8. Northwest Airlines hangar. 1940. Built by the City of Minneapolis with $90,000 in bonds. Northwest promised a twenty-year payoff of the bonds and used the hangar as their on-the-field maintenance building and offices. Their main overhaul base at this time was at St. Paul. A two-story brick addition was added to the west and south in 1941, and a small shop built by Van Dusen, formerly sitting between sites #9 and #10, was also moved alongside the hangar in 1942. The area north of this hangar was used for runups of Northwest's aircraft, and subsequently well-spattered with oil, coming to be affectionately known as "The Pig Farm." A vertical spotlight on the 34th Avenue side functioned as the weather bureau's ceiling finder into the 1960's.[29]

Some space was leased to Honeywell in the 1940s. The hangar was used by North Central Airlines in the late 1950s, the FAA in the late 1960s, Mesaba Airlines in the 1980s and more recently by the FAA.

9. Government Hangar. 1942. Erected by the *Defense Plant Corporation* for use by *Minneapolis Honeywell Regulator Company*, under contract to the government to run tests of a new autopilot

Summer 1941. The lull before the storm. Progress has been made that includes perimeter taxiways and additional hangars along 34th Avenue. Note the complexity of the Naval base compared to the next photo. (Noel Allard)

system. The hangar was used by Northwest Airlines during the 1950s, and later by De Ponti, who ran an air freight service from there. Today, the building is leased from the Metropolitan Airports Commission by *Page Airways*.[30]

10. Public Service hangar. 1928. Built by *Mid-Plane Sales & Transit Company*. Shortly after opening, Mid-Plane merged into *Universal Air Lines* who used the hangar until *Northwest Airlines* moved into it in 1930. De Ponti leased the building in 1933 and bought it in 1936. He also added a small office structure on the 34th Avenue side, which would eventually be sold to Tom Hillis and moved to a city lot at 7308 Portland Avenue. It has been used as a private residence since about 1940. De Ponti's cost to build it was just $600.[31]
In 1937, De Ponti sold the hanger to the *Hedberg-Friedheim Company*, cement contractors, who leased it first to Ben Freeman, Minneapolis shoe store owner. Freeman's pilot, Mel Swanson, was ever-present during this period, taking sightseers for rides in Freeman's Ford Trimotor. The plane was also used to fly parachute jumpers during weekend airshows. Merrill Kuehn and Ralph Arone, Minneapolis bar owners, also sub-leased the hangar from Hedberg-Friedheim for a period. They hired Bill Shaw to manage their business, and give flight instruction and sight-seeing rides. Keuhn went on to develop an interest in flying, got his license and joined Northwest Airlines, eventually retiring after a career with them.[32]
Next tenant was A. C. McInnis, who came along to sub-lease in 1938, holding the hangar until it was sub-leased to the Army, who turned it over to Minneapolis Honeywell for experimental research in 1942. The hangar was then moved a short distance to the south to make way for construction of the larger government hangar. While the Hedberg-Friedheim hangar had originally been aligned north-south, with the door facing the terminal building, it was now rotated 90 degrees to open onto the ramp on the east side. Dimensions of this hangar were 80x100 feet. It no longer exists.

11. Park Board warming house. 1929. This building was the unofficial office of the new airport director, Larry Hammond during 1929, while the terminal, then under construction, was being finished.

12. Terminal and Administration Building (The Ad Building). 1930. Originally two stories tall and without a control tower. It did have several offices on the main floor, including both a private and a business office for Larry Hammond, director of the airport. There was a dining room and lunch counter, a newsstand/cigar stand. Northwest Airlines had a ticket counter and waiting room. Public restrooms were in the basement along with several storage rooms. It was in one of the latter, actually a coal bin, that entrepreneur, G. B. Van Dusen, got his start in 1940, with a parts supply business.
The second floor held an office for the Department of Commerce, space set aside for future airways radio service, with a pilot's lounge and dormitory rooms filling the remainder. The roof held weather instruments, and a nearby garage housed the airport fire cart, ambulance and utility vehicle.[33]
In 1937, a third floor was added to the terminal, with seven bedrooms for travelers, and ten dormitory rooms for pilots. In 1938, a glass-enclosed tower was built. The building was used for all these functions until 1963, when a new tower was built alongside to take care of increased field traffic control, and a new larger terminal was built on the east side of the field. The old terminal, minus its control tower, still stands and is used by the National Weather Service and various private businesses.[34]

13. Park Board hot dog stand. Erected in the 1930's to serve refreshments to weekend visitors. Another stand was erected at the same time on spot #7.

14-15. *Universal Air Lines* hangars. 1928. Universal Aviation Corporation was the parent of *Universal Air Lines* and the *Universal Flying School* located at this site. The airline and flight school moved out in 1929, going to Chicago to start the mergers that would yield *American Airlines*. They left the hangars empty and unleased. Frank Armstrong, S. L. Gish, and P. G. Koch bought UAL's equipment and took on the name, *Minnesota Aviation Company*, but moved soon to the old airmail hangar in the center of the field. There, with De Ponti and Mohawk, they continued their operation.
In 1930, *Northland Aviation Company* moved in. They offered the whole gamut of services including; sight-seeing, charter flights, and a full-fledged ground school and flying program. Paul Paine was the CEO; Elmer Hinck, Ray Goetze, and Delmar Snyder were instructors. Paine had a small wind-tunnel built in a classroom for students to use in their studies. Northland was the only government approved flight school in the Northwest in 1933.[35]

Other businesses rented space in the Universal hangars and in the brick additions built facing the ramp to the east. *Interstate Air Credit*, the first aviation financing company in the northwest had an office there, manned by Harry Shaeffer and Harvey Cook. The *Ace High Flying Service* run by Ken Nisum also quartered in the building. In 1935, the *Hedberg-Friedheim Company* bought the two hangars and leased to *Hanford Airlines* and Northland. Hanford started business in Sioux City, Iowa, and moved their maintenance base to Wold in 1935, remaining through a merger into *Mid-Continent Airlines*, and later into *Braniff Airlines* in the 1950s. Hanford utilized a variety of aircraft, including Lockheed Vega's, Stearmans, Travel Air monoplanes, Ford Tri-motors and Lockheed 10A's. Gene Shank was chief pilot, and Walter Bullock worked there as a line pilot while he was laid off from Northwest in the mid-1930s. In 1937, De Ponti bought the buildings from Hedberg-Friedheim for $47,000. He used the hangars for the same purposes as his predecessors; training, storage, and rental, but added a Piper Cub distributorship. In 1938, he was still leasing space to both Mid-Continent and Northwest Airlines in these hangars. Just prior to World War Two, these hangars became home to Vern Georgia's *Minnesota Skyways*. Georgia had a CPT contract to teach college students to fly.

16. De Ponti bridge. 1938. Constructed by De Ponti to add space between the hangars for more storage and maintenance. After the outbreak of World War II, De Ponti's shop was designated a certified repair station, keeping wartime train-

ing program aircraft in license and airworthy. In 1942 and 1943 De Ponti leased the entire complex to *Northwestern Aeronautical Corporation*, which was under contract with the government to build and assemble Waco CG-4A troop gliders. De Ponti crews did the assembling. De Ponti continued to operate from this complex until 1953 when he moved his business to the big ice research hangar at the field's north end. The hangars were then leased by *North Central Airlines* during the 1960s and are currently being used for maintenance and storage by the *Metropolitan Airports Commission*.

17. Beacon tower. A 50 foot tower with windsock and an 8,000,000 candlepower beacon. The beacon had a self-changing bulb system and revolved at 6 r.p.m. It stood until the 1960s.[36]

18. Skelly Oil station. 1930. A fuel stop for both aircraft and automobiles. The *Skelly Oil Company* leased the station to Lyle and Willis Strong, who hired Charles Lee "Skelly" Wright as operator. He not only ran the station, but became a pilot, and flew for Northwest Airlines, beginning in 1943. He was assigned to the ice research project, the Honeywell autopilot project, and the static electricity research project. The Strong brothers also became Northwest Airlines pilots.

19. De Ponti hangars. 1940. Hangars were designed by barnstormer Bob Crain, and erected by De Ponti to keep up with his growing responsibilities to the government. Two of these hangars were

1944. Compare this view with that of the previous. Note the wartime buildup. (James Borden)

moved after the war to position #26. There, one of them burned down. The third hangar was razed to clear the line of sight from the control tower to the intersection of runways 4-22 and 29L-11R.

20. *North Central Airlines* hangar. Built on the site of two of the original three 1940 De Ponti hangars. Used during the 1960s. In the 1970s, the airline moved across the field to new facilities. This hangar still stands, being used by *Viking International Airlines*.

21. Braniff hangar. 1950s. Built by *Braniff Airlines* as maintenance and office facility. Razed after Braniff moved off the field.

22. *Mid-Continent Airlines* hangar. 1941. Built using City of Minneapolis bonds. It was here, in 1942, that Mid-Continent modified the Doolittle B-25's. Mid-Continent went on to perform other bomber and fighter modifications for the government during the war. After its merger into Braniff in 1952, that airline used this hangar until Braniff moved. The hangar was razed.

23. Army Air Force Transport Hangar. 1944. Used by the Air Force until a swap in the 1970's with the Naval Reserve. At that time, the Air Force moved to the north side of the field to take over the former Naval Reserve Air Base, and the Naval Reserve, relegated to a field training unit with no aircraft, moved to the Air Force's smaller facility.

24. *Air-O-Inn.* Favorite watering hole for people from all walks at Wold during the 1930s. Owned and operated by Jack Hohag, his wife and brother. The Inn featured an outside patio, a pastoral surrounding of fields and trees, and a bar with the traditional propeller over it. Parts of the bar were moved in the 1950s and still exist, having been incorporated into the bar at the Everett McClay VFW Post #126 at 2731 East 78th Street in Bloomington, just south of the airport, and a favorite watering spot in its own right.

An aerial view of the Navy research hangar under construction in 1944. The massive size is apparent by comparison to the semi-trailer truck in the lower left corner of the picture. (Metropolitan Airports Commission)

25. *Mercury Aviation-General Mills* hangar. 1950s Razed for new hangar construction.

26. De Ponti hangars. 1950s. Moved here from position #19. South hangar burned from spontaneous combustion of cardboard stored inside.

27. *Twin City Flyers* operations shack during early 1950s. Business was owned by Raymond Hense. Building razed. Author, Noel Allard, had his first airplane ride here in 1953.

28. Hohag farm. Most of the airport property was originally part of the Gus Hohag homestead on the Minnesota River bluffs. Gus sold part of his land to the Snelling Field, Inc. and the rest to the Park Board in 1928. His son, Jack, and Jack's family continued to live in the family farmhouse on 34th Avenue and 70th Street, (Post Road), granted staying rights until such time that the parents passed away. Jack operated the Air-O-Inn across the road for many years. His sons, Robert and Earl, became Northwest Airlines pilots. Upon the death of the Mother and Father, the small lot became airport property and is now ramp space.

29. Shakopee hangars. 1950s. So-called because they were so far south of the field that they, "might as well have been in Shakopee." These hangars were built by Northwest Airlines for their maintenance base and general offfices in the 1950s. De Ponti bought them in 1960 when Northwest moved across the field to new quarters. He then leased space to Honeywell, Braniff Airlines, and Eastern Airlines. The hangars were razed for taxiway construction in the late 1970s.

30. Golf driving range. 1940s. One of the special features of this driving range was the "skeeter chaser," an aircraft fuselage with engine, which was run at idle during business hours, providing a breeze to keep mosquitoes away...so the story goes.[37]

31. Air Guard hangars. Present position of two of the original three hangars built for the *109th Observation Squadron* in 1921. They are now offices.

HOLMAN FIELD

As Wold-Chamberlain Airport became the airport representing the city of Minneapolis, Holman Field had a no less colorful background as the main reliever airport, and representative airport of St. Paul.

The airmail played a great role in the development of the St. Paul airport. By the year 1918 it was obvious that mail could be sent by air and arrive at its destination much sooner than if shipped across country by truck as was the current practice.

The Federal Superintendent of Airmail met on 5 November, 1918, with representatives of both Minneapolis and St. Paul, including businessman, D. C. Cushman Rice of St. Paul, St. Paul Postmaster, Otto Raths, Minneapolis Postmaster, E. A. Purdy, and

State Senator, William F. Brooks, who represented the Aero Club of Minneapolis. The cities were to make a joint request that airmail be carried between the Twin Cities and Chicago. No action was taken at that meeting. The Federal Government lacked sufficient aircraft to honor all requests coming to them from around the country. They did, however, promise that service would start sometime in the future.

Minnesota Adjutant General, W. F. Rhinow, understanding that the airmail was coming to the Twin Cities, met with St. Paul and Minneapolis interests on 11 December, 1919 to designate a general flying field to cover both cities. Speedway Field had been in general use, and it was assumed that it would suffice as the major airport, being centrally located only a few miles from each metropolitan area.

Speedway Field was selected to accept the airmail. When the first trial airmail flight arrived at Speedway Field from Chicago on 10 August, 1920, aboard a military Martin bomber, a stop at St. Paul was not included. St. Paul would soon need a field nearer to its business interests. Both Minneapolis and St. Paul had Post Offices, and since the federal government was supporting the airmail operators, it made sense to locate an airfield near each Post Office.

St. Paul businessmen and the *St. Paul Association of Commerce* led by Colonel Lewis Brittin, tried in vain to interest Minneapolis in searching for a more central location for a new major airport to service both cities. Minneapolis was satisfied, however, with the location of the now renamed Wold-Chamberlain Field, for their own interests, and simply refused to negotiate with St. Paul.

In 1925, the search for an airport located closer to St. Paul businesses focused on Curtiss-Northwest Field, owned by William Kidder. St. Paul would have turned Curtiss-Northwest Field into their major airport, but Minneapolis refused to accept airmail delivered there. St. Paul, likewise, refused to accept airmail delivered to Wold-Chamberlain. With this squabbling, St. Paul withdrew its interests in Wold in the latter part of 1926.

That year, Brittin memoed the St. Paul Association his thoughts on the future of aviation, and the need for a St. Paul Airport. He saw a great expansion of passenger travel and mail transport, basing his thoughts on two main facts; one, the plan of the Ford Motor Company to produce large three-engined passenger transports; and second, that the large com-

Looking East across St. Paul Airport during the stopover of the Ford Reliability Tour, 9 August, 1926. Participating aircraft are lined up about where the present day terminal ramp is located. (Minnesota Historical Society)

mercial transport had proven itself reliable enough to become widely used. He stated that if St. Paul could provide itself with a major airport, it would be possible for the city to become a stop on the highly-touted, upcoming, Reliability Air Tour, thus promoting the City of St. Paul with national headlines.

A citizen's group led by the *St. Paul Aviation Club* and the *Aviation committee* of the *St. Paul Association of Commerce*, along with several other businessmen, succeeded in lobbying the city to purchase land for an airport. The land selected was then know as Riverview Flats, opposite Indian Mounds Park on a bend in the Mississippi River. The committee worked out a lease with the landowner, the *Abbott-Miller Company*. The St. Paul Association then leased the property with the intention of establishing a municipal airport in that spot. Mr. J. Parker Van Zant of *Stout Air Service, Inc.* of Detroit, was commissioned to lay out an airfield. His job was to make it attractive as an airmail stop to the *Dickinson Air Service* of Chicago, who had garnered the federal contract to fly the mail between there and the Twin Cities.

Van Zant's recommendation was for a field with a north-south sod runway of 3500 feet and an east-west strip of three thousand feet. With further lobbying by the Association, especially by William Kidder and Colonel Brittin, the city floated a bond issue of $295,000 on 21 June, 1926 and land procurement began. It was agreed that the city would own and manage the field, to be known as St. Paul Airport. The Public Works department immediately set about the grading and dredging necessary for leveling the field.

One of the first activities to occur at the St. Paul Airport was the establishment of a U. S. Weather Bureau office on the field. In 1926, Bennett Swenson moved in to set up the first weather station in the Twin Cities, making routine observations throughout the day and phoning his findings to regional offices in Omaha and Cleveland, as well as Northwest Airways at Wold-Chamberlain. A small building, actual-

Holman Field. May, 1927 photo shows the combination United States Weather Service office and office of Airport Master, Francis Geng. The buildings were former voting booths used by the City of St. Paul. (L. C. Seamer via Tom Kuhfeld)

ly a former voting booth, served as his office. He could be proud of his modest facility, since at the time, the field had no runway or landing lights, no beacon, no fire apparatus, no radio communications, and no food service. By 1927, Mac Emerson would join Bennett as weather service technician, and take over in 1928 when Swenson departed for Washington, D. C. to become a forecaster in the main office of the Weather Bureau.

By early 1927, a municipal hangar had been built. It was 100x100 feet in size and featured a 10-ton metal door 16 feet high by 80 feet wide that rolled up overhead. The hangar contained enough space for offices, shops, a stockroom, and a fire cart, besides being big enough to house a Ford Trimotor. Benches were placed along the airfield side from which spectators could watch the comings and goings. The hangar is still on the field immediately east of the terminal building and, at this writing, the home of *Wings, Inc.*

Another bond issued was raised in 1927 that provided for airport improvements. It was noted that the field was below flood level and most of the monies were targeted for raising the level of the field with fill material dredged from the river alongside. Provision was also made to create two paved runways.

Northwest Airways had begun making regular daily mail stops at St. Paul. On 5 July, 1927, Northwest Airways carried their first airline passenger to Chicago. That person could look forward to a twelve hour trip in a Stinson Detroiter aircraft, a ship of modest comfort, seating three passengers in addition to the pilot. The flight included several mail stops.

On 29 August, Francis J. Geng was appointed Airport Master, under the direction of the Department of Public Utilities. The first flying rules were written and adopted, governing all flying in the vicinity of the airport.

Francis Geng was an unlikely person to have garnered the job as Airport Master. He had been trained as an aviation mechanic in the Navy, but fell ill and was given a medical discharge. He returned to St. Paul where he trained as a jeweler and went into that line of work. In 1927, when the City announced an examination for the position of Airport

The Holman Field terminal building, newly finished in 1941. (Northwest Airlines via Vince Doyle)

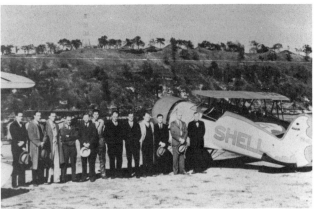

Jimmy Doolittle and a crowd of dignitaries stand alongside his Shell Oil Company Travel Air, Model R, at Holman Field in the 1930s. Doolittle is fourth from left, others are unidentified. (Northwest Airlines via Vince Doyle)

Master, Geng, the jeweler, applied. . . and was accepted, taking over the job officially on 28 August of that year. For an office, he was lucky enough to be able to share one of the voting booth shacks with the weather service. There were no airplanes based at the field at that time, it being used merely as a stop for the airmail, dropping off businessmen, or as a gas stop for transient pilots.

When the municipal hangar was built, Geng induced several itinerant pilots to base their aircraft there, including Mark Hurd, Thunder Johnson, Fred Whittemore, and Deke DeLong. The field didn't see substantial use until the Northwest Airways started using it. The 109th Observation Squadron of the Air National Guard moved into a new city-built hangar in 1929.

Aircraft were refueled from a fifty-gallon tank on a steel cart, according to Geng. If an aircraft the size of a Ford Trimotor were coming through, Geng would have a gasoline tanker come to the field. At that, fuel was less expensive at St. Paul. One memo from Northwest Airways Operating Manager, Walter Bullock, in 1931, advised the airline's flight crews that, "Pilots coming from points into the Twin Cities, stopping first at Minneapolis, requiring gasoline, will put in only enough at that point to safely bring them to St, Paul, as gasoline costs us practically double at Minneapolis than at St. Paul."[38]

Geng saw the airport change over the years, during which time he welcomed a friendly poker game with regular and visiting flyers to relieve the monotony. He made many friends, finally retiring in 1961, after 34 years in charge. One of his favorite stories concerned Thorwald "Thunder" Johnson. Thunder had been on a trip to St. Cloud and back, bringing some animals along as a publicity stunt. Among the animals was a monkey, which had been strapped into the front seat of Thunder's Waco biplane. When the ship touched down at St. Paul, Geng ran out and shook hands with the monkey, greeting him with "Hello, Thunder, how are you?"[39]

March of 1928 saw the installation of the field's first beacon light. It was not at the field, however, it was installed atop the Merchants National Bank Building in downtown St. Paul, at 4th and Robert Streets. The beacon, of one million candlepower, four hundred feet above the ground, was visible for up to fifty miles. Lighted beacons had been set up by the Department of Commerce at ten mile intervals to mark the federal airways. Sometime later, the beacon would be relocated at Indian Mounds Park, where it stands to-day, one of the country's few remaining beacons of its type still operating.

In May, the airfield was designated a Customs Airport by the U. S. Treasury Department. It was here that visitors from Canada were supposed to stop on trips to the U. S. interior. E. S. Flynn, of the U. S. Customs Service at St. Paul warned Canadian authorities that airplanes from Canada were not allowed to land at any other airport in Minnesota except St. Paul, unless making a forced landing. He warned especially against making unauthorized landings at Wold-Chamberlain.

On the first of September, coordinated air-rail service was started. The intent was to provide a cross-country traveler with single ticket passage the entire distance of the country by traveling certain stages aboard an airplane, and others by rail. The service included Northwest Airways and a consortium of railroads; the Great Northern, Northern Pacific, Milwaukee, and St. Paul and Pacific, providing the City of St. Paul with a link to both coasts.

All this activity had a beneficial effect on the use of the airfield. During 1928, nine thousand persons embarked or disembarked from St. Paul, with 1892 plane arrivals, and the same number of departures. Though most passenger flights were of the sight-seeing variety, still Northwest and Jefferson Airways accounted for nearly fifteen hundred passenger arrivals and twelve hundred departures. Flight training was also carried out with 1326 student flights conducted by *Great Northern Aviation Corporation*, a flight school, and the *Twin City Flying Club*.

In 1928 and 1929, additional land was purchased by the city to enlarge the airport. The river was partially dredged near the municipal hangar and a seaplane ramp installed. Fill from the dredging was used to raise the entire field a few feet, hoping to make it "floodproof." It was anticipated that further dredging from the eastern side of the airport would create a whole open area for the landing of seaplanes, to be known as "Hydroplane Bay." There also would be a park created and a bathing beach built for the public, along with a perimeter road around the east side that would connect with Concord Street, providing two accesses to the airport. The plan was never consummated.

In 1929, the City built a hangar for the 109th Observation Squadron, and in 1930, a large hangar for Northwest Airways, bringing both groups from Wold-Chamberlain. The facilities were leased back to the State and Northwest. In 1930, a second municipal hangar was built, larger than the first, 115x200 feet in size, at the cost of $75,000. Among the tenants in the municipal hangars were flight school/service companies including the *St. Paul Flying Club*, *Lexington Air Service*, and later, *Northwest Air Activities* owned by Alex Rozawick, Ralph Arone, and Dennis Scanlan, Jr.

From 1933 to 1939, the field was continually upgraded. Several WPA (Works Progress Administration) projects acted to improve the drainage, increase the number and length of runways, and add additional aprons, taxiways, and lighting. A terminal

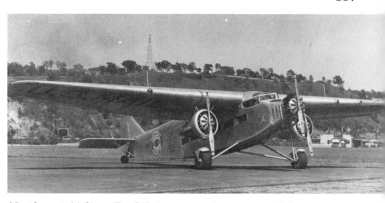

Northwest Airlines Ford Trimotor on the ramp at Holman Field. This publicity shot was made for an Airwheel Tire ad for Aero Digest Magazine. Note the beacon tower at the crest of Indian Mounds Park, across the river. (Northwest Airlines via Vince Doyle)

building was begun in 1939, between the municipal hangar and the Northwest hangar. It would be finished in 1941 and cost $250,000.

AIR TOURS AND VISITING CELEBRITIES

The idea of an air tour of the country was generated in 1925 by Harvey Campbell, a member of the Detroit Board of Commerce. His thinking followed the success and great publicity of the Glidden automobile tours. Calculating that an air tour would have widespread appeal and promote aviation, he would show that the aircraft was now a reliable form of transportation.

The Reliability Air Tours that followed came to be known as the Ford Reliability Tours. The Ford name is associated with these tours from the original 1925 provision of a trophy by Edsel Ford. The tours started at Henry Ford's new company airfield at Dearborn, Michigan, and included several Ford Trimotored aircraft among the contestants.

The 1926 version of the Tour did make a stop at St. Paul Airport on 9 August, as Colonel Brittin had hoped. It was sandwiched between stops at Milwaukee, Wisconsin, and Des Moines, Iowa. Twenty-five airplanes were entered in this tour, which was actually a handicap race. Well-known flyers who stopped at St. Paul with the Tour included: Eddie Stinson, Walter Beech, Johnny Livingston, Harold Pitcairn, and Vance Breese. The stop at St. Paul was an overnight stop. Leader of the tour coming into the city was Louis Meister, flying a Buhl-Verville Airster. Walter Beech, in a brand new Travel Air, model 4000, was second to land. Beech and his navigator, Bryce Goldsborough, had been using a set of new-fangled instruments to help them fly a straight line from stop to stop.

Their Travel Air was actually a sophisticated research ship owned by the *Pioneer Instrument Company*, and fitted with experimental instruments such as: a ground speed and drift indicator, venturi-driven airspeed indicator, an "air log" instrument to measure miles traveled, pitch indicator, turn and bank, wind-driven generator, two standard compasses, and the new "earth inductor compass." (The later would gain fame the following year when used by Charles Lindbergh to navigate across the Atlantic Ocean.)

1943. The war is on. A Northwest DC-3 with war bonds advertising, flies east over the Holman Field where a huge bomber modification program is in progress. (Northwest Airlines photo)

It would, therefore, come as no surprise that Beech and Goldsborough won the overall Reliability Tour, having taken the most direct routes of any contestant, and finishing back at Dearborn with an average speed for all flying hours of 124. 1 mph, over no less than 2585 total air miles.

The 1927 Reliability Tour did not stop at St. Paul, skipping it this year by sliding across Iowa from Moline, Illinois to Omaha, Nebraska, on its round-trip to Dearborn. In 1928, however, the Tour returned, making a stop at St. Paul on July 24th. This time, the Tour had been expanded to cross the entire western part of the country. The gaggle of twenty-four competitors made its way from Detroit to Texas, then to California, north to Tacoma, Washington, then back east. The leg from Fargo, North Dakota to St. Paul was led by Johnny Wood, with Frank Hawks second in a Ford Trimotor.

At each stop around the map, the group was feted with dinners, airshows and mind-boggling entertainment. At St. Paul, on the night of their stop, the contestants were treated to dinner by the *St. Paul Aviation Club*. St. Paul's own Phoebe Omlie was a tour contestant in her Monocoupe 70. Though she finished the tour in 24th out of 25 places, it was due mostly to the rather slow speed of her small airplane. Phoebe was no doubt compensated for her effort by the gala festivities and outstanding publicity along the way. The winner was Johnny Wood in a Waco 10.

In 1929, the Reliability Tour once again stopped at St. Paul, this time for two days, beginning on 18 October. This year, the tour covered the East Coast, from Dearborn, dipping as far south as Jacksonville, Florida, before returning north to stop at St. Paul, then continuing on to Dearborn. Some twenty-six airplanes sailed into St. Paul, with Johnny Livingston leading the way. Twenty other planes, while not in competition, accompanied the contestants.

That night, all were treated to a dinner-dance sponsored by the *St. Paul Aviation Club* and held at the *St. Paul Automobile Club*. Aviation promoter, Julius Perlt, Colonel Brittin and St. Paul businessman, Milton Rosen, were responsible for organizing the event. Once again, Phoebe Omlie was the only woman entrant with her Monocoupe, and was accorded a standing ovation for her efforts. The only other Minnesotan on the tour was Faribault's, Dale "Red" Jackson, flying a Curtiss Thrush. He eventually finished in a respectable 12th position. The two day

stopover at St. Paul was the occasion of an open house for the airport. In all, over 300,000 people are said to have attended events during the period. The final Air Tour occurred in 1930, with no stop being made at St. Paul.

St. Paul Airport was also the departure point for Goodwill Tours to Canada in 1928, 1929 and 1930. The Goodwill Tour was a local flying tour from St. Paul to Winnipeg, Manitoba, Canada, sponsored by the *St. Paul Association of Commerce* with the cooperation of the American Legion's *Square Post* and the *Contact Club of the Americas*. The endeavor was geared to promote friendly relations between sister cities through the transfer of goodwill messages and the exchange of small gifts. To most of the participants it was a thinly-disguised chance to have a good time, similar to that being had in the national air tours. It was also a chance for great publicity, and favorable public relations for Northwest Airways and the small businesses that sponsored various planes and pilots.

The first Goodwill Tour got underway on 26 May, 1928, with fifteen planes and pilots participating. Speed Holman flew a Northwest Airways Stinson Detroiter as the "Pathfinder," leading the way. The first stop for all tourers was Wold-Chamberlain Field where a huge airshow took place. The next stop was Little Falls, then on to Crookston, where the participants helped celebrate the opening of the Crookston Airport. Eleven of the tour aircraft had competed in a race to Crookston, with Thorwald "Thunder" Johnson, winner in his Eaglerock airplane. Gene Shank was second place finisher, and Jack Anderson, third.

Major Ray Miller, Commandant of the 109th Observation Squadron, flagged off the race starters at Little Falls, then took off himself for Crookston with two other Air Guard airplanes, overtaking the contestants, and landing at Crookston to supervise the finish. That evening, the flyers were treated to a dinner at Crookston and the following day, an open house and airshow was provided for the public. Departure for Winnipeg followed that afternoon with the flyers arriving at Winnipeg to be treated to yet another dinner that evening.

The 1929 Goodwill Tour included 25 aircraft and pilots, with departure from St. Paul Airport again led by Speed Holman, flying the "Pathfinder," this year a new Hamilton Metalplane, rented by the *St. Paul Dispatch and Pioneer Press*. Tour officials and newsmen flew with Holman. They included Julius Perlt, aviation secretary of the *St. Paul Association of Commerce*; R. J. Dunlap, Managing Editor of the Dispatch/Pioneer Press; and Fred Fellows of the St. Paul Association.

Messages of goodwill were carried from Minnesota Governor Christianson and St. Paul Mayor Hodgson to the Premier of Manitoba, and the Mayor of Winnipeg. The tour overflew St. Cloud to commemorate the opening of the new A. G. Whitney Memorial Airport there, and then overflew Alexandria before stopping at Grand Forks, North Dakota. At Grand Forks, there was an airshow in which Speed Holman borrowed the Waco Taperwing of Chad Smith and put on an outstanding aerobatic exhibition. Dinner and the usual ceremonies followed and departure was the next day.

At Winnipeg's Stevenson Field, the group took part in another celebration, again including aerial acrobatics and formation flying. Most of the intended airshow events were dropped, however, when the weather turned stormy. The airplanes departed the next day into strong headwinds for the return to St. Paul. In 1930, the Canadians reciprocated by sending a group from Winnipeg to St. Paul. No less than 39 flyers and their aircraft arrived on 24 May, following a stopover at Fargo, North Dakota. The *St. Paul Aviation Club* had arranged a reception and a parade. Manitoba Premier, John Bracken, and the Mayor of Winnipeg, both made the flight down to their sister city.

On 15 July, 1930, thirty planes again left the St. Paul Airport bound for Winnipeg on the third annual Goodwill Tour. They returned after three days of banquets and airshows.

The field at St. Paul was visited over the years by a great number of celebrities. Many of the most famous flyers of the country were among them: Sir Hubert Wilkins, arctic and antarctic explorer; Commander Richard Byrd with his pilots Bernt Balchen and Floyd Bennett; Lincoln Ellsworth the explorer; trans-Atlantic flyers Coste and Bellonte; air racers and record setter, Frank Hawks; Casey Jones; Clyde Pangborn; George Haldeman; Ruth Elder; Roscoe Turner; Art Goebel; Wiley Post; Amelia Earhart; Canadian World War One Ace, Billy Bishop; designers Alexander de Seversky and Walter Beech. Jimmy Doolittle, who traveled the country representing the Shell Oil Company, was a frequent visitor.

During the late 1920s, many small airlines started business, using St. Paul as either their headquarters, or a stop on their routes. Such was the case of *Jefferson Airways*, started on 13 July, 1928, using a single Ford Trimotor as equipment, and providing a run between St. Paul and Rochester. Their schedule lasted only a single year. On 20 July, *Chicago Airways* began a route between St. Paul and Chicago. In 1929, *Yellow Cab Airways* was formed and its routes ran between St. Paul and Kansas City, Missouri. Julius Perlt of the St. Paul Association was a principal in this airline, and was instrumental in getting St. Paul on the Yellow Cab route map. 1930 saw the field being used as the eastern terminus of *Mamer Airlines*, started by Nick Mamer. Julius Perlt was involved in this airline as St. Paul agent.

Northern Air Lines, a division of *Universal Airlines*, began making a St. Paul a stop on their schedule between Minneapolis and Chicago. They discontinued the flights in 1929. In 1932, *Hanford Airlines* began making stops in St. Paul. Using the municipal hangar as their northern terminus, they flew between St. Paul and Sioux City, Iowa, and on to Omaha, to the south, or Bismarck to the north. More about these airlines later in this chapter six.

During 1933, airline schedules showed that Northwest Airways operated six flights out of St. Paul to Minneapolis each day. St. Paul was now hooked up with Rochester, Milwaukee, Chicago, Fargo, Jamestown, Billings, and Winnipeg, as well as points as far south as Kansas City.

St. Paul began building a large hangar for Northwest Airways in 1930, to be used as main office,

overhaul facility, and maintenance base.

In May of 1931, Northwest Airways was shocked by the death of its operations manager. Speed Holman, performing an impromptu aerobatic routine at the opening of the Omaha Airport, was killed when he failed to recover from an outside loop. On 22 May, 1932, the St. Paul Airport was officially renamed *Holman Field* in honor of the fallen hero. A dedication ceremony took place with Governor Floyd B. Olson presiding. A seven ton granite block was placed at the entrance to the airport. On it a plaque to Holman's memory was attached. Governor Olson eulogized, "The memorial dedicated here today typifies the man—huge, rugged, enduring. Charles Holman achieved greatness through the qualities of modesty, simplicity, kindliness, and fearlessness, all of which are memorialized in the rugged simplicity of this monument to his memory."[40]

The bronze plaque on the stone read, "1898 - 1931, Charles W. Holman, "Speed." He belonged to the heights and the heights claimed him. Presented by the St. Paul Aviation Club, 1932."

1940 view of a tranquil Holman Field. The calm before the wartime storm. (Vince Doyle)

This monument is still on the field, now standing in front of the terminal building. The field is officially listed on the Metropolitan Airport Commission's books as St. Paul Downtown Airport-Holman Field.

Northwest inaugurated seaplane service from St. Paul to Duluth beginning 30 May, 1931, using a Sikorsky S-38 twin engined amphibian aircraft. Loading passengers at the seaplane dock on the river, they were flown to Duluth, where they landed in the harbor. Pilots, John Woodhead and Jerome Sparboe made the majority of the flights. A second S-38 was added, but this service proved to be less popular than expected and was dropped in less than a year.

The continual dredging and filling operation of the river took its toll. Northwest Airlines, renamed after the airmail cancellation of 1934 and the fiasco that followed, began experiencing difficulties in managing their schedules around the work in progress. On 31 December, 1937, Northwest discontinued flights into St. Paul. Their main offices had already moved back to Wold-Chamberlain. It wasn't until 10 May, 1941, that Northwest would again fly into St. Paul. At that, they still suffered from the weather. On 26

May, they announced that, of the 96 scheduled flights during the first two weeks of resumed operations, bad weather had forced cancellation of 40. On the first of November, they decided to cancel all further flights and maintain their schedule solely from Wold-Chamberlain. A month later, however, the world would be plunged into World War II, and Northwest's fortunes would, once again, be linked to Holman Field.

The airport and St. Paul businesses had been taking it on the chin for some time prior to the war. In 1936, U. S. Postmaster, J. A. Farley, had cancelled the airmail contract with Hanford Airlines, necessitating Hanford's dropping St. Paul as a stop on their route. When the St. Paul Aviation Club protested to Washington, the Post Office Department responded with the statement that since St. Paul was already being served by Northwest, with four daily round trip flights between the cities, there were enough passenger seats in and out of the airport. Not only that, but there were thirteen daily mail trucks between St. Paul and Minneapolis and train service for those commuters needing transportation, so there would be no reallocation.

THE AIR GUARD AT ST. PAUL

In July of 1930, St. Paul finished construction of a hangar for the Minnesota Air Guard. The 109th Observation Squadron immediately packed up their gear and moved out of Wold-Chamberlain to their new quarters. They began their relations with St. Paul by hosting a hangar dance in the new facility.

In January of 1941, the 109th was called to federal service, and transferred to *Beauregard Landing Field* near Alexander, Louisiana, departing from their quarters at Holman Field. (More on the Air Guard can be found in Chapter Seven.)

On 26 February, 1942, The Army assumed command of all operations at Holman Field. They, in effect, took over the entire airport for military use, moving all civilian operations off the field as well as bringing to a halt, all passenger flights in and out. As mentioned previously, the civilian pilot training program operators were told to move off the field, Northwest Airlines had dropped their activities at the airport, and now the Air Guard was gone as well. At this time the Government began construction of a huge hangar to be used for bomber modifications.
(The complete story of the Modification Center is related in Chapter Seven.)

OTHER AIRPORTS IN THE TWIN CITIES AREA

We have already mentioned the earliest airports in the metropolitan Twin Cities area, namely the Earle Brown Farm, Curtiss-Northwest Flying Field, and Clarence Hinck's field in Fridley. For the sake of continuity, a brief mention of each follows:

The Earle Brown Field came into being when Earle Brown, an early homesteader in the area northwest of Minneapolis, in the community of Brooklyn Center, and also an early member of the Aero Club, placed his 580 acre farm and buildings at the disposal of the Army in 1918, to be used as a training site. Though

Curtiss-Northwest Airport was originally called Curtiss Twin City Airport. The view shows Larpenteur Avenue and the nicely manicured fields to the north as well as typical weekend activity. (Bob Lemm)

the Army declined the use, because they had many more sites at their disposal, the University of Minnesota, the Dunwoody Institute, and the mechanic's school at the Overland Building in St. Paul, did accept Brown's offer. The latter two groups were in the process of teaching both Navy and Army aviation cadets. A hangar was erected there and several cadets cycled through each month, for either flying lessons or practical mechanical classes. When the Armistice was signed in November of 1918, the Navy training program ceased. During that time, Enos Ashley had begun operating from the field as the *Ashley Aeroplane Corporation*, selling aircraft and offering sight-seeing flights. Walter Bullock was chief pilot and manager of the company. The field was abandoned as early as 1920.

Curtiss-Northwest Field, located on the southeast corner of Snelling and Larpenteur Avenues, near the State Fair Grounds in St. Paul, was managed by William Kidder, who ran a healthy fixed-base operation there. His activities included the sales of surplus Curtiss Jenny aircraft, sight-seeing flights, commercial delivery, charter flights, and flying lessons.

Kidder's first pilots were: Bill Regan, Vernon Omlie, Charles Keyes, Marvin Northrop, Art Halloway and Ray Miller. Chet Jacobson and Ed Ballough were hired later as business expanded. Kidder, himself, described the opening of the airport in 1918:

"I will never forget the first Sunday we flew our planes at our new field opposite the Fair Grounds. I had two pilots to do the flying that day and thought that would be sufficient, and that I would sell rides to the customers who came to the field. One of the newspapers in Minneapolis and one in St. Paul ran a little story about the opening of Curtiss Northwest Airport.

It seemed like everyone in the Twin Cities was at the field. The roads were blocked with cars for miles and the St. Paul police and the county sheriffs had a terrific job to do, for it was a madhouse. We were carrying passengers so fast in those two planes that I had to get two other pilots to help out and we kept them flying until long after dark by building bonfires on the field so they could see to land. At that time, we were charging $15 for a short flight and we took in several thousand dollars that opening day."[41]

In June of 1921, a fire destroyed the office, a small

Clarence Hinck's hangar at Fridley Field in 1920. The name Federated Flyers Airport on the roof has been hand-inked on the photo for publicity purposes. (C. W. Hinck family)

Harry Holcomb stands in front of his Waco RNF at Robbinsdale Airport. The Ellis Log Cabin Restaurant is in the background. (Marv Sievert)

hangar alongside and all of Kidder's records. In 1928, the field was purchased by the William S. Kling Company and leased to Roth-Downs Airways, the franchise Travel Air distributor. The field closed before 1930. By that time, activity had shifted to the downtown St. Paul Airport, which was closer to the business community.

Fridley Field was started in 1918 by Clarence Hinck upon the signing of a lease between himself and pioneer homesteader, D. H. Fridley. The lease was to run five years. The field was located at 45th Avenue and Main Street in the community of Columbia Heights, north of the main downtown area of Minneapolis. Hinck built hangars and based his activities there from 1918 until he moved to Robbinsdale late in 1923.

These three fields, along with Speedway Field, in use from 1920, were the very first organized airfields in the state. Many other farm fields had been used for isolated landings and takeoffs during this period, but did not become regularly used. In the later 1920s, a new set of fields began to witness lively activity as the airplane became available to a growing number of local pilots. Already mentioned was Robbinsdale Airport, located north of the metropolitan area. Specifically, it was bounded by Fairview Avenue on the north, and approximately 44th Avenue on the south, Broadway Avenue (the old Jefferson Highway) to the east, and the Don Voge family farm to the west. (Now the site of Glen Haven Cemetery.)

The landing area was around fifteen hundred feet in length in the northwest-southeast direction, and there was a nine hundred foot east-west area, not generally used, but available in an emergency. The field got its start in 1920 when Walter Bullock and

Enos Ashley bought the land to be closer to the city than they were at the Earle Brown Farm field. Clarence Hinck ran the field from 1922 to 1924 and Marvin Northrop ran it during 1925. Operator, Gene Shank, became the new owner in 1926, and opened *Pioneer Airways* and later *Shank Flying Service*. Many of the pilots who became instructors, airline pilots, and aviation businessmen in subsequent years took their first flying lessons from Shank at the Robbinsdale Airport.

The next owner of the airport was Harry Holcomb. He bought Shank's Flying Service in approximately 1934, when Shank joined Hanford Airlines. Holcomb changed the name from Shank Flying Service to *States Flying Service* and continued to offer aircraft sales, service, instruction, and sight-seeing. Holcomb would later become a welding instructor for *Minneapolis Aviation Vocational School* at Wold-Chamberlain Field under Jim Follmuth. Brothers, Gordon and Robert Lindstam, and Dave Buckman, bought the States Flying Service from Holcomb in 1938 and continued through World War II with a similar line of service. The Lindstam brothers went to work for Northwest Airlines, Dave Buckman went to work in the Wold-Chamberlain Airport control tower. Most civilian flying was halted at Robbinsdale during the war. In January, 1945, the Minnesota Department of Aeronautics refused to re-license the field because of its proximity to residential housing and it was closed.

Don Voge, whose family owned the farm on the westside, adjacent to the airport, is probably the best

Dr. George Young's Stinson HW-75 at Robbinsdale Airport, circa 1940. (Hinck family)

142

Niels Sorensen has a smile on his face for the cameraman while flying his Buhl Pup over the Oxboro Airport, September, 1937. (Niels Sorensen)

remembered of Robbinsdale's flyers. His personal exploits are documented in the Thrill Show chapter of this book. When Voge's parents died following the war, he constructed an auto racetrack that covered both the family and airport property. It became known as Crystal Speedway, opening in 1948 and continued through 1949.

Another of the really colorful Robbinsdale characters was Dave Dover. Dave occasionally invited some of the flyers to engage in a game of hedge-hopping and buzz-jobs that left nearby farmers shaking their fists. Equally as colorful as Voge and Dover was Dr. George Young, who kept a Stinson HW-75 airplane at Robbinsdale. Dr. Young had owned a pair of amphibian airplanes prior to the Stinson, and had some bad experiences with them, including having one damaged in a windstorm, and making several hard landings that earned him a bad reputation.

Amateur aircraft designer, Orville Hickman, worked as a mechanic for Harry Holcomb at Robbinsdale airport during the middle 1930s. It was at this airport that several of Hickman's designs made their first flights.

Near the Robbinsdale airport was one of the more famous watering holes frequented by flyers, *Ellis's Log Cabin Restaurant*. From its beginning as a chicken shack in the 1920s, through the building of

Slim Enger with his Waco 9 at Oxboro-Heath Airport in 1933. (Niels Sorensen)

the original log cabin, the restaurant was the hangout of all the aviators and sight-seers from Robbinsdale, who stopped by for a hamburger or a Coke. When prohibition ceased, the Log Cabin tavern became a favorite stop. Today, the log cabin still exists, though the family of George and John Ellis, the original owners, have not been involved since 1950. Not quite as famous today, but equally as well-attended was the *Blue Moon Cafe*, a block north of the Log Cabin. A great many of the Robbinsdale flyers spent their non-flying time in one or both of these restuarants.

An organization called the "Zero-Zero Club" was formed by the regulars of Robbinsdale. It was an association of pilots with an interest in having a good time, even when the weather was "zero-zero," (referring to ceiling and visibility unsuited for flying). Club members frequented both the Log Cabin and the Blue Moon, and adopted a ditty written by Clarence Hinck:

When skies are fair,
We take to the air,
With one hand firm on the throttle.
When the day is over,
We land in the clover,
And transfer our hand to the bottle.

Though the wives had another name for the group, the "nothing-nothing club," it became very popular, with each newly-soloed student pilot being asked to join.

Besides the Lindstam brothers, other instructors at the old Robbinsdale Airport were Mark Madigan, Al Swanson, and Lloyd Franke.

(University, Victory, Flying Cloud, and Southport Airports are discussed in the chapter of this book dealing with the CPTP and WTS wartime training programs.)

Pietenpol at Oxboro Airport. The house in the background still stands at 10009 Lyndale Avenue South. (Jim Ladwig)

The Bloomington Airports

OXBORO AIRPORT. Often called Oxboro-Heath, after the original name of the community in which it was located, (now part of Bloomington), or just Lyndale Airport. Oxboro was located between what is now Highway 35W to the west and Lyndale Avenue to the east; and between 100th and 102nd Streets. It was located on land originally leased in 1931 by Harry Jaunty as a landing field. Though not a flyer himself, Jaunty built a hangar on the northeast corner of the field and let the *Oxboro Flying Club* use it.

Members of the Club and frequent visitors to the field were Wallace L. Neuman, Gilbert Enger, Ingvold J. "Slim" Enger, F. A. "Al" Schauss, Gerard M. Justen, Clarence J. "Happ" Walerius, Naomi E. Hansen, George F. Cornelius, Sam Kelsey, and William C. Weeks.

This Heath Parasol airplane unceremoniously bit the ground on landing at Nicollet Airport when it ran across the ruts of the road in the background, and bent the left gear. The hat on the ground was thrown there in disgust by the pilot after the incident, or so the story goes. Circa 1935. (Jim Ladwig)

Marvin Heinzel stands with his beautiful Cessna AW at Nicollet Airport in 1941. (Jim Borden)

Brothers, Wally and Al Neuman, cousins to Jaunty, took over the field in 1933. Wally was an instructor and gave lessons in a Curtiss Robin. Al furnished non-official flight instruction in a Waco 9 aircraft, despite the fact that he wasn't a licensed instructor. Al's Waco eventually wound up going through a barn, courtesy of Don Voge, the housecrasher!

In 1932, the first hangar, and two planes kept inside, were lost when the hangar burned to the ground. Schauss's Salmson-engined homebuilt parasol aircraft was one of the unlucky victims.

Many of the Oxboro flyers began moving to a slightly larger field near Nicollet Avenue in 1935. Others, such as Niels Sorensen, stayed on until sometime in 1937. Sorensen and Frank "Bubs" Christian purchased a Buhl Pup aircraft that year. It was powered by a Szekely engine and kept tied down at Oxboro. When Niels and Bubs finally moved, it was to the Christian family farm at 66th Street and Bloomington Avenue in Richfield. The Buhl changed hands several times, finally ending up in Indiana some years later, where it was seen with Luscombe wings.

Sometime before the 1932 fire at Oxboro, a small metal T-hangar was moved in from Brainerd and set up on the field. It would have a colorful history.

When the flyers began to move, the metal hangar was taken down and moved to Robbinsdale Airport. Following World War II, when that airport was closed, the hangar was moved to the new Crystal Airport. In 1949, to make room for additional runways at Crystal, the hangar again went on the auction block and Ken Muxlow, a flyer from Bloomington, bought it. Once more it was disassembled, and this time, moved to Flying Cloud Airport, where it still stands, and is still owned by Muxlow. It is certainly the most moved, if not the oldest hangar there today.

NICOLLET AIRPORT. This airport was located east of Nicollet Avenue between 90th and 93rd Streets. It featured a very short east-west landing strip and a lesser used north-south. The land had originally been purchased for $4000 by Wally Russell and Pat O'Conner from its original owner. With the exodus from Oxboro Airport, Al Neuman came to Nicollet in 1935 and started a business. He eventually was able to convince the Civil Aeronautics Authority (CAA) that he had somewhere near the number of hours that his logbook indicated, and he became a licensed instructor.

Many of the flyers using this strip remembered the area to have been encircled by potato fields with several dump areas where garbage and other trash was occasionally burned. The plumes from the dump fires made a very visible beacon with which to locate the field.

It was at this field, from 1939 until 1941, that Elmer Hinck based his cross-country training airplanes during the Civilian Pilot Training Program (CPTP) program. Later, as a result of the Navy's takeover of all airspace south of Wold-Chamberlain Field as far as the present Apple Valley, this airport was closed, civilian planes moved elsewhere.

During the first few months that Nicollet Field was in operation, the State of Minnesota was campaigning to license all aircraft based within the state. There was much resistance to this idea. Many believed it was unnecessary duplication of governmental regulation. Aircraft already had to have a federal license and identification numbers. However, until such time that aircraft were also licensed by the state, they were in violation of state law and authorities sought to prevent their being flown.

The aircraft in question were mostly homebuilts, and therefore, did not have a federal type certificate due to the fact that they had not been subject to manufacturing specifications and testing. Most were, however, airworthy aircraft. Some of the unlicensed ships were older production aircraft that did need serious overhaul or repair, but were kept flying, never-the-less. A number of planes of both categories found their way to a home at Nicollet Airport, which was an unlicensed airport.

Relations with nearby homeowners weren't the finest at Nicollet in the mid-1930s. One irate homeowner, tired of the noise, had a blank warrant sworn out for the arrest of these pilots. The first unlucky aviator who happened to land while the sheriff was there, was Sam Kelsey in his Mohawk Pinto. Kelsey was asked to show his license. He had none. The licensing agent where Sam had applied was not yet supplied with the actual certificates. When Kelsey was brought before the local magistrate, he did have a receipt for his license fee and showed that to the judge. The case was dismissed. Kelsey later sued the homeowner and eventually collected a judgement of $200 for wrongful arrest.[42]

CEDAR AIRPORT. Cedar was located close to Wold-Chamberlain, west of Cedar Avenue, between 86th and 88th Streets, with landing strips running in every direction. It was here that Wally Neuman came in 1937, as a result of the evacuation of Oxboro Airport. Neuman joined forces with Wally Dale, and later Russ Abbott, to run the field.

The threesome, operating as *Cedar Flying Service*, offered flight instruction, charter flights and sightseeing. Instruction was in 40 and 50 horsepower Cubs through the late 1930s. The Cedar Flying Service booklet professed, "Come out and try a sample of flying. Ten full minutes and you actually fly the plane yourself. This trial flight will cost you only $1.00."[43] The booklet stated that there were no Army, Navy, Marine or Airline aircraft to hinder flight instruction at Cedar airport.

However, in 1941, CPT instructors would bring the training aircraft from Nicollet Field to pick up their students at Cedar. They did not want students flying out of the rather small and unlicensed Nicollet Field.

Cedar Airport, south Minneapolis, 1936. Cedar Avenue is in the foreground and 86th Street runs off to the right. A crowd has gathered for a weekend airshow in this aerial view looking southwest. (Eugene Rosing via Chet Peters)

One of the flyers using Cedar Airport was Howard Beamish. Beamish owned an Aeromarine-Klemm, and later a Wright J-4 engined American Eagle. Another flyer was Hans Bjelleness. "Jello" built a hangar at Cedar and kept a five-passenger Stinson there until it was requisitioned by the military. The plane was turned over to the Navy in 1942 for sub-patrol out of Pensacola, Florida.

The area around Cedar airport was generally planted in grain crops except for the runways. A heavily wooded area bordered the field to the north, along Cedar Avenue. Not far from the southern end of the airport, on the northeast corner of the intersection of Cedar and Old Shakopee Road, was another

Cedar Airport, 17 July, 1945. This photo shows a lot of activity and the large number of airplanes based there. It is thought that this photo was taken for the state hearing, called to close the airport. (Metropolitan Airports Commission)

of the legendary watering holes favored by local flyers, the *Black Cat Club*. Stories of its parties and girls are prevalent among the nostalgia set. Across the intersection, *Stott's Club* on the southwest corner was also popular.

Some of the other pilots using Cedar Airport were; Chet Peters, the Strand Brothers—Don, Ray, and Sparky, Al Cassidy, Mel Lee, Len Otrembo, Al Schauss, and Norm Sten. Sten, Dale, and Russ Abbott owned a Fairchild KR-21 until 1941, when Sten bought out the others. Al Schauss kept a homebuilt Model A-powered biplane hangared at Cedar Airport.

In 1940, Wally Dale sold his partial ownership of the airport to his sister, and at the same time married Frances Pryzymus, a well-known lady pilot. Wally joined the FAA and the family moved to Milwaukee where he was assigned as a control tower operator.

The Christian brothers landing field at 66th and Bloomington, mentioned previously, was used by brothers, Ben and Bubs Christian, and Niels Sorensen, from approximately 1937 until 1941. The Christians sold Porterfield aircraft at nearby Wold-Chamberlain Field. Niels, who had been instructing at Cedar Airport in 1940, also instructed for A. C. McInnis and Elmer Hinck at Wold. In the Naval Reserve for several years, Niels went on active duty with the Navy in 1941, and was stationed at Pensacola.

Another field at 76th and Lyndale was run by Jimmy Piersal sometime in the 1920s, but details on this field are not available.

Still another metro airport was the Pierce Airport near Anoka. Originally a landing strip owned by Hartwick T. Hanson and called Hanson's Airport, the strip was operational from about 1928 until well into the 1950s. Hanson's airplane and hangar were hit by a windstorm on 11 November, 1931. Hanson quit flying after that, penning a final, terse entry in his logbook, "Ship and hangar blown to hell by cyclone

Cedar Flying Service booklet. Circa 1941.

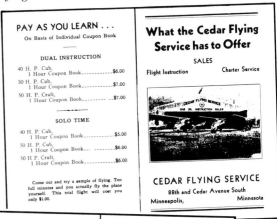

- complete washout."[44] Further information about this airport is unavailable.

An airport two miles west of Elk River was graded and levelled with a WPA (Works Progress Administration) program in 1934 and 1935. In 1938, a flying club using a J-3 Cub operated from a pasture alongside the never-finished airport. No further details are available on this field.

NAVY PRACTICE FIELDS:

During the wartime period, the Navy Reserve Primary Training Squadron, home-based at Wold-Chamberlain Field, was split into two sections for best use of local airspace. NRAB (Naval Reserve Air Base) Minneapolis, Training Squadron 1A was stationed at Wold, NRAB Minneapolis, Training Squadron 1B was stationed at South St. Paul Airport. This field later became Fleming Field.

Each base had its designated practice area. The routes and associated practice landing strips were numerous over the southern portion of the Minneapolis, St. Paul area and places south of the cities. A map and listing of those landing strips is included in the Navy-Marine section of Chapter Seven.

South St. Paul Airport was originally used by the *Hook-em-Cow Flying Club* run by Alex Rozawick in 1939. The field was then purchased by A. C. McInnis as a CPT base in 1940, and taken over by the Navy in 1942. The Navy built several large wooden-hoop-raftered hangars and other buildings, including a simple platform control tower. They paved a large apron in front of the hangars to make space for the 100 training planes based there and paved two fifteen-hundred foot diameter soil-cement circles on the airfield. From these circles, landings and takeoffs could be made into the wind, no matter from which direction it was blowing. The circles are still there, now providing flooring for newly constructed hangars.

The field was named Fleming Field after Marine Captain Richard E. Fleming, who died in a dive-bombing attack on a Japanese cruiser at the Battle of Midway.

ST. PAUL AIRPORTS

Two small airports retain the nostalgia among the older sport pilots of St. Paul, Onion Airport and Lux-inger's. Both were used by the same flyers, who may have kept their ships tied down at one or the other, but did most of their flying on the east side of St. Paul.

ONION AIRPORT. Probably the most remembered strip on the outskirts of the city was the unlicensed, Onion Airport, or the "Onion Patch." It was located to the west of Beaver Lake, between Stillwater Road to the south, and railroad tracks to the north, and encompassed several acres. Today, it is a housing development. Onion Airport got its nickname from a location among fields used for growing onions by the Wally and Eldon Kern family, farmers who had homesteaded the land.

Onion Airport existed from approximately 1931 to 1937. It had landing strips in various positions over the years, depending on where the onions were planted. At times, there were two parallel north-south strips. with rows of onions growing between. A strip

running east-west was kept unplowed, to be used in the event of strong crosswinds on the main strips.

A haven for homebuilders, Onion Patch was peopled with colorful characters. The airplanes and some pilots, like their counterparts at Nicollet Field in Minneapolis, were unlicensed. A few of the more illustrious pilots were Gordon Kindlein, Hilbert Nieman, Ray Haberman, Ben Wiplinger, Slim Zettler, Herman Jensen, Johnny Hallman, Charlie Ferraro, and Don Sanford.

Johnny Hallman was a natural inventor and engineer. He developed his own modifications to the Model A Ford engine, popular with the Pietenpol homebuilders. (See Chapter Four.) He also designed and built his own parasol aircraft to use the engine.

Gordy Kindlein had a similar inclination. Kindlein built a hangar at Onion Airport by simply constructing an A-frame over a burned machine shed. He built two homebuilts and flew them from the strip until the start of World War II. When civilian flying was halted, his last creation was brought to the Kindlein home in St. Paul. There, the neighborhood children played in it until it was finally junked out. Kindlein never had a Private license, but often gave other pilots air instruction.

Ben Wiplinger bought an unfinished Pietenpol from another local builder and continued the construction of it, installing a Model A engine. Though it was designed for dual controls, Wiplinger had covered over the unfinished front cockpit, and since he had not yet learned how to fly, let Burt Nieman put some hours on it. Wiplinger soon decided that the only way he would ever get to fly his own airplane was if he opened up the front cockpit, and got some dual time. He took tin snips and cut away the cowling, set up a bench made of two by fours in the front and got a couple of hours of instruction from Nieman. He later soloed himself.

Wiplinger exchanged the Ford engine for a German-made Siemens-Halske, 5-cylinder radial. Sometime later, he had the exciting adventure of having the propeller come loose while cruising over St. Paul, but he managed to land before the prop actually came off.

The Pietenpol was a popular homebuilt airplane in the 1930s, even as it is today. Ray Haberman had a Model A Pietenpol that he switched to Velie engine power. When it was ready to fly, he enlisted Gordy Kindlein to test fly it out of Ray's backyard in St. Paul. Haberman eventually sold the plane to a party in the state of Oregon.

By far the most colorful character of the lot was Burt Nieman. Not only a very active flyer, but also an inventor with inexhaustible energy, Nieman was always building something. He was an auto mechanic by trade, and also a professional wrestler. He had purchased a Velie Monocoupe early in his flying career, but stalled it and spun into the ground at St. Cloud, breaking his back and injuring his feet severely in the process.

Though he was told he would never walk again, he not only walked, but resumed wrestling in small towns around the area. His friends could tell of his famous overhead-airplane-spin with an opponent in the wrestling ring. Nieman's Monocoupe airplane was rebuilt and Nieman flew it many more hours.

Nieman also gave flying instructions, though it is

unclear whether he ever had an instructors license, or even a Private license for that matter. Once he was giving Ray Haberman some flight time in Ray's Pietenpol, and Ray remembers that Nieman had to get into the airplane in his stocking feet because the compartments for the rudder pedals had very limited room and Burt had large feet. When they landed at Wold-Chamberlain some time later, Burt walked around in his stocking feet as they made the rounds, visiting the Wold regulars. [45]

Some of Burt's other designs and inventions are spelled out in Chapter Four.

LUXINGER'S AIRPORT. The second of the well-used St. Paul private airports. Luxinger's was located on a one hundred-sixty acre site north of old Highway 12, now Interstate 94, between County Road 71 to the east and Manning Avenue to the west. It was active from roughly the same period as Onion Airport, 1931 to 1941.

As mentioned before, flyers using this field were the same ones who used Onion Airport. Some of them were unlicensed, and many of the planes, which were mostly homebuilts, were also unlicensed. Like their counterparts in Minneapolis, the owners of unlicensed aircraft flying from fields in St. Paul, were under pressure to be licensed by the State. Major Ray Miller, as both Commander of the 109th Observation Squadron of the Minnesota Air National Guard, and as chairman of the new Minnesota Aeronautics Commission, sought to enforce the Aeronautics Act of 1933 that required all planes based in Minnesota to be licensed.

Miller's method of achieving compliance was often through use of his "troops," the Guardsmen, who, while doing a lot of flying across the State, were often able to spot unlicensed aircraft. Miller was a stickler about this subject, and it had a detrimental affect on private flying. As mentioned before, homebuilt aircraft could not get a federal license, and since this was one of the requirements for Minnesota licensing, owners of those aircraft were fugitives from the law. The pilots hopped from airport to airport, avoiding Wold-Chamberlain and Holman Field, to keep out of the state's eye.

A sizeable movement was started to have the Aeronautics Act's regulation repealed. A delegation led by Bernard Pietenpol, Doctor George Young, and Burt Nieman, with as many as 100 other protesters, held meetings around the state to gather support and eventually brought suit against the Minnesota Aeronautics Commission and the Attorney General, Harry H. Peterson. Their actions were enough to influence Judge J. C. Michael declare the law unconstitutional.

World War II interrupted civilian flying, and of course, homebuilding as well. Following the war, enthusiast groups managed to get the rules changed to allow the licensing of homebuilts.

Between 1935 and 1937, many St. Paul pilots sought refuge at various out-of-the-way airfields, including a strip at Lake Jane, near North St. Paul, and another across the St. Croix River at Holton Hill, near Somerset. Many flyers sold their airplanes out-of-state for whatever they could get for them. The punishment for flying an unlicensed aircraft was a $500 fine and ninety days in jail! The sight of Miller or one of his

staff pulling up to Onion Airport would send many a pilot scurrying for the woods, even an occasional member of Miller's own troops, the Air Guard.

Final disposition of the situation came in July of 1941. According to the *St. Paul Dispatch* of 23 July, 1941, six unlicensed aircraft at Luxinger's were grounded by the State Aeronautics Commission, one of which was the Whitey Sport of Charlie Ferraro, which lay abandoned in trees on the property until sometime in the 1960s. The situation was unfortunate. Many airplanes were grounded forever.

Another St. Paul landing field, almost lost to memory, was located northeast of White Bear Lake. It was active during the 1920s when it was home for the *Harold G. Peterson Airplane Company*. Peterson built a wooden hangar in which a J-1 Standard was kept. By the 1930s the hangar was gone and the strip abandoned.

A farm strip at St. Paul Park, owned by the Lloyd Belden family, was a popular stopping-over spot on a Sunday afternoon. No further information is available regarding this strip.

EARLY AIRPORTS IN OUTSTATE MINNESOTA

As mentioned in earlier chapters, the very first organized airports in Minnesota were clustered around the metropolitan area of the Twin Cities. It was there that the impetus for such activity was strongest, what with the coming of the air mail and various business needs. It was there that the most entertainment dollars were to be spent. Thus, the barnstormers concentrated their activities at the major cities, and the businessmen who were to make their living from aviation found financing, supplies, and a ready market for their wares.

Not until Lindbergh crossed the ocean did interest in aerial activity become sufficient for smaller communities to designate landing fields and airports to support local flying. With some exceptions, most of Minnesota's airports were products of the very late 1920s and 1930s, postdating Lindbergh's flight.

Motivation to improve those early airports and provide others for communities that would be growing, was furnished by the WPA (Works Progress Ad-

Elmer Sell, on the right, proudly stands between the two products of his franchises, the Piper Cub and the Plymouth automobile. The owner of the Plymouth, standing to the left, has most likely signed up for some flight time as well as a new car. Sell's Flying Field in Carver County was the county's only airport through the pre-war years. (Charles Sell)

ministration), in the 1930s. Communities as International Falls, Hibbing, St. Cloud, and many others, got needed funds and manpower from that agency to expand facilities. An act passed by the state legislature in 1944 expedited the completion of many of the airports started during the preceeding ten years of WPA. This push would be responsible for the fine statewide network of airports that would come under extensive use following World War II.

Since we have discussed the Twin Cities in some length in previous chapters, we can now focus our interests on an alphabetical survey of the counties. It should be noted that this is not an exhaustive listing of all the primitive landing fields in each county. It would not be possible to relate the developmental details of each airport, as many of the earliest fields were nothing more than farm strips that became the locally accepted places for aviators to gather, to purchase fuel from a local service station, or to tie down for the night. The names and locations of most of these old fields have been lost to mind with the passing of their users. In many cases, no records were kept, nor was there news media coverage of the activities taking place.

Aitkin County. Located in the center of the State. No information on early airports is available.

Anoka County. One of the seven counties of metropolitan Minneapolis and St. Paul. Here was located Clarence Hinck's first airport on property leased from D. H. Fridley, after whom the present community is named. More information on C. W. Hinck in Chapter Three. The present Anoka County Airport was established in the early 1950s.

Becker County. In the north-central portion of the state. Detroit Lakes is the major city. Local aviators used a field on the Hohaug Farm near the city. In 1929, A. P. Foster and Harold Rathbun built a small hangar there, and in 1936, the city purchased the field, with the WPA constructing a runway. By 1938 the field was all but abandoned.

Many pilots encouraged the city to re-establish a regular field. Impassioned rhetoric by L. H. Rennewanz in the *Becker County Record*, 1 December, 1938, helped get the job done. After a chuck hole in a local field disabled his plane, it was vandalized overnight by local youths. He pleaded, "...someone is going to see the advantage of an air service and sponsor this project, and whoever it may be, will profit by the undertaking. We have the field; we have the means; we have the desire to fly; to put an air service in Detroit Lakes. We need a joining of the three."

In 1944, the city council opened a refurbished airport west of town, and named Lester Brown of Fargo, North Dakota, the manager.

Beltrami County. In the northern portion of the state. Bemidji is the major city. Flying began in the Bemidji area as early as 1919, with barnstormers and exhibitions. The first airfield used was inside the County Fair racetrack. In the early 1920s the Christ Larson farm about two miles west of the city was used as an airfield. In 1927, the American Legion took the lead in formally establishing it as an airport,

which was used until 1930. At that time, a field closer to the city was promoted by the Legion and came to be known as Bemidji Flying Field from 1930 until 1933. Still another field, called Bemidji Municipal Airport, was located north of Highway 2, and saw use between 1933 and 1945. The first hangar there was built as a WPA project.

The latter airport was the site of a CPT program, and in 1940, was undergoing $150,000 in improvements. Forrest Rising was airport manager and flight instructor.

Benton County. Located in the middle of Minnesota. Sauk Rapids is the major city in the County. No information on airports is available.

Big Stone County. Located near the South Dakota border in the middle of the State. Here, the cities of Graceville and Ortonville are located. At Graceville, Pat Kapaun started an airport on his own property in the 1930s and maintained it himself, for some 32 years. The Graceville Airport of today was dedicated in 1971 to Kapaun and Herb Wilson, two of the earliest flyers in the county.

The Ortonville Airport site was selected in 1933 by Ed Martinson and Ferd Grosenick, city councilmen; and long-time pilot and barnstormer, Jack Alfred Anderson. In 1934, the city council purchased 120 acres of land from the Federal Land Bank for $2900 and established two grass runways. With WPA labor and $35,000 in funds from the federal government, the city made improvements, and in 1941, put up a hangar. The field remains today and is named Martinson Field after its prime founder.

Blue Earth County. Southern Minnesota. The largest city is Mankato. There, in 1928, funds were solicited for the establishment of an airport. Local businessmen had high hopes that an airline could be established. It would operate from that port, east to La Crosse, Wisconsin, and west to Rapid City, South Dakota. At the very least, they hoped for the city to become a stop on the airline's proposed cross-country air route, called Mindakota Skyways. A 107-acre airport, managed by Lawrence Sohler was dedicated there 29 September, 1928. At the dedication, Captain Ira Eaker, representing the U.S. Air Corps, spoke to a large crowd. Air races took place and a large number of airplanes were displayed for the public. The hoped-for airline never matured.

Brown County. Located in the southern portion of the state. Includes the cities of Springfield, Sleepy Eye, and New Ulm. New Ulm's Airport originated in a resolution passed by their city council on 13 May, 1929, to purchase property for its development. A tract of land comprising 46 acres was procured and the payment was made from city funds. Interestingly enough, in 1932, a lawsuit was brought against the city and its councilmen, charging unlawful action in purchasing and improving the property. A citizen lawsuit sought to recover the entire costs amounting to $12,000. Some of the council members, at the time of purchase, were also stockholders in the land corporation from which the property was purchased.

The lawsuit was dismissed by the court, stating that

all parties had acted in the best interests of the citizens of New Ulm, and the flying public.

The airport existed until 1943, when a new, larger site was proposed, and in 1944, financing was available. The intervening war brought plans to a halt, and not until 1948 was a new airport built in New Ulm.

Carlton County. Along the east central portion of Minnesota. Largest city in this county is Cloquet. No information on early airports is available.

Carver County. This county is one of the seven-counties of the metropolitan Twin Cities. Most cities are rural, with Chaska and Chanhassen, the largest; Waconia, Norwood-Young-America, and Victoria, among the smaller. In Carver County, Elmer Sell's airfield was the major landing spot. Sometimes called the Mayer Airport, from its location on the Sell farm near the community of Mayer.

Elmer Sell, a member of a pioneer family, had an airplane as early as 1931, and flew it from a farm field near his own family farm. On that field, he built a hangar. In 1935, Sell rented some land from his Father, O.D. Sell, and began using a log house and a log barn for hangars. The joke about the "log cabin hangar" having been there since pioneer times, may not be exactly true, but it was, indeed, the oldest hangar in the state.

It was from the farm field that Elmer Sell took off on barnstorming tours and sold rides on weekends. In the 1930s Sell acquired a Piper aircraft dealership and sold Piper Cubs. He not only sold airplanes, but also autos, through a De Soto-Plymouth distributorship. *Sell's Motor and Flying Service* in the town of Mayer also handled Philco radios, Gibson refrigerators, outboard motors, and tires. Sell did machine shop work and cabinetry as well. He became a member of the Minnesota Aeronautics Commission in the 1930s, and was dispatched around the state inspecting proposed airport sites.

With the outbreak of World War II, Sell's airport was first guarded by a "home guard" of 14th Infantry soldiers from Fort Snelling, and later by two permanent guards, hired by the city. In 1942, the airport was closed for the duration of the war. Resurrected again after the war for a short period, the strip was gradually abandoned as the old pilots migrated away from the area. The log hangars were long gone, and a newer hangar, built after the war, was burned by the Mayer Fire Department as a training exercise in 1962.

Cass County. Located in the very central portion of the State. No information on early airports is available.

Chippewa County. In western Minnesota. Montevideo is the largest community, but no information is known about an airport in its vicinity. Gus Imm managed what was known as the Northern Airport in the community of Maynard, Minnesota, not far from Granite Falls. Gus held a Waco franchise there in 1927. He built a hangar and used it as a base for his barnstorming forays.

Chisago County. Located at the eastern edge of the State just above the metropolitan Twin Cities area. No information on early airports is available.

Clay County. On the western edge of the State. Moorhead is the principal city. No information available.

Clearwater County. In the north central portion of the State. No information available.

Cook County. The very northeastern-most county in Minnesota, includes the Grand Marais area. No information available.

Cottonwood County. In the southwestern part of the State. Includes the cities of Windom and Mountain Lake. No information available.

Crow Wing County. In the central part of the State. Includes the bigger city of Brainerd and one of the state's more popular resort areas. As early as 1920, entrepreneur Henry Rosko had brought a hydroplane to Brainerd, where he and his brother converted 160 acres of farmland at the south edge of the city into a private airport. They built two small hangars and some sheds, and soon purchased a Waco 10 aircraft. In 1931, the city took an option to purchase the land and built a larger hangar. The *Brainerd Flying Club* was established there. As needs for a larger airport grew, the city dropped their purchase option and the field was sold to Burton Garrett in 1945. That year, the city acquired 900 acres on Highway 210 and by 1947 had built a sizeable airport, that is still in use today.

Dakota County. Dakota County airports, including South St. Paul and Navy practice fields are discussed in Chapter Seven.

Dodge County. Southeastern Minnesota. No information available.

Douglas County. Includes the resort city of Alexandria. No information available.

Faribault County. Located on the extreme southern border of the State. Largest city, Blue Earth. No information available.

Fillmore County. Located in the southeastern corner of the state. This county encompasses the cities of Spring Valley and Rushford. Cherry Grove, near Spring Valley, was the home of Bernard Pietenpol and his airstrip was in use from the early 1930s.

Freeborn County. In southern Minnesota. Albert Lea is the largest city within this county. Earliest airfields were farm strips, with one on the Leonard Wolfe farm near Glenville, south of Albert Lea, being the first strip to see much activity. As other flyers began to congregate, a strip was established on a farm west of town, owned by the Ruble family. There, at least three T-hangars were built and flight training was given during the period just prior to World War II. The airport was used for only a couple of years, then was phased out when the county acquired land north of the city in approximately 1938. The city then built the present Freeborn County Airport. Earliest flyers were Bob Stiehler, Harley Ladlie, Frank Jensen, Irv Rofshus, Leonard Wolfe, and Edward Dusek.

Goodhue County. Southeast corner of the state. Red Wing and Cannon Falls are the principal cities. No information available.

Grant County. West central Minnesota. Elbow Lake is principal city. Most aviators in this county used the Fergus Falls Airport in Ottertail County to the north.

Hennepin County. Airports in this county have been discussed earlier.

Houston County. The very southeastern-most county in Minnesota. La Crescent, Spring Grove, and Caledonia are principal cities, but none had a municipal airport prior to World War II. Earliest pilots in this county are generally regarded as being Melvin Trehus and James Sylling. Melvin was said to have owned over 50 airplanes in his lifetime, and made a living, flying from farm to farm, selling machinery as well as airplanes, to the farmers. Sylling was himself a farmer, who had bought Pietenpol's first homebuilt airplane. The plane never flew for lack of an engine.

Hubbard County. In the middle of Minnesota. No information available.

Isanti County. Middle eastern portion of the state. No information available.

Itasca County. Grand Rapids and Coleraine are the principal cities in this county. The Coleraine Airport was dedicated on the 4th of July 1929. The airport was built on a former mine pit, filled in and graded over. Like most airport dedications, it occurred amidst a great deal of fanfare, with dignitaries and visiting pilots from other communities. Seventeen year old Gordy Newstrom was there. At the time, Gordy was a fishing guide at Marcell, Minnesota, and the dedication event firmed his decision to go into the aviation business. That business eventually included the establishment of *Mesaba Aviation*, today's *Mesaba Airlines*.

The Itasca County story really is a story of bush flying and the resort business. Wesley Barkla, from Coleraine, was flying an Eastman flying boat from Trout Lake near Coleraine, hopping passengers and moving fishermen from one place to another. C. R. "Dusty" Rhodes, with his Ryan monoplane on floats, hopped pasengers from his base on Trout Lake, near Grand Rapids, during the late 1920s as well. Rhodes adventures in the area became legendary.

Otis Lodge, on Lake Sisse-Bak-Wet, (later known as Sugar Lake), to the southwest of Grand Rapids, became very well known for its famous fishing, and the famous cooking of Eleanor and Art Otis. Following Lindbergh's flight in 1927, Art Otis developed a landing strip on his property and encouraged fishermen to fly in. The popularity of the place increased, and by 1937, Otis was routinely welcoming

At Itasca County, Coleraine Airport dedication, 4 July, 1929. The lineup of visiting flyers included Gordy Newstrom in the OX-5 Eaglerock at far left, a long-nosed Kinner Eagle, and a Hisso Eaglerock in the foreground. (Gordy Newstrom)

Air Guard and Navy pilots who stopped there for lunch in their military aircraft. Even a Ford Trimotor, with visitors from the twin cities, dropped in occasionally. Otis Lodge became the mecca for fly-in fishermen, and backed by the enthusiasm of his clientele, Art Otis took up flying.

The Grand Rapids Airport was newly opened in 1931. A WPA program enabled the city to develop what had previously been known as Wheaton Field. The airport started operation with a 1600 foot north-south landing strip. Ted Tinquist soloed from this field and went on to gain several ratings, becoming a spokesman for aviation in the area. He opened his own flying service, *Tinquist Aviation*, selling out in 1948 to Gordy Newstrom.

Jackson County. Located in the bottom row of Minnesota counties. The city of Lakefield had an airport on the former Krueger farm property as early as 1929. The field was located about half a mile north of the railroad depot on 40 acres of land with intersecting northwest-southeast, and northeast-southwest runways. It held a large hangar that was built by the local American Legion Post.

Charles Rodina, who is accepted as Jackson County's first pilot of record, leased the Krueger farm in 1929. When the Lakefield Commercial Club heard that the sister city of Jackson was planning to build a municipal airport, they urged that the Rodina field be purchased by Lakefield for the same purpose in an attempt to beat Jackson to the draw. The expectation was that the municipal field would become the stopping point for passenger and airmail planes flying

Sugar Lake spreads in front of Otis Lodge, and the large grass airfield lies behind it. What fly-in fishermen could resist in 1939? (John Otis)

from Minneapolis to points south. The Lakefield City Council took no action, and Jackson grabbed the headlines. The Rodina field was still be used until 1939 or 1940, however.

The city of Jackson located their airfield about a half mile north of the city in September of 1929 and convinced the local American Legion Post to erect a hangar. This location did become a flag stop for *Hanford Airlines*. A flag stop is normally overflown, but when mail or paying passengers are to be picked up, the pilot is "flagged down" to a landing by use of a flag or other easily seen signal, laid out on the runway. The fare to Minneapolis from Jackson was $8.00.

Occasionally, one of Hanford's Lockheed Vegas would get stuck in the mud while taxiing at Jackson. In one instance, a pair of elderly farmers were watching the recovery of a Vega by a man with a team of horses. One farmer remarked to the other, "That's the only way you'd ever get me into one of those things."[46]

Kanabec County. Located in the central portion of the state. Mora is the principal city. No information available.

Kandiyohi County. Located in the south central part of Minnesota. The principal city is Willmar. New London and Spicer are other large cities. Willmar opened the county's first official airport in 1934. It leased 110 acres of land from F.E. Gillette, whose farm was located west of the city in an area known as "Ramblewood." A WPA project and a federal grant totalling $19,830, allowed for the grading and improving of the site. In September of 1934, the airport was dedicated.

A pair of T-hangars were constructed soon after the airport opened and the luxury of luxuries, an open-topped touring car, was secured as an airport hack. A large airshow occurred at the airport in 1937 with well-known pilots of the area taking part in such events as stunt flying, handkerchief pickups, and providing air rides. In the 1939-1940 era, field lighting and a beacon were added, and a Federal Airways Communications station opened. The airways station was decommissioned in 1950.

In 1941, a large 100x144 foot hangar was erected under *National Youth Administration* contract and was known at the time as one of the finest buildings of its kind. The field was kept open for flying through

Lac Qui Parle County. The Madison Airport, having been improved for the WTS program in 1943. (Beverly Plathe)

the war, thanks to the efforts of local businessmen. In 1945, John Rice took over operation of the airport, and with his wife, Mary Jane, spent 38 years administering to the needs of the flying public from this spot.

Kittson County. The farthest northwestern county of Minnesota. No information available.

Koochiching County. Located in the northern row of Minnesota counties. International Falls is the principal city. The story of Koochiching county is the story of bush flying and seaplanes. Prior to World War II, what is now the International Falls Airport was a grass strip alongside Highway 11. Forrest Rising operated *Riverview Flying Service* there, using a Curtiss Robin for sight-seeing flights, and employing Dave Powell as a flight instructor. The present airport was established in 1945. Following the war, operator Glen Van Etten soon sold out to Francis and Jim Einarson, who continue operations there to this day.

Lac Qui Parle County. Located at the far southwestern area of Minnesota. Madison is the chief city. First local person to own an airplane was Ole Kravik in 1919. It is recorded that he flew from the County Fairgrounds. In the late 1930s the CAA set up airway beacons across Minnesota on the route from Minneapolis to Watertown, South Dakota, locating two of them in Lac Qui Parle County. One was near the village of Lac Qui Parle, itself, the other in the hills west of Madison. An early airport was located at Madison with the hopes that being on the airway, would bring air traffic to the city.

The airline traffic never materialized, but the airport was established and a hangar built.

In 1944, Bud Frye came from Jackson, Minnesota, to open a WTS program at the airport. He would continue there as FBO for 32 years. The Jackson airport is still in operation.

Lake County. In the arrowhead area of Minnesota. No information available.

Lake of the Woods County. The northernmost county of Minnesota, encompasses Baudette, Lake of the Woods, and the Northern Angle. Much of the flying in this area was from lake surfaces, or in the wintertime, from the ice or snow-covered fields. Pioneers such as Rudy Billberg, Pete Klimek, Roy Duggan, and Don Hanson, are legendary in their use of fields around Warroad and Roseau, flying mail and supplies to the hardy souls who inhabited cities on the border, such as Angle Inlet and Oak Island.

In March of 1933, Peter Klimek was contacted by no less than President Roosevelt, himself, to supervise the construction of airports between Baudette and Brainerd. He reported to Governor Floyd B. Olson's staff in St. Paul, where he was given the State's support in this project. The governor told Klimek that an airport at Baudette would have to be cut from timberland in order to provide jobs for at least 80 persons.

Klimek returned to Baudette and began the task of building an airport there. He arranged a site on the banks of the Rainy River and had a hangar constructed. Today, Baudette is a point of entry from Canada.

Le Sueur County. Located in the southern portion of Minnesota. Le Center, Le Sueur, Waterville, and New Prague are the major cities located within this county. No information available.

Lincoln County. Located in the southwestern portion of the state. No information available.

Lyon County. Southwestern corner of Minnesota. Principal city is Marshall. The Marshall Airport was established during the 1930s. It was the only southwestern Minnesota municipal airport to remain open to private flying during the war years. In 1942, there were 325 transient aircraft operations from the field. The WTS program was operating from there during the 1942-1943 period. In 1944, a grant was solicited from the State to improve the airport facility, with the town matching the $150,000 requested.

Mahnomen County. Northwestern portion of the state. Principal city is Mahnomen. No information available.

Marshall County. Far northwestern part of Minnesota Lake Country. No information available.

Martin County. Southern border county. Principal city is Fairmont. The *Aviation Improvement Association of Fairmont* announced to the community in May of 1928 that they would purchase a plot of land some 2000x300 feet along Highway 9, on what was then the E.E. Leonard farm, to be used as their municipal airport. It was about a half mile north of the city. Marcellus King and John Walatka gave instructions at the field and gathered a large clan of flyers around them. The airport was closed in the early 1930s.

The group migrated to a farm owned by the Alsworth family, near Sherburn, and began using one of the alfalfa fields. Operations there continued for the next ten years. The Alsworth boys, Lloyd and Leon "Babe" Alsworth, learned to fly and went on to careers in aviation, Leon in Alaska, and Lloyd as FBO at Fairmont.

The next airport to open was the Stade Airport near Fairmont. It opened in 1940, south of the city, and across from the municipal golf course. It had an east-west sod runway of 3,000 feet, and a shorter north-south strip. Eventually, several hangars were built there and a flight school opened. This airport lasted until after World War II when the present-day airport was built east of the city.

During the 1940s many private airstrips were established on farms in this area of flatland, giving rise to the *Minnesota Flying Farmers* organization.

McLeod County. South central Minnesota west of the Twin Cities. Glencoe and Hutchinson are the principal cities in the County. Neither city had any established airports prior to World War II.

Meeker County. South central Minnesota. Principal city is Litchfield. It is known that the Grove City Airport, in October of 1927, was the scene of a large airshow, which featured races and brought big crowds to see flyers and airplanes from all parts of the state. Though the airport was hardly more than a farm field belonging to the Alfred Larson family, it was called the Grove City airport by the local newspapers. Flying did continue for some time from this location.

Mille Lacs County. Central Minnesota. Principal cities are Milaca, and Princeton. No information available.

Morrison County. Central Minnesota. Little Falls the principal city. No information available.

Mower County. Southeastern Minnesota. Principal city is Austin. Austin's airport was established on 6 August, 1928, on property adjacent to a golf country club. William Stout, magazine writer and aviation advocate, who had spent two years of his boyhood in Austin, gave the dedication address before some ten thousand spectators. Stout advocated expanding the airport in the future, adding fuel pumps and hangars, and indicated that, "Distances are cut so short by air travel that a flier thinks nothing about going 50 or 100 miles to land at a field where he can get a hot dog. If facilities aren't good here, aviators will avoid Austin like motorists now look out for a bump in the road."[47]

In May of 1930, E.W. Decker presented the city of Austin with his farm of 160 acres, to be used for a new airport on the condition that it be named after him. It was so named and was located within a mile of the original airport at the outskirts of the city. Through the years, the airport has expanded to the present airport of today, and is now called the Austin Municipal Airport.

The airshow performer and racing pilot, Marcellus King, was an FBO at the Austin airport, opening *Austin Aero Service* in 1937, and began instructing pilots. Most of the senior pilots of southern Minnesota logged hours with Marc King, including: Cedric Galloway, John Lafferty, John Vasey, and Glenn Hoveland. Many went on to become instructors themselves.

Murray County. Southwest Minnesota. Principal cities are Slayton and Fulda. No information is available, except that in 1935, the city received $1700 profit from grain crops grown on its 160 acre airport tract.

Nicollet County. Southern Minnesota. Principal city is St. Peter. No information available.

Nobles County. Southwestern Minnesota. Main city is Worthington. Airport dedicated 24 August, 1930. Speed Holman, Florence Klingensmith, and Jack Kipp did aerial stunts for the dedication, and races were held in which Gus Imm and Jim Zarth took first places. Parachutress, Nona Malloy, performed a jump. Northwest Airways' CEO, Colonel Lewis Brittin, presented the local American Legion Post with an air trophy on behalf of the state Aeronautics Commission. The honor was for having been selected a major promoter of aviation that year.

Norman County. Northwestern Minnesota. Principal city is Ada. No information available.

Olmstead County. Southeastern Minnesota. Rochester is the main city. Northwest Airways' Colonel Brittin had asked, as early as 1927, that Rochester build a landing field to receive airmail from his line. The first airport in the community was Graham Field, dedicated in 1928. It was founded by the *Rochester Airport Company* with A. J. Lobb as President. Seeking an airport south of the city, the corporation purchased 285 acres of land, erected a hangar and a passenger "station." The airport obtained a federal A-1-A rating, one of the highest ratings available. The *Mayo Properties Association* later took over control of this corporation.

Rochester Airways was formed by Lester Fiegel, H.J. Postier, Dr. T.J. Moore, Jess Herron, and Arlie Stanki with capital of $15,000. They rented a 40-acre farm field from Albin "Ob" Seim, one mile west of St. Mary's Hospital, and constructed a hangar.

The group bought several small airplanes, including two Travel Air biplanes, a Standard, a Jenny, and a Monocoupe for rental and instruction. They also purchased a Hamilton Metalplane aircraft from Northwest Airways with the intention of starting ambulance and charter service between Rochester and other southern Minnesota communities. Unfortunately, the Hamilton met with an accident, and the group was forced to dissolve.

Universal Air Lines began Minneapolis to Rochester to Chicago scheduled flights in 1928. *Jefferson Airways* flew their first passenger flight from this field to Minneapolis in a Ford Trimotor on 13 July, 1928.

The airport was officially dedicated on 11 June, 1929 at the city's diamond jubilee, with Speed Holman performing a stunt routine, and Army and Navy flyers showing formation flights. Dr. C. H. Mayo gave the dedication speech relating that Rochester always built for the future.

In July of 1939, more land was acquired, bringing the total to 370 acres, and by then, four runways had been constructed, each of 3500 feet length. One hundred-ninety border lights were emplaced as of 1940 and a 2 million-candlepower beacon was installed on the *Mayo Clinic* tower a short distance away.

1936 view of Rochester Airport. (Gerald Sandvick)

Northwest Airlines made four daily stops and *Mid-Continent Airlines* used the field as terminal for a run to Kansas City. The airport manager was Don Swenson.

On 5 August, 1940, the renovated airport was rededicated in an event that saw Northwest Airlines President, Croil Hunter, acknowledging that the Rochester airport was the only U.S. airport built and equipped without federal, state or county money. Famous woman aviator, Jacqueline Cochran, attended the ceremony.

In September of 1941, the CAA opened a radio range station at Rochester, with John C. Hannon in charge. In 1943, the *Mayo Association* purchased the county poor farm to the south and three farms to the east to expedite runway expansion and by 1945, the corporation had deeded the airport to the city.

Otter Tail County. West Central portion of the State. Fergus Falls is the principal city. Gus Imm established the first airport near Fergus Falls, about four miles west of the city, in 1926. It was on the Wendell Road leading toward Wahpeton, North Dakota. He leased the property and built a hangar, using a farmhouse for an office. Imm barnstormed from the field in the summers and flew pipeline patrol for the *Ottertail Power Company* during the winter. Art Kantrud and partners, Rueben Anderson and Cliffe Bonde later leased the airport and continued to offer flight instruction.

The airport was named Einar Mickelson Field in 1947. Mickelson was born in Carlisle, Minnesota and joined the Navy in 1940. He was sent as an observer to China and subsequently joined the *American Volunteer Group*, (AVG). In July of 1942, he joined the *Chinese National Aviation Corporation*, (CNAC) as a transport pilot, flying supplies from Calcutta to China over the "Hump," as the mountains were called. On one of these flights, his aircraft disappeared and was never found. The Fergus Falls Airport remains on the same site where originally established.

Pennington County. Located in northwestern Minnesota, Thief River Falls is the major city. No information available.

Pine County. East Central Minnesota, on the Wisconsin border. Pine City and Sandstone are the largest cities. No information available.

Winter 1940-1941 view of the Rochester Airport. This contrasty photo gives a clear idea of the runway configuration just prior to World War II. (James Borden)

Pipestone County. Southwestern Minnesota. Pipestone is the largest community. No information available.

Polk County. Northwestern Minnesota. Crookston is the largest city. No information available.

Pope County. West central Minnesota. Glenwood is the largest city. No information available.

Ramsey County. Metropolitan St. Paul. Airports were discussed earlier in this chapter.

Red Lake County. Northwestern Minnesota. It was noted in the *Red Lake Falls Gazette* of 20 June, 1929, that the American Legion and the city had made arrangements for the purchase of the old fairgrounds to provide a landing field for the community. The field was to be graded and scraped, and Lorenzo J. Savard was to erect a hangar at the field. Savard was the owner of the first airplane in Red Lake County.

Redwood County. Southwestern Minnesota. Redwood Falls is the largest community. No information available.

Renville County. South Central Minnesota. Olivia, Bird Island, and Hector are the larger cities in the County. In 1928, the first field, established south of Hector, was called South View Airport, and managed by Glenn Clark and I. R. Hable. In the early 1940s Hector was proud of its reputation as the state's most "air-minded city." Indeed, in 1941, 40 percent of the community's men, between the ages of 18 and 40 years, were either licensed pilots or student pilots. (Population 1044, 45 pilots, 75 students). The airport at that time was a rolling field, two blocks from the city's main street, rented and operated by the *Hector Flying Club.*

Rice County. South central Minnesota. Includes the cities of Faribault and Northfield.

The first Faribault airport had already been established by August 1929, for on the 9th of that month a major air carnival called "Airport Day" was held in conjunction with the stopping of many planes on the *Minnesota Air Tour.* The plan was to stimulate public interest in improving the present airfield. To that end, pilots from around the state were invited. An airshow featured Speed Holman, parachute jumper Nona Malloy, and other acts, including: races, passenger flights, flour bombing, and balloon busting. The presence of Thorwald Johnson, local endurance flight pilot, was an added feature. Faribault's pride, Dale "Red" Jackson, was not able to attend due to being on tour elsewhere. He was a celebrity following a record endurance flight in St. Louis just a few days previously. A beauty pageant awarded the title of "Queen of the Air" to Faribault native, Catherine Treanor. Another highlight was the arrival of Don Finke in a Pietenpol homebuilt airplane from Cherry Grove. The airshow was followed by an airport concert.

Farm fields near Faribault were used for landing strips during the early days. One popular field was that which the American Legion Post rented in 1931. It comprised 80 acres, and stood south of the present location of the Spitzak home. This field was never developed, and in 1934, the Legion gave up. Soon after, Lawrence Merrill and Lloyd Schreiber rented some land south of the city, on old Highway 3. They put in an east-west strip of 1320 feet and a north-south strip of 2640 feet, each 300 feet wide. The two flyers bought an airplane and did a little commercial flying, and eventually built ten hangars there.

During the pre-war period, the *Faribault Sky Club* was established at this airport by George Holey. After Holey's departure from Faribault in 1939, the club foundered, but was reorganized in the following year as the *Faribault Flying Club.* This was only the second flying club of its type in the state, with ten members owning shares of a single airplane, a Piper Cub.

In 1944, the city of Faribault bought and developed 90 acres of property belonging to Henry Jackson along the Shieldsville Road. This site became the present airport with improvements being undertaken following the World War II period.

Rock County. The most southwestern county in Minnesota. Luverne is the county's largest city. Several early airports were but farm fields, including one near the foot of Blue Mounds historic site near Luverne. Another, simply known as the McDowell airport was in Springwater Township to the west and during the later 1920s saw quite a lot of flying activity. Both were closed during the 1930s.

Roseau County. Northwester Minnesota. Includes the cities of Roseau and Warroad. No information available.

Scott County. South of the Twin Cities Metro area. Largest city is Shakopee. No airports were developed in this area, though some flying was done from fields in the Murphy-Hanrahan Park area during the 1930s. Today's Flying Cloud Airport, in Hennepin County is across the river from Shakopee.

Sherburne County. Central Minnesota. Includes

The beautiful Fokker Universal, owned by the Pure Oil Company was fitted with a radio amplifier in its belly for broadcasting commentary from the air. Seen here at St. Cloud's Whitney II airport dedication in June 1935, the ship was nicknamed the "Voice of the Sky". (A.T. Hennek)

the city of Elk River. No information available.

Sibley County. South central Minnesota. Gaylord is the principal city. No information available.

Stearns County. Central Minnesota. St. Cloud is the major city in this county.

In Brooten, to the far west of the county, an attempt at getting an airport organized occurred as early as 1928. Carl Ben Eielson, one of the pioneer flyers of North Dakota and Alaska, had a mishap while landing at Brooten. That prompted local businessman, Olney Solberg, to approach the city's *Commercial Club*, as a member of the American Legion Post, requesting the establishment of an airport. It is unknown how long this airport was in existence, but by the 1940s it had been abandoned.

St. Cloud, itself, had a colorful history. In June of 1928, a barnstormer by the name of Sven Peterson established the Northside Airport, just northwest of the old Great Northern railroad roundhouse. He leased property and made arrangements to build a hangar. The field held a 2600 foot landing strip, but a power line across the middle of the field permitted only 1600 feet to be used. The city attempted to purchase the property, and Northern States Power agreed that if they did, the company would remove the power line.

In 1929, however, Mrs. Alice W. Whitney offered the city another parcel of property for use as an airport. This property was a 143-acre parcel between the city and the town of Cable to the southeast. She sweetened the offer with $650 in cash, making her gift total over $11,000. Her wish was that the airport be known henceforth as the A. G. Whitney Memorial Airport. Most early flyers in this area called it the Whitney-Cable airport.

This airport officially opened amid fanfare on 23 May, 1929. The ceremonies included a three-day airshow and open house at the field. Cross-country races, aerial demonstrations, stunting contests, parachute jumping, and a fly-over of the Minnesota Air Tour, hopping from airport to airport during this period. The weekend had its down side, too, however. The expected crowds did not materialize, nor did many of the participants as promised. Managers of the field, the *Air-O-Ways Corporation* were castigated by the local press for the lack of attending personalities and the unadvertised entry price of 75 cents, quite a lot of money at the time.

By 1930, there was a hangar on the field and fuel was available. Barnstorming was a regular weekend event with some fliers coming up from the Minneapolis area to hop rides. Al Luckemeyer, the airport manager, had hired Millar Wittag to give instruction, provide charter flights and sight-seeing in Luckemeyer's American Eagle biplane.

Flying during this period also continued at the Northside airport. Cliff Trossen, Jack Kipp, Delroy George, Sven Peterson, Ray Russell and Chet Heinzel were basing their planes and gliders at that site. Florence Klingensmith was a frequent visitor. In 1933, the runways at Northside Airport were improved with some grading. Two runways were widened to 100 foot widths. This qualified the field for federal recognition.

That same year, Whitney Field at Cable was condemned by the new State Aeronautics Commission as unsuitable for federal improvement funds. It recommended that the city find a third site for their official airport. This prompted Mrs. Whitney to offer another piece of property owned by her family for the purpose. It was located within the city limits on sixth avenue between 17th Street North and the Sauk Rapids bridge. She had actually offered it before, at the time the city selected the Cable site, but it was not accepted then because of its proximity to the new St. Cloud Hospital.

The city agreed to return the former Whitney-Cable property to the family in exchange for the new site which would also be known as the A. G. Whitney Memorial Airport, like its predecessor. This property did meet the federal requirments. The city went ahead and acquired additional property adjacent to the donated site and building progress got under way. This field became known as the Whitney II site. This airport was officially dedicated on 28 June to 30 June, 1935. In a solemn ceremony, Mrs. Whitney mixed water from the Seine River in France with Mississippi water and soil from the St. Cloud airport, with appropriate speeching. A plane carried Nathan B. Fish, Commissioner of Improvments, aloft, and he scattered the mixture over the field. The symbology of linking continents by air was drawn. Dignitaries were present including well-known pilots, Jimmy Mattern and Art Goebel, the later of which did some aerobatics.

Well-known woman pilot, Edith Campbell, from the area, was named "Sky Queen." Planes from the 109th Aero Squadron, Air National Guard, performed, and Sven Peterson won a dead-stick landing contest, while Betty Goltz performed a parachute jump.

In 1938, B. G. Vandre became airport manager, opening *Van's Air Service*. He would handle the CPT training for the airport in the pre-war period.

The current airport is on none of the previously mentioned sites. Rather, it is located on property to the southeast of the city of St. Cloud, and dedicated in 1970. It is known as the St. Cloud Municipal Airport.

Steele County. Southeastern Minnesota. Largest community is Owatonna. In Owatonna, the old Cashman Field was used by Glenn Degner to operate his *Southern Minnesota Aviation Company* during the 1930s. He promoted construction of a new airport, which was opened following World War II.

Stevens County. West central Minnesota. Morris is the largest community. No information available.

St. Louis County. Northeastern Minnesota. Duluth is the principal city in St. Louis County. Flying in the Duluth area was somewhat extensive from several airfields, and from the lake and harbor area. The first flight on record is that of exhibition flyer John Geistman who demonstrated a Curtiss Pusher in 1912, from the area where Wade Stadium now stands. In 1913, Duluth grain entrepreneur, Julius Barnes, got interested in flying machines and purchased a Benoist Flying Boat. He hired Tony and Roger Jannus to fly it in public demonstrations and offer rides. The plane was moored at the *Duluth Boat*

Club facility on the bay. Barnes, himself sought to become licensed and wanted the Jannus brothers to teach him to fly, but business interests in Duluth convinced him that it was too dangerous. In fact, Barnes hid his ownership of the aircraft at first, by listing William D. Jones as owner, to protect his own reputation.

The Benoist, christened "Lark of the Lake," operated for three months in the summer of 1913 and much flying was done over the city and around the harbor. With the colder weather approaching, business became unprofitable in the Port City and the Jannus brothers, with Barnes blessing, took the plane to Florida, where it was used to inaugurate the first scheduled passenger airline in the U. S., the *St. Petersburg-Tampa Airboat Line*. The aircraft returned the following summer to carry on with sight-seeing flights during June and July. Late that year the plane was shipped to Russia where the Jannuses were to train Russian flyers. Both brothers were killed soon afterward in flying accidents.

One of Duluth's pioneers was famous propeller manufacturer, Ole Fahlin. Coming from Sweden, Ole began his aviation career in 1925, as a barnstormer in Duluth. He carried passengers from a field owned by the Louis Anderson family near Pike Lake, and from another field near Belknap Avenue in Superior. Fahlin later headed for California, where he became famous for his propellers, but the Anderson field would become Duluth's unofficial airport until 1930. The field was used by the 109th Air Guard as a base from which to stage gunnery runs over Lake Superior.

City fathers were interested in establishing a formal Duluth airport as early as 1926, when members of the *Chamber of Commerce* and the *Junior Chamber of Commerce*, as well as the *American Legion*, took up the call. One of the recommended sites was the St. Louis County workfarm northwest of the city. In May of 1927, *Arrowhead Airways* established its base of operations at the Superior end of the old Arrowhead Bridge, on the Twin Ports Flying Field. A. J. Hase owned the operation and hired Eddie Middagh as his chief pilot.

Very soon, Fred and William Trump organized Trump Air Lines as a passenger carrier from Duluth to Minneapolis, using Anderson Field. In 1929, the workfarm's 640 acre site was officially procured by the City of Duluth as its municipal field. The passing of a $100,000 bond issue by the state legislature enabled construction and grading to begin in August of 1929, and by November, two runways were completed.

Activity still continued at the Anderson Field with a branch of Minneapolis-based *Mid Plane Sales and Transit* opening there under the management of Harvey Williamson. Daily air service between Duluth and the Twin Cities followed, beginning in June of 1928. Mid Plane's Ryan aircraft was put on floats to operate out of St. Louis Bay, but in August, crashed into the bay, killing Williamson and ending the operation.

Lt. R. J. Sergent, another Duluth entrepreneur who was connected with Minneapolis' *Great Northern Aviation Corp.*, opened the *Sergent School of Aeronautics*, which offered flight instruction and scenic flights. A. J. "Jake" Pfaender was hired as

chief pilot. This operation was also based at Anderson Field, but soon transferred operations to the Superior Belknap Avenue airport. In 1930, the company faded into oblivion due to lack of business.

Meanwhile, Detroit businessmen, Edward F. Schlee and William S. Brock, who had been making headlines with record flights, began developing small airlines around the upper midwest and opened two such operations in Minnesota. One was *Canadian-American Airlines*, based out of St. Paul, the other, *Arrowhead International Airlines*, based at the Anderson Field in Duluth. The inaugural Duluth flight occurred on 11 September, 1929. Schlee and Brock's goal was to provide passenger service between Duluth and the Canadian resort areas. They purchased five speedy Lockheed Vega aircraft and hired two transport-rated pilots, J. Warren Smith and Jake Pfaender, with the intention of hiring and training other pilots for the rest of the fleet. The Vegas were soon put on floats to operate from the harbor.

Some of the locals who took their training from Arrowhead were Victor Filiatrault, Bill Magie, and the first woman pilot to solo from the new workfarm airport, Ann McDonald. When the Vegas were taken off floats, they were based at the municipal field. The first hangar was built at the new facility in the spring of 1930. *Land-O-Lakes Airways* was established at the field, incorporated by local businessmen, C.J. Yoho, Otto Altman and Elmer Stovern. They began building their own hangar immediately. Some of their flight students were Guilford and Cavour Hartley, Rueben Bloom, Dean Tresise, Hank O'Hara, Jules Berndt, Clem Gunderson, Morton Larson, Dr. Huderle, and Ed Porter.

On 11 January, 1930, a group of U. S. Army Air Corps pursuit planes arrived at the field, on their way to winter maneuvers at Spokane, Washington. They used the field for cold weather refueling and winter starting exercises.

The Superior airport was also very active during this period, with a glider club, plus *Head-of-the-Lakes Airways* being formed there and much pleasure flying taking place.

The Duluth municipal field was named the Williamson-Johnson Airport, dedicated to the memory of Harvey Williamson and Conrad Gilbert Johnson. Johnson was a Duluth native who was killed in the World War I. The dedication ceremony occurred in September 1930, with great fanfare. Flyers such as Minnesota's own Freddy Lund, Florence Klingensmith, and Speed Holman, flew exhibitions and the ceremonies were favored by a stop of the *Ford Reliability Tour*, which included some fifty aircraft competing in the nationwide tour.

In 1931, *Land-O-Lakes Airways* failed, but a new operation was started with Gil and Cavour Hartley joining Jake Pfaender in the *Hartley-Pfaender Air Service*. The Hartleys would also fund the design and building of the Cloquet Trainer aircraft discussed elsewhere in this book. That same year, Northwest Airways of Minneapolis began flying their Sikorsky S-38 amphibian flying boats between St. Paul and Superior Bay, offering speedy passenger service between city centers. Service ceased in December due to extensive costs, but was resumed later using single-engined Hamilton Metalplanes from the Williamson-

Johnson Airport.

The *Duluth Aviation Club* was formed in 1932 and was to have a very positive influence on aviation development and shaping of public opinion in the area. The Club organized an airshow that included closed-course racing, stunting, and passenger flights. At least 15,000 persons attended the 1932 airshow at the Williamson-Johnson Field to watch the events. This big show was followed later in the year by a second airshow with similar results. So successful were the events, that the *Western Air Show Company* was formed by local businessmen to promote airshows in other communities. At least twenty shows were booked during the next year. The Duluth Aviation Club also promoted goodwill flying tours to supplant the previously successful automobile tours of neighboring communities. Cloquet and Aitkin were among the towns visited.

Earl O. Olson was hired as airport manager in 1941, at which time five hundred-fifty WPA workers were constructing runways and taxiways, and making other improvements. Aviation was healthy in the Duluth area from this time forward, with the CPT/WTS program coming along in 1940.

(Some of the above information regarding Duluth aviation and airport development is excerpted from material written by Marvin Zack. Marvin was a lifelong Duluth resident, aviation historian, and writer, before his accidental death in 1990. His written history of the area was generously provided by Mrs. La Verne Zack.)

In Hibbing, the first landing field was the St. Louis County Fairground, and named the Banks Airport after a flyer who lost his life in an air crash. In 1927, R. F. Davis and partners leased 160 acres of farmland from John McHale and formed the *Minnesota Flying Service, Inc.*, operating it as a flight school and charter service. The city of Hibbing purchased the land in 1931 and dedicated it as their municipal airport. L. Millar Wittag operated a flight school there from the mid-1930s and continued with a CPT/WTS program at the beginning of World War II.

In 1941, between 300 and 400 men were employed in a WPA project to finish an improvement program to pave one 3,900 foot runway and extend a second to 3,800 feet at the Hibbing Airport. Additional runways were planned. A pair of hangars came under another WPA contract.

At Ely, the County Board decided in 1929 to purchase land for an airport and subscribed $15,000 for its purchase. In 1931, they added $6,000 for improvements to the field, which was then deeded to the County. In 1929, *Scenic Airways*, operating a Challenger Robin from the airport, provided summer passenger flights among the resorts and lakes.

Stunt pilot, Malcolm Dunlop of Duluth was killed during an aerobatic performance at the 1932 airport dedication. The Ely airport and a floatplane base some miles away were very active during the 1930s, with at least thirty-six aircraft being based at one or the other. William Leithold was one of the most active flyers at this location, and carried on his activities well after World War II.

Swift County. West central Minnesota. Benson and Appleton are the largest communities. In February of 1920, Ed McElligott is listed as head pilot and general manager of *McElligott Aviation* with airport and general offices at Appleton. It was his intention of opening a flying school and doing the usual barnstorming, charter flying, and maintenance work as an FBO from the field. He intended to build a number of hangars. McElligott was one of the pioneer flyers, having flown since the end of the World War in 1919. He appeared at the Swift County Fair in 1919. Relationship of his early airport to the airport of today is unknown.

Todd County. Central Minnesota. Long Prairie is the major community. No information available.

Traverse County. West central Minnesota. Wheaton is the major community. No information available.

Wabasha County. Southeastern Minnesota. Wabasha is the largest city. No information available.

Wadena County. Central Minnesota. Wadena the largest community. No information available.

Waseca County. Southeast Minnesota. Waseca is the largest city. An airport operated by Howard Deichen was located at the south edge of town. A north-south strip required a long final approach right down main street when landing to the south. Deichen's strip was used until well after WWII.

Washington County. One of the Twin Cities metropolitan counties. Airports are discussed earlier in this chapter.

Watonwan County. South central Minnesota. Major communities are St. James and Madelia. No information available.

Wilkin County. Western central Minnesota. Breckenridge is the major city. No information available.

Winona County. Southeast Minnesota. Winona is the major city. It is known that Max Conrad began using a field on property belonging to his future in-laws, the Biesanz family. A field adjacent to it was procured by the Department of Commerce, Bureau of Aeronautics, to be used as a signal beacon site and emergency field for planes operating on the cross-country airway running through that area. It had the designation of 25B and Max was paid $30 a month to tend the light and watch over the field.

Since the two fields were adjacent, Conrad simply used the larger Government field for an overrun of the Biesanz field. Occasionally the tailskids of his airplanes would plow through the white crushed rock circle that was the government field's aerial marker. Max would have one of his hired hands, Ken Brommer, patch up the damage.

The Biesanz field was but a mere 20 acres or so, three miles west of the city of Winona, but was increased in size to 1800 x 2500 feet by the time it was dedicated as Conrad-Templeton Field on 5 August, 1929. At that dedication, the Governor of Minnesota,

Theodore Christianson, and several other legislators spoke words of wisdom. Eight military planes from Michigan's Selfridge Field, and some from the 109th Aero Squadron of Wold-Chamberlain, were on display.

Wright County. Central Minnesota. Buffalo is the major city. Maple Lake, Annandale, Delano, Howard Lake and Cokato are other communities. No information available.

Yellow Medicine County. Southwestern Minnesota County. Granite Falls the major city. There were no regular established airfields in this county prior to World War Two.

A 1936 recap of Minnesota airports, prepared for the Minnesota Aeronautics Commission by the *Abrams Aerial Survey Company* of Michigan, indicated that there were 14 existing airports listed in good or fair condition. Several additional airports were under construction, including fields at International Falls and Springfield.

The 1937 *U. S. Airport Directory* listed the following fields in Minnesota as approved airports: Alexandria, Austin (Decker), Bemidji, Brainerd, Canton, Coleraine, Crookston, Detroit Lakes, Duluth (Grand Lakes Flying Field), Duluth (Williamson-Johnson Field, now Duluth International), Ely, Glenwood, Grand Rapids, Gull Lake, Hibbing, Lake City (Underwood), Little Falls (Camp Ripley National Guard Field), Mankato, Marshall, Minneapolis, Robbinsdale, Rochester, St. Cloud, St. Paul, Slayton, Tamarack (Snader), Virginia, Waseca, Winona (Conrad), Winona (Government adjoining Conrad Field), and Worthington.

Not listed in this survey were fields at Park Rapids and Willmar which had been listed in a Minnesota tally of the same year.

In a memorandum to the Aeronautics Commissioner by Forrest Wheeler of the Commission staff, in May of 1937, improvements for each field were spelled out. He also commented on the fact that many communities felt that their local fields should come under the direct supervision of the Commission as opposed to local control. Reasons for this varied, from the desire for state funding, to the wish for air mail stops, radio beams, commercial airline stops or enhancing their ability to draw recreational traffic through improvements.

Wheeler also offered some very appropriate thoughts regarding the times. He stated, "In making a survey of this state, one is impressed with the number of men born since the beginning of the World War, into an air-minded world. These young men have recently reached the age where they are buying planes and taking courses in aviation. This is a new generation, free from the discouragements of the

pioneer aviators. They wish to travel about the state as their means will permit, and are now commenting on the lack of landing fields in a safe condition."[48]

This report mentioned appropriations granted by the state and work being undertaken on airports at Baudette, Detroit Lakes, Glenwood, Grand Marais, Moorhead, Ortonville, Two Harbors, and Warroad. It also mentioned an appropriation for airmarking, then being undertaken by the Women's group, the 99's.

Other notes mention an airport at Cloquet, and the abandonment of a field at Wadena.

By 1942, the Aeronautics Commission acknowledged the problem of convincing communities that they should provide for an airport. Communities were sluggish in their site selections, and asking for state help in making surveys. Likely, some communities even suffered from lack of a funding base to develop an airport, or from the lack of local engineers. In this period, immediately after the start of World War II, each community experienced differing problems. In some, such as Brainerd, a search for a new field of larger proportions caused the shut down of operations at the former site. In Buffalo, the state was told that the town could not afford an airport. In Benson, the field operator was inducted into the Army and the field ceased operations. In Mankato, city officials had practically refused to see the value of an airport, according to the Minnesota Aeronautics Commission.

New sites were being selected, however. Most of the original airports now found themselves cramped into expanding communities. Larger and more powerful aircraft and military training needs resulted in runways being too short, with severe cross-wind conditions for students, and overloaded facilities. It was a period of looking for new sites for most communities. Most suffered at the same time from a shortage of funds, caused, in part, by the intense war effort already underway. Through all of this, the Aeronautics Commission kept the pressure on local officials.

The situation with airports in the late 1930s and early 1940s gradually straightened itself out. By the time post-war aviation was at its peak, most of the communities that could support an airport, had located a fitting site and improved it with hangars, surfaced runways, shops for maintenance, etc. Communities that could not support an airport had gone by the wayside, and remain so to this day. It is unlikely that new airports will be built, due to the value of land and the interference with community life caused by the noise and activity at airports in today's world. Great foresight on the part of some community leaders in the 1930s, and the constant urging by the Aeronautics Commission brought about the wonderful airport system we enjoy in Minnesota today.

[1] *Minneapolis Star*, 19 March, 1953.

[2] Theodore Wirth, *The Minneapolis Park System*, 1883-1944, The Minneapolis Park Board, 1945, Pages 294-300.

[3] Ibid.

[4] Ibid.

[5] Ibid.

[6] Ibid.

[7] Gerald Sandvick, "Early Airport Development and the Emergence of the Metropolitan Airports Commission," *Hennepin County History*, Vol. 43, No. 3, Fall, 1984. Pages 3-17.

[8] Theodore Wirth, *The Minneapolis Park System*, as above.

[9] Ibid.

[10] Charmion Brown, "History of Wold-Chamberlain Field," *Airport News*, Issues of 3, 12, 19, 26, August; 2, 19, 16, 23 September; 7 October, 1933.

[11] *Aero Digest*, May 1931. Pages 90-91.

[12] Ibid.

[13] *Aviation*, "Rolling It Down," January, 1938. Page 22.

[14] Michael J. H. Taylor and David Mondey, *Milestones of Flight*, Janes Publication, 1983, Page 96.

[15] *Airport News*, 26 August, 1933. Page 1.

[16] *Minneapolis Journal*, 20 July, 1934.

[17] *Minneapolis Star*, 14 July, 1938.

[18] *Minneapolis Star*, 29 August, 1938.

[19] *Minneapolis Star*, 11 May, 1939.

[20] Interview with Stan Ketcham by Noel Allard, 5 April, 1986.

[21] Ibid.

[22] Gerald Sandvick, *Hennepin County History*, as above.

[23] Bill of Sale from Confer, Libby, and Heinrich to Rhodes, 1923, copy in possession of the author.

[24] Theodore Wirth, *The Minneapolis Park System*, as above.

[25] Interview with Angelo De Ponti by Noel Allard, 11 November, 1988.

[26] Theodore Wirth, *Minneapolis Park System*, as above.

[27] Charmion Brown, *Airport News*, as above.

[28] *The Minnesota Flyer*, January, 1978.

[29] Theodore Wirth, *Minneapolis Park System*, as above.

[30] Ibid.

[31] Charmion Brown, *Airport News*, as above.

[32] Interview with Merrill Kuehn by Noel Allard, 9 November, 1988.

[33] Theodore Wirth, *Minneapolis Park System*, as above.

[34] Charmion Brown, *Airport News*, as above.

[35] Ibid.

[36] "Minneapolis' Municipal Airport," *Aero Digest*, May 1931, pages 90-91.

[37] Interview with Roger Poore by Noel Allard, 31 October, 1988.

[38] Interoffice communications, 28 September, 1931, from Walter Bullock, operations manager of Northwest Airways, to all line pilots, copy in possession of author.

[39] Interview with Francis Geng by Anne Holey, for Air Museum of Minnesota, 12 June, 1965.

[40] *Minneapolis Journal*, 23 May, 1932.

[41] Interview with William Kidder and Thorwald Johnson by George and Anne Holey, for the Air Museum of Minnesota, 8 October, 1957.

[42] Interview with Kenneth Muxlow by Noel Allard, 2 October, 1989.

[43] Brochure, *Cedar Flying Service*, Wally Neuman and Wally Dale, circa 1939.

[44] Hartwick T. Hanson's pilot's logbook, entry dated 11 November, 1931, copy in possession of J. D. Christian.

[45] Interview with Ray Haberman by Noel Allard, 25 May, 1988.

[46] Interview with Robert Johnson by Noel Allard, 13 June, 1988.

[47] *Minneapolis Journal*, 7 August, 1928.

[48] Report to the Aeronautics Commission by Forrest Wheeler and Captain A. W. Nelson, May, 1937, Aeronautics Commission records, Minnesota Historical Society, St. Paul, 45.J.5.4.f. Ray Miller Papers.

SIX

1920s — 1930s: AIRLINES AND AIR COMMERCE

On the morning of 7 June, 1926, howling gales swept the upper Midwest, saluting the start of the first regularly scheduled commercial air transportation between Minneapolis-St. Paul and Chicago. It was not an auspicious beginning. Four pilots were ready to depart from Maywood Field near Chicago and carry mail via LaCrosse to Wold-Chamberlain Field at Minneapolis, while two others at Wold-Chamberlain were preparing to fly the opposite route. The four that departed Chicago flew into the teeth of the gale, and two made forced landings in southern Wisconsin, one due to a broken gas line and the other because the wind had begun to shred the fabric covering the wings. A third plane made LaCrosse, but was so far behind schedule that darkness precluded going on, and the fourth pilot, veteran Emil "Nimmo" Black, navigated some of the roughest air he had ever seen and finally arrived in the Twin Cities nearly eight hours late.

Two Minneapolis airmen scheduled to fly to Chicago, William S. Brock and Elmer Lee Partridge. Brock loaded his mail sacks, took off at 3 p.m., and using tail winds to his advantage, made Chicago in a little over four hours. Elmer Partridge followed, but nine miles southeast of the airport the savage winds clawed his aircraft from the sky. The dead pilot's undamaged mail bags were sent on to Chicago by train.[1]

The airline that absorbed this opening day tragedy was variously, and informally, called Dickinson or C. D. Airlines after its founder, Charles "Pop" Dickinson. Dickinson was a colorful figure who had made his fortune heading a Chicago seed company and then

Charles "Pop" Dickinson's Air Mail ship #2, a Laird LCB, makes a stop at Wold-Chamberlain. The pilot, Billy Brock, in the cockpit, is helping load mail sacks. (Elmer Tivetny via Jerry Kurth)

retired to go into the aviation game, largely for the fun of it. "I am," he said, "sixty-seven years old, and I might as well spend my money for Uncle Sam and the public. That is what I say when they ask me why I want to lose money in aviation. I am trying to open the way for commercial flying."[2] Dickinson had been involved in aviation for several years, promoting air shows and races, but had become a pilot himself, only after age sixty. His instructor, ironically enough, had been Elmer Lee Partridge. The bewhiskered Dickinson looked more than a little like Santa Claus, and the resemblance did not stop with physical appearance.

Throughout the summer of 1926 he poured more money into the Chicago-Twin Cities air mail route than he ever got back. Despite the fact that his aircraft were emblazoned with the slogan "celerity, certainty, security," he was beset by constant problems. In late June, he had to make a mail flight himself because of a pilot shortage. Two of his pilots had quit, saying his aircraft simply were not safe to fly. Two others, however, vowed "never to quit the old man," and Dickinson fumed that "these pilots have more temperament than an opera singer."[3]

One of the loyal pilots was Billy Brock, but even he had reason to wonder about his dedication. At the end of a late June mail run from Chicago, he was amazed to see several head of assorted livestock grazing the runways of his destination. He circled to chase off some pigs and sheep and then swooped in past a goat and donkey and stopped "close enough to a Jersey cow to milk her." He wired back to Dickinson that he drew the line at trying to land on the back of a cow. Not wanting to lose another valuable pilot, Dickinson complained to the Police Chief who, in turn, issued nineteen warrants threatening the owners with ninety days in the workhouse for allowing their animals to stray on the airfield.

In mid-August, Dickinson threw in the towel. He had been operating at a daily loss of money, accidents had reduced his fleet to a single Laird biplane, and most of his pilots had quit. The Post Office Department was, therefore, given the required forty-five day notice that he was giving up the air mail contract and would cease operating at the end of September.[4]

Dickinson's abortive mail service was not the first air mail attempt in Minnesota. Indeed, air mail service began when the U. S. Government embarked on air mail activities in the Spring of 1918 with one experimental route from Washington to New York, flown by Army pilots and aircraft. In August, however, the Post Office Department took over opera-

The first airmail arrives at Wold-Chamberlain, August, 1920. An experimental run, it proved the concept sound, though its future would be rocky. (Vince Doyle)

tions and began to develop an ambitious plan for a transcontinental air mail route. Equipment consisted of several aircraft types, but most numerous was the de Havilland DH-4. This was a World War I British design built under license in the U. S. and powered by a 400 h.p. Liberty engine. The de Havillands were modified for mail service by replacing the front cockpit with a rainproof mail compartment and rigging the controls so that the pilot flew the machine from the rear seat. Thus modified, the aircraft could carry 400 pounds of mail for about 300 miles at a cruising speed of just over 100 m.p.h. The DH-4 was an obsolete aircraft to which pilots attached the morbid sobriquet "flaming coffins" because the gasoline tank was close to the pilot and if it ruptured in a crackup, the results could be unfortunate.

The transcontinental air route was opened in several stages between May 1919 and September 1920, and followed a line from New York westward through Cleveland, Chicago, Omaha, Cheyenne, Salt Lake City, and Reno to its termination in San Francisco. The Post Office operated the route continuously until 1926, when a new law mandated turning operations over to private carriers. During 1924, portions of the airway were even lighted with beacons to allow night flying, with the result that by the mid 1920s, air mail transportation was on a solid footing in the U. S. Over the long transcontinental route, the airplanes could beat the fastest mail trains by about 22 hours.

The driving force behind the air mail was Assistant Postmaster General, Otto Praeger, whose goal was to tie as many cities into the system as possible. In 1920 he made the decision to add two feeder routes which would tie into the transcontinental trunk line. One of these would link St. Louis to Chicago, and the other would run from Minneapolis-St. Paul via

The new Airmail Hangar and an expectant crowd await the first inbound trial airmail flight, August 10, 1920. (Vince Doyle)

LaCrosse to Chicago. Praeger came to Minneapolis in early May, 1920, to coordinate the planned service with local postal officials and to inspect the Twin Cities' landing field. The airmail service would be, he said, "for experimental purposes," and then added, prophetically, "I would rather see it let on contract as this would help commercial aviation, which we must foster."[5] The entry of private carriers into mail transportation would not come for another half dozen years, but the Post Office itself was now ready to give the Twin Cities its first regular air service.

Communities that were included in the airmail routes at that time considered it an enormous honor, and there was in the Twin Cities an outpouring of civic pride. William F. Brooks, a state senator, and head of the Twin Cities Aero Corporation, a group of businessmen organized to promote aviation, felt the new service would greatly aid economic activity. Business could be done with more speed, more money could be made in interest on accounts in banks out of the area, and Minneapolis-St. Paul would just be in a better commercial position.[6]

A good landing field was available at Speedway Field, the present site of Minneapolis-St. Paul International Airport. There remained the matter of a hangar to shelter and service the eagerly awaited mail planes, but enthused civic groups in Minneapolis and St. Paul raised $15,000.00 in each city, and by early August an 80 by 90-foot hangar, the airport's first structure, had been built.

The arrival of the first mail plane on 10 August, was the centerpiece of an aerial circus. Several local pilots met the twin engine Martin bomber south of the airfield and escorted it in. Shows of aerobatics followed, and there was even a parachute jump by Speed Holman, who was a newly-hired member of the Larabee Brothers operation at the airport. The arrival of the mail, however, was only a demonstration run. The airmail service was stretched thin, and no matter how eager for regular runs to start, the Twin Cities would wait another three and one-half months."[7]

The anticipated regular service finally began on 29 November, 1920, when William T. Carroll, a young ex-army pilot and a Minneapolis native, arrived from Chicago shortly after 2 p.m. with 175 pounds of mail. On the same day, E. Hamilton Lee, who had pioneered the Chicago-St. Louis route, made the first regular mail flight from the Twin Cities to Chicago. Both flights were uneventful although Lee did encounter fog most of the way.[8]

Over the next seven months, Post Office pilots would fly the mail daily, except for Sundays and holidays, through some of the worst winter weather in the nation. They were engaged in a dangerous occupation. Forced landings due to weather or mechanical failures were commonplace, and close encounters with disasters were simply a part of the job. A few days after Christmas 1920, E. Hamilton Lee was heading for Minneapolis at extremely low altitude.

"I stayed close to the ground to avoid the wind," he explained later. "I was so close to the ground I had to slip around the hills...I got so close to the Mississippi River that I almost touched the ice." Near Winona, two men evidently watched

the low flying aircraft with alarm, and the pilot, unwisely it turned out, watched them watching him. "I was wondering why they were running and watched them so intently that I did not look to see where I was going. When I struck the telephone wires...I knew it was something serious." With "at least 150 feet" of telephone wire snarling the propeller, Lee's machine went straight into a looming woods and was totally wrecked. The dazed, but otherwise unhurt Lee crawled out, hailed a nearby farmer, and got a ride into Winona, where he and his mail bags finished the trip to the Twin Cities by train. The airmail pilots prided themselves on showing the understated elan that a later generation would call "the right stuff," and E. Hamilton Lee's summary of his crash upheld the traditions of the fraternity. "It was a real thriller," he concluded, "but I wouldn't care to go through it again... Am I going to get out of the game? I should say I am not. I probably will not discontinue low flying, although I am going to try to. However, there is so much pleasure in it, that most of us take a fling at it at some time or another. The funniest part of the affair is that it did not make me very nervous. When I was in an accident a year ago, it took me about a week to get over it, but I could start out on a trip again today if it were necessary.[9]

Unfortunately such mishaps did not always end in semihumorous close shaves. During this period, airmail pilots were being lost at an average of one each month, and in one terrible week in February 1921, two crashes killed four airmen on the Twin Cities to Chicago route alone.

Shortly before noon on 3 February, pilot Kenneth Stewart and his mechanic, George Sampson, took off for Chicago flying a twin engine version of the de Havilland DH-4. They had climbed to 1,500 feet, and near Mendota an engine quit. The de Havilland could not fly on a single engine, but Stewart attempted to turn in the vain hope of getting back to the airport. Losing altitude rapidly, the aircraft nose dived into a field at a 40 degree angle. Its descent had been observed at the airport, and E. Hamilton Lee jumped into his ship and made for the crash site which he circled until a ground party could arrive. The de Havilland was a total loss, and Stewart was dead. Sampson was rushed to a St. Paul hospital, where later in the day he said, "Poor Stewart, he tried hard but it wasn't any use. I never got such a jar in my life as when that ship hit the ground, but I expect to be up and around again soon." The mail was picked up and sent on to Chicago. It was announced that there would be no break in the daily schedules because of the accident.[10]

Six days later, a J.L.6 mail plane left Chicago but landed at Lone Rock, Wisconsin, to outwait a heavy snow squall. Resuming its flight toward the Twin Cities, it arrived at La Crosse for a fuel stop and circled the field as the pilot began to descend from 2,000 feet. At about 500 feet, the aircraft suddenly went into a dive and burst into flame on impact. Killed were mechanic Robert B. Hill and pilots Arthur Rowe and William T. Carroll.

The crash caused a number of shockwaves that af-

fected the airmail service both locally and nationally. Carroll's death was an especially bitter pill since he was something of a local hero. Born in Minneapolis and a World War I veteran, he had flown the first regular airmail flight into Minneapolis and, though an experienced pilot, was but 22-years-old. St. Paul Aero Club President, L.P. Ordway, issued a strong statement accusing the Post Office of mismanagement and of foisting dangerous airplanes on its pilots. Minnesota Governor, J. A. Preus, sent a telegram to Postmaster General, Albert Burleson, saying that the killing of the three flyers was tantamount to manslaughter and that, while Minnesota needed airmail service, it would be better to discontinue it than sacrifice more lives.[11]

The problem was that the de Havillands were wearing out, and the J.L.6 had a troubled past. The J.L.6 was a modification of the German Junkers F-13 and for its day was a radical design. A low wing monoplane with a cantilever wing, it was built entirely of aluminum. It could carry over twice the payload of the de Havilland on half the horsepower and use low grade gasoline. It seemed that the J.L.6 was the answer to greater efficiency, and the Post Office had bought eight of them. If the manufacturer's claims seemed too good to be true, they were. In August and September 1920, in-flight fires destroyed two aircraft, killed four men, and nearly killed several others. The J.L.6 was withdrawn and supposedly fixed, the trouble having been identified as a faulty gas line. Not wanting to give up on its miracle plane, the Post Office in late 1920 ordered them back into service. They were unpopular with the pilots, and Carroll had expressed reservations about the aircraft prior to his fatal flight. The probable cause of the tragedy was gasoline leaking from a faulty fuel line which caused an in-flight fire and loss of control. In any event, the J.L.6 was now withdrawn for good.[12]

The accident soon became a national issue when Minnesota Congressman, Halvor Steenerson, raised the point of aircraft safety, questioned the legal authority of the Post Office to operate airmail at all, and then moved to slash $800,000.00 from the airmail budget. Since Steenerson happened to chair the House Post Office Committee, his opinions were of more than passing interest to those involved in the airmail service.

The Post Office fought back by blaming the accident on pilot error. Carroll was inexperienced with the J.L.6 and, it was implied, had used incorrect flying procedure. The J.L.6 was not unsafe, it was further argued, and in any case the decision whether to fly an airplane ultimately rested with the flyers. Finally, one of the airmail chieftains upheld the greatest of all bureaucratic traditions when he opined that "If the people are going to blame anyone for the use of made over airplanes, the responsibility must be put on congress for that body refused to appropriate money for new airplanes while the army and navy have large numbers..."[13]

The crash near LaCrosse had the effect of lifting the lid from a kettle of doubt and criticism that had been brewing over the airmail service for some time. Congressional consideration of the airmail budget was imminent, and the whole enterprise in February 1921 was in danger of cancellation. The airmail, however, had its defenders as well as critics, and in the end probably saved itself with a spectacular 33 hour transcontinental mail delivery. Flying day and night through terrible weather, exhausted pilots brought the mail from San Francisco to New York in less than half the best train time. The low reputation of the airmail was reversed, and Congress voted funds for it to continue.

It was not enough to save the first airmail route in the upper Midwest, however. Four men dead and eight aircraft lost had made the Twin Cities to Chicago route a costly one, and the Post Office needed its resources for the all important, transcontinental route. On 4 March, 1921, the Wilson Administration was replaced by that of Mr. Harding and shortly thereafter, the new airmail chief, Edward H. Shaughnessy, announced the cancellation of all feeder routes as a budget saving measure.

The ultimate reason was that, in 1921, aircraft could not make a case for themselves over the relatively short distances on the feeder routes. Airline historian, R. E. G. Davies, has summarized the situation: "Most business mail was dispatched towards the end of the day and so the normal overnight rail service was quite adequate to ensure delivery by the first post next morning. But this did not apply on the 2,600 mile transcontinental route, where airplanes could save considerable time, if operated efficiently."[14]

At noon on 30 June, 1921, the last airmail flight arrived at Twin Cities Municipal Field with a load of 18,000 letters, and Minnesota's first scheduled air transportation service came to an end. A foundation had been laid, however. Civic pride and enthusiasm for having air service had been drummed up, airfields had been constructed, and, most of all, the aviators had shown that scheduled service could be flown even in upper Midwestern winter conditions. For the next five years there would be only hit and miss attempts to use aircraft for transportation. Whiskey running from Canada was popular in these Prohibition years, and the airplane was a splendid vehicle for quick border crossings.

Air transportation, as a regular reliable business, did not return to Minnesota until 1926. The 1920 airmail flights were a false dawn, but Dickinson's short-lived attempt in that year marked the true dawn of air commerce in the state.

When Dickinson gave up, a new company was formed to take over his air mail contract. The new company was the sole bidder to replace Dickinson on the Chicago to Minneapolis route and on 1 October, 1926, it began doing business as *Northwest Airways, Inc.* The new airline would carry only mail at first but would soon graduate to passenger service.

There had been a number of factors that retarded the use of airplanes for passenger transportation. Indeed, given the highly sophisticated passenger airlines of contemporary America, it is interesting that in the early years of air transport, the U. S. was slow to use the airplane for passengers but quick to employ it for carrying certain cargo. The main reason for this was geographical. While distances in the U. S. are large, there are no long over-water routes to hinder efficient railroad service, and well before 1920, major cities were linked by an excellent rail system. In contrast, airplanes and airports were still in their

Colonel Lewis H. Brittin, the driving force behind the establishment and operation of Northwest Airways. (Frank Geng via James Borden)

Northwest's Croil Hunter. Hunter was responsible for pushing the Northwest route system to the west coast. (James Borden)

infancy. The airports of the 1920s were apt to be a few acres of more or less level sod and some drafty sheds. The aircraft were, to put it mildly, uncomfortable: soundproofing was accomplished by stuffing cotton in one's ears, ventilation by opening a window, and service from the flight crew was usually little more than the co-pilot walking back, collecting tickets and giving a waxed bag and vial of ammonia to anyone who looked green around the gills. Even the larger aircraft could not carry enough passengers to be profitable. The standard airliner of the late twenties, the Ford Trimotor, in high density seating, could carry twelve or fourteen.

Finally, aircraft of the period were slow. Although the Ford and other types might have cruising speeds of over 100 m.p.h., when stops were figured in, the average speeds over a route were more like 80 m.p.h. As one historian has aptly observed, "This was not a spectacular improvement over express trains and certainly not enough to draw large numbers of passengers away from the luxury of the typical American Pullman trains."[15] The result was that for the first half dozen years of the 1920s, air transport throughout the U. S. was almost exclusively devoted to airmail development directly run by the government.

The reason for this surge of airline activity in 1926 was the passage, by Congress, of the Air Mail Act of 1925. Commonly called the Kelly Act after its sponsor, Representative Clyde Kelly of Pennsylvania, the new law was basic to the evolution of American air transportation. It authorized the postmaster general to determine air routes, contract with private air carriers to fly mail over those routes, and pay them a subsidy for so doing. No other event so clearly and directly encouraged private companies to enter into air transportation, and it was not long before passengers were being carried along with the mail. When that happened, the modern airline industry, already warming up, was ready for takeoff.[16]

The immediate result of the Kelly Act was that the Post Office, starting in late 1925 sought bids from companies to fly the mail over a nationwide system of Contract Air Mail routes, or CAM's as they quickly became known. CAM 9 was advertised in October 1925, with the requirement that the mail plane leave Chicago after the arrival of the inbound flight from New York and then proceed to Minneapolis-St. Paul

The first aircraft purchased by Northwest Airways, a Stinson Detroiter, purchased from the Stinson Aircraft Company in 1926. (Bob Lemm)

in the morning by way of Milwaukee and La Crosse. A return flight via the same cities was scheduled for the afternoon. In January 1926, Charles Dickinson was awarded the CAM 9 contract which gave birth to the airline he operated from June until September.

Dickinson's announcement that he would give up the CAM 9 route created a small problem and a large opportunity for Lewis Hotchkiss Brittin.

Brittin was an engineer by trade. Born in Connecticut in 1877, and educated in the east, he became an Army Captain during the Spanish-American War and later a Colonel on the General Staff. He came to Minneapolis in the early 1920s to supervise construction of a large wholesale distribution complex known as the Northwest Terminal Company. The successful completion of that won him another project which was overseeing the construction of a power dam on the Mississippi River. The availability of power from the dam, in turn, induced the Ford Motor Company to build a plant in St. Paul. With the Ford plant and the dam so closely connected, Brittin naturally worked with Ford's chief engineer, William B. Mayo. With the completion of that project, Brittin went to work for the St. Paul Association and it was as head of that organization that he actively promoted the development of an airport for that city.

Brittin quickly began to contact investors in order to raise the capital necessary to create a new airline and bid on the Minneapolis to Chicago mail contract. Brittin was eager to get someone to continue airmail service to St. Paul because he worked for the St. Paul

Association and the businessmen of the city wanted the airmail to continue. Brittin was well-placed in St. Paul business circles and he also contacted William Mayo of the Ford Company. The upshot was an invitation to come to the Detroit Athletic Club and meet with a group of interested businessmen. By August 1926, sufficient capital had been raised from the combination of St. Paul and Detroit investors to incorporate Northwest Airways in Michigan.[17]

The new company now sent a bid to the Post Office which was accepted on 4 September, although the actual contract was dated 7 September. As it turned out, Northwest was the sole bidder. The contract called for six round trips per week from Chicago to the Twin Cities via Milwaukee and LaCrosse, and the airline would be paid $2.75 per pound of airmail carried.[18]

The officers and directors of the new airline were drawn from the ranks of the Minnesota and Michigan businessmen who had provided the capital to start it, but the key position was that of vice president and general manager. That post was taken by Lewis Brittin, who, for the next eight years, would be the operating head of Northwest. The ground staff included Andrew J. Hufford, Chief Mechanic, and three assistants, plus Julius Perlt, Brittin's clerk and general right-hand-man. Perlt had worked for Brittin at the St. Paul Association office and now came with him to the airline. He recalls Brittin as having been "dynamic, intelligent, honest, a gentleman, tough in working toward his goals but wonderful to work for."[19]

The flight section of the company was as modest as the non flying compliment. Three pilots were hired, with Charles Holman as chief pilot, and Robert W. Radoll and David L. Behncke completing the flight staff. The earliest existing financial voucher is dated 30 November, 1926, and shows that each pilot earned $75.00 per week. Indeed, the entire list of Northwest employees numbered nine with a monthly payroll of $838.43. Brittin is not listed and did not draw a salary from the airline. For the first several months, he continued as head of the St. Paul Association and was paid by and operated out of the office of that organization.

One of Brittin's first orders of business was to undertake the first buy of airplanes in Northwest's history. He ordered three Stinson Detroiters which could carry mail and three passengers at 85 m.p.h. They were biplanes, but featured completely enclosed cabins which was something of an innovation in 1926. The Detroiters, however, could not be delivered

Dickinson's ill-fated Air Mail ship #3, the Partridge-Keller biplane, designed and built by Elmer Partridge, rolls into Wold-Chamberlain Field on 7 June, 1926 after a wild ride from Chicago. Partridge had replaced an airsick Merrill Riddick at Watertown, Wisconsin, and flown the leg into Minneapolis, having been blown north of his route, and actually having made an emergency landing at Robbinsdale, where he rolled the tire off his right wheel rim. After catching his breath, he succeeded in making it to Wold. Note the tire missing from his wheel. (James Borden)

The remains of the Partridge-Keller ship in a field south of the Twin Cities, where Partridge crashed after fighting the winds and turbulence on 7 June, 1926. Partridge died in the wreck. (James Borden)

Northwest Ford 5AT roaring through wispy clouds between the Twin Cities and Chicago in 1934. (Joe Quigley via James Borden)

Hamilton H-47 Metalplane at Milwaukee County Airport, 1938. Still in service after nine years, the Hamilton was a workhorse. (Noel Allard)

until November, and Northwest was scheduled to begin operations on 1 October. William Kidder, who operated the airport at Snelling and Larpenteur, thereupon agreed to lease two of his airplanes to the new airline; a 90 h.p. Curtiss Oriole, and a W.W.I. vintage Thomas-Morse Scout. With these two open-cockpit biplanes, Northwest started flying the mail on 1 October, 1926. The first Detroiter arrived on 1 November, and was flown in by Dave Behncke. Speed Holman and Eddie Stinson, himself, brought the second and third new airplanes into Minneapolis the following day. The ships were pressed into service immediately.[20]

For the next nine months, Northwest flew the mail profitably without major mishap, although minor mishaps were common in that age when forced landings, due to weather or mechanical malfunctions, were common. Since the airline was being paid $2.75 for each pound of airmail carried and since the government did not closely scrutinize just what was being mailed, cargo was sometimes slightly bizarre. Kidder had several old propellers and said "we revarnished them, had them lettered "USE AIR MAIL" and mailed them to different postmasters for window display. These propellers in their crates weighed close to 100 pounds so every time we mailed one of those props we realized about a hundred dollars profit."

When pilot, Dave Behncke, decided to move his residence from Chicago to St. Paul, he was told to package all his belongings, put stamps on them and fly them up. Several profitable trips were made until a mattress slung under the wing broke loose over LaCrosse. Kidder said later, "There was quite a 'to-do' over that."[21]

Northwest's first passenger flight was made with only mild embarrassment on 5 July, 1927. With appropriate fanfare to mark the historic occasion, a Stinson took off from St. Paul with Speed Holman at the controls and headed toward Chicago. The passengers were Byron G. Webster of the St. Paul Association, and L. R. S. Ferguson, president of the St. Paul City Council, whose intention was to carry the civic greetings and good will of their city to folks at stops along the way. The first stop, however, was unscheduled. Over Hastings, a clogged fuel line forced a landing and the problem was quickly fixed. The Stinson could not, however, lift itself, Holman, the mail, the fuel, and two passengers from Hasting's small field, so Webster and Ferguson were sent back to St. Paul by automobile. Holman then took off, flew back to St. Paul, collected his two undaunted passengers and tried again.

The second try went better. A brief stop was made for lunch and ceremonies at La Crosse, and the trio then battled heavy winds and rain eastward across Wisconsin. Milwaukee was reached, albeit somewhat behind schedule, and an uneventful hop to Chicago completed the trip. The next day passengers were carried on the scheduled flights in both directions including a Miss Hazel Hart of Brooklyn, New York, who became the airline's first female passenger. Northwest was now in the mail and passenger carrying business for good.

For the rest of the decade of the 1920s, the Northwest story was one of steady growth. In early 1928, routes were extended to include weekly service to Winnipeg, via Fargo, and later in the same year, service was scheduled from Milwaukee north to Green Bay. By early 1929, two flights per day were being run to Chicago and *Aviation Magazine* could report that, as of April, Northwest had flown 9,200 passengers without injury to anyone or loss of a single mail pouch.[22] On the more purely financial side, the spring of 1929 saw the airline become almost an entirely Minnesota company when Twin Cities businessmen bought out the original Detroit investors and established the airline's corporate headquarters at the Merchant's Bank Building in St. Paul.

With the hard work of St. Paul banker, Richard C. Lilly, the elite of the Twin Cities business community were convinced to come up with $160,000 cash to pay off the Detroit business interests who had made the initial investment in the airline. The new Board was a "Who's Who" of the Twin Cities business community, with but a single director, William B. Mayo, of the Ford Motor Company of Detroit, remaining.

The rest of the officers included Lilly as president; Arthur R. Rogers, president of the Rogers Lumber Company, chairman of the board; Colonel Brittin, vice-president and general manager; Harry C. Piper, of Lane, Piper and Jaffrey, vice-president; Julian Baird, vice-president of the Merchants Bank and Trust Co. of St. Paul, secretary and treasurer. The board of directors included many other luminaries.

By the end of the decade, Northwest had added larger, "state-of-the-art," aircraft to their fleet.

In 1928, the company purchased its first large passenger aircraft, Hamilton Metalplanes and Ford Trimotors. Both were similar in construction: corrugated duraluminum skin riveted to aluminum trusswork fuselage, and corrugated aluminum skin fastened to aluminum truss ribs and spars for the wing. The difference lay in the number of Pratt & Whitney engines, three Wasps for the Ford and a single Hornet for the Hamilton. Passenger capacities were fourteen for the Ford and six for the Hamilton.

The first Ford was delivered on 30 August, 1928, two days before the first Hamilton. Colonel Brittin requested that Operations Manager, Speed Holman, report the comments of his line pilots on their first trips in the Hamiltons. On 27 October, the trip summaries were turned in:

From Fred Whittemore: In accordance with your request that a report be made on the performance of the Hamilton on my two trips over the mail route, I submit the following in condensed form.

My first trip was made on October 22 when I left Minneapolis and landed at the regular mail stops enroute. Nothing need be said of the ship's performance at Minneapolis or St. Paul fields as both are of such size as to eliminate all doubt as to landing and takeoff. Landings at Madison and Milwaukee, Wisconsin, where obstructions on the north make landings normally difficult, were made without undue cause for stalling in. Takeoffs from the same fields presented no difficulties and a marked improvement over the Stinsons under the same proportional peak loads was noted. The trip from Milwaukee to Chicago was made at night to note the visibility and I was more than pleased to note the wide range of vision.

The return trip was made over the lighted beacon route the following morning and landings were made at all intermediate fields as well as the regular mail stops, and three landings were made between La Crosse and Minneapolis in open fields on the regular course.

On my second trip made on October 25th, I left Minneapolis with about 1200 pounds of sand and full tanks of gasoline and landings and takeoffs were made at all fields. The ease with which the Hamilton lands and handles on takeoffs and in the air is nothing short of remarkable and is in my estimation a real ship for the combined air-mail and passenger service.[23]

Whittemore went on to note his only complaint; with the engine in front of his nose, the visibility would be made better by the removal of an exhaust collector ring that ran between the two top cylinders, and its relocation elsewhere.

Line pilot, John Malone reported that he believed the ship could be landed without difficulty in any field in which the Stinson could land, and had better takeoff performance than the Stinson. He also advocated the rearrangement of the exhaust collector ring, and adjustable rudder pedals for tall and short pilots.[24]

Pilot, Homer Cole's report stated, "My first impression of the landing speed of the Hamilton was that it seemed to be high, that is, around 75 to 80 miles per hour. After flying it for several hours and after making the numbers of landings on the two trips, I found that my impression was wrong and that the ship lands at a very reasonable speed and I feel that it lands at approximately the same speed as the Stinson. My first landings were made with the nose down, but I later discovered that the nose of the ship could be, quite definitely held up, with no tendency

Sheet metal work being done to the wing of a Hamilton Metalplane at the St. Paul maintenance hangar. (Northwest Airlines via Vince Doyle)

whatever to stall or fall off, this of course, tending to make a very slow landing."[25]

He also noted that he would prefer a better arrangement of the exhaust system.

Speed Holman then submitted a summary of these reports on the Hamilton Metalplane to Colonel Brittin with his own comments, "From my personal experience with it, I feel certain that it is highly suitable for a combined air mail and passenger plane due to its great strength and high speed. It cruises nicely at 1600 r.p.m. at about 110 miles per hour, which is about 20 miles per hour faster than our present mail planes. The landing speed is about 60 to 65 miles per hour, as close as I can tell.

"In conclusion, I want to say that the more experience I have with it, the better I like it, and think that it is O.K. in every respect for the purpose for which we desire it."[26]

Northwest eventually owned nine of the airplanes, obtained between September, 1928 and June of 1931. The Hamiltons performed yeoman service, with no accidents during their careers with Northwest. One was written off after being destroyed in a hangar fire at Fargo when a fire pot being used to heat the engine, exploded. The last Hamilton was still in service as late as 1941.

The Ford Trimotors, of which there were five dur-

Classic Northwest Airways Ford Trimotor photo shows the overhaul and maintenance hangar with the passenger ticketing and waiting room in the foreground. This historic building was demolished in 1988 to clear space for a new runway approach at Holman Field, St. Paul. (Northwest Airlines via Vince Doyle)

Interior of the maintenance hangar looking west a couple of years later than the previous picture. The hangar now holds three Lockheed 10A's, the Waco Taperwing, a Lockheed Orion in gleaming white paint, a Hamilton in the near foreground, and the engine run-up test stand, a Pheasant biplane fuselage. (Northwest Airlines via Vince Doyle)

ing the same period, were the 747's of their day, carrying the heavy passenger loads over the major route segments. Their introduction was also accompanied by much hoopla. The first Ford was purchased with $65,000 worth of Northwest Airways stock bought by Transcontinental Air transport (TAT). Northwest purchased the first 5-AT Trimotor model to be manufactured by the Ford Motor Company.[27]

Altogether, the Fords were an attractive answer to fast, reliable, cross-country transportation. They flew with a full passenger load on almost every trip, seating 14 in quiet comfort (compared to what had come before). The Ford's luxury included a restroom, and for the first time, a steward accompanied the pilot, and cheerfully handed out box lunches, magazines, pillows, and chewing gum (to relieve the discomfort of air pressure differences in the ears as the plane climbed and descended). In ten months, Northwest racked up a million passenger miles with the Fords and Hamiltons.

"A million miles without an accident." The slogan had a wonderful ring to it, and a promotional booklet with that theme was published. But just as the booklet come off the press, Northwest suffered its first fatal accident.

On 25 June, 1929, pilot Eddie Middagh was taking off from St. Paul Airport in a Ford Trimotor. As was

On April 12, 1932, Mal Freeburg had a propeller blade snap while airborne in this Ford Trimotor. Vibration shook the engine loose from its mounts but Freeburg waggled the wings and dropped the engine into the Mississippi River, then made an emergency landing at Durand, Wisconsin. The landing was all the more difficult as the left tire had been slashed by the broken prop blade on its departure. (Carl Magnuson)

the custom with a light passenger load, he was using only the two outboard engines, the center engine was simply not needed. At this most inopportune time, one of the two operating engines suddenly quit. There was not enough altitude to turn around and glide back to the airport and the edges of the bluff at Mound's Park stared him in the face. All Eddie could do was to aim the plane at the large clear area of the park where children normally were playing and couples strolling. The crash resulted in a single fatality, that of Eddie Middagh.

With beacon lights having been installed by the federal government across the country, Northwest bought three special-design Taperwing mailplanes from its own Waco agency and launched night airmail to Chicago. (Northwest, taking every opportunity to make a dollar in those early years, held a Waco dealership). A new group of pioneer pilots came on board to operate the burgeoning schedule. Walter Bullock had been on board for a few months and was joined by Leon S. "Deke" DeLong, R. L. "Lee" Smith, Les Smith and Mal Freeburg.

Freeburg, who occasionally stripped down to his BVD's to keep cool while flying the mail on hot summer nights, was following the Burlington railroad tracks to Chicago on the night of 12 July, 1930, when he spotted a flaming railroad trestle over the Chippewa River near Trevina, Wisconsin. He knew the train schedule by heart and knew that ahead of him the Burlington "Blackhawk" passenger train was barrelling along at 70 miles per hour and due to cross the trestle in a matter of minutes.

He raced ahead toward the oncoming train, blinking his landing lights and diving at the train, but the engineer did not show any sign of stopping the train for a crazy barnstorming pilot, so Mal zoomed by once more and dropped his landing flares along the right-of-way. This caught the engineer's attention and he brought the train to a stop within sight of the flaming bridge. One of the passengers on that train was pro golfer, Bobby Jones. He was on his way to the U. S. Open Golf Championship at Interlachen Golf Course in Minneapolis, where he would win the event, and in the processs, nail down one third of the only

Mal Freeburg (far right) receives the first Congressional Airmail Medal of Honor from President Franklin D. Roosevelt at the White House on December 13, 1933 for stopping a railroad train from running across a burning trestle bridge. Left to right; W.W. Howes, 2nd Assitant Postmaster general; J. M Donaldson, Deputy 2nd Asst. Postmaster General; Clyde Kelly, Congressman from Pennsylvania; and Freeburg. (James Borden)

Grand Slam in the history of golf.

Freeburg was in the hot seat again on the night of 12 April, 1932, when the propeller blade of his Ford Trimotor's left engine snapped. Before it could be shut down, the engine set up such violent vibrations that the 500 pound motor jerked itself out of the engine mounting and hung precariously from the struts, threatening to plunge like a bomb, on the city of Wabasha, below.

Joe Kimm, the co-pilot on the flight remembered, "everybody knew a Tri-motor would fly on two engines, but nobody had any idea how badly the ship would be unbalanced with one outboard motor removed altogether. And we had passengers on board."[28]

With great delicacy and precision, Freeburg gently turned his stricken plane toward the Mississippi River, holding his breath until he was well out over the water. Then he banked to the left and whipped the controls back and forth. The motor shook loose and dropped harmlessly into the "Father of Waters." To add to the seriousness of the situation, the broken propeller blade had slashed the landing gear tire as it departed from the engine. Never-the-less, Mal gingerly put the Trimotor down on an emergency field at Durand, Wisconsin, with hardly a bump, much to the passengers', and the co-pilot's, admiration.

For his heroics, Freeburg was given the first Congressional Air Mail Medal of Honor by President Franklin Delano Roosevelt in 1933, in ceremonies at the White House.

In early 1931 Northwest signed an agreement with Transcontinental Air Transport to become a member of a national network that eased passengers along from one end of the country to the other. Northwest set up its airline schedules so that it could connect with trains at each end of the line, Chicago and St. Paul. Passengers could leave New York, Philadelphia and Washington on evening trains that would put them in Chicago just after lunch the next day. They could then board a Northwest Hamilton or Ford and be in the Twin Cities in just a little over three hours. Train time between Chicago and St. Paul was normally twelve hours.

In St. Paul, they could catch the afternoon train west aboard the Great Northern, Northern Pacific or the Chicago, Milwaukee and St. Paul (the Milwaukee Road). Similarly, from the west, passengers on trains arriving in St. Paul early in the morning could make the flight on Northwest to Chicago and catch the noon trains going east. In either direction, the time saving with the Northwest leg was eight hours.

In the back of Colonel Brittin's mind was a plan to see his airline stretch across the west to the shores of Puget Sound. Brittin knew it would be a struggle, especially during the Depression, as the federal government was becoming more and more stingy with airmail contracts and subsidies. Government officials also looked upon the route across the northern tier of states as an impractical idea, with the mountains being a natural barrier and the weather too rugged. Unfortunately, this group of naysayers included the U. S. Postmaster General, Walter F. Brown. Brown was convinced that there should be only two routes across the country, both of which would be farther south.

The situation meant that cities like St. Paul, Min-

Interior of Northwest's St. Paul maintenance hangar looking east. In the foreground, Frank Toll, Northwest's painter is preparing to paint the Northwest insignia on the side of an H-47 Hamilton Metalplane, circa 1932. In the background is a Ford Trimotor, another Hamilton and, tucked between them, a Waco Taperwing used for night mail. (Northwest Airlines via Vince Doyle)

neapolis, Fargo, Bismarck, Billings, Helena, Spokane and Seattle, would be destined for second-class service, with no direct routes to the Coast. Brittin drummed up support in North Dakota to lobby for a route to Fargo, Grand Forks and Bismarck. When this route was granted, the cities were "on the map." Bismarck, in gratitude, named its airport "Brittin Field," but the honor was mixed with tragedy, when Speed Holman was killed at Omaha in May 1931.

Speed's place on the Northwest staff would be taken by Chad Smith, older brother of pilots Lee and Les Smith. The operation manager's position was vacated again within four months, when Smith died on the operating table during an appendix operation. His place would next be filled by Walter Bullock.

The Holman and Smith tragedies were temporary setbacks in Brittin's push westward. The year ending 30 June, 1931 showed that over 7,000 passengers had been boarded in the preceeding twelve months, with over a quarter million pounds of mail being carried. At $2.75 a pound, the mail had generated $687,500 gross income.[29]

The next destination in the route expansion was Winnipeg, to be served from Fargo. For this, Northwest signed its first "Air-Link" partner, Western Canada Airlines, in May 1931. Northwest needed them to service the route into Canada as the Canadian government had not yet signed an agreement authorizing Northwest to fly directly into that country.

In 1930, Northwest moved from Wold-Chamberlain

168

Northwest Stinson SM-2AB Junior is parked at the Janesville Airport, between flights, in this view from 1931. (Dick Palen via Sherm Booen)

to their new $100,000 terminal and maintenance facility at the St. Paul Airport. With new shops and room to expand its own maintenance, it could handle any repair or overhaul, including 350 hour major engine overhauls, and 100 hour propeller overhauls. A few things were still done the old-fashioned way. When Wasp and Hornet engines were overhauled, they were attached to an old Orville Hickman-designed Pheasant biplane fuselage that was rolled out onto the ramp, chained to the ground and the engines run-up and tested. Jim LaMont was maintenance supervisor and reporting to him were Lou Koerner of the ship department and Hank Aune of the engine department.

The times were colorful. Passenger travel was in its infancy, and there was little to distinguish the pilots from regular folks. They often had a drink in the bar with the passengers prior to a flight and nobody seemed to think it unusual. The following are parts of various memos from Northwest's operations managers Speed Holman, Chad Smith and Walter Bullock, which show the simplicity of operations of those times.

23 June, 1930. To all pilots and stewards. "As a result of various tests conducted by the Department of Agriculture, it has been ascertained that burning tobacco dropped from aircraft will, under certain circumstances ignite underbrush, dry timber, etc.

"There now exists in the Air Commerce regulations a prohibition in the matter of dropping or releasing objects from aircraft which will endanger life or damage property. Burning tobacco, such as cigars or cigarettes, are definitely within the meaning of the provision."

The beautiful Lockheed Orion, bright white with black inset panels on the wings. The Lockheed provided speedy service between the Twin Cities and Spokane in the middle 1930's. (Northwest Airlines via Vince Doyle)

12 August, 1930. To all pilots. "In the past most of us have left the pilot's cockpit in some of our line ships with the engine running. This is a practise that is forbidden by the Department of Commerce and I think we should take steps to eliminate it. It (taking care of paperwork or other business) may be done in one of two ways, either by the pilot remaining in the cockpit and having reports handed to him to sign, or possibly better still have someone on the ground climb on the wheel on small ships or on the step on the Hamilton, reach in and handle the throttle until the pilot returns. I think pilots operating through fields where we have no company representative can make arrangements with some local person to do this for us." Charles Holman.

3 January, 1931. "Pilot should take friendly and courteous attitude toward passengers whether or not they appeal to them personally, also optimistic and enthusiastic attitude toward air travel." Chad Smith.

1 July, 1931. All pilots and co-pilots. "The pilots' uniform for hot weather flying will be the same as prescribed last summer. This is uniform trousers, black belt, white shirt, black four-in-hand tie and uniform cap. Suspenders are taboo." Chad Smith.

3 July, 1931. To all pilots. "There has been some complaint that some of the pilots have been careless in the way they taxied away from the passenger station at Fargo, and in some instances have blown dirt over passengers and spectators at that point. It is suggested that the planes be taxied well away from the passenger station and, where possible, turn towards the passenger station instead of away from it, so that the dirt is blown out into the field." Chad Smith.

28 September, 1931. To all pilots. "All pilots coming from outside points into the Twin Cities stopping first at Minneapolis requiring gasoline will put in only enough at that point to safely bring them to St. Paul as gasoline costs us practically double at Minneapolis than at St. Paul." Walter Bullock.

4 February, 1932. To all pilots. "Hereafter we are going to discontinue the practise of putting gum and cotton packets in the seat receptacles on our ships and it will be necessary for the pilot and co-pilot to distribute them to our passengers." Walter Bullock.[30]

In 1932, Northwest equipped its aircraft and stations with two-way radio communications when they purchased $50,000 worth of radio gear from Western Electric. Soon afterward, they introduced radio service for the passengers. From a Philco Transitone radio aboard the Ford Trimotor, passengers could plug a set of headphones into a jack at each seat and listen to such events as the World Series or college football games.

Route expansion was still uppermost in Brittin's mind. To counter the critics, and prove the northern tier route safe and reliable, he and Croil Hunter made a series of proving runs to Washington state. On 4 March, 1933, the Post Office Department approved a route from Bismarck to Billings, Montana, provided Northwest cancel an equal number of miles from their Wisconsin and Illinois schedules so as not to gain additional air mail revenue.

Newly elected postmaster, James A. Farley, however, threatened to cancel the last-minute authority. He had decided to cut airmail revenue nationwide by 25% and allow no further issuance of airmail contracts in a fiscal tactic to control the government's Depression budget.

Northwest had gained a step on its route to the West Coast, but United Airlines, which operated a route to Seattle along a more southerly corridor through Salt Lake City, had been siding with the government to block Northwest from competing to the north. Now, suddenly, United applied for the northern route as well.

Next, Brittin tried for a 447 mile link from Billings to Spokane. Postmaster Farley rejected the application. Northwest offered to discontinue airmail flights to Duluth, Green Bay, Madison and Rochester to offset the mail revenue once more. Farley approved this. The fact that the U. S. Department of Commerce had appropriated $655,445 for light beacons every ten miles from Minneapolis to Seattle, gave weight to the argument for approving the northern route.

Both Northwest and United lobbied in Washington. Authority there was divided, the Department of Commerce, charged with supervising the airways and the Post Office Department in charge of airmail. Brittin suspected that United would try to go around the Post Office Department and get approval of the route for themselves by requesting the Commerce Department to approve a passenger route to Seattle, planning to acquire the airmail contract after they were well entrenched.

Brittin had a habit of working on Saturdays while lobbying in Washington. On Saturday, 2 December, 1933, discovered United's ploy. United had, in fact, filed a request to initiate passenger service between Spokane and Seattle the following Monday, 4 December, just two days away.

Brittin went directly to Stephen Cisler, superintendent of air mail service, on Saturday afternoon, and insisted that Northwest had a "moral priority" on the route as it had been advocating it for some time while United had been publicly opposed to it. Cisler agreed with Brittin and promptly approved Brittin's request to acquire the route. To implement the plan immediately, Brittin phoned Croil Hunter back in St. Paul, and the two scheduled the first flight over the new route for the next day, Sunday, 3 December, 1933. Pilot Nick Mamer, flying one of the Taperwing Wacos, roared past Mt. Rainier the next day and nailed down Northwest's claim to the route. The Twin Cities and Chicago were now linked to Seattle through the upper states.

In Washington, at that time, Senator Hugo Black, heading a congressional investigating committee, began to examine the "spoils" of the government's granting exorbitant airmail contracts to the largest airlines. Northwest was not one of those large airlines at that time, but became involved in the problem in a bizarre way. The Black committee had subpoenaed records from the office of Washington attorney William P. McCracken, Jr., who represented half a dozen airlines, including Northwest.

Brittin knew that important Northwest documents were among those files subpoenaed. He went to McCracken's office and withdrew Northwest's papers from the files, tore them up, and dumped the scraps in the trash. Investigators discovered the situation, retrieved 300 pounds of trash and laboriously pasted them back together. Although there was no damning

Sikorsky S-38 flying boat carried Northwest Airways passengers between St. Paul and Duluth from 1931 until 1935. (Don Erickson)

evidence in the reconstructed documents, McCracken and Brittin were charged with contempt of congress. Brittin subsequently spent ten days in jail and gave up all involvement with Northwest.

But there was more turbulent air for Northwest. On 9 February, 1934, President Roosevelt, on advice from his postmaster, James Farley, cancelled all airmail contracts. He ordered the Army to carry the mail.

It was customary for Northwest's Treasurer, E. I. Whyatt, to add his own comments to the monthly Treasurer's report presented to the Board of Directors. Whyatt's March memo about February begins:

"February 1934 will be a month long remembered by Northwest Airways. On the 9th we received a telegraphic order from the Postmaster General annulling our mail contracts as of midnight, February 19th. This meant the elimination of 75% of our income and required drastic reduction of expenditures to preserve the company's liquidity. With this in mind, several important steps were taken:

1. Service was curtailed.
2. 70% of employees were laid off.
3. All remaining employees were given a salary cut of 50%."[31]

In addition to the above steps, the Fords were taken out of service and the more economical Hamiltons, Orions, and Travel Air cabin planes were substituted. Certain routes were discontinued. Later in the month some were reinstated, but employees hired back were hired at half their previous salary.

Businessmen complained to the President that 300,000 stockholders of various airlines across the country were left in the lurch. Colonel Charles Lindbergh complained that the largest portion of the U. S. commercial aviation had been condemned unjustly without a trial. The most dramatic backlash to Roosevelt's plan was the unpreparedness of the Air Corps.

For ten days, the nation had no airmail service at all while the Army got it's act together. Then, flying obsolete planes with little or no night experience, the service barely maintained 60% of the former commercial schedules. What's more, there followed a series of crashes with the loss of many lives. The situation shook the nation.

In April, two months later, Farley, under great pressure, ordered all airlines to reorganize and rid their ranks of any official who had participated in the "spoils system," after which they could submit new bids for the mail routes. Northwest reorganized as Northwest Airlines, Inc. on 16 April, 1934. When the routes were awarded, despite the fact that it had retained the route from Fargo to Seattle, Northwest was

The Lockheed 10-A was a workhorse. Northwest bought the first three aircraft off the Lockheed production line in 1934. This aircraft has not yet been modified to a sloped back windshield, still having the original pointed style, as it came from the factory. (Northwest Airlines via Vince Doyle)

staggered to find that it had lost its key route from St. Paul to Chicago, and the route from the Twin Cities to Fargo and Pembina.

In December of 1934, Hanford TriState Airlines, which had won both former Northwest routes by bidding very low for the airmail contracts, was on the verge of bankruptcy. Northwest had also been operating in the red, but purchased the contracts from Hanford for $46,000, and rehired some of its own former pilots who had been laid off during the cancellation and gone to work for Hanford. Now Northwest had its full route system back.

Back in February 1929, the route from Minneapolis, St. Paul to Chicago made stops at La Crosse, Madison and Milwaukee. There was a single flight each way each day. A one-way trip took approximately four hours, including stops, and cost $30.

In August of 1929, the route map still showed Minneapolis as the western-most point of the route picture, and Chicago the easterly. Planes on these routes were given dramatic names such as the "Grey Eagle" for the Fords, the "Black Bird" for the Stinson Detroiter, and the "Silver Streak" for the Hamilton. The Grey Eagle operated between Minneapolis and Chicago by way of Rochester, the Silver Streak between Minneapolis and Chicago by way of La Crosse, Madison, and Milwaukee. The Black Bird operated from Chicago to Green Bay with stops at Milwaukee, Fond Du Lac, Oshkosh, and Appleton. Single flights each direction between cities occurred each day. Ford

Loading mail and parcels into the nose of a Lockheed 10-A at St. Paul. (Don Erickson)

Trimotors and Hamiltons were used on the Minneapolis to Chicago route and the original Stinson Detroiters were used between Chicago and Green Bay.

In August 1930, the route had expanded to include stops at Elgin, Rockford and Janesville but still included a single flight each way each day.

By May, 1931, the routes had expanded again, and now included Fargo, Grand Forks and Pembina, North Dakota. The use of Western Canada Airlines to add a Pembina-Winnipeg route was included on Northwest's schedule. Several flights each day between Minneapolis and Chicago were also provided. The schedule for July 1932 shows further expansion to the west with Valley City, Jamestown and Mandan being served. Duluth was also on the schedule, being served by Sikorsky amphibian.

A Sikorsky S-38 had been purchased in April, 1931 to be used to service the city of Duluth. Duluth had no large airport at the time and Northwest chose to operate from the harbor, utilizing the shore facilities of the Duluth Boat Club. Eventually an airport was built that could handle larger aircraft. The original Sikorsky and a second one, purchased for spare parts, were sold by 1935.[11]

August, 1933, saw extensions to the west as far as Billings, with stops at Bismarck, Glendive, and Miles City. August of 1934 brought the route to its extent past Billings, to Butte, Missoula, Spokane and Wenatchee, prior to the terminus at Seattle. Equipment had changed from Ford Trimotors to speedy Lockheed "Orions" and Lockheed 10A "Electras".

Like the Sikorsky amphibians, the Orion's career with Northwest was short. Three were purchased to provide service between St. Paul and the far west until the next generation of airliners came on line. The Orion was a follow-on to the famous Lockheed Vega, a popular personal cross-country airplane, the favorite of aviatrix Amelia Earhart.

The Orion was a plywood masterpiece with wooden wings and a molded fuselage. A 550 h.p. Pratt & Whitney Wasp engine gave it a great cruising speed of nearly 230 m.p.h., yet it landed at only 50 m.p.h. with a full load on board. It had landing lights imbedded in the wing leading edge, landing flaps, retractable landing gear and could carry a pilot and five passengers in considerable comfort. But for all its comfort and innovation, it was a stopgap measure until the first "modern" airliner could be delivered.

In 1934, Northwest had signed an agreement with the Lockheed Corporation of California to purchase the first ten-passenger Lockheed 10A Electra. It gave them a marketing edge. The monocoque all-metal aircraft was "high-tech" compared to the Ford Trimotor and the Hamilton which it replaced. It was faster, smoother, and quieter; its seats, more comfortable, and with only two Wasp engines, it was more economical. Passengers and flight crews grew to love it.

With a sophisticated set of cockpit instruments, the provision for a directional gyro and a Sperry artificial horizon, together with two-way radio, trim tabs on both rudder and elevator, ball bearing mounted control surfaces, and wide-stance landing gear, the ship was easy to fly. The baggage compartment in the nose provided 40 cubic feet of cargo space, and the fuselage, which hunkered down deeply into the wing structure, presented a small frontal area to the wind making the plane extremely efficient.[33]

A trip on the Lockheed Electra to Seattle in 1936 was romantic. Witness one account by author, Kenn C. Rust, writing in the *American Aviation Historical Society Journal:*

Northwest Flight 1, a silver Lockheed 10A, after taking on 10 passengers, mail and express, departs Chicago Municipal Airport at 7:00 a.m. The pilot is one of the top pilots on the line, Mal Freeburg, and the co-pilot is Art Haid. The Electra passes over small farming towns in northern Illinois and southern Wisconsin and soon crosses the icy Wisconsin River near Madison. As it does, Mal climbs to 8,000 feet to take advantage of a 40-m.p.h. tail wind. He is flying visually, not following the radio beam on this cold winter's morning. Down below, the temperature is near zero, in the cabin and cockpit of the Lockheed, it is a highly comfortable 76 degrees.

Reaching the Mississippi, the plane follows its left bank for nearly an hour. Then a light flashes in the cabin to tell the passengers to fasten their seat belts, the retractable landing gear is lowered with a hum, the flaps go down with a whine, and Mal deftly sets the trim Lockheed down at Minneapolis at 9:00 a.m. - 20 minutes ahead of schedule, thanks to the tail wind.

Following a meal stop and a crew change at Minneapolis, diminuative Carl Leuthi is now the pilot, Lee Wright the co-pilot, the plane takes off at 9:35 a.m. and heads northwest. It flies over hundreds of Minnesota's famed lakes and such places as Sauk Centre, made famous by novelist Sinclair Lewis, and Osakis, favored hunting grounds for Andrew Carnegie. To the left of the flight path is the string of airway beacon lights pilots follow at night.

Over the western part of the route, Rust continues:

As soon as the passengers finish a light supper and the plane is refueled [at Spokane], Nick [Mamer] takes off at 5:45 p.m., climbs, and sets the plane on the beam for its final destination, Seattle. Ahead in the distance, clouds cloak the high Wenatchee and Cascade Mountains, and Nick begins climbing to 11,000 feet to get over them. The early evening is so clear, that as the climb begins, passengers looking out to the right can make out, a hundred miles north, the Huckleberry Mountains through which the Columbia River flows westerly before turning south. Soon the plane is over the gorge of the southward flowing Columbia as the Lockheed approaches the Wenatchees. Fifteen minutes later, headed for Snoqualmie Pass in the Cascades, snow-capped Mount Rainier is clearly visible to the south. Mount St. Helens and Mount Adams can just be made out in the twilight. As Snoqualmie Pass is negotiated, blizzards can be seen raging around some peaks.

With the highest of the Cascade Mountains behind him, Nick Mamer starts letting down into the vast valley ahead to the west, with Puget Sound at its center and Seattle just this side of the sound. Below, the lights of scattered houses

A Lockheed 14-H loads up at Chicago in April, 1940. The Model 14 was not well liked. Three crashed with loss of life, including this one. The airplane was replaced in service by the famous DC-3. (Sid Davies)

appear, become more numerous and give way to lighted streets. The gear goes down, the flaps are extended and gently, with the touch of an expert, Nick Mamer sets Flight 1 down at Seattle. The time is 7:25 p.m. - five minutes ahead of schedule after the 14-½ hour flight from Chicago.[34]

Since the airmail scandal and the departure of Colonel Brittin, Croil Hunter had been the general manager of Northwest Airlines. Hunter, a native of Fargo, North Dakota, and a graduate of Yale, had served as a 1st Lieutenant in the 338th Field Artillery in World War One. He learned to fly in Minneapolis and was a former member of the Minnesota Aeronautics Commission. He came to Northwest in 1932 as traffic manager and was based out of the Chicago office. He succeeded Col. Brittin as general manager following the airmail situation in 1934.

Hunter assumed the reigns from Brittin with the same goals, the same mindset and same zeal. He pushed for the westward movement, and he authorized the purchase of the Lockheed Orions and 10A's. In July 1937, Hunter took a giant step, purchasing a newer model airliner, the Lockheed Model 14 "Sky Zephyr."

A single 10A had crashed in Idaho with loss of life in 1936, but the Model 14 was destined to be "snake-bitten." Within a year of its purchase, the first ship would be written off at Bozeman, Montana, on 10 January, 1938, killing pioneer pilot Nick Mamer, co-pilot Art Haid, and eight passengers. It was the first loss of life for a passenger on any Northwest aircraft. Structural failure was the cause, the vertical

Plush interior of the Lockheed 14-H. The net luggage racks overhead are evident as are the comfortable padded seats. (Don Erickson)

172

stabilizers having separated in flight. The next May, vice president of operations, Fred Whittemore, was killed when a brand-new Model 14 hit a canyon wall near Glendale, California. The aircraft, not yet belonging to Northwest was on an acceptance flight back to the Twin Cities. Two other Zephyrs would be lost during the next two years. These wrecks were accompanied by many minor accidents, and both pilots and the flying public grew skeptical of them. Fortunately their time with the airline was drawing to a close.

In 1938, Croil Hunter had placed an order with the Douglas Company for its brand-new DC-3 aircraft. In April, 1939, the first DC-3 was put on the line. Northwest would purchase 29 of the hard-working aircraft before World War II ended. The DC-3 would feature a stewardess, among other flying amenities.

Northwest came out of the airmail situation of 1934 in the red, but in the following years, revenue passenger miles rose, as did airmail and freight. In 1934, passenger boardings totalled a little over 12,000, but by 1941 had risen to 149,212.[35]

Flying cross-country required flights at greater altitudes than the simple flights across lowlands between Chicago and the Twin Cities. Northwest crews had reported feeling drowsy during the flights across the Cascades into Seattle when flying at 13,000 feet. Croil Hunter brought up the subject to Dr. Charles Mayo of the Mayo Clinic, at a party in 1938. Dr. Mayo assigned three of his top physiologists and surgeons to investigate the matter. Doctors Walter Boothby, William Lovelace, and Arthur Bulbulian, by using a pressure chamber at the Mayo Clinic, verified that lack of oxygen above 10,000 feet would cause drowsiness and slowed reaction times.

Dr. Bulbulian, who was an expert in reconstructive facial surgery, designed a latex rubber oxygen mask that would fit over the nose, yet leave the mouth area open for eating and talking, a workable solution for both flight crews and passengers. The innovative team had designed the mask with a small bladder "lung" that mixed oxygen with regular air in just the right quantities for normal breathing.

In its first test on 27 July, 1938, pilot Mal Freeburg, his wife, the team of doctors, and other Northwest personnel, flew to Los Angeles at 20,000 feet. The masks worked extremely well and the flight stirred so much interest that news reporters making the return flight to the Twin Cities, asked pilot Mel Swanson to remove his mask for a few minutes to watch his lips and fingertips turn blue.

The "B.L.B." mask, as it was known, was named after the three doctors, and its use spread to other airlines as well as Northwest. Eventually, the military used the same mask as the basis for developing an entire line of World War II high-altitude oxygen masks to be used by fighter and bomber crews.[36]

A week after Pearl Harbor, the government took control of all civil airlines and commandeered many aircraft from the nation's airline fleets. All the country's airlines were affected.

The Canadian government had built many small airstrips across the expanse of western Canada by 1941. Though the string of airports, itself, was practically invulnerable to enemy attack, they were woefully inadequate to handle the amount of traffic

New Northwest DC-3 leaves the ground at Minneapolis in 1939. Many DC-3's were commandeered for military work during the war, some sold to the Chinese, and some continuing in use until as late as 1957. (Vern Georgia collection)

necessary to build and supply bases in Alaska, needed to defend against a Japanese invasion of North America. And there was no highway beyond a point at Fort St. John in northern British Columbia.

The War Department asked Northwest to set up an aerial route over the forests, mountains, and frigid, trackless wastes of northwestern Canada and to ferry into Canada and Alaska huge quantities of men, ammunition and supplies. The request was due to Northwest's experience in flying over similar rugged country between Billings and Seattle. Northwest did not hesitate. After a survey flight headed by Frank Judd, superintendent of the newly created Northern Division, Edmonton, Alberta, was chosen as the jumping off point for Alaska by way of Grand Prairie, Alberta; Dawson Creek, Fort St. John, and Fort Nelson, British Columbia; and White Horse and Dawson in Yukon Territory.

Giant fuel tanks were cut apart, flown in to new airstrips, and welded back together as were trucks and other heavy equipment. Buildings of varying sizes were erected; a network of radio navigation and weather stations was created, and a mountain of supplies brought in. Maintenance crews worked outside in the bitter cold; it was the most rugged winter in history as the men surmounted one challenge after another.

On the route to Anchorage and Fairbanks, it was a case of "can do" and "make do." At Whitehorse, Ar-

Chad Smith took over as Northwest Airways Operations Manager following the death of Speed Holman in 1931. Smith, one of three brothers to fly for Northwest, died in the hospital from complications of an operation in 1932. (Walter Bullock family)

Frank Judd beside a Lockheed 10-A. Judd would go on to become Superintendent of the Northern Region during the war and later, Vice President of Operations and Maintenance and Engineering. (Northwest Airlines via Vince Doyle)

A mechanic works on Fred Whittemore's Waco at the St. Paul base. In the background a visiting Fokker Super Universal shares hangar space. (Northwest Airlines via Vince Doyle)

Fred Whittemore became Operations Manager in 1934. A resplendent figure, always sharply attired, he kept a company Waco JYM always shined up and ready for himself to fly. (Northwest Airlines via Vince Doyle)

thur "Art" Petersen, later Western Region Manager of Flight Operations, ran into extreme difficulties while trying to set up a base as part of the military contract operation:

> *When I picked out a location, I discovered it was impossible to buy any property in a hurry. This was not a time to quibble, so I simply took squatter's rights to about 50 acres of Canadian government land.*
>
> "*Croil Hunter and a group of company officials arrived a short time later on an inspection trip and Croil asked me: 'Pete, do you have a lease on this property?'*
>
> *Sure, replied Petersen.*
>
> *Let's see it, said Hunter.*
>
> *Petersen walked into the john, ripped off an armload of toilet paper, walked back to Hunter and slammed it down on the table. He laughed: "Here's your lease.*[37]

Less than three weeks after the survey flight, the first northbound cargo flight for Alaska left the Twin Cities on 15 March, 1942. Soon troops were being ferried in regularly. When a 25-bed military hospital in Nome burned to the ground, two Northwest crews were dispatched to St. Louis, and within 48 hours, a complete new hospital was winging its way to Nome.

In June, 1942, Japanese forces invaded the Aleutian Islands. Carrier-based planes bombed the U. S. Naval installation at Dutch Harbor on rocky Unalaska Island on 3 June 1942, keeping American forces occupied while attack troops swarmed ashore and siezed the outer islands of Kiska, Attu and Agattu. It marked the war's only invasion of the North American continent.

Northwest, the "grandfather operator," with nine other airlines assisting, prepared to supply the troops and material to retake the islands. Northwest briefed the others, supervising all radio-weather contacts, major maintenance, loading and refueling. Northwest also briefed Army Air Corps crews on instrument procedures and navigational aids, and how to cope with the tricky fog, snow, winds, and mountains. Two Northwest Captains, Roman Justiss and Lloyd Milner, were awarded the Air Medal for their work in teaching the Army fliers instrument techniques, a singular honor, normally reserved strictly for the military.

Air Medals were also awarded posthumously to two other Northwest pilots who lost their lives while hauling supplies during the Alaskan campaign, Frank Christian and Raymond Dyjak. Ironically, although Northwest flight crews were actually flying under

military command in the 11th Wing of the Air Transport Command, and wearing ATC (Air Transport Command) uniforms, they were not eligible for military benefits during or after the war.

By the spring of 1943, a 100,000 man U. S. and Canadian force had been assembled in Alaska, and on 11 May, Allied units, led by the Seventh Infantry Division, annihilated the Japanese defenders on Attu. Three months later, Kiska and Agattu were also retaken and the Aleutians were once again in U. S. hands.

In addition to the modification center mentioned later, Northwest was also called upon to aid the government in other ways. The Vandalia, Ohio, Test Center was one such project. Known as the Accelerated Testing Center, it was opened in January of 1943. Its principal mission was to "de-bug" all new aircraft models produced for the military by test-flying them, writing engineering reports and getting changes made on production lines. Superintendent of the facility, E. Ben Curry, noted that three aircraft of each new type were delivered, with bomber, reconnaisance, fighter, and even gliders being tested.[38]

Northwest established a flight test laboratory under the Air Transport Command that provided both ground and flight personnel to operate a research project on aircraft icing. In June of 1942, Wold-Chamberlain was the site of de-icing experiments carried out by Northwest, utilizing a B-25 bomber nicknamed "Flamin' Mamie." It was a basic B-25, but rather than its engines having standard exhaust pipes, they had collector systems that accommodated a heat exchanger. With the ability to manufacture a great deal of heat, the Northwest crews could seek

Position report passed through the cabin to passengers aboard a Lockheed 14. There were no Captain's announcements in those days. (Gale Frost)

NORTHWEST AIRLINES		12-38
Position Report		
Over *Miles City, Montana* at *2:20* ~~a.m.~~ p.m.		
Altitude *4000* ft. above sea level	Out side Temp. *+3* °F	
Making *185* M. P. H.	Will arrive *Billings* at *3:05* ~~a.m.~~ p.m.	
Weather ahead *Cloudy*		
Captain *Gene Shank*	First Officer *Tom Chastain*	

Please Pass to your fellow Travelers

out the worst icing conditions anywhere in the country and fly into them, using the plane's generated heat to blast the ice off wings and tail surfaces. Small generators in the propeller hubs provided an electric heat system to de-ice propellers.

As a direct result of this testing, wing and tail leading-edge de-icing boots were fitted to all B-24 Liberator bombers that flew against Germany and Japan during the war.

Northwest also worked with the Honeywell Company to develop the C-1 autopilot. This device was built to hold a bomber steady on its bomb run, dramatically increasing bombing accuracy. Northwest also provided planes and crews for perfecting the Honeywell designed B-3 Turbo Supercharger Regulator System which improved engine performance at high altitudes.

A Jefferson Airways' Ford Trimotor, with engines idling in the frigid temperatures, has delivered a group of fishermen, their gear and dog team to a Northern Minnesota lake, 1929. (F. Paul Wright photo, Minnesota Historical Society)

In 1943, the Naval Research Laboratory asked Northwest to join a research program to investigate a means of eliminating electrical interference with voice communications and radio signals. Once again, Northwest provided the airplanes and crews to do the job.

For two years, Twin Cities residents wondered what was going on inside a huge multi-million dollar hangar constructed on 34th Avenue and 60th street. They never dreamed that under a Naval Research Laboratory contract, inside the building a million-volt generator developed, at the University of Minnesota, was zapping test aircraft suspended from the hangar ceiling, with man-made bolts of lightning. New radio antennas and static discharge "wicks" were developed. The wicks are used to this day on virtually all aircraft trailing surfaces to dispell static electricity.

A program at the Fargo airport between Northwest and the Air Transport Command's Alaskan Wing, established a special service facility there. Aircraft headed for the northern region were modified for cold weather. A mix of "old-timers" and new hires installed oil dilution systems, wing de-icer indicators, cabin heaters, oxygen lines, and the pressurized ignition harness. Invented by one of Northwest's engineers, Carl E. Swanson, the wire harness was sealed and pressurized with engine bleed air to keep electrical energy from jumping from wire to wire in the partial vacuum of high altitudes, thus increasing the efficiency of the engines.

Northwest established an Airmen's Transition Training Program (ATTP) at Billings, Montana for the Air Transport Command. Courses began in February of 1943 with a 107-man faculty conducting a ground school that provided flight training and specialized mechanical courses to some 700 military students.

One of the more colorful events in Northwest's wartime work was its participation in a mass flight of aircraft to India. It came in April 1943, in response to the military's call for help to bring 30 Curtiss C-46 Commando aircraft, carrying 90 tons of urgently needed war material, from Miami, Florida to Karachi, India. The planes were to be flown over the "Hump," as the Himalaya Mountains were called.

Northwest contributed 15 pilots to this four-and-a-half-day, 15,000 mile odyssey, the longest mass flight of transport aircraft ever undertaken to that time. Pilots Walter Bullock, Les Smith, Frank Judd, Harold Barnes, Charles Wheelock, Skelly Wright, Warren Schultz, Earl Hale, Lyle Strong, Ed LaParle, Joseph Osowski, Robert Ashman, Jack Bain and Jerry Thompson took part. Every aircraft arrived safely.[39]

While the story of Northwest through World War II is both distinguished and dramatic, it must be remembered that that company had the financial security of a mail contract. In the dozen years that preceeded the war, several attempts were made to create airlines in the state.

The first Minnesota firm to start an airline without the security of a mail contract was, appropriately enough, one that had been involved in transportation for several years. The Jefferson Highway Transportation Company's President, Edgar F. Zelle, had been in the bus business since his graduation from the University of Minnesota in 1923. In the spring of 1928, he purchased a Ford Trimotor with the intention of operating two flights each day, morning and afternoon, from St. Paul to Minneapolis to Rochester and return. The purchase price for the airplane was $45,000 and it was seen by the company as the first step toward supplementing their bus service with an airline.[40]

By late May, *Jefferson Airways, Inc.,* had been created as a division of the bus company and a Minneapolis man, Arthur R. Helm, hired as operating manager. Helm, a former sales manager of the Russell Miller Milling Company, went to Detroit to observe the construction of a Ford Trimotor, to take flights, and generally gain aviation experience. The

Canadian-American Airlines "City of Winnipeg" Travel Air Model 6000 is ready to go at the St. Paul Airport in this 1929 view. The line was the first to fly regular schedules and charters between the Twin Cities and Winnipeg. (Minnesota Historical Society)

Ford was actually delivered to Jefferson in early July, 1928, and prospective passengers could marvel that it had individual chairs, a washroom with running water, clear glass windows that could be opened in flight by the passengers, electric lights, and even cabin heat, so that Minnesotans need not bundle up for winter flying.[41]

Since the flying time from the Twin Cities to Rochester was but 45 minutes, the company's hope was that the air service would be "used extensively by the large number of doctors traveling through the Twin Cities to Rochester from all parts of the country." Between the scheduled flights, sightseeing hops would also be given.[42]

Scheduled service was inaugurated on Friday, 13 July, 1928, and, if busy physicians were not yet lining up for the flights, a dozen Rotarians flew to Rochester to have lunch with brother members of the Rochester Rotary Club. Not surprisingly, bus transportation from the air field to downtown was built into the process. Later that day, four Minneapolis businessmen took the afternoon flight to spend the weekend playing golf with friends in Rochester, and flew back on Sunday.[43]

Throughout the summer and autumn, Jefferson operated their early example of a commuter airline. Then, in December, Zelle announced that he was dropping the air service stating, quite simply, there was not sufficient business to make the airline profitable. The reason, no doubt, was that the Ford could carry 14 passengers and there just not enough people willing to pay the $20.00 round trip fare. The Ford Trimotor cruised at about 100 m.p.h. but when airport to downtown time was factored in, the time saving was probably not significant over land transportation. Jefferson kept the Ford Trimotor for a time, evidently giving sightseeing flights, but in 1929, it was sold to the up-and-coming firm, Embry Riddle in Cincinnati, and Jefferson left the airline business.[44]

Just a year after Jefferson left the airline business, another ground transportation company attempted to run air service to the Twin Cities. This time it was *Yellow Cab Airways* which was incorporated in Des Moines in the spring of 1928. Started by the head of the local Yellow Cab Company, Russell Reel, the firm began with the usual assortment of small airplanes but in the summer of 1928 took delivery of a Fairchild 71. This was a modern aircraft, a high wing monoplane carrying seven passengers over a range of about 900 miles. All of the company's aircraft were painted in the standard Yellow Cab colors with yellow wings and a black fuselage.[45]

Reel's plan was apparently to offer local service in central Iowa at first, but to expand into a more regional market by creating a route from Kansas City to Minneapolis via Des Moines and Mason City. The reason that Yellow Cab thought it could make a profit on a passenger line was that it planned to make connections with other, larger airlines. As Reel put it, "Through its connections in Des Moines and Kansas City, the new line will offer faster service to the south and southwest. It connects in Des Moines with the transcontinental mail line for the west. At Kansas City it meets Universal Airlines for St. Louis, the Southwest Air Fast Express and the Central Airlines for cities in Oklahoma and Texas, and the Western

Air Express for Los Angeles. By the new line, a passenger can leave St. Paul at noon, spend the night in Kansas City, and arrive in Los Angeles at 6 p.m. the next day. It can cut 8 to 12 hours off the all rail time to California."[46]

The following spring, this route was begun with Yellow Cab's Fairchild making its first flight to Minneapolis on 6 May. No inaugural flight in those days happened without a ceremony, and the Fairchild landed at Wold-Chamberlain Field, piloted by Art Goebel, a nationally-famous flyer, who had won the 1927 Dole Race from California to Hawaii. Goebel had four passengers on board: Ross Arnold, who would be the regular pilot of the new run; an official of Yellow Cab; a Des Moines Register reporter; and a Miss Dorothy Kellog of Lead, South Dakota, once a University of Minnesota student, then attending Drake University. Exactly why she made the flight is unrecorded but she did say that flying was great fun and that she had been "excused from one class to make the 900 mile round trip to Minneapolis." Goebel praised the Minneapolis airport as splendid, compared to many in the country, and said it was a real pleasure to land in Minneapolis.

The group was met by a delegation of local business people and they all had a brief lunch during which they "chatted hurriedly about air transportation, landing fields, the speed of the modern age, and flying in general." One of the local men, however, felt that the airfield was too far from downtown, and opined that he wanted to "...see the day when this city has one on Nicollet Island to say nothing of amphibians landing in the Mississippi only a few minutes from the loop."[47]

One member of the local delegation that met the flight was Julius Perlt. Perlt worked for the St. Paul Association and was still involved with aviation activities on their behalf. Yellow Cab had planned its route to terminate in Minneapolis, but in June 1929, Perlt flew to Des Moines to meet with Russell Reel and ask him to extend service over the short hop to St. Paul's municipal airport. Perlt recalled years later that Reel readily agreed, as it was simply a matter of getting as much business as possible.[48]

Yellow Cab operated their airline during the summer of 1929. The published timetable indicated that flights would leave Kansas City at 9 a.m. Monday, Wednesday, and Friday, arriving in the Twin Cities at 1:30 p.m. The reverse route was flown on Tuesday, Thursday, and Saturday, and stops were made at Des Moines and Mason City in all flights. Fares were $12 to Mason City, $18 to Des Moines and $33 to Kansas City and each passenger was allowed 25 pounds of baggage. The schedule also contained a section explaining to passengers "What Holds the Airplane Up?" and instructing them on "How to Get Real Enjoyment from Your Flight." This latter section ran to a series of eight specific points, the first being "Don't Worry. There is Absolutely Nothing to Worry About." Other advice included a plea for passengers to be patient as the pilot taxied across the field to take off into the wind, and a reminder that banking and turning in the air were quite natural motions. "Take turns naturally with the plane. Don't try to hold the lower wing up with the muscles of the abdomen...it's unfair to yourself and an unjust criticism of your pilot."[49]

Yellow Cab's plan to connect with other air routes at Des Moines and Kansas City may have looked good on paper but it did not work out. In the autumn of 1929, Yellow Cab ceased operation of the air route, although it did continue aviation activities around Des Moines for a time. The problem, again, was that with only passenger revenue coming in, an airline just could not turn a profit. Given the excellent and comfortable rail service to points south, Yellow Cab could not lure travellers away from the trains. The additional cost, discomfort, and perceived risk, as compared to the trains, did not make air travel worth the time savings to most travellers. With no mail contracts forthcoming, Yellow Cab Airways could not produce a positive balance sheet and it passed from the scene.

Early air route expansion in Minnesota was not limited to attempts to link the Twin Cities with more populous areas to the south. Several attempts were made to expand to the north with the most obvious possibilities for passenger business being routes to Duluth and to Winnipeg. Northwest Airways operated a tentative route to Winnipeg in 1928, but it was discontinued after a three month trial. Not until an airmail contract became available in February 1931 did permanent daily service begin to Winnipeg and, based on its earlier performance, Northwest was the airline that won the government contract.[50]

In August of 1929, however, a new airline was formed to try to succeed on the Winnipeg route that Northwest had dropped a year earlier. Several Minneapolis and Winnipeg investors formed *Canadian-American Airlines, Incorporated.* Using six passenger Travel Air monoplanes, the new airline began operating about 1 September, 1929. The route provided for daily flights both north and southbound from St. Paul to Winnipeg, with stops at Minneapolis, St. Cloud, Alexandria, Fergus Falls, Fargo, and Grand Forks. The fare to St. Cloud was $10.00, and $40.00 all the way to Winnipeg, with prorated fares for the intermediate stops. Scheduled flying time was 5 hours, 20 minutes.[51] Canadian-American could have been just another local airline attempt, except that in October something happened that was indicative of the mania for mergers that was then sweeping the airline industry.

In October, 1929, controlling interest in Canadian-American was acquired by the Schlee-Brock Aircraft Corporation of Detroit. William S. Brock, a famous flyer, was president of the company and E. F. Schlee was the vice-president. Although a Detroit firm, several officers and members of the board of directors were Minnesota men, and the reason for their interest in controlling the embryonic airline was simple. Several towns in Minnesota and North Dakota had requested airmail service and the Post Office was considering advertising a contract to carry airmail from the Twin Cities to Pembina, from which connections could be made to Winnipeg. Canadian-American intended to bid when the contract became available.[52]

The Schlee-Brock firm had already been operating a small line called Arrowhead Airways between Duluth and Port Arthur, and they now combined the two under the Canadian-American name. At the same time, the new company made plans to introduce the

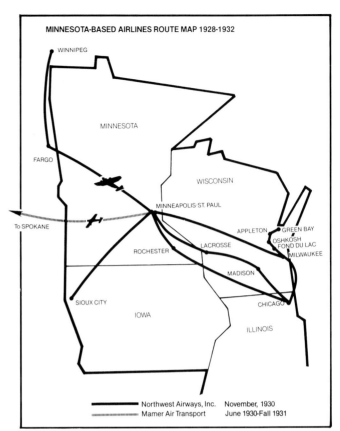

MINNESOTA-BASED AIRLINES ROUTE MAP 1928-1932

——— Northwest Airways, Inc. November, 1930
·············· Mamer Air Transport June 1930-Fall 1931

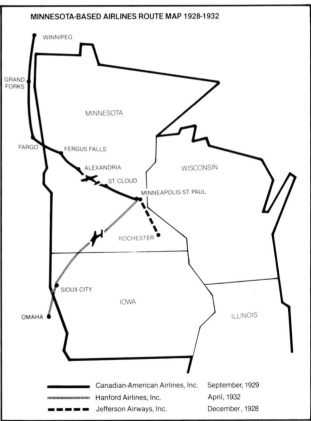

MINNESOTA-BASED AIRLINES ROUTE MAP 1928-1932

——— Canadian-American Airlines, Inc. September, 1929
·············· Hanford Airlines, Inc. April, 1932
– – – – Jefferson Airways, Inc. December, 1928

Lockheed Vega, a modern six-passenger monoplane that was much faster than previously used aircraft. Canadian-American's plans were nothing if not grandiose. Their intention, evidently, was to add routes linking Winnipeg to Port Arthur and Minneapolis to Duluth, thus completing a triangle. Connections could be made on other carriers for Montreal, San Francisco, and Los Angeles. It was announced that the new

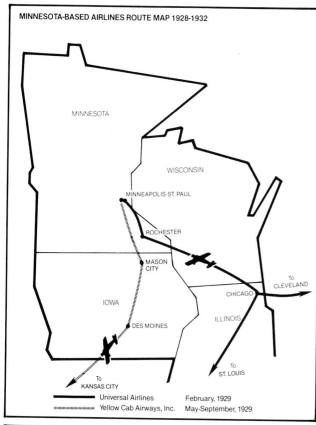

MINNESOTA-BASED AIRLINES ROUTE MAP 1928-1932

━━━ Universal Airlines February, 1929
·········· Yellow Cab Airways, Inc. May-September, 1929

MINNESOTA-BASED AIRLINES ROUTE MAP 1939

▬ ▬ ▬ Northwest Airlines, Inc.
·········· Mid-Continent Airlines, Inc. August, 1939

line would make it possible to fly from Winnipeg to Rio de Janeiro. Aircraft would use skis in winter and wheels or pontoons, as appropriate, in summer, and the possibility of flying fishermen and hunters to the Canadian wilderness was contemplated.[53]

All came to naught, however, because no airmail contract was forthcoming, at least not until 1931, when Canadian-American had passed from the scene.

Like other airlines before it, Canadian-American could not pay its bills on passenger revenue alone, and the onset of the depression in late 1929 was probably the final blow. The company ceased operation in January 1930.

There was one other airline company with strong roots in Minnesota in the late 1920s that is of historical interest. It was a splendid example of the merger mania that hit the industry at that time. It is of interest, too, because once the merger dust had settled, it had become a major component of American Airlines, which remains today a major air carrier. It is difficult to trace the roots of Universal Airlines, but the allusion to small fish being eaten by big fish, devoured by giant fish is irresistible. While the exact origins of the individual companies are sometimes obscure, two things should be kept in mind. The period from late 1928 through 1929 was an era of incredible growth and change in the airline industry. This was a nationwide trend and the fervor in which people believed in, and invested in aviation companies was awesome. The result was a shakedown in the industry that left some successful independents, such as Northwest, and most of the early airlines consolidated into the so called big four: Eastern, United, American and TWA.

In late July 1928, it was announced that three small Minneapolis firms; *Air Transport, Inc., Northrop Airplane Company,* and *Mid-Plane Transit Company* would merge under a holding company called *Northern Aeronautics,* with a new company, *Northern Air Lines,* to actually conduct the passenger operations.[54]

These three companies had been created just six months earlier, in January 1928, under the aegis of the Minneapolis Civic and Commerce Association. The association had an aviation committee, a common practice in these Lindbergh boom months, to foster the growth of aviation in the area. It was through the association, it seems, that several Minneapolis businessmen, investors, and aviation people were brought together. Of the three companies, Air Transport is the most obscure, but it probably intended to get involved in air freight and possibly passenger flying. The Northrop Airplane Company was established by two Minneapolis men, Clyde S. Yarnell and Marvin A. Northrop, the latter a prominent aviator and secretary of the Civic and Commerce Association's aviation committee. Their intention was to operate a flying school, and to become an airplane sales agency or distributor. They quickly leased hangar space at Wold-Chamberlain Field and made arrangements with Speed Holman and Leon S. "Deke" DeLong, two moonlighting Northwest pilots, to fly for them.[55]

The third company, Mid-Plane Sales and Transit, was capitalized by its investors at $100,000 and incorporated in Delaware. Its aim was to operate passenger services in the upper midwest, and its principal officers were two men who were mainly investors, and two who were experienced in aviation. The former were James L. Pierce, who became secretary-treasurer, and M. J. Scanlon, a lumber company officer, who became president. Rufus R. Rand was named Mid-Plane board chairman and Mark M. Hurd became vice-president and general manager.

178

A Hanford Airlines Lockheed 10-A. perches on the snowy Wold-Chamberlain runway in 1935. (James LaVake)

A Lockheed 10A of Mid-Continent loads on the ramp at Wold-Chamberlain. (Hal Swanson)

Hurd had been a pilot in World War I and had become a well known flyer in this area during the 1920s. Rand was at this time a vice-president with Minneapolis Gas Light Company, but he was well known in aviation circles. During the First World War he had served with the Lafayette Escadrille. Because he was a pilot and a war hero, his advice on aviation matters was often sought by businessmen, and Rand had remained active in aviation activities after the war.[56]

Mid-Plane, using six-passenger Fairchild 71's, actually began airline service in late June 1928, with scheduled flights from Minneapolis to Fargo. Somewhat quixotically called the "Presidential Express," the airline carried passengers for $25, and the flight time for the whole route was 2 hours 45 minutes, including intermediate stops at Fergus Falls and Alexandria.[57]

This was the situation when the merger of the three Minneapolis companies was announced in July 1928. Several businessmen, including Rand and Yarnell, took part in the negotiations but, most significantly, Louis H. Piper and Harry C. Piper of the Lane, Piper and Jaffray brokerage firms, were also involved.[58] Louis Piper had far more in mind than the merger of three small air service companies.

On 30 July, 1928, a group of investors, mostly bankers and brokers from Chicago, St. Louis, and Minneapolis, incorporated a firm called *Continental Air Lines Corporation.* The excuse was to bid on a small mail contract between Cleveland and Louisville, but within a few weeks, the name was changed to *Universal Aviation Corporation.* 245,000 shares of stock in Universal had been bought up by the syndicate of bankers, and Universal was now capitalized at $2.3 million. Universal immediately

Mid-Continent Model 14-H Lodestar in front of the terminal building at Wold-Chamberlain. Mid-Continent employee Ken Brommer shows off the new Oliver tractor purchased as a tug. Note the zeppelin windsock. (Ken Brommer)

began buying a host of other aviation companies, partly paying cash, and often using stock transfers. The goal was to forge a number of diverse companies into a large, unified aviation enterprise in the Midwest, which would be linked together under the Universal Aviation Corporation, a huge holding company. Since these were the great boom months in aviation, the original investors, who paid under $10 per share, stood a fine chance of enormous profits.

In mid October 1928, Louis Piper was named president of Universal, and in early November the weekly magazine, *Financial Chronicle* listed Universal's board of directors. Some of the more interesting Minnesota names on the list were, R. L. Griggs, a Duluth banker, A. H. Rand, president of Minneapolis Gas Company, his son, Rufus Rand, Harry Piper, G. Nelson Dayton, and A. F. Pillsbury.[59]

During the months from August, 1928, to March, 1929, there was a flurry of activity as the financiers bought, sold, and reorganized dozens of aviation companies, large and small, and the aviation men who actually ran the companies started, altered, and dropped passenger services, which sometimes changed weekly. It was a period as confusing as it was dynamic. Some notion of the complexity of tracing the financial dealings was noted in a 1935 report which indicated that Universal began acquiring companies, paying for the stock so acquired partly in cash and partly in the stock of Universal Aviation Corporation. To figure out exactly how much cash, or the equivalent of cash, was paid into the Universal system, and remained in the various companies, is a puzzle which is almost impossible to solve.

For example, Northern Airlines, Inc., was organized in 1928, and except for ten shares of its stock issued for cash, totaling $1,000, 990 of its shares were issued to Northern Aeronautics, Inc., in return for the transfer of an account receivable from Universal Aviation Corporation, amounting to $72,000, which had been given in the first place by Universal to Northern Aeronautics in return for the assumption by the company of the obligation to repay certain advances totaling approximately $98,000, made by individuals, while Northern Aeronautics, in turn, issued its 5,000 shares of no par stock to Universal Aviation Corporation in exchange for stock of Universal Aviation Corporation and approximately 1,000 shares of stock of Mid-Plane Sales and Transit Company. Who got what and who got paid?[60]

Compounding the difficulty of assessing who was really doing what was the crossover among officers and directors. Rufus Rand, chairman of Mid-Plane, was a director of Universal, and James Pierce and Mark Hurd, both Mid-Plane officers, became directors of Northern Aeronautics. Paul Goldsborough, president of Northern, was the Minneapolis manager of Universal, and a certain P. G. Kemp, of Chicago, was a director of Northern and the office manager of Universal.[61]

By November, 1928, Universal owned nine companies and was still growing. Some of these, such as Northern in Minneapolis and Egyptian Airways in St. Louis, flew passengers and operated flying schools, but the significant part was Universal's forging of a major airline with three arms radiating from Chicago as the hub. One major acquisition had been the Robertson Aircraft Corporation of St. Louis, which had the all-important mail contract from Kansas City to St. Louis to Chicago, and carried passengers, too, on the St. Louis to Chicago route. Robertson then operated as a division of the Universal Air Line System. The second arm was a new line from Cleveland to Chicago via Toledo, and the third was the Chicago to Minneapolis route with a stop at Rochester. The latter was operated by Northern Air Lines which was now one of Universal's divisions.[62]

Universal, during its short life, was nothing, if not innovative. During August, the Northern Division operated float planes from Lake Calhoun to Duluth Harbor, and continued the Minneapolis to Fargo route although both were dropped by year's end.[63]

In late November, 1928, radio equipment was installed in aircraft on the Minneapolis to Chicago run so the flight crews could receive hourly weather reports, and in February, 1929, some surprisingly modern passenger comforts were being tried. Certain aircraft were equipped with galleys to serve hot meals in-flight and passengers between Chicago and Minneapolis, at that time, experienced the first use of in-flight motion pictures.[64]

Despite these innovations, Universal had the same problem that all other early airlines had in this area and that was Northwest's firm hold of the vital Minneapolis to Chicago mail contract. Without the government revenue from the mails, Universal's Northern Division was doomed and the announcement was made in April 1929 that passenger service would be dropped, and the aircraft and equipment shifted to other divisions. Universal would maintain its presence in the Twin Cities only through the operation of flying schools.[65]

The holding company itself lasted only a little longer, before being taken over by an even larger holding company. In March, 1929, the Aviation Corporation was founded. Better known as *AVCO,* its board of directors was composed of seventy men drawn from the wealthiest families and biggest businesses in the nation. A stock offering immediately brought in a staggering working capital of $35 million, and AVCO began to buy up everything in sight. Within the year, they had purchased several individual airlines and two smaller holding companies; *Southern Air Transport and Universal Aviation Corporation.*

The first offer to trade AVCO stock for Universal stock came in March 1929. Universal president, Louis Piper, issued a statement that, despite certain rumors to the effect that Universal had entered into

Handbill supplied by Dayton's Dry Goods Store in 1909 during exhibition of a Curtiss Pusher aircraft in their third floor exhibition hall. (Noel Allard)

agreements to combine with other companies, "we feel it is necessary to deny that any such agreement has been made." Two weeks later, though, it was all official and the *Financial Chronicle* could report that Universal stockholders were "being offered in exchange for their holdings, stock in the Aviation Corporation on a share-for-share basis. The offer being contingent on the acceptance of the proposal on or before May 20 by holders of at least 51% of the outstanding Universal stock." Things went a bit more slowly than hoped, and the date was extended, but by 25 May, the requisite 51% of Universal shares had been deposited with AVCO. AVCO's balance sheet for 30 June, 1929, shows nearly 100% ownership of all of Universal's subsidiaries.

Universal continued for a time as an operating subsidiary of AVCO, but AVCO itself was a holding company. In January, 1930, in order to better operate its diverse air routes, AVCO created its own new

1919. Dayton's delivery service brought this JN-4 to towns across Minnesota, dropping off merchandise in a well-publicized use of the airplane for promotional purposes. (Dayton-Hudson Corporation)

10 May, 1920. Dayton's merchandise has arrived at the Minneapolis Parade Grounds from New York. Note the covers over the cockpits to protect the cargo, from a downpour a few minutes earlier. Standing by the airplane is William Kidder, pilot Chick Keyes, and one of the Dayton Company executives. (Minnesota Air National Guard Historical Foundation)

operating arm which was *American Airways,* and Universal disappeared from the scene shortly thereafter.[66]

One other airline established a presence in Minnesota during the 1930's. In 1928, *Tri-State Airlines* had been formed in Sioux City, Iowa, but toward the end of that year was purchased by Arthur S. Hanford and renamed *Hanford Tri-State Airlines.* In 1930, Hanford began passenger service between Sioux City and Minneapolis, and by mid-1934 had been awarded two airmail routes, was flying Ford Trimotor and Lockheed Vega aircraft, and had moved their base of operations to Minneapolis.[67]

In December of 1934, however, Hanford's Chicago to Winnipeg airmail route was sold to Northwest and the Hanford general office returned to Sioux City. Until the outbreak of World War II, Hanford continued to operate routes from Minneapolis into South Dakota, Nebraska, Missouri, and as far south as Tulsa, Oklahoma. In August of 1938, the name was changed to *Mid-Continent Airlines* to better reflect the territory served. It was Mid-Continent, who during World War II, modified the Doolittle B-25 bombers, the story of which can be found in Chapter Seven.

Ray Miller helps unload Dayton's merchandise from the wingless J-1 Standard, parked on Nicollet Avenue in front of the department store. (Minnesota Air National Guard Foundation)

By the early 1930's, however, the foundations of commercial air transportation in Minnesota had been laid. During the decade before World War II, Northwest Airways (Northwest Airlines, after 1934) would not just keep, but strengthen its dominant position. The company would have its problems to be sure. There were fatal crashes and a scandal that would send Lewis Brittin to jail briefly and force his resignation. Northwest, however, remained efficient, modern, reliable, as safe as most for the time, and above all, profitable. Passenger revenue steadily grew and the company kept its firm hold on the mail contracts that were so vital to the profits of the early airlines.

AVIATION IN THE MINNESOTA BUSINESS COMMUNITY

Many Minnesota companies were quick to realize the benefits that aviation offered, such as the rapid movement of mail from one locale to another, the ability to bring entertainment right to the people, and the provision of new opportunities for profit.

We can examine some of the earliest applications of the latter principle and witness how the business community used the airplane to enhance profits.

William Kidder, the owner and manager of Curtiss-Northwest Airport in St. Paul, was one of the earliest businessmen to recognize the many different ways that aviation could bring profits. Already mentioned were his aircraft sales, flight training, and entertainment features. One of the more profitable ventures for him was the rental of airplanes and pilots.

It was only a natural that he rent aircraft and pilots to the Dayton's Dry Goods store of Minneapolis. Dayton's, itself, was fully aware of the appeal of this new means of transportation. In fact, it is interesting that Dayton's Department Store Company has used aviation-oriented advertising for nearly 83 years.

It was a mere six years after the Wright Brothers first flight, in November of 1909, that the Dayton Dry Goods Company, through the enterprise of President, George D. Dayton, secured an aeroplane for display in their 3rd floor exhibition room, at the downtown Minneapolis store. The ship was a Curtiss, billed as "an exact counterpart of the Herring-Curtiss machine which won the International Races at Rheims [France] and Brescia [Italy]."[68]

Thus Dayton's introduced the aeroplane to Twin Citians. The introduction was all the more significant when it is remembered that the first important aviation event in the U. S. did not occur until the following year; the famous 1910 Dominguez Field Air Meet in Los Angeles, California. Actually, the very first airshow in Europe was held at Rheims, France, only three months earlier, and indeed, the first Minnesotan to fly, had only done so a few months before.

The first time Minnesotans would get a chance to witness an airplane in flight would not occur until the 1910 State Fair! Little wonder that Dayton's exhibit of an aeroplane in their auditorium would be attention-getting, and historic.

A *Minneapolis Journal* news story indicated that "The factory that made this [plane] already has orders for ten more, and nearly all of them for private persons taken with the idea of a little flying on their own account."[69]

1924. A young Speed Holman with his modified Thomas-Morse Scout. He convinced the Washburn-Crosby Company to advertise their flour products on the side of his airplane. He flew the ship in cross-country races gaining publicity for both himself and the milling company. (Noel Allard)

The event showed that Dayton's management was wise to innovative marketing ideas for attracting business. The Department Store tied-in the exhibition of the airplane by featuring, in their adjacent bookstore, two of the very first aviation books ever published. The books, *Vehicles of the Air*, by Victor Lougheed (later to change his name to Lockheed); and *The Conquest of the Air*, by Alphonse Berget, had been published earlier that same year, and are treasured editions in any historian's library today.

The innovative use of the airplane by Dayton's also found it being used as a marketing tool. In 1919, mail order merchandise was delivered around the country by means of trucks. That year, the Dayton Company signed a contract with William Kidder of the Curtiss-Northwest Airplane Company, to fly merchandise orders across the state by air, carrying parcels to many Minnesota communities such as Elk River, Bird Island, St. Cloud, Little Falls, Brainerd, Arlington, and others; a total of 24 cities where items had been ordered by individuals. The Company specified that their name be painted on the aircraft sides and that they would pay $1.00 per air mile for the service.

The service and its publicity sparked enough enthusiasm, that, in May of 1920, Dayton's planned a major historic event. They again contracted with Kidder for use of his airplanes and pilots. This time, the plan was to fly two plane-loads of merchandise from New York to Minneapolis. Kidder's fee for this service was $1750, a large investment in aerial commerce by Dayton's executives, George Dayton, and advertising manager, Hugh Arthur.

Kidder's pilots, Ray Miller and Charles Keyes, took off for New York's Roosevelt Field in a pair of J-1 Standards. Arriving at the field on 5 May, 1920, they loaded between 700 and 800 pounds of merchandise, half into each of the front cockpits of the two ships. Their return trip took them through Poughkeepsie, Albany, Syracuse, and Buffalo, New York; Erie, Pennsylvania; Cleveland, Ohio; Valparaiso, Indiana; Genoa, Illinois; and Madison, Camp Douglas, and Eau Claire, Wisconsin. Additional stops were made in between, and the planes did not fly at night.

The pair of planes landed at the Parade Grounds across from the Dunwoody Institute in Minneapolis on 10 May. Miller arrived under minimal ceiling conditions and Keyes landed an hour later during a downpour. When the rain subsided, the wings were removed from the airplanes and they were paraded down Nicollet Avenue to the front of Dayton's store between 7th and 8th Streets, where an official welcoming committee provided a ceremony, and the unloading began.

The actual flying time had been 23 hours and 40 minutes for Miller and Keyes, they had covered 1600 miles at an average speed of 67 miles per hour. That was quite respectable considering that the pair had bucked winds, storms, hail, and fog for the last several hundred miles. Miller related his tribulations, "Flying through that rain storm today was the worst part of the trip. I couldn't see anything. The rain covered my goggles and I had to tear them off. Then it beat into my eyes and blinded me. When I flew over Hudson, Wisconsin, my altimeter showed 500 feet. A few minutes later, there was a tree straight ahead of me. I zoomed up as hard as I could, but I brushed the branches. I could have pulled off twigs if I'd leaned over."[70]

Earlier in the flight, the weather being more pleasant, Miller had stopped in Van Wert, Ohio, to pay a visit to his mother.

The actual merchandise carried consisted of ladies' "waists" (corsets), silk underwear, handbags, neckwear, gloves, perfume, jewelry, etc. Most of the load was womens-wear, but some men's silk shirts were also included. The merchandise was valued at $10,000, but the publicity was worth much more. Dayton's tied in newspaper advertising, in-store promotions, and handout postcards. The merchandise, itself, was tagged with cards which read, "By Airplane from New York to Minneapolis for the Dayton Company. This merchandise was carried 1500 miles in the air, the longest trip ever made with freight by an airplane up to this time."[71]

Though sold at regular prices, the souvenir tags were urged to be kept as proof of the means by which specific merchandise had been purchased. A May 13th *Minneapolis Journal* ad indicated that "scrupulous care will be taken that these tags are used only on the goods that actually come by air." You can bet they were sold out very shortly.

The flight was of special interest to U.S. Postmaster, A. E. Purdy, who wrote to Dayton's to ask that details of the mileage, fuel consumption, landing fields, and weight of goods carried, be forwarded to him. He

Speed Holman with the National Lead Battery Company's Laird in 1927. Promoting the company's product through racing, brought attention, and increased sales to the battery company, now Gould, Incorporated of Inver Grove Heights. (Jim Borden)

would be using the figures in his planning of the soon-to-be-issued airmail contracts for a cross-country airmail route.

Dayton's continued to utilize the airplane for promotional purposes. In the Fall of 1920, Dayton's advertising manager, Hugh Arthur, contracted again with Kidder for taking the airplanes, still painted with the Dayton's name on their sides, around Minnesota, to appear at County Fairs. The contract price paid Kidder was 50 cents per air mile. 29 communities like Little Falls, Park Rapids, Fergus Falls, and Princeton, were visited from August 23rd to October 2nd; 29 locales. The pilots, Ray Miller and Chuck Keyes, were admonished when visiting County Fairs, to do no aerobatics, hop no rides, but merely to "fly one of the airplanes over and adjacent to the Fair Grounds ...and to distribute such advertising matter as the party of the second part shall direct."[72]

Though Miller and Keyes were not intentionally to take part in aerial displays other than flying past, on at least one occasion, Miller was asked to fill in for a missing act. Kidder advised George Dayton that he had okayed it in a letter to him, "At Fergus Falls, Miller also helped out the Fair Secretary in a way that we had not planned for him to advertise. The Fair Secretary had Charles Hardin, the wing-walker and parachute jumper, billed to do his act and the plane he was to use for the purpose was out of commission so that the minute Miller landed, both Hardin's manager and the Fair Secretary got after Miller to carry Hardin while he put on his parachute act. I understand he did so to their entire satisfaction."[73]

Kidder, ever the businessman, wrote to Hugh Arthur, that he could easily send the planes to various other towns between Fair dates and further the advertising value of the Fair tour. On one occasion, when the planes had been scheduled for a three-day layover in Wheaton, Kidder had Ray Miller fly to Fargo instead, claiming in his invoice to Dayton's that there were better protective facilities there, and of course, charging Dayton's for the extra mileage. He stated in his invoice to the Dayton Company, "I think that the different trips the Dayton Company has put on, have demonstrated in a pretty good way the utility of the airplane." He pointed out all the side trips the aircraft had made in addition to their main stops, and the value of the advertising to Dayton's.[74]

Dr. George Young's Sikorsky S-39 Amphibion seaplane docked somewhere at Lake Minnetonka during the 1934 to 1937 period. Publicity through his appearance at many public functions made the radio station very popular. (Minnesota Historical Society)

The Young-Quinlan Company's truck is shown here loading mail-order merchandise into one of Pop Dickinson's airplanes, a Laird flown by Ed Ballough. The exact date is unknown, but summer of 1926. (Minnesota Historical Society)

Ever aware that rapid movement of merchandise was a marketing plus, Dayton's continued to be innovative. In 1944, they applied, but were turned down for a request to operate helicopters from their downtown Minneapolis department store roof for the purposes of pickup and delivery.

Mentioned in other sections of this book are details of how various other companies used aviation for publicity purposes. Already reported are the uses of aircraft on the barnstorming circuit, such as the St. Paul Dispatch Flying Circus, and the Minneapolis Journal Flying Circus. Also mentioned is the National Lead Battery Company (now the Gould Company). This enterprising corporation, influenced by Speed Holman's popularity, purchased a Laird model LC-B in 1924 and had its name painted on the sides, along with a splashy white flying eagle and the name "National Eagle." Of course, Speed was their company pilot.

Speed's record-setting, long-distance flights around the country were sponsored by the battery company until Speed, with Northwest Airways help, purchased the airplane himself, in 1928.

Aircraft sales agencies also put their names on aircraft sides to publicize their franchise or dealership aircraft. Such was the case of the Minnesota Aircraft Corporation, the Eaglerock distributor for this area. Lyle Thro was the chief pilot for the firm, which was based at Wold-Chamberlain in 1929, and also an officer of the company.

In the later 1920s, Dr. George Young, a very promotion-minded individual, used aircraft for promoting his business, the radio station WDGY. The station call-letters were his initials. He is mentioned elsewhere, but some further consideration of his use of the airplane is warranted here.

Young, who among other things, was, a Doctor of Optometry, had his name painted in huge letters on the underside of the wings of his Sikorsky S-39 "Amphibion" aircraft. His initials/station call letters were painted on the sides. On or about 1923, Young started the radio station in his upstairs apartment, using a shipboard radio from a Navy sub-chaser as a transmitter. His was the only station regularly on the air during the period of the 1920s. WDGY has been in the Twin Cities radio market ever since that time, although passing through the hands of several different owners.

Young was responsible for many radio innovations, one of which was the first use of advertising on the air. He also derived much publicity from the appearance of his airplane at social functions, and his habit of making the headlines by one sort of mishap or another. Whether of his own doing or that of mother nature, the mishaps certainly added to his promotional efforts.

Young parted with the Amphibion in 1938, and subsequently purchased a Stinson 105, on which he also painted the radio station call letters. It was flown from Robbinsdale airport and used to give flight instructions, by various local instructors.

The Tracy Oil Company previously mentioned, utilized an autogiro to promote its interests, bringing it to airshows around the region. At these shows, it was flown for owner H. K. Webb, by either Millar Wittag, Jack Robinson, or Major Mulzer. The autogiro was the subject of great curiosity in the period of the 1930s and was worthy of much publicity wherever it went.

Willoco Oils of St. Paul also used the airplane in much the same way. In 1928, they painted their name on a Waco 10 and kept it before the public while traveling through their sales territory, selling Willoco Brand lubricants. In addition to the publicity, the airplane sped sales reps, like E. L. Gutterson, from point to point in a minimum of time. The Waco 10 was already a well-known airplane, having been the very ship that Gene Shank had used to set his loop record of 515 loops in February of 1928. It was fittingly, if not rather grossly named, the "Spirit of Lubrication."

The following are examples of other companies who used the airplane for business.

Many of the flight schools and aviation businesses in the metropolitan area have been mentioned previously. There were a great many others which began to crop up about 1930. It would be almost impossible to determine the total number of schools and flight services operating within the state and write something significant about them. Many left no records or are only mentioned in newspaper articles. Some not previously mentioned, are worth naming:

Ace High Flying Service, operating from Wold-Chamberlain Field. 1933.

Alexandria Air Transport, Inc. Alexandria, Minnesota. 1934.

Arrow Flying School, Wold-Chamberlain 1930s. Fred Kloskin was an associate.

Arrowhead Airways, Duluth. 1927. A.J. Hase, president. Ed Middagh, chief pilot. Established at Twin Ports Flying Field at the Superior end of the Arrowhead Bridge between Duluth and Superior.

Arrowhead International Airlines, Duluth. 1929. One of the regional airlines established by Edward F. Schlee and William S. Brock, Detroit businessmen. The airline offered regular passenger service between Duluth and Port Arthur, Ontario and the Canadian resort areas.

Atwood-O'Hara Air Service, Duluth. 1932. Sight-seeing flights and fishing trips arranged into Canada and points north. Established by Henry O'Hara and Mr. Atwood.

Brown-Morgan Flying Service, Wold 1931. J. C. Brown and Wilbur E. "Billy" Morgan were principals. Advertised "Night Flights a Specialty." When Morgan joined Northwest Airlines in 1935, Peter Lohmar took over operation of the company, until he, too, joined the airline in 1940.[75]

General Air Transport, Wold-Chamberlain. 1930s. Jerry Bringhurst, owner.

Great Northern Aviation Corporation, St. Paul Airport. 1929. Mark Hurd organized this company and was president; Glenn M. Waters, executive vice-president; Loye W. Chandler was vice-president (formerly President of Minnesota Aircraft Corporation which was purchased by GNAC); Glenn S. Locke, vice-president; Marcus F. Day, secretary; and F.T. McCahill, treasurer. The corporation opened flight schools at St. Paul, Duluth, Cloquet and Coleraine. They were granted an Eaglerock dealership, which was located at Wold-Chamberlain Field. The company planned to operate airports, service aircraft, sell accessories, and conduct aerial photography. Carl Leuthi and Lyle Thro were instructors. The company failed in July of 1930, due to lack of business and capital.

Great Northern Flying School, 1929. Originally the flight and ground school portion of Great Northern Aviation Corp., organized by Mark Hurd, with Paul D. Paine and L. P. Bardin. The school's offices were located at 917 Hennepin Avenue in Minneapolis. Reorganized in 1931, Hurd and Ray Norby benefitting from financing by Rufus Rand. The company then conducted business out of the old airmail hangar at Wold-Chamberlain Field.

Hartley-Pfaender Air Service. Duluth, 1931. Brothers Cavour and Guilford Hartley joined with A. J. "Jake" Pfaender, to originate this flight school and scenic flight operation.

Head of the Lakes Airways. Duluth. 1930.

Kelly Aviation Service, Taylors Falls. Late 1930s.

Kingston-Rhodes Airways, Inc. 1932. Eveleth. M. S. Kingston, a banker from Virginia, Minnesota, financed this passenger and cargo carrying operation, often cited for illegal transport of game furs and importing of spirits from Canada. C. R. "Dusty" Rhodes was the chief pilot.

Kenyon Transportation Company. Morris, Minnesota. 1930. Jess Kenyon, owner.

Land-O-Lakes Air Service. Duluth. 1930. Incorporated by Duluth businessmen, C. J. Yoho, Otto Altman, and Elmer Stovern. Jake Pfaender was chief pilot. Aircraft consisted of a 5-passenger Stinson, a Waco 10, and a Great Lakes 2T-1A. Charter flights and flight lessons were offered.

Mid-Plane Sales and Transit. Minneapolis, Duluth. 1928. Started by Mark Hurd. A branch in Duluth was operated by Harvey Williamson, who was killed flying the organization's airplane later that year. The Duluth Airport was named in his honor.

Minnesota School of Aviation. Wold-Chamberlain. 1933.

Minnesota Aircraft Company. Wold-Chamberlain. 1930. Eaglerock distributor. Lyle Thro and Loye Chandler were principals.

Moon Flying Service. Wold-Chamberlain. 1933. Al Moon, owner.

Northern Minnesota Flying Service. Hibbing & Virginia. 1931.

Northland Aviation Company, Wold-Chamberlain. 1932. One of the first government-approved flying schools in the area. Northland moved into the Universal hangars at Wold, following that company's departure for Chicago. Northland perfected a flight curriculum and offered training for solo, private, limited commercial, and transport licenses. They also issued mechanics ratings. Instructors were Elmer Hinck, chief pilot; Ray Goetze, Delmar Snyder, Clarence Harmon, and "Casey" Jones. Stub Chrissinger was parachute instructor. Paul Paine, was listed as "principal." Orville Hickman was reported to be the operations manager, and was designing an aircraft to be sold as a proprietary product of Northland. Jerry Stebbins was chief ground instructor.

Northwest Aviation School, Wold-Chamberlain. 1928. Officers: A. W. Nelson, president; Tom Lane, vice-president; F. R. Haselton, medical advisor. Faculty included, Trevor Williams, Joe Westover, John Malone, Robert Rentz, M. Sam Furber, Tom

A good close-up of the Federal ski mounting on a Northwest Airways Hamilton Metalplane. Date is about 1931. Note the straps and bungee cord arrangement. Captains Frank Ernst and Clarence Bates check out the installation. (Northwest Airlines via Vince Doyle)

Strickler, Paul Kanuit, Joe Ohrbeck, Art Halloway, Daniel Foote, Charles Weiss, and A. Emerson. Most of the faculty and officers were military personel of either the Naval Reserve Squadron or the 109th Observation Squadron.

It is apparent that the organization was intended to be run like a military operation. Students were expected to attend from 7:30 a.m. to 9:30 p.m. on Tuesdays, Thursdays and Fridays. The rigid curriculum provided strictly regulated study periods, and test requirements. The school provided silver wings upon graduation, and published the fact that "those with only mediocre ability will not be permitted to complete the course."[76]

Northwest also offered a home study course and a flying club for graduate students to build up their flying time.

Rochester Aviation Co. Ambulance and charter service between Rochester and other areas in southern Minnesota. The company purchased a former Northwest Airways Hamilton Metalplane in 1935, but it was destroyed shortly afterward.

Roth-Downs Airways, Inc. Curtiss-Northwest Field. 1928. St. Paul Airport. 1929. Travel Air and Driggs distributor. B. W. Downs, president.; H.L. Rothchild, secretary; Elmore Wall, chief pilot; Leon Dahlem, associate.

Scenic Airways. Ely. 1931.

Sergent School of Aeronautics. Duluth. 1928. Started by Lt. R. J. Sergent, formerly with Great Northern Aviation Corporation. Sergent was a flight school and mechanics training school.

Southern Minnesota Airways. Fairmont. 1931.

Trump Airlines. Duluth. 1927. Fred and William Trump, owners. Company offered passenger service between Duluth and the Twin Cities.

Valley Airways Co. Thief River Falls. 1931.

Minnesotans were quick to cash-in on the needs of the thriving aviation community from the beginning. A sampling of those companies is mentioned here. Companies which have already been described in previous chapters are not mentioned here.

The Marvin A. Northrop Aeroplane Company of Minneapolis, later the Marvin A Northrop Airplane Company, was one of the region's outstanding supply houses supporting the activities of homebuilders, aircraft rebuilders, and repair stations. Northrop's main business location was at 500 Washington Avenue North. In time, he expanded until he had as many as five warehouses near downtown Minneapolis, and warehouses in other locales.

His companies provided anything that had to do with aircraft, including entire airplanes, which he bought and sold from Wold-Chamberlain Field, to instruments, propellers, engines, tires, hardware, parachutes, clothing, etc. He produced the first parts catalog in the country, mailing thousands to repair stations around the nation, as well as government air-

Cessna DC-6B flown by Bill Hazelton for the Mark Hurd Air Mapping Company in 1938. The airplane was modified to include a huge fuel tank in the cabin giving the aircraft a six to seven hour endurance while making aerial photos. (Forrest Lovley)

fields, military bases, and pilots. He held an early Ryan aircraft franchise.

Northrop started his first business after coming from duty as sales manager for Bill Kidder's Curtiss-Northwest Company in the later 1920s. Almost every early flyer can tell a Marvin Northrop story. In the field of keeping the area's airplanes flying, he was legend.

The **Federal Ski Company** pioneered the manufacture of skis for aircraft use. Francis John Ditter had been working in an auto repair shop since his high school days. He was mechanically inventive and designed and built his own airplane in 1930, learning to fly from local pilots, among them Walter Bullock. Ditter was also an avid hunter and fisherman. It was natural that he came up with the idea of producing low-cost skis for small aircraft, and was encouraged by Bullock. He designed the first pair in the 1920s, working out of a small shop on North Washington Avenue in Minneapolis.

The first skis were made of wood. Oak and other woods were cut and tapered, then soaked for several days in hot water to make them soft, and finally pressed into forms to give them a ski shape with upturned front tips. Testing was done and an CAA approval issued to the Federal Ski Company.

As interest in the skis evolved, the idea spread throughout the aviation industry. Northwest Airways, whose routes often took them into snow-covered fields between the Twin Cities and Pembina, North Dakota, or from the Twin Cities to Chicago, had ski sets made up for the Hamilton Metalplanes then in service. These skis were made with a wooden platform and a sheet metal cup into which the airplane's wheels were rolled. Straps went over the wheels to secure them to the base. History records no unfavorable incidents with them, so it is assumed they worked well enough.

The majority of skis were sold to sportsmen. The wooden ski was replaced by a metal ski version prior to World War II. Emmett Boucher, took a job as engineer with Federal Ski as an engineer prior to the war and witnessed the growth of the company. He vividly remembers stamping the first metal skis and experimenting with different metals for the bottoms. The more successful skis were made of Dural aluminum sheet, even though various types of steel,

and even brass, were tried.[77]

By 1940, the company was manufacturing six models of metal skis to accommodate aircraft with weights up to 4600 pounds. A 1940 *Flying Magazine* ad indicates that a series of combination wood/metal skis in fourteen sizes were available in addition to the metal models and various customized versions.[78]

Federal Ski Company held contracts with the Army, Navy, Coast Guard and foreign governments during this period and went on during and after the war to supply the U.S. military with most of the skis it would use, including those used by the Byrd Expeditions to the North and South Poles. One of the major distributors of Federal Skis was the Marvin A Northrop Airplane Company.

The main distributor of Federal Skis during the 1940s period was the **Van Dusen Aircraft Supplies** Company, based at Wold-Chamberlain Field. Van Dusen handled a line of aircraft supplies, including propellers, windshields, wheels, paints, instruments, hardware, refinishing materials, radios, flying wires, etc.

As mentioned in the chapter on Wold-Chamberlain Field, G. B. Van Dusen started his company in 1940 using a small room in the basement of the original terminal building at the airport. Before long, his clientele included fixed-base operators scattered throughout Minnesota and the midwest region. He hired Sig Gudmundson as salesman, and equipped him with a Stinson, model 105 airplane with which to fly from one dealer to the next, taking orders.

Van Dusen was one of the civilian businesses required to move from the big airport when the war started in 1941. He moved to an office and warehouse in downtown Minneapolis. During the war, business continued. Following the war, Van Dusen established sales offices worldwide. The company endures to this day.

The **Loague and Loague Parachute Company** bought out Stub Chrissinger's parachute interests and customer goodwill sometime during the 1940s. Loague and Loague packed parachutes for the navy training squadron at South St. Paul Airport during their use of that field in World War II.

Typical of many local companies which manufactured materials for aviation use during the wartime period was the **Setchell-Carlson Company** of St. Paul. S-C's main business since 1931 had been the manufacture of portable and console model home and car radios. With the start of the war, Setchell-Carlson was permitted to finish assembling a backorder of civilian radios then under production, but since raw material supplies would be curtailed, to be used instead in the production of war materiel, they were to cease manufacturing.

The military offered a contract to produce a quantity of radios to be used in ferrying military aircraft across the oceans. After the production of these, the company turned to producing parts for groundbound and shipboard communications gear under subcontract to other manufacturers.

Minneapolis Honeywell developed the C-1 autopilot for military aircraft use during World War II. The Honeywell story can be found in Chapter Seven.

Munsingwear also contributed its share to the war

ANGELO "SHORTY" DE PONTI 1909 - 1991
PIONEER MINNESOTA AVIATION BUSINESSMAN

Angelo De Ponti
(Floyd Homstad)

Angelo De Ponti always was an entrepreneur. At age nine, he held a newspaper route and delivered telegrams for the Western Union Company. He also took a job as a lamp-lighter, with two routes in St. Paul, where it was his job to light as many as 240 gas streetcorner lamps each evening. This job earned him $10 a month.

As a teenager, he worked in a bicycle shop, where he learned to understand things mechanical. He furthered this interest by joining a road-construction crew, working at Winona, Minnesota, and at Fountain City, Wisconsin.

Fascinated by the sight of an airplane flying overhead during those formative years, he began visiting Curtiss-Northwest Field in St. Paul, and Speedway Field in Minneapolis. Though not a lot of activity at either airport in those days, there were no fences, and an interested young man could hang around and watch the older men repairing or servicing airplanes. The youngster was usually put to work...running errands, degreasing parts, sweeping floors, sorting nuts and bolts...but it was a chance to be near airplanes. By age fifteen, De Ponti was spending most of his time at Speedway Field.

De Ponti's first full time job came in 1928 with Universal Air Lines. He worked as a lineboy for $10 a week at their Minneapolis-based Universal Flying School. Later that year, he decided to strike out on his own, leasing space from Universal to sell aircraft parts to local aviators. His first company was *Min-*

The old Airmail Hangar inside the racetrack, 1937. De Ponti's first operation. Sales, service, and storage. (Angelo De Ponti)

nesota Aero Salvage Company.

In 1929, Universal Air Lines closed their hangars and the tenants were required to move. A group of men bought the Universal equipment, named themselves *Minnesota Aviation Company*. They leased space in the old airmail hangar from Northwest Airways in the infield of the still-existent auto racetrack. De Ponti and his partner, Anton Jacobson rented space from Minnesota Aviation.

In 1930, Northwest Airlines made some big moves. They opened a main service base at the new St. Paul Airport, and moved their Minneapolis space across the field to the west side, where they took up residence in the northmost of Universal's old hangars. This gave De Ponti, now nicknamed "Shorty", the opportunity to lease the entire airmail hangar himself. Increasing his supply of aircraft and engine parts (particularly OX-5 parts) to keep up with demand, his business boomed. He also took flying lessons and got his license in 1930.

The *Mohawk Aircraft Company*, sub-leasing space for assembly of their airplanes, began to experience financial troubles. Shorty bought their inventory of parts and assemblies when the company folded. Mohawk had manufactured airplanes in the Prospect Park area off University Avenue, between Minneapolis and St. Paul, but leased space at the airfield to assemble their planes. With their departure from Speedway Field, De Ponti had more room, and could offer flying instruction, rental space, and service, as well as parts. He hired Elmer Hinck as chief pilot. In addition to instructing, Hinck put on weekend aerobatics over the field to attract customers to the flight school and for sight-seeing hops.

Shorty incorporated under the name *De Ponti Aviation Company* for the service, maintenance and flying instruction, but kept the name *Minnesota Aero Salvage Company* for parts sales until 1933, when he renamed that division *Minnesota Aviation Sales and Service Company*.

The next milestone for De Ponti came in 1933, when he bought the westside hangar from Northwest Airways. It was the northmost building on 34th Avenue, just north of the new terminal built three years earlier. De Ponti continued to use the old airmail hangar as well, keeping it for storage space. During the 1930s, on De Ponti's flight line, according to the Minnesota section of the *U. S. Aircraft Register*, one

could have seen an Overland Sport biplane, a Waco GXE and an Eaglerock A-14. By 1936, he had acquired a Travel Air 6000 which Elmer Hinck used for weekend parachute drops and hopping passengers; a Fleet 2; an American Eagle; a Robin; a Waco JYM Taperwing (known as the Whittemore Waco because Fred Wittemore, a colorful Northwest Airlines pilot, had previously owned it); and a New Standard.

In 1937, the flight line included a Rearwin 7000, and one of the first Taylor Cubs. Most of these planes were housed in the old airmail hangar, with floor space at the westside hangar being allocated to rentals. De Ponti also purchased a Ford Trimotor from the Phillips Petroleum Company. It was soon lost in a fire at Sioux City, Iowa. He purchased a second Trimotor and used it for charter and sight-seeing. Carrying three persons for $1.00, he could make money hauling a full load in the Ford, and making the trip very short.[79]

In 1937, De Ponti acquired the Piper Aircraft distributorship for the region that included Minnesota, North and South Dakota, Montana, and parts of Wisconsin. A 40 horsepower Cub was selling for under $1,000 and sales were plentiful. So good were the sales, in fact, that for a time in 1937, Shorty ceased to offer flight training to concentrate on sales alone. Having one of the first ten Piper franchises in the country assured De Ponti of business success. In 1940 and 1941, he was top sales outlet in the entire country, with Cubs being either ferried in from Pennsylvania, or shipped by train, six to a boxcar.[80]

By 1937, De Ponti also needed expansion room. He arranged a swap with the *Hedberg-Friedheim Company*, present owners of the Universal hangars. For $47,000 and title to the former Northwest hangar, he acquired the two Universal hangars. De Ponti, now with major facilities, took on the Texaco oil franchise and his ramp became the favorite refueling stop for many visiting fliers. The University of Minnesota Flying Club rented ramp space from him.

It was on this ramp that a freak accident occurred on 22 May, 1937. Shorty's brother, Albert, who worked for him as an all-around helper, ticket-seller, mechanic, and serviceman, was struck by a stray

De Ponti's 1933 home, the "public service hangar" on the west side of Wold-Chamberlain field. (Refer to diagram, position 10). Formerly owned by Northwest Airways, De Ponti's Ford Trimotor is on the ramp. (Dick Palen)

bullet from the gun of a soldier practicing at the nearby Fort Snelling rifle range. The bullet struck the concrete ramp, ricocheted through the fuselage of an airplane being loaded by Albert and pierced his chest, grazing his main heart artery. At first, nobody realized exactly what had happened, and it was not until he was hospitalized, that the situation was discovered. At Rochester, where Albert was then taken, physicians refused to remove the bullet, judging it to be too dangerous to remove, lodged alongside a main heart artery. It was never removed, and Albert came back to work following a period of recuperation.

By 1938, De Ponti offered a wide range of aviation instruction as indicated in a multi-page brochure. For example, two mechanics courses were available, a 16-week and a 51-week version at $175 and $380 respectively. The student could get a 5% discount by paying with cash. Training included a solo flight course, called the "Amateur Course," made up of four weeks of ground school and 35 hours of flight instruction, for $360; the full Private Pilot's course of 12 weeks of ground school and 60 hours of flying, for $630; a Limited Commercial course with 16 weeks of ground school and 60 hours of flying for an additional $650. The Limited Commercial was a highly desirable rating as it allowed the carrying of passengers for hire

Overview of De Ponti's post-war shops and service area, the original Universal Air Lines hangars. Cubs predominate on the ramp, shared with Northwest Airlines DC-3's and others. The portion with "visiting ships" on it is the bridge between the original hangars. Photo shows the brick frontage on the two hangars, rented out as offices. De Ponti also erected the

three smaller hangars to the left and it was in this hangar complex that Waco CG-4A gliders were assembled during World War II. The large hangar behind the complex is the Air Force hangar constructed in 1944. (Dick Palen via Angelo De Ponti)

188

The Air Force ramp in 1956. F-80's and T-33's share space with a B-29, a C-46, and a C-47. Shorty is in the foreground with the Commanding Officer of the detachment and the Shell Oil Company representative. De Ponti provided fuel under contract to the military. (Angelo De Ponti)

(though within a ten mile radius of home base,) or acting as corporate pilot, co-pilot, or demonstration pilot. In other words, the license provided the opportunity to fly for pay.

De Ponti also offered a Transport Pilot's course of 210 flying hours and a 50 week ground school. This last course included the complete syllabus of all the previous classes joined together. Cost was $2,250. Aeronautical Radio was also offered. A third class radio operator's license then, as now, was required by the government for all aircraft crew members operating aircraft radios.

In the late 1930s, De Ponti bridged over the space between the two former Universal hangars and built three additional smaller hangars to the south of them. (Refer to diagram of early buildings on Wold-Chamberlain Field) The bridge cost De Ponti $25,000. He had owned or leased every building on the airport except the military hangars at one time or another.

De Ponti abandoned the airmail hangar in 1941. It was cut up and moved to Northport Airport in White Bear Lake, for use in the government WTS program.

When the war broke out, De Ponti's entire operation was turned over for military use. His Cubs were taken immediately for the CPT and WTS programs around the state. His facility was designated an official government repair station to support those same programs. *Northwestern Aeronautical Corporation* of St. Paul was awarded a large Army contract to manufacture Waco CG-4A troop-carrying gliders.

The big hangar known as the "ice research hangar" was built in 1944. It's size is evident in this dramatic view from about 1970. Note the Constellation airliner on the ramp and the small size of the waiting room at lower left. (Dick Palen via Angelo De Ponti)

Northwestern leased parts of the old Universal hangars from De Ponti and also his three newer south hangars for glider assembly. De Ponti was contracted to build the fuselages, landing gear and tail assemblies for the gliders. He did this at off-airport facilities located in South Minneapolis, near 53rd Street and Lyndale Avenue. He made up jigs from Waco drawings and turned out 1325 fuselages and assemblies at that location in a residential neighborhood.

From Lyndale Avenue, most gliders were shipped to Wold-Chamberlain by truck where they were covered, painted, and mated with wings manufactured by the *Villiaume Box Company* in St. Paul.[81] Some were then crated and shipped to the east coast where they would await shipment to England for the future D-Day. Many were towed away by C-47, C-46, or even by P-38 aircraft, according to stories. Fifty larger Waco CG-13 gliders were also assembled at the airport, along with two CG-4A's, designated XPG-1's. The later were modified to include a pair of 150 horsepower Franklin engines; the purpose, to test the feasibility of making the gliders independent of tow planes. Though the test flight on 12 May, 1943 and subsequent flights were successful, the Air Corps dropped the project with no further testing.

De Ponti's repair services were used to keep many of the CPT/WTS aircraft in the State flying, but it was the refueling service for the military that kept him the busiest. Not only did he fuel the Doolittle B-25's before they departed Wold-Chamberlain for training fields to the west, but it was Doolittle, himself, that encouraged Shorty to add to his enterprises, tipping him off that the military would be providing Shell oil and fuel for some operator to service Army Air Force planes. Shorty listened to the advice and took on the Shell Oil franchise, for a time holding both Shell and Texaco franchises. He often polled his customers for their preferences. When he discovered that the majority preferred Shell, he dropped Texaco products.[82] The Shell Oil franchise would be very good to De Ponti over the following years.

By 1944, De Ponti was refueling all the transient Army Air Force aircraft that stopped at Wold-Chamberlain. The Navy Reserve had their own fueling facilities on their ramp. Air Force business amounted to nearly 150 aircraft per day. At the peak of his wartime payroll, De Ponti employed as many as 450 persons.

Many colorful and well-known local aviators and technicians worked for Shorty during these early years. Among them was another "Shorty." This man, Harold "Shorty" Hall, was from Cambridge, Minnesota. He had started with Northwest Airways as a handyman, then worked for Universal Air Lines. When Shorty De Ponti moved across the field to the airmail hangar, Hall came along and took a job with him, hawking sight-seeing rides during weekend activities, sorting parts, and managing De Ponti's tool room. After De Ponti became the Piper Cub distributor, Hall worked as his sales manager. During the wartime period, Hall worked with the glider assembly group.

Among the many persons in De Ponti's crew was a crack mechanic, Jerry Stebbins. Stebbins is

1959 photo shows three prominent Minnesota aviation personalities clowning around. At left is Clarence Hinck; center, Marcellus King, barnstormer and businessman; and Angelo "Shorty" De Ponti. (Angelo De Ponti)

remembered by most of today's senior aviation folks as one of the most outstanding mechanics in the state. As chief mechanic at De Ponti, he supervised all repair and maintenance services, as well as the other mechanics. He was a stickler for airworthiness, and would ground any airplane he felt needed maintenance. Shorty acknowledges that once, when Stebbins had eight of nine training planes grounded, the two "had words."[83]

Edith Campbell Finholt, who worked for De Ponti as part-time mechanic and part-time secretary, says of Stebbins, "he held the place together." Slightly older than the rest of the crew, he was a father-figure. Edie continues, "he let me grind a few valves and let me think I really knew what I was doing. He'd give me jobs to do, but always would watch over me." Stebbins would tell her who it was okay to talk with, to walk with, and to fly with. When the boys in the shop would laugh or ask her what she was doing, he'd tell them to leave her alone. "When Shorty De Ponti was in trouble, he'd go to Jerry for advice. He was a sweetheart, one of my favorite memories..."[84]

Edie, herself, was unique. A woman involved in what was supposed to be a man's line of work. She was born in St. Cloud, attended the *North Dakota School of Sciences* at Wahpeton, North Dakota, where she enrolled in aviation courses taught by Art Sampson. She was the only woman in those classes.

She came to Minneapolis and applied for a job with De Ponti, and he fell for her. She handled bookkeeping and secretarial duties for many years and took flying lessons from Elmer Hinck along the way. She received her Limited Commercial rating in 1936, and her full Commercial license in 1939, becoming only the 18th woman in the U. S. to do so.

Edie brought in a lot of business with her charming personality, standing in for publicity photos and demonstrating Cubs to prospective buyers. She delivered many of the Cubs personally, and flew many more to the field from the factory at Lock Haven, Pennsylvania. She married a dashing young Northwest Airlines pilot named Ted Finholt, much to the dismay of many jealous suitors at De Ponti's.

EPILOGUE: ANGELO DE PONTI

With the ending of World War II, there came a rush of veterans, eager to spend their hard-earned GI benefit checks on flight training. Once again, De Ponti resumed a flight training program and picked up where he had left off with Cub sales. He found that the Cub still sold like crazy. His sales soon averaged 150 to 200 units per year. In all, De Ponti's Piper relationship lasted 24 years, and his territory eventually covered eight states.[85]

In 1946, De Ponti overhauled some Lockheed F-5G aircraft (photo P-38's), sold on the civilian market as surplus. He modified one such plane for Northwest Airlines pilot, and homebuilder, Walter Bullock, to fly in the Bendix cross-country race from Van Nuys, California, to Cleveland, Ohio. Bullock finished the unlimited category in ninth place.

In 1950, Shorty moved two of his three small south hangars from their spot near the old Universal complex to a new location, even farther south, across 66th Street and just south of a hangar constructed by Northwestern Aeronautical. There he used them mostly for storage, including non-aviation related materials. One of his hangars burned down when corrugated cardboard boxes filled with empty tin cans spontaneously kindled, destroying the hangar. In 1953, De Ponti consolidated his operations in the big ice research hangar built during the war by the navy, leasing it from the Metropolitan Airports Commission. The ex-navy hangar was an immense edifice. The hugeness of the hangar matched the entrepreneurial spirit of De Ponti, both were big!

The hangar was 80 feet high, 300 feet deep and 330 feet wide. It had eight 65 foot high doors, each with its own electric motor to move it. The hangar's full-span rafters were of laminated wood, supported by concrete pillars. Heating costs in the deep of winter could climb to $3,000 per month and the simple act of opening the doors to pull an airplane in during mid-winter could cost $500.[86] But then, fuel was cheap...and Shorty was a distributor.

De Ponti also occupied two other hangars at the north end of the line on 34th Avenue. The northernmost had been built by Northwest Airlines with city bonds in 1940. The next one south had been built for Honeywell by the government in 1942. De Ponti was invited to take over these hangars, and to "fix them up" as he said.[87]

In 1960, Shorty De Ponti again followed Northwest Airlines in ownership, this time purchasing the three "Shakopee hangars", to the south of 66th Street and west of 34th Avenue. Shorty then rented space to Honeywell, Eastern Airlines, and Braniff Airlines, for cargo and storage. De Ponti paid $500,000 for the three hangars. Meanwhile, his fuel trucks continued to service the Air Force and Air Guard ramps.

In 1970, De Ponti serviced 2930 charter flights, which delivered 50,000 persons to the Twin Cities and departed the same number. He handled over 4,000 flights by regional carriers, and nearly 5,000 flights by business or pleasure fliers, all from the Green Concourse of the new terminal. This was a new ramp segment built on the field's east side in the early 1960's. Shorty pumped 4 million gallons of gasoline during the year, with his storage capacity being over 300,000 gallons. Though a competing fueling service had come onto the field and had garnered contracts with most of the major carriers, it didn't put a dent in De Ponti's business.[88]

In 1971, however, he faced a serious challenge. He and the Metropolitan Airports Commission gambled that traffic would double in the next few years. De Ponti bet $350,000 of his own money in the purchase of additional equipment to augment a 130 vehicle fleet of service trucks. He contracted to handle the entire operation of the Green Concourse, Gate 35. The contract covered maintenance, fueling, and baggage handling of all aircraft using that gate.[89]

De Ponti maintained a contract with Pan American Airlines to refuel their London to Los Angeles flights if they needed a stop along the way on their return flights. At this time, De Ponti was leasing six hangars from the Metropolitan Airports Commission for $100,000 a year.[90]

The pace finally caught up with Shorty in 1973. Not only was he getting tired, but he could see the unions coming, something he was dead-set against. He sold his franchise back to Shell Oil. Page Airways picked up the franchise and still holds it. In his time at Wold-Chamberlain, Shorty saw no less than fifty-three businesses start up and close down, while his own flourished. He retired to his handsome home in White Bear Lake, Minnesota, where he and his wife, Bernice, had lived since 1968. Bernice was no stranger to aviation, having worked for Shorty since 1946, and marrying him in 1953.

Angelo "Shorty" De Ponti was one of the most successful Minnesota aviation businessman ever to start business in the state. In the beginning, Shorty admitted, "...if you could pay the $50 a month rent, you paid it...and we couldn't sometimes. I paid (Elmer Hinck and Jerry Stebbins) $125 a month, if I had it, otherwise, we'd just empty out the pot and split it up."[91] Never-the-less, De Ponti's entrepreneurial drive parlayed a small parts business into a very lucrative Piper franchise and Shell Oil distributorship, bringing him wealth and respect.

effort, manufacturing, among other things, half-wool, half-cotton underwear for high altitude bomber crews and combat troops, jungle hammocks, airplane wing covers, tents, and knitted caps.

Munsingwear also owned a controlling interest in the David Clark Company, whose work with the Mayo Foundation during the war, helped develop the "G" suit which was used to keep pilots from blacking out when ejecting from their aircraft at high altitudes.

The **Ford Motor Company** plant in St. Paul also played a role during World War II. From that plant came oil pumps for Pratt & Whitney aircraft engines, supplied to Ford's Willow Run bomber manufacturing facility in Michigan.

The name Mark Hurd and aerial surveying are synonymous in Minnesota. Hurd, a University of Minnesota graduate in Chemical Engineering, spent his World War One years in the Signal Corps aviation section, then went into the business community, where he formed several corporations. Mid-Plane Sales and Transit was incorporated in 1927 at Wold-Chamberlain and soon merged with Air Transportation Company into the large, Universal Aviation Company.

In 1930, Hurd set up the **Aerial Photographic Service Corporation** in Chicago to make aerial surveys, but soon returned to Minneapolis, and in 1932, Hurd and John Holmberg began operating an aerial mapping company called **Holmberg and Hurd Aerial Mapping Company**. They flew assignments for the Minnesota Highway Department, the Minnesota National Guard, and the U. S. Forest Service. In 1934, Holmberg moved to Chicago, and Hurd continued the corporation under his own name. One of Hurd's 1930s assignments was to photograph the city of Minneapolis to make a mosaic of the entire city. Another job was to provide the federal government with aerial proof of the farm acreage not being planted by farmers who had put their land into the soil bank program.

In 1939, Hurd organized another company, the **Mark Hurd Manufacturing Corporation**, to manufacture a better aerial camera. The camera had a 9 inch x 9 inch format. Hurd designed a new shutter and mounting.

Having remained in the Air Force Reserve after World War I, Hurd was called to active duty following Pearl Harbor, sent to England and put in charge of photographic materials and equipment. Hurd's group was awarded five battle stars while attached to Patton's 5th Army in France. After the war, Hurd reorganized the company into the **Mark Hurd Mapping Company** and continued tinkering, manufacturing several additional camera models. The company's fleet included six P-38's, a B-17, two Beechcraft AT-11's, a Ventura patrol bomber, and two Mosquito bombers, plus a Stinson L-5 observation aircraft and two Cessna 180's.

Contract followed contract and the company expanded, eventually establishing offices in many states and Puerto Rico. The company exists today and continues as a leader in aerial mapping.

AIRMAIL COMMEMORATION DAY

The history of airmail in Minnesota can be traced back as far as October, 1911. At that time a scheme had been hatched to carry a load of mail aboard a hydro aeroplane from one of Minneapolis' lakes, down the Mississippi River to New Orleans. The story of Hugh Robinson's abortive flight can be found in Chapter Two.

As early as 1919, a trial airmail flight was made under the auspices of the Duluth and Minneapolis chambers of commerce and the Minnesota Motor Corps. On 22 February, Lieutenant Walter Bullock and Major William C. Garis, members of the Motor Corps section of the Minnesota Home Guard made a trip to the port city and back with a small cargo of mail. More on this flight is found in the story of the Minnesota Air Guard in Chapter Seven.

In 1938, the U. S. Post Office Department authorized a National Air Mail Week. The celebration took place during the week of 15 May through 21 May, and each state was to decide its own means of honoring the Air Mail Service's 20th anniversary. Minnesota's state chairman of Air Mail Week, John R. Coan, ar-

May 19, 1938. Air Mail Week celebration at Wold-Chamberlain. Flyers from all over the State have landed, bringing air mail from many communities throughout Minnesota. (Vern Georgia)

ranged for experienced flyers from each community to pickup mail from their city and others, along a route that would bring them all to Wold-Chamberlain Field around noon on 19 May for a major celebration. Coan's invitation to each selected flyer, read as follows:

Dear Pilot:

Enclosed herewith you will find:

1 form N.A.M. 6 (Certificate of Authorization)

1 Form 2702-A (Trip Report)

1 Schedule of special flights

1 Guest ticket

The certificate will be carried with you and will show your authority for picking up mail on your particular flight.

The Trip Report will be carried on the flight and will be turned in at the end of your flight, after having been filled in by the pilot.

The Schedule of Special Flights shows the time of your arrival at the Wold-Chamberlain Field at Minneapolis. You should work out your schedule so as to arrive here at that time, and at the same time, allow sufficient time at each pickup point for a brief civic celebration. Communicate immediately with the Postmaster at any point where you will pick up mail and advise him of the time you will make the pickup at his city. This is important and should be done without delay, as the time is very short, and he will be awaiting this information.

The guest ticket will entitle you to a buffet lunch at the Wold-Chamberlain field as a guest of the Minneapolis Civic and Commerce Association.

CAUTION: No pilot should attempt to land at the Wold-Chamberlain field at any of the following times: 9:45 a.m., 9:52 a.m., 10:15 a.m., 10:35 a.m., 10:55 a.m. Regular passenger planes are scheduled to land or takeoff at that time.

With best wishes to each of you in this big experiment, I wish to take this means of thanking you for your assistance in making National Air Mail Week a success.

Very truly yours,
John R. Coan
State Chairman
National Air Mail Week[92]

The certificate of authorization cleared each pilot taking part, to pickup mail at specific airfields spelled out on the form. Pilots were required to declare an oath of allegiance to the post office department in order to handle the mail.

The following list of flights and arrival times at Wold-Chamberlain has been copied from a schedule in the collection of the Freeborn County Historical Society. It is interesting in that it is a veritable who's who of aviators in Minnesota at that time:

Special flights and pickups scheduled in Minnesota on 19 May, 1938

1. Roosevelt-Franklin[sic]-Delano-Minneapolis
   Jack O'Meara — 4:30 p.m.
2. East Grand Forks-Warren-Stephen-Hallock-Roseau-Greenbush & Badger-Middle River-Thief River Falls-Red Lake Falls-Fosston
   Lester Jolly — 4:25 p.m.
3. Breckenridge-Fargo, ND
   John Danicourt
4. Baudette-Minneapolis
   Peter J. Klimek — 12:00 a.m.
5. International Falls-Minneapolis
   Forrest Rising — 11:55 a.m.
6. Hibbing-Minneapolis
   ... Murray — 11:45 a.m.
7. Virginia-Minneapolis
   Gil Hartley — 11:35 a.m.
8. Cloquet-Moose Lake-Minneapolis
   Roscoe O. Raiter — 11:25 a.m.
9. Duluth-Minneapolis
   David Rall — 11:40 a.m.
10. Pine City-Minneapolis
    William L. West — 9:30 a.m.
11. Bemidji-Park Rapids-Minneapolis
    John Walatka — 11:20 a.m.
12. Cass Lake-Minneapolis
    Wm. A. Haller — 11:15 a.m.
13. Grand Rapids-Minneapolis
    Douglas Smith — 10:30 a.m.
14. Alexandria-Minneapolis
    ... Rilling — 11:10 a.m.
15. Sauk Centre-Minneapolis
    Dean Brown — 11:00 a.m.
16. St. Cloud-Minneapolis
    Edith Campbell — 10:25 a.m.
17. Little Falls-Minneapolis
    Bill Morse and Cavour Hartley — 12:00 a.m.
18. Litchfield-Minneapolis
    Ed Croft — 9:35 a.m.
19. Tracy-Redwood Falls-Willmar-Minneapolis
    Jack Robinson — 12:05 p.m.
20. Montevideo-Minneapolis
    Wally Seebach — 11:35 a.m.
21. Hutchinson-Minneapolis
    Al Brandt — 9:40 a.m.
22. Maple Lake-Minneapolis
    Mark Madigan — 9:05 a.m.
23. Buffalo-Minneapolis
    Budd Stahel — 10:35 a.m.
24. Elk River-Minneapolis
    F.J. Christian Jr — 9:10 a.m.
25. Anoka-Minneapolis
    ... Schwyzer — 9:15 a.m.
26. Glenwood-Osakis-Robbinsdale
    James C. Pipo
    Robbinsdale-Minneapolis
    Harry Holcomb — 8:45 a.m.

Air Mail Week celebration. The 7-Up skywriting Laird Super Solution, restored by Bob McManus is perched on a float, where it has been paraded down the ramp to the admiration of a large crowd. (James LaVake)

27. Center City-Minneapolis
    Ray Petersen   10:20 a.m.
28. South St. Paul-White Bear Lake-Mpls.
    Bill Shaw   9:30 a.m.
29. Mayer-Minneapolis
    Elmer Sell   9:25 a.m.
30. Glencoe-Minneapolis
    M. R. Lee   10:05 a.m.
31. Waconia-Minneapolis
    I. Stahlke   10:20 a.m.
32. Worthington-Adrian-Minneapolis
    James Zarth Jr.   12:15 p.m.
33. New Ulm-Minneapolis
    O.P. Gestad   11:00 a.m.
34. St. James-Lake Crystal-Minneapolis
    Roy L. Graham   11:20 a.m.
35. Monterey-Triumph-Minneapolis
    Melvin Marple   11:25 a.m.
36. Sherburne-Minneapolis
    Roy K. Reed   11:10 a.m.
37. Truman-Minneapolis
    E.B. Wilkinson   9:55 a.m.
38. Mankato-Minneapolis
    H.R. Schlesselman   9:40 a.m.
39. Winnebago-Minneapolis
    Gordon Paschke   10:00 a.m.
40. Le Sueur-Minneapolis
    R.W. Fleischauer   9:30 a.m.
41. Le Center-Minneapolis
    Jack Lysdale   10:30 a.m.
42. Mason City,IA-Minneapolis
    E.J. Kraemer   11:45 a.m.
43. Waseca-Minneapolis
    Howard Deichen   10:30 a.m.

A copy of the Post Office Department's certificate of appreciation to the participating pilots of commemmorative flights, May, 1938. (John V. Kipp)

44. New Richland-Minneapolis
    F.H. Briese   11:15 a.m.
45. Albert Lea-Minneapolis
    E.A. Evans   9:55 a.m.
46. Faribault-Northfield-Minneapolis
    L.E. Merrill
47. Blooming Prairie-Minneapolis
    R.R. Reidel   11:15 a.m.
48. Waterloo, IA-Minneapolis
    ... Harris   12:20 a.m.
49. Austin-Minneapolis
    Marcellus King   10:25 a.m.
50. Pine Island - Zumbrota - West Concord - Kasson - Rochester
    Jos. A. McKeown
51. Preston-Chatfield-Rochester
    Jos. A. McKeown
52. Caledonia-Minneapolis
    Cletus Hoffman   10:25 a.m.
53. Winona-Minneapolis
    Max Conrad   10:30 a.m.
54. Red Wing-Minneapolis
    George Holey   9:05 a.m.
55. Lake City-Minneapolis
    Clayton Brown   9:30 a.m.
56. Hastings-Minneapolis
    H.A. Gogolin   9:10 a.m.
57. Farmington-Minneapolis
    R.K. Rowley   9:15 a.m.
58. Oxboro-Minneapolis
    Wm. [sic] (Wallace) Neumann   9:05 a.m.
59. Cannon Falls - Randolph - Lakeville - Minneapolis
    John V. Kipp   10:10 a.m.
60. St. Peter-Minneapolis
    D.S. Berent   10:10 a.m.
61. Hopkins-Minneapolis
    Elmer Hinck   9:00 a.m.
62. Chaska-Minneapolis
    Willis Strong   9:25 a.m.
63. Tamarack-Excelsior
    John J. Wolf   12:00 a.m.
64. Madelia-Minneapolis
    Les I. Petterson   10:40 a.m.
65. Olivia-Minneapolis
    Cornelius Kraemer   10:50 a.m.
66. Forest Lake-Minneapolis
    A.C. McInnis   10:40 a.m.

Authorized by John R. Coan, Chairman, Minnesota Air Mail Week Campaign.

As might be expected, with all of the activity centered at Wold-Chamberlain Field following the flights, the event was a huge field day. A great crowd attended, and watched a dandy airshow. The 7-Up Laird of Bob McManus was mounted on a float which paraded the length of the field, and arriving aircraft provided the spectacle. The 109th Air Guard performed some precision flight maneuvers, and everyone enjoyed the day. There is no indication that any of the pilots taking part had difficulties with their aircraft and there were no bad incidents.

Each participating pilot was issued a certificate from the U. S. Postmaster General, James A. Farley, thanking him for his efforts and commemorating the occasion.

═══ ☆ ═══ National Air Mail Week ═══ ☆ ═══

POST OFFICE DEPARTMENT

CERTIFICATE

KNOW ALL MEN by these presents, that in recognition of his service and in appreciation of his cooperation, this Certificate is presented to

J. V. Kipp

who, on May 19 , 1938, cooperated in the National Air Mail Week campaign to commemorate the Twentieth Anniversary of the Inauguration of Scheduled Air Mail Service, by flying a plane-load of air mail on a flight sponsored by NATIONAL AIR MAIL WEEK COMMITTEE.

from   CANNON FALLS,MINNESOTA   to   MINNEAPOLIS, MINNESOTA.
via   RANDOLPH AND LAKEVILLE

PILOT   JOHN V. KIPP   executed the oath of office of an air mail pilot prior to making this flight. He performed it in a most satisfactory and commendable manner, transporting the mail with certainty, celerity, and security.

James A. Farley

POSTMASTER GENERAL

Business and Commerce   Documentation

1 Donald B. Holmes, *Air Mail*, New York, Clarkson N. Potter, Inc., 1981, pp. 152-153. A version of part of this chapter first appeared in *Minnesota History*, 50/3, fall 1986.

2 *St. Paul Pioneer Press*, 12 January, 1926, p. 1.

3 *New York Times*, 23 June, 1926, p. 3.

4 *New York Times*, 27 June, 1926, Sect. 2, p. 19.

5 *Minneapolis Journal*, 9 May, 1920, p. 11.

6 *Minneapolis Journal*, 9 May, 1920, p. 11.

7 *St. Paul Pioneer Press*, 8 August, 1920, p. 6 and *Minneapolis Journal*, 15 June, 1920, p. 15.

8 Holmes, *Air Mail*, p. 115.

9 *Minneapolis Journal*, 29 December, 1920, p. 17.

10 *St. Paul Pioneer Press*, 4 February, 1921, p. 6.

11 *St. Paul Pioneer Press*, 11 February, 1921, p. 1.

12 *Minneapolis Journal*, 25 February, 1921, p. 11 and Jackson, *Flying the Mail*, pp. 60-62.

13 *St. Paul Pioneer Press*, 12 February, 1921, p. 1 and 2.

14 R.E.G. Davies, *A History of the World's Airlines*, London, 1964, p. 41.

15 Davies, *A History of the World's Airlines*, p. 39.

16 The literature on airline development and the story of the air mail is voluminous. See, for example, R. E. G. Davies, *A History of the World's Airlines*, London, 1964; Carl Solberg, *Conquest of the Skies*, Boston, 1979; and Donald Dale Jackson, *Flying the Mail*, Alexandria, Va., 1982. There are also numerous histories of individual airlines.

17 Biography File (Brittin), National Air & Space Museum (NASA), Washington, D. C.

18 *New York Times*, 5 September, 1926, Section 1, p. 10, and Senate Documents, no. 70, p. 195.

19 Interview of Julius Perlt by Gerald Sandvick and Noel Allard, 29 January, 1985, notes in author's possession. On company salaries, here and below, see Northwest Airways, voucher No. 21, 30 November, 1926, in Northwest Airlines, Inc. Records, division of library and archives, Minnesota Historical Society, St. Paul.

20 David R. Lane, *Aircraft in Northwest Airlines' History*, Bloomington, Minn.; David Galbraith, "The Aircraft History of Northwest Airlines," *American Aviation Historical Society Journal 21* (Winter, 1976): 241-256.

21 William Kidder Manuscript.

22 Here and below, see *St. Paul Dispatch*, 5,6 July, 1927, both p. 1; *Journal*, 6 July, 1927, p. 11. The passengers were Byron G. Webster of the St. Paul Association and L. R. S. Ferguson, president of the St. Paul City Council.

23 Reports from line pilots and Operations Manager, Charles W. Holman, to Colonel Lewis Brittin, all dated 27 October, 1928, copies in possession of author.

24 Ibid.

25 Ibid.

26 Ibid.

27 Kenneth D. Ruble, *Flight To The Top*, published by Northwest Airlines, 1986, page 20.

28 Interview with Joseph Kimm by Kenneth Ruble for the book, *Flight To The Top*, 1976.

29 Kenneth D. Ruble, *Flight To The Top*, Northwest Airlines, p. 40.

30 Memorandum written by various Operations Managers to the line pilots of Northwest, 1930-1933, from Dan and Pat O'Keefe collection of Russ McNown material, copies in possession of author.

31 Memo accompanying March, 1934 financial report to the Board of Directors of Northwest Airlines by E.I. Whyatt, NWA Treasurer. Memo dated March 28, 1934. Copy in possession of author.

32 David Galbraith, "The Aircraft History of Northwest Airlines", *American Aviation Historical Society Journal*, Winter, 1976, pages 240-256.

33 Fred W. Whittemore, "Northern Transcontinental Airway thru Twin Cities", *Minnesota Techno-Log*, University of Minnesota, January, 1934, pages 75-78.

34 Kenn C. Rust, "Early Airlines," Chapter 10, *American Aviation Historical Society Journal*, Winter, 1986, pages 305-307.

35 Kenneth D. Ruble, *Flight To The Top*, Northwest Airlines, page 72.

36 "Northwest Tests Inhalators," *Aviation Magazine*, April, 1939, page 62.

37 Interview with Tom Nolan by Kenneth Ruble for the book, *Flight To The Top*, 1976

38 Interview with E. Ben Curry by Kenneth D. Ruble for the book, *Flight To The Top*, 1976.

39 Some of the preceeding material is taken from work done for this book by author, Kenneth D. Ruble, Venice, FL., 1986.

40 *Minneapolis Journal*, 28 March, 1928, p. 27.

41 *Minneapolis Journal*, 24 May, 1928, p. 19.

42 *Aviation*, 18 June, 1928, p. 1772.

43 *Minneapolis Journal*, 13 July, 1928, p. 15 and July 15, p. 4.

44 *Minneapolis Journal*, 6 December, 1928, p. 18 and William T. Larkins, *The Ford Story*, 1958, p. 26.

45 *Aviation*, 2 July, 1928, p. 46.

46 *St. Paul Pioneer Press*, 6 June, 1929.

47 *Minneapolis Journal*, 7 May, 1929, p. 10.

48 Interview with Perlt, 6 March, 1985.

49 Yellow Cab Timetable, in possession of the authors.

50 Davies, p. 98.

51 Canadian-American Timetable, 20 August, 1929.

52 *Aviation*, 26 October, 1929, p. 356, and *Aero Digest*, November 1929, p. 214.

53 *Commercial West*, 2 November, 1929, p. 14.

54 *Minneapolis Journal*, 29 July, 1928, p. 1.

55 *Aero Digest*, February 1928, p. 268, and *Minneapolis Journal*, July 29, 1928, p. 1.

56 *Minneapolis Journal*, 29 July, 1928, p. 1. The information on Rufus Rand is from the classic biographical work on LaFayette Escadrille pilots, James Normal Hall and Charles Bernard Nordhoff, *The LaFayette Flying Corps*, Boston, 1920, p. 399.

57 *Aviation*, 2 July, 1928, p. 44.

58 *Minneapolis Journal*, 29 July, 1928, p. 1.

59 *Aviation*, 20 October, 1928, p. 1265, and *The Financial Chronicle*, 3 November, 1928, p. 2554.
For the complex story of the Universal Aviation Corporation and the Aviation Corporation of America as related here and below, the best general accounts are in R. E. G. Davies, *Airlines of the United States Since 1914* and Henry Ladd Smith, *Airways*, New York, 1942.

60 *American Airlines History*, pp. 8-9.

61 *Minneapolis Journal*, 25 July, 1928, p. 1; July 29, 1929, p. 1, and 1 November, 1928, p. 1.

62 Universal Airlines System Timetable, 15 November, 1928.

63 *Aviation*, 25 August, 1928, p. 605.

64 *Aviation*, 24 November, 1928, p. 1629 and 9 February, 1929, p. 414. Bilstein, *Flight Patterns*, p. 1.

65 *Aero Digest*, May 1929, p. 192.

66 *Financial Chronicle*, 16 March, 1929, p. 1732; 9 March, 1939, p. 1576, 23 March, 1929, p. 1927, 17 August, 1929, p. 1126.

67 Here and below, Robert D. Orr, *A history of Aviation in South Dakota*, unpublished Master of Arts thesis, University of South Dakota, 1957; Hanford Airlines timetable, 1 June, 1938; Mid-Continent timetable, 1 November, 1938.

68 Handbill distributed at Dayton's Dry Goods Store, November, 1909, during display of Curtiss-Herring Aeroplane. Copy in possession of author.

69 "Curtiss Airship Is On Exhibition, *Minneapolis Journal*, 18 November, 1909, page 1.

70 *Minneapolis Journal*, 10 May, 1920.

71 Merchandise tag from Dayton's Dry Goods Store, May, 1920. Copy in possession of author.

72 Contract between William Kidder and Dayton's Dry Goods Store, 24 August, 1920. Copy in possession of author.

73 Ibid.

74 Letter from William Kidder to Hugh Arthur of the Daytons Company, 21 October, 1920. Copy in possession of author.

75 *Airport News*, Volume 1, number 8.

76 Northwest Aviation School brochure, 1934, page 7. Copy in possession of author.

77 Interview with Emmett Boucher by Noel Allard, 18 December, 1987.

78 Ad appearing in *Flying and Popular Aviation Magazine*, December 1940, page 70.

79 Interview with Angelo De Ponti by Noel Allard, 9 October, 1974.

80 *Wings*, "It's Been a Long, Long Time", article by Angelo De Ponti, Volume 1, Number 4, March, 1946. Pages 18, 26, 27, 36.

81 Ibid.

82 Interview with Angelo De Ponti by Noel Allard, 9 October, 1974.

83 Interview with Angelo De Ponti by Noel Allard, 11 November, 1988.

84 Interview with Angelo De Ponti, 9 October, 1974.

85 Ibid.

86 *The Minnesota Flyer*, January, 1978.

87 Ibid.

88 *The Minneapolis Star*, Business News, February 12, 1971, page 18a.

89 Ibid.

90 Interview with Angelo De Ponti by Noel Allard, 9 October, 1974.

91 Interview with Angelo De Ponti by Noel Allard, 11 November, 1988.

92 Letter from John R. Coan to each pilot taking part in National Air Mail Week commemmorative flights. 13 May, 1938, copy in possession of author.

SEVEN

1920s — 1940s: THE MILITARY CONNECTION

THE MINNESOTA AIR NATIONAL GUARD

The single engine biplane, a Curtiss Oriole, was beating its way southwest into the teeth of a fierce headwind. As pilot Ray Miller and mechanic Joe Westover looked down from their open cockpits, they were doubtless wishing they were almost anywhere else.

It was Tuesday, 24 January, 1922; the pilots were 5000 feet over Minnesota's North Shore near the town of Little Marais, and they were two men with several problems. The ground temperature was well below zero, and at their altitude and airspeed, the wind chill was indescribable. They had left Port Arthur bound for Duluth, but the 60 m.p.h. headwind so slowed their progress, that the day was turning to dusk when they noticed their fuel pump had quit and the few gallons in a gravity-fed tank was now their total fuel supply. Lake Superior was jumbled ice and open water, the shore was uneven rocks and woods, and there was no such thing as an airfield anywhere near.

Miller, though, remembered an inland lake near-by and grabbed his only chance. He swung the Oriole inland and within a few minutes was over Lax Lake, a long body of water with a hard frozen surface. In the fading daylight they spotted a trapper's cabin on the shore and set their ship down as close to it as possible. The high hills ringing the lake made for a difficult approach, but Miller slipped past them and stretched it out over the lake. "We got our worst fright when we hit the snow which was two to four feet deep," he said. "There was no crust on top of the snow and the wheels sank deep into it. As the machine dashed the snow, we were nearly blinded. Finally the ship stopped with a jerk in a deep drift."

The two fliers took refuge with the trapper who apparently offered hospitality and, most important, warmth. According to the pilot, "We were half frozen when we landed," and the trapper's shack looked like a palace. "Everything he had was at our disposal and we rested in front of a huge fire." Since it was January on Lax Lake, "the trapper was as surprised as we were happy to land on the lake."

At dawn the two aviators arose and so did new troubles. Since they had been expected in Duluth on the previous afternoon, officials there were ready to call out a search party. The assumption was that they had either crashed or made a forced landing since they had last been seen passing over Little Marais and had not been heard from since. On Lax Lake the overnight temperature had dipped to 30 below, and

the Oriole's engine was so stiff that Miller said, "I could hang on the prop and never budge it." Westover built a fire and began heating large stones to pile on the engine to heat it. They heated water and oil on the stove in the shack, poured it into the airplane, and then found a supply of gasoline of dubious quality. The gasoline, however, belonged to a settler two miles from the lake, so the trapper's horse was hitched to a small sled and the gasoline dragged back to the aircraft in several small cans. After filtering out the dirt and rust particles, they had half a tank's worth, enough to get to Duluth.

It was mid-afternoon when they got the engine started, and then came the real task. They tried to tramp out a path in the snow, but it was still over the wheels and the tip of the prop was swishing through the drifts when they made their takeoff run. "I didn't dare raise the tail to the normal starting position," Miller recalled, "because if I did, there was a good chance that the propeller would smash. In this position the plane bounded from drift to drift until finally I felt it take to the air. How it was done I'll never know."

As they staggered into the air, they barely cleared the trees and hills, but they were off and set a course for Duluth. Miller's flight log book for that day contains the entry "Lax Lake to Duluth - 70 minutes."

The fact that the Twin City aviators spent a day struggling against nature and balky machinery on a frozen lake is only one episode in a larger story and the story itself is an historic one. Major Ray Miller, the commanding officer, and Lt. Joe Westover, the engineering officer of Minnesota's Air National Guard squadron, were up north because Governor J. A. O. Preus had ordered them to be. The unit was the first Air Guard squadron to be officially created by the Federal government, and the flight north in that frigid January in 1922 was the first time the squadron had been called to active duty by the civil authorities.

Miller and Westover were on a humanitarian manhunt. In late December, James Maher, a Cook County Commissioner, disappeared from his open boat in Lake Superior. The search area ran from Grand Marais, Minnesota, to Port Arthur, Ontario, and a water or land search was difficult at best. Indeed, a Duluth based unit of the National Guard, a tank company, was unable to get beyond Grand Marais due to snow blocked roads. An air search was ordered by the Governor, and Squadron Commander Miller decided to make the flight himself along with the unit's chief mechanic.

Thus, in mid-January they flew from Minneapolis

to Duluth and on to Port Arthur where they landed on the frozen bay with almost no gas remaining. For the next several days they flew search missions out of the Canadian city in conditions of great danger. Cold, wind, lack of emergency landing places, and exhaustion took their toll. Maher was not found, the search was called off, and on 24 January, Miller and Westover were headed home when they force-landed on Lax Lake.

Miller later said that on the flight to Port Arthur, the temperature was 42 below on the ground and over 60 below at their altitude. In the exposed open cockpits, Miller froze his face badly and said, "the skin on the entire side of my face was cooked as if it had come into contact with a hot stove and my nose and chin were one aching scab for over two weeks." Westover's hands were frostbitten in several places. Miller's summary comments on the historic search are descriptive of the hardships. "I never dreamed of the intense cold that could prevail in this country. At no time were we comfortable. Most of the time we were so cold we were without sensation. Handling the ship was automatic on my part, as many times I could not feel the controls...I am glad to be back and I hope the trip does not have to be repeated under the same circumstances."[1]

In general, Ray Miller got his wish, for these circumstances were not to be repeated. In the coming years, however, the Air Guard squadron would be called to duty many times to serve the state and nation. The search for a lost County Commissioner was not the last time the squadron would get great press coverage for its efforts and be seen by the public as undertaking heroic tasks. Indeed, a characteristic of the nation's pioneer Air Guard squadron during its formative years was a finely tuned sense of the need for good publicity. Even before the ordeal of Miller and Westover, the squadron had made spectacular flights that served to make it well known to the people of Minnesota and to key officials in the national government.

The Minnesota air unit was officially recognized by the federal government in January, 1921, and designated the 109th Observation Squadron. Interest on the part of National Guardsmen in creating aeronautical units goes back farther, however, than this first official acknowledgment of an Air National Guard Squadron.

The U. S. Army purchased its first airplane directly from the Wright Brothers in 1908, and militiamen were not long in showing their interest. As early as 1909, the Missouri National Guard tried to form an aero detachment with members drawn from the St. Louis Aero Club. In 1911, the California Guard formed a short-lived aero section and one of their officers actually took instruction and earned an aviators license. There were other tentative experiments in Ohio and Nebraska, and as the clouds of World War I rolled closer to the United States, the New York National Guard created two aero squadrons. In 1915, Capt. Ray Bolling, a U. S. Steel lawyer, became commander of the 1st Aero Company, New York National Guard, and the unit recruited a full complement of officers and men and operated at least two aircraft. The Company was actually called into federal service during the Mexican border emergency of 1916, but

in their ten weeks of active duty they got no closer to Mexico than their base on Long Island. The 2nd New York Aero Company was formed at Buffalo in 1916, but disbanded later the same year. It is significant that the influential magazine *Aviation*, reported that the Company was "never mustered into Federal service, it owned no airplanes, it received none from New York, and none from the Federal Government."[2]

The common thread in these various experimental aero units is clear. There was never official funding or acknowledgment that the units were a part of the National Guard structure. Any aircraft operated were privately owned, and either donated or flown by the owner. Most of all, none of these early units lasted. The most successful of them, New York's 1st Aero Company, operated for about 18 months, and when the U. S. entered the War, it was disbanded. The fact was that the War Department had no interest in giving the National Guard aviation units, and the National Guard Headquarters had neither the money nor equipment to do so.[3]

The state that would finally give birth to the first National Guard aero squadron also had an earlier air unit which, as in other places, was recognized by the state but never by any national authority. In this case, however, there is a direct linkage of key officers between the Aviation Section of 1918 and the 109th Observation Squadron of 1921. The roots of modern National Guard aviation are found in an obscure outfit called the Aviation Section of the Minnesota Motor

Lt. Col. W. C. Garis and Major Ray Miller at Bolling Field, Washington, D. C., having arrived on their quest to obtain the nation's first Air National Guard Squadron charter. Federal recognition of the Minnesota Air Guard unit was issued on 17 January, 1921, designating it as the 109th Observation Squadron. (Minnesota Air National Guard Historical Foundation)

Summer encampment, 1922. New Curtiss JN-6 aircraft were supplied by the War Department to be housed in the three newly constructed hangars built in the center of the former auto racetrack near Fort Snelling. This photo shows the old racetrack, trees having overgrown its edges, and its prominent sand dune area at the northeast corner in the foreground. (Augustus Whittier Nelson)

Corps of the Minnesota Home Guard.

In the spring of 1917, Minnesota's 34th Division was federalized and left the state as part of the general call-up of Guard forces for the war with Germany. It was observed that the state produced 16% of the entire world supply of iron ore and now had no military units to guard docks, mills, iron ore ranges or public utilities from mischief by enemy agents or pro-German sympathizers. To correct this seemingly dire situation, the Minnesota Home Guard was created by order of Governor Joseph Burnquist in late April, 1917. The activities of the Home Guard were many, varied, and beyond the scope of this essay. Suffice it to say they were, in effect, a replacement National Guard, and took into their ranks "men who, for one reason or another, could not at that time offer their services to the United States."[4]

Thirteen months later, another volunteer military unit was created as a part of the Home Guard. It was called the Motor Corps, Minnesota Home Guard, and it was unique in the nation. The idea came from a prominent Minneapolis automobile dealer named Winfield R. Stephens who was given command of the unit and made a Major. In a memo dated 5 June, 1918, Stephens said that the state required quick transportation of its troops "in case of riots, strikes, and disloyal exhibitions." The Corps would be organized and operated along strictly military lines. To be worthy of joining, a man must be "one hundred per cent American" and "a man who had not less than a five passenger car at his command at all times."[5]

Enough volunteers materialized to quickly fill the ranks of the Motor Corps, and in September its first official activity was held. At a three day encampment near Lake City, the members lived in tents, pulled K. P. duty, practiced driving in formations and columns, and even rehearsed "dismounted riot formations...brandishing riot sticks and yelling at the top of their voices."[6]

At first glance this may seem vaguely ludicrous, but it should be remembered that there was a wartime spirit of citizens doing their bit, and a month later serious forest fires ravaged the Moose Lake area. The Motor Corps was called out and spent several hot, dirty, and dangerous days transporting firefighters, supplies, survivors, and bodies.[7]

During the summer of 1918, the Aviation Section was created as a part of the Motor Corps. The first mention of the unit appears at the time of the September encampment with the roster listing an Aviation Section composed of three officers and 26 enlisted men. In October, during the Moose Lake fires, records show that several Aviation Section personnel were issued supplies ranging from deviled meat and ginger snaps to overshoes and blankets. The unit certainly existed, but there is no evidence that they undertook any flying activities. The commanding officer was John P. Ernster of Minneapolis, who was president of the Peoples State Bank.[8]

The Aviation Section did, however, make several well publicized flights in January and February, 1919. In early 1919, Walter Bullock was a Lieutenant in the aero unit. The nineteen year old Bullock was the premier aviator in Minnesota. In late 1918, he purchased an Army surplus Standard J-1, a 100 h.p. biplane trainer which could carry the pilot and a passenger. With this aircraft, Bullock made several flights off the ice of Lake Calhoun in January 1919. On at least one flight he had Major William C. Garis as a passenger. As Chief of Staff to the Adjutant General, Garis was the second ranking officer in the Minnesota National Guard. It is also noteworthy that on 21 January, the *Minneapolis Journal* published an aerial photograph of the Kenwood area of the City and the caption indicated that the photo was taken by Lt. Walter Bullock and Charles M. Pester who had flown over the city two days earlier. Pester is listed as a mechanic on the Aero Section roster.[9]

Although about one thousand spectators showed up to watch Bullock fly, the flights had more purpose than simple exhibitions. The Home Guard had always been considered a temporary organization that would be dissolved when the National Guard returned to the state at the war's conclusion. There was now a strong move underway to make the Motor Corps, including the Aviation Section, a permanent part of the National Guard. As early as October 1918, Governor Burnquist praised the organization's efforts and wrote, "it should be made a permanent state institution."[10]

A month later, the State National Guard Commander, Adjutant General Walter F. Rhinow, recommended to the Governor that an enlarged Motor Corps be made a permanent part of the National

Reveille. The U. S. flag is being raised in early morning at the Air Guard's base at Speedway Field, circa 1923. Note the control tower erected on top of one of the three new hangars. (MANGHF)

Guard, and that in the unit "also would be the Aviation Corps." — Rhinow was thinking of more than state action, too. "Minnesota," he insisted, "is now the only state with an aviation section in its state military units, and federal recognition would be highly desirable." To observe the flying activities and report back to Rhinow, Major Garis was detailed to fly with Bullock. Already in 1919, their goal was to have the first official Air National Guard squadron.[12]

This could not be accomplished, however, without the approval of the state legislature in St. Paul and the Militia Bureau in Washington. Since legislators listen to public opinion and like to spend money on programs of obvious practicality, Rhinow and Garis decided to get publicity and show the utility of airplanes at one stroke. They began planning the first flight between Minneapolis and Duluth.

The idea was that Bullock and Garis would fly to the Port City in early February and carry U. S. mail greetings between municipal officials. They would depart on 3 February, remain overnight, put on some flying demonstrations, and return the next day. Along the route, Northern Pacific railway agents would telephone the airplane's progress back to the Adjutant General's office where Lt. T. Glenn Harrison would keep note of the flight's progress.[13]

Blizzards and cold delayed the flight until 21 February, when, shortly before noon, the fliers took off from Lake Calhoun. They landed at Moose Lake for a courtesy call on the Mayor, continued north and circled Duluth where crowds had gathered to watch, and landed on the frozen bay about mid-afternoon. Although the flight was a first, Bullock reported that they had had no problems and that the air was as smooth as glass. The next morning, two Duluth Motor Corps officers and two young women of their acquaintance were taken aloft for rides. Bullock and Garis then headed south, making landings at Pine City and White Bear Lake and touching down on Lake Calhoun just before 4:00 p.m. The purposes of the flight were accomplished. The aviators made the roundtrip of over 320 miles with only the most minor problems, and the Twin Cities and Duluth newspapers gave prominent space to the flight.[14]

Unfortunately for Rhinow and Garis, the favorable publicity generated by the flight did not translate into legislative action. A bill to make the Motor Corps and its Aviation Section a permanent part of the Guard had been introduced in the 1919 session with the support of the Governor, Adjutant General, and a number of legislators, but by March, the bill seems to have died in the State Senate.

It probably failed for three reasons. The original bill called for an appropriation of $100,000, but a revised bill in early February raised this to $150,000, most of which was for uniforms and equipment. Obviously the price of having a Motor Corps was escalating. A second factor was the opposition of the State Federation of Labor. In early February, the secretary of that organization promised to have a thousand working men lined up to oppose the bill.[15] When it is recalled that the Motor Corps was a part of the Home Guard, the reason for Labor opposition is obvious. The Home Guard was called out to patrol the Twin Cities during the streetcar strike of December 1917.

The final and most damaging blow to legislative ap-

Though the windsock is hanging limp, this Thomas-Morse Scout, possibly Speed Holman's, was blown against one of the Guard's hangars in an unexpected storm during summer encampment on 28 July, 1927. (MANGHF)

proval was opposition of the National Guard itself. While the highest ranking officers clearly favored the Motor Corps, Guard members around the state were alarmed and were contacting their legislators. The simple reason was that they feared the expense of the corps would "keep down the allowance of the state funds for infantry and artillery and machine gun commands."[16]

Without state support the Aviation Section faded from the scene in the spring. Then, on 2 July, 1919, Army headquarters sent out orders concerning the organization of the National Guard that said "no special service units such as aero squadrons...will be organized at the present time."[17] Washington and St. Paul had both stopped the possibility of a Minnesota Air Guard squadron. As events emerged, however, it was a temporary setback. National and state policies were both going to change, and when they did, the Minnesota Guard officers would be ready.

In the months that followed World War I, congress considered, and finally agreed to, a reorganization of the Army and National Guard. The National Defense Act of 1920 established the structure of the nation's military forces that would endure through World War II. The most important provision for National Guard aviation was the stipulation that National Guard divisions would be organized identically to Regular Army divisions. Since each Army division was going to have an attached air squadron for reconnaissance, the National Defense Act effectively gave the green light to official creation of the Air Guard. As early as December, 1919, the Air Service, the Militia Bureau, and the War Plans Division reached agreement that should the proposed law pass "Divisional Air Units should be allowed for National Guard Divisions."[18]

The Defense Act became law in June 1920, and in the same month the Militia Bureau sent Circular No. 1 to the states. This document allowed the creation of aero squadrons in the Guard and reflected not only the new law, but new thinking in the War Department about the utility of National Guard air units. There was, at this time, a surplus of wartime airplanes and little commercial market for them. The aircraft and spare parts would need funds for storage, so it would save money to allocate them to the Guard.

Many also felt that the wartime pool of trained pilots and mechanics should not be allowed to disperse, and yet the Air Service was a fairly small organization. The National Guard could help here, too. Finally, as the lessons of the war were being studied, obviously that infantry divisions could make good use of an organic observation squadron. Such a squadron would be directly a part of the division and could observe and photograph targets, enemy movements, and the like in the divisional area.[19]

Adjutant General Rhinow and Assistant Adjutant General Garis had not forgotten their earlier experience and now saw a way of getting their aero squadron. In June 1920, Rhinow gave Garis the go ahead, and Garis checked and found no other militia air units. If they moved quickly, Minnesota could have the first in the nation. At this juncture, Garis almost certainly would have been eager to recruit a few experienced people to form the nucleus of the squadron. One of the leading pilots in the area was Ray Miller, who, it appears, was acquainted with T. Glenn Harrison. Harrison was a reporter with the *St. Paul Daily News,* but from July 1918 to March 1920, he had been a Guard Lieutenant and Captain in the Adjutant General's office. When Garis and Bullock had flown to Duluth, it had been Harrison who handled the ground observers' reports of their progress. Harrison took Garis out to the flying field where Miller worked and introduced the two men.[20]

It was probably in later June 1920, that Garis, Harrison, and Miller met at a speakeasy on Wabasha Street in St. Paul and there they agreed to form an aero squadron. It is interesting to note in this triple paternity of the squadron, that two of the three had been Guardsmen earlier involved with the defunct Aviation Section of the Motor Corps. In a 1956 interview, Ray Miller gave this account of that historic meeting: "Garis offered me the command, but I refused because I believed Garis had the better knowledge of organization and command of such a unit. He proposed that I be commanding officer because as he said 'Hell, I don't know anything about flying.' I told him 'you don't need to know anything about flying. Just run the outfit.' So Garis accepted and turned around and said 'you are the senior captain.' Both turned to Harrison and said 'You're the writing son-of-a-bitch, so we'll make you the adjutant.' So that was the real beginning of the First Minnesota Aero Squadron, later to be known as the 109th Observation Squadron. So we all had a few more drinks on the idea."[21]

Ray Miller became the unit's first Commanding Officer, a post he held for twenty unbroken years, until the squadron went to England in World War II. He was born in Ohio in 1891 and, like many aviators of the time, had an early love of automobiles and motorcycles. In 1917 he learned to fly at the Curtiss school in Newport News, where he soloed after only three hours of dual instruction. He then enlisted, went through Army instruction, and was commissioned as lieutenant. He was still in training when the war ended and he was discharged. The Curtiss Aircraft Company was establishing schools and dealerships to sell airplanes throughout the nation, and Miller negotiated a job with that firm.

In St. Paul, businessman William Kidder had the dealership and an airport at Larpenteur and Snelling Avenues where he operated the Curtiss Northwest Company. In May, 1919, Miller had become chief pilot for Curtiss Northwest.[22]

The officers wasted no time. On 11 July 1920, it was reported that the First Minnesota Observation Squadron was being organized and would use Speedway Field where they planned to build hangars. On the 14th, a newspaper account said that Garis was ready to brief the squadron officers on the organizational plan and training courses, that a board had been created to examine recruits, and that training would begin at once. Eleven days later, the *Minneapolis Journal* reported there were posters around town calling for "courageous, red blooded Minnesota youths to join the First Minnesota Observation Squadron."[23]

The projected strength of the unit was 22 officers and 81 men, and by mid-September all but a handful had been recruited. The squadron was organized, training programs were underway, and the whole outfit was awash in eagerness. What they did not have were the airplanes and ancillary equipment the federal government would supply once the unit got its coveted official recognition. To hurry the recognition process, impress federal officials, and gain public exposure, Garis and Adjutant General Rhinow again settled on staging a spectacular flight. This time, however, the destination would not be Duluth, but Washington. On 22 September, Rhinow sent a telegram to the Chief of the Air Service. Said Rhinow, "MINNESOTA VERY DESIROUS FOR ALLOTMENT OBSERVATION SQUADRON ... I HAVE DIRECTED COLONEL GARIS THE SQUADRON COMMANDER AND CAPTAIN RAY MILLER ALSO OF THE SQUADRON TO TRANSPORT ME TO WASHINGTON BY AIRPLANE CURTISS ORIOLE FOR THE PURPOSE OF PRESENTING TO YOUR DEPARTMENT AND THE MILITIA BUREAU MINNESOTA CLAIM TO AN OBSERVATION SQUADRON EXPECT TO BE IN WASHINGTON TUESDAY."[24]

The flight was sure to draw major attention because, as Miller said, "trips through the air from such a distance as St. Paul to Washington were just not done."[25] Since the squadron had no aircraft, an Oriole was rented from Curtiss Northwest. It could carry two passengers in the forward cockpit, with the pilot in a separate cockpit behind. On the wood fuselage was painted the inscription "Minnesota Observation Squadron - Minn. Nat'l. Guard." The morning of 26 September, the three left from Curtiss Northwest airfield after remarks by Governor Burnquist and a rousing cheer from the audience. Numerous fuel stops were made and, because publicity was a main goal, the Minnesotans were happy to be the objects of attention by local dignitaries along the way. The route took them to Madison; Chicago; Miller's hometown of Van Wert, Ohio; Cleveland; Buffalo; Albany; Poughkeepsie, New York, and at last, Washington, D. C. on 2 October.

In Cleveland, a ground crewman cheerfully informed them that the last Oriole passing through had crashed and killed three people, and in upstate New York wind and rain forced delays. Indeed, at Poughkeepsie, Rhinow decided to go on to Washington by train while Miller and Garis waited out heavy rain. When Miller and Garis arrived, they found Rhinow already at work. For three days the Minnesota delegation presented their case for early federal recognition. The most important meetings were with General Jesse M. Carter, Chief of the Militia Bureau, and Generals Mason Patrick and William Mitchell, respectively the Director and Assistant Director of the Army Air Service. Miller later recalled that when he and Garis met Billy Mitchell, "he turned to me and snapped, 'Captain, where did you get those wings?' 'I earned mine at Love field, Sir,' I replied. That broke the ice and we told him all about our ideas. He was definitely interested and promised to do all he could."[26]

Rhinow, Garis, and Miller could not have been more successful in their efforts to lobby the Washington officers. They met with cordial receptions, expressions of interest, and promises of support. Garis summarized it well when he wrote, "Our object in flying to Washington was to impress upon the officials there the fact that we have organized in Minnesota an aero squadron: that equipment for this squadron is needed and that Minnesota is in the habit of going after what she wants in an up to date fashion... We were told that any organization which would fly 3,600 miles for such an object was entitled...to a unit."[27] With their business completed, the Guardsmen returned home. Rhinow took a train because he did not want to risk being delayed again by weather. Miller and Garis flew back along nearly the same route as they had followed east. In New York they picked up Bill Kidder who had been there on business, and he flew back to St. Paul with them.

They returned with the promise of federal recognition and equipment that would include 13 airplanes, necessary parts and tools, and the equipment for an aerial photography section. Garis was right when he said, "We had a dandy trip."[28] The fulfilling of Washington's promises, however, depended on the squadron passing an official inspection and arranging to build hangars to protect the aircraft. In the meantime, squadron headquarters had been established at the St. Paul Armory, classes in aeronautics and engineering were being held at the Curtiss Northwest field, and the photo section was training in the Minneapolis Armory.[29] In October, the squadron held its first encampment when they went to Elk River for an overnight camp-out. With an eye toward public relations, the camp was open to visitors on Sunday and invitations issued to "relatives and friends of squadron members to attend and see how the men are treated."[30]

By mid-November, Squadron Commander Garis was ready for inspection. The Air Service in Washington was informed that "The Adjutant General of Minnesota is extremely anxious that the Federal Inspection necessary before Government recognition be made as soon after December 15 as possible, in order that the organization can be recognized before the next session of the State Legislature." The bureaucratic horse was not to be spurred, however, and the Air Service Headquarters replied that "Inasmuch as this is the first request for definite recognition" of an Air Service unit of the National Guard, the request had been referred to a committee to decide what procedure to use.[31]

What the 109th Observation Squadron was all about in 1928. Large format aerial cameras helped the Guard map sections of northern Minnesota including an area near Little Falls that would become Camp Ripley. Jack Malone, pilot; Art Lund, photographer. (MANGHF)

By late December, Air Service Major Ira Rader, 7th Corps Air Officer, had been detailed to make the inspection. He did so on 17 January, 1921, which became the official date of recognition. He reported that the unit had made a very creditable showing and had only a couple minor discrepancies in personnel assignments. The background and ability of the officers and men were particularly praiseworthy and he judged Speedway Field adjacent to Fort Snelling as an excellent site for aircraft operations. There were, however, two items of concern. One was that the state had not provided hangars, but, Rader pointed out, a bill had been introduced in the legislature to remedy that. The plan was to construct three hangars, one of which would be supply and repair shops and the other two would house airplanes. The second concern was over Garis. According to regulations, aero squadron commanders had to be qualified pilots, and Garis was not. He could not, therefore, be assigned to command the squadron even though he was the most senior in rank, and had done a great deal of the organizational work. Ray Miller thus became the first commanding officer and Rader observed that he was "a former officer of the Air Service and capable in my opinion of commanding the squadron. However, he has not the administrative ability of Lt. Col. Garis."[32]

Minnesota's squadron was now official and the Air National Guard had been born. If the squadron intended to fly, however, it still had to do so in borrowed or rented aircraft. In the weeks after getting federal recognition, Guard members turned their attention to the state legislature. Senator William Brooks of Minneapolis, a staunch supporter of aviation, had introduced a bill appropriating $50,000 to build three hangars at Speedway Field. The Guardsmen had always been confident that the state would provide hangars, but they now began a campaign to both insure and expedite passage of the bill. Articles appeared in the press explaining the usefulness of aerial patrols and photography in times of forest fires while other stories pointed out that for a $50,000 State investment, the federal government would give over $500,000 in equipment to the State. In mid-April the squadron invited the members of the House Appropriations and Senate Finance Committees for a tour of the air field. Half a dozen aircraft had been scraped together, and the legislators were all given rides during their inspection of the field. The bill passed shortly thereafter.[33]

The rest of the squadron's first year was absorbed in the routine of training and the start of hangar construction in the summer. The training program consisted of courses in engineering, photography, and military matters. Squadron members attended one 90 minute session each week with 75 minutes devoted to instruction and 15 minutes to drill. In the summers, Saturday afternoon drills were held at the airfield. An active social program of parties and dances also quickly developed. Most officers and noncommissioned officers were Air Service veterans, and many of the enlisted men were students at the University of Minnesota and St. Thomas College who wanted to get practical experience with airplanes.[34]

The Air Guard had grown to seven squadrons across the nation by January 1923, and the 109th, like the rest, was occupied with weekly drills, summer encampments, ceremonial activities, flying, aircraft maintenance and always more training. They were still flying World War I Jennies, but Ray Miller was eager to get more modern machines. It was inevitable that fatal crashes would occur, and in December 1925, the squadron suffered its first when Lieutenant Edward Michaud of St. Paul, crashed. Only six weeks later, Lieutenant Russell Olson's Jenny went into an unrecoverable spin over the airport. Olson was killed and his observer, Lieutenant William Nolan, was badly injured.

It was too much for Miller, always protective of his people, and he publicly complained that "These machines are obsolete. We have repeatedly asked for better machines but without success. Lieutenant Olson was flying...the JNS-1 (JN-6) training plane. They were built in the war and are now antiquated. When the wooden framework deteriorated, they were rebuilt in Dayton...We have made no public complaint about the machines as they are as safe as old airplanes can be made. But the fact remains that they are obsolete."[41]

Not until 1927 did the unit begin getting replacement aircraft, Curtiss Falcons and Douglas O-2Hs. They were both two seat observation biplanes and

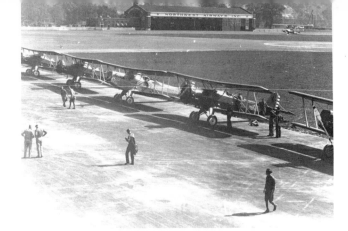

Flight line at Holman Field in 1931, following the Guard's move to St. Paul. Visible are O-38 and O-2H aircraft. In the background is the newly constructed Northwest maintenance hangar. (MANGHF)

represented no technological advance, but at least they were new. Miller's petitioning of the Militia Bureau may have helped get the new ships, for on one occasion he wrote that he had heard of a contract being let and said. "I suppose Minnesota, being the senior squadron, will have priority in the issue of this equipment. Have you any idea when we can expect it?" Washington replied that they were anxious that new aircraft be delivered, but that the original schedule had been "all shot to pieces" and that they did not know. Miller was assured, though, that the 109th was "right at the top of the priority list."[42]

It was not until August 1930, that the unit received aircraft that were modern for the time. The Douglas 0-38 was still of the two seat open cockpit biplane configuration but it had a 525 h.p. Pratt & Whitney aircooled radial engine that was a marked improvement in power, weight and reliability. The 0-38 would be the workhorse for the squadron until 1938. In fact, 1930 was a year of major changes for the unit. Not only did the new airplanes begin to arrive, but the base of operations was moved from Wold-Chamberlain Field to the St. Paul Municipal Airport.

The squadron had outgrown their original quarters and St. Paul had just made major improvements involving runway paving and lengthening, and new hangars. As Miller explained "Since our state-owned buildings were wooden and inadequate in size, and not fire-proof, we initiated a competition between the two cities with the idea that the city that came

Lieutenant Joseph Quigley, the Guard's master photographer, and Captain Joe Westover, pilot, pose beside an O-2H aircraft at Wold-Chamberlain Field in 1928. (MANGHF)

1933 photo shows less than graceful lines of the O-38B Guard aircraft, flown here by Captain William Canby, with Corporal L. Ekloff, observer. Photo taken over Brainerd during summer camp exercises from Camp Ripley. (MANGHF)

O-38 aircraft and flight crews standing tall for inspection at Camp Ripley in 1932. (Gerald Sandvick)

Douglas O-47 observation aircraft over Camp Ripley, 1939. The O-47 became the last generation observation aircraft operated by the 109th Squadron prior to World War II. (MANGHF)

through with the best proposition would inherit the home station of the squadron.[43] The Guard started their tenure in St. Paul by holding a dance in the new hangar, complete with "near Beer," since July, 1930 was still prohibition time.

The site of the annual summer encampments was also going to change. Usually held at the squadron's base in Minneapolis, more space was needed for flying, and plans were made to move to the National Guard's new training base at Camp Ripley which was then being improved. The first actual use of the new central Minnesota camp was in 1932.

By 1931 the Air National Guard was well enough established that it participated in Army Air Corps maneuvers for the first time. It was a major training operation involving 672 aircraft and 1400 officers and men. The Secretary of War had directed a major effort to acquaint the American people with the Army's air capability. To put that many personnel and machines together, however, the Air Corps "committed all, save one of the squadrons stationed in the United States, the instructors, students and planes of the Advanced Flying School, flights from 19 National Guard squadrons, and every transport plane it could lay its hands on."[44] Minnesota's squadron was ordered to participate and Ray Miller selected six officers to fly their 0-38s with him to Dayton, Ohio. In recognition of his seniority, Air Corps headquarters designated Miller as a group commander for the exercises. A local press account proudly explained that "He is the oldest in point of service of all National Guard aero squadron commanders," and that "The 109th has a rich record of experience."[45] The group also received an award of Excellence from the commander of the Air Corps, General Benjamin D. Foulois.

Hangar construction took several months and the buildings were finished in November. Some feeling for the bucolic setting of the early airport may be gotten from the *St. Paul Daily News.* When that newspaper published the first aerial photo of the completed hangars, the caption read, "An idea of the enormous size of the hangars may be gained upon close inspection of the picture by comparison with the cattle grazing near the buildings."[35] It was also in the autumn, 1921, when the Militia Bureau changed the unit's designation to the 109th Observation Squadron.

The officers of the 109th were exceptionally adept at publicity in the formative months. In early 1921 a Massachusetts Guard officer visited the squadron

and wrote that "Every opportunity is grasped to place the name of the organization before the public. For instance, at the recent Inaugural Reception, the Governor's Guard of Honor was made up of the officers of this organization, and every possible publicity was given to this fact in the Twin City newspapers. The adjutant...is the publicity man...and is also a reporter. Colonel Garis travels all over the state speaking to various organizations in order to arouse interest...The object of all this, of course, is to make the people of the state feel that this organization is of actual worth to the state."[36]

It should not be thought that the 109th was only concerned with public relations. Three times in the first full calendar year of operation the squadron was called to undertake missions that would demonstrate its actual worth to the state. The January 1922 search for James Maher was discussed earlier. The squadron still did not have its own airplanes so the Oriole that Miller and Westover flew was rented from Curtiss Northwest. Adjutant General's records show that the company was paid $1,250.00 for use of the airplane.[37] The Air Service was, however, in the process of delivering the long promised squadron equipment and by the spring, the unit proudly owned nine Curtiss JN-6H "Jennies."

The first flight with the squadron's own aircraft was on 9 April when Ray Miller took one of the Jennies on a test hop over the airfield.[38]

In July and August the squadron had an excellent opportunity to show the practical contributions it could make and, at the same time, make itself better known in all corners of the state. The U. S. Department of Agriculture and the University of Minnesota

A closeup of the aviation hangar at the National Guard's new summer training grounds at Camp Ripley, near Little Falls, Minnesota, 1941. (MANGHF)

Ouch! One of the 109th Douglas O-47 observation planes has made a beautiful landing at Wold Chamberlain in 1939, the only problem...the pilot forgot to extend the landing gear. Plane sustained minimal damage and was repaired...not so, the pilot's ego. (Vern Georgia)

An annual visitor to Camp Ripley. Charles Lindbergh, is seen here in 1939 with Major Ray Miller, at left, and Captain John Hinkens, at right. Lindbergh stopped each summer at the Camp when vacationing at his family home in Little Falls, landing at the military field in whatever aircraft he happened to be flying at the time. (Gerald Sandvick)

were involved in research to eradicate barberry. This shrub served as a host plant to wheat rust spores, a major problem in all wheat growing areas. Data was needed on where and how the tiny spores spread by means of air currents. The 109th was asked to cooperate and eagerly did so. For several weeks, two squadron Jennies flown by Miller and Lt. Trevor Williams sampled air currents. With them were Lt. Joe Westover and E. H. Ostrom, an agricultural agent. Glass plates were lightly coated with vaseline and exposed to the air at various altitudes. The plates were then sent to the University where spores that had been trapped could be examined. Not only was useful agricultural information obtained, but twenty towns throughout the state were visited. The squadron received prominent mention in papers such as the *Huchinson Leader* and *Olivia Times* as well as in Duluth and Twin Cities papers.[39]

Only a few days after the research flights were finished, several dangerous forest fires broke out. They were widely scattered through forests and peat bogs in St. Louis, Cass, Hubbard, and Aitken Counties. In this crisis air surveillance could be an obvious help. State Forester William T. Cox had established a headquarters in Duluth, and Miller assigned three aircraft and necessary support personnel. The fire area was divided into three sectors and a Jenny assigned to patrol each.

The pilots called to duty were Miller and

Aerial view of the new Camp Ripley at Little Falls, 1939. Note the ramps from the hangar at top of picture are under construction. Troops from National Guard and Air Guard were quartered in the field tents in the middle ground. 1932 marked the first summer encampment at the new facility. (Sherm Booen)

Lieutenants Trevor Williams and Ralph Jerome; each carried a forester as an observer. The foresters notes were attached to ribbon streamers and dropped to firefighters and settlers below. Cox later said, "An aero patrol squadron is invaluable for spotting fires. With airplanes in use, we have been enabled to obtain a birds-eye view of the situation and afford a closer planning of the fire fighting work." The squadron spent sixty one days on fire patrol. It was hazardous flying not only because of fire conditions but because any forced landing would have been in rough wooded terrain. Flying daily, each aircraft covered an average of 300 miles a day without a single forced landing which indicates a high level of competence possessed by the mechanics as well as the 109th pilots.[40]

The maneuvers were successful and the local men seem to have done well but there was a bit of public carping around the nation. Pacifist sentiment resulting from World War I was still strong, and 1931 was a depression year. There were complaints about the bellicose nature of the exercise, while others fretted over the cost to the taxpayers.[46]

That the 109th received good press about its participation was not unusual. From its creation, the unit had enjoyed a favorable public image due to the mystique of airplanes and aviators. This was enhanced by Ray Miller's willingness to keep his unit in the public eye and no celebration was too small for the 109th to show their flag. In 1931, for example, they helped celebrate the Payne Avenue Businessmens Association Festival and the arrival in St. Paul of the first coal barge of the season. In 1932, Miller went to Bemidji for two days in connection with a display at an American Legion Convention.[47]

Requests for squadron participation were sometimes turned down, though, and one refusal casts light on some of the problems a National Guard squadron faces in the years of lean budgets and scarce equipment. In July, 1938, Duluth was hosting a Northwest Territory 100th anniversary and Managing Editor Doug Fairbanks of the *Duluth Herald & News Tribune* wrote to ask if "maybe you could have your unit fly up here to participate." Miller's reply is enlightening. "A National Guard Squadron, such as this organization, is extremely short of airplanes. We

The Minnesota squadron had been activated in 1941 and its members sent overseas. When this picture was taken in the summer of 1943, at Ibsley, Southern England, the group was flying Spitfire, Mark V's, filling in as scramble-alert squadron for an RAF unit moved to a different station. (MANGHF)

Gosselies, Belgium, 1944. P-5l's flown by the 109th Tactical Reconnaisance Squadron, now part of the 67th Tactical Recon Group, were flying missions over the invasion area of Normandy, photographing the coastline, railroad marshalling yards, and highways. (MANGHF)

recently loaned three airplanes to the Cleveland, Ohio unit. The same three go to Nashville, Tennessee upon completion of the Cleveland camp. Thursday of this week we loaned two airplanes to Chicago, which leaves us a total to two airplanes. Wednesday, Thursday, and Friday of this week, one of our airplanes will be used on duty at Ripley in cooperation with an artillery regiment from Iowa, which leaves the balance of one airplane, and at the present time that ship is minus an engine. Now Doug, this is not a sob story, it is our condition at present.[48]

The life of the squadron was not entirely serious, and at one point they asked for and received special permission from the State Director of Fish and Game to remove birds from the airfield that had become "destructive and dangerous to life and property." That the birds in question were ringneck pheasants may account for the squadron's eagerness to act.

The job of squadron commander sometimes the bizarre as well as serious as was illustrated in a letter from a state senator from St. Cloud to Ray Miller. "On March 19, 1932...an airplane passed over the farm of the Loidolt brothers...in Benton County, flying at low altitude and scared a team of horses...hitched to a manure spreader, causing the team to run away...the team ran over and killed a valuable holstein cow and also badly damaged the manure spreader. The plane...was open biplane orange colored. I am informed that the airplane of the 109th squadron landed at Little Falls and was in charge of Lt. H. S. Paul. It is probable that this was the plane...the Loidolt brothers will make claim for the cow killed as well as damage to the manure spreader. I would like to have any information you may have so that the identity of the plane may be established." Miller replied that Lt. Paul had, indeed, gone to Camp Ripley near Little Falls on that date but that he flew at 2000 feet going up and 6000 feet returning. "It would be improbable that a ship flying at that altitude would frighten livestock. And judging from your description of the ship you must be mistaken in the identity."[49]

Through the 1930s the Air Guard trained at Camp Ripley each summer. By 1935 the squadron counted 22 officers and 97 enlisted men and in that same year, enjoyed a camp visit by Charles Lindbergh, whose boyhood home was near Little Falls. That year also brought a modified version of the 0-38 to the

squadron. It had a more powerful engine and, what must have been a Godsend in the winter, a plexiglass cockpit enclosure. The 0-38s were retired in 1938 and replaced with North American 0-47s. These had a 975 h.p. radial engine and were all-metal monoplanes with retractable landing gear. The same year saw the 109th once more pressed into forest fire spotting service, when major fires developed in the International Falls-Ft. Francis area.[50]

By 1940, Europe was again at war and in the United States a general call up of reserve forces came during the winter and spring, 1940-41. The 109th got its mobilization orders on 17 January, 1941, along with the rest of Minnesota's National Guard and the orders took effect on 10 February. By now squadron strength was 28 officers and 143 enlisted and they were ordered to report to Camp Beauregard, Louisiana.

In an attempt to build up a more concentrated air arm quickly, the War Department had decided that most Air Guard units would not remain organic parts of their own state's ground divisions. Most were sent to completely different camps which is what happened with the 109th. The effect was that the air units quickly lost their traditional state identification. This loss of state identification was reinforced for the Minnesota squadron by two changes of command within eight months. On 2 November 1941, Ray Miller was

Gosselies. The war is almost over for the 109th. This photo taken during the Battle of the Bulge in 1945. (MANGHF)

ordered to duty at Wright Field in Ohio, and command passed to Captain Gilman Holien. Holien was from St. Paul and had joined the unit as a private and advanced through the ranks. He died of pneumonia on 12 July, 1942. The new commander was Albert R. Defehr, a 1st Lieutenant who had learned to fly at Kelly Field, Texas, and had been assigned to the 109th in June 1941. With wartime transfers in and out added to all this, the squadron soon lost its Minnesota connection.[51]

Until August 1942 the unit trained and participated in maneuvers in Louisiana, Texas, and North Carolina. The ground echelon was then sent to New York where they departed on the *Queen Elizabeth* for Scotland, arriving at their permanent base at Membury, Berkshire, on 7 September. The air personnel arrived about a month later. In November the squadron was disbanded and personnel assigned to other units, but it was reestablished in May 1943. It had been the 109th Observation Squadron since 1921, but 1943 saw "Observation Squadron" changed to "Reconnaissance Squadron (Fighter)" and later in the year to the 109th Tactical Reconnaissance Squadron. During the war the unit flew Spitfires and then P-51 Mustangs on photo reconnaissance missions, first out of England and, after 8 July, 1944, from France and Belgium.

While the unit had a distinguished combat record during the war, the many changes necessitated by fighting it caused the 109th to be Minnesota's Air Guard unit in name only. Ray Miller was not reunited with the squadron that he created until after the war and he never did get overseas. On VJ Day he was a Lieutenant Colonel and the commander of an airbase at Rome, New York.

NRAB (NAVAL RESERVE AIR BASE) MINNEAPOLIS

In discussing the formation of the Navy/Marine reserve squadron at Wold-Chamberlain Field in Minneapolis, it is helpful to understand the background of all Naval flying.

Naval air service was launched in 1911 with the Navy's purchase of a two-seat hydroaeroplane from Glenn Curtiss in New York. Curtiss, himself, taught the first few naval aviators to fly in this plane, christened the Triad. By 1915, the Navy had begun forming local Naval militias across the United States, and advocated an aeronautical corps as a part of each. The next year, Congress passed the Naval Appropriations Act which established both a Naval Flying Corps and a Naval Reserve Flying Corps (NRFC). Glenn Curtiss offered the Navy reduced prices on flying boats and free flight training to one man per local unit.

These Militia units were very small, and ten state-

Three TS-1 fighters on the ramp at the new U. S. Naval Reserve Air Base at Wold-Chamberlain, 1929. Note the original hangar "A" in the background, and visible behind it is one of the Air Guard hangars which would soon become navy property. (Joe Hosek)

run units then in existence comprised only forty-eight officers and ninety-six enlisted men. An additional twelve Marine officers and twenty-four men filled out a companion service. The total Naval air fleet consisted of six aircraft.

Stimulated by fighting on the Mexican-American border, college men in some states began forming their own naval militia units, the first of which was known as the *Yale Group*, formed at Yale University in New York. It was led by F. Trubee Davison, a gung-ho young man who used his family influence to borrow an airplane and instructor from New York department store magnate, Rodman Wanamaker. In this plane the group was to learn how to fly. The Yale Group as a whole enlisted in the Naval Reserve in 1917. When America entered the war, the Group was assigned to anti-sub patrol along the New England coast. Davison went on to become 1st Assistant Secretary of War under Herbert Hoover in 1926.

Before 1917 ended, the Navy had established aviation training bases at Anacostia, in Washington, D. C.; Squantum, near Boston; and Fort Hamilton, New York, as well as at Pensacola, Florida.

By the end of the war in 1918, there had been a great expansion of the Naval Flying Corps and it numbered over 37,000 men of which over 30,000 were reservists. Then the doldrums set in.

In 1922, with demobilization and a return to pre-war isolationism, the force was drastically cut as was the funding from Congress. By 1923, Naval aviation was almost dead in the water. Heroic efforts by Rear Admiral William A. Moffett, championing the cause for a large ready force of naval aviators and sailors, held the line, but Congress vacillated over the need.

Closeup of a TS-1 with the Minnesota Gopher naval insignia on its side. The plane is being demonstrated at St. Paul Municipal Airport in 1929. Note the peculiar configuration of the lower wing as it attaches to the aircraft's fuselage. (Elmer Tivetny via Jerry Kurth)

The Navy "A" hangar in 1929. A wing has been added on the east side to the original configuration. The hangar underwent many modifications during it's lifetime. (Roland Sorensen)

Curious spectators examine a navy Curtiss N2C-1 Fledgeling from NRAB, Minneapolis which has suffered a forced landing at Northfield, Minnesota. The wingtip was damaged when it broke through a fence surrounding a ballpark. (Roland Sorensen)

Most reservists either joined the regular Naval Air Service, or dropped out altogether.

Anacostia and Squantum became the Reserve bases with Great Lakes, in Illinois, being added in 1923. Sand Point, in Seattle, opened in 1925. Still there was little funding. Congress finally adopted a five-year building program in 1926 which included a plan for training the Reserves. In the spring of 1928, four more Reserve bases opened, among them, Naval Reserve Air Base (NRAB), Minneapolis, at Wold-Chamberlain Field.[52]

The first naval aviation activity in Minnesota began with the formation of Naval Militias in the 1915 period. An item appearing in *Aerial Age Weekly Magazine* of 5 April, 1915, reported that Minneapolis had established a militia unit and its commander, Guy A. Eaton, was urging the formation of a similar group in Duluth, saying that he had already signed two officers and six men for the unit. They were to be sent to Pensacola for their flight training and would then return to Duluth.[53]

With the great wartime expansion, there arose a need for naval aviation technicians and mechanics. Dunwoody Institute in Minneapolis began a training course in March of 1918 with the prospects of training two thousand men per month. Lt. Colby Dodge was the commanding officer there. Pilot, Art Helm, was a member of the original group of cadets that took their training at Dunwoody. Years later, Art would remember the school and some of the events that occurred:

"I'd had a fight with my roommate and he'd thrown a bottle at me and cut my eye, so I was in sick bay for a while. Dodge was there also and had just been given some medication for a toothache and went to his room to nip on a bottle of whiskey along with the medication. He went out of his mind and cut himself all up with a safety razor. He called down to me and told me, 'Helm, get up here'. I got there and he was half naked and covered with fine cuts from his razor. He told me 'they came in the window and attacked me and I'm bleeding to death'. I gave him my Colt pistol to protect himself, but I'd secretly removed the bullets before I handed it over. That settled him down."[54]

Helm and three of his fellow sailors went together and bought a Curtiss MF flying boat and wished to keep it based at Lake Calhoun. Knowing that Park Commissioner, Theodore Wirth, took a dim view of flying activity on city lakes, they sought to butter him up by sending him a box of cigars, a box of candy, and a bouquet of flowers, along with their request to base the plane there. Wirth, acknowledging their gifts, never-the-less, held the line, and returned a letter stating that he "didn't smoke, had not a sweet tooth and was prone to hay fever...and no, they couldn't base their airplane at the lake."[55]

Despite the doldrums after the war, things did not totally die for naval aviation in Minneapolis. Naval Reservists began meeting at the old armory at 3009 Calhoun Boulevard, near Lake Calhoun in the city. At the Armory, they did their drilling and were taught ground school by instructors from the University of Minnesota. Training fell into three categories;

NRAB Minneapolis, 1936. FF-2's are on the line. The Navy took over the Air Guard hangars in 1930. (Jim LaVake)

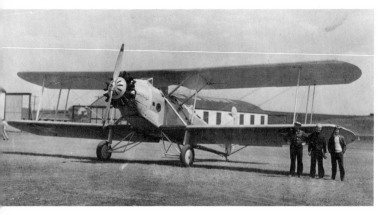

Martin T-4M torpedo bomber. Only a single aircraft of this type was stationed with the squadron from 1932 to 1935. (Joe Hosek)

Helldivers in flight over the Twin Cities, circa middle 1930s. Helldiver colors were silver with chrome yellow wings, red band around fuselage, and lemon cowls. The exception is the squadron commander's aircraft in the foreground with a red cowling. (Niels Sorensen)

a mechanics school for enlisted men under the direction of Ensign G. W. Fox; a student pilot's school under Ensign E. W. Morrill; and an officer's school under Ensign Earle D. McKay. For the flyers, the curriculum was eighty-five hours of ground school instruction in some ten subjects. In 1925, thirty-five students were given exams to select flight training candidates. Following their local courses, they were sent to Great Lakes, Illinois, for flight training.

The Calhoun unit ran a tight ship and managed to rank 2nd out of twenty-nine units in the country during spring inspections in 1928. Partially because of their good showing, the Navy Department designated Minneapolis as the location of a new Naval Reserve Training Base that same year.

With the establishment of a training squadron at Wold-Chamberlain, construction of an 80 by 90' hangar was undertaken. The unit moved from the Calhoun Armory on 4 June, 1928, and Lt. Frank E. Weld took command of the station and its newly designated squadron, VN-11RD9 from Earle McKay. The Minneapolis squadron was one of only ten reserve squadrons in the country, the only one not based on a body of water or on the coast. Sixteen pursuit planes were to be assigned.[56]

The new quarters were leased from the Park Board for $1.00 per year. Funding was scarce. Members of the unit drilled in civilian clothes, and often bought

NARB, Minneapolis, 1933. This picture shows the original "A" hangar with the three former Air Guard hangars to the east, and the original airmail hangar after it was moved from the middle of the airfield. The airmail hangar had an illustrious career and is in 1993 at Northport Airport near White Bear Lake. The road which runs behind the hangars is the remnant of the racetrack built in 1915 and removed in 1930. Curtiss Helldivers are parked on the ramp. (Roland Sorensen)

their own uniforms. Contributions by Twin Cities businessmen, including George Dayton, L. H. Piper, and Rufus Rand, were largely responsible for the $15,000 raised to build the hangar.

Lt. Frank Weld, a native of Minneapolis, had been with the squadron in its early days. He enlisted in the Navy in 1918, and was commissioned in 1919. One of the cadet commanders at the Calhoun Armory in the 1920-1922 period, Weld was transferred to Great Lakes, Illinois, where he became an inspector. His return to take over NRAB, Minneapolis in 1928, brought the group through its formative flying years. In June of 1931, he was succeeded by Lt. Matthew Crawford, another of the old Naval Militia members, and he, in turn, was followed by another early member, Lt. K. B. Salisbury of the mattress manufacturing family.

Drills were held one night a week and one Saturday and Sunday a month in hangar "A." (Hangar "A" was the original, and at that time, the only hangar belonging to the Navy). A large hot air furnace was located in the middle of the hangar and two Consolidated training planes were tailed into the hangar, one on each side. During drill periods in the next year, the members of the unit assisted in building wings onto both sides of the hangar for additional room. In 1931, the Navy assumed control of the three Air Guard hangars, located adjacent to Hangar "A." The Guard had abandoned them when they moved to the St. Paul Airport.

In June of 1931, the unit attained an efficiency score of 93.5, the highest mark of any of the existing twelve Reserve bases. At that time, there were nineteen flight officers and fifty-two enlisted men at NRAB, Minneapolis.

In 1932, the unit was the first in the country to complete major aircraft overhauls, while still operating on a shoestring Depression budget. Summer camps were spent at Camp Ripley at Little Falls, Minnesota, the Navy alternating with the Air Guard and Army in using the Ripley facilities. The unit's aircraft complement during the 1928 to 1941 period can be seen in the chart accompanying this chapter.

VN-11RD9 was awarded the Noel Davis Trophy in 1933 and in 1935 for being the most efficient squadron in the navy's Reserve fold, bringing more honor to the group. Up to this time, the Reserve had conducted no

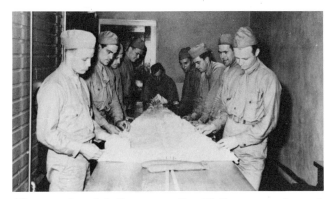

The parachute loft. Instructor, Ray Wellumson, at far end, instructs the cadets in proper parachute packing. (Roland Sorensen)

AVCAD class learning Morse Code, essential in this time period for navigation and communication. (Roland Sorensen)

flight training at Wold, merely proficiency flying and mission practise.

The Reserve became involved in the AVCAD program. (AVCAD, or sometimes NAVCAD stood for Naval Aviation Cadet.) The program's professed mission was to build a ready reserve of trained pilots capable of being immediately activated as full-fledged naval aviators in event of national emergency. It was to be a temporary establishment, expected to create officers until such time that the regular Navy could train enough full-time airmen. As one might expect, a product of the Depression, it was underfunded. War was not on the immediate horizon and the entire naval aviation section included only six hundred thirty-one officer aviators at that time.

AVCAD was an elimination program, offering a 30-day ground school and solo flight training course to college graduates. Having soloed and passed successfully, a year's training would be given each cadet at Pensacola, after which the cadet would spend three years with the fleet as an AVCAD, then be commissioned. Some AVCADs had enlisted as Marines. They would be carried on the roster as PFC's through their stay at Minneapolis, the Navy cadets carried as Seamen 2nd Class. A washout from the elimination program left the candidate free as a civilian, or eligible to join another service. During the Reserve's annual summer encampment at Fort Ripley, AVCADs also attended, undergoing their continuing training without a two week break in their schedule.

The Navy's hope was that the new officers would return to their home bases and remain in the reserves. The AVCAD Program was to produce five hundred officers nationwide in that first year. Minneapolis was one of the country's prime locations in this elimination program.

By 1938, with war now a definite possibility, it was evident that even the AVCAD program, as it was, would be unable to provide an adequate pool of naval aviators. A strong voice in Congress kept things moving ahead for the Navy. That voice belonged to Minnesota Congressman, Melvin J. Maas.

Maas was a driving force in the U. S. Congress. He spoke his mind, battling for military appropriations in this crucial pre-war period. He became a prominent member of the House Naval Affairs Committee in 1935 and introduced a Bill in Congress in 1936 that eventually became the Naval Reserve Act of 1938. It provided for Reserve expansion and proved expeditious. In 1939, he introduced another bill that

would take Private and Commercial pilots, have them trained in the reserves and sent to squadrons as full-fledged naval aviators. The idea did not get support, especially from the Navy, who believed only they could train their service pilots properly.

The 1939 Naval Reserve Act changed the AVCAD program to provide for the cadets being commissioned as Ensigns immediately after their year at Pensacola, eliminating the three-year trainee period with the fleet.

The Naval Reserve squadron was called to active duty at the station on 6 October, 1940, but there was still only mediocre support from congress. Not until the bombs fell at Pearl Harbor did mobilization on a large scale begin. On 7 December, 1941, the Reserve at NRAB, Minneapolis, totaled seventeen officers and one hundred twenty-two men in training. One year later, that number would grow to four hundred thirty-six as the station's mission was changed to that of Primary Training Base.

During the wartime period, the Navy Reserve Primary Training Squadron, home-based at Wold-Chamberlain Field, was split into two sections, for best use of local airspace. NRAB Training Squadron 1A was stationed at Wold, while NRAB Training Squadron 1B was based at South St. Paul Airport (later known as Fleming Field). Primary flight trainees would be bussed from their quarters at Wold-Chamberlain to South St. Paul. The map associated with this chapter is from a hand-drawn handout issued to all newly assigned squadron cadets.

Each base had its designated flying area. On the

A quick dice game develops between classwork for the sailors and marines at NRAB, Minneapolis. Base ambulance is parked in the background. (Joe Hosek)

Lt. Col. Patrick Mulcahy addressing the Marine squadron in the Reserve hangar at Wold. Major Mel Maas stands at left. (Vernon A. Peterson family)

Minneapolis side, those pilots flying from Wold were assigned area "A," those from St. Paul, area "B." The two areas were separated by an imaginery line running due north out of the Gopher Ordnance Works between Rosemount and Farmington.

In the "A" area, training flights were made in one of two circuits from Wold. The first being westward after takeoff into a major stunt practise area roughly above Eden Prairie. It included practise landings at Field A6 (later to be known as Flying Cloud Field), then back east along the Minnesota River to Wold-Chamberlain. Additional landings could be made at Cedar Airport (A1) just before reaching Wold. Note that in this circuit, all landing and practice patterns were made to the left. Pattern altitudes around the

Hand-drawn map handed to each cadet as a guide to the two practise flight areas. Note the stunt areas over Eden Prairie and Newport. (Niels Sorensen)

practice fields were five hundred feet. The field at A6 consisted of a sod strip running north and south, roughly where the paved north-south runway is today.

The second circuit out of Wold was a departure straight south, making a loop to the west, and turning north over Prior Lake to the Minnesota River and thence back to Wold. Along the way, landings could be shot at several unnamed fields identified with the designations, A2, A3 (later known as Southport, or sometimes "Paris Field"), A4 near Cleary's Lake, and A5 south of Shakopee. Note the pylon turn points south of the river. On this circuit, all landing and practice patterns were right-handed.

From South St. Paul, there were also two circuits. One departed straight east, through a stunt practice area, then looping south around the city of Hastings. It then followed the Mississippi River back north to the South St. Paul Airport. Along the way, landings could be practiced at designated fields, B1, B2, and B5, with pylon turn points as indicated. On this circuit, all patterns were right-handed.

The second circuit from South St. Paul dropped due south to a point west of the river, looped around practice fields B3, B6, B7, and B4, then returned to base via the river route. Patterns were all left-handed.

All pilots from either station were cautioned to avoid the Gopher Ordnance plant and it was noted that no training flights were to take place over the Twin Cities. Airspace to the north of the cities was relegated to civilian flight operations and the CPT/WTS training programs.

South St. Paul Airport was originally used by the *Hook-Em-Cow Flying Club*, run by Alex Rozawick in 1939. It was then purchased by A. C. McInnis as a CPT base in 1940 before being taken over by the Navy

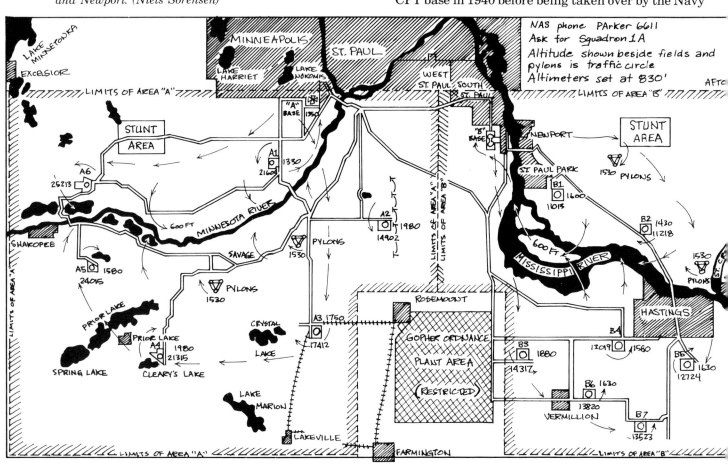

Closeup of the Marine and Navy emblems on the side panels of a Helldiver. The two were later combined into a shield symbolizing common usage of the aircraft by both services. (John V. Kipp)

Curtiss SBC-4 dive bomber seated its crew in closed cockpit comfort, enjoyed when the temperatures were cold. Note the combined Navy-Marine insignia on the cowling ahead of the retractable landing gear. SBC-4's were assigned NRAB, Minneapolis during 1939 and 1940. (Roland Sorensen)

in 1942. The Navy built several wooden-hoop raftered hangars and other buildings, including a simple platform control tower. They paved a large apron in front of the hangars to make space for the one hundred training planes based there and created two fifteen hundred foot diameter soil-cement circles on the airfield. From these circles, landings and takeoffs could be made into the wind, no matter from which direction it was blowing. The circles and the hoop-roofed hangars are still there today, with the soil-cement circles providing flooring for newly constructed private hangars.

Of all the wartime Navy practice fields, only Southport and Flying Cloud survived into the postwar period, with Southport closing in 1975.

Construction of additional navy facilities at Minneapolis got heavily under way in 1941, with a new hangar and administration building being built. A two hundred-bed student barracks was started, with galley and mess hall included. Construction of shops, a steam plant and other facilities had also begun. The total spent on new construction by the first of 1942 was over $950,000. More money was allocated in 1942, with five additional barracks, a classroom building, officers quarters, and before the year was over, a second classroom building being constructed.

Simultaneously with the work at Wold-Chamberlain, 1942 saw work begin on preparing the outlying fields for practice landings and other student work. By May, 1943, the Navy was using South St. Paul Airport. At Southport Airport in Apple Valley, and Flying Cloud Airport in Eden Prairie, runway paving was undertaken and operations buildings erected.

In 1943, with the war deepening, additional construction was started in Minneapolis on a Link trainer building, a guard house, photo lab, engine test stand, a one hundred twenty bed dispensary and storage sheds. A three hundred foot long drill hall was opened in the fall, and adjacent to it, another large building was erected to house an olympic-sized swimming pool measuring 164' x 75'. A cold storage building was next, followed by a barracks to accommodate some 225 Waves (women trainees) now assigned to the base. Even more building followed in the fall of 1943, with additional housing, hangars, and facilities.

In February of 1944, the Navy Department finish-ed construction of a giant research hangar that would become known as the Ice Research Hangar. In cooperation with the Army Air Corps, it would be instrumental in housing the research on precipitation and the development of de-icing equipment.

In January of 1943, the official name of the base changed to Naval Air Station (NAS), Minneapolis.

By May, 1944, cadet strength at any given time at NAS, Minneapolis, was 3580 in training. In May, total flying hours reached 27,500, with a record 1479.5 occurring on 16 May.[57]

One of the more illustrious naval cadets to take Primary at NRAB, Minneapolis, was George Bush. The man who later became President of the United States, came to Minneapolis on a very cold 5th of November, 1942. He flew his first few flights in NP-1 Spartans, before making his first solo with a total time of 11.3 hours in his logbook. Instructor, J. A. Boyle, made these comments in Bush's records:

"Satisfactory check. Taxied a little fast. Landings were average to above with the exception of one almost ground loop. Safe for solo." By the time Bush departed Minnesota on 19 February, 1943, he had accumulated 82.5 hours during sixty-one flights, of which 24.7 hours were solo time. He shipped out to Corpus Christie, Texas for his Advanced training.[58]

NAS, Minneapolis' mission changed over the years. From 1935 until July 1942, the base had been designated an "E" base, that is, authorized to conduct elimination training. From July, 1942 until October 1944, the base conducted Primary Flight Training

Grumman J2F-3 Duck flying over Minneapolis lakes during the pre-war years. Only one Duck was assigned, but was popular for flights into northern Minnesota. (Roland Sorensen)

An overall view of the building boom occurring during the war. Note that the city of Richfield has expanded virtually right to the front gate of the base. (Deno Sotos)

A view of the crowded ramp at South St. Paul. N2S primary training aircraft await the cadets in this 1943 view. Hangars in the background are used by Wipaire, Inc. (Roland Sorensen)

under the V-5 program, and in 1944 its mission was changed to that of a technical training center under the Naval Air Technical Training Command. Its job would be to train patrol service units in line maintenance of PB4Y Privateer aircraft. Accordingly, the beautiful N2S Stearman trainers and N3N's, (the "Yellow Perils"), were shipped out as the Privateers arrived. During the preceeding Primary Training period just ended, 4232 cadets had been trained.

Station Commanders for the period 1928 through 1945 were as follows:

Lt. Frank E. Weld, USNR	Nov 1928-Jun 1931
Lt. Matthew D. Crawford, USNR	Jun 1931-Nov 1931
Lt. Kenneth B. Salisbury, USNR	Nov 1931-May 1935
Lt. I.D. Wiltsie, USN	May 1935-Jun 1937
Lt. H.A. Hopping, USN	Jun 1937-May 1938
Lt. C.S. Smiley, USN	May 1938-May 1940
Lt. Kenneth B. Salisbury, USNR	May 1940-Aug 1940
LCdr. H.C. Doan, USN	Aug 1940-Jun 1942
LCdr. D.M. Campbell, USNR	Jun 1942-Dec 1943
Cdr. W.C. Grover, USNR	Dec 1943-Jan 1944
Cdr. K.M. Krieger, USNR	Jan 1944-Jul 1945
Capt. Wm. B. Whaley, USN	Jul 1945-Jul 1947

On 15 March, 1931, the Marines came to town. A Marine Training Detachment with Marine Air Reserve Squadron was assigned to NRAB, Minneapolis. The squadron was designated VO-7MR, an observation squadron. In command of the Detachment was 2nd Lt. Warren Sweetser, Jr., USMCR. He was relieved in 1932 by 1st Lt. Charles Schlapkohl, who

South St. Paul Airport, 1941. This postcard shows the two large soil-cement circles used for any-direction takeoffs and landings. (Marv Topness via Minnesota Flyer Magazine)

had been designated Inspector-Instructor, but took over command and remained commander until 1940.

In 1935, VO-7MR was redesignated VO-6MR, and in 1936, its mission changed from Observation to Scouting, becoming Squadron VMS-6R.

On 16 December, 1940, the Squadron's eight officers and thirty-two enlisted men were mobilized and assigned to San Diego, where they were absorbed into Marine line units. A few of them were serving at Pearl Harbor when the bombs fell in December of 1941. Others from the detachment remained at Wold-Chamberlain until 28 October, 1944, when the unit was deactivated. (It would be reactivated following the war.) The Detachment command passed from Schlapkohl to Captain Avery Kier in 1940, and to Major John V. Kipp, former local barnstormer, who commanded from 1941 through 1944.

The Reserve Squadron, itself, was commanded by Lt. Col. Melvin J. Maas, USMCR., from 1931 until 1940.

Maas was born in Duluth and his family brought him to St. Paul at an early age. He graduated from St. Paul Central High School and entered St. Thomas College. In 1917, he enlisted in the Marine Corps Aero Company and served in the Azores at the end of the war. In 1926, he ran for U. S. Congress, representing Minnesota, and was elected. Remaining in the Marine Reserves, he was nicknamed "Minnesota's Flying Congressman."

In 1931, Maas was assigned as commanding officer of the Marine Air Reserve Squadron at Wold Chamberlain. He continued in Congress until 1932, when he lost his seat. He was reelected again 1934 and served another ten years in Congress. During the interim period, while sitting as an observer in the gallery of the U. S. House, he heroically disarmed a man brandishing a pistol. For this he received the Carnegie Hero Fund Award in 1933. A man of many interests, he also drove in stock car races at the state fairgrounds during this time.

In 1945, Maas was sent to Okinawa, where he became Commander of Kadena Airfield and Awage Airfield. During his tour of duty he was wounded by shell fragments during an air raid. In later life, Maas became blinded by diabetes, but remain active in the Reserves. He passed away in 1964.

When Maas took over command of the Marine Reserve Squadron in 1931, it was in the midst of the

VO7MR squadron commander, Melvin Maas, poses in front of Helldiver at Camp Ripley during two-week summer camp in 1933. (Niels Sorensen)

Richard Fleming poses while a cadet at NRAB, Minneapolis. Fleming would later give his life in combat and the South St. Paul Airport would be named after him. (Roland Sorensen)

Depression and there was virtually zero funding for the unit. The new volunteers attended classes with the regulars for six months before they were inducted into the squadron. Almost no one had been issued a complete uniform; they bought their own shoes, and when drill pay was finally authorized, the men rushed out to purchase dress blue uniforms from the windfall. Fortunately the navy did provide training aircraft.[59]

Brothers, Ed and Goodwin Luck, enlisted in the Marine Air Unit in 1935, and Ed remembers, "My brother and I had similar duties. On the ground we were aircraft mechanics and in the air we were machine gunners in the rear seat. The Helldivers (Curtiss O2C-1's) had 30 caliber Lewis machine guns in the back. The mount held a single machine gun. Shooting had its moments. To shoot upward, the gunner had to squeeze down under the gun to point and aim. To shoot downward, the gunner hung about halfway out of the cockpit."[60]

Goodwin stayed in the Marines and became a pilot. Ed joined the Navy AVCAD program in 1937. He became a carrier pilot and ended his career at Point Mugu, California, after years as an engineer in the Sparrow missile program.

John V. Kipp joined the Marine Reserve Squadron while attending St. Thomas College in St. Paul. He barnstormed weekends at Wold between drills and then trained at Great Lakes, Pensacola, and San Diego. He became commander of the marine air unit at Wold in 1940 and stayed as C. O. until he was sent to the Pacific theatre in 1944. There, he flew five hundred hours on transport missions, sixty dive bomber and photo-reconnaisance missions. He was well decorated for his flights over enemy territory.

Probably the most noted Marine aviator to come from the local Marine unit was Captain Richard E. Fleming, USMC. Born in St. Paul, he joined the Marine's AVCAD program at Wold while in college. After his training, he was assigned to Marine Scout-Bombing unit VMSB-241. During the 1942 battle of Midway, he was leading a squadron of six SB2U Vindicator dive bombers on a sortie against the crippled Japanese heavy cruiser, Mikuma. On the bomb run, his plane was crippled by anti-aircraft fire. Though he managed to drop his bomb, his plane crashed against the after turret of the Japanese ship. Flames from the crash were sucked into the ship's air intake system and exploded fuel fumes in the engine room, knocking out the ship's propulsion. The ship was finished off by other American dive-bombers. Flem-

ing was posthumously awarded the Congressional Medal of Honor.

South St. Paul Airport was named Fleming Field in honor of the brave flier.

NAS, Minneapolis, would have its name changed again in 1963, to Naval Air Station Twin Cities. The active station closed down in 1970, swapped facilities with the Air Force Reserve, and remains to this day as the Naval Air Reserve Center, a detachment of Air Eschelon, Naval Air Station, Glenview, Illinois.

Interestingly, no less than eight Marine General Officers earned their stars after belonging to the local unit. They were Major General Arthur H. Adams, General Russell A. Bowen, Major General Avery R. Kier, General Alexander Kreiser, Major General Melvin J. Maas, Brigadier General Wyman F. Marshall, General Warren E. Sweetser and General Vernon A. Peterson.

NRAB, Minneapolis Aircraft, 1928 - 1944

Dec. 1928	1 TS-1, 1 NY-2
Apr. 1929	1 TS-1, 3 NY-2
June 1930	4 N2C-1
Dec. 1930	4 N2C-1
June 1931	4 N2C-1, 3 O2C-1
Oct. 1932	4 N2C-1, 6 O2C-1, 1 T4M-1
June 1935	4 N2C-1, 7 O2C-1, 1 T4M-1
June 1936	4 N2C-1, 5 O2C-1, 2 FF-2, 1 OJ-2, 1 OL-9
Nov. 1936	4 N2C-1, 5 O2C-1, 3 FF-2, 2 OJ-2, 1 OJ-9
June 1937	4 N2C-1, 2 O2C-1, 3 FF-2, 3 OJ-2, 1 OL-9

Lt. Col. John V. Kipp (center) takes a well-deserved rest on Guam after a flight from Iwo Jima. He had brought out the famous pictures and film of the Marine flag-raising on Iwo Jima. (John V. Kipp)

1946 view of Navy ramp with F-6F Hellcats, F-4U Corsairs, TBF Avengers, and SB2C Helldivers in abundance. (Metropolitan Airports Commission)

Nov. 1937	2 N2C-1, 4 FF-2, 3 OJ-2, 1 OL-9, 2 N3N-1
June 1938	4 FF-2, 2 OJ-2, 1 OL-9, 5 N3N-1
Nov. 1938	2 FF-2, 2 OJ-2, 1 OL-9, 5 N3N-1
June 1939	2 FF-2, 2 OJ-2, 1 SF-1, 1 J2F-3, 5 N3N-1
Nov. 1939	3 FF-2, 2 OJ-2, 4 SBC-4, 1 J2F-3, 4 N3N-1
June 1940	3 FF-2, 1 OJ-1, 3 SBC-4, 1 J2F-3, 1SNJ-2, 4 N3N-1, 1 N3N-3
Nov. 1940	3 FF-2, 3 SBC-4, 1 J2F-3, 1 SNJ-2, 4N3N-1, 6 N3N-3
May 1941	1 J2F-3, 1 SNJ-2, 4 N3N-1, 12 N3N-3
Sep. 1941	1 J2F-3, 4 N3N-1, 10 N3N-3
Oct. 1942	1 J2F-3, 11 NE-1, 18 NP-1,4 N3N-1, 11 N3N-3, 10 N2S-2, 21 N2S-3, 26 N2S-4, 3 SNC-1, 1 SNJ-4, 1 GB-2
Aug. 1944	248 N2S-1, 9 SNV
15 Oct. 1944	9 SNV, 1 GB-2
31 Oct. 1944	1 GB-2, 1 GH-2, 1 JRB-4, 2 NE-1, 2 PB4Y, 1 SNB-1, 9 SNV-2

Notes:

June 1937	Production assignment N3N-1 #0646, 0647, 0687, 0688
Nov. 1937	Production assignment N3N-1 #0691
June 1939	Production assignment SBC-4 #-23-1480, 1481, 1482, 1495
Nov. 1939	One FF-2 to come from NRAB Kansas City
Nov. 1940	Two SBC-4 ordered from Miami
Sept. 1941	Production assignment NP-1 #3777-3792 inclusive N3N-3 #2584, 2585, 2634, 2635

WARTIME TRAINING PROGRAMS IN MINNESOTA

THE CPT AND WTS

During the mid-1930s, news from Europe and Asia prompted people throughout the world to speculate that war was looming. In the United States, which had been pursuing a policy of non-intervention, there was a great deal of controversy, both among the civilian population and within government. There were those who were not willing that the U. S. become involved in hostilities. In Europe, it was an all-European war. In Asia, the warring Japanese and Chinese would also fight it out among themselves and not involve the U. S.

There were, on the other hand, those in government and in the civilian sector who knew preparations had to be made for both protecting our borders, and for going to the assistance of France, England and Russia. While the U. S. was recovering from a devastating depression, many industries were idling, with no orders for production, no jobs for America's workers, and no impetus to change its course.

The following paragraphs will provide an overall view of the national Civilian Pilot Training Program and the War Training Service:

The Civil Aeronautics Act of 1938 had created the Civil Aeronautics Authority (CAA) with a view toward stabilizing the airline industry and giving a shot in the arm to general aviation. Until now, small airports had been closing and light plane manufacturers faced bankruptcy. Robert H. Hinckley of Ogden, Utah, was a member of the CAA who projected some far-sighted thinking. He had a plan to see the general aviation industry make a turn for the better. He conceived the idea for the Civilian Pilot Training Program (CPTP, or simply known as the CPT).

The plan would provide flight schools with new students, and light plane manufacturers with a wider market for their wares. In talks with the military, the idea was given little regard, even though the plan would also be able to provide a ready pool of basically-trained pilots should war break out and the U. S. become involved. The military did not accept the idea in the beginning; in fact, they never got used to it. The thought of turning civilian trained pilots into service pilots was repugnant to them.

Never-the-less, the idea had merit for the private sector and there was support for a test program in congress. On 27 December, 1938, President Roosevelt announced the CPT program from the White House. The Civil Aeronautics Authority planned to train 20,000 pilots a year once the program had full funding. A test program was to get underway immediately at thirteen designated universities around the country that had an established aeronautics department. The University of Minnesota was one of the original thirteen.

Initial funding of $10,000 for the overall plan would come from the National Youth Administration (NYA). There would be no new institutions built, but rather aviation ground schools would be conducted by instructors from the colleges and universities; airwork provided by already existing fixed base operator flight schools of the universities' selection.

The training was open to both college graduates and undergraduate students from eighteen to twenty-five years of age, providing they had at least a full year's credits upon application. Students were required to be U. S. citizens and have had some physics classes. The fee charged by the university per student was $40. $20 went for a $3,000 life insurance policy (it would seem that the insurance industry got a boost too), $10 for a physical examination, and the other $10 went to the school. The CAA paid the college an additional $20 per student and the flight school was paid $270 to $290. Charitable institutions such as chambers of commerce and civic groups often set up fundraisers to provide the initial $40, so that the student would have no fee to pay. The CPT program was geared to give thirty-five to fifty hours of flight time to each student - enough to provide a private license.

President Roosevelt then asked Congress for $10 million dollars to finance the total program for 1939. Congress appropriated only $4 million, but it was still enough to expand the program. By the end of the 1939-1940 school year, 9885 private pilots had been turned out, along with 1925 instructors. By this time, nearly five hundred institutions of higher learning were involved.

In 1940, the CAA announced its plan to train 45,000 students in the coming year. Though the CAA was dissolved during the year, the program continued under its successor, the Civil Aeronautics Administration, which had become part of the Department of Commerce. As the program had originally been intended, private licenses became more numerous, and totalled nearly 80,000 by the summer of 1941! Moreover, the ownership of private aircraft had burgeoned, with the 1939 figure of 11,160 being hiked to almost double that by mid-1941.[61]

By this time, the military was feeling pressure from abroad. Britain had been begging for help, both for trained fliers and for equipment. General H. H. "Hap" Arnold, Chief of the Army Air Corps, knew full well that his main pilot training base, Randolph Field in Texas, and the Navy's main base at Pensacola in Florida, together, could only train a mere 750 service

pilots a year. He realized there would be closer to 100,000 per year needed if hostilities were to include the United States. His only hope for the future air corps was to enhance the Civilian Pilot Training Program. As the pressure for numbers began to be asserted, the CAA had found a friend in the War Department.[62]

At the same time, the enrolling of women, who had been accepted from the beginning of the program in a ratio of one for each ten students, was terminated, beginning in the summer of 1941. The 16,000 male trainees for that year were enrolled in primary, secondary, instructor and cross-country courses. Then, just as that summer's class of students were to graduate, the bombs fell on Pearl Harbor, and things changed virtually overnight. On 13 December 1941, hardly a week after the bombing, the CPT program was canceled. A new program called the War Training Service (WTS) took its place. Though the CAA would still manage the new program, the difference lay in the fact that no longer would ordinary college students be accepted, now all must come from the enlisted reserves. They were to wear uniforms, be fingerprinted, and given wings when they graduated. The training period was shortened to eight weeks. General Arnold provided a cadre of trained Randolph Field instructors to oversee the private operators, standardizing military etiquette and discipline.

During the summer of 1942, the WTS operated on seven levels:

Elementary. 240 hours ground school, 35-45 air hours. Graduates received a private license and the opportunity to advance to secondary training, or to volunteer for glider pilot training.

Secondary. 240 hours ground school, 40-50 air hours. Graduates were qualified to advance to cross-country.

Cross-country. 108 hours ground school, 45-50 air hours of both day and night flying. Graduates were eligible for either the Link instrument course or for flight officers course. Certain qualified students were sent directly to the Army Air Force as service pilots.

National Youth Administration (NYA) trade school project at Murphy's Landing, Shakopee, Minnesota. Hangar is under construction for aviation mechanics course. Roger Poore is standing in the foreground. (Roger Poore)

214

No more private flying! Elmer Sell's Airport in Carver County with state militia on guard to prevent flying, one week after Pearl Harbor. (Chuck Sell)

Link Instrument.	108 hours ground school, 20-25 air hours plus 15 hours in the stationary Link trainer. This prepared the graduate for the instructor course.
Instructor.	72 hours ground school, 50-60 air hours. Completion led to a commercial license and instructor rating plus assignment as a flight instructor somewhere in the system.
Flight Officer.	325 hours ground school, 20-25 air hours of single engine time, 21 hours of multi-engine, 20-30 hours Link trainer time. Graduates received commercial ratings with a flight officer designation and assigned to an airline under contract to the Air Transport Command (ATC), or special duty as an Army Air Force ferry pilot.
Liaison.	240 hours ground school, 55-60 air hours. Graduates went to the Field Artillery as aerial spotters.

By December, 1942, the program had been so successful, there was a backlog of qualified pilots. Recruiting was discontinued. In January of 1943, the military decided it was capable of all further training of pilots, but allowed the WTS to continue to train instructors and to provide a 10-hour basic screening program. Under the 10-hour course, the student was not allowed to solo, but merely qualify for pilot, navigator, or gunner, with further training being carried out by the military. By January 1944, instructor training was also cancelled, and by June, the 10-hour course was closed. The entire WTS program ground to a halt by the end of 1944, the military finally having taken on the entire job of pilot training themselves.

In 1939, the University of Minnesota had an established Aeronautical Engineering Department. Under the directorship of Professor John D. Akerman, the department offered courses in internal combustion engines, aerodynamic theory, structural theory, propellers, airship theory, meteorology, and navigation.

John Akerman joined the University staff in 1928, with already a colorful background. Born in Latvia, a protectorate of Soviet Russia, in 1897, Akerman graduated from the Imperial Technical Institute's

Aero School in Moscow in 1917 and went into the military. He trained as a pilot in France where he logged 2,000 hours. In 1925, he came to this country to earn his Aeronautical Engineering degree at the University of Michigan, and then went to work for the Stout Aircraft Company, where he designed the wing structure for the predecessor to the Ford Trimotor. (Ford had bought out the Stout Company during this period.) Akerman also designed the Hamilton Metalplane in 1928, and was chief designer at the Mohawk Aircraft Company in Minneapolis from 1928 to 1930. His activities during the 1930s were wide-ranging. He had taken part in the design of a huge wind-driven power plant, was consulting designer on Roscoe Turner's racing planes, was a consultant for the Porterfield, Boeing, and Bell aircraft companies, and a consultant for the Mayo Clinic at Rochester.

Akerman became head of the Aeronautical Engineering school at the University of Minnesota in 1931 and helped organize a flying club there. He also designed a tailless airplane which was licensed and flew in 1937.

Because of the Department's expertise, the University of Minnesota was selected as one of the CPT test program schools under President Roosevelt's direction. The program at the university was managed by M. A. Tinker of the University's staff. He selected the Hinck Flying Service at Wold-Chamberlain as the provider of the flight training for the university's twenty students.

Elmer Hinck, who ran the Hinck Flying Service, had a single instructor, Vern Georgia, who had been flying since 1924. With the requirements for one in-

Flight Instructor, Niels Sorensen, in front of Waco UPF-7 at Elmer Hinck's flight school, Wold-Chamberlain Field, May, 1941. CPT Secondary program. (Niels Sorensen)

structor for each ten students, Hinck sought another instructor, and hired George Holey. Holey would later become the CAA's regional director of all CPT and WTS programs. Hinck maintained four Piper J-3 Cubs for training. Two were used by each instructor, one for dual instruction, and the other for student solo work.

Holey remembered a long-running "feud" he had going with Vern Georgia. It stemmed from the fact that it was customary for students, upon soloing, to give their instructor a gift, usually a bottle of good whiskey. At the very time that Georgia's students were ready to solo, he became ill and Holey soloed several of them. Naturally, Holey was the recipient of the gifts. For years, Georgia hounded Holey, accusing him of "stealing" his students to get all the whiskey. The fact was, as Georgia knew well, that Holey did not drink.[63]

With the successful country-wide CPT test program completed, the second part of Roosevelt's and Hinckley's plan got underway in June of 1939. At this time sixteen Minnesota colleges were given the go-ahead to initiate training programs:

Albert Lea Junior College
Austin Junior College
Bemidji Junior College
Duluth Junior College
Eveleth Junior College
Hibbing Junior College
Itasca Junior College of Coleraine
Macalester College of St. Paul
The University of Minnesota
Rochester Junior College
St. Mary's College of Winona
St. Olaf's Teacher's College of Northfield
Virginia Junior College
Winona State Teacher's College
Worthington Junior College[64]

As the program expanded during the war, additional Minnesota schools secured training contracts with the CAA. Carlton College at Northfield; Concordia College at Moorhead; Hamline University in St. Paul; St. Cloud Teacher's College; St. John's College near St. Cloud; and St. Thomas College of St. Paul became involved. Schools other than colleges also participated, such as Alexandria High School, Marshall Public Schools, and the West Central School of Agriculture.

The CAA also provided that 5 percent of the training be given to non-college students, with civic and commerce associations sponsoring such programs.[65] The Brainerd Junior Chamber of Commerce and the St. Paul Association of Commerce are examples. In this program, fixed base operators were able to petition the CAA for contracts, by assembling blocks of ten students and having the required instructors and airplanes to do the job. It is not known exactly how many operators there were in Minnesota who performed this part of the program, but such an example was Ernie Evans at Albert Lea.

One of Evans' students at Albert Lea in 1940 was Sherman Booen. Booen, at that time was a high school graduate, not yet in college. His fees were paid by the CAA and he received both his ground school and flight training from Evans, eventually soloing in Evans Aeronca C. Booen later joined the Marine

Corps Reserve as an aviator and served in Korea. Following his service, he became a popular and very visible spokesman for general aviation through his weekly TV program "World of Aviation" and his monthly magazine, *The Minnesota Flyer*.

Flight instructors hired by the various FBO's involved with the CPT program had been instructing on their commercial and limited commercial licenses through 1939. Early in 1940, the CAA decided on a new course of action, to standardize flight instruction by testing all instructors and issuing a flight instructor rating. The re-rating program occurred over the entire country.

To get his re-rating, George Holey had to take written, oral, and flight tests. When he got his instructor's rating, Holey became the very first pilot in the country with the new rating. He then began taking instrument instructions at Rochester from Neil Chievitz, and acquired his instrument rating. This enabled him to instruct both the basic course and instrument training.[66]

Holey worked for Elmer Hinck at Wold-Chamberlain for six months. He was then offered a position as inspector with the CAA. He accepted and was sent to Chicago to take aerobatic instruction, returning to the Twin Cities with a brand-new Waco UPF-7 trainer. His new job would be to inspect and authorize all CPT and WTS flight schools, examining their instructors, airplanes and curricula. One of his most unlikely chores was to fly with each student "washout" from the various schools to make sure they had deserved the fate, and had been given a fair chance.

Holey was named District Superintendent for the CAA region which encompassed Minnesota, North Dakota, Upper Michigan and parts of Wisconsin.

Following is a rundown of CPT/WTS programs at Minnesota institutions from the best information available:

ALEXANDRIA. Alexandria Technical School sponsored a CPT program with A. C. McInnis providing the flight training at the Alexandria Airport. Don Pennertz was an instructor.

AUSTIN. Austin Junior College program was run at the Austin Airport by Marcellus King. He trained a single block of CPT students during the summer of 1941.

BEMIDJI. Bemidji State Teacher's College did not get into the program in 1939 due to lateness in filing an application, and the lack of complete facilities at

Vern Georgia stands beside a J-3 Cub from his flight school, Minnesota Skyways, Inc. at Wold-Chamberlain, 1941. (Vern Georgia)

216

WTS instructor's uniform insignia. (Joseph Williams)

WTS instructor's uniform shoulder patch. (Joseph Williams)

the Bemidji Municipal Airport. Dr. Charles R. Satt-gast, President of Bemidji State, did jump at the chance to get involved in 1940, assuring the CAA that the school could provide the proper ground school teachers and would employ Mr. Forrest Rising of the *Rising School of Aviation* at the airport as flight instructor. Sattgast even sent airport diagrams to the CAA Regional office in Chicago to help convince the government that Bemidji was ready.

There were stringent requirements for a training airfield. The CAA demanded a strip of no less than eighteen hundred feet in length in as many directions as necessary to provide a crosswind of no more than 22 degrees through 75 percent of the year. It was to have a width of three hundred feet or more if planes were to be parked alongside, and required a clear approach from any direction.

Sattgast was so sure that the Bemidji field fit federal requirments, that when the *Minneapolis Star Journal* announced a survey to determine locations for new airports throughout the state, Sattgast offered this, "It would seem that Bemidji is ideally located for an army or navy aviation station. We have both a landing field and a lake so that either naval or army planes could come in. It would seem also that Bemidji is ideally located for the protection of the iron mines in Northern Minnesota. In making a survey for the location of new aviation bases, it would seem to me that careful consideration should be given to this location."[67]

Sattgast appointed Dr. E. W. Beck as director of the new CPT program and sent a member of the faculty to the University of Wisconsin to study meteorology and navigation.

From 5 September, 1940, thru May of 1943, Bemidji State was responsible for training one hundred twenty-five students, in blocks of ten, fifteen, and twenty. All ground school instruction was given by members of the faculty over and above their regular teaching duties.

In June of 1943, Bemidji State offered a class in Pre-flight Aeronautics for fifteen high school teachers from throughout the state. The goal was to make them better able to teach their students about aviation in high schools.

BRAINERD. The Brainerd Junior Chamber of Commerce sponsored a non-college program. Burton Garrett was an instructor at the Brainerd Airport for

George Fairfield's flight school. The school used a Piper Cub and a Taylorcraft for training. Garrett took the year of 1941 to do private instructing and give sight-seeing flights in the Pine River area, but was back into the WTS program in 1942 at Grand Rapids.

CONCORDIA COLLEGE OF MOORHEAD. At Concordia, two classes of ten students were given the CPT courses, with the earliest class going on to secondary phase while the second block was in elementary in 1941. Dr. Konrad O. Lee of the Concordia physics department was also assigned the duty of coordinating the program. Flight training was given at the Hector Airport in Fargo, North Dakota, by instructors, Charles Klessig and W. T. Cates. In 1942, Concordia provided training for enlistees under the Navy V-5 program.

DULUTH. Duluth Junior College carried on a CPT/WTS program through the early war years. (The Junior College, originally part of the State Teacher's College system, and later known as Duluth State Teacher's College, was phased out in 1947, with the college site and assets being transferred to the University of Minnesota, Duluth.)

The Junior College originally authorized three flight schools for CPT training; *Northern Air Service,* owned and managed by Rueben Bloom; *Zenith City Air Service,* owned by Dean Tresise and May Slenna; and *Lakehead Airways,* owned by Nick Niemi, Gil Enger and Ken Cooley. By late 1939, Rudy Billberg was associated with Lakehead Airways. All ground school was taught at the college by Tracy B. Gardner. The air training was carried out at the Williamson-Johnson Airport (now Duluth International).

The enrollment in the CPT program was open to college students with at least one year's college credits, the curriculum included seventy-two hours of ground school, consisting of fifteen hours of aerodynamics, fifteen hours of navigation, five hours of engine function, fifteen hours of meteorology, and two hours of radio. Ninety-nine students had attained their private licenses by February of 1941, and by April of that year, one hundred twenty-two total.

Among Rueben Bloom's instructors at Northern Air Service was Bill Morse, already a bush pilot of some renown. From March through May 1941, Morse would instruct the elementary students in J-3 Cubs during the week, but rush home to Ely on weekends to fly resorters to their favorite fishing holes.

When the war started, participation in the Duluth program was restricted to enlisted Navy cadets in the V-5 program. Gordy Newstrom and Ned Powers instructed for Bloom during this period. Newstrom came on board fresh from receiving his instructor rating, when cadets were being soloed after eight hours of training. Newstrom recalled that, at the time, he was hardly more than a green cadet himself.

"There were fellows like Nick Niemi there, who were older than I was. Well, you know, you kind of play follow-the-leader when you've got a bunch together. You've got to do what George does, and do what Joe does. So, as I know, and as I've heard since, pretty near everybody did aerobatics with Cubs in those days. So I was out riding around with one of the cadets one day and did a couple of snap rolls with him. We had done some loops before and I told him, 'Now, don't you ever let me catch you doing this'. This was fatherly advice too late.

"There was quite a competition between those elementary students and the secondary students flying biplanes (N3N's) and doing aerobatics. I remember this cadet .... he was ready to finish up his course and had forty minutes of solo left to put in, and I told him, 'Now you go out and go through all those maneuvers and then you'll be ready for your flight check.' And I don't know ... he got tangled up with some of those secondary pilots and they egged him on and they egged him on, and finally he changed his mind about what he was going to do. I can recollect that I came back from a flight with one of the other cadets and you could see the icicles hanging all over the Duluth airport... that's the way it seemed to me. I just sensed something was wrong as soon as I got out of the airplane. One of the cadets told me to report to Mr. Bloom. So I went and reported to Mr. Bloom and he told me that this cadet of mine had put on one grandiose airshow right over the top of the Duluth airport. Well, it ended up with both of us getting an advisory board action. He got washed out, and I almost did."[68]

EVELETH. Eveleth Junior College program details not available.

HAMLINE. Refer to the end of this chapter on the Northport glider program.

HIBBING. The Hibbing CPT program was sponsored by the Hibbing Junior College. Flight instruction was carried out at Hibbing Airport by Millar Wittag Flying Service, owned by L. Millar Wittag, originally a flight instructor from Wold-Chamberlain Field in Minneapolis. At that time, the Hibbing airport was a sod field with a large municipal hangar built by the Works Progress Administration prior to World War II. There, using some of the municipal hangar facilities, Wittag set up a CPT program, and after Pearl Harbor, managed to get a WTS contract which he operated through 1942 and 1943. He borrowed money from banks in town to finance another large hangar and shop buildings.

Duluth Airport (Williamson-Johnson Airport) from the air during 1939. Note the single hangar. At least three operators held CPT contracts here during 1939 and 1940. (Minnesota Air National Guard Historical Foundation)

At the college, Shorty Davis taught the ground school classes in federal air regulations, meteorology, powerplant theory, and airframe theory. Some classes were also taught at the airport. Students enrolled in the CPT program took the the flight instruction in addition to their regular studies, sandwiching the ground school and flying time between academics.

Under the WTS program, Wittag bought three Waco UPF-7 airplanes, and was issued a fleet of Meyers OTW biplane trainers. Secondary aerobatic instructor, Carl Hickman, was sent to the east coast with a group of other instructors to bring back twelve N3N trainers. For teaching aerobatics, Hickman recalled that the N3N was the best of the lot.

Well-known author, Robert Stevens, was a student of Wittag's at Hibbing and went on to spend a career with North Central Airlines and Western Airlines from which he retired as a DC-10 Captain.

Millar Wittag also had a WTS contract to train glider pilots at Crookston, Minnesota. Robert D. Hodge, later a Minnesota game warden, was selected as a student in Wittag's program at Hibbing, and got his private license, his commercial and instructor ratings at Galesburg, Illinois, and returned to Crookston to teach the glider trainees. Using J-3 Cubs, he had his students practice 360 degree overhead approaches, 180-190 degree side approaches, and dead-stick landings. Al Johnson, another of Wittag's original students, also taught at Crookston. A

Hibbing Airport during the WTS. Lineup of Meyers OTW's and N3N's is interesting. Municipal hangar is at left, Millar Wittag's hangar and shops at far end. (Carl Hickman)

third student, Donovan Hogan, became Wittag's operations manager at Crookston.

Wittag stayed on at Hibbing, operating as *Arrowhead Air Service* after the war and died in a plane crash in the 1950s.

ITASCA JUNIOR COLLEGE. Itasca Junior College and *Tinquist Flying Service* teamed up to provide ground school and flight training for students at Grand Rapids Airport. Ted Tinquist and Lloyd Alsworth, owners of Tinquist Flying Service, gave the CPT flight training. They handled their first block of CPT students in 1941, just prior to Pearl Harbor. The curriculum called for night flying, and as Grand Rapids was too small for night landings, that part of the instruction was carried out by Millar Wittag at Hibbing.

When war was declared, Tinquist and Alsworth were offered a WTS contract almost immediately. By then, the Grand Rapids Airport was improved and all their training could be done there. Lloyd's wife, Evelyn, functioned as bookkeeper and secretary.

In their WTS program, one group of students came from North Dakota to be trained as liaison pilots. One block was Navy cadets. Most of the Grand Rapids students went into a pool from which they were assigned to the Army as glider, liaison, or ferry pilots. Those coming through in early 1943 as 10-hour elimination students were quartered at the Pokegama Hotel nearby, the only housing available.

Ground school was originally conducted at the college, but giving classroom time there and moving students to the airport for flight training was a logistics headache. It was eased when all instruction was given at the airport. The college sent over an instructor to help Tinquist and Alsworth. To expedite the classroom work, an old one-room schoolhouse, nicknamed the "old Cowhorn School," was purchased and moved to the airport. The last class finished in June 1943, with Tinquist then being assigned to a school in Fargo, North Dakota, and Alsworth being sent to Mankato.

Tinquist, Burton Garrett, and Harold Hanon were the instructors at Grand Rapids from January of 1942 until August of 1943. During that time, Garrett logged considerable hours. His log shows daily flying time in the six to eight hour range, and on 17 April, 1943, his log shows eleven hours and 30 minutes of instruction.[69]

MANKATO STATE TEACHER'S COLLEGE. At Mankato, the CPT program was under the auspices of the Mankato State Teacher's College. Flight training was conducted by Harold Schlesselman of *Mankato Aero Service* at the airport. Contracts issued to Schlesselman during the WTS program were for the Navy V-5 program. Some of the instructors were: Lawrence "Abe" Merrill, who taught in both the primary and secondary series, Keith Tillejohn, Arnold Waage, a mechanic who eventually got his instructor's rating, Don Lankammer, Cooper Stubbs, and Warren Fields. The CPT and WTS primary was done in Aeronca L-3 Defenders, the WTS secondary in Meyers OTW aircraft.

MARSHALL PUBLIC SCHOOLS. Not much is known about the Marshall CPT or WTS programs, except that the Marshall Public School (High School) was involved in teaching the ground school portion for both phases. Fred Hite was involved in the early programs, but was superseded by George Ice from South Dakota, who gave the flight training portions at the Marshall Airport. He was assisted later by Bernard "Bud" Frye and his wife, Ellen, who did the bookkeeping.

In the WTS phase, only elementary training was given. Enlisted Army Air Force students such as Fred Comb, now a retired Minneapolis construction contractor, went elsewhere for further training. In Comb's case, to Hibbing for secondary, and to Rochester for instrument and cross-country.

Instructor Bud Frye had been using a field near Madison, Minnesota for a remote practice field. When the city of Madison decided to build their own airport, they chose that field as the site, and Frye moved there in 1944 to manage the airport. He spent his career there, instructing students under the G.I. Bill after the war, and offering crop-spraying services.

ROCHESTER. Several flight schools were involved in the CPT and WTS programs at Rochester. The first was probably the school owned by Joe Atherton, and managed by Fred Hite. John Rice was an instructor. John instructed in the first CPT program there in 1939, then was sent to Wold-Chamberlain Field in Minneapolis to instruct for McInnis's flight school. There he got his aerobatic instructor's rating, and returned to Rochester to teach that subject in the secondary phase of the CPT. Aerobatics were taught in a Waco ASO. John once logged two hundred twelve hours in thirty-two days, passing sixteen students. When the time came to get additional aerobatic training aircraft, John was sent to Tecumseh, Michigan, to pick up the very first production Meyers OTW.

The OTW was a biplane trainer for which the government had high hopes. According to Rice, however, it had many problems. One of which was the poor positioning of the fuel gauge in the front cockpit, making it impossible to be seen at night from the rear cockpit. This problem caused John to force-land a Meyers on the flight to Rochester when he ran out of gas. The Meyers was also a sluggish aircraft when performing a slow roll. No matter how he tried, he couldn't do a smooth slow roll with it. On one occasion, when being checked out by George Holey, Holey chided him, "can't you do a slow roll better than that... here, let me show you how." After a few tries, George finally admitted, "You're right, John, it just won't do a slow roll."[70]

Atherton and Hite left Rochester and operator, Mario Fontana, picked up the next CPT program there, a cross-country block. He continued into the WTS period, with a glider training contract, then migrated to Iron Mountain, Michigan when the WTS ended.

Bill Shaw and Mel Swanson, who was a Northwest Airlines pilot, also ran a CPT program in the fall of 1941. Fred Hinze was an instructor in their cross-country contract, teaching the fine points to a block of ten students.

After McInnis had been relocated from Wold-Chamberlain to South St. Paul in 1942, he found the runway and night lighting inadequate for his cross-country aircraft, a Stinson SR-5 and a Stinson SR-6. Don Swenson, manager of the Rochester Airport, invited Mac to bring his program south and Mac did

St. Cloud, 1941. B. G. Vandre, with parachute, and John Nelson, his instructor, standing in front of a Howard DGA-18. (Myron Hall collection of Stearns County Historical Society, St. Cloud)

St. Cloud, October, 1939. First group of CPT students from St. Cloud Teacher's College in front of Van's Air Service Cub. At upper left is college program coordinator, John J. Weismann; B. G. Vandre is next to him. (Myron Hall collection of Stearns County Historical Society, St. Cloud)

just that. He sent Ed Croft and Henry "Red" Robinson as instructors, along with Margaret Yates, a ground school instructor, and several mechanics. Croft left the WTS when it folded in 1943, and went to work for Mid-Continent Airlines. He and Red Robinson stayed on at Rochester, and with Art Hoffman, another instructor, formed Gopher Aviation.

ST. CLOUD STATE TEACHER'S COLLEGE. The St. Cloud CPT program got started when Bernard G. Vandre ("B. G" or "Van"), a flight school operator from Wold-Chamberlain, received a contract to train a block of ten students from the St. Cloud Teacher's College. He taught these first students himself. When he secured a second block of ten students, he was required to have another instructor, so he hired itinerant flight instructor, Joseph Williams from Minneapolis, as his first employee. Joe was offered $2.00 an hour for instructing, or $100 a month minimum for his efforts, but did not sign a contract. Joe needed to be re-rated as an instructor. He got his flight check from George Holey, and took his written and flight tests from Dave Nelson of the CAA. He hitched a ride to St. Cloud and lived in a rooming house while he instructed for Vandre.

John J. Weismann was the college's CPT administrator. He selected staff teachers to instruct the CPT ground school. The school included seventy-two hours of classroom work in CAA rules and regulations, navigation, meteorology, theory of flight, and engine theory. When the first students took their written tests in the spring of 1940, few of them passed. One of the problems was that the instructors, while very well able to lecture on the theoretical aspects of aviation, could offer little practical instruction. Joe Williams was recruited to help coach the class through a second try at the written, and all students passed.

With the second block of students,the first woman trainee arrived. Rose Maher seemed like a good student, but Vandre, who held to the basic theory that women shouldn't fly, assigned her to Joe Williams. Maher, like most of the students had other interests, and held a job after school hours. Her schedule left her with too little time to spend at the airport and she was forced to drop out. The next block of students included lady flyer, Joan Trebtoske. She was also involved in many extracurricular activities which took up the majority of her time. She had been voted Miss St. Cloud for 1940, making her an automatic candidate for Aquatennial Queen, for which she eventually became the runner-up Princess. Vandre took her as his own student.

She also had a hard time finding enough hours to spend in the airplane and Vandre became exasperated with her for not being able to solo. He was ready to wash her out, but turned her over to Williams to follow through. Williams had more patience and Joan finally soloed and got her license. She joined the WASPs (Women Army Service Pilots) and ferried aircraft during World War II. Since she was not an officer, Trebtoske was not allowed to fly bombers, but was able to ferry P-39's, P-63's and P-47 fighters across the country. She learned cockpit procedures by crouching on the plane's wing while a pilot taxied the aircraft around. On her first solo in the P-47, she took the plane to 10,000 feet and the engine quit. Faced with the prospect of either bailing out or bringing it in, she chose to dead-stick it in to her home field. The landing was uneventful.

Following the war, she became a flight instructor and commercial pilot in the Twin Cities area, and later, at Pipestone.

When the third CPT group began in September 1940, Vandre had become a certified flight examiner and hired John Nelson as a second instructor to take his place tutoring the students. Nelson revived the

Reproduction of page from student, Al Ayer's, logbook during CPT program. Instructor was Jerry Kilian. (Joseph Williams)

Ident. No. NC 3/6/5	RATING SHEET		Note.—Keep time by stages.				
Make and model Howard	RESTRICTED COMMERCIAL COURSE		Ground Instr. Time	DUAL		SOLO	
Engine Dean. Hp. /85	**Stage D**			Hr.	Min.	Hr.	Min.
Time up a.m. p.m.			Time this flight		40		
Time down a.m. p.m.	Minimum, 13 Hours—Dual Check and Solo		Previous time	8	45	6	10
Date 8/21/41	Grade Maneuvers During Instruction		Total stage time	10	25	6	10
			Total course time	26	10	20	50

Dual or Solo, as Needed

Lesson No. 10. .... Flight test........

Check number in each column indicating student's characteristics

| W | 8 | 3 | 3 | 1 | 3 | 3 | 3 | 4 | 3 | 4 | | 3 | 3 | | | 3 | 4 | 3 | 3 | | 3 | 3 | 3 | 3 | 3 | 4 |

A	ATTITUDE	B	PHYSICAL TRAITS	C	MENTAL TRAITS	D	FLYING HABITS	7	Good timing.	E	SPECIAL FAULTS
1	Eager to learn.	1	Relaxed.	1	Alert.	1	Good coordination.	7	Good timing.	1	Cocky.
2	Cooperative.	2	Good control touch.	2	Careful.	2	Good speed sense.	8	Climbs too steep.	2	Disobedient.
3	Punctual.	3	Tired.	3	Consistent.	3	Poor coordination.	9	Skids on turns.	3	Overconfident.
4	Tardy.	4	Tense.	4	Erratic.	4	Nose too high	10	Slips on turns.	4	Overcautious.
5	Indifferent.	5	Rough on controls.	5	Forgetful.	5	Nose too low.	11	Lands too fast.	5	Irresponsible.
6	Hard-headed.	6	Airsick.	6	Mechanical.	6	Dives in glide.	12	Reacts slowly.	6	Reckless.

Above instruction given.

Above ground and flight instruction received.

Jerome H. Kilian 20393 *Alven Guy Ayers*
(Instructor's signature) (Cert. No.) (Rating) (Student's signature (first, middle, and last names) must be signed exactly the same on all forms)

220

old custom of the student providing the instructor with a "gift" upon solo, and advised his students that, when they thought they were getting near soloing, they should carry a bottle of whiskey with them in the airplane at all times so they would be prepared. Williams students heard this and didn't realize that Nelson was only kidding. On the day that the first six of Williams students soloed, he was taken to dinner by one and given five bottles of whiskey by the others... all this, and he didn't even drink.

On the first of February, 1941, the fourth group of nineteen students arrived. There were two women, as authorized by the CAA, and some of the students came from the other college in St. Cloud, St. John's College. At the same time, Vandre was also granted a contract to teach a CPT secondary program and ten former students returned to take this training. Vandre bought a Warner-powered Waco RNF for the job and Jerry Kilian was hired as instructor for secondary. By this time, Williams was giving all the ground school for both programs. He also flew two hundred fifty hours with eight Primary CPT students and several local students, and sat out another three hundred hours of "supervised solo." For this responsibility, Vandre raised Joe's salary to $3.00 per hour.[71]

During the early period of the CPT program, St. Cloud State students were transported from the college to the airfield aboard a well-used two-door 1932 Plymouth Coach. It was a familiar sight, bouncing down the gravel road to the airstrip, bulging at the seams with students, it's frame, buckled from some un-remembered incident, nearly dragging on the ground.

Incidents during training were rare, but colorful. On one takeoff, Joe Williams snagged a frozen snowball, left after Vandre dragged the snowy airfield with a simple log timber. The frozen "rock" bent the landing fear, but Joe made an uneventful landing anyway. He then faced a chewing out from Van and a humbling trip to Wold-Chamberlain to have De Ponti's repair shop fix the axle.

Another time, the instructors watched horrified when a young student from Tennessee took off on his first solo cross-country... heading 90 degrees from his planned flight direction. Almost out of sight, the student recognized his error, and corrected his heading much to the relief of the witnesses. The same student landed downwind on one of his early solo landings and was made to spend the rest of the day standing in the doorway of the flight shack, and explaining to everyone how "the bird that flies into the bag gets caught," a reference to the fact that the "bag" or windsock, has a large end and a small end. Every pilot should know that he is to fly as if he were flying out of the big end of the windsock on landing, or into the wind.

At least a fifth block of students went through the CPT program at St. Cloud before the war turned it into the WTS. The CPT accounted for eighty-two Primary students and twenty-three Secondary students, with several of them working as instructors during the later WTS. The WTS program lasted seven months at St. Cloud and trained forty persons.

Captain John E. McElroy became the military commanding officer at St. Cloud, supervising all military aspects of the training. He was once accosted by an angry local resident. The woman complained that one of "his boys" was carrying on with her daughter. The Captain responded by saying, "Madam, we keep our boys in the dormitory six nights a week. If you could keep your daughter home that one other night, the whole problem would be solved."[72]

St. Cloud also benefited from a third program under the military. The Army Air Forces College Training Program (AAFCTP), began in January of 1943, while the WTS was still occurring. Besieged by new recruits into the Air Corps, this so-called "10-hour elimination program" was something different. Vandre and seventeen instructors kept busy screening trainees to channel them into one of the Air Forces categories of pilot, navigator, or gunner. Obviously, it went on a perceived skill level because the students had only flown ten hours each, and not been allowed to solo. They were sent on their way to other Army Air Forces training facilities.

The ten-hour program was a large program, with students being temporarily housed at Lawrence Hall on the St. Cloud State campus, and at St. John's College north of the city. Every three months, some five hundred fifty students were pushed through. Vandre's instructors flew nearly 18,000 hours in the year and a half duration of this program. Everything came to an end for the WTS at St. Cloud in the spring of 1944.

VIRGINIA JUNIOR COLLEGE. The Virginia Junior College sponsored the CPT program in this community. One of the instructors was Harry Upham. It is unknown if there was a WTS program.

WINONA TEACHER'S COLLEGE and *ST. MARY'S COLLEGE OF WINONA.* Conrad Aviation, owned by Max Conrad, provided the flight training for both programs. In all, Conrad set up seven CPT programs. Besides the two in Winona, he also set up a program in De Pere, Wisconsin; one at South Bend, Indiana, in conjunction with Notre Dame University; one at Eau Claire, Wisconsin; and one at St. Thomas College in St. Paul. Once the CPT programs were cancelled with the start of the war, Conrad closed the five schools outside Winona to concentrate his efforts in one spot. He enlarged his facilities there to include a huge addition to his hangars with a lunchroom/restaurant, classrooms, offices, shops, and dormitories for the students. He based a total of thirty aircraft there, a mixed fleet that included Taylorcrafts, Pipers, Aeroncas, Stinsons, and a Ryan Brougham.

A 1943 fire consumed Conrad's entire facility, ending his WTS involvement in the V-5 Navy program.

WORTHINGTON. At Worthington, the local Chamber of Commerce sponsored a non-college CPT program, while the Junior College sponsored another for its students. Marvin Knudson of the college staff was coordinator of both and enlisted Jack Lysdale, operator at the Worthington Airport, to handle the air training. Ground school classes were taught, beginning in October of 1940, at the college by C. W. "Cy" Amundson, who also taught an Aviation Mechanics course for non-CPT students there. Classroom work included two hundred forty hours, with Amundson teaching twenty-four hours of meteorology, thirty-six hours of navigation, and sixteen hours of CAA regulations; Don Olson giving thirty-six hours of mathematics; O. I. LeBlanc providing twenty hours of international morse code; R. E. Tucker, thirty hours of physics; and Vic Moeller and A. T. Sanderson providing forty-eight hours of physical training and drill.

For their program, the Chamber of Commerce paid the college $40 for each of their students to include them in the ground school, and they paid Lysdale $400 for each student receiving his license. The government paid for one of each five students, but also matched funds donated by the Chamber and other organizations.

By 1942, Lysdale was certified as a flight examiner and aircraft inspector. He received a WTS contract to train Naval enlistees in the V-5 program. In February of 1943, the Navy program listed thirty students. Lysdale was instructing eighteen Army glider pilot trainees simultaneously and had three instructor students. In addition, with the airfield being opened to private flying (one of only seven allowed in the State), there were twelve civilian flight students. Some of Lysdale's instructors were Robert Young, Pat McGrath, Ken Noll, and Bob Gilmore.

Perhaps more fortunate than most communities, Worthington's airport programs had a very verbal public relations man, instructor Bob Gilmore. Gilmore wrote a frequent column in the Worthington newspaper, entitled "Propwash." One such column of 18 February, 1943, is indicative of the good work Gilmore did:

"At almost any other city but Worthington, flyers off duty because of bad weather are a harassed lot. In the middle of a hot pool game, you'll see one suddenly begin to tremble, miss the side pocket altogether, drop his cue and rush off to a telephone.

'Gimme the airport, quick!' he'll shout. 'Emergency!' After a short pause, during which he silently gnaws three fingernails down to the second knuckle, he'll mutter into the mouthpiece, 'what's the pitch on the weather, Mitch?' at the same time glancing furtively around to make sure there's no Jap spy behind him thumbing through an American slang dictionary.

"Worry over the weather is a common flyer's affliction. Many airports spend huge sums on barometers (whose delicate insides are always getting stuck and recording 'dry and clear' in the midst of deluges), wind velocity instruments always in need of oiling, and toy balloons that are supposed to measure something or another but always disappear before you've time to look in the instruction book and find out what.

"Flyers at airports having these instruments invariably end up looking silly with one finger licked clean from holding it in the air to get the real truth. Which serves them right.

"But here at Worthington airport, no flyer worries about the weather. Our pool games are unruffled, if unskilled, and our fingers are always uniformly dirty. The secret behind our calm, accurate, and unworried weather appraisals stands majestically at the lake end of 3rd Avenue, belching from its ten foot mouth 240 feet in the air the gassy remains of fuel which fur-

nishes the Worthington city heat, plus electricity for all of Worthington, Brewster, the REA, southwestern Minnesota Sanitorium, and the village of Rushmore.

"That power plant chimney serves a noble purpose in furnishing an outlet for so much hot air (please, we're not talking about the hot air from the power plant) is undeniable. But of its far nobler purpose as barometer, weather vane and wind velocity indicator for the airport, much remains to be said.

"On cold winter mornings, when sleep is the most important commodity in life, Worthington airport instructors throttle their alarm clocks and head for the nearest window to study the chimney. A brief glance is sufficient to send them hurrying out to fly or gratefully, back to bed.'"[73]

The article goes on to state that the rules indicate that when the chimney appears in sharp outline, two miles from the field, visibility is good for flying. When it disappears, flying stops and the instructors and students rope themselves together and proceed to the pool room, led by a seeing-eye dog. If the smoke curls lazily up from the chimney, they can fly all they wish. If the smoke hurries away horizontally, hold onto their hats and fly with the aid of experienced students. When the smoke runs down the chimney's side, stake down the airplanes, tin roofs and underweight students.

The humor in Gilmore's columns was interspersed with profiles of the instructors, students, and cute stories about training. This was obviously good public-relations between the program at the airport and the townfolk.

In April of 1943, unable to provide expanded facilities for an increased number of students planned by the government, the Worthington WTS program ended. Lysdale was asked by George Holey to take over the McInnis operation at Victory Airport, located near 77th Street and West River Road in Brooklyn Park, north of the Twin Cities. There, McInnis had secured a University of Minnesota contract to screen 500 students at a time in the ten-hour elimination program. The figure later escalated to 1,000 every week! Student flyers were housed at the university and bussed to the airport.

But, McInnis was in trouble. His replacement in the program was inevitable. At Wold, he had been a well-respected fixed base operator. Forced to move when the Navy took over the airport in 1942, he organized the airport at South St. Paul, then only a cow pasture with a small hangar used by the Hook-em-Cow Flying Club. Once McInnis settled there, he built a large hangar, and used it as his base for training forty students. It was not long before the Navy cast its eye farther from Wold-Chamberlain, looking for auxiliary fields for their training flights. They wanted South St. Paul. McInnis was forced to move a second time, and settled at what he called Victory Airport, as much a victory for himself for finding a place to operate, as a site from which to train flyers for victory in the war effort.

A number of things worked against McInnis. Partly his own love of life, and his love for partying kept him from spending adequate time on record-keeping and up-dating his fleet's maintenance. He spent less

Snow rolling tractor at Stanton during the winter of 1942-1943. (C. W. Hinck family)

and less time at the airport. Compounding this lack of time was the fact that he had been hired by Northwest Airlines in April of 1943 as a line pilot. Lysdale bought McInnis' business at Victory Airport and simply picked up where McInnis had left off, eventually giving nearly 2,000 students their evaluation in the 10-hour program without an accident. Some of the instructors at Victory included Howard Sokol, Jim Leonard, and Neil Thompson. Carlos Clark was employed there as a mechanic.

With the declaration of war, civilian flying had been curtailed at most Minnesota Airports. The *St. Paul Pioneer Press* of 4 January, 1942 indicated that at twenty-eight airports, pilot training would continue. At the same time, a five hundred-man Minnesota Defense Force consisting of local reservists, legionnaires, and townsfolk, would be posted at all other airports by State Adjutant General, Ellard K. Walsh. With fifty airports closed and some five hundred sixty aircraft grounded, two thousand private pilot's licenses were effectively "suspended."

In many cases, general aviation pilots were told to remove the propellers, or even the magnetos from their airplanes. These stringent measures didn't last long. By 1943, the actual guards were no longer posted, but the rationing of gasoline and the appropriation of most civilian aircraft made civilian flying virtually non-existent. Around the country, general aviation aircraft were bought up by the government and given to the training schools. First the Cubs, Taylorcrafts and Aeroncas, then the larger cabin planes and sport planes.

A week after Pearl Harbor, the CPT program ceased to exist. Student training, however, continued under the CAA. Students were now invited to enlist in one of the services to continue their training under the WTS. Army and Navy advisors were put in charge of all individual programs. The mobilization built like a ground swell, rolling over the entire country. Everybody, and every organization, set its mind to producing material and manpower to wage war. Almost immediately, the Navy was given full authority over the area of Wold-Chamberlain Field.

Since the early pre-CPT programs sponsored by the University of Minnesota, six operators had contracts for training student pilots at Wold. Prime among them were Vern Georgia, A. C. McInnis, and the Hinck brothers. Although no new CPT contracts were to be issued, many operators were still finishing the training of students under the existing contracts. On 1 June, 1942, the Navy informed all these civilian

operators that they had one month to vacate the premises and move to other sites.

Vern Georgia had a contract with St. Thomas College of St. Paul. The administrator, John Madigan, was most insistent that Georgia not cancel his contract. Thus, Georgia packed his bags and equipment quickly and moved to Albert Lea. His WTS contracts were part of the Navy V-5 program.

McInnis, as mentioned previously, moved first to South St. Paul, then to Victory Airport. Niels Sorenson, Claire Morrill, and Lloyd Johnson were some of McInnis's instructors.

Clarence Hinck made plans to move the Hinck Flying Service to the Stanton Airport near Northfield. He had a large school that offered elementary training in J-3 Cubs, secondary in UPF-7's, and cross-country in a Stinson Gullwing. Among instructors were Ben and Frank "Bubs" Christian.

Clarence traveled to Washington, D. C., to secure a contract to train Army glider pilots, and planned to handle that operation at Monticello.

The Stanton operation opened 26 October, 1942. Both Carlton and St. Olaf Colleges of Northfield, sponsored the training under a Navy WTS contract. All classroom work and physical training were conducted at Carlton, with students being housed in the football stadium where toilet and washroom facilities were available. Flight training was given at the Stanton Airport in N3N's, Waco UPF-7's and Howard DGA-18's. Al Falck was named manager of operations at the field. Many stories about the winter weather came out of the training period 1942-1943. Instructor Glen Slack related one near-disaster:

"This fellow was hand-propping one of the Howard DGA-18's. There was a mix-up in signals and the engine popped. I saw his red winter cap going up fifty feet in the air and I thought it was his head. I almost kissed him when I saw he was okay. The prop had hit him in the elbow and broke his arm. We found his wallet fifty feet from the airplane. The prop had also hit him in the fanny, tearing out his pocket, but not hitting the flesh. He had put his hand on the propeller hub to push away, and it had cut a circle in the palm of this hand. He was a lucky person, even though he was disabled after that."[74]

The program at Stanton closed in January of 1944 with the instructors moving on to other jobs; some to fly with the airlines, others to spend a career in the military. Mechanic, Orville Hickman, an aircraft designer in the 1930s, left in 1943 to run the maintenance shop at the University of Minnesota Airport. In his logbook, instructor Claire Morrill logged four classes of primary students, putting in over one thousand hours in the process. He also logged five classes of Secondary students for another seven hundred eighty hours and a class of instructors for which he logged one hundred fifty hours.

When the Navy instructed all civilian operators to cease flying at Wold by 1 July, 1942, five airports were affected; Wold-Chamberlain, Cedar Airport, Nicollet Airport, South St. Paul, and St. Paul's Holman Field. The Navy claimed a training area roughly bounded by a line extending from Long Lake to the west of Minneapolis, east to the St. Croix River, south to Hastings, and west to Prior Lake. A cry went up from many sources that the displaced CPT operators as well as four civilian operators would be put out of business.[75]

There was a petition by concerned businessmen to Governor Stassen asking for a one hundred sixty acre site somewhere near the cities for the ten operators and their fleet of eighty-eight aircraft. The Minnesota Aeronautics Commission favored developing several minor airports around the outer perimeter of the cities for civilian flying. The Commission asked Governor Stassen to give them specific instructions as to what was to be done and they asked for emergency funds to the tune of $100,000 and the cooperation of all State agencies involved.

With the Governor's approval to proceed with their plans, the Commission took action to establish the University Airport north of the Twin Cities, already a landing field for some time, as the official home for the WTS orphans. There, flying would be allowed only in a northerly direction so as to avoid the sensitive Northern Ordnance ammunition plant, immediately to its south. It was further indicated by the Commission that the only flying at that site would be conducted by those contracted to the government. Though the state backed the program, the Commission was stymied for a while by the Navy, who had claimed all airspace, and the Army, which was nervous about the proximity of the defense plant. Repeated begging by the state finally won approval of the plan.

At the same time the Navy was evicting civilians from Wold-Chamberlain, the Army was taking over St. Paul Holman Field. They would eventually establish a giant B-24 bomber modification center there, with Northwest Airlines flight operations as well as all civilian operators being moved out. Northwest would be the modification contractor, however, and manage the huge program.

Lexington Flying Corporation, owned by Otho "Al" Brandt, had a CPT contract at Holman Field prior to the start of the war. Macalester College of St. Paul administered the contract, with its president, Dr. Charles J. Turck, himself, the head of it. Brandt instructed with a fleet of Aeronca Defenders, and kept them flying nearly all the time. During one of his cross-country classes, a tremendous snow storm blew in, piling the snow deeper than the airport plows could handle. One of the local mechanics, Orville Tosch, came up with an ingenious idea. He offered to make a set of skis out of barn door parts. Al told him to go ahead and see what he could do. The next morning, when Al opened the hangar door, there stood an Aeronca Defender with neat "skis" mounted on it. Tosch had made the skis out of barn door tracks, bending up the front ends. They were mounted on tripods of welded steel tubing. Tosch was at work on a second pair, and now, as far as Al Brandt was concerned, the airport maintenance crew could take its time in clearing the runways.

During the fall of 1942, Brandt was faced with the move from Holman Field. "The government had plans and it was useless to argue to stay. I was in the middle of a CPT class when we had to move and I didn't know what to do. I argued. I had a government program too. That was the way it was, though, I was frozen to train these students by the government, I couldn't quit, I couldn't even join the Air Corps

Monticello, Minnesota. Destruction similar to that occurring at Northport during the September, 1942 windstorm. Truly a bad year for Taylorcrafts. (C. W. Hinck family)

myself.

"So we had to go to University Airport. They didn't have any runways. We got busy and got a road grader and made some runways. We were out of operation for some time until we got this airport fixed up so we could use it.

"The government put the pressure on the contract holders to get going there, yet their own inspectors nit-picked about the size and condition of the runway installation. Here is the war effort screaming for pilots, and the CAA is being real picky about whether this runway is safe or not. I finally said to them, 'Look you guys, we got a war going on... we can't spend a whole winter fixing up runways. They are good enough the way they are to operate from.' Finally, they okayed it and we started flying again.

"I had to transport the students there by bus. I had to buy a bus and two station wagons. We picked the students up and we took them back to Macalester."[76]

When the program changed to the WTS, Brandt's contracts still came from Macalester College. He worked on the 10-hour elimination program. Students came in groups of sixty-six at first, and there were no women among them. By 1944, the group sizes had increased, occasionally to one hundred thirty-two at a time.

Teaching ground school at the College, among other instructors, were Paul Paine, and one Hubert H. Humphrey, who would later achieve fame in the political field.

In addition to the glider pilot training program at Monticello, mentioned in the Clarence Hinck biography earlier in this book, there was another similar program located between Stillwater and White Bear Lake, at Northport Airport. Thomas North, owner of *North Aviation Company*, ran this one. Besides originally having a CPT series with secondary, cross-country and instructor courses, North received a contract with the 15th Army Air Force Glider Training Department, to train glider pilots.

A military staff to oversee the latter operation was quartered at the plush Lowell Inn at Stillwater. Students were first housed in the Stillwater High School gym, and later in barracks constructed on the airfield. Several satellite fields were leased for the glider training, including a field approximately where

Northport, 1941. Instructor Sam Hamilton is giving a class on aerodynamics. Students from left: Chester Pingrey, Harry Hayashi, Vince Doyle, and Richard Koplitz. (Vince Doyle)

Northport, 1941. A lesson in starting engines by the "armstrong" method. Instructor, Paul Scanlon, offers instruction, while student Herb Splettstoesser does the pulling. (Vince Doyle)

the Lake Elmo Airport is today, and another known as the Flynn Farm, a couple of miles farther east, toward Stillwater. At the Flynn Farm, Taylorcraft L-2A's were used for teaching future glider pilots the fine art of landing approaches, including downwind and dead-stick landings. The farmhouse was used as an office and the barn for minor maintenance on the airplanes.

At Northport itself, another section of glider instruction was also being given in L-2A's and the regular WTS training was also taking place. Tom North owned a Stinson SR-8E Gullwing and a Waco VKS cabin biplane which he used for cross country and navigation training. He also had a fleet of Waco UPF-7's for secondary aerobatic training. In 1942, the old airmail hangar from Wold-Chamberlain Field was trucked in, section by section, and reassembled. On its top was constructed a small control tower to handle field traffic. The hangar was used for service, storage and maintenance. Today, this hangar still stands on tilled farmland, delapidated, and not being used for any purpose.

One of the more unusual programs carried out at Northport was the South American pilot training program. On 12 May, 1943, under a WTS contract, ten Latin American students were brought to Northport for training. They came from Brazil, Argentina, Peru, Chile, Venezuela, and Mexico, after winning competi-

A short-bladed "run-in" prop is being used on this UPF-7 at Northport after an engine overhaul. (Roger Poore)

tions for the honors in their respective countries. They would earn commercial and flight instructor's ratings and carry the skills back to their native countries to train countrymen as service pilots.

They spoke some English when they arrived, but Stillwater High School teacher, Irene Hedberg, was charged with providing additional language training. A second wave of South Americans followed the first. Each was given one hundred hours of classroom training and forty hours of flying instruction in a seven month stay.

Northport, like Monticello, experienced a monster mid-summer storm in 1942. A straight-line wind front slammed across the airport, piling North's entire fleet of thirty L-2A's into a soggy mess. Most were totally destroyed and later scavenged for parts. Magically, however, within a few days, the government provided a new group of trainers, probably pulling them from satellite fields around the area.

Though Northport's glider program had the best safety record of six midwest schools, it did suffer at least one fatal accident. A Taylorcraft, flying from the Flynn Farm crashed, killing both student and instructor. Whether the student "froze" at the controls, as is rumored, or wing icing caused the crash on a wintry fall morning, the cause was not clear. Several Waco UPF-7 accidents resulted in only minor injuries.

Hamline University of St. Paul provided ground school for the WTS students at Northport, with K. H. Bracewell, the Coordinator; Aircraft Maintenance taught by Malcolm Smiley; Structures and Theory by Sam Hamilton; Navigation by John M. Gran; other subjects by Louis King. Sam Hamilton later drove back and forth between the college and the airfield to teach the practical subjects.

Some of North's instructors were John Rice, Milan Gersting, Russell Neff, LaVerne Pfeiffer, Don Minar, Frank Kraft, Lloyd Louckes, Lloyd Alsworth, Merrill Hawkins, Carlton Hess, and Louis Long. Mechanics included Ken Maxwell, Harry Hayashi, Roger Poore, Gene Kunde, John Benson, Bill Bakker, Bill Bolduc, and Wally Lindquist. At a time when Japanese-Americans were being persecuted and sent to detainment camps around the country, the presence of Hayashi at Northport was unique.

During the six months from June to November,

Northport Airport, 1942. Control tower erected atop the old airmail hangar brought up from Wold-Chamberlain Field. Note the operator with light signal gun. (Roger Poore)

1942, three thousand cadets, at the rate of two hundred fifty every two weeks, received their training at Northport, going on to advanced training at bases in the south.[77]

Tom North continued to train pilots under the WTS program until 1943 when his contracts ended. He then joined Northwest Airlines as a co-pilot.

As District Superintendent of all CPT and WTS programs in the region, George Holey wore many hats. After Pearl Harbor, a regulation came down that all students, now enlisted men in the Army Air Force, would have to be fingerprinted, and George was assigned to visit each training operation to set up the procedure. Often he conducted the fingerprinting himself. He tells of an incident where he set up a fingerprint line, checking each individual's record card as he printed him. A student came through one day and a quick check of his records told Holey that this man was not of legal age, but only seventeen. "I looked up at him and asked him what the hell he was doing. It was a real cold day, and he fainted in front of me. He must have been so terrified that it happened. Some of the other students took him outside and revived him. I apologized.

"About a year later, he came to see me in my office. He said, 'I've got a chance to go into the Air Force, now what happened to me back there, do you think they'll hold it against me?' I said I didn't think so- just not to open the door. If they did give him a rough time, I told him to have them get a hold of me. They never did, so I suspect he had no trouble.

"I was giving aerobatic flight tests. One time I went to Milwaukee and flight-tested ten Secondary students in aerobatics, all in one day. I was goofy by the time I was through.

"I continued to give those tests through the war. I also did most of the washing out. The chief instructor would give me the data on the students. I'll never forget up in Duluth, a young fellow was up for washout. I did wash him out, and he just begged me to authorize another five hours, which I did, and named the instructor to help him. About a year later, a young second lieutenant walked into my office at Wold with a new set of wings. 'Mr. Holey, I don't suppose you remember me. I'm the fellow you gave a second chance to in Duluth. Look here, I have something to show

Northport Airport, 1942. Taylorcraft L-2's lined up waiting for glider pilot students during the military glider program. (Roger Poore)

you.' We walked out of the old terminal building at Wold, and there sat a shiny new B-17... and he was the Captain.'"[78]

With students flying around all over the cities, Holey also had to field many complaints. "There was a complaint from a citizen. I asked what her name was, but she wouldn't give me that. I asked where she lived and she wouldn't tell me that either. I told her I couldn't help her unless she could give me the details. I asked her the reason she would not give the information. She meekly told me that she was in a nudist colony up north of Anoka."[79]

To get around, the CAA provided George with a brand-new Waco UPF-7, painted in the usual CAA colors, bright orange and black. George remembered that many times the sight of his airplane would get violators of restricted airspace, or pilots fooling around, buzzing residential areas, to turn tail and run.

In 1944, the military services, flush with new recruits and a plethora of CPT/WTS trained pilots, had reached saturation. The WTS programs closed down. If it would seem like a blessed event, it was not. The cancellation of the government program meant the stoppage of income for most civilian flight schools.

A hue and cry went up across the land. In Minnesota, a group of operators sent a delegation to Washington to lobby for continuance of the McCaren Bill which authorized the original programs, now due to be shut down. The group was led by B. G. Vandre of St. Cloud, and one of his WTS instructors, R. J.

Northport Airport, 1942. A mess! Some of the damaged L-2's following a 1942 windstorm that struck the northern portion of the metropolitan area. The entire fleet was damaged. (Roger Poore)

Northport Airport, 1942. Tom North's fleet consisting of one Stinson Gullwing and one Cabin Waco, plus a group of Waco UPF-7's for the CPT Secondary program. Note the absense of the airmail hangar which had not been moved in at the time this photo was taken. (Milan Gersting)

Goodrich. Goodrich testified before a Senate Committee, "My purpose here is to represent the contractors, the colleges, and the 175 instructors in the Minnesota area who are engaged in training Army and Navy flight personnel. It would seem to us a good thing to further training through continuance of the CPT Act, as the history of the Act of 1939 has spoken so well for itself when the Armed Forces needed pilots so badly at the commencement of hostilities and before, they admittedly, did not have them."[80]

He went on to state, "If the war ended today, CPT's use has been significant. But contrary to rumors started that peace is near when training slows up, as is happening as a result of this, the CPT is still useful.

"First of all, how can we forecast the fortunes of war with enough accuracy to say that we have enough trained men?"

He stated that it was possible that this training should be part of the life of every qualified young man in war or peace, and indicated that trained pilots would furnish the backbone of the post-war aviation industry. The impact on the colleges and the communities who would have to pay for the facilities built up by the government and now about to be abandoned. His main thrust, however, was regarding the effect of the cancellation on the instructors themselves.

"What about the flight instructors in this program? These men are all highly trained by public expense. They form a nucleus for post-war aviation, but now that their period of usefulness is supposedly over, their only recourse is to join the Army in a *non-flying* capacity, while those with much less experience, perhaps are still receiving flight training (I refer to Liaison, Women's Ferry Command, ATC, etc.). Those [of us] who are combat age and those who are not, are willing to go into active flying duty, but feel that it is a waste of public expenditures to go in as a foot soldier and discard all this flight experience. It is my sincere hope that now that we have this wealth of trained men, they can be kept active in furthering the war effort and in development of post war aviation in a flying status by continuing the CPT Act as proposed here today."[81]

Goodrich then related how he had enlisted in the Reserves at the urging of the government to become a combat pilot, as he had already obtained his private license at his own expense. Instead, they made him a flight instructor in the WTS. As such, he had spent his last two years. He responded to an Air Corps Major's public statement that these no-longer-useful instructors be trained now as mechanics, by saying that the government was still advertising for new flight enlistees, why not use the instructors instead?

The Senate Committee stalled him off, suggesting that he go to his Congressman to inform the legislator about the community impact of cancellation, which Goodrich did. Next he met with his congressman and a representative of General "Hap" Arnold's staff to determine why Minnesota, especially, had been the first to be cancelled. This officer simply implied that the first schools to be closed were those farthest from the active military training bases. Further, each instructor would be evaluated by Air Corps personnel to determine his qualifications for further military duty. Goodrich was told of three scenarios; one, if the instructor was of the age and physical qualifications to become a pilot candidate, he would be sent on as such; two, if he was not within those requirements, he would be sent to an Air Corps technical school; and third, if unqualified for the first two, he would be sent into the Army as a "G.I."

There were feelings in military circles that the CAA had overstepped its bounds in competing with the services as a training entity. If the CAA wanted to keep training men, they were welcome to do so, but not for the military. The military felt that the CAA would be glutting post-war aviation and instructors should not be deferred from present military obligation. One staff officer even indicated that the military wanted to train men who had never touched an airplane before. He even told Goodrich in no uncertain terms, that it was military-trained men who would form the nucleus of post-war aviation!

Thus the War Training Service came to an awkward end in late 1944. It did not die quietly, but left repercussions. For one thing, government subsidies had been barely meeting the costs of some operator's expansion and expenses. Some, like Al Brandt, had been promised a review of their fees by the Contract Termination Board of the CAA. The reviews were put off, and put off, until the program came to an end. That left Brandt with no avenue of appeal, and he, like a great many, never realized a profit from the WTS program.

A few other interesting aviation-related government training programs occurring just prior to and during World War II and bear mentioning:

During the late 1930s, the National Youth Administration (NYA) built a "campus" on the site of what is now Murphy's Landing in Shakopee, Minnesota. There, in 1938, they offered aviation mechanics as a trade school course. A hangar was built on the grounds as were shops for woodworking, engine overhaul, fabric covering, and a machineshop. An old Navy airplane was brought in to give the students some hands-on practical training. The hangar still stands, now the Murphy's Landing restaurant.

In 1942, a move on the part of the Minnesota Aeronautics Commission was made to try to interest Governor Harold Stassen in establishing "camps" for flight training of young people. In a letter from Acting Director William M. Beadie, of the commission, to Lester R. Badger of the governor's staff, Beadie

Victory Airport as it looked in 1978. At that time, the big hangar and other buildings were being used by the Foldaside Door Manufacturing Company. (Noel Allard)

recommended setting up ten such camps, located outside of the Twin Cities, as WPA projects using State Civil Defense Funds. Each camp would have the facilities to house and train thirty to sixty students at the cost of $1.00 a day. If this plan worked out, the State would produce nearly two thousand pilots each year. The idea was soon overshadowed by the tremendous buildup of the WTS.[82]

St. Paul Vocational School also offered an aviation mechanics course taught by Franz Sjowall. The course was known as War Production Training, prepping the students for work in war production plants.

Though women had been excluded from most training programs after the war started, an interesting program did develop at the University of Minnesota. Sponsored by the Curtiss-Wright Corporation, the University was one of seven institutions in the country at which Curtiss-Wright sought to train workers for their defense plants. Women were selected from all parts of the country with one hundred two coming to Minnesota to become "Curtiss-Wright Cadettes." Their schooling was provided at no charge with the provision they would pledge to work for Curtiss after graduation. They were furnished board and room and spending money of $10 a week. Shevlin Hall on the University campus was converted to a dormitory by replacement of the men's urinals with toilet stalls, painting the bunk beds pale green and lining the halls with pink wooden lockers.

The women studied 40 hours a week on such subjects such as drafting, structures, mechanics, aerodynamics, machine shop, stress analysis, materials testing, aluminum fabricating and even riveting. These fledgling engineers made quite an impact on the campus male population, especially when they started wearing blue jeans to classes, a situation unheard of in those days. The reason was to have the extra pockets for their slide rules and other tools. In ten months of studies, the women earned credits equalling two and half years of college. Nearly one hundred of the group graduated and went to work for Curtiss, most at Columbus, Ohio. Many spent their working career as an engineer in the aerospace industry.[83]

MODIFYING THE DOOLITTLE RAIDERS

World War II broke into America's lives with crushing impact on Sunday morning, 7 December, 1941. It was a dark hour for American pride. Stunned and demoralized by the loss of a vast portion of our great naval fleet, the citizenry went into shock. The government was momentarily at a loss as to how to retaliate. In the next few days, however, it became charged with a fervor to strike back in a telling way.

The "sleeping giant," as a Japanese admiral had alluded to the U. S., was awakened with a rush of action on the government's part, and great patriotic feelings among its citizens. Almost immediately, all political, business, and personal energies shifted into high gear to produce war materials.

President Franklin D. Roosevelt met almost daily with the chiefs of the various armed services, badgering them for ideas as to how best to raise a military strike that would regain a feeling of national pride. In January of 1942, barely three weeks after Pearl Harbor, an idea was advanced among the military staff for the launch of medium bombers from an aircraft carrier at sea, against the Japanese home islands. The idea was offered to the Navy Chief of Operations, Admiral Ernest King, and it soon made the rounds to Army Air Force chief, General Hap Arnold.

Arnold then looked in on a newly-promoted Lieutenant Colonel named James H. Doolittle, working in an office in the same building. He questioned Doolittle as to what kind of an airplane could take off from a very short space at gross weight and fly a mission of 2300 miles. Doolittle, who did not know of the overall idea, had few choices. He quickly calculated that the Douglas B-23 bomber and the North American B-25 were the only two candidates. When he learned of the 75 foot width of the takeoff runway, the B-25, with its 68 foot wingspan was the only choice. When Doolittle found out the details of the plan he realized that the bombers wingtips would pass by an aircraft carrier's island structure with only a few feet of clearance.

Even though President Roosevelt had yet no inkling of the plan, the mission was set. Arnold gave Doolittle complete command over the "B-25 Special Project," as it was called. Doolittle's first order of business was to request from the Air Service Command, a single B-25B aircraft to be made available for the planning and engineering tests. The mission would require long-range fuel tanks to be installed. This B-25B would be the first plane to be modified.

Doolittle quickly checked with several airlines regarding their capability of handling such a "rush" request. Of American, Chicago and Southern, United, Northwest, and Mid-Continent Airlines, only Mid-Continent was willing and able to make the modifications in such a short time. Mid-Continent was a company with a high certified mechanic-to-apprentice mechanic ratio, a clean bill of health in the quality of their operation, the mechanical soundness of their aircraft, and their business acumen. Moreover, their maintenance base at Wold-Chamberlain Field in Minneapolis, where the work would be accomplished, was located in the northern portion of the country, far

The first B-25B's have arrived at Mid-Continent Airlines hangar at Wold-Chamberlain Field in early February, 1942 to be modified for Jimmy Doolittle's proposed raid on Tokyo. At least four are seen here, in this snapshot by a Mid-Continent employee, as they are parked next to the airline's hangar on 34th Avenue. (Ken Brommer)

away from the potential of spy activity, and able to handle a project of great secrecy without fanfare.

Mid-Continent's well-qualified mechanics worked in a large, newly-constructed hangar at the south end of Wold-Chamberlain, far from the scrutiny of airline passengers or visitors. Doolittle was no stranger to the area, having been a Shell Oil Company representative for several years prior to the war, making periodic calls on his franchisee, Shorty De Ponti. When Doolittle arrived at Mid-Continent's shops on 10 February, 1942, to check on the environment in which the bombers would be immersed, he conferred at length with Supervisor of Maintenance, Benjamin F. Krouse. Doolittle plotted out the timing that was required for the modifications. He wanted twenty-four aircraft modified with long-range fuel tanks...and he wanted the work completed by the 3rd of March, barely a month away. A tall order!

Krouse immediately jumped to the task. There were no blueprints to go by. Every fitting and fuel line would have to be engineered on the spot, drawings made as they went along. Quickly, the production schedule was set in motion. An order had already been placed by officers at Wright Field with the U. S. Rubber Company for collapsible neoprene rubber fuselage fuel tanks. They had even been delivered before Doolittle's visit. Custom-built 275 gallon bomb-bay tanks would have to be constructed of 20-gauge steel by hand. Mid-Continent sub-contracted for them with the McQuay Company of Minneapolis, at that time producing automotive radiators.

Military Police from Fort Snelling appeared overnight to patrol the area. Workers were advised not to talk about the project with anyone off the property. Though they were never informed as to what target the bombers would be hitting, what they saw and what they heard should be kept confidential, even from their own families.

Very soon, B-25's were landing at Wold. It was the first time that this airplane had been seen in the area and public interest was aroused. Military Police kept visitors away, however, including the media...and cer-

tain airport officials. When Airport Manager, Larry Hammond, decided to pay a visit to inquire why some of the fences had been taken down, he was unceremoniously kept at bay with a warning rifle shot! Commissioners, tower staff, and even airport manager, soon learned that even *they* had no business near the Mid-Continent hangar.

Though Mid-Continent still had an airline to operate, forty mechanics per shift, in three shifts, worked on the bombers. One aircraft was nosed into the hangar, a second ship tailed in alongside. Occasionally, they were pulled outside to make way for a Mid-Continent plane that needed some maintenance. Krouse pushed his workers hard, often inciting hot tempers, but the work rushed along.

The neoprene fuselage tanks were fitted and piped via hose to the bomb-bay tanks, then into the main fuel transfer system. Each 160 gallon neoprene tank was a vexing problem, the smell of neoprene gagged the mechanics who had to work in the confined spaces inside the airplanes.

The actual task of making the installations lasted a scant two weeks, with nearly two aircraft per day being completed. The last B-25 rolled out on 28 February, 1942, ran up its engines, and took off to the north, into a strong wind.

Just like that, the bombers that had so suddenly come...were gone! In less than a month, Mid-Continent had engineered the modifications, completed them and sent two dozen B-25's on their round-about way to California where they would be tested and the crews trained. Sixteen of these aircraft would takeoff from the U. S. S. Hornet, 650 miles east of Japan, led by Jimmy Doolittle. Just six weeks after their departure from Wold-Chamberlain, on 18 April, 1942, they would be dropping bombs on Tokyo and other cities in Japan in America's first retaliatory strike.

Mid-Continent handled other government contracts in the following years, including the installation of Sperry autopilots in B-26 bombers, ferry tanks in B-17's, and modifications to F-5's (photo P-38's) and P-51's. They also did some contract work on other B-25's.

The story that the Doolittle raiders were further modified at Holman Field in St. Paul, is not true. A group of B-25C's were modified there under the Lend-Lease program, destined for the Netherlands. Mid-

Continent's contribution is not highly publicized in Tokyo Raid literature, but their magnificent effort in a one-month period of early 1942 stands out as exemplary. Minnesota can be quite proud of that. More of Mid-Continental history is related elsewhere in this book.

Much of the above information is excerpted from an unpublished manuscript written by T/Sgt William R. Ellis, 934th Tactical Airlift Group, USAF Reserve, Twin Cities Air Force Reserve Base, Minneapolis-St. Paul International Airport.

TROOP GLIDER MANUFACTURING

Some very far-sighted thinking derived the plan for the use of glider aircraft to land supplies and troops behind enemy lines during World War II. Far-sighted because, while the glider itself was not a new invention, its use for this purpose was conceived at the very beginning of the war, even though it would not be used until much later.

With the war in its infancy, the War Production Board was contracting with private corporations which had the ability to manage many facets of military production. The Waco Aircraft Manufacturing Company of Troy, Ohio, had designed a small troop carrying glider during the winter of 1941-42. The Army Air Forces designated it CG-4, intending it to carry fifteen combat troops, or combinations of troops and supplies. They assigned blocks of the gliders to be built by various manufacturers besides Waco, including Cessna, Timm, Ford, and a hastily-formed corporation in St. Paul with literally no aviation experience of any sort, named Northwestern Aeronautical Corporation.

Northwestern Aeronautical was incorporated in February of 1942 by three lawyers from the offices of Doherty, Rumble and Butler in St. Paul. Francis Butler, Jack C. Foote, and Irving Clark were the founders. They named as President, John E. Parker an entrepreneur from Washington, D. C. Though none of the four had any prior experience in aviation, or manufacturing, Parker did have friends in the contracting office in Washington, and was able to convince the government that he could pull together the expertise to handle a contract for glider production.

Northwestern would not construct any of the glider components, but would sub-contract that portion to

Waco CG-4A glider under tow, has just lifted off the runway at Wold-Chamberlain Field. (Villaume Company)

companies with manufacturing experience and aviation know-how in the Twin Cities. Then, Northwestern would handle the assembly portion of the contract in rented facilities at Wold-Chamberlain Airport in Minneapolis. The two companies selected for the actual manufacturing were the Villaume Box and Lumber Company of St. Paul, and the De Ponti Aviation Company of Minneapolis.

Villaume was a pioneer St. Paul company. Eugene Villaume had come to St. Paul from France in 1873 as a woodworker. In 1881, he and his brothers established the Villaume Box and Lumber Company at the base of bluffs on the Mississippi River's westside. The company grew and acquired other small companies, eventually becoming well-known for the quality of their woodworking, cabinetry, and store fixtures. They produced church interiors for local and out-of-state churches. The mahogany doors and trim on the top twenty-five floors of St. Paul's First National Bank Building, as well as the interior of the nearby Northern States Power Building, the Ramsey County Courthouse and the St. Paul City Hall were done by Villaume craftsmen.

It was no wonder, then, that Villaume was selected to produce the all-wooden wing and control surface structures for the Waco CG-4 gliders under Northwestern Aeronautical's contract, despite the fact that they, also, had absolutely no prior experience in the aircraft industry.

In addition to the $7 million glider wing contract, Villaume was also to produce shipping crates for the gliders under a separate $1.5 million contract. In the following year, Villaume would also contract with the

A "snatch pickup" is under way. Spectators watch as a C-47 roars past at full throttle, snagging a line which is attached to a yet stationary CG-4A in the background. The glider will be tugged into the air from a standstill. (Floyd Homstad)

The two gliders produced in the Twin Cities share the ramp in front of De Ponti's hangars at Wold-Chamberlain. Probably the initial CG-13 with tailwheel needs the crowd of manhandlers to move it. CG-4A is at left. (Villaume Company)

Waco CG-13A-NW shown during a practice load/unload exercise. Note the nosewheel configuration and the large perforated flaps. (Villaume Company)

government to manufacture $1.8 million worth of ammunition crates for the Army Ordnance Division, and K-ration cartons.[84]

Villaume's property included 50,000 square feet of space in fourteen caves in the river bluffs. Company literature indicated that the caves could double as storage space and air-raid shelters. The company operated three Moore Dry Kilns with a drying capacity of a million board feet. They also boasted of a complete woodworking plant with saws, shapers, sanders, planers, routers, jointers, etc. They hired and trained their own work force, which at peak production, totaled 1500 persons.

Villaume required start-up expertise, however. Glider expert and head of the newly chartered Gliding, Soaring and Aeronautical Education Department of the Minnesota Aeronautics Commission, Ted Bellak, was loaned to advise on such things as setting up a production line, interpreting drawings, and building jigs.[85] Stunt man and airplane rebuilder, Chuck Doyle, who also had a commercial glider license, was put on the payroll at Villaume as inspector. His job was to select the spruce planks that would be machined into wing spars, birch and mahogany for the ribs, and oversee the casein gluing operation that fastened the various rib parts together. His knowledge would help assure the integrity and airworthiness of the components.

Though the Villaume plant was equipped with all the woodworking machinery needed to do the job, it was somewhat antiquated, relying on overhead shafts and great pulleys to delivery power to the saws and shapers. Though adequate for the cabinetry and crate business, it did have some problems in the delicate area of precision aircraft parts. For example, a drill press was being used to drill holes in the butt-end of wing spars for the purpose of attaching the heavy-duty steel wing-to-frame brackets. It would not sink a perfect perpendicular shaft all the way through the massive spar. The drill was "crawling" with the exit hole being somewhat offset from the entry hole, causing misalignment with the bracket, and creating many rejected parts. Doyle helped engineers solve the problem by putting a stop in the drill head so that the hole was drilled only half-way through. With all the holes drilled halfway, a dowel was mounted in the drill base, and when the spar was turned upside down and set on the dowel, the other half could be drilled with perfect alignment.[86]

Wings, rudders and elevators, built in Villaume's west-side plant on Indiana Avenue, and crates built on the east side in another of Villaume's facilities, were shipped to Wold-Chamberlain Field for assembly. The assembly point was a series of hangars that Northwestern Aeronautical leased from Shorty De Ponti.

Meanwhile, in a quiet, residential neighborhood in South Minneapolis, near 53rd Street and Lyndale Avenue, the De Ponti Aviation Company was also constructing the glider fuselages, horizontal and vertical stabilizers and landing gear. From Waco-supplied drawings, jigs were built and steel tubing was welded together to form the glider airframes. The frames were built up in three sections; nose section, main body section, and tail section.

Worker, Floyd Homstad, who had been a stable-boy for Shorty De Ponti, caring for De Ponti's horses at a nearby farm, became a fuselage welder. Like all new welders-to-be, he learned the art at an in-plant school taught by instructor, Wenzel Broash. Upon completion of the classroom work, with a welder's certificate in hand, he stepped right onto the production line, working either a single or double shift, without a break, for a solid year...nearly the entire time on tail sections alone.[87]

Ironically, Homstad soon entered the military, became a pilot, and ended up towing these same gliders into Burma to supply the 14th Army. He flew the C-47, making "snatch pickups." He relates, "There was a winch in the airplane that payed out at a certain rate and you'd grab that cable with all the power on and you'd still hit the windshield. The glider pilot really has to be careful so the towplane doesn't stall. When you snatch them, you just pull up, and the glider pilot lowers his nose at first, then goes back to level flight to pickup speed. I had a double tow (pulling two gliders) at night one time and lost an engine on takeoff. The glider pilots saw that...and cut off immediately. I circled around and landed. They (the glider pilots) were on the ball that time!"[88]

The De Ponti fuselage building had been an auto showroom and repair shop before the war, under the ownership of the O. I. Borton Motor Company. (Borton has a Volvo dealership only blocks farther south of that location today.) As each glider fuselage was finished, it was primered with zinc chromate paint, squeezed out the doors at one end of the plant, and loaded onto a waiting flatbed truck for its trip to Wold-Chamberlain.

At peak production, nearly three hundred persons were employed, turning out as many as two hundred gliders a month.[89]

At Wold, in the De Ponti hangars, Northwestern Aeronautical assembled the gliders with their own work force. There, using the expertise of Northwest Airlines Chief Mechanic, James B. "Big Jim" La-Mont, the assembly line was synchronized with all steps of assembly coming together at the right time. In the south-most hangar, slip-case envelope wing and fuselage covers of unbleached muslin were sewn. They were fitted to the wings, fuselages, and tail components. The large covered units then moved next door to the second hangar where they were painted. John Storm, who worked in the paint department, relates the procedure from there: "The first coat of clear nitrocellulose dope was brushed on, lightly sanded, and a second coat was sprayed on. Following this, they started spraying the olive-drab on the tops (of wings and fuselages). Some were painted olive-drab underneath as well, some were painted grey underneath. There were no silver coats. Between each of the two olive-drab coats, the parts were sanded. One man laid out the insignia with chalk on a stencil, then painted the insignia. The old insignia with a red meatball in the middle changed to a plain blue circle with a white star and bars."[90]

Women workers did all the taping, laying tape strips along all the stress points on fuselages, wings and surfaces. They also did the sanding between paint coats, while teams of men did the spray painting. When a wing came into the spray booth, it was pushed under a scaffold. Two men stood below the scaffold, one on each side to paint the lower half, while two men on the scaffolding painted the upper portion.

As the glider fuselages were finished, they were moved into the third of the smaller hangars where they were mated with tails, and interior components were installed. Then the major assemblies were moved into the larger bays of the former Universal hangars where they were either crated for rail shipment to southern or eastern training bases and storage depots; or they were fully assembled. In the later case, they were pushed outside and lined up waiting for tow planes to pull them out of the field.

For the crews that worked this part of the production, it was a three-shift, around-the-clock operation. Wages were $31 a week for workers, with the Government exacting a 5% "Victory Tax" on top of federal and state taxes.

In the beginning, there was a strict division of labor, with men doing the doping, women the taping and sanding. In a move to integrate the work force, Northwestern Aeronautical tried to move the women into the painting operation, mixing the paint crews with members of both sexes. There were negative reactions among the males, some refusing to work.

Urban McMiller, assistant production manager, and manager of planning and control for all three of Northwestern's facilities, had to deal with this problem. His schooling at Dunwoody Institute had been in Industrial Management, ("Foreman training" he called it).[91] His studies included labor laws, environmental concerns of lighting, ventilation, heating, safety, occupational diseases, morale, and wage scales. He was well equipped to handle employee relations plus the myriad of other problems that we think are new today, such as: employee dressing rooms, safety shielding of machinery belts and shafts, and handling of toxic chemicals such as the lacquer paints. He and the staff successfully integrated the work-force.

Despite these "people" problems, there was a high regard for the work ethic. With the glider's final coat of paint, it was as handsome as many of the civilian aircraft produced before the war. The truth of this fact is apparent in photos of gliders taken during this period. John Storm acknowledges, "We were cognizant of the fact that these gliders had to be flown, and if they didn't have a nice finish, they wouldn't fly as well. People worked very hard."[92]

Northwestern's facilities also produced a larger troop and vehicle-carrying glider, the Waco CG-13A, seating thirty troops, and able to carry a jeep or artillery piece. The first CG-13A had a tail-wheel, but only a single item was produced in that configuration. Forty-nine additional CG-13's with nose wheels came off the line after that. The whole nose section of this larger glider, including the flight controls and crew seats, swung upward to allow for loading and unloading.

An unusual powered version of the CG-4A was built at the facilities and assembled at Wold-Chamberlain. The Army Air Force designation was XPG-1. Shorty De Ponti indicated that two were built; but Air Forces records show only a single one. The XPG-1 did fly successfully on 12 May, 1943, but the Air Forces did not follow-up with a production order.

Air Force records list an additional 10 powered gliders built at Northwestern Aeronautical, designated PG-2A, another derivative of the CG-4A. No information about them, or confirmation that they were even built, has come to light. This model, might however, account for De Ponti's recollection of a second powered glider.[93] Evidence indicates that plans were under way to hang detachable engines on the larger, CG-13 glider as well, but again, details are not available.

According to various sources, from 1325[94] to 1559[95] gliders were turned out by Northwestern Aeronautical through the spring of 1944. In all, the Government purchased 13,912 CG-4A gliders and twelve additional powered versions from fifteen different manufacturers, with the largest numbers being built by Ford (4190). Other manufacturers were Commonwealth (1470), Waco (1074), General (1112), Gibson (1078), Pratt and Read (956), and Cessna (750).

Exactly where the aircraft produced by Northwestern Aeronautical went upon completion, whether

XPG-1 prototype. Publicity photo on day of test flight, 12 May, 1943 shows the 150 h.p. Franklin engines mounted under the wings. (Angelo De Ponti)

for training, or storage for the eventual D-Day, is unknown. Due to great far-sighted planning on the part of the War Department, and the dedication and conscientious craftsmanship of hundreds of Minnesota men and women, the ships were ready when needed.

THE MOTORLESS FLIGHT PROGRAM

One of the more colorful and lesser-known wartime programs within the State of Minnesota was undertaken in 1941 to establish classes in Minnesota's technical schools, whereby students would be taught the fundamentals of general aviation knowledge through the construction of glider aircraft.

Governor Harold Stassen backed the project, testifying before the state legislature to procure funding. Initially set at $15,000, the legislature later increased the amount to $35,000. The man hired for implementation of the program was Theodore G. Bellak.

Bellak's background ran deep in gliding and soaring. Born in New Jersey, he had spent nearly half of his twenty-nine years studying the principles and practice of soaring. He had even spent a year in Europe in the 1930s, observing and learning from gliding experts in Belgium, Holland, and Germany. In this country, he had worked for the Du Pont Sailplane Company and the Frankfort Sailplane Company, where he and Stanley Corcoran had designed the "Cinema II" glider. During World War II the military purchased many Cinema II's for training purposes.

Bellak's interest in soaring took him across the country on behalf of the Soaring Society of America, searching out the best soaring sites. He became so adept at the sport, that he, along with soaring experts Chet Decker and Emil Lahecka, were booked to perform formation glider aerobatics at the 1938 National Air Races at Cleveland, Ohio. On 4 July, 1939, Bellak set an overwater soaring flight record in his personal glider, the "Minimoa," winging some 56 miles across Lake Michigan from Sturgeon Bay, Wisconsin, to Frankfort, Michigan.

In 1936, at Chelsea, Michigan, he set up the first federally sponsored program to establish a vocational school class in aeronautical knowledge and glider construction, setting the stage for his coming to Minnesota.

In 1941, at the request of the Minnesota Aeronautics Commission, he came to the state to become Director of the commission's Gliding, Soaring and Aeronautical Education Division. A program to promote general aviation knowledge was sponsored by the Aeronautics Commission with cooperation of the National Youth Administration (NYA), a federal institution. It was to be guided by an oversight committee chaired by Governor Stassen, with Doctor Maurice Walsh of the Mayo Clinic, Leonard Olson of the State Department of Education, and George Selke, President of St. Cloud State University, as members.

Students would learn general aeronautical knowledge, the fundamentals of flying, and aircraft construction. What better way to apply these principles than to have them construct gliders and fly them. Bellak embraced the theories of committee member Walsh's well-circulated booklet, "A Practical Method of Pilot Selection," in which it was professed that a glider pilot would become a better "instinctive" powered pilot than a person without the same background. Thus, Bellak would advocate glider training for all future pilots, including those entering military service, which would be a natural outcome of this program.

Bellak placed an order for three Cinema II sailplane kits from the Frankfort Sailplane Company. These kits were assembled by students in a warehouse near the Mississippi River, on Hennepin Avenue, in downtown Minneapolis. Bellak designed a special trailer to be built by students at the NYA school in Shakopee, Minnesota. The trailer was used to transport gliders around the state for training and demonstrations.

During this period, Bellak crossed the State, giving demonstrations in his own sailplane to various student groups, civic organizations and air show audiences. He was towed to Litchfield, Minnesota, behind a Piper Cub flown by local barnstormer and Marine pilot, Jack Kipp, putting on one such exhibition the day before Pearl Harbor.[96]

With the war having started, there was a new urgency to the program. A licensed A & E (Airframe & Engine) mechanic was needed to supervise the glider construction. Bernard Pietenpol was among applicants for the position, but Robert Heermance was hired.

In January of 1942, Bellak proposed the idea and was given the go-ahead to write a curriculum and implement a similar glider construction program in thirteen high schools around the State.[97] Those schools were: Albert Lea, Appleton, Austin, Washington High School of Brainerd, Morgan Park High School of Duluth, Eveleth, Minneapolis Central, St. Cloud Tech., St. Louis Park, St. Paul Central, Virginia, Winona, and Worthington.

In February, Bellak authorized Professor John Akerman's Aeronautical Engineering Department at the University of Minnesota, to begin design and construction of a simple glider of original design, capable of being built in the various schools. George Baggs was the project engineering supervisor. Bellak later test-flew the glider prototype, securing the first airworthiness certificate ever issued to a U. S. university.[98]

The high school curriculum included such topics as the history of motorless flight, aerodynamics, design and construction of gliders, launching methods, tools, drafting, etc. The course was a free elective for junior and senior high students under the governor's Executive Order Number 8, dated 10 December, 1941, which stated, "...in the view of the state of war and emergency, the Minnesota Glider Program is hereby expanded for the purpose of contributing to the defense of the state, and increasing the aeronautical ability of the youth of the state and nation."[99]

Obviously, students trained in aeronautical knowledge would be a valuable asset in the war effort, not only as a pool from which combat pilots could be trained, but also in the aircraft manufacturing industry, now shifting into high gear.

By July 1942, plans had been made to start high school courses in the fall semester. Bellak busied himself with continued trips around the state. One such trip brought him to Monticello, Minnesota, where the Army glider pilot training program was under way. There he gave a demonstration to cadet pilots. He would later be stung by legislative and public skepticism of the school glider program, when accidents occurring in the military program were translated to involve all glider programs.

The media played up military training accidents, includng fatalities, as "glider program" accidents. An angered Bellak wrote a clarification to the news media: "Because these accidents have not been presented to newspaper readers as airplane accidents, they tend to be construed as glider fatalities. This erroneous interpretation, caused by lack of a plainly worded statement that the accidents occurred in powered airplanes (Taylorcraft L-2's, Piper L-4's) used as gliders by idling their motors, result in a damaging attitude toward the Minnesota State Gliding and Soaring Program...

"To date, there has never been a fatal accident in a glider in the state...for your information, the following distinction between these two programs should be borne in mind in order to write articles which are not confusing..."[100]

He went on to explain that the high school program was producing non-airborne, pre-flight glider trainers, and students would also be flying in certified and bonafide gliders such as the Cinema II's. The Army program was substituting powered planes for gliders, and the two did not compare. He stated that the glider could stay aloft much longer without power, thus providing a great margin of safety to the pilot, while the powered aircraft with idling or shut off engine, had no such capability.

Other problems cropped up. With the wartime aircraft industry expansion, parts and materials were hard to come by. Certain materials were under a priority-use basis, and top priority users were supplied first. When it came to rubber tires and lacquer paint, for example, the glider program fit into a low-priority category. Governor Stassen traveled to Washington to beg for a higher priority rating for his pet program, but was unsuccessful. The state finally got the needed materials, but through a private source: Van Dusen Aircraft Supplies.[101]

Bellak found time to act as consultant to Northwestern Aeronautical Company and the Villaume Box and Lumber Company of St. Paul on glider construction requirements.

Each of the high schools involved with the program did construct a pre-flight glider. Most gliders were fitted with a short twenty foot wing, which would allow a student pilot to make ground runs under tow behind a vehicle, thus getting the feel of handling controls at relatively low speeds. The idea was to select the most promising students, and encourage them to pursue pilot training after school graduation. To enhance this prospect, they would be given "morale rides" in the Cinema II gliders later.

With the haste and hustle of military programs throughout the country, the glider program in the schools was often an overload for the facilities. Problems were experienced such as lack of space in the school shops, indifferent instructors, class conflicts, and lack of materials, tools, time, and money. Nevertheless, the program persisted through two semesters, ending in June of 1943. The new governor, Edward Thye, lacked the enthusiasm of his predecessor, feeling that perhaps the school boards should sponsor the program if they were so disposed. A legislative advisory committee lopped the program from the Civilian Defense Program to which it had been attached, and did not submit a funding request in their budget proposal.[102]

At that time, assets were listed as: thirteen pre-flight gliders, three trucks, three full-sized gliders (two stored at the Fairgrounds, one at Franklin and Lyndale Avenues in Minneapolis), one Piper Cub towplane at the Miller Vocational School in Minneapolis, one glider at the University of Minnesota in Professor Akerman's Department, two experimental gliders under the control of the NYA in Minneapolis, and various raw materials, tow ropes, and other small items.[103]

With the cessation of funding, Bellak was available for military duty. He joined the Navy in 1943, serving as a pilot and flight instructor in New Orleans. He later became public relations director for Breck High School in Minneapolis and was one of the first employees of the Medtronics Company. He remains active at this time and lives in retirement in Hawaii.

The motorless flight program was a short but unique chapter of Minnesota's contribution to the war effort. That it died so abruptly is not to fault the concept or the program, but rather it is indicative of the rapid mobilization of manpower and training processes, plus the enthusiasm with which Americans joined together to make an impact on the war front.

PROPELLER MANUFACTURING AT THE MINNESOTA STATE FAIRGROUNDS

In their search for manufacturing sites for war production at the start of World War II, the Facilities Division of the U. S. government's War Production

Map showing the buildings on the Minnesota State Fairgrounds under control of the military for propeller manufacturing 1943-1945. (Gregg Beckett)

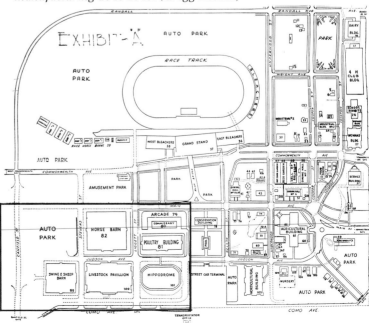

Board noted that many state fairgrounds included buildings of good size that could be converted to use as manufacturing facilities.

The War Production Board had determined that by using readily available buildings and modifying them for contractor use, five to six months of construction time could be saved, with the corresponding savings of human life on the war front. The Minnesota state fairgrounds in St. Paul had several structures suitable for this purpose.

The Board would create a propeller manufacturing plant to be run by the A. O. Smith Corporation of Milwaukee, Wisconsin. The Smith Corporation enjoyed a solid reputation as a blacksmithing and metal-working company for years, producing such items as auto and truck chassis, pressure vessels, and oil refinery machinery. The U. S. government would lease the fairgrounds property, and the Smith Corporation would manufacture the propellers.

The area that the government wanted was a 49-acre site between Como Avenue and Main Avenue, from Canfield Street on the west to the streetcar terminal area at the east, and centered on the old Hippodrome. The area encompassed seven buildings, including the Arcade, Commissary, Swine-Sheep Barn, Poultry Building, Horse Barn, Livestock Pavilion and the Hippodrome. It was a sizeable chunk and the real heart of the fair's exhibition area.

On 6 April, 1943, the government entered into negotiations with the Agricultural Society of Minnesota, who owned and operated the state fair.[104] From the start, the fair board was uneasy about the usurpation of their property. They well understood the massive amount of modifications that would be necessary to convert the exhibition buildings to a manufacturing facility, and determined that, in ad-

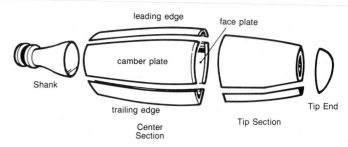

Illustration showing the several parts of propeller blades manufactured by the A. O. Smith Company under military contract in the old Hippodrome at the Minnesota State Fairgrounds during 1943 to 1945. (Gregg Beckett)

dition to any rental contract that the government would put forth, there would also have to be a separate agreement for the rehabilitation of the premises at the end of their occupancy.

Negotiators for the fair board were President A. H. Dathe and his consulting engineer, K. C. Wright; for the government, George E. Powers of the Minneapolis office of the Reconstruction Finance Corporation; Mr. McElroy, Field Engineer for the Defense Plant Corporation; and for the A. O. Smith Company, President W. C. Heath. Minnesota native, Colonel (and later, General) Edwin W. Rawlings, would take a later part in the negotiations on behalf of the Army Air Force.[105]

The Smith Corporation took photographs and measurements, then returned to Milwaukee to make their appraisal for the military. On 7 April, 1943, a tentative agreement was reached whereby the government was to pay the Fair Board $75,000 per year rental, with an agreement for rehabilitation.[106] The fair board needed a signed document so they could make their plans for the 1943 Minnesota State Fair. Negotiations dragged on, however, with agonizing slowness. The fair board phoned and wrote almost daily for word of the final papers.

On May 6, the Board decided that they would have to go ahead with the Fair, assuming they would not have the facilities, subject to the military intentions. They decided that they would hold Sheep and Swine judging in tents on other portions of the Fairgrounds and cancel both horse and cattle competition altogether.

Indeed, much hinged on the government's orders. There were tons of materials stored for other agencies in the Livestock Building's basement, for example, including machinery and equipment belonging to the Treasury Department. That would have to be moved elsewhere. The material would eventually go into the basement of the Horticulture and Industrial Buildings, which would necessitate moving materials from there to yet another location, with the game of musical chairs seeming to have no end.

A railroad spur needed to be extended from the Great Northern's Como Yards to the Hippodrome area. That disruption would be only a part of the mess.

On May 7, Colonel Rawlings made an announcement to the Press that the agreement had been made, but the papers still weren't forthcoming.[107] Wrangling continued. The fair board had always insisted on the right to approve all building modifications and the Army Corps of Engineers, who would handle the construction contracting, disagreed. When Army officers stomped out of a meeting in early May, the fair

Photograph of exploded display model of A. O. Smith blade made at Minnesota State Fairgrounds. This artifact is on view at the EAA Air Museum, Oshkosh, Wisconsin. (Noel Allard)

board drew up a $90,000 "loss of rental" invoice to present to them for losses they had suffered during the lengthy negotiation. The Army Air Force finally settled the matter, overruling the Corps of Engineers objections, agreeing that the Board should have a voice in the modifications.

Finally, on June 15, the agreements were signed. Minnesota Governor, Ed Thye, officially handed the property over to the Army.[108] Work started immediately on building and grounds alterations. John Nash, Chief Engineer for the Smith Corporation was the first to arrive, setting up his office in the Commissary. The Arcade Building windows were sealed with concrete blocks, the Commissary was divided into temporary office space for the many engineers and draftsmen arriving daily. Next, the Poultry Building was partitioned off into offices to be used for inspectors, first-aid station, and personnel departments.

Beginning with the Swine and Sheep Barn, then the Livestock Pavilion, and finally, the Hippodrome, new floors were laid. Floors had to be heavily reinforced for huge 15 to 20-ton drop forges that would soon be installed. Pads for the monster presses would be seven to eight feet thick.

A new power house with its 80-foot smokestack, dominated the area of the eastern parts of the Horse Barn and the Livestock Pavilion. A power sub-station was built in the parking lot north of the Swine-Sheep Barn, as were other outbuildings. In the Livestock Pavilion, the cattle stantions and half the balcony were also removed and the dirt floor excavated to a depth of three feet, and replaced with concrete. Seven boilers that had been in the building were moved to the Commissary Building where they would be hooked up to provide power for the whole complex.

In the Horse Barn, a concrete floor was laid and the anchor stalls removed. More than 100 offices were built there. The Hippodrome had all the seats removed and its dirt floor also excavated some three feet with heavy-duty concrete replacing it. The west end of the building was cut open, as was the east end of the Livestock Pavilion, and a covered workway was built between them. An overhead crane, running the entire 880 foot length of both buildings was installed.

Miles of electrical conduits ran both inside and outside the buildings. A myriad of pipes routing natural gas, propane gas, high-pressure steam, and water, connected the facilities.

Machinery was installed as each building was finished. In the Hippodrome, large gas-fired furnaces were brought in. They would be used to heat steel ingots to two thousand degrees centigrade. The steel itself, 4340 molybdenum, softened by the heat, would then be stamped by immense drop-forges into eight different pieces for a single propeller blade. The eight pieces included a shank, a center section, a tip section, and a tip end.

The shank was tapered. It was flanged to fit into a propeller hub for final use. The center section was composed of four separate pieces; leading edge, camber plate, face plate, and trailing edge. Here, at the Minnesota Fairgrounds, these four center-section pieces were "bump-welded" together. Each piece began one-quarter inch longer than the finished part would be. In the bump-welding process, these pieces were again heated red hot and slammed together, interlocking their molecules and making them, in reality, a solid single piece.

The tip section started life as a length of tubing. It was placed into a machine that stretched and formed it in a hollow airfoil shape that mated to the end of the center section. This ingenious machine had been invented by a pair of Scandinavian blacksmiths who operated it entirely by themselves. The machine was off-limits to other members of the work force, including government inspectors. It worked very well, turning out perfect parts consistently. A trailing edge was bump-welded to the hollow section. The rounded tip end was a separate solid piece; the eighth and final part.

When quantities of all of these parts were finished, they were crated and loaded into boxcars at the railroad siding outside and shipped to Milwaukee. There, they were treated against corrosion, both inside and outside, heated, and welded together into finished propeller blades. Shipment to the Army completed the job.

Contracts between the A. O. Smith Corporation and the government have not surfaced, but a memo from the government, dated 22 August, 1944, indicates that the facility was originally designed to produce ten thousand blades per month, but, as that was overly optimistic in terms of the military's needs, the schedule was reduced to five thousand blades per month, including six hundred blades for P-47 aircraft, and three hundred blades for SB2C-1 aircraft.[109]

The blades were seven feet long when finished, but longer blades could be manufactured by simply adding additional center sections.

Contemporary newspaper accounts speak of three thousand to thirty-five hundred persons employed at the plant, but as the news media had very little access to the plant through the production period, and according to employee recollections, it seems more likely that there were only several hundred. The plant was in operation around the clock, seven days a week.[110]

Having come in as Construction Inspector for the Corps of Engineers, as building modifications were being made, Grege Beckett got his chance to stay on as Inspector-in-Charge, managing quality control for the government.[111] He and his staff of nearly 40 persons spot-checked parts as they came off the end of the production lines. The Smith Company had their own quality control personnel, whose job it was to pass or reject a part from the press. Normally, questionable parts never made it to the end of the line, but Beckett's staff, never-the-less, did pull some suspect parts each day. To decide on the shipping of these, a "Salvage Board" met each morning in the conference room, and the parts were laid on the table. There was give-and-take between quality control people and the Smith Quantity-Control Department, whose job it was to get as many parts out the door as possible.

The inspection department had at their disposal, several techniques for spotting flaws and problems in the metal parts, including magnetic inspection, fluorescent dye inspection, or x-ray internal analysis.

Beckett reported quantities and problems each day to the Army at Wright Field. The military kept a close eye on their manufacturing plants, lest newly constructed aircraft be standing without propellers. Army Air Force Chief of Staff, Hap Arnold, made a single visit. His job was a wickedly-tiring series of trips around the country to inspect hundreds of aircraft and aircraft parts manufacturing plants. His demanding schedule found him traveling day and night, by plane or train, accompanied by a retinue of junior officers. Their job was to tend to the details and paperwork of each inspection and confer with Arnold.

On his visit to the fairgrounds, the haggard General made a brief walk-through with his entourage in trail, then motioned to Beckett to step into Beckett's private office. Against his juniors insistence, and Smith Company officials desires that they be in on all discussions, Arnold closed the door behind himself and Beckett.

Plant employees and supervisors, as well as Arnold's advisors, stood anxiously outside, pondering what sort of ominous problem was being discussed, and what actions they would have to take. Once inside, however, Arnold whispered to Beckett, "Cover for me for fifteen minutes, I simply have to take a nap." The astounded Beckett could do nothing but sit at his desk and shuffle papers while Arnold lay dozing on a couch, out of sight of the others. At the end of a short period, and with some effort, Beckett woke the General and helped him to the door. "Thanks" was the General's only remark, as he picked up his party outside and left the building. No one was to know the actual content of Arnold's private meeting with Beckett.[112]

Even during late 1943 and early 1944, plans were being drawn up by the Fair Board's engineer, K. C. Wright, concerning changes to the grounds and buildings that would be necessary for re-use by the fair after the war. Included in their plans was the option for the Army Corps of Engineers to be responsible for the reconstruction of the leased properties, or simply pay the fair board to have the work done themselves.

In March of 1945, the fair board got down to specifics. They indicated to the government a reconstruction estimate of $2.7 million.[113] The fair board secretary stated in his minutes that "the amount of work which will be necessary to rehabilitate the buildings for the exhibition of livestock is so stupendous as to stagger the imagination."[114]

On 3 September, 1945, propeller manufacturing ceased and the plant was officially shut down. It was the day after the Japanese signed surrender documents.[115]

It was the fair board's fervent hope that they would be able to reoccupy the buildings in time for use for the 1946 Minnesota State Fair, but if the board thought it took a long time to get a document in the beginning, they were twice as dismayed at the length of time it took for the government to agree to restore the buildings to their original condition.

Not until 22 January, 1946, did the Army Engineers make their first offer to the Board. The offer was a paltry $1,618,000. Besides the inadequate amount, they wanted to subtract $350,000 for materials that they planned to leave on the grounds, telling the fair board they could sell them to make up the difference.[116] The board's only other option was

to accept the settlement and remove the material themselves.

The board did not accept either offer. Their construction advisors, the Fegles Construction Company, who had done most of the construction work for the Army, prepared an estimate of $3,888,385 for the work. In the end, the Fair received only $1,702,000 and was allowed to sell some of the leftover machinery for salvage.[117]

It was determined that the Hippodrome could not be brought back into shape to be used for exhibition, as it was now structurally unsafe due to modifications and acid-corroded structural members. In September 1946, the old Hippodrome was razed. It made way for a new Hippodrome to be built. That structure, today, is the fairgrounds most prominent landmark.

THE NORTHWEST-ST. PAUL MODIFICATION CENTER

On 26 February, 1942, the Army assumed command of all operations at Holman Field. They, in effect, took over the entire airport for military use, moving all civilian operations off the field as well as bringing to a halt all passenger flights in and out. The Air Guard had been mobilized and moved to a field in Louisiana, but the civilian organizations displaced included the CPT/WTS operators and Northwest Airlines.

In March, of 1942, with the war underway, bombers were being built at plants around the country. Most, at that time, were being shipped to America's ally, Britain. The Ford Motor Company of Detroit was contracted by the federal government to build a large bomber construction plant at Willow Run, Michigan. Ford's engineers had been to California and studied production techniques at other aircraft manufacturing facilities and returned to set up the most efficient production line in the country. It ran so efficiently that B-24 heavy bombers were soon coming down the assembly line at the incredible rate of one ship per hour, eighteen hours a day.

The fact was, however, that with such assembly line speed, theatre modifications and retrofitted items were unable to be incorporated onto the aircraft coming off the line. The Army Air Force then contracted with civilian modification centers in various locations across the country to make the changes. Such was the

Inside the modification hangars at Holman Field in 1943. Looking down the line of B-24's very much resembles the Ford production lines at Willow Run, Michigan. Photo was likely taken during an air raid drill as there are no workers visible. (James Borden)

case with the Modification Center at St. Paul.

"The Mod," as it was called, was certainly one of the more spectacular operations that Holman Field was to witness over the years. The Army had taken over all facilities at Holman, including Northwest's former maintenance hangar. They contracted with Northwest Airlines to manage the Modification Center and leased the hangar back to them. For Northwest, this would be one of the biggest of ten military projects they were commissioned to perform. Northwest was responsible for hiring and training its own staff and workers. Ralph Geror was put in charge of the entire program, from the staffing to the arrangements of work flow through the various modifications to be made. E. Ben Curry succeeded Geror as program manager a few months after the center opened.

Modifications began only a few days after Northwest had committed to handle the program. A group of B-25 medium bombers arrived and under Army Air Forces supervision, certain changes were made, some outside and some inside Northwest's former hangar. The B-25 bombers were destined for delivery to the British, and would be based in North Africa to fend off the advances of German General Rommel. Others were to go to the Netherlands. The 109th's former hangar was also leased for additional space when B-24 Liberator bombers started to arrive for extensive modifications. With work being done all over the field, temporary shelters were erected outdoors and a maze of air hoses and electrical cables stretched across the grass between wooden planking. Work started immediately on a 600-foot long hangar, wide enough for

B-24J roars across Holman Field at 25 feet altitude testing the AN/APN-1 radar altimeter to be used for making blind landing approaches. (Kermit Larson via Glenn Horton)

two rows of bombers to flow through. The hangar was completed by December of 1942 and construction of a second similar hangar was soon begun.

At the peak of bomber modification, six thousand persons were in Northwest's employ, all trained as skilled craftsmen and craftswomen. Housewives, teachers, salesmen, cab drivers, secretaries, and retired persons were hired. Northwest hired nine blind employees. The blind workers were to become specialists in sorting parts for re-use from the huge

In this July, 1945, aerial view of Holman Field, 82 B-24 Liberator bombers can be counted. These ships are in the process of being modified for vaious theatres of war. Only other aircraft on the field are a DC-3 and a military C-45. (Markhurd Corporation)

238

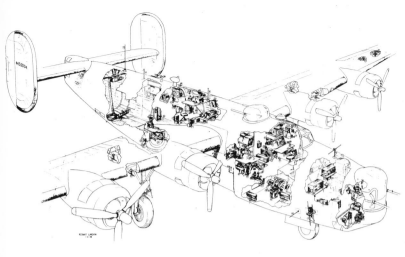

Illustration of B-24 modifications for the L.A.B. radar bombing variant being performed in the Mod hangars at Holman Field. Drawing by Kermit Larson. (Ted Gruenhagen)

amount of items collected in the nightly floor sweepings. Unerringly, they could feel the differences in sizes of nuts and bolts, screws and washers. The cost savings of restocking these parts, made to precise military specifications, more than made up for the salaries of the handicapped workers.

A self-contained city soon materialized at Holman Field, with a full service cafeteria, shops, offices, a field post office, a fire departement, a small bus route, and even a newspaper called *Field and Hangar*. Classroom training was done in a three week blitz, and included instructions on how to drill and rivet. Crew chiefs were selected and were responsible for further training their own crews. The chiefs would be required to sign off the work when it was finished, before Army Air Force officials made the final inspections.

As B-24 aircraft arrived at the field, they were signed over to Northwest, actually becoming Northwest's property for the duration of their time at Holman Field, according to the June, 1945, issue of *Field and Hangar*. They were then positioned on the field in groups according to their assigned modifications. Certain items were removed from each plane, including radios, radars, navigational instruments, autopilots, bomb-sights, tool kits, coffeee urns, first aid kits, and anything else classified as "secret" or prone to theft. These items were stored in lockers and were reinstalled when the aircraft were ready to depart for combat.

When the planes were scheduled for modification, they were towed into the open end of one of the massive hangars. During summer months, planes were moved in at one end and out at the other, at eight-hour intervals. In the wintertime, to minimize heat loss, the huge hangar doors were opened only once during the third shift when activity was at its lightest.

There were eight stations within each hangar. A plane progressed through each station on an eight hour interval. At each, a different crew had its own work to do. A workbook accompanied each plane and every line item on dozens of pages had to be checked off when work was completed and before the plane could be sent to the next station. Work not accomplished during the eight hour period at one sta-

tion or another was finished outside. There could be no slowups inside the hangar to wait for a job to be finished.

As each plane was towed out the south end of the big hangars, it was given a radio and compass check and taken to the gun pits farther south, where its guns were test fired. Then it was moved across the field to an area near the former 109th Guard hangar where it was spotted in one of six "nose hangars." There, the engines were run up and adjusted if necessary. Next, it was brought into the 109th hangar where it was given a pre-flight check. A test flight by Northwest Airlines flight crews, doubling as test pilots, was next. The test flight was generally from St. Paul to Fargo, then to Duluth, and back to St. Paul. Occassionally, the guns were test fired again over Lake Superior. Upon the plane's return, it had to pass final inspection by Army Air Force inspectors and was signed back to the Army; in effect, "repurchased" from Northwest.

The planes were then parked until Air Transport Command ferry pilots could pick them up and fly them to embarcation points on the East Coast. Some of the bombers were flown to Brazil for later flight to Dakar, West Africa, and would be at their combat stations in a mere two days.

Modifications made at St. Paul included the installation of H-2X radar units beginning in December of 1943. H-2X radar was an innovation that worked, not unlike today's LORAN, to provide a combat navigator with a precise "fix" of his location, allowing him to bomb through clouds. The H-2X modification required twenty-eight hundred man-hours alone and took twenty-five days to complete.

Other B-24's were modified as C-109 flying tankers. They would haul huge quantities of gasoline over the "Hump" in Burma to supply allied forces in China. Still others were modified to include installation of special camera gear as photo and weather reconnaissance planes, and winterization modifications. Some were painted a pink color to blend in with the desert of North Africa.

Navy PB-4Y's destined for anti-submarine patrol in the Pacific, were also modified, receiving a special radar system that would help them spot submarines cruising the ocean.

The pace was altogether unbelievable. E. L. "Ted" Gruenhagen was the Production Scheduling Director. He recalls the pace:

I can remember we didn't miss a production schedule in eleven months, and I didn't have a day off. I worked as much as thirty-six hours at a stretch. Many times, I'd almost meet myself coming and going. Once I fell asleep at the wheel of my car. Still, I was lucky not to be laying out there at the Battle of the Bulge.

That was a hectic period. We'd have an AAF tech order as to what to do. We'd have a mock-up crew show the production crew how to do it. I worked directly with the modification center engineering department, and with the chief engineer of the Ford Willow Run bomber plant where the planes were built. He had designed the production line there. He would come up here and check our procedure and then go back and put the modifications on the regular produc-

tion line at Ford's plant.

Our work was under military inspectors. We eventually got a 32-year old production officer. We really went to town after he came. There was none of this 'bad rivet on the oxygen bottle bracket' stuff. After a test hop, he'd sign it off, saying that the plane would be shot down before the rivet job failed.[118]

Altogether, 3286 B-24 bombers were equipped with one or more of ten major modifications for the Army Air Force. The Northwest crews were justifiably proud of their work. The Mod Center won several commendations from the government for their effort, efficiency and quality, including the prestigious Army-Navy "E" award.

MINNEAPOLIS HONEYWELL

In the days immediately preceeding World War II, the Minneapolis Heat Regulator Company (which became Minneapolis Honeywell) had no aviation related business products. They were, however, well known in the field of thermostats for home and commercial heating systems.

In 1940, Honeywell's top management, aware of the urgency of preparing for an obvious wartime state, requested of the Minneapolis Lab Group, a team of engineers known as the "Brain Trust," to look for ways in which Honeywell could contribute to the war effort. Early in 1941, members of the Lab Group were invited by the Army to demonstrate several electronic devices they had prepared to the Army Air Forces staff at Wright Field, Dayton, Ohio. The devices included pressure switches, a remote position controller, and an aircraft cabin temperature control.

Nothing was heard immediately from Wright Field, but a month later, Honeywell was asked to study the use of their remote positioner to steady aerial cameras. A prototype device was successfully constructed and tested. The Army was definitely interested. In May of 1941, the Army again called to suggest that Honeywell make up an electronic remote controller based on their cabin temperature control. The ultimate use of the controller, although Honeywell did not know it at the time, would be to stabilize the secret Norden bombsight.

The Norden Company had already produced their own automatic pilot for the same purpose, to accompany their sight, but it functioned with cable controls running the length of the bomber, operating the control surfaces. Such cables were prone to shrink and stretch depending on the temperatures encountered at various bombing altitudes. In this event, fine control of a bomber's attitude on a bomb run was jerky and demanded constant adjustment by the crew.

Honeywell would produce a smooth operating system based on potentiometers taking their inputs from gyroscopes and controlling an aircraft's ailerons, rudder and elevators by electronic command of their servo motors, negating the need for cable controls during the bomb run sequence. In effect, they produced a workable fly-by-wire control system to be used in high altitude precision bombing and useful in the event of disabled control cables. Indeed, according to Sherm Booen, who worked as a Honeywell field representative, testing the device, and training combat crews in its operation, the Honeywell autopilot was capable of auto-landing the aircraft, and did so numerous times during the ensuing war years.

The Honeywell C-1 Autopilot, as it came to be called had its basis in the remarkable "balanced bridge" system developed originally by Honeywell for the heating thermostat. In the thermostat, once set at a pre-determined temperature, any decrease in temperature would "unbalance" the bridge, causing a circuit to switch on a heating system. When the temperature climbed to the pre-set number, the system would again be balanced, and another signal would switch off the heater.

In adapting the system to an aircraft autopilot, virtually the same circuitry was used. When the autopilot was calibrated, if the aircraft deviated from a wings-level attitude, an unbalance signal was generated by spinning gyros that would electronically call for movement of the proper control surface to level the aircraft, bringing the plane again to a balanced position. The beauty of this system, as attached to the Norden bombsight, was that a bomb crew's bombardier could fly the airplane from his position in the aircraft's nose by simply aligning his bombsight.

Testing the first model of the autopilot was done on a B-17B with only the elevator being hooked to the device, and the original flying cables used for control. The nervous pilot, Captain Don Diehl of the Army Air Force had Honeywell technician, George Borell, bring along a set of bolt cutters on the test flight. In the event of a malfunction, Borell was to simply cut the offending connection. No such action was necessary, the device worked perfectly.

The government ordered a full three-axis set immediately and loaned Honeywell a B-17 for development tests, minus the secret bombsight. The first fully capable production autopilot was installed after just five months and a mere sixty hours of flight testing. The Army signed a contract for over 35,000 units which were eventually installed on every B-17 and B-24 shipped to Europe.[119]

The brain trust worked out of Honeywell's "ghost rooms" at their downtown Minneapolis plant. The rooms got their name when white sheets were draped over secret projects being moved from one room to another. The group also produced a device that tied into the C-1 autopilot called the "formation stick." This small joystick, mounted alongside the bomber's

The master panel of the Honeywell C-1 Autopilot and its gyro system. This panel was a familiar sight in the cockpits of all U. S. bombers in World war II. (Honeywell, Inc.)

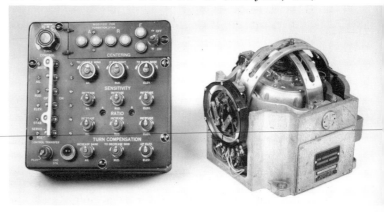

240

pilot, allowed him to fly the plane in formation with only wrist movements, alleviating the tiresome jockeying of the control wheel.

Though the automatic pilot was Honeywell's most important contribution to the war effort, the company also produced electronic turbo regulators which efficiently controlled the input of air into the carburetors on a bomber's engines, maintaining the proper fuel-air mixture as it changed altitudes during a combat mission. This unit was a vast improvement over previous controls and Honeywell was to produce over eighty thousand of these units before the war was over.[120]

One of the Honeywell "brain trust," John Sigford, designed a machine that could produce perfect gun-sight reticles (the piece of optical glass on which the cross-hairs of the sight were etched). Within one year, Honeywell had produced over fifty-five thousand excellent reticles.[121]

Another device pioneered by Minneapolis Honeywell was the fuel quantity indicating system that used a two-electrode probe inserted into an aircraft's fuel cell. By utilizing the trusty balanced bridge system of increased or decreased capacitance between the electrodes, the amount of fuel in each cell could be accurately measured. This device was designed in 1942, adapted from a still earlier mechanism used to detect icing on a bomber's wings during high-altitude operations.

WORLD WAR II ACES AND OUTSTANDING AIRMEN

In other sections of this book, the reader has been introduced to the flyers of the Air Guard and their activities in World War II. The reader has also been informed of the activities of certain Navy and Marine Corps fliers. In this section, we will concentrate on Air Aces and other airmen of achievement who were Minnesotans. Though impossible to account for every airman's activities, the following is a sampling of Minnesotan's contributions.

Most of the fighter pilots and bomber crews were young men at the start of World War II. Hardly any of them were twenty years old, and most had never flown an aircraft prior to 1940. When the war started, it opened in the European and Asian theatres with America isolated from the turmoil and wishing to take no part in the fighting. Many politicians and civilian personalities, including Charles Lindbergh, advocated that America stay out of the war.

It was clear to many Americans, however, that their allies in Europe, particularly Britain, were taking a beating at the hands of the Luftwaffe, and many young men wished to go to their aid. Since the United States had not geared for war, nor had it put any effort into combat pilot training, there was no way this could be effected. Or was there?

A St. Charles, Minnesota, youth, Arthur Donahue, found a way to fly and fight in the conflict. Getting his first flight instruction from Max Conrad at Winona, Donahue felt that it was America's war just as much as England's. He applied for a U. S. Air Corps Reserve commission, but the process was agonizingly slow to develop. He heard that American

pilots were being hired for non-combatant jobs with the Royal Air Force and went to Canada in June of 1940 to investigate. Donahue was hired and immediately shipped off for England. Once on the Continent, the door was open to his becoming a fighter pilot, though the U. S. Government had publicized the fact that by doing so, an American might lose his citizenship.

Never-the-less, Donahue was trained and commissioned a Pilot-Officer, equal in rank to an American Second Lieutenant, before he was even sent to advanced pilot training. He transitioned to Spitfires, and became one of the first American pilots to be posted to the front lines when he was sent to 64 Squadron. As a member of this squadron, Donahue was shot down and badly burned on one of his first sorties. Upon recovery, he was posted to 71 Squadron, one of several "Eagle Squadrons," composed almost entirely of American pilots, who by now had been reaffirmed of their U. S. citizenship. The unit was stationed at Church Fenton, 180 miles north of London, where there was little action other than aerial patrolling. Donahue transferred back to his original squadron as a Sergeant-Pilot. He was sent to Gibralter, then to the Far East. Leading a mission against the Japanese in Java, Donahue held his squadron pilots back while he dropped down to destroy an anti-aircraft barge. He was hit by a fragment of a 20mm shell on his first pass, and to stem the bleeding of a serious leg wound, stuffed a glove into it while he continued his firing passes. He was awarded the Distinguished Flying Cross for this action.

Donahue returned to England to command 64 Squadron, where he scored the last two of his five aerial victories. Over the English Channel on 11 September, 1942, his aircraft was hit while attacking a Junkers Ju-88, and he ditched in the English Channel. Weather conditions were severe and the British air-sea rescue service never found him.

Before his death, Donahue wrote a book about his experiences, which is listed in the bibliography in this book.

James J. Michaud, born in White Bear Lake, took pilot training in the U. S. Army Air Forces, soloing in February 1943. He was sent to North Africa as a member of the 12th Air Force, and flew 127 fighter and ground attack missions in Italy and Southern France. Michaud was credited with detroying fourteen enemy aircraft either on the ground or in the air, plus two hundred railroad cars, eleven locomotives, one hundred motor vehicles and twelve heavy artillery positions. Michaud served in the Air Guard following the war.

Robert D. Hanson, an Army Air Force pilot with the 474th Fighter Group, flew one hundred three combat missions over Europe in P-38 Lightning aircraft and received the Distinguished Flying Cross. Hanson flew armed escort, bombing, and reconnaissance missions and shared, with another member of his squadron, the destruction of an Me-109 over Merey, France on 18 July, 1944.

Wayne C. Gatlin enlisted in the aviation cadet program in 1942 and was sent to the 360th Fighter Group at Ipswich, England, in 1944. He logged fifty-five missions in P-47's and P-5l's, and was credited with destroying a German Me-262 jet fighter and damaging a second one. Gatlin joined the Air Guard following the war, was stationed in Duluth, and served in Korea in 1951. He returned to Duluth and rose through the ranks of the Guard to become Chief of Staff for Air, of the Minnesota Air Guard.

John R. Dolny flew 10,000 hours, logging 211 combat missions in A-36's, P-40's and P-47's from bases in Italy during World War II. While attacking a German convoy near Rome in March 1944, his plane was hit by ground fire and he was forced to bail out, fortunately over friendly territory. He earned the Distinguished Flying Cross, the Air Medal, Purple Heart, and Croix de Guerre. Dolny joined the Minnesota Air Guard following the war and commanded the 133 Fighter Interceptor Wing at Wold-Chamberlain, and its successor, the 133 Tactical Airlift Wing, later retiring as a Major General.

Harrison B. "Bud" Tordoff was born in New York but has lived in Minnesota since the end of World War II. He joined the Army Air Force as a flight cadet in 1943 and was assigned to the 8th Air Force. In his 85 combat missions, flown in both P-47's and P-51's, he was credited with 9-1/2 enemy aircraft destroyed, of which five were in the air.

One of Tordoff's victories came against a German Me-262 jet fighter. Though the Mustang was the fastest Allied fighter, the jet was over a hundred miles per hour faster. Tordoff attacked the jet from a position of advantage above and behind, diving his aircraft at top speed to close on the adversary and shoot it down. Tordoff, speaking at a World War Two history lecture on 11 January, 1990 at Fort Snelling, related how the combat occurred:

It was in March of 1945, we were escorting B-17's over Central Germany...pretty deep in. There had been heavy Me-262 activity in the air, we saw some of them making passes at the bombers. They were incredible. They would go twice as fast as we could. We were at about 25,000 feet and the bombers were alongside us and these jets would come up the bomber stream going twice our speed. They could do what they wanted to do. The problem was that they had very little fuel and could fly only for about twenty minutes at full power.

We found out where they were coming from very quickly from photo recon...so whenever they were in the air, we would delegate some P-51's to go and hang around their bases, and we knew that sooner or later they would run out of gas. The day I got involved with them, I was leading the second section of our squadron. I looked down and saw two planes coming way below us at right angles and I knew they would pass under us. I thought right away that they were Me-262's. I called to my group and we dropped our wing tanks and I dove vertically down about eight or nine thousand feet and I was at 16,000 when I leveled off behind them. I was still too far behind them to fire and not getting any closer despite my dive. I simply began shooting while kicking the rudder and pumping the stick trying to get a hit. I could see white flashes on the left jet unit of the one I was closest to. They were maybe 100 yards apart. Then the jet I'd shot at started to leak fuel, I could see it stream-

ing out. It began to dive and I chased it.

After a while more and more stuff started coming off the jet. My guns had jammed but I thought I had my gun camera grinding away for the record. Finally, about 3,000 feet above the earth, the German jet burst into flame, pulled straight up and the pilot bailed out. The jet stalled and dove into the ground. My gun camera didn't function, so I didn't get the pictures, but my wingman corroborated my story.

Tordoff's last two aerial victories were Me-109's and his final ground tallies were an Me-109, a Dornier Do-217 and a Junkers Ju-188, all blasted where they were parked, on the ground at Bad Aibling, German airdrome in far southern Germany.

Kenneth Dahlberg moved to St. Paul as a High School student. He entered the Army in 1941 and was assigned to the Coast Artillery. He joined the aviation cadet program in 1942, went through the prerequisite schools and spent some time as an instructor on P-40's and AT-6's. Dahlberg shipped to England and was assigned to the 354th Fighter Group of the Ninth Air Force at Lashenden, Kent, flying P-51's. Dahlberg scored an aerial victory on his fourth mission. When performing a dive-bombing assignment, he spotted an Me-109 and immediately shot it down.

In June of 1944, Dahlberg was restationed in France. In one hectic dogfight, Dahlberg was shot down, and secreted back to friendly lines by a French family. He ran his score of aerial victories to fourteen before he was shot down again, making a forced landing with his P-47 in enemy territory. This time he was rescued by an Army tank commander who had seen him come down. Dahlberg's last mission was on 14 February, 1945. His aircraft was hit by an 88-millimeter German anti-aircraft shell and he had to bail out once more. Though injured, he evaded German search parties for a day before being captured. He attempted escape, but was caught and beaten. He remained in a prisoner of war camp until the end of the war.

Dahlberg had flown both the P-47 and the P-51 and at a recent World War II history lecture, was asked to give his opinion about which was the better aircraft, he replied: "I don't know. The P-51 was the dream plane and I guess I liked it the best. But in my last mission in a P-51, I shot down four German aircraft, and in my subsequent first mission in a P-47, I got four more. So if you can find a good target, it doesn't make any difference...they were both good."[122]

Navy Ace, Herbert Houck, from Corona, Minnesota, took his elimination training at the Naval Air Station, Minneapolis, in June of 1936. After schooling at Pensacola, Newport in Rhode Island; San Diego, and Fort McNair in Washington, D. C., he taught navigation, instrument flight, and fighter classes at Pensacola.

In combat during 1943, Houck was flying F6F Hellcat fighters from the U. S. S. Essex. On a November day, while the carrier was supporting bombing missions against Japanese shipping in the harbor at Rabaul, fighters and dive bombers on the Essex were refueling and rearming. Japanese dive bombers appeared over the ships and began to attack. Houck managed a dangerous takeoff from the carrier deck, despite the fact the ship was weaving wildly and spent anti-aircraft shell casings were rolling under his wheels. No sooner off the deck, than a Jap bomber slid into Houck's sights. He wasted no time in dropping it into the ocean. Attacked by another wave of enemy torpedo planes, Houck shot down two more.

On a mission to Truk in February 1944, while escorting torpedo bombers, the carrier's Hellcats went in to strafe Japanese airfields. Houck nailed two more enemy aircraft in the landing pattern, making him an Ace and earning him the command of Carrier Air Group Nine.

The Hellcat, armed with a 500-pound bomb, made a fine dive bomber. Accompanying other dive and torpedo bombers on 7 April, 1945, Lt. Commander Houck and his Air Group attacked a group of Japanese ships. Among them, the battleship Yamato. When the battlewagon was blown sky high, Houck's camera recorded the scene. The group also sank a cruiser and several destroyers on the same mission. In all, on that six month combat cruise, Essex Air Group Nine sank or damaged forty ships, and shot down one hundred twenty-nine enemy aircraft, for the loss of only nine aircraft of their own.

Houck's following tours of duty on the carriers Lexington and Yorktown provided him an additional 42 combat missions, many against Tokyo. Houck received two Navy Crosses, the Silver Star, six Distinguished Flying Crosses, and ten Air Medals. After the war, Houck further distinguished himself in the Navy, including a 1960s tour as Commander of the aircraft carrier Shangri-La.

Recognition is given to the wartime contribution made by several African-American airmen from Minnesota. Four outstanding Black airmen who went on to play important roles in military aviation following World War II were from this state.

Harold H. Brown was born in Minneapolis and graduated from North High School in the class of 1942. He passed his Army Air Force examinations and was sent to flight training at the Tuskegee Army Airfield at Tuskegee, Alabama, in 1943. This location near the Tuskegee Institute was designated as the only military flight training facility available to qualified black pilot candidates. Brown was rated as a pilot and commissioned a Second Lieutenant in 1944. He was stationed in Italy as a member of the 99th Fighter Squadron of the 332nd Fighter Group, based at Ramitella.

On his 30th combat mission, Brown's P-51 Mustang fighter was shot down and he was interred as a prisoner at camps in Nurnberg and Moosburg, Germany. Following the war, Brown returned to Tuskegee Army Airfield and became an instructor. Later on, Brown was transferred to the Black Fighter Wing in Ohio, where he remained until 1949, when the organization was disbanded and the airmen were absorbed into other regular Air Force groups. Brown served on active duty during the Korean war as a flight test pilot for the Far East Material Command. Lt. Col. Brown's last assignment was with the Strategic Air Command at Lockbourne AFB, Ohio, as an aircraft commander and instructor-pilot on B-47 bomber aircraft.

Stanley L. Harris was a graduate of St. Paul Washington High School and attended the University of Minnesota before military duty. He was accepted

The book, *Fighter Aces* by Raymond F. Toliver and Trevor J. Constable (McMillan Co. NY, 1965) lists 34 Minnesota World War II Air Aces:

Victories	Name	Service	Hometown
15.5	Donald M. Beerbower	Air Force	Hill City
15.5	Richard A. Peterson	Air Force	Alexandria
14	Kenneth H. Dahlberg	Air Force	Wayzata
13	John R. Strane	Navy	Duluth
12	Eugene A. Trowbridge	Marine Corps	Bloomington
11	Francis J. Lent	Air Force	Mpls.
10.5	William J. Hovde	Air Force	Crookston
10	John M. Smith	Navy	Owatonna
8.5	Arthur G. Johnson, Jr.	Air Force	Litchfield
8	James B. Tapp	Air Force	Eveleth
7.5	Kenneth J. Dahms	Navy	Winnebago
7	Samuel V. Blair	Air Force	Mpls.
7	William J. Hennen	Air Force	Mound
7	Clarence O. Johnson	Air Force	Ada
7	Warren A. Skon	Navy	St. Paul
7	Robert J. Stone*	Air Force	Tracy
6.5	Chas. H. Haverland, Jr.	Navy	Hibbing
6	Raymond H. Callaway	Air Force	Grove City
6	Ronald W. Hoel	Navy	Duluth
6	Thomas H. Walker	Air Force	Mound
5.33	Hipolitus T. Biel	Air Force	St. Paul
5.25	Thomas Haywood	AVG (Flying Tigers)	St. Paul
5	Jack A. Bade	Air Force	Elk
5	Richard L. Bertelson	Navy	Eden Prairie
5	Arthur G. Donahue	RAF	St. Charles
5	Cecil J. Doyle	Marine Corps	Marshall
5	Edwin W. Hiro	Air Force	Chisholm
5	Herbert N. Houck	Navy	Cromwell
5	Hayden M. Jensen	Navy	St. Paul
5	Morton D. Magoffin	Air Force	Deerwood
5	John L. McGinn	Air Force	Luverne
5	Forrest F. Parham	Air Force	Kensington
5	Ross F. Robinson	Navy	St. Paul
5	William J. Stangel	Air Force	Waubun
5	Harrison B. Tordoff	Air Force	St. Paul

*Not listed in the Toliver/Constable book as a Minnesotan.

into the Army Air Force in 1943 and sent to Tuskegee Army Airfield where he completed pilot training and was commissioned. He was assigned to the 301st Fighter Squadron of the 332nd Group (all black unit) in Europe. He flew 77 combat missions as attack and ground support pilot, earning the Distinguished Flying Cross. After the war ended in Europe, Captain Harris was assigned duty as an instrument flight instructor at Tuskegee AAF.

Following his wartime service, Harris entered the University of Minnesota where he earned an engineering degree and went to work for the Honeywell Company. In 1960, Harris moved to Sunnyvale, California to accept an engineering position with Lockheed Missile and Space Corporation.

N. Walter Goins, Jr. was born in St. Paul, where he attended Central High School. In 1942, after two years at Macalester College, Goins was inducted into the Army at Fort Snelling, and was soon promoted to Sergeant. In 1943, he volunteered for Officer Candidate School, was commissioned as a Lieutenant in the Army Air Force. He entered pilot training at Tuskegee AAF in November, 1945 and completed the twin-engined course for pilot training. He remained there as Flight Test Maintenance Officer for B-25 aircraft after the war ended. Goins was released from active duty, but served in the Air Force Reserves until 1955.

Henry P. Bowman was a graduate of Minneapolis Central High School who enlisted in the Air Corps in April, 1941. He was one of the first black enlisted men to be assigned directly into the newly-formed 99th Pursuit Squadron, which was being organized at Tuskegee AAF where he took his training. Commissioned, he was assigned as armament officer for the 100th Fighter Squadron of the 332nd Fighter Group which saw combat in Italy.

Following the war, Bowman served on active duty until 1949 with the 332nd Fighter Wing, located at Lockbourne AFB, Ohio. During the Korean War, Captain Bowman was a crew member on a B-29 aircraft. In 1962 he retired from active duty, to go to work for the University of Illinois. In 1980, Bowman held the position of vice-president in the Hilton Hotel Corporation, Los Angeles.

CIVIL AIR PATROL IN MINNESOTA

With the mobilization and departing of the Minnesota National Guard and the Air Guard in 1940, ming of a State Guard. In May of 1941, the State Guard, a civilian force dedicated to providing a "last line of defense" in case of local emergency, was formed. The State Guard was, in effect, a civilian replacement for the absent National Guard. It was able to provide its own air arm composed of private pilots and their aircraft.

Minnesota Adjutant General, Ellerd Walsh, commissioned the Minnesota Wing of the Civil Air Patrol as the official air arm of the State Guard on 8 December, 1941, a week after the national Civil Defense Authority authorized its creation, and just a single day after Pearl Harbor. The first units were sworn in at the old Air Guard hangars at St. Paul on 4 January, 1942.

A Wing headquarters was established at the Minneapolis Armory under the command of Lt. Col. Les Schroeder, who was also the director of the new Minnesota Department of Aeronautics. Schroeder selected trusted civilian aviation leaders from around the state to be his deputies. The first unit to become operational was designated Squadron 711-1, located at St. Paul's Holman Field under the command of O. A. Brandt. The second was 711-2 from Minneapolis under R. Saddigg, the third, 711-3, was a St. Paul squadron under Lt. J. E. McGuiigan, and was composed entirely of women members, the first of this composition in the nation. The fourth Squadron of the original group was 711-4 based at Robbinsdale Airport under the direction of Lt. Gordon Lindstam. This unit would be the first in the United States to develop a cadet squadron.

Fourteen additional squadrons were soon formed, including units in Mankato, Worthington, Bemidji, St. Cloud, Alexandria, Duluth, and Grand Rapids. All of them continue to this day.

The Minnesota Civil Air Patrol command structure divided the state into thirds. Horizontal slices divided the Northern group based at Hibbing under Captain Millar Wittag, the Central group based at St. Cloud under Captain B. G. Vandre, and the Southern group based at Mankato under Captain Harold Schlesselman.

One of the first wartime assignments for the CAP was to set up guards at all the local airports around the state, ostensibly to prevent sabotage. It was conceivable that a subversive organization could load a bomb aboard a private aircraft and drop it on a war factory. Though the damage would be slight, the effect could cause panic among the population.

In Cleveland, Ohio, a CAP Commander did stage such a raid to show that it was possible. He dropped flour bombs on a factory in the middle of the night, publicizing his deed the following morning. It surely made an impact on the local citizens.

All CAP members, especially the pilots, had to have background checks by the FBI. All were fingerprinted and given identification cards. While other private pilots were grounded, their aircraft often immobilized by the required removal of propellers, CAP members continued to fly and give flight instruction.

From 1942 to 1945, Minnesota CAP personnel carried out courier missions totaling thousands of hours. They transported military officers, war department inspectors, government personnel, and materials from one location to another. Volunteers were given per diem reimbursements and a moderate aircraft rental was paid for the use of their aircraft. Minnesotans also took part in observation missions such as forest fire patrol, target-towing duties for anti-aircraft gun crews at Camp Ripley, and blackout exercise patrol.

In April 1942, the Robbinsdale Squadron created a junior organization within the CAP, designating them Civil Air Patrol Cadets. Within eight months the idea had caught on nationally. In August of 1942, the cadet squadron began, using Minneapolis Central High School as their meeting place. Later, they moved to the downtown Minneapolis Armory. Each original cadet was sponsored by a senior member to provide personal guidance and training. The cadets were responsible for additional cadets that began to join in large numbers. Cadets learned military subjects such as leadership, drill, guard duty, communications, and flying subjects such as meteorology, aircraft structures, and aerodynamics.

In May 1943, the CAP was transferred from the U. S. Department of Civil Defense to become an official auxiliary of the US Army Air Forces. They were then authorized to wear the same khaki uniforms as the Air Forces plus their own unique three-bladed propeller badge and insignia. Until 1943, all aircraft used by CAP members were privately owned, but at that time, the Air Forces assigned Taylorcraft L-2M, Stearman PT-17's and Vultee BT-13's to various units. Unfortunately, these were recalled during the period from late 1944 through 1945.

The first encampment occurred in 1943 when the CAP seniors exercised with the State Guard at Camp Ripley. CAP aircraft provided realistic training for anti-aircraft gun crews by flying simulated attack missions. One hundred fifty cadets from Minnesota took part in the first cadet encampment in 1944 at Truax Field near Madison, Wisconsin. Cadets were trained by Air Forces personnel from the field and many were lucky enough to receive their first ride in an airplane.

In 1944, young men of age 17 were allowed to enlist in the Army Air Force Reserve and train with the Civil Air Patrol until reaching their 18th birthday. At that time, they would enter formal military service and be sent to military training schools as flight cadets. During this period, as many as one hundred of these enlisted reserve cadets filled out the ranks of the Robbinsdale Squadron to bring its strength to nearly two hundred fifty members.

In Minnesota, the Civil Air Patrol continues as a strong organization to this day. It's prime peacetime mission is Search and Rescue, with both seniors and cadets assisting governmental, military, and law enforcement agencies to locate everything from downed aircraft, to lost hunters, children, and senior citizens.

Background on the Civil Air Patrol was provided by Lt. Col. Thomas J. O'Connor, Director TTN, Minnesota Wing, Civil Air Patrol.

Minnesota Air Guard   Documentation

[1] The story of the search for James Maher is drawn from Ray Miller's pilot's log book, a letter from Miller to William Kidder, 29 March, 1922, and the transcript on an interview with Miller, taped 2 June, 1956, all in the Miller Papers Collection, Minnesota Air National Guard Museum, Minneapolis. Contemporary press accounts are to be found in *The Minneapolis Tribune*, 26 January, 1922, p. 1, *The St. Paul Pioneer Press*, 26 January, 1922, p. 1, and 29 January, 1922, p. 6, and *The Duluth News Tribune*, 25 January, 1922, p. 1, and 26 January, 1922, p. 1.

[2] "New York Aero Companies Demobilized," *Aviation*, 1 October, 1916, p. 161.

[3] On the early attempts to create National Guard air units, see Jim Dan Hill, *The Minuteman in War and Peace*, Harrisburg, PA., 1964, p. 519-523, and Rene Francillion, *The Air Guard*, Austin, TX., 1983, p. 11-16.

[4] State of Minnesota, National Guard, Adjutant General's Annual Report for 1917-1918, p. 253. Minnesota Historical Society, Archives and Manuscripts Division.

[5] W. R. Stephens to W. R. Curtiss, 5 June, 1918. Adjutant General's Papers, Minnesota Home Guard. Minnesota Historical Society, Archives and Manuscript Division.

[6] State of Minnesota, National Guard, Adjutant General's Annual Report for 1917-1918, p. 292. Minnesota Historical Society, Archives and Manuscripts Division.

[7] *The Minneapolis Journal*, 27 October, 1918, p. 4. (Magazine Section).

[8] Minnesota Motor Corp, Roster of Encamped Units 21-23 September, 1918 and Miscellaneous Receipts, Adjutant General, Minnesota Home Guard. Minnesota Historical Society, Archives and Manuscripts Division. Ernster is listed in *The Minneapolis Journal*, 27 October, 1918, p. 4, and in the 1918 Minneapolis City Directory.

[9] *The Minneapolis Journal*, 21 January, 1919, p. 12, and 25 January, 1919, p. 1. The Aviation Section roster is found in *How Minnesota Gave to the United States the First Military Motor Corps*, Minneapolis, 1919, p. 117. Minnesota History Collection, Minneapolis Public Library.

[10] *The Minneapolis Journal*, 27 October, 1918, p. 1.

[11] *The Minneapolis Journal*, 24 November, 1918, p. 10, sect. 1.

[12] *The Minneapolis Tribune*, 27 January, 1919, p. 9.

[13] *The Duluth News Tribune*, 4 February, 1919, p. 2.

[14] The accounts of the flight to Duluth in 1919 were carried in *The St. Paul Pioneer Press*, 23 February, p. 1; *The Minneapolis Journal*, 2 February, p. 1, 21 February, p. 25, 22 February, p. 2, 23 February, p. 1, *The Duluth News Tribune*, 3 February, p. 1, 22 February, p. 1, and *The Duluth Herald*, 3 February, p. 9, 6 February, p. 2, 21 February, p. 1, 22 February, p. 11, 24 February, p. 2.

[15] *The Duluth Herald*, 3 February, 1919, p. 1.

[16] *The Duluth News Tribune*, 28 February, 1919, p. 4.

[17] Memo, 2 July, 1919, War Department to Military Bureaus, National Archives and Records Administration (NARA) RG 18 (AAF), General Correspondence 1919-1921.

[18] U. S. Army Air Service, internal memo, 12 December, 1919, NARA, RG 18 (AAF), General Correspondence 1919-1921. On the National Defense Act of 1920, see Hill, *Minuteman in War and Peace*, Chapter 3.

[19] Hill, *Minuteman in War and Peace*, p. 525-526.

[20] Transcript, 2 June, 1956 interview with Miller, Miller Papers, Minnesota Air National Guard Museum and T. Glenn Harrison's Officer's Record, Adjutant General's Office, St. Paul, MN.

[21] Transcription, 2 June, 1956 interview with Miller, Miller Papers, Minnesota Air National Guard Museum.

[22] Transcription, 2 June, 1956 interview with Miller, and "Ray Miller: A Biographical Sketch by Mayme Miller Shoemaker (Miller's Sister)," both in Miller Papers, Minnesota Air National Guard Museum, and "Who's Who in American Aeronautics," *Aviation*, 4 July, 1921, p. 18.

[23] *The Minneapolis Journal*, 11 July, 1920, p. 1. 14 July, 1920, p. 13, and 25 July, 1920, p. 1 (city life section).

[24] Telegram from Rhinow to Chief of the Air Service, 22 September, 1920. NARA, RG 18 (AAF), General Correspondence 1919-1925.

[25] Transcription, 2 June, 1956 interview with Miller, Miller Papers, Minnesota Air National Guard Museum.

[26] Transcription, 22 June, 1956 interview with Miller. The trip received wide press coverage in 1920. See *The St. Paul Daily News*, 21 October, p. 15, *The St. Paul Pioneer Press*, 27 September, p. 1, 2 October, p. 1, 13 October, p. 22, 24 October, p. 4, *The Minneapolis Journal*, 3 October, p. 8, 28 November, p. 11, *The New York Times*, 11 October, p. 4, and *Aerial Age Weekly*, 18 October, p. 181.

[27] *The St. Paul Daily News*, 21 October, 1920, p. 15.

[28] *The St. Paul Pioneer Press*, 13 October, 1920, p. 22.

[29] Garis to J. B. Woolnough, Inspector Minn. N.G., NARA RG 18, (AAF), General Correspondence 1919-1925.

[30] *The St. Paul Pioneer Press*, 22 October, 1920, p. 9.

[31] 7th Corps Air Officer to Chief of Air Service, 17 November, 1920 and Chief of Air Service to 7th Corps Air Officer, 23 November, 1920. NARA RG 18(AAF), General Correspondence 1919-1925.

[32] 7th Corps Air Officer to Chief of Air Service, 31 January, 1920. NARA RG 18(AAF), General Correspondence 1919-1925.

[33] *The Minneapolis Tribune*, 18 April, 1921, p. 8 and *The St. Paul Daily News*, 24 April, 1921, p. 3.

[34] "Organization of the Minnesota Observation Squadron of the State Militia," 24 February, 1921, Report by Lt. B. J. Osborn, Mass. N.G., NARA RG 18(AAF), General Correspondence 1919-1925.

[35] *The St. Paul Daily News*, 17 November, 1921, p. 11.

[36] Adjutant General, Special Orders No. 187, in *The Air National Guard in Minnesota 1921-1971*, Minnesota Department of Military affairs, St. Paul, 1970.

[37] Adjutant General's Voucher Register 1921-1926. Minnesota Historical Society, Archives and Manuscripts Division.

[38] *The Minneapolis Tribune*, 10 April, 1922, p. 9.

[39] *Huchinson Leader*, 11 August, 1922, p. 12, *Olivia Times*, 3 August, 1922, p. 1, *Duluth News Tribune*, 30 July, 1922, p. 11, and *The St. Paul Pioneer Press*, 6 August, 1922, p. 3.

[40] *Duluth News Tribune*, 19 August, 1922, p. 1, and State of Mn, Adjutant General's Biennial Report, 31 December, 1922, p. 17. MHS Archives & Manuscripts Division.

[41] St. Paul Dispatch, 18 January, 1926, p. 1.

[42] Miller's letter, 7 March, 1927 and Militia Bureau letter, 11 July, 1927 in Miller Papers, MN. Air National Guard Museum Library.

[43] Miller letter, 31 July, 1939 in Miller Papers, MN ANG Museum.

[44] Maurer Maurer, *Aviation in the U. S. Army 1919-1939*, Office of Air Force History, 1987, p. 246.

[45] St. Paul Pioneer Press, 10 May, 1931, p. 11.

[46] Maurer, p. 248.

[47] Letter to Miller, 19 October, 1931 and Mn. Adjutant General, Special Order, in Miller Papers, MN. Air National Guard Museum.

[48] Letter to Miller, 12 July, 1938 and Miller's letter, 25 July, 1938, MHS Manuscripts Division, Aeronautics Dept, Mn National Guard, Ray S. Miller Correspondence 1938-1939.

[49] Letter to Miller, 10 April, 1932 and Miller's letter, 4 May 1932 in Miller Papers, MN ANG Museum.

[50] Mn. Dept. of Military Affairs, *The Air National Guard in Minnesota 1921-1971*, 1971, p. 66 & 72.

[51] Here and below see Historical Record and History of the 109th Observation Squadron July 1920-May 1945, in MN ANG Museum library.

NRAB, Minneapolis   Documentation

52 Peter Mersky, USN (Ret.), *U. S. Naval Air Reserve Diamond Anniversary*, 1986, Government Printing Office, Washington, D. C.
53 *Aerial Age Weekly*, 5 April, 1915, p. 53.
54 Interview with Arthur Helm by Noel Allard and James Borden, 27 April 1987.
55 *Contact*, publication of the Minneapolis Aero Club, Vol. II, No. 5. p. 30.
56 Gordon Genser III, *Marine Air Reserve*, Twin Cities, unpublished story, Minneapolis.
57 Interview with Arthur Helm by Noel Allard and James Borden, 27 April, 1987.
58 M. W. Cagle, VADM, (USN, Ret.), *Naval Air Foundation Journal*, Vol. 10, No. 2., Fall, 1989.
59 Ibid.
60 Letter from Goodwin Luck to Noel Allard, 6 March, 1986. Other general reference material:
   Naval Air Reserve Training Command Golden Anniversary 1916-1966, edited by John E. Dougherty, (Brig. Gen'l, USAF), 1967.
   NAS, Twin Cities 1928-1970, NASTC Public Affairs Office, 1970.
   Skyblue Warrior, final Issue, "A History of the Minnesota Marine Air Reserve, Richard Fleming Chapter of the Marine Corps Officers Association", Sherm Booen, editor. 1970.
   Gladys Zehnpfennig, *Melvin J. Maas, Gallant Man of Action*, 1967, T. S. Denison Co., Minneapolis.
   Lt. Col. Edward C. Johnson, (USMC), *Marine Corps Aviation - The Early Years, 1912-1940*, 1977, History and Museums Division, Headquarters USMC, Washington, D. C.

CPT Training Programs   Documentation

61 Patricia Strickland, *The Putt-Putt Air Force*, CPTP and WTS Programs, 1939-1941, Air Education Staff DOT/FAA, 1970.
62 H. H. Arnold, *Global Mission*, 1949, Harper & Row, Reprint TAB Books, 1989, pp. 180-182.
63 Interview with George Holey by Noel Allard, 3 June, 1988.
64 *St. Paul Pioneer Press*, 3 November, 1940, page 16.
65 "The Civilian Pilot Training Program 1939-1940," Dr. Charles K. Sattgast papers, 1933-1940, A. C. Clark Library, Bemidji State University, 1/15 Aeronautics.
66 "A Veteran Pilot Remembers," paper given by George Holey at Minnesota Historical Society Annual Meeting, 12 October, 1985.
67 Dr. Charles K. Sattgast Papers, letter to *Minneapolis Star Journal* 17 August, 1940 by Sattgast to Tourist Editor.
68 Interview with Gordon Newstrom by George and Anne Holey for Air Museum of Minnesota, 1965, Minnesota Historical Society, p. 10-11.
69 Interview with Richard Garrett by Gerald Sandvick, 23 August, 1989,
70 Telephone interview with John Rice by Noel Allard, 3 July, 1989.
71 Interview with Joseph Williams by Noel Allard, 28 June, 1986.
72 Van's Air Service Reunion Booklet, 31 July, 1977, St. Cloud, MN.
73 Robert Gilmore, "Propwash," column in *Worthington Globe* newspaper, 18 February, 1943.
74 Interview with Glen Slack by Noel Allard, 26 October, 1987.
75 Report to Governor Stassen, 6 June, 1942, by Minnesota Aeronautics Commission, Minnesota Historical Society, Aeronautics Commission papers.
76 Interview with Al Brandt by Noel Allard, 11 April, 1988.
77 Anita Buck, "Army Glider Pilot School at Stillwater," *Historical Whisperings*, Washington County Historical Society, July 1987, Vol. 41, No. 2.
78 Interview with George Holey by Noel Allard, 30 August, 1986.
79 Interview with George Holey by Noel Allard, 3 June, 1988.
80 Report to Governor Edward J. Thye, from Les Schroeder of the Minnesota Aeronautics Commission, 21 February, 1944, Testimony by R. J. Goodrich of St. Cloud before Senate Committee in Washington, D. C. MHS., Mn/DOT Aero. papers. Records 73-E-1-6F.
81 Ibid.
82 Letter from William A. Beadie to Lester R. Badger, 26 February, 1942, MHS, Mn/DOT Aeronautics papers 73.E-1-6F.
83 Jean Geelan, "Curtiss-Wright Cadettes," *Tower Talks*, Co-op newspaper for Prospect Park neighborhood of St. Paul, November 1979, Vol.6, No. 8.

Glider Manufacturing   Documentation

84 Villaume Company brochure, circa 1950, copy in possession of author.
85 Resume, Theodore G. Bellak, circa 1960, copy in possession of author.
86 Interview with Charles P. Doyle by Noel Allard, 1 February, 1989.
87 Interview with Floyd Homstad by Noel Allard, 26 June, 1987.
88 Ibid.
89 Interview with Angelo De Ponti by Noel Allard, 9 October, 1974.
90 Interview with John Storm by Noel Allard, 28 June, 1988.
91 Urban McMiller, personal resume circa 1946, copy from Joanne McMiller in possession of author.
92 Interview with John Storm by Noel Allard, 28 June, 1988.
93 James C. Fahey, *U. S. Army Aircraft, 1908-1946*, 1946, Ships and Aircraft, Falls Church, Virginia.
94 Angelo De Ponti, "It's Been a Long, Long Time," *Wings*, March 1946, publisher, Emmett L. Duemke.
95 James C. Fahey, *U. S. Army Aircraft, 1908-1946*.

Motorless Flight   Documentation

96 Governor's General Order Number 12, State of Minnesota, Office of Civilian Defense, State Capitol, 4 April, 1942. Records of the Aeronautics Department 45.J.5.6F, Minnesota State Archives, Minnesota Historical Society.
97 Theodore G. Bellak, resume, circa 1960s. Copy in possession of author.
98 Theodore G. Bellak, correspondence with the author, 12 February, 1989.
99 Governor's General Order Number 12, (as above).
100 Statement by Ted Bellak appearing in Governor's General Order Number 12.
101 Department of Aeronautics Correspondence, 45.J.5.6F, Minnesota State Archives, Minnesota Historical Society, folder entitled "Public Relations."
102 "Glider Plan Fund Is Given Death Blow By Committee," a clipping in the papers of Professor John D. Akerman, University of Minnesota Archives.
103 Department of Aeronautics Correspondence, 45.J.5.6F, Minnesota State Archives, Minnesota Historical Society, folder entitled "Public Relations," list dated 18 June, 1943, directed to Les Schroeder, Commissioner of Aeronautics.

Propeller Manufacturing   Documentation

104 Board Meeting Minutes, State Agricultural Society of Minnesota, 6 April, 1943, SAM 86, Roll 7, page 10. Minnesota Historical Society.
105 Ibid, 6 April, 1943, page 9.
106 Ibid, 6 May, 1943, page 17.
107 Ibid, 8 June, 1943, page 26.
108 Ibid, 21 June, 1943, page 38.
109 Memo to A. O. Smith Corporation, re: RCS Project 96B-4, from Product Essentiality Division, War Production Board. Facilities Committee Document #487, National Archives, Washington, D. C. Record Group 179, WPB 315.1422.
110 *Minneapolis Tribune*, 29 February, 1944. *St. Paul Pioneer Press*, 29 February, 1944.
111 Interview with Grege Beckett, 3 January, 1989,
112 Ibid.
113 *Minutes*, 28 March, 1945, SAM 86, Roll 7, page 216. MHS.
114 Ibid, 28 November, 1945, SAM 86, Roll 7, page 257. MHS.
115 Ibid, page 258.
116 Ibid, 22 January, 1946, SAM 86, Roll 7, page 16.
117 Ibid, 27 March, 1946, SAM 86, Roll 7, page 45.

Mod Center   Documentation

118 Transcription, interview with E. L. Gruenhagen, 27 March, 1986.

Honeywell Documentation

119 "Research Comes Of Age in 1941," *Honeywell World*, Centennial issue, 7 January, 1985, pages 20-22.
120 Ibid.
121 Hank Dinter and Diana Lutz, "How Honeywell Got Its First Avionics Contract," *Scientific Honeyweller* Volume 7, number 1, Spring 1986, pages 1-7.

Aces and Airmen   Documentation

122 Kenneth Dahlberg, lecture in the World War II Roundtable series at Fort Snelling State Park, 11 January, 1990.

EIGHT

MINNESOTA ORGANIZES AND REGULATES

As aviation matured in the two decades after 1920, the intractable problems of noise and safety began to be apparent. The safety issue was paramount. The public was obviously willing to turn out and pay to see stunt flying but such flying was a risk for the pilot and, potentially, for the crowds below. Aerial mishaps, especially those due to engine failure, were not uncommon and fears of fatal accidents were clear and real.

As early as 1919, Cavour S. Langdon, President of the Minneapolis Civic & Commerce Association, wrote to the city's most prominent air show company, Federated Fliers, run by Clarence Hinck, saying "we have received complaints regarding the flying of ships over the city and especially over places where large crowds are congregated."[1] What was proposed were voluntary rules mutually agreed on by local aviators that they would not fly under 3000 feet or stunt with passengers while over Minneapolis. Hinck warmly endorsed the idea of safety and regulation that would promote it but added that 3000 feet was not necessary except over the center of the city and that he hoped the complaints were not directed at the show that Federated Fliers had performed over the city on Armistice (Veterans) Day.[1]

With public concern seemingly widespread it was inevitable that state governments would begin to extend their legislative and regulatory powers. As early as 1918, Connecticut passed a law to register and regulate aircraft, and in 1919, several states prohibited using airplanes for hunting or "molesting birds" (Michigan). By 1921 state laws dealing with licensing, registration, insurance, and land acquisition for airfields were common. The first act by the Minnesota Legislature came in that year.[2] In January, Representative Thomas E. West of Minneapolis introduced House File 277, a bill "to regulate the traffic of aircraft over cities of the first class," which meant Minneapolis, St. Paul, and Duluth. It was a straightforward low flying law and met no opposition. The original 1000 foot minimum altitude was amended to 2500 feet on 5 April, when it passed the House on a 90-0 vote and was sent on to the Senate. For no readily apparent reason, the Senators changed 2500 to 2000 feet on 15 April and five days later passed the bill 46-0.[3]

The 1925 Legislature made the first stab at actual regulation when it required an aircraft registration certificate ($10.00) and a state pilot's license ($10.00), but the law was vague and said the money collected "shall be retained and disbursed...for purposes of administering the provisions hereof." The Adjutant General's office was the department charged with enforcement, probably because, thanks to the Air National Guard squadron, it was the only state agency that even remotely had anything to do with aviation. The measure was not widely acknowledged or enforced and, in 1929, the legislature tried again. This time the law was more detailed to the point where every state licensed airplane "shall have the letter M painted in one color in sharp contrast to the color of the aircraft on the lower surface of the right wing and the upper surface of the upper left wing, the top of the letter to be toward the leading edge, the height to be at least four-fifths of the mean chord; if more than thirty inches, the height of the letter need not be more but shall be not less than thirty inches."[4]

The 1929 session did, however, pass the most significant legislation yet, and nationally respected *Aviation* magazine reported that, "Three important aviation measures were passed by the Minnesota legislature during the session just concluded." One was the revamped licensing and registration act, another gave municipalities the power to condemn land if needed for airport property, while the final one authorized the larger cities to issue bonds for airport construction and maintenance. The latter was limited to not more than $500,000. Curiously enough, the agency that would enforce licensing was no longer the Adjutant General but the registrar of motor vehicles. One other legal matter was dealt with when a "right to flight" provision was adopted. While landowners owned the airspace above their property, flight through that space was declared lawful, unless at such a low altitude as to be dangerous or to interfere with things.[5]

The new bonding authority was a major help to the first class cities and was certainly an element in the airport modernization of the 1930s. The regulatory law, however, remained essentially meaningless. Neither the motor vehicle registrar, nor the Adjutant General's office before it, had been given strong enforcement powers and their focus was not aviation. They had other things to do and until some kind of aeronautics agency was created and given legal teeth, state government's role in promoting and regulating aviation would languish. That this was the case can be seen in the activities of the 1931 legislative session.

Legislative records indicate that several bills were introduced in the spirit of fine-tuning the powers of cities and villages over airport acquisition and funding. The House by now had an Aircraft and Airways Committee that gave any aviation proposals their first hearing. Citizen testimony before the committee shows a strong interest by the aviation community to have the state government regulate and promote their activity effectively. On 28 January, for example, Dr. William McCadden, a Minneapolis dentist and aviation enthusiast, advocated state regulation and so did R. R. West, also of Minneapolis, President of the Minnesota Aircraft Association. Others, including Speed Holman, appeared at the 4 February committee meeting and "urged that laws be enacted that would mean something in Minnesota." Committee Chairman John A. Weeks then appointed a subcommittee to study the matter. For the next several weeks the committee heard comments and drew up legislation and, on 11 March, unanimously approved a bill. The bill mentioned a regulatory commission although it appears that its powers would have been limited to approving air races, exhibitions and the like. The committee may have favored the idea, but no regulatory law came out in 1931. In the depth of the depression, the state budget was tight and "A bill for an act to regulate aeronautics and making an appropriation therefore," probably stumbled over its last four words.[6]

The 1933 Legislature, however, did create the state agency that so many aviation people wanted. Wishing for state regulation may, at first, seem odd but there were several factors at play. If the power of state government could be applied to aviation it would not be just to regulate but to promote as well. This meant state authority and, not incidentally, state money to mark airways, establish beacons, and improve airports, and the law that passed did, indeed, intend to "foster" aviation. Regulation was also needed because this was still an age of amateur airplane builders and pilots who learned by trial and error. Not most aviators, of course, but there were enough unlicensed planes and pilots to make news when accidents happened. Those involved with the growing airlines and other aviation business ventures were anxious to rid aviation of a daredevil image and the licensing power of the state could help.

The national government already had done this when Congress passed the Air Commerce Act of 1926 creating the Aeronautics Branch of the Department of Commerce. Under the authority of the Aeronautics Branch, pilots were already required to be licensed and aircraft to be certified, but the problem was interstate commerce. It was, and is, a long accepted constitutional principle that Congress can regulate interstate commerce, but purely intrastate commerce is left to each state. If a Minnesotan did not fly an unlicensed aircraft out of the state, the national Aeronautics Branch could do nothing.

In the spring of 1933, Robert G. Marshall of Minneapolis, introduced the bill in the Senate, and H. M. Carr, Chairman of the Aircraft and Airways Committee, introduced it in the House. The bill was for "regulating aeronautics and making an appropriation therefore." In an action that would have great consequence for the future, the House Airways Committee, on 11 April, deleted the words "making an appropriation therefore," and the next day the Senate Aviation Committee did the same. On 18 April the bill went to the floors of both chambers and passed the House 70-1 and the Senate 40-0.

The new law created a five member Aeronautics Commission to be appointed by the Governor, who would also designate one of them to chair the Commission. The lengthy law gave the Commission broad powers to demand that pilots and aircraft operated in the state comply with Aeronautics Branch licensing rules. To fly in Minnesota a pilot needed a federal license and he had to register it with the state. The same went for airplanes and a $10.00 registration fee was imposed for both an aircraft certificate and pilot's license. The Commission could also make "reasonable rules" to regulate flight schools and set airport standards and could hold investigations, issue subpoenas, and compel attendance and testimony of witnesses. Violations of the law or the Commission's proper regulations was a gross misdemeanor that could cost an offender up to $500.00 or 90 days incarceration, or both if a court saw fit.[7]

Minnesota finally had an aviation law that had teeth but the Legislature had done two things that would cause problems. One was the deletion of the appropriation clause, for the new Aeronautics Commission had no source of revenue other than the $10.00 fees it would collect to register licenses. The other was that the law defined airports and emergency landing strips as being, respectively, 1800 x 500 and 1000 x 220 feet, which many private pilots would find excessively limiting.

The first order of business was to get the Commission up and running, and Governor Floyd B. Olson appointed five prominent men: Lewis H. Brittin, who headed Northwest Airways, would Chair the Commission, and the other four were Ray Miller, Commander of the Minnesota Air National Guard unit; John D. Ackerman, head of Aeronautical Engineering at the University of Minnesota; Richard L. Griggs, President of Duluth's Northern National Bank; and Dr. William McCadden who, as noted above, had been pushing for the now realized law. The Commission held its first meeting on 3 October, 1933, in St. Paul's Lowry Hotel, got organized, hired Mrs. Leona Cline of St. Paul as secretary, and pondered the money question.[8]

Getting the funds to carry out the Commission's responsibilities would remain a major headache for years to come, because the Legislature consistently refused to fund the new body. At this first meeting it was decided that the Commission would contact the major civic organizations in Minneapolis, St. Paul, and Duluth and ask for contributions. It was a doomed idea from the start. A 26 October letter to McCadden indicated that the Minneapolis Junior Chamber of Commerce was "very receptive" to the proposal but that they were heavily involved with other major projects and, consequently, with great regret, were "forced to pass up this opportunity."[9]

The Commission's second meeting was in the Silver Room of the Lowry Hotel on 12 December, 1933, and money was only one problem. Complaints about regulation were coming in. Harold Colbes from Fairfax wrote to say the new law "will cripple the aviation industry" and that the airfield definitions in the law would prevent "so-called barnstorming or carrying passengers for hire." He pointed out that he favored safe regulated air commerce, but that a pilot should be able to fly without a license as long as passengers were not carried. Ted Jonson of St. James believed the Commission should enforce federal rules and nothing more, arguing that under the new state law he could not "carry a passenger from St. James to any other spot in Minnesota unless it happened to have a registered airport...If anyone can show me how this is helping aviation, I'll be for it." Paul Nalewaja of Long Prairie wrote that in his view "it would be illegal to land nearly anywhere. I do not see why the freedom of the people should be so infringed upon. As far as safety measures, why, a pilot will not land in dangerous fields for his own reasons."[10]

In addition to complaints from individual private pilots, there were others who objected to the landing field definitions. B. G. Vandre, who ran a flight school and air taxi service at Alexandria at that time, also said that unlicensed pilots should be able to fly solo and that it would be illegal to land nearly everywhere. "Now gentlemen," he added, "I am not doing any barnstorming, but I make my living by doing aerial taxi work and student instruction. I am compelled to fly to many cities that have not airports or landing strip but that have many good fields to land on that are not registered. By passing this regulation, it is going to make it impossible for me to continue operations along with many others and will eventually kill commercial flying..."(sic). Larry Hammond, who headed the Pilot's and Airplane Owners Association at Wold-Chamberlain Field, spoke for several dozen others saying, "overall the law was a good one," but objected to rules that would keep barnstormers from earning a living. It is interesting that on the issue of unlicensed pilots, his organization was "divided between washing them out or allowing only solo flights in such planes." Ackerman's reply to Vandre represents the Commission's interpretation that the law meant "that the taking off and landing should be done on a piece of clear land of proper size" and that Vandre could do all the barnstorming and taxi service he wanted.

The Commission did not meet again until mid-March 1934, and at that time a new and troubling development had arisen. Several airline heads had been accused of illegal collusion in obtaining airmail contracts in the later 1920s, and Commission Chairman, Lewis Brittin of Northwest Airways, was one of them. A U. S. Senate investigating committee chaired by Hugo Black was delving into it all and, to make matters worse, Brittin allegedly had destroyed some documents and was under fire for contempt of Congress. Needless to say, he was tied up in Washington and his mind was not totally on Aeronautics Commission business. On 6 March, Griggs wrote to Governor Olson saying that Brittin's unfortunate absence made it desirable to name a Vice-Chairman so the Commission would have a head. He further indicated that general office expenses could not be met and Leona Cline, who was thoroughly competent and efficient, could not run the office under the circumstances. In January, Griggs had sent her a personal check for $50.00 to defray office expenses and in February he wrote to her, "I know it embarrasses you where you have contracted bills, and you know I will do everything I can...but there must be some other plan for the future. We cannot go on without money.[11]

The Commission limped along with a few fees coming in and by using a portion of W.P.A. funds that the state had been given for airport improvement. In February, Brittin was found in contempt of Congress and served a brief jail sentence and he resigned from both Northwest and the Aeronautics Commission. The Governor moved Ray Miller into the Chairman's slot and later in the year the new Northwest Airlines head, Croil Hunter, filled the Commission's vacant seat. During the 1935 legislative session, Miller tried for funding, approaching J. R. Schweitzer and A. J. Rockne, the Chairmen of the all-important House and Senate Appropriations Committees, respectively, saying the Commission had done its best to do the legislature's will despite the fact there was no appropriation to do so. In a letter of May 1935, Leona Cline described the attempt as a complete failure.[12]

There is no doubt that Leona Cline and the Commissioners were carrying out more than their duty. Eve Hope Miller later said, "Ray personally furnished stationery and was always digging into his own pocket." Miller's irritation can be seen in his reply to an April 1935 letter from H. A. Lindberg of the Duluth Aviation Club who made several criticisms of the Aeronautics Commission. None of the Commissioners, said Miller, "have benefitted personally, but all have given generously of their time and money to administer this law as their oath of office requires. It would seem to me that if your organization is so much interested as you pretend to be in the promotion of aeronautics in this state you might at least offer something constructive rather than destructive criticism." Cline was reduced to begging free airline tickets to attend the annual meetings of the National Association of State Aviation Officials.

The 1935 meeting was in Detroit and American Airlines refused her request for a complementary ticket but Pennsylvania Airlines came through. The 1936 meeting was in Hartford, Connecticut, and this time Cline wrote directly to the legendary President of American Airlines, C. R. Smith. She expressed her eagerness to attend the convention, saying, "As the Minnesota Aeronautics Commission has been functioning without an appropriation since its enactment, my only means of transportation is in the method I am now forced to take. This letter is in the form of an appeal to you for transportation for myself, from Chicago to Newark and return as well..." Smith replied that "We shall be very glad to have you fly with us..." On 29 December, 1937, Leona Cline received a letter apparently from the Department of Administration saying, in its entirety, "We regret to inform you that due to a shortage of funds, it is necessary to terminate your service effective December 31st. Two weeks salary will be paid in lieu of notice."[13]

The Commission's 1937 request for funds got nothing although $5000.00 was appropriated by the Legislature so the state could prepare a display for the 1939 World Triennial Poultry Congress.[14]

Despite the many problems, they were trying hard to do their duty and as Miller said "In view of the lack of an appropriation, the Commission has continued to function in its duties, and needless to say has accomplished much despite such a handicap."[15] To inspect and certify aircraft, they had divided the state into 17 districts drawn along county lines and in each district secured the cooperation of volunteers that were "men whose interest in, enthusiasm for and knowledge of aviation, as an art and business, makes them willing to act as inspectors and qualifies them to do so intelligently and effectively." The Commission had also, by the end of 1934, officially grounded all unlicensed aircraft, and owners who wanted to get licenses were being helped to do so. For those operators "who have chosen to act in defiance of the law," the Commission was using its enforcement power. "Warrants had been sworn out in a case of violation, two fliers charged with operating an unlicensed aircraft, the case was tried, a conviction secured, followed by a workhouse sentence of sixty days, but a stay...was issued."

During its first year the Commission licensed seven airports, a flying school, and of the state's 248 licensed pilots, 210 had registered under the new law. Miller's first annual report also added that most licensed aircraft were now registered with the state and that the number of unlicensed ships had declined substantially. He concluded that while there was more or less natural objection and criticism of he and the Commission at first, it was being greatly reduced as aviators better understood they had a common purpose.

But the road to common purpose had still another pothole. Hilbert L. Niemen had sued the Commission, claiming their powers were unconstitutional and he was supported by the members of the Minnesota Aviation Association, one of whom was Marvin Northrop. The attorney for the pilots and aircraft owners of the Aeronautics Association was Clarence T. Lowell and, in a 31 December, 1934 letter to one of the suit's backers, Northrop said that Lowell's central argument was that the law, "does not provide for the licensing of the planes in this State but transfers all that licensing authority to Washington, which is an invasion of State rights." He added that 33 states had similar laws and that, "if we can upset it, it will cause you no end of pride to think that you had contributed toward the lightening of the burdens of private flying."[16]

The case was heard by Judge James C. Michael in the State District Court in Ramsey County and his opinion was published on 22 January, 1935, and the result might be called a split decision. The plaintiffs had, of course, made several arguments and most were dismissed including their complaint that the law was an unwarranted delegation of legislative power to the Commission. Of this, Judge Michael said, "I do not think the objection is sound, because the act in terms only authorized the Commission to make "reasonable" rules and regulations, besides Section 18 gives any aggrieved party the right of appeal to the District Court."[17] He called the law a "valid enactment" except the two sections requiring pilots and aircraft to have valid Aeronautics Branch licenses. These he declared unconstitutional, essentially buying the plaintiff's argument. He pointed out that the legislature had required a federal license but had given the Commission no power to grant a state license, which was an abdication of authority, "to a foreign sovereignty over which the Legislature or Courts of Minnesota have no jurisdiction."

The Legislature could, however, require a license granted by the federal Aeronautics Branch or by the Minnesota Aeronautics Commission. If that were the case, then, "the local citizen has no grounds for complaint." Judge Michael attached a memorandum to his decision saying that, "I cannot escape the conclusion that this was an inadvertent oversight on the part of the Legislature," and advised that the law could quickly be amended since the Legislature was currently in session. This was quickly done and the 1935 Legislature expanded the Commission's powers to issue and revoke state licenses for pilots and their machines.

During the last half of the decade, the Commission sputtered along with the legal authority needed to regulate aviation in the state but no money to do it. The impossibility of cracking down on unapproved flying is demonstrated by the fact that the Commission's first court prosecution did not come until 1941. A young Minneapolis man, Archie Canfield, had bought a homebuilt airplane and crashed on takeoff in Scott County, narrowly missing an auto in the process. Prosecutor Edward J. Devitt told the Court that this was the first case since the 1933 law was passed, because lack of appropriation meant "they haven't been able to effectively enforce the terms of the act." Because of this, he recommended leniency for Canfield who got a suspended sentence, forty dollars in court costs, and a stern lecture from Judge Joseph Moriarty. At a June 1937 meeting, the problem of funding "was thoroughly discussed," but discussion is all that came of it. A few weeks earlier, John Ackerman had left the body, and Governor Elmer A. Benson appointed Stanley E. Hubbard, Sr., a Red Wing native who was a long time pilot and activist in Twin Cities aviation programs.

Between 1937 and 1941, the Commission appears not to have met as a body and simply fell into disuse although the individual members continued to work and plead for legislative alms. In 1939 Ray Miller again went to the legislature with an emergency request for $7000.00, saying that because of no funds, there was little enforcement of the law and the state was becoming a "dumping ground" for unlicensed airplanes. It will come as no surprise that the legislative committee "took the request under advisement, but expressed the belief that it could not provide the money unless it could be set up as a WPA project."[18]

The autumn of 1941 saw an enormously changed aviation scene in the state. The country was preparing for the chance of war and pilots in heretofore undreamed of numbers would be needed. Federal money was pouring in for training and airport construction and the moribund Aeronautics Commission was reactivated to manage it all. In September, Governor Harold Stassen called the first Commission meeting in years, and his first action was to appoint Stanley Hubbard permanent chairman. Of the previous members, Croil Hunter and Ray Miller were still aboard, but the other two terms had expired and, it will be recalled, Miller had been called to active duty the previous February and was in Louisiana with the Air Guard squadron. The meeting was attended by the Governor, Hubbard, Hunter, and two members recently appointed by Stassen. Dr. Maurice L. Walsh was a Rochester pilot and Leslie L. Schroeder, born in White Bear Lake, was also a pilot and aircraft owner. The latter had his law degree from the University, had been Athletics Department business manager there for twenty years, and would two years later become head of all state regulated aeronautics.

The resurgent Commission decided to hold regular meetings and vigorously get to the business of licensing, certifying, and, especially, providing planning assistance to communities that were building airports. A three person staff was hired to handle the daily affairs of the body, including William L. Beadie as acting director, and Ted Bellak to organize a glider training program. It was estimated by 1942 about 80 airports would be under construction and that 8 million dollars in federal money would come to the state for basic pilot training facilities.[19]

The federal money, however, was for airports, not staff and other Commission expenses. For that the Legislature was needed and even that picture looked brighter, at least for a moment. In April 1941 an act had been passed that appeared at long last to fund the Commission with $10,000. A state per-gallon tax on aviation gasoline existed and the Legislature decided the Commission should be funded by it. The State Petroleum Division, which collected motor vehicle gasoline taxes too, would turn the aviation portion over to the Commission. In a singularly peculiar move, however, the lawmakers also decided that consumers could apply for a refund of the tax within four months of buying gas for their airplanes, and the law read that the Commission got the first $10,000 in *unclaimed* gasoline taxes. Of course nearly everyone claimed their refund and nothing like $10,000 was available. It also turned out the sales records for aviation fuel were not segregated from other sales receipts at the Petroleum Division and it was thus "practically impossible without an exhaustive survey, to audit and estimate to determine what money should be justly paid into the Commission fund." William Beadie was more than a little frustrated when he wrote that the Petroleum Division "after some months of auditing, reported that there was $111.00 of unclaimed tax available for our use."

The reconstituted Commission continued to limp along on fees it collected for licenses, and Hubbard wrote to the Governor that "the Commission is helpless if sufficient funds are not available for continued operation of an office...$10,000...is relatively little to accomplish the construction of 8 million dollars in military airports."[20]

If Minnesota was going to use the powers of its state government to promote and regulate aviation, it was abundantly clear that something dramatically different had to be done. In 1943, the winds of change were in the air, and when the legislature finished its session in the spring, the changes that it had made were so sweeping that the new laws would mould Minnesota aviation for at least fifty years.

Three factors explain the new willingness to remodel the role of state government. The most obvious was that the ten year old system of a five member Commission had worked only marginally well. The Commission had been given broad responsibilities but never an appropriation to carry them out and the five members, it will be recalled, were unpaid citizens. They may have been dedicated and knowledgeable about aviation, but Griggs had a bank

to worry about, Hubbard a radio station to run, Ackerman a University department to fret over, and Miller an insurance and bond business plus an Air Guard squadron to occupy his time. The various men who had served as Commissioners had done their best but it was an impossible job. A second factor was the new reality of wartime expansion. Some sort of central state agency run by a director with a decently qualified staff of experts was needed to help local communities plan and build the facilities where flight training would occur.

A final component in the new equation was that by 1943, many Americans were already thinking about life in the post-war world. It was widely believed that there be an explosion of aviation activity and every state wanted to be ready. Newspapers and magazines were full of articles predicting an airplane in every garage. To be "air-minded" was to be in favor or progress. There were predictions that 32 percent of Americans wanted to own an airplane, and 7 percent definitely would buy one. This meant airports for as many a 15 million private planes in post-war America.

A state agency to plan for, and later regulate and manage, the anticipated post-war boom seemed imperative. On 20 January the *Cottonwood County Citizen* reported that Aeronautics Director Beadie had spoken to 60 Windom citizens who had braved subzero cold and stiff winds to hear him say the world was going to be airminded and that, "the city without landing facilities is going to be very much behind the times."[21]

Events moved rapidly in the spring of 1943. On 5 March, Minneapolis Representative Vernon Welch, Chairman of the Aircraft and Airways Committee, introduced an airport bonding bill and a week later two or more major aviation bills. The bonding bill would allow the state to issue bonds and spend other money to build and maintain airports. The legislature, it will be remembered, previously let cities do this, but for the state to do so would have taken a constitutional amendment.

The bill had already been discussed in committee and had drawn wide support from such diverse people as John Ackerman, Les Schroeder, A. E. Floan of Northwest Airlines, Alderman Albert Bastis of Minneapolis, the President of the twin cities chapter of the National Aeronautic Association, the President of the Northwest Good Roads Association, and the mayor of Ortonville. After the usual amendments to clean up details and language, the bill passed the House on 22 March and went to the Senate. The Senate passed a slightly different version and the bonding bill, therefore, went to a conference committee. The committee of three members from each chamber hammered out the differences and the bill passed on 20 April.

Since it was a constitutional amendment, the voters would have the final say in November 1944, at the next general election.[22]

The other two aviation measures were aimed at a vital revamping of the way in which aeronautics and airports would be managed. On 29 March, Representative Welch introduced them both as H.F. 1386 and H.F. 1387. The former would effectively abolish the Aeronautics Commission and replace it with an

Aeronautics Department headed by a single Commissioner. Les Schroeder had advocated this approach to the Aircraft and Airways Committee in February. It was an approach that other states had already taken and the new Aeronautics Department would now be organized in a way similar to the Highway Department. The bill was a straightforward bureaucratic reorganization measure that many supported and it passed the House unanimously on 16 April. The Senate adopted the measure with only one dissenting vote on the same day. The Senate bill differed in detail and the usual conference committee procedure came into play. Four days after initial passage, the conference committee compromise was accepted by both the House and Senate. The new law gave the Commissioner of Aeronautics broad powers to set rules and regulations, organize the Department, and "prepare plans for an airways system...which will serve the best interests of the State as a whole."[23]

The third of the important 1943 bills was by far the most controversial. In the standard English of legislation, it was intended to, "provide for the organization and administration of public corporations for acquiring...developing, maintaining...and operating airports. The "public corporation" the bill created was the Metropolitan Airports Commission. There had long been a degree of competition between St. Paul and Minneapolis airports but it was becoming increasingly obvious that one main airport made more sense. Both cities had their own, of course, and who would give up what and to whom?

In late December 1942, a report surfaced that Minneapolis was considering building a large airfreight field west of that city. St. Paul mayor John McDonough said he thought it was foolish for the two cities to compete and waste money and that the plan should be stopped. "I believe," he said, "we should ask the Legislature to appoint a metropolitan airport commission, much on the order of the old Metropolitan Drainage commission." In January 1943 the *St. Paul Dispatch* editorialized that, "The two cities will get farther in post-war commercial aviation if they pool their resource and influence....If in the opinion of competent authorities, Wold-Chamberlain field will meet the specifications of the future, then that field would be acceptable, and the proper steps should be taken." In February the St. Paul City Council indicated their full support.[24]

By the time the 1943 legislature met, it was an idea whose time had come. The idea was widely discussed, and during February several meetings were held in Governor Stassen's office to work out something acceptable to both cities. Names vary, but meeting were representatives of the respective mayor's and city attorney's offices. Since the Minneapolis Park Board legally owned the airport, they were included, as were Beadie from the Aeronautics Commission, and William Green, the assistant Attorney General, who was charged with actually drafting the bill. As it went through the inevitable round of committee hearings, there was a bit of wrangling but, for the most part, common purpose was evident. All agreed that the commission should have a like number of members from each city, but Minneapolis wanted the commissioners to select their chairman while others wanted the Governor to make the selection.

Before the House Appropriations Committee, William Green said the whole idea of the bill was that, "other states are getting huge appropriations from the federal government, and that due to lack of unity between St. Paul and Minneapolis, Minnesota was being overlooked." With both mayors and other city officials behind it, the bill easily passed the full House and Senate in mid-April, and Governor Stassen signed it on 20 April, 1943.[25]

The law went into effect in the summer. Stassen had resigned and gone into the Navy in late April and Edward J. Thye was now Governor as the Metropolitan Airports Commission began to function. The MAC consisted of nine members, four from each of the two cities and one Chairman who could not be from a county contiguous to Hennepin or Ramsey, all appointed by the Governor. Duluth banker Lewis G. Castle was selected as the first Chairman. They were the governing body of the new public corporation and had authority to develop and operate airports in the metropolitan area, which was defined as all airports within a 25 mile radius of each of the two city halls.

The first major piece of business for the MAC was to do a study of long range airport requirements and, appropriately enough, Charles Doell, chief engineer for the Minneapolis Park Board, and George Shepard, St. Paul city engineer, were given the task. Their report of 31 December, 1943 established what would late be taken for granted. Because of its proximity to both cities and because of the large investment already made there, the report concluded that, "Wold-Chamberlain Field is recommended for development as the major air terminal for the metropolitan area. By August 1944 both Wold-Chamberlain and Holman Field had been turned over to MAC. Due to the requirements for extensive public hearings and various legislative changes, MAC would not legally declare Wold-Chamberlain the major airport for another 42 months, but by the end of the War, the pattern of future metropolitan airport development was becoming apparent.[26]

The new Aeronautics Department was up and running as of 1 July, 1943, and Governor Thye appointed Les Schroeder as the first Commissioner. His first task was to hire a staff and organize the Department. The legislature had appropriated $100,000 for the biennium to help do it. Wartime manpower shortages, however, made it slow going and Schroeder had only gotten a staff of 12 together when the 1945 legislature, in effect, froze his staff hiring. The freeze had to do with nothing more than budget technicalities but, said Schroeder, "it was heartbreaking." The Department ended 1945, ironically enough, with enough money but not enough people to adequately staff its seven divisions organized to license, inspect, regulate, plan, operate, manage, and account for the money the legislature had appropriated.[27]

It may be remembered that the history-making 1943 legislature passed three significant acts creating MAC, the Aeronautics Department, and giving state government authority to sell bonds for airport financing. The latter, a constitutional amendment went to the voters in the November 1944 general election. Under the state constitution, an amendment thereto needs a majority of the votes cast in the election, so that a voter who votes for other matters but neglects the amendment effectively votes against it. Throughout the history of the state, this provision has sometimes made it difficult to pass amendments. In November 1944 Minnesotans gave the aviation amendment nearly 62-25 approval or 139,392 more votes than the amendment needed to pass. It was a tremendous vote of confidence by the people of Minnesota for the future of aviation in their state.[28]

Minnesota Organizes and Regulates   Documentation

[1] Here and below see letter to Federated Fliers, 21 November, 1919 and letter to Langdon, 24 November, 1919, Hinck family correspondence, copy in possession of the author.

[2] *Aviation*, 5 December, 1921, p. 685.

[3] House Journal (HJ) 1931, p. 129 & 1057 and Senate Journal (SJ) 1921, p. 1118. All legislative records are in Minnesota Historical Society, Division of Archives and Manuscripts.

[4] HJ 1925, p. 1052 and JH 1929, p. 686.

[5] *Aviation*, 4 May, 1929, p. 1521; HJ 1929, p. 685; and "A History of Aeronautic Laws In Minnesota," Aeronautics Department Subject File, (73E1.7B). All Aeronautics Department and Commission files are in Minnesota Historical Society, Division of Archives and Manuscripts.

[6] HJ 1931, p. 442 and House Committee Book, 1931, Committee on Aircraft and Airways.

[7] SJ, 1933, p. 1075, 1373, 1684; HJ 1933, p. 1668, 2050, and Minnesota Statutes, Chapter 430.

[8] *St. Paul Daily News*, 23 October, 1933, and Minutes of Meeting of Minnesota Aeronautics Commission, 3 October, 1933, Aeronautics Commission subject files.

[9] Minutes of Meeting of Minnesota Aeronautics Commission, 3 October, 1933 and Letter to McCadden in Aeronautics Commission subject files.

[10] Here and paragraph below see letters in Aeronautics Department subject files, Ackerman correspondence.

[11] Here and paragraph below see letters in Aeronautics Department subject files, Miller correspondence and Griggs correspondence.

[12] Here and paragraph below see letters in Aeronautics Department subject files, general correspondence and Miller correspondence.

[13] Interview with Eve Hope Miller, 9 May, 1989, and Aeronautics Department subject files, Miller correspondence.

[14] House Committee Book, 1932, Appropriations Committee.

[15] Here and below see "1st Annual Report of the Minnesota Aeronautics Commission, 1 January, 1934 - 31 December, 1943," Minnesota Air National Guard Museum (ANGM) library, Miller papers.

[16] Letter, Northrop to Wallace T. Hanson, 31 December, 1934, Hinck family correspondence, copy in possession of the author.

[17] Here and below see Niemen v. Brittin et. al., District Court, 2nd Judicial District, No. 212715, 22 January, 1935, and "History of Aeronautic Laws in Minnesota."

[18] *Minneapolis Times-Tribune*, 30 August, 1939, p. 10. The Canfield case was apparently the first prosecution that resulted in a fine and sentence, even if suspended. Minnesota v. Canfield, Scott County District Court, 12163, 21 November, 1941.

[19] Aeronautics Commission minutes, 2 September, 1941; letter and report, Hubbard to Stassen, 4 April, 1942; Aeronautics Department files (78E16F and 56D78F) and Legislative Manual, 1945.

[20] Beadie letter, 30 April, 1942 and Hubbard letter, 4 April, 1942, Aeronautics Department subject files, Dept. of Administration (73E16F).

[21] Joseph Corn, *The Winged Gospel, America's Romance With Aviation, 1900 - 1950*. p. 108; *Cottonwood County Citizen*, 20 January, 1941, p. 1.

[22] House Committee Book, 1943, Aircraft and Airways Committee and HJ 1943, p. 326, 1784.

[23] HJ 1943, p. 1194, 1781; SJ 1943, p. 1480, 1666; *Minneapolis Star-Journal*, 12 March, 1943, p. 1.

[24] *St. Paul Dispatch*, 10 December, 1942, 16 January, 1943, 5 February, 1943.

[25] House Committee Book, Appropriations Committee, 9 April, 1943 and St. Paul Pioneer Press, 3 April, 1943, p. 4.

[26] Chapter 500, Laws of Minnesota 1943, Sect. 360 and "Aviation Progress and Airport Problems in the Twin Cities," Metropolitan Airports Commission, 1957, copy in possession of the author.

[27] Schroeder, "Brief Outline of the Scope of the State's Aviation Problem," 9 December, 1946, Aeronautics Department subject files (42B77B).

[28] "Aviation Amendment Draws Record Vote," Aeronautics Department subject files (42B77B).

NINE

WHO'S WHO IN MINNESOTA AVIATION PRIOR TO 1945.

In the following Who's Who, we have done our best to account for the more illustrious aviation figures of the period prior to 1946. It was not our intention to include the names of every pilot who flew during that time, but to include the ones that drew publicity for one deed or another, and of whom the rest of the aviation community repeatedly told stories or otherwise held dear. We apologize for names that do not appear on the roster that are historically significant. Unfortunately, there were those for whom there was simply no available biographical information. Lack of a single research source prevented an intense search for all birth and death dates.

We are confident that the following information is as accurate as could be gleaned from hundreds of sources over a period of nearly twenty years. We welcome additional documentation and new information.

Abbott, Russ
One of the owners of Cedar Avenue Airport in the mid-1930s.

Akerman, Professor John D. 1897 - 1972
Born in Latvia, Soviet Union. Akerman migrated to Russia when the Germans took over Latvia, and learned to fly there in 1916. He moved to France, where he flew for the French Air Force, before coming to the U. S. in 1918. He received an Engineering degree from the University of Michigan and worked for Stout-Ford until 1927 and for the Hamilton Metalplane Company for a while after that.

He began work for the Mohawk Aircraft Company in 1928, where he did engineering redesign of the Mohawk airplane and joined the University of Minnesota in 1929, becoming head of the Aeronautical Engineering Department in 1930, when the Department was separated from the rest of the Engineering School. He stayed until 1958, and during that time, authored many books and articles on structures and meteorology. He was a consultant to the Boeing Company and a major part of the team that designed the B-29 wing.

Professor Akerman was instrumental in starting the University's Rosemount Aeronautical Research Center, and headed that until 1962. He served as one of five Commissioners of the 1933 Minnesota Aeronautics Commission. Akerman was inducted into the Minnesota Aviation Hall of Fame in 1990.

Alsworth, Leon "Babe"
Born in Southern Minnesota, Alsworth took up flying in 1932, inspiring many local flyers, including his brother, Lloyd. In 1934 he went to Bemidji, where he ran the airport for some time. In 1938 he flew to Fairbanks, Alaska, and decided to stay. He became one of the more prominent Alaskan bush pilots, and Port Alsworth, a city near Bristol Bay north of the Aleutian Islands, is named after him.

Alsworth, Lloyd A. 1906-1992
Born in Sherburne, Minnesota. He soloed in 1932, and flew privately until World War II, when he became a CPT/WTS instructor at Grand Rapids and Mankato, Minnesota. During the late 1930s, an airstrip on his family's farm near Fairmont became the regular hangout of local flyers.

After World War II, Lloyd managed the airport at Fairmont and ran a flight school there for twenty-five years, instructing and licensing over 3500 pilots.

Amundson, C. W. "Cy"
Cy began teaching Industrial Arts in the Worthington Public Schools in 1928. He taught aircraft construction and built a Pietenpol airplane in class. As a certified ground school and mechanic instructor, he taught during the CPT/WTS programs at the Worthington State Junior College and at St. Thomas College prior to World War II.

Anderson, John A. "Jack" 1889 - 1972
Born in Ortonville, Minnesota. Anderson began flying in 1919, and what was to have been his first solo flight was made with passengers in the plane. He barnstormed with Clarence Hinck's Federated Flyers through 1923, and then bought an implement store. He applied to all the airlines of the day for a full-time pilot's job during the Depression, but was not hired. He eventually found work in 1929 at the Universal Air Lines flight school at Rochester as an instructor. During the early 1930s Anderson continued barnstorming, became chief pilot for the local Alexander Eaglerock distributor, Minnesota Aircraft Company, and worked the family farm. In the late 1930s he was elected Big Stone County Registrar of Deeds.

Anderson, Olof A. "Ole" 1903 -
Ole Anderson was born in Linkoping, Sweden. After working in Swedish aircraft factories, he migrated to America and became a resident of North Dakota. He barnstormed the Dakotas and Minnesota, joining Northwest Airlines in 1941. Anderson helped pioneer the Northern Routes through Canada and Alaska. Ole retired in 1963, making his home in Minnesota. He was inducted into the Minnesota Aviation Hall of Fame in 1992.

Ausley, Robert W. 1918 -
Born in Oregon, Ausley moved with his family to the coast of Alaska in 1919. He was introduced to flying in 1927 when he was given a plane ride by Noel Wien. Ausley got his commercial license in 1940 and began flying for Pollack Flying Service out of Fairbanks. He worked for Wien Alaska Airlines and for Lavery Airways before the war.

During World War II, Ausley was hired by Northwest Airlines. He flew supply and troop transport missions along the Aleutian Islands and returned to make Minnesota his permanent home.

Backus, David H. 1893 -
Born in St. Paul, Backus enlisted in the Norton Harjes Ambulance Service in World War I and was sent to the battlefront in France. There, he transferred to SPAD 13 of the French aviation section where he was taught to fly, and eventually to the American 94th Aero Squadron as a pilot. He was involved in seven combats in which he shot down three German aircraft. He received the Croix de Guerre and Distinguished Service Cross with Oak Leaf Cluster.

Ballough, Ervin E. "Eddie" 1892 - 1948
Born in Florida. Ballough became an instructor with the Royal Canadian Flying Corps in World War I, He worked as aerial delivery boy for the New York Bamberger Department Store, and once landed his airplane on the roof of a building as a publicity stunt. He came to Minnesota in 1920 and went to work for Bill Kidder at Curtiss-Northwest Airfield in St. Paul as an instructor. One of his pupils was Charles "Speed" Holman.

Ballough flew newsman, Stanley Hubbard Sr., on many newsgathering flights, flew powerline patrol for Northern States Power Company, and brought the Dempsey-Gibbons boxing match newsreel movies from Shelby, Montana, to the Twin Cities. With aerial photographer, Paul Hamilton, Ballough is credited with having mapped the Twin Cities from the air. He was hired by Charles Dickinson of Chicago to fly airmail flights in 1926, and left the Twin Cities.

Barnes, Philip J. 1894 -
Born in Minneapolis, Barnes learned to fly in 1917 at the Curtiss School at Newport News, R. I. Commissioned in the Navy, he became a dirigible pilot and held two flight records for the craft, set between 1914 and 1919. He was loaned to the British as a dirigible pilot, flying convoy patrols over the Atlantic. He was a member of the Allied Armistice Commission on Aircraft, returning to Minneapolis in 1921. Barnes was a member of the Aero Club of Minneapolis.

Barnhill, Jean
In 1934, Barnhill was the only woman college senior in the United States majoring in Aeronautical Engineering. On receiving her degree, she continued fellowship work for a Master's degree. At the same time, she held a Transport Pilot license and took part in national air racing events. She led the U. of M. Flying Club to second place in the first National Intercollegiate Air Meet, held at Purdue University in 1935. She took second place in both bomb-dropping and spot landing events.

Barrus, Earl 1916 -
Barrus was a Minneapolitan, having attended Washburn High School. He learned to fly at Wold-Chamberlain Field, getting his license in 1936. He began making parachute jumps to earn spending money and performed at county fairs and at the Minnesota State Fair. He also performed other stunts such as the rope ladder transfer from car to plane, and the Crazy-Cub act. He worked for Jess Bristow Air Shows and Bob Ward's Hollywood Daredevils. Barrus made two hair-raising balloon ascensions, suspended below a group of hydrogen-filled weather balloons and jumping with a parachute from them. One ascension was at Chippewa Falls in 1938, the other at the Minnesota State Fair in 1939.

Barrus' most daring stunt was a housecrash at the 1939 County Fair at Wausau, Wisconsin, in which he cracked a vertebra, but was never hospitalized. His career took him into the Coast Guard, and then to American Airlines.

Bean, John R. 1918 -
Bean began flying in the late 1930s with Max Conrad's flight school. He did some barnstorming during the period and joined Northwest Airlines in 1942. He was a candidate for the Carnegie Medal.

Behncke, David L. 1897 - 1953
Behncke was hired as a pilot for Northwest Airways in 1926. He became the number two man behind Speed Holman. Behncke was laid off and went to work for National Air Transport, another of the fledgling airlines of the period. He had always been concerned about the welfare of the airline pilots, and called a group together to form a union among the airlines in 1931. That union is today known as ALPA, the Air Line Pilot's Association.

Bellak, Theodore G. 1912 -
Born in New Jersey. Bellak studied soaring as a teenager. He helped organize a sailplane company and designed a sailplane in Michigan. He set an overwater soaring record in July, 1939, by soaring fifty-six miles across Lake Michigan from Sturgeon Bay, Wisconsin, to Frankfort, Michigan. Bellak was hired in 1941 to direct the Gliding, Soaring and Aeronautical Knowledge Division of the Minnesota Aeronautics Commission. He developed curricula for thirteen high schools around the state to teach juniors and seniors the fundamentals of motorless flight and glider construction. He toured the state lecturing about soaring, and giving demonstrations, and served as a flight instructor in the U. S. Navy during the later part of WWII.

Bennett, Ashley C.
Bennett, with partner, Ralph Wilcox, attempted to fly the first airplane built in Minnesota from Lake Minnetonka in 1909. Except for short hops, it did not fly.

Berent, Donald -1943
From Minneapolis, Don Berent was one of the colorful pre-World War II stuntmen that performed at county fairs and weekend airshows at Wold-Chamberlain Field. As a partner of Danny Fowlie, his premier stunt was landing one plane on top of another. Berent flew an old Waco biplane with wheel supports attached to the upper wing and Fowlie would land a Cub on them. The pair later did the stunt with two Cubs that could be locked together to perform some minor maneuvers while attached. Berent flew later for Cons-

airway, a military contract air service out of San Diego, to supply material to Hawaii, Australia, and the South Pacific during the beginning of the war.

Berg, Ernest 1894 - 1987
Born in Sweden, Berg was a barnstorming pilot in the 1920s, performing stunts and giving passenger rides throughout the Midwest. He joined the Army Air Force and during World War II, helped with construction of air bases in Burma and India, and flew one hundred eighty hours of combat. Berg's wit and talents for ventriloquism kept his unit in laughs. After the war, he played a key role in the Minnesota Air National Guard's expansion.

Billberg, Rudolf G. 1916 -
Born in Roseau, Minnesota, Billberg is one of Minnesota's top bush pilots. He took up flying in the Northwest Angle, crossing Lake of the Woods and covering the Warroad area. In 1937, Billberg found his way to Alaska and took a job with Wien Alaska Airways in Nome. He returned briefly to Duluth to work in the CPT program, was hired by Northwest Airlines in 1942. In 1945 he went back to Alaska. Billberg continued to fly off and on for various airlines, flew fire fighting missions and charter flights.

Billeter, Earl
One of William Kidder's early pilots. In the 1920 - 1923 period, Billeter flew the first air ambulance and aerial hearse flights in the nation for Kidder. He also delivered Dayton's merchandise around the state.

Blackstone, Al
Al Blackstone was a colorful wing-walker of the early 1920s. He started his career with the St. Paul Dispatch Flying Circus, teamed with Speed Holman. The pair did routines in which Blackstone would hang by his feet or by one hand from the wing of a biplane, stand on his head on the wing, and finally parachute from the plane. His antics were witnessed by thousands at county fairs and open air picnics around the region. After Holman's death in 1931, Blackstone carried on with this flying circus. At the same time, he drove marathon auto endurance runs as promotional events for car dealerships.

Bloom, Ruben L.
Duluth Airport operator during the CPT/WTS program period of World War II.

Bolduc, Wilmer E. 1922 -
An aircraft mechanic since the later 1930s, Bolduc worked on most of the old airplanes and became a specialist on the OX-5 engine. He earned his Private license in 1940 and worked for Mac McInnis. He then went to work for Tom North at North Aviation at White Bear Lake during the WTS program of World War II. Bolduc became an Air Force mechanic during the war and continued afterward until his retirement as an FBO at Crystal Airport.

Booen, Sherman P. 1913 -
Born in Glenville, Minnesota. Booen was greatly interested in radio and electronics in his college years and worked for radio stations in Dubuque, Iowa, and Albert Lea, Minnesota prior to World War II. He learned to fly in the early CPT program at Albert Lea. In 1942, the Air Corps assigned him to the Air Material Command at Dayton, Ohio, where he provided final inspection of airborne radar units and trained flight crews in its usage. He was reassigned in 1943 as a Honeywell autopilot liaison rep, orienting crews to the new system of the autopilot coupled to the Norden bombsight.

Booen was released from active duty in 1945 and went to work for radio station WDGY, where he created a radio program called "World of Aviation." At the same time, he received a Marine Corps commission. Following active duty in Korea in an air traffic control group, he returned to work for WCCO Television and put "World of Aviation" on TV. Booen also founded and edited the Minnesota Flyer Magazine.

Bour, Anthony A. 1909 -
Bour soloed in 1929 and flew many of the early biplanes, owning his own Waco 10 in 1930. He joined the 109th Observation Squadron of the Air Guard in 1928 and was sent to maintenance school. He served as a crew chief on Guard airplanes until the unit was federalized in 1941, and he was sent to officers candidate school. Bour was commissioned and shipped out to the 9th Bomb Squadron in the China-Burma-India theatre where he served as maintenance officer. He moved up to take the Group Maintenance Officer's position in the 7th Bomb Group. Following the war, he became affiliated with the Air Force Association, the EAA, Air Guard, and Confederate Air Force.

Bowman, Elmer 1905 -
Bowman was born in Iowa and moved to Owatonna as a youth. He rebuilt a Jenny and learned to fly. When a partner cracked up the Jenny, Elmer designed and built his first homebuilt airplane, resembling a Curtiss Robin. The plane flew well and was soon sold. His second homebuilt airplane was similar to the first and was also sold at the onset of World War II. Bowman designed and built another more radical aircraft after World War II. This plane was more a flying wing than a conventional airplane. Lacking an engine, the plane never flew.

Brandt, Otho A. "Al" 1903 -
Brandt was born in Ohio, learned to fly there, went to work for the Waco Aircraft Company, and became involved in barnstorming. At the Waco Company, he was associated with airshow pilot Freddie Lund. Brandt became an instructor for the St. Paul Flying Club in 1935, and formed Lexington Flying Corporation in 1938. At the St. Paul Airport and later, University Airport, he trained military flight cadets under the WTS program. After the war, he formed Brandt Aero Service at St. Paul. He operated a flight school, charter service, aerial applicator service and was an Aeronca distributor. In 1961 he was hired as production test pilot for Champion Aircraft at Osceola, Wisconsin.

Brittin, Col. Lewis H. 1877 - 1952
Born in Connecticut, Brittin was schooled as an engineer. He earned the title of Colonel as an officer in the Army Corps of Engineers. He came to Minneapolis and managed several industrial plant installations, including the Ford plant, and the lock and dam at St. Paul. Brittin became Vice-President of the St. Paul Association of Commerce. In 1926, he headed a campaign to buy out the faltering airmail line between the Twin Cities and Chicago. When the purchase was complete, he served as Northwest Airways Vice-President and General Manager until 1934. Under Brittin, the airline acquired a large modern aircraft fleet and expanded air routes. Brittin is a member of the Minnesota Aviation Hall of Fame.

Brooks, Senator William F. 1863 -
Brooks was an aviation-minded State Senator, who sponsored aviation legislation, promoted aviation tours and flying exhibitions with the intention of making the Twin Cities the aviation hub of the country. He started the Aero Club of Minneapolis in 1920, helping to build a large aviation reference library. He became President of the Twin City Aero Corporation which purchased the defunct Speedway Field from its creditors, making it available to the Minneapolis Park Board for an airport. His strong sponsorship of aviation is one of the major building blocks of Minnesota's aerial heritage.

Brown, Raymond 1905 - 1988
Brown received his flying license in 1927, much influenced by the flight of Charles Lindbergh. Brown had, in fact, been one of the airport crowd that helped Lindbergh get off the ground at Roosevelt Field in New York. He worked for the Ireland Aircraft Company, Huff-Daland Corporation, and Coastal Airways as a pilot. He became a ground-school instructor and in 1940 went to work for the Civil Aeronautics Board. When Brown requested to be stationed in Alaska, they gave him Minnesota instead, indicating that the two were just about the same. In 1944, he joined the Minnesota Department of Aeronautics, earning a reputation as a colorful and feisty General Aviation Inspector. He made his permanent home in Minnesota and retired to live on a private airstrip where he restored a classic airplane and constructed a homebuilt.

Buckman, David
Buckman was hired by the Minneapolis Park Board as one of the early control tower operators after the tower was opened at Wold-Chamberlain in 1930. When the St. Paul tower was opened in 1940, he was transferred there, and was later sent to Milwaukee. During the late 1930s, he and a group of flyers organized the Zero-Zero Flying Club at Robbinsdale airport.

Bullock, Walter R. 1899 - 1986
Bullock witnessed the airmail flight from Minneapolis' Lake Calhoun in 1911, then hung around early pioneer Alex Heine's shop, watching him build airplanes. Bullock went to Newport News, Virginia, in 1916 and received his flying license from the Curtiss School. He barnstormed for the next few years, while building and rebuilding planes. He started Robbinsdale Airport in 1920; flew part-time for "Whiz-Bang" publisher, Captain Billy Fawcett; and was hired in 1927 at Northwest Airways for Speed Holman while the latter was in a cross-country air race. Bullock stayed on and eventually retired in 1960. During the war years, Bullock flew for the Northwest Ice Research Program, and also in the Northern Region. After the war, he competed in the 1946 Bendix air race,

finishing ninth. He built or rebuilt a dozen aircraft after the war, at least three of which are in the San Diego Air/Space Museum at this writing. Bullock was inducted into the Minnesota Aviation Hall of Fame in 1988.

Burke, Eugene 1895 -
Burke wanted to enlist in the Marines, but instead took flight training with the Royal Canadian Flying Corps during World War I. He was commissioned, but saw no action. He returned to barnstorm in Minnesota and went to work for the Larrabee Brothers at Speedway Field in Minneapolis.

Butchart, Dana 1898 -
Born in Hibbing. Butchart was a World War I night bomber pilot in the RAF, having joined the Canadian Flying Corps in 1917. He returned to Minnesota to barnstorm, then ran the Hibbing Airport for 35 years.

Butters, William
Flight instructor for the Larrabee Brothers at Speedway Field in the early 1920s. Among his students were Vern Georgia and Speed Holman.

Callaway, Raymond L. 1916 -
As an Army Air Force pilot, Callaway served nineteen months with Chennault in China. His record in the 8th Fighter Squadron, included six Japanese fighters destroyed in the air, one probably destroyed, and three damaged. He received the Distinguished Flying Cross, Air Medal, and Purple Heart.

Canby, William C. "Punk" 1892 -
Canby served in the U. S. Air Service from 1917 through 1919. He enlisted in the 109th Observation Squadron in 1928 and was sent to active duty in 1941 with the unit. He was discharged in 1945 and rejoined the 109th Fighter Squadron at Wold-Chamberlain Field, taking a final discharge in 1948.

Chamberlain, Cassius "Cash" - 1939
Chamberlain was a Northwest Airlines pilot, hired in January of 1931. He was killed in the crash of a Lockheed 14 at Miles City, Montana, in 1939.

Chamberlain, Cyrus Foss 1896-1918
A native of Minneapolis, where his father was Chairman of the First and Security National Bank, Chamberlain joined the French Lafayette Flying Corps in June of 1917. He attended French school and was posted to Escadrille SPAD 98. Slightly older than his squadron mates, he was often more reckless than the rest. During the German offensive in the spring of 1918, his squadron flew air superiority missions over the front lines and on 13 June, his group dove from 12,000 feet on some German aircraft. They had been lured into a trap and other German fighters attacked. Chamberlain was killed by machine gun fire from an enemy ship. He was posthumously awarded the Croix de Guerre. Wold-Chamberlain Field was dedicated in his honor in 1923. Chamberlain is a member of the Minnesota Aviation Hall of Fame.

Chrissinger, Lyman "Stub" - 1943
Parachute jumper, rigger and airshow/thrill show jump coordinator of the late 1930s. His handling of chutes and jump equipment is legendary. Chrissinger was president of the Rip Cord Club, an association of jumpers that met regularly to socialize. He recruited, trained, and cared for many of the colorful women jumpers of the period. He rented parachutes, was a government licensed repacker, and was ever-present at any jumping event, several times coordinating the State Fair thrill show jump routines.

Christian, Benjamin 1913-1948
Christian began flying in the 1930s and was a part owner with Niels Sorensen of a Buhl Pup aircraft, flying it from his farm strip at 66th Street and Bloomington Avenue in Richfield. Ben and his brother, Frank, along with Niels Sorensen, formed Twin City Aviation Service, holding a Porterfield aircraft franchise. Ben joined Northwest Airlines in 1942 and worked the Northern Region. He was killed in a DC-4 crash near Edmonton, while enroute from Anchorage to Minneapolis in 1948.

Christian, Frank, Jr. "Bubs" 1915-1944
Frank Christian began flying in the 1930s with his brother, Ben. He flew from the local Twin Cities airports such as Oxboro and Nicollet, and the family farm in Richfield. He joined Northwest Airlines at the beginning of the war and flew in the Northern Region. He was killed, along with 13 others, while bringing a C-47 back from the Aleutian Islands to Adak, Alaska, when the plane was caught in a snowstorm with 90 m.p.h. winds.

Clousing, Lawrence A. 1906 -

Born in Minneapolis, Clousing got an engineering degree at the University of Minnesota, then earned his Naval wings in 1927, spending ten years in the Navy. At one time, Clousing spun a Loening amphibian aircraft into the ground near Long Beach, California, but was uninjured. In 1938, he joined NACA (National Advisory Council for Aeronautics) and worked at Langley Field and other research centers. His logbooks showed literally hundreds of aircraft types tested for both the Army Air Corps and Navy. He was manager of de-icing tests conducted with a Lockheed 12-A fitted with engine-exhaust-heated de-icing boots along the wings and tail surfaces. In 1940 and 1941 NACA brought the plane to Minneapolis seeking icing conditions, there being none available at its home base in California. For his outstanding service as test pilot, Clousing was honored with the Octave Chanute Award in 1947.

Cohn, Benedict 1913 -1987

Cohn spent a career with the Boeing Company beginning in 1936 after graduating from South High School in Minneapolis and receiving an engineering degree from the University of Minnesota. He was chief of aerodynamics, supervising the Boeing wind tunnel, and later became director of engineering there.

Cole, Homer 1898-1977

Cole was born in Niagara Falls, Ontario. He joined the Norton-Harjes Ambulance Corps and served in World War I in France and Belgium. He joined the British Royal Flying Corps and worked in their air mail service. In 1928, while barnstorming in the United States with future brother-in-law, Walter Bullock, he was hired by Speed Holman to fly for Northwest Airways. Four years later, he helped form the Air Line Pilots Association as one of the "key men" from Northwest. In 1934, he became an American citizen. Cole left the airline in 1936 to take a job with the Bureau of Air Commerce (now the FAA). He was one of the first air traffic controllers and retired from the FAA in 1966.

Conrad, Max 1903 - 1979

From Winona, Minnesota, Conrad was a college athlete. He took up flying and opened his own flight school, operating from a farm strip that many years later would become the Winona city airport. During the pre-war years, he contracted with several colleges to run flight training in conjunction with their CPT programs. At one time he had seven of these programs. He started an airline between Rochester, the Twin Cities and Duluth, but found it impossible to maintain fixed schedules. He worked for the Honeywell Company as corporate pilot following World War II and began making deliveries of Piper aircraft around the world.

Conrad eventually recorded well over two hundred solo ocean crossings, of both the Atlantic and Pacific, and began making record-breaking flights. His most ambitious trip was to include a flight around the world via the poles. His journey across the north pole went well, but he had to abandon his plane at the south pole when it suffered engine problems. Minnesotans grew to love this hard-working and intense individual and nicknamed him "The Flying Grandfather." Conrad is a member of the Minnesota Aviation Hall of Fame.

Cook, Harvey

Harvey Cook was one of the partners in Interstate Finance. That company was based at Wold-Chamberlain during the 1930s and provided the means for uncounted numbers of would-be aircraft owners to finance their purchases. Along with partner, Harry Schaeffer, they played a great role in getting Minnesota aircraft and flying businesses started and keeping them viable.

Croft, Edwin H. 1907 -

Born in St. Paul, Croft was raised on the family farm across the road from the Curtiss-Northwest airport. Watching planes daily, got him enthused about flying. He opened an auto repair shop in St. Paul and gave visiting pilots low prices on their repairs. Croft barnstormed an OX-5 Travel Air and taught in the CPT and WTS programs at Wold-Chamberlain for Mac McInnis, and later at Rochester. He started Gopher Aviation at Rochester. In 1943, Croft joined Mid-Continent Airlines and stayed with them after a merger with Braniff Airlines, retiring as a senior Captain. In post-war years, Croft helped major corporations, such as 3M, Pillsbury, and Peavey, set up flight departments. Croft is a member of the Minnesota Aviation Hall of Fame.

Cummings, Wallace C. "Chet"

One of four partners who started the Mohawk Aircraft Company in 1927. Besides being vice president and chief engineer, he was also chief designer, and produced the Mohawk Pinto airplane. The Pinto became the first Minnesota design to achieve an approved type certificate. Cummings had also worked for the Alexander Aircraft Company in Denver as a designer.

Curry, Ezra Benham "Ben" 1896 - 1991

Curry joined the Norton-Harjes Ambulance Service in 1917 and went to France, where he signed up with the U. S. Signal Corps. He was commissioned and sent to Bradley Field in New York. There he held the position of engineering officer. He returned to the University of Minnesota and received a Mechanical Engineering degree in 1920. He went to work for the Milwaukee Railroad, then the WPA service, and was hired by Northwest Airlines in 1943 as general manager of the St. Paul Modification Center. He was later sent to Vandalia, Ohio, to oversee the Northwest modification center there.

Dahlberg, Kenneth 1917 -

Dahlberg was a flight instructor for the Army Air Force at Yuma Air Base and Luke Field in 1943 - 1944. Sent to the European theatre in 1944 as a member of the 353rd Fighter Squadron of the 9th Air Force, he flew both P-51 and P-47 aircraft, downing fourteen German aircraft. He was shot down three times himself, the third time resulting in his being taken prisoner, and spending the remainder of the war in a prison camp. He won the Distinguished Flying Cross (DFC), Bronze Star, fifteen Air Medals, the Purple Heart, and a Presidential Citation for his valor during the war. Following the war, he was a squadron commander with the 109th Fighter Squadron, Minnesota Air National Guard.

Dahlem, Leon 1902 - 1978

Dahlem learned to fly in 1924 as a Naval cadet, after attending the University of Minnesota. He barnstormed, then helped form the Mohawk Aircraft Company in 1927, serving as its first president. He was called to active duty with the Navy in 1928, at which time he flew from the original aircraft carrier, the Lexington. Following his service period, he flew for Kohler Airways, operating Loening amphibians across Lake Michigan. Dahlem later took a job as test pilot and instructor for the Driggs Aircraft Company of Lansing, Michigan. He flew actively until 1934, and remained in the Minnesota wing of the OX-5 Aviation Pioneers.

Dale, Wallace S. 1913 - 1972

Dale learned to fly in 1936. He and his partners started an airport on Cedar Avenue in Minneapolis and he became an instructor there. He took part in local airshows. Dale married woman pilot, Frances Pryzmus. In 1940, he left to work for the CAA as a control tower operator in Louisville, Kentucky. Cedar Airport was sold to his Aunt, Rose Dale.

Daugherty, Earl

Early pilot and aerial photographer for the Minneapolis Star and Tribune.

Deichen, Howard F. 1900 - 1970

Deichen was issued the third Minnesota pilot's license in 1926 by examiner Ray Miller. He flew in the Waseca area. Deichen owned a Curtiss Robin in which he brought the parents of endurance flyer, "Red" Jackson to St. Louis to make an aerial encounter with their son while the latter was in the midst of an endurance flight in 1929.

DeLong, Leon S. "Deke" 1894 - 1965

DeLong went to France as a foot soldier in World War I, but asked for a transfer to the Signal Corps following the conflict. He was given flight training, but quit the service and barnstormed, working for Marvin Northrop until he joined Universal Air Lines in 1927. In 1928, DeLong was hired by Speed Holman to work for Northwest Airways. He and Mal Freeburg became regular pilots on the Milaukee-Green Bay passenger run. In 1930, DeLong was made manager of flight operations and helped forge the route system to the West Coast. He was the only Northwest Captain to fly until age 65, volunteering to retire. Later, all pilots were required to step down at age 60.

De Ponti, Angelo "Shorty" 1908 - 1991

Born in St. Paul, De Ponti took his first job with Universal Air Lines in 1928, but quit the following year to start his own business. Though a pilot, De Ponti made his reputation as an entrepreneur, his company providing storage, flight training, fueling, sight-seeing, charter and aircraft sales. At one time or another, he either owned or leased almost every one of the original buildings on Wold-Chamberlain Airport.

At the beginning of World War II, De Ponti received a contract from Northwestern Aeronautical Corporation to build Waco CG-4A gliders, which he did at a plant in South Minneapolis. He leased portions of his space at Wold to Northwestern to assemble the gliders, providing the welded fuselages and tail surfaces. Wings and other components were manufactured by Villaume Box Company in St. Paul. De Ponti held both Texaco and Shell Oil franchises and provided the major fueling facilities at Wold through the post war years. In the 1960s, along with the Metropolitan Airports Commission, he developed the Green Concourse at the airport. De Ponti retired in 1973, one of Minnesota's most successful aviation businessmen. He is a member of the Minnesota Aviation Hall of Fame.

Ditter, Francis J. 1899 - 1977
Born in Yakima, Washington, Ditter came to Minnesota as a child. In his youth, he became interested in flying, received his license in 1928, then went barnstorming. He opened an auto repair shop in downtown Minneapolis, but the fumes from automobile exhausts made him quit the business. He began to manufacture wooden skis for aircraft while still working on autos, and after quitting the auto business, began full-scale manufacturing as Federal Ski Company. Through the 1930s the company continued to manufacture various models of wooden and aluminum skis. Northwest Airways put his skis on their Hamilton aircraft, Admiral Byrd equipped his South Pole planes with Ditter's skis, and the military bought them in quantity. The company was sold to the Fluidyne company, which is still manufacturing the same lines of skis.

Doan, Lester H. 1908-
Doan got his Transport Pilot's license in 1932 and barnstormed in the mid 1930s. He was hired by Northwest Airways in 1938 after working for Stout Airlines and Century Airlines. In February of 1939, he and Mal Freeburg set an altitude record of 23,000 feet in a Lockheed Model 14 over Midway Airport in Chicago. Doan flew with the Northwest Airlines ATC program in the Northern Region during World War II, and later was recalled into the Air Force. He assisted in establishing Homestead Air Force Base in Florida during that time. He retired from Northwest Airlines in 1967.

Donahue, Arthur - 1941
From Lewiston, Minnesota. Donahue learned to fly at Max Conrad's school in Winona, then entered the Royal Air Force, as a member of the Eagle Squadron. (Americans flying for the British in the Battle of Britain.) Art became the first American to die in that Battle, when he was shot down over the English Channel. During his training days, he authored an exciting book on flying with the British, entitled *Tally Ho!*

Doyle, Charles P. "Chuck" 1916 -
Doyle was born a daredevil, learning to fly while still in high school. He bought his first airplane when he was a senior and rebuilt it during the following winter. He started parachute jumping and made dozens of jumps as early as 1935, including several at the Minnesota State Fair. On his motorcycle, he leaped over cars, crashed through burning walls, and changed from it to an airplane as a thrill show performer. He joined a barnstorming troupe in 1937 and traveled around the country, making several housecrashes in the south.

When the war started, Doyle was hired by Northwest Airlines and gave up the thrill shows, but kept rebuilding airplanes, skywriting, and towing banners. He had learned the skywriting trade from the first skywriters in the 1930s and still performs the art at this writing. He has had a hand in most of the aviation enterprises undertaken in the Twin City area, including part ownership of Southport Airport; restoring five warbird airplanes now in museums around the country; helping to bring an antique Grand Champion Hamilton Metalplane back from Alaska; and restoring a Curtiss Pusher. He is an inductee into the Minnesota Aviation Hall of Fame.

Duggan, Roy R. 1905 -
One of Minnesota's legendary bush pilots, Duggan learned to fly in the late 1920s and went barnstorming. He found his way to Roseau, Minnesota, where he went to work for an airmail contractor flying mail to the remote post offices on Lake of the Woods. He purchased several planes, including an eight-place Travel Air monoplane and flew passenger charters regularly as well as the mail flights. He worked for Ruben Bloom at Duluth during the CPT program, and after the war continued to fly sight-seers and mail in the Northwest Angle.

Duryea, David G. 1910 -
Duryea, from St. James, Minnesota, started flying in the late 1920s after having a few air rides with Freddie Lund. Duryea borrowed an airplane from a friend and soloed himself. He owned an auto repair garage in St. James, but got the notion he would like to make a career out of flying, and sold the business. He traveled to New York and worked for several companies, eventually operating a flying service for an aircraft brokerage firm at Flushing Airport.

Duryea then became a world traveler, flying for the Shell Oil Company on aerial surveys of the Pacific. He joined the Flying Tigers in Burma and flew combat missions into China. In 1942, he was sent to England as technical representative for the Republic Aircraft Corporation, providing maintenance support for Republic's Thunderbolt fighter. He stayed with Republic until 1957, when he went into the restaurant business.

Eklof, Londor E. 1910 -
Born in Minneapolis, Eklof joined the 109th Observation Squadron in 1929, took up flying, and earned his license in 1933. He barnstormed through the Midwest until 1937.

Enger, Gilbert
Gil Enger and his brother, Slim, lived across the road from Oxboro airport in Bloomington. Both brothers began flying and Gil barnstormed during the late 1930s. He was hired in 1942 by Northwest Airlines and flew in the Northern Region under the ATC service. Gil Enger was killed on a flight from Fairbanks to Edmonton in June of 1943, when his C-46 transport plane went down without a trace.

Fairbrother, M. W. "Lee"
Fairbrother began his career as a stuntman, making many parachute jumps in the late 1930s. He joined the RAF in 1940 and became a test pilot at Farnborough, spending 30 months with the British. He returned to the U. S. and, in 1942, was hired by Northwest Airlines. He retired in 1970. Fairbrother competed in the Bendix Trophy Race in 1946, flying a P-38 to 16th position. In 1947, he competed with a P-51 in the Kendall Trophy Race, an event of the National Air Races, finishing 4th. He raced in 1948, but did not finish, and again in 1949, taking 7th spot in the Sohio Trophy Race.

Farmer, Weston E. - 1981
One of the editors of Fawcett Publications' *Modern Mechanics Magazine* in the 1930s. Farmer took a special interest in aviation, and was responsible for the consistent publishing of homebuilt aircraft plans. His columns were so well received that the company published a compendium of those plans in special anthologies entitled *The Flying and Glider Manual* from 1929 to 1933.

Finholt, Edith Campbell 1916 -
From St. Cloud, Minnesota, Finholt began her aviation career in 1934 by attending the North Dakota School of Sciences in Wahpeton. She was the only woman student in the Aviation Mechanics class taught by Art Sampson. She signed up for flight training at De Ponti's flight school in Minneapolis and also worked as his secretary. Finholt earned her Limited Commercial license in 1936. In 1939, she joined with other local women flyers to form the Minnesota chapter of the Ninety-Nines, and two years later was asked to become executive secretary for the Minnesota Aeronautics Commission.

Finke, Donald K. 1910 - 1991
Finke learned to fly in 1928 and worked with Bernard Pietenpol in the construction of Pietenpol's first airplanes. Finke test hopped the first Pietenpol Model A Aircamper in 1929 and became a Northwest Airlines pilot in 1942. He flew the Northern Region during the war, and retired in 1970.

Fleming, Captain Richard E. - 1942
Fleming was born in St. Paul. He enlisted in the Marine Reserve at Wold-Chamberlain Field as an AVCAD (Aviation Cadet). After his training, he was sent to the Pacific. During the Battle of Midway, Captain Fleming was a member of VMSB-241 of Marine Aircraft Group 22, flying from the Midway Island. On 5 June, 1942, while leading a group of six SB2U Vindicator torpedo bombers in an attack against the Japanese cruiser Mikuma, Fleming's plane was hit by anti-aircraft fire and crashed into the cruiser's rear gun turret. Flames from the crash were sucked into the ship's air intake system and detonated fumes inside the engine room, killing all the men inside.

The Japanese ship limped away and was finished off the next day by planes from the carriers Hornet and Enterprise, making it the heaviest warship lost by Japan since the war's opening. Fleming was posthumously awarded the Congressional Medal of Honor for his valor. South St. Paul Airport was renamed Fleming Field in his honor shortly afterward.

Flynn, Nicholas A. 1912 - 1992
One of Minnesota's most outstanding aircraft mechanics was born in St. Paul. Soloed by Bill Shaw at Wold-Chamberlain Field, Flynn went to work for C. W. Hinck as a mechanic. He worked at Mon-

ticello during Hinck's military glider training program, then was tranferred to Stanton Airport at Northfield. After he worked for Northwest Airlines for a short time, he went back to work for Hinck at Monticello. He later opened his own shop on land he purchased from Hinck adjacent to the field and spent the rest of his career there.

Follmuth, Earl "Jim" 1916 - 1983
Follmuth worked for Vern Georgia at Albert Lea as a mechanic in the WTS program. Following the war, he came to Wold-Chamberlain Field to work as an instructor for Angelo De Ponti. He left De Ponti to work for the University flight facility at Anoka County, and then took a position as engine instructor at the Aviation Vocational Technical School in Minneapolis.

Ford, Richard F. 1914 - 1985
Ford was a Minneapolitan whose interests in flying began as a high school boy, hanging around Robbinsdale Airport. After learning to fly in the CPT program, he became an Army Air Force Ferry pilot, flying C-54's across the mountains between India and China. After the war, Ford became an FBO at Crystal Airport.

Foster, Benjamin 1891 - 1973
A wingwalker with the St. Paul Dispatch Flying Circus in the early 1920s. Foster was a good friend of Speed Holman. Hired by Speed as a mechanic and machinist for Northwest Airways in 1928, he later headed the machine shop, and during World War II, worked on the Northwest Airlines modification program at St. Paul and Vandalia, Ohio. He was sent to Alaska to set up a repair shop there for transient military aircraft.

Foster, Charles
Manager and booking agent for the St. Paul Dispatch Flying Circus, and a brother to Ben Foster.

Fowlie, Daniel - 1946
One of the best acrobatic pilots to come from Minnesota. Fowlie began his daredevil career at the age of fifteen, when he started parachute jumping. He learned to fly and was very active during the 1930s and 1940s as a stunt pilot. He performed skywriting for Bob McManus, crashed houses, made dozens of parachute jumps, and perfected the act of landing one aircraft atop another. During World War II, he ferried military aircraft around the country. Tragically, he was killed in an automobile accident.

Freeburg, Mal 1906 - 1963
Mal learned to fly in 1926 and established Freeburg Flying Service at Shenandoah, Iowa. He went with Northwest Airways in 1928. In 1930, while flying a mail plane, he spotted a burning railroad bridge and flew back and forth in front of an oncoming train, dropping flares to warn of the danger.
In 1932, shortly after takeoff in a Northwest Ford Trimotor, a prop blade broke on the left side engine and the engine shook loose from its mounts. As it hung from its various cables and hoses, Freeburg flew over the Mississippi River and managed to shake the engine off entirely, avoiding the danger of having it fall into a populated area. He then made an emergency landing in a farm field in Wisconsin with no injuries to the passengers or crew. In 1933, President Roosevelt presented him with the first Civilian Air Mail Medal of Honor. Freeburg was Northwest Airways operations manager in 1933. He retired in 1952, and was elected to the Minnesota Aviation Hall of Fame in 1990.

Freeman, Ben
One of the more illustrious businessmen at Wold-Chamberlain Field in the middle 1930s. Freeman owned a shoe business in Minneapolis and a hangar at the airport. He purchased a Ford Trimotor and hired Mel Swanson to fly it. The plane, its pilot, and owner were all well known to aviation fans during that time. The ship appeared at many airshows and over the State Fairgrounds, dropping parachutists, and hopping riders.

Fuller, Cora May 1894 - 1972
From the Fairmont area, Fuller was the first woman to fly in Martin County, receiving her pilot's license in 1931.

Gallaway, Cedric 1910 -
Born in Austin, Minnesota. In 1924, Gallaway entered a bicycle race for which the first prize was an air ride with aviator Art Smith, performing at the Mower County Fairgrounds. Gallaway won the race and the ride. He went on to solo and received his license in 1930, buying a Great Lakes biplane. He barnstormed for several years in Southern Minnesota, and then moved to California in the late 1930s, going to work for the Lockheed Company.

Garis, Lt. Col. William C.
As Assistant Minnesota Adjutant General, he flew to Washington, D. C. in 1920 with Captain Ray Miller and Adjutant General W. F. Rhinow in an Oriole aircraft to meet with the Militia Bureau, where they successfully petitioned for the first Air Guard charter in the U. S. Garis help nurture the growing Guard unit during the early years.

Garrett, Burton 1905 - 1983
Garrett's career in aviation began in 1927. He barnstormed through the southwest in 1928, flew with a number of private companies, then worked briefly for Boeing Air Transport on the Chicago-Omaha and Chicago-Cheyenne runs. He moved to Minnesota in 1938 and flew charter flights out of Pine River. During the war, he was a CPT instructor in Brainerd, Grand Rapids, and Bemidji. In 1944, he owned and operated as FBO at the Brainerd airport, and following the war, he started Garrett Flying Service at Pine River, retiring in 1965.

Gere, George "Bud" 1912 - 1932
Designer and builder of the homebuilt airplane that has his name, the Gere Sport of 1932. Gere was killed in a powered iceboat accident at White Bear Lake.

Gehror, Ralph 1912 - 1982
Gehror went to work for Northwest Airways in 1926 at the age of fourteen. In 1938, he became foreman of the engine shop and later manager of the Mechanical Division. He was Mod Center Superintendent during World War II.

Geng, Francis J.
Geng served in the Navy during World War I, coming to Minnesota in 1919. He was hired in 1927 as the "Airport Master" at the St. Paul Municipal Airport and stayed on as Airport Director until 1961. During that time, he saw the airport grow from a swampy field with no facilities, into a large metropolitan airport. His 34 years as manager made him legendary in Minnesota aviation circles.

Georgia, Vernon 1903 - 1982
Georgia was a school chum of Speed Holman. They hung around together, and went to work at the Security Aircraft Company at Speedway Field together. Georgia learned to fly in 1920 and designed his own homebuilt aircraft. He opened a flight school at Wold-Chamberlain Field in 1940 called Minnesota Skyways. He was forced to leave Wold during the military buildup there, and went to Albert Lea to run a WTS program. Following the war, he joined North Central Airlines and retired as Assistant Manager of Procurement in 1969.

Grace, Richard 1898 - 1965
Born in Minnesota, Grace started flying in 1917 with a commission in the Navy. He saw action in France, flying British seaplanes and Handley-Page bombers. Attached to a fighter group, Grace was shot down in combat. He recuperated and was transferred to a base in Italy, where he flew Italian flying boats. After the war, he came to Minneapolis and joined with Clarence Hinck in the Federated Fliers Flying Circus. A gifted pilot, he performed aerial stunts, including crashes into the ground. In the early 1920s he moved to Hollywood, where he continued his stunting, car and airplane crashing for the Fox movie studios. His most famous crash scenes are in the Academy Award winning movie of 1927, *Wings*.
Grace joined the Air Force during World War II and served 11 months as a test pilot at Yuma, Arizona, testing P-39's and P-51's. He did a stint in Ferry Command and then was assigned to a bomb group in England as Assistant Group Operations Officer. Grace was with several bomb groups through the war. With forty-seven crashes and eighty broken bones, Grace had survived two careers; stunt man, and wartime pilot. He wrote three books about his experiences.

Greiner, Jack B. 1920 -
Jack began flying from Wold-Chamberlain after having been a ticket-seller for many of the old barnstormers, and as a general laborer at Hanford Airlines. He barnstormed with Danny Fowlie and Don Berent, and did some house crashes and motorcycle stunts. He went to work for American Airlines in 1942.

Gruenhagen, Theodore L. 1911 -
Born in Litchfield, Minnesota, Gruenhagen's aviation career began as a boy mechanic helping build a homebuilt airplane at Grove City. He worked for the Waldron Aircraft and Manufacturing Company at Robbinsdale, and then for Mohawk Aircraft Company. From 1929 to 1933, he worked for Alexander Aircraft at Denver, Colorado, then for Travel Air in Wichita. During the war,

he was hired by Northwest Airlines as head of production scheduling at the bomber modification center at Holman Field.

Gudmundson, Sigurd 1918 - 1991
Gudmundson began his career as a ticket-seller for barnstormers and later as a mechanic for A. C. McInnis at Wold-Chamberlain. He went to work as a counter clerk for G. B. Van Dusen in 1940, spending the remainder of his career as salesman for that company. He was Van Dusen's first employee and opened their office in Waterloo, Iowa. Gudmundson flew across the country in Van Dusen aircraft, servicing customers in many States.

Hall, Harold "Shorty" - 1977
Born in Cambridge, Minnesota. Hall worked for Universal Air Lines at Wold-Chamberlain, sold tickets for local barnstormers, then took a job as manager of the tool crib for Shorty De Ponti at Wold. He worked for Shorty on the glider manufacturing contract during World War II. Following the war, Hall held an Ercoupe distributorship and managed the airport at Bemidji. In 1962, he opened Aero Sales at Fleming Field, selling aircraft parts and supplies.

Hallaway, Arthur G. 1883-1973
A lumberjack as a young man, then a telephone lineman, Hallaway took work with the Curtiss Company in New York during World War I. He became an expert mechanic and went to work for Bill Kidder at Curtiss-Northwest Field in St. Paul. Ray Miller induced him to join the newly formed 109th Observation Squadron in 1923. In 1941, he went on active duty with the Army Air Force and was a technical inspector at San Angelo and San Antonio, Texas.

Hallgren, Walter A.
Hallgren was a Royal Canadian Air Force pilot in World War I and was shot down twice by German aircraft. He came to Minnesota and joined Clarence Hinck's Federated Fliers Flying Circus, and barnstorming the country. He took a job with Universal Air lines at Wold and was killed in an accident while flying for them.

Hamilton, Paul W. 1899 - 1963
Born in Minneapolis, Hamilton was Minnesota's first specialized aerial photographer. Interested in cameras from his high school days at North High, he worked for the Eastman Kodak Company, and then the Minneapolis Tribune, where he became experienced in all types of photography and lab work.

Hamilton built his first aerial camera and mounts, and worked for the Curtiss-Northwest Company and the Federated Fliers in 1924 and 1925. For Bill Kidder, he photographed Minneapolis from the air, the photos being sold to the *Minneapolis Star Journal*, the first such pictures ever made. He provided aerial photography of Duluth for Northern States Power Company, forest fire photography, surveyed the Mississippi River, and all of Crow Wing County. He also conducted air-to-air photography of many barnstorming scenes for the Federated Fliers and the Tribune.

Hamilton joined the 109th Observation Squadron and organized the photography section for them. He worked for the Fairchild Aerial Survey Company in New York in 1926, but returned to Minneapolis the following year to begin an advertising photography career, and prior to World War II, set up the fine arts photo lab at the Minneapolis Institute of Arts. He was associated with the Civil Air Patrol and Air Force Reserve photo sections.

Hamilton, Samuel R. 1904 - 1979
Sam Hamilton was one of Minnesota's most respected aviation ground school instructors. He began his career in teaching at St. Paul Johnson High School in 1939, was drafted by the CAA to teach during the CPT program at Northport. At the same time, he taught at Hamline and Macalester Universities. In 1943 he was hired by the Aeronautical Engineering Department of the University of Minnesota as ground school instructor and assistant professor of aeronautical engineering. During that period, he rewrote the DC-3 manual for Northwest Airlines. He continued at the U. of M. until his retirement in 1969.

Hammond, Laurence C. 1892 - 1968
Born in Richfield, Minnesota, Hammond learned to fly at Kelly Field in 1918 with the U. S. Air Service. He was sent to France with the 88th Observation Squadron where he saw action over the front lines. In 1928, the Minneapolis Park Board hired Hammond as the first director of the Minneapolis Airport. His office was a Park Board warming house as there was no administration building until 1930. He continued in his position of Airport Director through World War II when the Metropolitan Airports Commission took over the airport. Hammond was among the first airport managers around the country, and as such, had to solve problems with no background of experience. He is considered a major factor in the successful development of Wold-Chamberlain Field. Hammond became an inductee into the Minnesota Aviation Hall of Fame in 1990.

Hannaford, Foster, Jr.
During his time in Minnesota, Hannaford lived at White Bear Lake. He was a colorful character involved with barnstornming in the local area. He took lessons from Max Conrad, checking out in a Ford Trimotor. He owned several unique aircraft, including a Northrop Alpha and a Boeing Trimotor. He was an entrepreneur, always looking for a new scheme. With the threat of war looming, Hannaford retreated to Canada. Under investigation by the draft board, Hannaford responded that he had gone to Canada to seek a commission in the RCAF. He later tried to establish an airport at New Brighton. According to his request of the Aeronautics Commission, he planned to train Canadian Air Force personnel there. He was not granted a license.

Harden, Charles
Parachute jumper in the 1920s. Listed by the Minneapolis Tribune as one of the state's best aviators in 1922.

Hartley, Cavour

Hartley, Guilford - 1983
Flying businessmen brothers from the Duluth area. Among the first businessmen in the state to purchase aircraft for corporate use. In August of 1931, the pair, along with Jake Pfaender, formed the Hartley-Pfaender Air Service at Duluth. They also invested in the Cloquet trainer aircraft. The Hartleys wowed the public by attending events in their matched Beechcraft Staggerwings. Gil became a Northwest Airlines pilot in 1942, but returned to business four years later.

Haugland, Owen - 1929
From Buffalo, Minnesota. Haugland learned to fly in the early 1920s and became fascinated with long distance flights. In 1929, he made five record flight attempts. The first three with Gene Shank were unsuccessful in setting a new refueled endurance record, as was the fourth, flown with Thorwald "Thunder" Johnson. The fifth attempt, conducted while others were being held elsewhere in the country, continued for seven days aloft, the plane being flown alternately by Haugland and Preston Crichton. The plane was refueled regularly over the Wold-Chamberlain airport. The record attempt came to an unfortunate end when Crichton stalled the airplane during a message drop to the ground, and spun in. Both pilots were killed.

Hazelton, Chester W. "Bill" 1910 -
A native Minnesotan, Hazelton learned to fly in 1932 and joined the Mark Hurd Aerial Surveys Company in 1938 as an aerial photographer. During World War II, he was with Pratt & Whitney, working in their installation department, and returned to the Mark Hurd Company again after the war. During his career, Hazelton logged thousands of hours at high altitudes, with a cameraman as passenger. In 1939-40-41, he flew a mapping project for the U. S. Geological Survey that covered all of Northern Minnesota. He also flew mapping projects in Alaska and Puerto Rico.

Heine, Alexander T. 1884 - 1960
The first flyer to fly over the Minneapolis loop area. In 1911, Heine graduated from the Curtiss Flying School at Newport News, Virginia. Returning to Minneapolis, he built several Curtiss-type aircraft at a shop near the old Wonderland Amusement Park on Lake Street near 36th Avenue. He flew from a field near Fort Snelling and he was photographed flying around the Courthouse tower in downtown Minneapolis in 1913. His activities were responsible for getting Walter Bullock interested in flying by allowing the latter to stand on the airplane's landing skids while it was taxied and hopped off the ground. Heine also instructed the airmail pilot, E. Hamilton Lee, who flew the first inaugural airmail flight from Minneapolis to Chicago in 1920. Lee became one of United's senior captains.

Heine built as many as eight aircraft and exhibited them around the country, carrying passengers and stunting. In later years, he was a machinist for the Milwaukee Railroad.

Heinzel, Chester H. 1913 -
Born in St. Cloud. A model airplane builder, Heinzel and Ray Russell, built a glider in 1930. In 1935, Heinzel bought an OX-5 Eagle from Spide Jones and took flying lessons from Sven Peterson, barnstorming for a while after receiving his Private license. In 1936, he taught his cousin, Marvin, to fly and threw a football

from his airplane in 1937 to start the St. Cloud Teacher's College homecoming football game. In World War II, he was in the U. S. Army Band. Heinzel flew privately after the war.

Heinzel, Marvin L. 1912 - 1981
Born in Sauk Rapids, Minnesota. In 1932, Heinzel learned to fly and began selling his services as a charter pilot in the St. Cloud area. He barnstormed and did some stunting, then flew as an aerial photographer in Tulsa, Oklahoma. He returned to fly for Millar Wittag at Hibbing during the CPT program. In 1940, he joined Pan American Air Ferries, ferrying aircraft to the British through South America, and by 1942, was flying on Pan American contracts in the Aleutians. In 1944, he went with Trans World Airlines. Heinzel flew for several airlines after the war, and eventually opened his own aerial mapping business in Alexandria, Virginia.

Helm, Arthur 1896 - 1992
Helm took his first plane ride with Walter Bullock at Lake Calhoun in Minneapolis. He became a Navy cadet at Dunwoody Institute and learned to fly at Pensacola. He served at Rockaway, New York, where he worked on the NC-4 flying boat and rode in it on a test flight with 50 other workers. He flew Naval patrols over the Atlantic Ocean and returned to Minnesota, where he was a member of the Naval Reserve Squadron at Wold-Chamberlain in the late 1920s. During World War II, he was Commanding Officer of the Naval Air Station at Roosevelt Field, New York.

Hennessy, Thomas P. 1914 -
Born in Winona, Minnesota. Hennessy took flying lessons from Max Conrad's school, going to work for Max after getting his Limited Commercial license. He joined the Hell Divers Flying Circus in 1935. Performances by this group took him through the Midwest and into Texas. He went to work in Cincinnati for the Aeronca Corporation's flight school, and enlisted in the Air Corps in 1936. He flew for Northwest Airlines in 1937 and became a Captain in 1941. A commissioned Air Corps Reserve officer, he was called to active duty in 1942 and assigned to Ferry Command in Michigan. In 1944, he was shipped to Europe and established an instrument training program for the Fifth Air Force, later becoming Deputy Group Commander for the 90th Bomb Group, flying combat missions. He returned to Northwest Airlines following the war and retired in 1966.

Henry, Robert M. "Red" 1918 - 1975
Born in Kenyon, Minnesota, Henry started flying with Max Conrad in 1937. In 1939, he started the "Hook 'Em Cow" Flying Club. He was a flight instructor in the WTS program and later in the Army Air Force during World War II. Henry took a job with Pan American Grace Airways, flying through South America, but returned in 1959 to work for Gopher Aviation in Rochester. He went to work for the Van Dusen Company for a number of years, and finally opened his own flight school at Fleming Field.

Hickman, Orville
Hickman came to Minnesota in 1928 with the Waldron Aircraft and Manufacturing Company. At that time, he had a background as an aircraft designer. Working for Waldron, and later, the Starling Aircraft Company, he designed several aircraft. Though the aircraft were intended for quantity production, none of them made it that far. Hickman's last design in Minnesota was a racing plane which was sold to a party outstate. He was one of the colorful characters that flew out of Robbinsdale airport. Hickman worked in the CPT and WTS programs, being the chief mechanic at Stanton Airport and later, at University Airport. Following the war, he left Minnesota, returning to his hometown in Kansas.

Hillis, Thomas N. 1908 - 1986
Hillis was a native of Fergus Falls, Minnesota. He joined the 109th Observation Squadron as a mechanic and learned to fly in 1929 from the Northwest Airways flight school. He bought an OX-5 Thomas-Morse Scout biplane from the airline and went to work for them that same year as a mechanic. He graduated to the right seat as co-pilot and finally the left seat as Captain in 1941. When Hillis retired in 1969, he had flown every aircraft that Northwest had owned up to and including the Boeing 707.
In 1930, Hillis bought the small building that Northwest had used for an office since 1926. It had stood alongside their hangar on 34th Avenue. He moved the building to 73rd and Portland where he used it as his home. That building is still a private residence at this writing.

Hinck, Clarence W. 1889 - 1966
From Litchfield, Minnesota. "C. W." Hinck enlisted in the Navy in 1917 and was a student at Dunwoody Institute's Naval Training School. He became friends with the Commandant, Lt. Commander Colby Dodge, and they, along with Dick Grace, started the Federated Fliers Flying Circus. Operating from a field in Fridley, Minnesota, Hinck staged thrill shows at county fairs for many years. He opened a flight school at Wold-Chamberlain prior to World War II, operated by his brother, Elmer. He also contracted with the military to open a glider pilot training school at Monticello, Minnesota, and another at Stanton, Minnesota, near Northfield.
Clarence was President of the Minnesota chapter of the National Aeronautics Association, a Commander of the American Legion, a Seabee dealer, and was founder and first president of the Minnesota chapter of the OX-5 Aviation Pioneers of America. He continued to be involved with aviation until his death in 1966. Clarence Hinck became a Minnesota Aviation Hall of Fame inductee in 1990.

Hinck, Elmer M. 1892 - 1940
Born at Litchfield, Minnesota, Elmer Hinck went to France during World War I as a foot soldier. Returning to Minnesota, he went to work for his brother, Clarence in the Federated Fliers Flying Circus. Hinck learned to fly, and became a stunt pilot as well as a wing-walker. He joined the Universal Air Lines aviation school at Wold-Chamberlain as an instructor, then was with Northland Aviation, eventually opening a school financed by Clarence. When flight schools had to leave Wold at the beginning of World War II, Elmer moved to Nicollet Airport. He was killed in a crash at Monticello, Minnesota. At the time of his death, he was considered one of the top instructors in Minnesota, having taught hundreds of students to fly and logging over 15,000 hours in the air. Elmer Hinck was inducted into the Minnesota Aviation Hall of Fame in 1991.

Hincks, Agnes Nohava
From Lonsdale, Minnesota. Hincks became a registered nurse and was practicing in Illinois. In 1933, one of her patients told her that American Airways was looking for nurses to work as hostesses on their airplanes. Agnes was hired as one of the airline's first four hostesses, later to be known as stewardesses. She was "retired" when she got married and became pregnant in 1937.

Hodge, Robert D. 1925 -
Warden pilot with Minnesota Department of Conservation. Hodge started flying in 1941 at Hibbing, in the CPT program, and stayed on with Millar Wittag as an instructor. He was sent to Crookston as a glider pilot trainer and then joined the Army Air Force where he flew as a ferry pilot during the war.

Hohag, Jack M. 1921 - 1987
Patriarch of the Hohag family that homesteaded property to the south of Speedway Field, and sold most of it to the airport association in the 1920s. Hohag retained the home lot through the years and deeded it to the airport upon the death of his wife, which occurred in the 1970s. Jack Hohag also owned the Air-O-Inn, a favorite spot for airport people in the late 1920s and early 1930s. The Inn was located at 66th Street and 34th Avenue, a quiet, converted gas station with bar and restaurant. It featured tables under the trees outside, with open fields between it and the airport. Hohag's sons, Robert and Earl, flew as Northwest Captains. Robert from 1929, and Earl from 1942. Son, William Hohag became a Northwest mechanic.

Holbrock, Clyde M.
Holbrock grew up in Minneapolis and went to Canada when World War I started, joining the Royal Canadian Air Force. He was trained as a fighter pilot and sent to France, where he shot down one German aircraft, and was shot down three times himself. He escaped twice and was taken prisoner the third time, finishing the war in a German prison camp.

Holcomb, Harold "Harry" 1898 - 1966
Holcomb learned to fly a Jenny. He graduated from the University of Minnesota with a degree in Engineering and held a mechanics license in addition to his pilot's license. In 1931 he bought the Robbinsdale Airport and was known to all local flyers for his friendly service, flight instruction, and advice. When Robbinsdale Airport was closed after World War II, he went to Crystal Airport and remained there with his shop until he retired.

Holey, George 1912 - 1989
Holey was born in Montgomery, Minnesota, and learned to fly at Wold-Chamberlain in 1929. By 1930 he had secured his Transport Pilot's license and went to work for Sohler Flying service at Mankato. He did some barnstorming and instructing at Faribault. When CPT training started, Holey worked as an instructor for Elmer Hinck at Wold and then was hired by the Civil Aeronautics Administration as District Supervisor, supervising all CPT programs in the Region. He inspected and licensed all flight

schools, and often gave the students their flight tests.

In 1945, he was called on by the Minnesota Department of Aeronautics to serve as aviation representative under Les Schroeder, charged with rewriting all of the Minnesota Air Regulations. After the war, Holey certified all veterans training at Minnesota flight schools. His deep interest in Minnesota's aviation heritage led him and his wife, Anne, to develop an aviation history collection which included numerous recorded interviews with pioneer aviators. The collection was given to the Minnesota Historical Society. George's interest also helped enable this book to be written.

Holman, Charles W. "Speed" 1898 - 1931
Holman was born in Minneapolis and grew up a daredevil. Early pranks and motorcycle racing earned him the nickname "Speed." He learned to fly at the Security Aircraft Company at Speedway Field in 1920, did some parachute jumps and received his first airplane as a gift from his father. Stunting and cross-country racing became his passion. His name became a household word, and when the newly organized Northwest Airways looked for its first pilot, they hired Speed. He became Operations Manager and pioneered air mail routes across Wisconsin and into North Dakota. His airline career was punctuated by wins in national air races, including the prestigious Thompson Trophy Race in 1930, part of the National Air Races in Chicago.

Holman set a looping record that stood for many years; visited every corner of the State, lobbying the cities to build airports; was considered one of the country's top aerobatic pilots; and every fragment of his life was spectacular. Such was his death during an impromptu aerobatic performance at the dedication of the Omaha Airport. His funeral was the largest in state history, with a hundred thousand persons turning out along the funeral route and at the cemetery. Holman is a member of the Minnesota Aviation Hall of Fame.

Holmes, Forrest 1917 - 1987
Born in Minneapolis, Holmes got his pilot's license in 1930 at Cedar Airport. He worked for the Mohawk Aircraft Company and bought one of their airplanes, then designed and built an airplane to his own specifications, powered with a Henderson motorcycle engine. In 1930, Holmes joined the Naval Reserve Squadron at Wold-Chamberlain as a mechanic, and turned down an offer to go to work for Northwest Airways. When the Depression was over, he made his living by flying around the country repairing trucks. In later years, Holmes restored a Fairchild PT-19 aircraft.

Hubbard, Stanley E., Sr. 1897 - 1992
A native of Red Wing, Minnesota, Hubbard took his first flying lessons in 1916. He soon enlisted in the U. S. Cavalry and took part in World War I. Following the war, he settled in Louisville, Kentucky, and opened an airport that became known as Bowman Field. He started an airline, Kentucky Aviation Flight Company, one of the first commercial passenger carriers in the U. S. He designed an aircraft for quantity production, but was unsuccesful in seeing it produced. He tried his hand at starting airlines in New York, and then in Florida, but was only marginally successful. Hubbard is a member of the Minnesota Aviation Hall of Fame.

In 1922, he returned to Minnesota and began barnstorming. He lobbied the Park Board to take over Speedway Field. When the Minnesota Aeronautics Commission was formed, Hubbard was appointed a commissioner, and took over as chairman from Ray Miller in 1941, following Miller's call to active duty in the Air Force. Hubbard was instrumental in enacting the regulations that govern flying in Minnesota to this day. In 1943, he helped organize the Metropolitan Airports Commission.

In 1924, Hubbard bought radio station, WAMD in Minneapolis, and later bought station KSTP. He pioneered the use of aircraft for gathering news from the far corners of Minnesota, and eventually formed Hubbard Broadcasting, Incorporated, one of Minnesota's most familiar institutions.

Hufford, Andrew J.
Hired as the first mechanic for fledgling Northwest Airways in 1926, Hufford came with experience. He had been the chief mechanic with Sir Hubert Wilkins on the latter's first trip to the North Pole in 1926. Hufford was a passenger in the Ryan M-1 aircraft flown by Vance Breese in the 1926 Ford Reliability Tour. In 1929, Hufford became chief of the Northwest engine shop.

Hunter, Croil - 1970
From Fargo, North Dakota, and a graduate of Yale University, Hunter played a significant role in Northwest Airlines history. A veteran of World War I, he was hired in 1932 by Northwest Airlines' President, Richard Lilly, to act as the airline's Traffic Manager. He dove into the westward expansion of Northwest's routes with

vigor. His enthusiasm and energy brought him the title of General Manager, and in 1937, he was elected President of Northwest Airlines. He had ramrodded the routes on to the west coast, and helped Northwest weather the stormy period of the airmail cancellation of 1934.

In World War II, Northwest jumped in to serve the nation by carrying personnel and supplies through Canada and Alaska, to the Aleutian Islands, helping to build military bases and erect defenses against a Japanese invasion. The Northern Division was then merged into the Army's Air Transport Command in 1942 and other airlines brought in to help with the buildup. By 1946, Hunter had helped the airline to establish a base at Anchorage, pioneering the routes to the far east, to Tokyo, Shanghai, Manila, and finally, Seoul. Hunter stepped down in 1954 and turned over the reins of office to Donald Nyrop.

Hurd, Mark M. 1892 - 1969
Hurd graduated from the University of Minnesota in 1914 with a degree in chemical engineering. He enlisted in the Signal Corps and was sent to France, where he served as an aerial observer and photographer. Following the war, he opened an aerial survey business in Chicago, and returned to the Twin Cities with the Fairchild aircraft franchise. Here, he was issued Minnesota pilot's license number five. He organized Mid-Plane Sales & Transit company at Speedway Field and was soon bought out by the Universal Air Lines organization. In 1920 Hurd became manager of the Aero Club of Minneapolis, set up the welding and aircraft mechanics courses at Dunwoody Institute, and became a charter member of the National Aeronautics Association as well as the newly formed AOPA. (Aircraft Owners and Pilots Association.)

Hurd also organized Great Northern Aviation at Wold-Chamberlain with training schools in St. Paul, Duluth, Cloquet, and Coleraine. His next enterprise was Aerial Photographic Service Corp, which later became the Hurd Aerial Mapping Company, whose contracts included those with the Minnesota Highway Department, the National Guard, and the U. S. Forest Service. He developed improvements in aerial cameras, and aerial photo techniques. In World War II, he was assigned to General Patton's office, in charge of aerial reconnaisance. Following the war, Hurd returned to Minnesota and formed Mark Hurd Aerial Surveys. Hurd is a member of the Minnesota Aviation Hall of Fame.

Imm, Gustav O. 1900 -
Imm was born in Astrovo, Poland, and came to Minnesota in 1922. He worked as a printer in Jordan, Minnesota, and took flying lessons from Lawrence Sohler at Mankato. He bought a Jenny before he had soloed and when he received his license, (number 14 in Minnesota), moved north to establish the Northern Airport on a farm near Maynard, Minnesota. He held a Waco sales franchise and took part in local air races. In 1927, he was lured to Fergus Falls and flew powerline patrol for the Ottertail Power Company. Imm took over operation of the airfield at Fergus, built a hangar, and did some barnstorming on weekends. In 1937, Imm moved to the St. Paul Airport, taking a job in the insurance industry. He instructed at the 29 Palms Air Academy in California during World War II. He quit flying in 1953 following the crash of the plane he usually flew. The crash had taken the life of his cousin, State Representative Val Imm. Imm is a member of the Minnesota Aviation Hall of Fame.

Jackson, Dale "Red" 1906 - 1932
Jackson was born in Iowa, but his family moved to Faribault, Minnesota, when he was in his early school years. After obtaining his flying license in 1928, he barnstormed across the U. S. and set a barrel roll record of 417 rolls in 1930. He flew as a member of a stunt flying team with Freddie Lund, a prominent pilot.

In July of 1929, Jackson and Forest O'Brine, a flyer from St. Louis, got immersed in the refueled endurance flight craze and persuaded business interests from St. Louis to sponsor a record-setting flight. In a Curtiss Robin aircraft, they circled over that city for over 420 hours (17-1/2 days) in the air, refueling forty-eight times in flight. When this record was broken, the pair went aloft a second time, and in August of 1930, set a second record of over 647 continuous hours in the air. Jackson was killed two years later while testing a Curtiss amphibian aircraft.

Janes, Phillip H. - 1964
Janes learned to fly in New York in 1926, spent several years barnstorming and stunting, then became an FBO at airports in New York, Vermont and New Hampshire. Janes went to work for the Civil Aeronautics Administration, was stationed in Cleveland, and in 1949, was transferred to Minneapolis as General Aviation Safety Inspector. After a period assigned to Kansas City, Janes returned to Minnesota as Deputy Director of the Metropolitan Airports Commission. Janes also served 22 years in the Naval Reserve.

Jenks, Joan Trebtoske 1922 -
A St. Cloud CPT student who went on to join the WASP (Women Air Service Pilots) in World War II. As a ferry pilot, she flew P-39's, P-40's and P-63's from factories to embarkation stations around the country. She became a 1st Lieutenant in the Air Force after the war, was a Civil Air Patrol Major, and instructed for John Lysdale at Pipestone for ten years.

Johnson, Conrad G. - 1918
Born in Duluth, Johnson was a student at the University of Minnesota when World War I was declared. He enlisted and was sent to the Princeton Aviation School where he graduated and was sent to the combat front in France. He flew aerial missions for nearly a year before being shot down by German anti-aircraft fire in the Argonne on 23 October, 1918. The Duluth Williamson-Johnson Airport is named in his honor.

Johnson, Erling - 1976
Johnson started flying when he was 16 years old, and soloed at the McInnis school at Wold-Chamberlain. He purchased a Waco Model RNF and began carrying passengers. He then worked for Hinck Flying Service, and later, General Air Transport. He instructed in the CPT program and joined Northwest Airlines in 1942.

Johnson, Gerald 1906 -
Johnson was a Minneapolis parachute jumper during the 1930s. He specialized in jumps at county fairs, and at Wold-Chamberlain on weekends. On 8 June, 1935, he set a national record for the most parachute jumps performed in a single day, with fifteen. He started the ordeal at 9:00 a.m. and finished at 9:00 p.m. that evening. He was flown aloft by Elmer Hinck and would make two jumps, one after the other, then would rest while Stub Chrissinger, Betty Goltz, and Stella Kindem repacked parachutes for him. By the time the day was over, his legs had been taped from the knees down to relieve the pain of the repeated landing shock.

Johnson, Leroy
LeRoy Johnson worked for the Minneapolis Park Board from 1924. In 1928, the Park Board offered him the opportunity to become assistant to airport director, Larry Hammond, which he accepted. He took over the position of director on Hammond's retirement in 1957.

Johnson, Lester I. 1905 -
Johnson worked for the Mohawk Aircraft Company in 1928. It was his job to transport the unassembled aircraft from the factory near the Midway district between St. Paul and Minneapolis, by truck, to Wold-Chamberlain, where the parts were assembled and the Mohawks test flown. He was hired by Northwest Airlines and spent thirty-two years there as mechanic, crew chief, foreman, and supervisor. He was also a mechanic with the Naval Reserve from 1929 until 1969.

Johnson, Thorwald "Thunder" 1903 - 1973
Born near Oslo, Norway, Johnson was only nine years old when the flying bug bit him. He came to Minneapolis in 1910, and learned to fly as a teenager. He barnstormed, raced, and attempted some endurance records during the 1920s and early 1930s. He worked at times for the Federated Fliers, for Dick Grace, and Harold Peterson at White Bear Lake. Johnson went to the Ford Motor plant in Detroit in 1928 to learn Ford Trimotor systems and brought a Trimotor back to the Twin Cities, where he flew it some fifteen hundred hours for Jefferson Airways. He achieved his Transport Pilot rating, and flew as pilot for Hanford Airlines from 1932 to 1936. In 1936 he went to work for the CAA, and finished his career with that agency.

Jones, V. L. "Casey" - 1972
Casey was one of the top ground school instructors in the Twin Cities area. His students could be counted on to pass their exams and do well in the aviation business. He joined the Marine Air Reserve at Wold in the 1920s and taught students in his own home, serving them soft drinks and popcorn as well as the instruction, accepting pocket change as compensation. During his tenure as ground school instructor at the Marine station, he emphasized his lessons with hand-drawn cartoons. He left Minnesota in the 1930s and taught in Georgia, Oklahoma, Illinois, New York, Arizona, and Texas. He was elected to the OX-5 Hall of Fame in 1971.

Judd, Frank C. 1909 - 1984
A graduate of Minneapolis' West High School in 1929, Judd learned to fly, and joined Northwest Airways in 1932. During World War II, he was Superintendent of the company's Northern Division, heading the survey flights and in charge of all operations in Canada and Alaska. In April of 1943, he and fourteen other Northwest pilots took part in a mass cargo flight from Miami, Florida to Karachi, India, a four and a half-day, 15,000 mile odyssey. He became Western Regional Manager in 1945 and later Vice-President of that region. Following the war, he held the positions at Northwest of Vice-President of Operations, Vice-President of Maintenance and Station Operations, and Vice President of Maintenance and Engineering.

Kantrud, H. Arthur
From Otter Tail County, Kantrud and two partners, Rueben Anderson and Cliff Bonde, had an air service at Gus Imm's Wendell Road Airport south of Fergus Falls as early as 1927. In 1928, this airport was abandoned and the men moved to a new site on Fergus Falls' west side. Kantrud hired B. G. Vandre to instruct and barnstorm for him, and remained as a fixed base operator until 1939, when he went into the hardware business in town.

Kapaun, Patrick 1909 - 1963
Kapaun was one of the first flyers in Big Stone County, beginning in the mid-1930s. For 32 years, he gave the city of Graceville and its flyers use of an airstrip on his own property, free of charge. He was an informal instructor who took prospective students for their first introduction to flying, letting them fly his airplane. In later years, Kapaun got his seaplane rating and had Toqua Lake licensed as a seaplane base. The Graceville Airport is named in his honor.

Keller, Archie C. 1918 -
Keller joined the Army Air Force at the start of World War II and was trained as a fighter pilot. He went to Casablanca where he was stationed with the 33rd Fighter Group, 60th Fighter Squadron, flying P-40's. To reach his base, he was catapulted from a baby flat-top (aircraft carrier), the HMS Archer. He shot down four German Stuka aircraft over North Africa and then was shot down himself, falling into enemy hands. As he was being transported to a prison camp by German motorcycle, the cycle was strafed by Allied aircraft, and the cycle driver, his German guard, killed. He was wounded in the wrist, but was taken to an Allied hospital, treated, and returned to action five months later, as a P-47 instructor. He joined Northwest Airlines following the war, and flew thirty-three years for the airline, until his retirement.

Kelsey, Samuel
Kelsey was one of the local Twin City pilots during the 1930s who flew from the Oxboro Airport, and when it was closed, moved with the gang to fly out of Cedar and Nicollet Airports. He associated with Wally and Al Neuman, Wally Russell, Al Schauss, Wally Hanson, and Ken Muxlow. Kelsey owned a modified Pietenpol in 1934, and several years later bought a Mohawk Pinto, modifying it by adding wheel pants, and a cowled Siemens-Halske engine.

Kenyon, Jess - 1932
Kenyon was a wealthy Morris, Minnesota, hotel owner. He decided to get into flying and bought a Ford Trimotor, hiring various pilots to fly it on barnstorming trips, on which he almost always went along, often with his entire family. In four years of these trips, Kenyon covered thirty-three States, Canada, and Mexico, his plane carrying thousands of passengers. Thunder Johnson and Paul Quinn were Kenyon's pilots.

Ketcham, Stanley 1910 -
Born in Montevideo, Minnesota, Ketcham learned to fly at Oxboro and Robbinsdale Airports in 1938. He joined the Marine Air Reserve at Wold-Chamberlain and took a home-study course on radio operating. A bulletin board notice informed him that the Park Board was hiring a control tower operator for the new tower at Wold, and he responded. He got the job in July, 1938, because of his persistance and his knowledge of "radio operating." Ketcham began with little knowledge of what to do, little cooperation from the local pilots, and rapidly changing radio usage, traffic conditions, and government regulations. With the advent of World War II, the job became much bigger, with increased Naval training traffic. He retired in 1973.

Keyes, Charles "Chick"

One of Bill Kidder's pilots at Curtiss-Northwest Airport. Keyes, along with Ray Miller, flew to New York in 1920 to bring back dry goods for the Dayton's Department Store. Keyes delivered movie films around the state for the Finkelstein and Rubin theater chain, and chemical pesticides to various cities in Minnesota.

Kidder, William A. 1886 - 1974

Kidder earned his pilot's license in 1917 at the Curtiss school at Newport News, Virginia. He opened Curtiss-Northwest Airport at Snelling and Larpenteur Avenues in St. Paul. He received the first Aerial Transportation license from the State of Minnesota in April of 1919 for the Curtiss-Northwest Aeroplane Company. He bought 75 Jenny aircraft from Curtiss and had them shipped by rail to St. Paul, selling them as each was assembled. Kidder offered sight-seeing and charter flights, merchandise transportation, and exhibitions. He was clearly the first major Minnesota FBO, and his airfield, along with Brown Field and Hinck's Fridley Field, were the first Twin Cities airports.

Kidder rented aircraft to the newly organized 109th Observation Squadron of the Air National Guard in 1921, and to the fledgling Northwest Airways to get them started in 1926. He served in an advisory capacity to Colonel Brittin in forming Northwest Airways. Kidder saw the airplane as a machine that allowed transportation, entertainment, photography, and crop dusting to be done as never before. In later years, he wrote an unpublished autobiography which contains a wealth of history and good tales of flying in those days. From 1918 to 1925, his field was undoubtedly the center of aviation in the State. Kidder is a member of the Minnesota Aviation Hall of Fame.

Kimm, Joseph E. 1911 -

Kimm started his aviation career as a model airplane builder, with Walter Bullock as his club's advisor. That led him to seek employment in the aviation business, and he was hired in 1929 by Speed Holman to work for Northwest Airways. He began as a steward. After graduating from Northwest's flight school, he was hired as a pilot at age 19, and retired in 1971, a career of 41 years as a pilot for the airline, a record that has stood until the present time. Kimm was co-pilot on a 1933 flight to prove the northern transcontinental air route between Chicago and the Pacific Northwest. On board the flight was Amelia Earhart. Kimm also figured in another important cross-country flight, that of 1956 to celebrate the 30th anniversary of Northwest. The airline had procured a Ford Trimotor and restored it in Northwest's old colors, and with Kimm and Deke DeLong at the controls, flew it from New York to Seattle, making twenty stops during ten days of celebrations.

King, Marcellus A. 1907 - 1969

Though born in Iowa, King became a popular adopted Minnesotan. He had learned to fly in 1928, when he began barnstorming, and purchased a Monocoupe aircraft in which he flew stunt exhibitions at county fairs. In the mid-1930s he entered national air races and it is said, once set a record, flying upside down from New York to Chicago. He became the airport manager at Fairmont, Minnesota, then moved to Austin, where he started Austin Aero Service in 1937. He instructed there in the WTS program, and later the G.I. training program until 1947, when he took up crop dusting. King later moved to Alaska to help his sons with an air service there. He returned to Minnesota in the 1950s to continue in the aerial survey business for the remainder of his career.

Kipp, John V. 1907 -

Born in Madelia, Minnesota. Kipp took his first plane ride with Speed Holman in 1928. By 1929, he had his Commercial License and went barnstorming in a Curtiss Robin aircraft. He often accompanied Florence Klingensmith on barnstorming trips. He joined the Marine Reserve and became an officer while attending St. Thomas College in St. Paul. He pursued a career in High School Administration at Harmony, Wadena, and Randolph, Minnesota, also coaching school sports teams to state championships. He instructed flying at Wold-Chamberlain prior to World War II, then was called to active duty in the Pacific, becoming Commander of Marine Air Group 13.

Kipp flew the historic flag-raising films from Iwo Jima to Guam, the first leg of their trip to the United States. He was awarded the Air Medal, three Gold Stars, and the DFC for bombing missions in the Pacific. Following the war, he became part owner of Southport Airport in Apple Valley, then moved to Florida, where he returned to school administration. Kipp is a 1992 inductee into the Minnesota Aviaton Hall of Fame.

Klausler, Walter W. 1906 -

Klausler earned his reputation as a thrill show promoter. His 1930s shows featured both aviation and auto racing acts. In the

aviation realm, his featured stars were Don Voge and Wally Neuman. Klausler promoted dozens of house crashes in states around the country, using Voge, and aerial stunts by Wally Neuman. He was a friendly competitor to Clarence Hinck, vying for Fair dates.

Klimek, Peter J. 1907 -

Born in Little Falls, Minnesota, Klimek was another flyer who got his first air ride with Speed Holman, and became enthused about flying. Klimek's parents owned a resort near the Minnesota-Canadian border and decided to buy an airplane to give rides to resorters. Klimek learned to fly the plane and spent a number of years flying sight-seers, airmail, and search missions in the far northern portions of Minnesota. During the airmail cancellation of 1934, Klimek was the only American who retained a government airmail contract, bringing mail across Lake of the Woods to the Northwest Angle.

In the 1930s, Klimek was in charge of construction of the Baudette Airport, then worked for the Forestry Service. He instructed in the CPT program in Iowa, and was called to active Naval duty in 1941, joining the Naval Air Transport Service. His service in the Pacific included flying the "brass hats" (Admirals Mitscher, Halsey, Nimitz, and Spruance) from island to island. Following the war, he retired to the Minnesota resort area, to own a lodge at Wheeler's Point on Lake of the Woods, and sell surplus aircraft.

Klingensmith, Florence G. 1906 - 1933

Klingensmith was born in Moorhead, Minnesota. She moved to North Dakota at an early age and took up flying. She convinced Fargo businessmen to loan her money to purchase an airplane, and then began touring the region, barnstorming and putting on flying exhibitions. She was to be seen nearly every weekend at Wold-Chamberlain Field during the summers of 1930 and 1931, taking up sight-seers. Over the field, she set a women's loop record of 1078 loops in June of 1931. She then began entering air races, winning a number of them. Her short, but highly visible career, ended in 1933 when she was killed while racing a Gee Bee aircraft in the Chicago National Air Races.

Kloskin, Frederick P. 1911 -

Kloskin was a member of the 109th Observation Squadron in the 1930s, and owner of the Arrow Flying School at Wold-Chamberlain Field. Prior to World War II, he was the Minnesota Civil Air Patrol Wing Commander. In 1946, he enlisted in the 233rd Air Service Group and was discharged in 1949.

Koerner, Louis E. 1900 - 1973

Born in Pennsylvania, Koerner began his career as a mechanic in 1918. He joined Northwest Airways in 1928 under "Big Jim" LaMont, and retired as Manager of Maintenance in 1965.

Krause, Walter H. "Rocker Arm"

From Ormsby, Minnesota. Legendary mechanic.

Krouse, Benjamin F. 1909 - 1968

Born in Ohio, Krouse worked for the Douglas Company in California as a welding and sheet metal mechanic. He came to Hanford Airlines in 1935 and stayed after it became Mid-Continent Airlines in 1939. He became Mid-Continent's superintendent of maintenance in the late 1930s. Krouse oversaw the modification of the Doolittle B-25's from January to March, 1942. It was his decisive planning and action that got the aircraft modified in a two month period and on their way to the event that made history. By 1945, Krouse was gone from the airline, to work for Honeywell as a project engineer.

Ladwig, Harold 1908 - 1960

Hal Ladwig began flying in 1930, but didn't muster enough hours to solo until 1934. He then bought a wrecked OX-5 Waco 10 and rebuilt it. Ladwig flew from the Oxboro and Nicollet Airports, taking odd jobs to pay for his flying. He worked for Al Brandt's Lexington Flying Service at University Airport as a CPT instructor prior to the war. His colorful career after the war included flying as stunt pilot for World Airshows, doing a Crazy Curtiss Junior aircraft act.

Lafferty, John D. 1914 - 1990

Born in Illinois, Lafferty came to Minnesota as a youngster. He received his Private license in 1937 after taking lessons from Marcellus King at Austin, Minnesota. Lafferty began taking up sight-seers to earn enough for additional flying time. He instructed during the pre-war CPT program, then journeyed to California, where he taught at the famous Pancho Barnes "Happy Bottom Riding Club" flight school. During the war, he instructed in BT-13 trainers, and was eventually transferred to B-29's where he acted as flight engineer. After the war, he continued to fly for fun, rebuilding Stearmans and a multitude of other classic and homebuilt aircraft.

La Mont, James B. "Big Jim" 1889 - 1964

La Mont started his working career as a steamboat captain in New York. He went to work for Glenn Curtiss at Hammondsport, New York, as a motorcycle mechanic and factory worker. Jim La Mont helped Curtiss rebuild the Langley Aerodrome, an airplane that preceeded the Wright Brothers airplane, to help prove that the Wrights did not own the idea of flying. La Mont also helped Curtiss build the famous "June Bug" early airplane. La Mont met aviatrix Ruth Law, and became her regular mechanic, going with her on tour through the United States, Europe, and Japan. La Mont also worked as a mechanic for Lincoln Beachey, and later for Matty Laird at Chicago, building the Laird airplanes. It was there he met Speed Holman, who hired him to work for Northwest Airways in 1928.

During the war, La Mont was loaned to Northwestern Aeronautical at St. Paul, to advise them on, and oversee production of, Waco military gliders they were building under contract to the Army. In 1946, La Mont retired from Northwest with the title of Superintendent of Inspection in the maintenance department. La Mont is a 1991 inductee into the Minnesota Aviation Hall of Fame.

LaMotte, Joseph

In 1941, LaMotte was a mechanic for the Fontana School of Aeronautics at Rochester, Minnesota. He then went to work for Northwest Airlines and retired as Superintendent of Engine Overhaul and Procurement.

Lane, Lt. Thomas D. 1894 -

Born in Omaha. Lane enlisted with the University of Minnesota contingent of Marines in 1917. He began flight training at Miami but was mustered out at war's end in 1919. He returned to the U. of M. to finish his engineering degree, but switched to law. He joined the 109th Observation Squadron of the Air Guard in 1924. Lane flew with Speed Holman on cross-country flights until 1928, then joined Universal Air lines as manager of their flight school at Wold-Chamberlain, and as airline dispatcher. He remained in the 109th until 1937.

Larrabee, Weldon
Larrabee, Wilbur 1897 - 1963

The Larrabee brothers opened the first fixed base operation at Wold-Chamberlain Field, (then Speedway Field), in 1920, when they started the Security Aircraft Company. Their hangar was built on the concrete racetrack, using it as flooring. They provided airplanes and pilots for both the St. Paul Dispatch Flying Circus and the Minneapolis Daily News Flying Circus during the early 1920s. The operation was sold to Dusty Rhodes in 1923.

Weldon was the business partner of the pair. He was also a song writer and musician whose band was frequently booked for local parties. Several of Weldon's songs were published. Wilbur and Weldon went to California to seek their fortune in the west. Wilbur, however, returned to St. Paul, where, after the war, he became associated with the law firm of Walston and Company.

Wilbur had been a U. S. Air Service pilot in World War I, and after starting the Security company, flew and acted as wingwalker for weekend airshows. He made a record 130-mile flight between Minneapolis and Duluth in 1919, and a 1921 flight between Minneapolis and New York in sixteen hours and twenty-two minutes. He was a member of the 109th Observation Squadron.

LaVake, James 1915 - 1991

Born in Minneapolis, LaVake learned to fly in Minnesota in 1931. He worked as a photographer and a writer for the Minneapolis Tribune and the St. Paul Dispatch-Pioneer Press. He owned several airplanes, including a Monocoupe, a Stinson SM8A, and a J-5 Waco. As one of the first local business pilots, he flew for the Mason Furnace Company. In 1938, he obtained his Instrument rating and was hired by Eastern Airlines, from which he retired in 1975. In addition to his hobby of photographing airplanes and airmen, he was a railroad photographer. Several of LaVake's aviation photos are found in this book.

Leavitt, Claire E.

Leavitt started flying lessons in 1932. She received her license and became well-known in the area as parachute jumper, utility pilot, and air race competitor.

Leighton, Elmer F.

Hired in 1926 as the first mechanic to work under Andy Hufford at Northwest Airways.

Lerdahl, Herman I. 1906 - 1983

Born in Cyrus, Minnesota. Lerdahl was smitten with aviation in 1930 following a barnstorming ride with Noel Wien at Virginia, Minnesota. He got his first job in the flying business in 1935, when he joined his brother, Ed, at Fairbanks, Alaska, in an effort to open a charter flight service. In 1936, he went to work for Noel Wien. In 1941, Lerdahl was hired by the Morrison-Knudson Construction Company as company pilot. The M-K company was under government contract to build military defenses. Lerdahl went to work for Northwest Airlines in December of 1942 and retired after a career there.

LeVier, Anthony "Tony" 1913 -

Born in Duluth, LeVier's family moved to California when he was six years old. He soloed in 1930, received his Transport Pilot's license at age 19, barnstormed through the West, and participated in air races in which he regularly flew the Schoenfeldt "Firecracker" racing plane. He won the 1938 Bendix Race, and took 2nd in the 1939 Thompson Trophy Race. During the war, he worked for Lockheed, and was sent to military bases to teach fledgling pilots how to fly the P-38. He became one of the country's best-known test pilots, testing the P-80 jet, the F-90 supersonic jet and the F-94.

Lilly, Richard C.

In 1929, Twin Cities based interests bought Northwest Airways. Lilly, President of Merchants National Bank of St. Paul, was elected President of the airline. He remained as President until 1933, when he was replaced by Shreve Archer, and became Chairman of the Board. It was Lilly who put Croil Hunter on the Northwest payroll as Traffic Manager.

Lindbergh, Charles A. 1902 - 1974

Lindbergh grew up on a farm in Little Falls, Minnesota. His father was a State Congressman from 1907 to 1917, representing the sixth district. After graduation from Little Falls High School in 1918, the younger Lindbergh spent two years in engineering studies at the University of Wisconsin, then succumbed to the urge to fly and enrolled in a flight school in Nebraska, becoming a wingwalker, parachute jumper, and barnstormer. He purchased a surplus Jenny and continued barnstorming. In 1924, he entered the Army flying school at San Antonio and became an airmail pilot after his training.

Lindbergh convinced St. Louis business interests to fund his attempt at a transatlantic solo flight, and in 1927, made the crossing, immediately becoming the most important aviation figure in the world. In the latter part of 1927, he made an 82-city tour of the United States, inspiring thousands of young men and women to get into the flying. He met and married Anne Morrow and in 1932, their first child was kidnapped, amid sensational publicity. The Lindberghs retired to France, and while there, Lindbergh assisted with the development of an artificial heart.

During the 1930s, Lindbergh, on behalf of the U. S. Government, inspected the status of aviation in European nations, reporting back on the strengths and weaknesses to U. S. intelligence. He went on record as favoring non-involvment in a European conflict by the U. S. and faced severe criticism. After America entered the war, Lindbergh served as technical advisor to the government, and test pilot for United Aircraft. He flew fifty combat missions in the Pacific and shot down a Japanese aircraft. Eisenhower commissioned him a Brigadier General in the Air Force Reserve. He won the Pulitzer Prize for the book about his record flight, *Spirit of St. Louis*. Lindbergh is a member of the Minnesota Aviation Hall of Fame.

Lindstam, Gordon H. 1910 - 1987

Lindstam began flying at Oxboro Airport in Bloomington in the middle 1930s. He and his brother, Robert, moved to Robbinsdale Airport when Oxboro closed, and bought States Flying Service where they conducted flight training, service and charter work. When the business outgrew Robbinsdale, Gordy Lindstam purchased land to the north, opening Crystal Airport. He went to work for Northwest Airlines in 1941 and retired in 1970.

Lindstam, Robert F. 1915 - 1975

Brother to Gordon Lindstam, Robert began flying at the same time, the middle 1930s. At Robbinsdale, the brothers ran States Flying Service. Robert, his brother Gordon, Dave Buckman, Ray Hanson and Stan Ketcham started the "0-0 Flying Club" at Robbinsdale. Robert was a member of the Air Guard and one of their photographers during the early 1930s. He joined Northwest Airlines in 1942 and retired in 1971.

Longeway, Forrest H. - 1965

Longeway is the legendary 1930s Department of Commerce flight inspector whose territory included Minnesota, where he was officed.

He was responsible for giving virtually all the early flight examinations from the start of Federal licensing; including Private, Limited Commercial, and Transport license tests during the 1930s. He was a tough examiner, often intimidating the student to find out if he would become flustered under pressure. Longeway was also a member of the 109th Observation Squadron in the 1930s.

Lowinski, Eldon
FBO and crop-duster from the Sleepy Eye area. Lowinski acquired over 40,000 hours of flight time in his logbooks.

Luethi, Carl F.
Luethi came to the Twin Cities as a young boy in 1919. He graduated from West High School in Minneapolis, and received a degree in engineering at the University of Minnesota in 1927. He joined the Naval Reserve and after completing his flight training, was sent to join the Pacific fleet, flying from aircraft carriers as an observation pilot. He then returned, obtained his Transport Pilot's license, and was hired in 1931 as Chief Pilot for Minnesota Aircraft Corporation at Wold-Chamberlain. He began instructing at St. Paul for the Twin City Flying Club and was hired by Northwest Airways. In 1934, Luethi made the initial trip from Minneapolis to Seattle in a new Lockheed Orion aircraft, initiating speedy 200 mile per hour service between the cities. He retired in 1963.

Lund, Frederick M. "Freddie" 1897 - 1931
Born in Alexandria Township, Minnesota. Lund grew up on the family farm and attended school at Nelson, Minnesota. He left the farm to take up work as a mechanic, and when World War I was declared, joined the Air Service and trained at San Antonio. He was sent to the 4th Pursuit Squadron at Toul, France. Stricken with tuberculosis following the war, he returned to the states, not expected to live. He struggled back to strength and joined the Gates Flying Circus as a stunt flyer, working for a while in Hollywood, as a movie double, where he earned the nickname "Fearless Freddie."
Lund joined the Waco Aircraft Company as a test pilot and flew around the country performing stunt exhibitions, representing Waco. Fred performed the first outside loop ever done in a commercial airplane. He was World Aerobatic Champion in 1930. His wife, Betty Lund, was a well-known woman stunt pilot. Lund died in October, 1931, when his plane was cut in two in a mid-air collision during an air race in Kentucky. Lund is a member of the Minnesota Aviation Hall of Fame.

Lundquist, Gilmore J. P. - 1987
Lundquist was a native Minnesotan. He joined the University of Minnesota Flying Club in 1930 and learned to fly gliders. He aided Professors John Akerman and Jean Piccard in aeronautical projects. Joining the Air Corps in 1939, Lundquist became a B-25 pilot. He flew during World War II in North Africa, Sicily, Italy, and in the China-Burma-India theatre. He spent twenty-eight months in combat, flying in ten campaigns. He also flew in Korea and also in Vietnam. In 1961, Lundquist was Chief of Aerial Reconnaisance for the Air Force, playing a key role during the construction of the Berlin Wall and the Cuban Crisis. Following his military career, he opened Eagle Aviation at Faribault.

Lysdale, Jack P. 1913 - 1992
Lysdale began flying in 1929 while working as a Standard Oil station operator. In 1936, he went to California to work for the Ryan Aircraft Company but returned to Minnesota and opened a fixed base operation at Mankato. In 1940, he moved to Worthington, where he instructed students in the CPT program. By 1941, he was appointed a CAA licensing inspector and was managing the airport. The following year, Lysdale became a certified flight instructor. He was transferred to Victory Airport north of the Twin Cities to continue WTS training, and after the war worked for the Reconstruction Finance Corporation, disposing of surplus military aircraft.
After the war, Lysdale relocated to South St. Paul Airport and rebuilt military aircraft, including several B-17's, BT-13's, and Cessna T-50's, selling them on the civilian market. He continued as FBO at South St. Paul, and was the airport manager at the time of his death.

Maas, Brig. General Melvin J. 1898 - 1967
Born in Duluth, Maas was the first man from St. Paul to enlist in 1917 when the United States entered World War I. He joined the Marines, and was trained as a foot soldier, but transferred to the First Marine Aeronautic Company in 1918 and shipped to the Azores, where his unit's mission was to locate and destroy enemy submarines. As an observer, he held the rank of Sergeant. He was sent to officer's school at Quantico, Virginia, but the war was soon

over and he returned to Minnesota. Maas was Commanding Officer of Marine Reserve Squadrons based at Wold-Chamberlain; Observation Squadron VO-7MR from 1931 to 1935; Observation Squadron VO-6MR from 1935 to 1937; and Scouting Squadron VMS-6R from 1937 to 1940.
Maas entered the business world upon graduation from the University of Minnesota, and was elected to Congress, serving in Washington as a member of the House Sub-Committee on Military Affairs. He spearheaded the program of "airmarking" in which prominent buildings of each major city in the United States had the town names painted on them as signposts for aerial wayfarers. Bills that Maas introduced in Congress in 1938 helped strengthen the Naval Reserve program in the United States.

MacDonald, George A.
Vice President and Chief Pilot for the Mohawk Aircraft Company, MacDonald was a graduate mechanical engineer who had obtained his pilot's training in the Naval Reserve. He flight-tested most of the Mohawk aircraft after they were assembled. Both MacDonald and Speed Holman were reported to have had to bail out of a Mohawk during spin testing episodes in the unstable aircraft.

Mace, Captain Gage
Mace was carried as a Captain Observer on the original roster of the 109th Observation Squadron of the Minnesota Air National Guard in 1921. In 1930, he was elected President of the Minnesota Aircraft Association succeeding Speed Holman. At the time, he was General Manager of the Northwest Division of Universal Air Lines.

Magnuson, Carl G. 1907 - 1988
Born in Minneapolis, Carl made his first solo flight in a Waco 10 in August of 1929. He had been working for the Enos Ashley Motor Company on Franklin automobiles in Minneapolis. (Ashley had also been in partnership with Walter Bullock as an FBO at the Earle Brown Farm Airfield.) Magnuson was part owner of an OX-5 Thomas-Morse airplane, but it was wrecked before he ever flew it. He then bought a Curtiss Robin and flew it from 1931 until 1934. During the early 1930s, Carl did auto mechanics work out of his home in North Minneapolis, taking University of Minnesota engineering courses.
In 1938 he joined Northwest Airlines as a mechanic and worked in the engine shop. In 1942, he was a full-time maintenance instructor for the airline, then was sent to the Northern Region, where he organized classes in maintenance at Edmonton, Alberta, Canada. In 1943, he returned to Minneapolis where he became Superintendent of Line Maintenance in the engine department. Magnuson retired from the airline in 1974, but continued to work as a consultant to various domestic and foreign airlines, setting up maintenance programs.

Malone, John F. "Jack" 1896 - 1984
Born in Woodstock, Minnesota. Malone studied mechanics at Dunwoody Institute in Minneapolis. He was one of the first to enlist when the U. S. entered World War I. He joined the aviation section and trained in mechanics at Kelly Field, Texas. He was assigned to the 4th Aerial Squadron and then was accepted for pilot's training. In 1919, he was discharged and returned to the Twin Cities, finding work with the Security Aircraft Company at Speedway Field. He joined the Federated Fliers Flying Circus and did stunt flying until 1924. He was a member of the 109th Observation squadron from 1921 through 1936. In 1928, he was hired by Northwest Airways and began flying their Hamilton Metalplanes on airmail routes. He left the airline with the layoff following the airmail cancellation of 1934.
Malone re-entered the Army Air Force in World War II and retired after the war with the rank of Colonel.

Mamer, Nicholas B. 1897 - 1938
Mamer was born in Hastings, Minnesota. He joined the U. S. Air Service and served in Panama. Following his discharge, he worked as a parachute jumper, motorcycle racer, and pilot for the Federated Fliers Flying Circus. Mamer fell in love with the Pacific Northwest and by 1923 was flying forest fire patrol for the U. S. Forest Service there. In 1927 he competed in the New York to Spokane Air derby, placing third, behind Speed Holman and Ed Ballough. He made a round-trip between St. Paul and Seattle in October, 1928, as a test flight for the proposed opening of an airline between the two cities.
In 1928, he started Mamer Air Transport, an airline flying between Seattle and Spokane and extended the route to Minneapolis in 1930. Mamer set a record in August of 1929, flying a Buhl Airsedan from Spokane to New York and return, refueling in midair and setting a non-stop record for the 7200 miles. Despite his personal fame, his airline lost an airmail subsidy in a bidding war

in 1930 and Mamer went to work for Northwest Airways, flying the northwest routes he knew so well. He was killed in January of 1938 when his Lockheed Model 14 lost its vertical stabilizers in flight over Bozeman, Montana, and crashed.

Marshall, Brig. General Wyman Fiske 1893 - 1983
Marshall began his flying career in Iowa in 1926. He was an airport operator, airline executive, and barnstormer. He joined the Department of Commerce in 1929 as Chief of the Licensing Division, test-flying many aircraft to certify them for Type Certificates. He served with the Marines at Grosse Isle, Michigan. He came to Minnesota to become Eastern Division Superintendent for Northwest Airlines in 1939, and was promoted to Operations Manager in 1942. From late 1942 until 1944, he served on active duty in the Marines, where he was assigned to South Pacific Combat Air Transport, carrying VIP's and wounded soldiers from the battlefield airstrips to command posts and hospitals.

Following the war, Marshall returned to Northwest Airlines as Executive Assistant to the President, became General Operations Manager, then Vice-President of Operations in 1946. He resigned in 1948 to return to the military, retiring from active duty in 1953, at which time he was a Brigadier General in the Marine Reserves.

Mau, Arnold
Mau began flying at Fergus Falls in 1927. He bought a Monocoupe aircraft for his personal flying and later took a job with the Otter Tail Power Company, flying pipeline patrol during a 54 year career with the company.

Maxwell, Kenneth 1914 -
One of Minnesota's most experienced mechanics and propeller experts, Ken Maxwell came to the Twin Cities during the height of the Depression seeking work. He began his aviation career in 1933, taking the mechanics course at Northland Aviation at Wold-Chamberlain. He went to work for Hanford Airlines, and then Mid-Continent. In the latter 1930s, he worked for McInnis Aviation. In 1941, Maxwell worked as a mechanic for Tom North at Northport Airport, near White Bear Lake and later for Orville Hickman at University Airport. When the WTS program ended during World War II, he went into the maintenance department at Northwest Airlines, where he learned the details of propeller overhaul. Following the war, he bought the assets of Tom North's business at Northport. He moved to Crystal Airport in 1951 and prospered in the service and propeller reconditioning business. He can be found there at the time of this writing.

McFail, Wellington P. 1899 -
McFail was born in Minneapolis, joined the Army Engineers and was sent to France to fight in World War I. Following the war, he began flying with Mid-Plane Sales & Transit, and later took up barnstorming, traveling throughout the country. He found his way back to Minneapolis, where he took a job with Universal Air Lines. Universal transferred him to Chicago. After a merger into American Airlines, McFail worked for that Company until his retirement.

McInnis, Adrian C. "A. C." or "Mac"
McInnis began flying from Wold-Chamberlain in the early 1930s, opened a flying school at the airport and taught CPT students there until the field was closed to civilian operations at the start of World War II. He then opened for business at South St. Paul Airport, but was chased from there also, moving to Victory Airport to instruct for the Government's WTS program. McInnis joined Northwest Airlines in 1943 and was with the airline until 1959.

In 1939, McInnis planned a non-stop flight to Florida from Minneapolis in a J-2 Cub fitted with a large external fuel tank. The plane lifted off, but was unable to climb with its added burden and mushed into a haystack south of the Minnesota River, barely fifteen minutes after its start. McInnis is one of the most colorful of Minnesota's aviation characters. In his pre-war advertising brochure, McInnis lists himself as "The most popular flight instructor in the Northwest."

McMahan, Claire B. "Cowboy" 1895 -
Born in Stephen, Minnesota, McMahan grew up on a ranch. He became a rodeo cowboy and acquired the nickname, "Cowboy." He turned his thoughts to aviation in 1916 when he witnessed a local barnstorming exhibition. In 1919, after taking some lessons from itinerant flyers, he bought a Thomas-Morse Scout airplane. There is some doubt as to whether he actually flew it, for it was a high performance ship in its time and he had little experience. He came to the Twin Cities where he took lessons and learned to fly. He purchased a J-1 Standard, but cracked up on his way home to Montana. Undaunted, he bought another Standard, and some time later, an American Eagle which he entered in the 1927 Transcon-

tinental Air Derby. In this race from from New York to Spokane, he finished in seventh place.

McMahan qualified for his Transport license, and took a job with Yellowstone Airways at Billings. He moved to Minneapolis and went to work for Universal Air Lines, flying passenger and mail runs while instructing at Wold-Chamberlain. His adventures took him to St. Louis where he flew pipeline patrol and, liking the work, opened his own pipeline patrol company in Monroe, Louisiana. During World War II, McMahan flew in the Army Air Force Ferry Command.

McManus, Robert J. "Red" 1914 - 1972
Born in St. Paul, McManus learned to fly in the 1930s. He became one of the first skywriters in the country, and as son of the president of the 7-Up Bottling Company franchise in Minneapolis, did much of the company's promotion in that fashion. He owned several Laird and Waco aircraft, all equipped for smoke writing, and at one time owned the Laird Solution racer. During World War II, he flew with the Air Transport Command and returned to Minneapolis after the war, being elected President of the Minnesota Bottling Company. He was close friends with stunt pilots, Danny Fowlie and Don Berent, and a probable influence in Chuck Doyle's taking up skywriting a couple of years later. In 1957, McManus retired to Florida where he opened a bait and tackle shop. He is buried at Fort Snelling.

McMiller, Urban M. 1900 - 1976
McMiller moved to Minneapolis from Wisconsin at age ten. In 1917 he enlisted in the Royal Canadian Flying Service, but being underage, was not accepted. A year later, he joined the Marine Corps, becoming a First Sergeant at Paris Island where he started flight instruction in 1920. He cracked up a Marine JN-6 Jenny in Santo Domingo when he ran out of gas. Following his discharge from the service, he came back to Minnesota, where he went to work for the Mohawk Aircraft Company. When the company folded during the Depression, he worked as an auto and seed salesman. McMiller and Clint Blomquist built a glider in the early 1930s.

In the 1940s, McMiller went into the manufacturing business, making logbook covers and seats for Piper Cub aircraft being sold by the Van Dusen Company, motor scooter seats, and collapsible canvas car-top carriers.

McNown, Russell J. 1902 - 1964
Born in Wisconsin, McNown learned to fly as an Air Service cadet in 1919. He barnstormed the Midwest and in 1929 worked as a delivery and demonstration pilot for the Hamilton Metalplane Company. Speed Holman hired him as a pilot in 1930 to work for Northwest Airways and McNown helped develop the early mail and passenger routes between Chicago and the West. He was one of the few Northwest Captains who never flew as co-pilot. During World War II, he was called to active duty in the Army Air Force and served in Ferry Command, delivering planes to the Aleutians.

Merrill, Lawrence E. "Abe" 1908 -
Merrill began flying in 1929 and barnstormed through the Midwest and South in an OX-5 Eaglerock. He taught in the CPT program at Mankato and went on to instruct at St. Cloud and Albert Lea in the WTS program, where he also served as an Inspector. During World War II, he became a Flight Officer Service Pilot in the Air Transport Command. Following the war, he established Merrill Aviation Co. at the new Faribault Airport, operating there until 1953 with partners Stu Shaft and Ralph Temple.

Michaud, Col. James C. 1923 -
Born in White Bear Lake, Michaud saw action as a member of the 12th Air Force in World War II. He was attached to a ground attack squadron, flying P-51's, A-36's and P-47's in North Africa, Italy, Southern France, and Germany. He flew 127 missions, destroying fourteen enemy aircraft, including three aerial victories. He joined the Air Guard following the war, and is active today on the Board of the Air Guard Museum.

Mickelson, Einar - 1944
From Fergus Falls, Mickelson entered the Navy in 1940 and trained as a flyer. In 1941, he volunteered for duty with Chennault's forces in China and became a member of the American Volunteer Group, the "Flying Tigers." After his tour with the AVG, he joined the CNAC (Chinese National Aviation Corporation), and transported supplies from India across the "Hump" to China. He developed a colorful background, marrying a Russian woman. Stories of his efforts in flying huge quantities of gasoline and ammunition through bad weather, facing Japanese flak and fighter opposition, into China enhanced his reputation. He was lost on such a mission over Japanese held territory in 1944. The Fergus Falls Airport is named after him.

Middagh, Edward H. - 1929

Born in Minneapolis. Middagh enlisted in 1917 in the 337th Field Artillery and was sent to fight in France. His arrival in France coincided with the end of hostilities and he returned to the States. He worked in the auto accessory business in 1922, but became interested in flying, and took lessons at the Rhodes School of Aviation at Speedway Field. He bought a Jenny airplane, but crashed in it when a rider jammed the controls. He obtained another airplane and flew with the St. Paul Dispatch Flying Circus, giving exhibitions around the Northwest. In 1927, he became Chief Pilot for Arrowhead Airways of Duluth and later ran an airfield at Superior, Wisconsin. In 1928, he joined Northwest Airways. In June of 1929, with a load of passengers aboard, one of his Ford Trimotor's engines failed after takeoff from St. Paul and the plane struck the ground in Indian Mounds Park. He was the only fatality and Northwest Airways first fatality in a million miles of passenger flying.

Miller, General Raymond S. 1891 - 1961

Ray Miller began flying in 1917, learning the skill at the Curtiss School at Newport News, Virginia, after World War I. He came to St. Paul and went to work for Bill Kidder at Curtiss-Northwest Airplane Company as a general working pilot, flying charters and sight-seers, and giving instruction.

In 1920, as a pilot and member of the Minnesota National Guard, he and others in the unit decided to apply to Washington for a charter to create an Air Guard section. Miller, Minnesota Adjutant General William F. Rhinow and Lt. Colonel William C. Garis, Assistant Adjutant General, flew to Washington, D. C. in a Curtiss Oriole rented from Bill Kidder where they were successful in receiving the charter.

The new 109th Observation Squadron was formed and in years to come, earned a respectable reputation for its help throughout Minnesota in time of need. Miller served as head of the Minnesota Aeronautics Commission in the 1930s and was active in licensing Minnesota's aircraft and pilots. He commanded the Guard squadron until World War II, when he was called to active duty and sent to Wright Field. He was called again to active duty during the Korean War, and retired from service in 1951. He continued to provide inspiration for the Air Guard until his death. Miller is a member of the Minnesota Aviation Hall of Fame.

Milner, Lloyd A. 1912 -

Lloyd was born in Minneapolis and learned to fly in 1931. He was active at Robbinsdale Airport in the 1930s, and received his Aircraft and Engine mechanics license. He went to work for Hanford Tri-State Airlines in Sioux City, Iowa. He worked for Northwest Airlines in 1937 and was transferred to Billings, Montana. Milner worked his way to the left seat Captain's position by 1942 and flew with Northwest's Northern Division in Alaska and Canada, receiving an Air Medal for his efforts. He was one of the pilots to fly on the Northwest Airlines Orient Survey flights. He was retired in 1972, but stayed in Hawaii to fly air tours and air taxi in the islands.

Moberg, Ralph J. 1903 - 1991

Moberg learned to fly in 1942 in Bemidji. His first airplane was an OX-5 Travel Air that he never had a chance to fly. It was crashed by a friend before the lessons started. In 1943, Moberg started a seaplane base at Bemidji and gave float flying instruction.

Moe, Volney

Early Marine Corps Reserve flyer, entered the service in 1932.

Morgan, Wilbur E. "Billy" 1904 - 1993

Morgan came to the Twin Cities from New York. He received his private license in Florida, and came to Minnesota in the early 1930's. He barnstormed and took part in the 1933 air races at Wold-Chamberlain. With J. C. Brown, started Brown-Morgan Flying Service at Wold-Chamberlain. In 1935, he went to work for Northwest Airlines and retired in 1964.

Morrill, Claire F. 1916 - 1988

From Randolph, Minnesota. Morrill learned to fly at Wold-Chamberlain in 1934, taking lessons from Ray Goetze. He went barnstorming with Jack Kipp and then worked for Clarence Hinck during the CPT and WTS programs. In 1944, he injured a leg in a crackup at Stanton Airport and was unable to fly afterward. He spent the rest of his working career with the Chicago Northwestern railroad.

Morse, William L. 1913 -

Born in Little Falls, Minnesota. Morse soloed in 1935 and worked for Clarence Hinck's Federated Fliers as a wing-walker and parachute jumper. He also worked in 1935 and 1936 for Shorty De

Ponti at Minneapolis and flew the airmail from Little Falls to the Twin Cities in the Airmail Commemoration ceremony of 1938. He did bush flying out of Ely, and prior to World War II, taught in the CPT program for Ruben Bloom at Duluth, returning to the resort business on weekends. He joined the Army Air Force in 1942, was assigned to Ferry Command, and was later commissioned. At one time, he bailed out of a burning P-39. After the war, he returned to fly resorters to their favorite fishing spots in Ely. At this writing, he has over 18,000 hours of float flying.

Muxlow, Kenneth 1909 -

Muxlow came to Minneapolis in 1928 to attend Dunwoody Institute. He learned the mechanic's trade and went to work for the Ford Motor Company at St. Paul, where he made his career, retiring in 1969. During the World War II period, he was an inspector on the modification line at the Northwest Airlines Holman Field Modification Center. Muxlow began flying in the 1930s and owned a Pietenpol airplane and a Star Cavalier. He bought the first production 1934 Cessna Airmaster after the war and still owns and flies it to airshows and breakfasts.

Neff, Russell

Neff was a well-known flyer of the 1930s. He learned to fly in 1928 at St. Paul and was a member of the 109th Observation Squadron. He owned a Waco floatplane and flew it between the Twin Cities and northern Minnesota lake country where he ferried fishermen to their favorite fishing grounds, and took up sightseers. With the Wolf Flying Service at Mora, Minnesota, Neff used the floatplane to advantage, making newsworthy emergency trips, spotting forest fires, and rescuing downed flyers.

Nelson, David R.

Senior CAA Inspector during the 1940s period in the Twin Cities area. With this responsibility, he checked out most of the CPT's Secondary and Instructor students, issuing their licenses.

Neuman, Al - 1943

Neuman, Wallace I. "Wally"

The Neuman brothers began flying in the 1920s, running a field at 100th Street and Lyndale Avenue, called Oxboro Field. In approximately 1937, "Wally" moved his operation to Cedar Airport, closer to the twin Cities. He was an instructor and many of the local pilots who started flying during the late 1930s received flight instruction from him. He, Russ Abbott and Wally Dale, operated Cedar Flying Service, sold fuel and oil, sight-seeing flights, instruction, and charter.

Brother, Al, moved to Nicollet Airfield when Oxboro Field was closed and joined with Wally Russell and Pat O'Conner in operating that field. Al owned a Hisso-powered Waco that he enjoyed flying and earned the nickname, "Hisso Al" by many of the locals. He later moved back to Cedar Airport with his brother.

Newstrom, Gordon K. 1912 -

Born in Minneapolis. Newstrom was inspired by Lindbergh's epic flight in 1927, and became interested in flying, although the family resort business kept him too busy to take lessons. When he met "Dusty" Rhodes in 1929, he saw a way to marry the resort business and flying. He continued his job as a fishing guide, and learned to fly. He became a WTS instructor, first at Duluth, and later at Albert Lea. In 1941, he took over as FBO at the Coleraine Airport, incorporating Mesaba Aviation.

Business was good and Newstrom branched out to Grand Rapids, Onamia, Isle, Deer River and Brainerd. He sold the business in 1970, and it become an airlink for Northwest Airlines.

Nieman, Hilbert

From St. Paul, Nieman is legendary among Minnesota aviators. His colorful homebuilding inventions, his often questionable building techniques, his crackups, and the fact that he was a professional wrestler added to his reputation. He operated an auto repair garage and flew a Monocoupe airplane. He led a group of pilots who resisted state aircraft licensing for many months after it became mandatory in 1933. Nieman invented a ram-jet powered helicopter that was capable of driving on city streets. It drove well, but never flew successfully. At the time of his death, he was working on a perpetual motion machine.

Niemi, Nicholas S. 1898 - 1949

Niemi taught himself to fly in a Curtiss Robin he bought as a wreck. He owned and operated Lakehead Airways in Duluth through World War II and continued afterward, and was killed on a charter flight in Wisconsin.

Nisun, Kenneth 1906 - 1937
Nisun was the owner of the Ace High Flying School at Wold-Chamberlain Field during the early 1930s. He flew a Travel Air cabin monoplane for the Midwest Oil Company and was well-known around the Minneapolis area. He was killed in a crash in Ohio.

Nolan, Thomas
Nolan was a long-time employee of Northwest Airlines. He held the position of Field Dispatcher during the hectic period that Northwest flew the Northern Division, contracted to the Air Transport Command. Nolan was appointed Cargo Superintendent, with the responsibility of shipping and handling supplies and materials shipped to Edmonton, Canada, for dispersal to Allied troops and bases.

Norby, Raymond 1907 - 1939
Norby joined the Navy at the age of 16. At 18, he was racing automobiles in northern Minnesota. He started the Great Northern Aviation School at Wold-Chamberlain Field in 1931, and took electrical engineering courses in New York during the 1933 to 1935 period. He was commissioned in the Navy and was a Link Trainer instructor at Floyd Bennett Field. In 1936, he was hired by Northwest Airlines and became Chief Pilot of the Eastern Division. He and Cash Chamberlain were killed in the crash of a Northwest Lockheed 14H at Miles City, Montana in 1939.

North, Thomas H. - 1960
In 1939, North started an airport which he called Northport, near White Bear Lake. The property had been used by the White Bear Flying Club and the Stillwater Lumberjacks Flying Club. North got a contract to provide CPT training for students at Hamline University in St. Paul. The CPT became the WTS and North garnered several WTS contracts. Among them was a contract to teach South American college students how to fly, with the expectation that they would go back to their native countries and instruct their fellow countrymen. North also received a contract from the Army Air Force to train glider pilots, which he did at Northport and at satellite fields near Stillwater and White Bear Lake. In 1944 he was hired by Northwest Airlines, but left in 1956.

Northrop, Marvin A. 1895 - 1950
Born in Mankato. Northrop enlisted in the Army in 1918, and upon discharge, became Sales Manager for William Kidder at Curtiss-Northwest Airport. He barnstormed a little after dropping out of college at the University of Minnesota, then opened the Marvin A. Northrop Aeroplane Company, Inc. The Company supplied parts and assemblies of aircraft to homebuilders, rebuilders, and repair stations. Northrop produced the first aircraft parts catalog in the nation. He became well-known within the aviation community and spoke on behalf of aviation around the State. He was appointed to serve as the export advisor to the Minneapolis Park Board, and again as aeronautical advisor to the state legislature.

Northrop ran the Robbinsdale Airport in 1925 and 1926. His company held the only regional Ryan aircraft sales franchise in the late 1920s. He went to Europe in 1928 to buy surplus aircraft parts there, having borrowed a small sum of money from the brokerage firm of Lane, Piper and Jaffrey. While Northrop was away, Piper went through with the incorporation of the Northrop Company, leaving Northrop, himself, out. Northrop returned, and brought suit against the brokerage firm to reclaim his business, or at least be paid for it, but was unsuccessful. Undaunted, he started over as the Marvin A. Northrop Airplane Company and continued with his former line of surplus parts sales. He also sold White motor trucks. After World War II, he maintained his business, selling engines, aircraft tires, wings, and even airport crash vehicles.

Northrop was an educated man whose interests ranged from American history, to gardening, to opera, travel and archeology. He died in an accident at his warehouse on Washington Avenue, when he was crushed in the building's freight elevator. In a bizarre and still unexplained turn of fate, the coroner termed his death a suicide.

O'Conner, Patrick
O'Conner had flown with Ray Miller during the 1920s and this association got O'Conner enthused about aviation. He started his own flying at Oxboro Airport and, in 1935, paid $4000 for the property that became known as Nicollet Airport. His partners were Al Neuman and Wally Russell.

Odekirk, Glenn 1905 - 1987
Born in Waseca, Minnesota. Odekirk became a railroad brakeman, but later a mechanic and flyer. In 1926, he built an automobile from parts and drove it on a 15,000 mile odyssey across the United States. He met airplane designer and oil-drilling machinery baron, Howard Hughes, in 1933, while working for Pacific Airmotive, a firm contracted to Hughes. He became Hughes'

right-hand-man, and helped design the Hughes H-1 racing plane. He also did the administrative work to set up the entire Hughes Corporation. After that, he became Hughes most trusted advisor and administrator. It was Odekirk that hired the original engineering staff for Hughes to begin the design of the "Spruce Goose."

Odekirk and Hughes shared the ability for hard work and intense living. It was Odekirk that piloted their late-night flights to night spots in Los Angeles and elsewhere. It was Odekirk that personally patched Hughes skull wounds after the 1943 crash of a test plane in Lake Mead that killed two other persons. Odekirk was at Hughes side again in 1946 when Hughes was critically injured in the crash of another experimental plane near Beverly Hills. Odekirk spent 35 days in an adjoining hospital room, taking care of Hughes business, and was the only one allowed to see him. Odekirk remained a close advisor to Hughes until the billionaire began to withdraw from society in the late 1960s.

Ohrbeck, Joseph E. 1898 - 1979
Ohrbeck graduated from Minneapolis' West High School in 1918 and enlisted in the Army Aviation Service. He was commissioned a Lieutenant and qualified as a pursuit pilot in 1919. Returning to the Twin Cities, he joined the 109th Observation Squadron of the Air Guard. At the University of Minnesota, he learned architectural drafting and practiced that until 1928, when he became an instructor for the Mid-Plane Sales & Transit Company at Wold-Chamberlain. He was also the ground school instructor at Dunwoody Institute. At the end of 1928, he went to work for Northwest Airways.

Ohrbeck served as both Eastern and Northern Region Manager for Northwest, and was one of the first four Northwest pilots to be called to Army service when the Army took over the flying of airmail in 1934. In June of 1943, Ohrbeck's son, Richard, was hired as a co-pilot for the airline and the pair became the only father-son cockpit crew flying a scheduled airliner in the United States. Ohrbeck retired in 1959.

Olson, Earl "Ole" 1898 - 1972
Olson was born in Duluth. He learned to fly and barnstormed in a Jenny in 1919, returning to Duluth a few years later. In 1928, Olson helped choose the site of the Duluth Airport and was airport maintenance superintendent in the 1930s, finally taking the manager's job in 1939. He saw the Williamson-Johnson Airport turn into a major port, now called Duluth International. In 1958, Olson was named Outstanding Airport Manager by the American Airport Officials Association.

Omlie, Phoebe Fairgrave 1902 - 1975
Fairgrave graduated from St. Paul Mechanic Arts High School in 1920. She went to Curtiss-Northwest Airport and tried to find someone to take her up for a parachute jump. Ray Miller, one of the pilots there at the time, would not take her, but insisted she go home and strengthen her muscles. She took his advice, but returned, making her first jump from a plane flown by Vern Omlie, who would become her future husband. She made many jumps and performed wing-walking with Omlie on a barnstorming tour of the South. They married and Phoebe learned to fly. She was quite skillful and entered women's air races and cross-country tours, winning the Women's Air Derby from Santa Monica to Cleveland, and the Dixie Derby from Washington, D. C. to Chicago in 1930.

From 1932 to 1936, she campaigned for President Roosevelt by flying around the country advertising and speaking on his behalf. He appointed her Special Advisor for Air Intelligence to the National Advisory Council for Aeronautics. She opened a flying school in Memphis and later joined the CAA, from which she retired in 1952. Omlie is a member of the Minnesota Aviation Hall of Fame.

Omlie, Vernon C. - 1936
One of the early pilots working for William Kidder at Curtiss-Northwest Airport in St. Paul. He instructed Phoebe Fairgrave, who would become a well-known woman pilot and racer, took her barnstorming with him around the country, and married her. He joined the 109th Observation Squadron as a pilot and was a Lieutenant in 1921. Omlie also flew along the barnstorming trail with Clarence Hinck and the Federated Fliers.

Opsahl, Alvin B. 1904 -
Born in Minneapolis, Al Opsahl began flying with Gene Shank at Robbinsdale Airport, and soloing in 1925. He barnstormed with Clarence Hinck's Federated Fliers and with the Del Snyder and George Babcock Flying Circuses during the 1925 to 1928 period. His career led him to work for the U. S. Airmail Service, flying for the Post Office Department and making the first night flight from Chicago to Omaha and on to Cheyenne, Wyoming. He was hired by Northwest Airways in 1928 as a mechanic, becoming chief inspector at St. Paul, and later moved to Seattle to take over the same job there. He retired in 1964.

Opsahl, Clarence W. "Nippy" 1908 -
Brother of Al Clarence Opsahl, also worked for the Federated Fliers, then the Del Snyder and George Babcock Flying Circuses. He drove the semi-trailer truck with auto polo cars from city to city, competed with them at county fairs and did some motorcycle racing for the groups. He got his mechanics license in 1927 and asked Speed Holman for a job with Northwest Airways, being hired as a mechanic, to service the Northwest Ford Trimotor aircraft in Chicago. He learned to fly and got his Transport license, became a co-pilot, and then a Captain in 1938. He flew in the Northern Division and moved to Seattle after the war. Clarence retired in 1968.

Otis, Arthur R. 1894 - 1979

Otis, Eleanor - 1987
Art Otis was born in St. Paul. He took over his family's farm homestead on Lake Sissibakwet in 1912, moved the farm cabin across the lake to a different site and became a potato farmer. Intrigued by the walleyes that local fishermen were catching, he conceived the idea of renting boats, tents, and picnic tables to tourists, along with the cottages he built. Art Otis married Eleanor, the local schoolteacher, and in 1927, cleared an airstrip on his property. There followed years of soliciting pilots to fly in and providing them with free or reasonable food and rooms. He got his own flying license, and with Eleanor, the pair flew their J-3 Cub on an air tour to Florida in 1947. Otis Lodge was one of, if not the first, fly-in fishing resorts in Minnesota.

Paine, Paul D.
Paine worked for Northland Aviation at Speedway Field. He became a Minneapolis Vocational School aircraft mechanics instructor prior to World War II.

Palen, Richard 1917 - 1972
One of Minnesota's premiere aerial photographers. Palen's interest in aviation photography was evident during the late 1930s, and brought him fame over the years. He was a parachute rigger during World War II, President of the Minnesota OX-5 Chapter, National Director of the Air Force Association, and a Colonel in the Civil Air Patrol.

Palmer, Captain George M.
Palmer was First Sergeant of Company I, First Minnesota Infantry, during the conflict with Mexico in 1916. He and Charles Hardin, of Fergus Falls constructed a balloon and barnstormed it around the region. Palmer joined the Signal Corps and was one of the first officers commissioned at Kelly Field in Texas during the 1920s. He was one of the first six airmen taught to fly there, and became an instructor. He commanded the 1st Bombardment Group whose mission it was to make the test bombings of the the the captured German battleships Frankfort and Ostfriesland off Langley Field, Virginia. Palmer was with the 109th Observation Squadron for many years.

Parker, Fred
Parker was the first Minnesotan to successfully build and fly his own airplane, when his second design, a monoplane, was flown 29 August, 1910.

Pennertz, Donald W. 1913 -
Pennertz was born in Forest City, Minnesota. He learned to fly in 1932, did some barnstorming, and taught in the CPT and WTS programs at Wold-Chamberlain, Alexandria, Fargo and Jamestown. He flew for Northwest Airlines during World War II.

Perlt, Julius L. 1903 - 1991
Born in St. Paul, Perlt graduated from the University of Minnesota in 1925, having been a medal-winning gymnast. In 1926, he went to work for the St. Paul Association of Commerce and promoted all manner of aviation activities, including the Ford Reliability Tour stops in 1926, 1928 and 1929. He worked closely with Colonel Lewis Brittin to get the airmail contract for Northwest Airways, and became Northwest's first office manager. In 1929, Perlt lobbied the City Council to purchase land to build the St. Paul Airport and organized the St. Paul to Winnipeg Goodwill Tours.
Perlt also became secretary of the St. Paul Aero Club, and an officer of both Yellow Cab Airlines and Mamer Airlines that used St. Paul as a base of operations. He remained with the St. Paul Chamber of Commerce and the Visitor's Bureau througout his career, while working for the Brede Company. He was very well known as the announcer of the University of Minnesota's Gopher football and basketball games at Memorial Stadium and Williams Arena. Perlt is a member of the Minnesota Aviation Hall of Fame.

Peterson, Lt. Harold G. 1894 -
Born in Hutchinson, Minnesota, Peterson built a glider at Redwood Falls and flew it successfully in 1912. He joined the Air Service in 1917 and learned to fly at Chanute Field, Illinois, where he taught aerobatics until 1919. He was posted to the Border Patrol in the Southwest. There he became somewhat of a hero, having been captured by Mexican bandits, and rescued in spectacular fashion. He and Dick Grace headlined the Federated Fliers Flying Circus in 1919, performing stunt flying and sight-seeing hops. Peterson opened the Harold G. Peterson Airplane Company at a field near White Bear Lake and ran it from 1920 through 1922. He was a member of the Minneapolis Aero Club.

Peterson, Sven H. 1906 -
Born in Sweden, Sven came to Minnesota in 1916. He learned to fly in the early 1920s and based himself at St. Cloud. He staged weekend airshows that brought aviation to the attention of citizens of that area. His sight-seeing flights often lasted throughout the full daylight hours. In 1933, he was appointed a district representative to the Minnesota Aeronautics Commission, supervising aerial activities in his region. He helped build the St. Cloud Northside Airport and helped start a flying club there, teaching several persons to fly. He is considered St. Cloud's foremost early flyer. Peterson is a member of the Minnesota Aviation Hall of Fame.

Pfaender, A. J. "Jake" - 1991
Pfaender was a very active pilot in the Duluth area. He had learned to fly in St. Paul in 1926 and did some barnstorming, along the way earning his mechanics license. In 1928 he was hired as chief pilot for R. J. Sergent's School of Aeronautics, instructing and passenger hopping. He moved from one FBO to the next, working for Arrowhead International Airlines in 1929, Land-O-Lakes Airways in 1930, and in 1931 joined the Hartley brothers in the Hartley-Pfaender Air Service. Pfaender was the test pilot for the Cloquet Trainer aircraft in 1932.

Piccard, Jean 1884 - 1963

Piccard, Jeanette 1895 - 1981
Jean and his twin brother Auguste Piccard, were born in Switzerland. They were both taken with science, Jean becoming an organic chemist and Auguste, a physicist. Jean came to this country in 1917 to work at the University of Chicago. He married Jeannette, a native of Chicago, in 1918, and the couple returned to Switzerland to teach for several years, coming again to the U. S. in 1926. Jeannette became a licensed balloon pilot and in 1934, piloted a gas-filled balloon from Dearborn, Michigan, on a research flight that set a women's altitude record which lasted until 1963. The couple came to Minnesota in 1935 and Jean was hired by the University of Minnesota's Aeronautical Engineering Department, to work with Professor John Akerman.
Jean helped build a helium balloon constructed of cellophane in 1936. The first successful flight of one of these balloons was from Memorial Stadium at the University of Minnesota. Jean and Jeannette made many flights in similar balloons, carrying scientific instruments to very high altitudes. Jeanette won the Harmon Trophy for a stratospheric flight in October of 1934. She was the first woman to fly in physiological space (over 45,000 ft). She became headline news in 1974 as the first woman priest in the Episcopal Church. Jean retired from the University in the 1950s.

Piersol, James V. 1900 - 1962
Early flyer and friend of Walter Bullock. A mechanic, he flew on the 1927 Ford Reliability Tour as a crewman and also accompanied the Tour in 1929 and 1930.

Pietenpol, Bernard H. 1901 - 1984
Born in Spring Valley, Minnesota, Pietenpol is Minnesota's premiere homebuilder. He learned to fly in the 1920s, constructing his first homebuilt plane in 1923 with a Ford Model T engine. In April of 1929, he brought a Model A engined airplane to Minneapolis to show to the editor of Modern Mechanics Magazine. The plane sparked interest and plans for it were published. Copies of this model, called the Air Camper, are still being built and flown today. Pietenpol also designed a single seater of similar styling, which could be powered by a Ford Model T engine.
Pietenpol was a self-taught engineer who designed his own airfoils and made his own stress analysis. He taught in the CPT program before the start of World War II, and after the war, returned to his hardware business at Cherry Grove, Minnesota. He continued homebuilding activities, selling his popular plans and helping other homebuilders with their projects. Pietenpol is a member of the Minnesota Aviation Hall of Fame.

Pothen, Frank M. 1910 -
Brought up in the Murdock, Minnesota area, Pothen was inspired by Lindbergh's epic flight and enrolled in a mechanic's school in Chicago in 1929. In 1930, he became a student at the Wahpeton School of Sciences in North Dakota, where Art Sampson taught him to fly. He earned his Transport license in 1936, and taught in the CPT program prior to World War II at Willmar. After the war, he managed the Wadena Airport, instructing students and servicing itinerant flyers.

Powers, Ned R. 1918 -
Born in Coleraine, Powers began flying in 1938 and got his Private license at Grand Rapids in a Waco 9. With an Instructor's rating, he and Gordy Newstrom taught at Ruben Bloom's CPT program at Duluth. Powers started a flight training operation at Coleraine after the WTS program was finished in 1944, and convinced Gordy Newstrom to take it over. Powers became a CAA inspector and worked out of the Des Moines and Minneapolis offices, where his volunteer chaperoning of local airshows earned him the nickname, "Ned the Fed." After his retirement, he opened an aerobatic school at Grand Rapids, Minnesota, where he instructs at the time of this writing.

Pryzymus, Frances (Lennon, Dale) 1910 -
Born in Ivanhoe, Minnesota. Frances Pryzymus' interest in flying was sparked at age eight. Having to leave the family to seek her own living during the depression, she began working in the Veteran's Nursing Home at Fort Snelling. She took flying lessons in her spare time, and in 1930, earned her Private license. She progressed through Limited Commercial, Commercial and Transport ratings. She met and married a hospital patient, Jack Lennon, who died a few years later of World War I injuries. She continued to fly, and in 1940, married Wally Dale, part owner of Cedar Airport in Bloomington. When Dale took a position with the CAA, the couple moved to Louisville, Kentucky. Frances was one of the earliest members of the Minnesota 99's.

Quigley, Joseph E. 1892 -
One of the foremost of Minnesota aviation photographers. Joe enlisted in the Minnesota National Guard in 1916 and became a Captain in the 109th Air Guard during the 1930s, responsible for the major portion of the fine large-format photos that document the guard's activities. He was activated with the Guard unit in 1941 and discharged a Major in 1946.

Quist, Paul P. 1915 - 1989
Born in Minneapolis. Quist learned to fly at Fergus Falls. He soloed in 1931 and barnstormed with Harold Kittleson and Gus Imm. He was airport manager at Fergus Falls and flew with his father in the Ford Reliability Tour in 1928. He flew out of Cedar Airport prior to World War II and went to work for Northwest Airlines, where he became Superintendent of Material Control from 1942 to 1944. He then enlisted in the Navy and was assigned to the Department of Naval Aviation Medicine, studying night and high-altitude flight. Following the war, he helped start West Central Airways at Fergus Falls, and flew charter through 1979.

Radoll, Robert W.
A former barnstormer, Radoll was one of the first three pilots hired by Col. Lewis Brittin to fly for Northwest Airways. He resigned a year later.

Rand, Rufus R. 1892 - 1971
A member of the family which owned the Minneapolis Gas Company, he joined the Lafayette Flying Corps in World War I. Rand returned to Minnesota, and in 1929 invested in the Mohawk Aircraft Company, becoming the company's receiver when it went into bankruptcy in 1931. Rand owned the last few Pinto aircraft built by the company, and sold them off to pay the bills. Rand was associated with the Universal Air Lines Corporation. He built the Rand Tower office building in downtown Minneapolis in the 1930s and was a Regent of the University of Minnesota. He was a State Commander of the American Legion and officer of the Minneapolis Gas Company. During World War II, he served as Executive Officer in charge of security at a bomber base in England and was one of the twelve founders of the Air Force Association.

Rask, Peter S. 1896 -
Rask learned to fly during World War I and was hired by Clarence Hinck to fly for the Federated Fliers in 1920. He was also a member of the 109th Observation Squadron from 1929. He was activated with the Air Guard from 1941 through 1945. He remained in the Reserves, and was discharged a Colonel in 1953.

Rawlings, Edwin W. 1905 -
Raised in Tracy, Minnesota, Rawlings attended Hamline University in St. Paul before entering the Air Corps, receiving his commission in 1930. He served at bases in Hawaii and Texas, becoming an administrative officer. After Pearl Harbor, Rawlings commanded the Aircraft Production Section of the Air Material Division. In 1947 he became the first Air Force Comptroller as a 2-star General. In 1951 he became Commander of the Air Material Command, retiring in 1959. He was the youngest 4-star General in the Air Force at age 40. Rawlings is a member of the Minnesota Aviation Hall of Fame.

Rentz, Robert J. 1897 - 1985
Born in Minneapolis, Robert Rentz was an aviation mechanic during World War I and began flying at Kelly Field in the class of 1924. Lindbergh was a fellow classmate. Rentz flew with Northern Airlines between Chicago and Minneapolis after the war. He joined the 109th Observation Squadron and flew with them from 1920 to 1931. In 1928, he worked for Mid-Planes Sales & Transit. In 1929, he bought a Ford Trimotor and started an airline between Brownsville, Texas, and Mexico City, the line later being sold to Pan American Airways.

Rentz was hired by Universal Air Lines as Operations Manager of the Robertson Division in St. Louis in 1931 and was transferred to Fort Worth, Texas. Called to active duty in the Army Air Force, one of his assignments was to move a Combat Cargo Group to China. Rentz continued with American Airlines, flying out of San Francisco. He had a gift of gab and pioneered the in-flight narration of the history and beauty of the land being flown over, for the passengers' benefit. He retired in 1960 with over 26,000 hours in his log.

Rhinow, General Walter F. 1880 -
Walter Rhinow joined the U. S. Army in 1898. Seeing action with the U. S. Border Service in 1916 and after a promotion to General, became the Minnesota Adjutant General, serving from 1917 to 1927. During his tenure, the 109th Observation Squadron, Minnesota Air National Guard, was formed. He not only furnished his support for the establishment of the new unit, but made the trip to Washington, D. C. aboard a rented Curtiss Oriole to petition for the unit's charter before the Militia Bureau.

Rhodes, Clarence H. "Dusty" 1885 - 1983
One of the most colorful characters in Minnesota's aviation lore, Rhodes was born in Verndale, Minnesota. He took his first airplane ride in Chisholm in 1920, came to Minneapolis to take flying lessons from the Security Company at Speedway Field, and was issued Minnesota Pilot's license #6 by Ray Miller. He started the Rhodes School of Aviation at Wold, a flying school and exhibition company, then bought the Security Company, inheriting the St. Paul Dispatch Flying Circus. He loved the north country and settled at Virginia, Minnesota, where he made a business of flying fishermen and sightseers over the Arrowhead country and into Canada. M.S. Kingston, a wealthy banker from Eveleth, financed a Ryan monoplane on floats for Dusty to operate as Kingston-Rhodes Airways.

Rhodes found that better profits could be made by transporting illegally-taken beaver pelts into Canada where high prices were being paid; and Canadian whiskey back into Minnesota. His career was most dramatic, with many stories being told of his smuggling episodes, narrow escapes from game wardens, fist fights, and interceptions by armed Mounties. Despite the notoriety, Dusty lived to be 98 years old.

Rice, John L. 1911 -
John learned to fly in 1937 at Hector, Minnesota, where he was born. He earned his instructor's rating and instructed in the CPT at Rochester, where he taught aerobatics in the Secondary program. He taught at Grand Forks, North Dakota, and Northport near White Bear Lake, Minnesota. When World War II was declared, he went to Texas to teach Army Air Force cadets. From 1943 to 1945, he worked for Mid-Continent Airlines, and in 1945, became the manager of the Willmar Airport. John's wife, Mary Jane, was also a well-known pilot, who began her flying career in 1935. The Rices continued managing both the airport and a busy Mooney franchise until John's retirement in 1983. Along the way, he built a Pitts biplane, rebuilt a Waco UPF-7 and a Waco HRE cabin biplane.

Riddick, Merrill
In 1922, Riddick was listed as one of the State's top pilots by the Minneapolis Tribune.

Riedl, John, Sr. 1914 - 1987
Riedl learned to fly at Robbinsdale Airport in 1936. He studied Aeronautical Engineering at the University of Minnesota and taught in the CPT program. He and a partner bought land and

opened an airport at Nisswa in 1946. (Since closed.) He became the Brainerd Airport Manager in 1954. Following his death, the Brainerd Airport terminal was named after him.

Rising, Forrest R.
First flyer in the area of International Falls. Connected with Riverview Flying Service.

Ritchie, Bertram F. 1903 -
Born at Howard Lake, Minnesota, Ritchie started with Northwest Airways as a steward. He took flying lessons from Northwest pilot, Chad Smith, in company training planes, received his license, and was hired as a pilot by Speed Holman in 1931. He began as a co-pilot on Ford Trimotors and Hamiltons, and became a Captain. He and Joe Kimm bought a Mohawk Pinto airplane which they flew to build time for their Transport licenses. During the war, Ritchie was one of the Northwest Airlines flight crewmen who flight tested B-24 Liberator bombers modified at the Mod Center at St.Paul.

Rittenhouse, Lt. David 1894 -
Born St. Paul. Rittenhouse entered the University of Minnesota, but did not graduate, rather, he joined the Norton-Harjes Ambulance Corps and found his way into the French Army. He became an enlisted Naval cadet at the Dunwoody Institute in 1917, and was trained as a Naval aviator at Key West, and Pensacola. He saw duty with the U. S. fleet as an observation pilot. In 1923, Rittenhouse won the Schneider Trophy, flying a Curtiss CR-3. He flew in the Trophy race again in 1924 with the Curtiss R2C-2, but did not win. During World War II, he was Production Manager for the Grumman Aircraft Corporation.

Robinson, John "Jack"
A stunt pilot in the 1930s and company pilot for the Webb Oil Company flying their Stinson Reliant airplane.

Rodina, Charles
Rodina, of Jackson, Minnesota, rented ground and built a hangar there in 1929, becoming the area's first regular flyer. He had learned to fly in California and bought an airplane in Denver on the way back home. Rodina continued to fly until World War II.

Rozawick, Alexis K. 1919 -
Born in St. Paul, Rozawich graduated from the University of Minnesota's Aeronautical Engineering School in 1938. At age fourteen he soloed an airplane and at age sixteen, leased the City Hangar at Holman Field. He started his own businesses prior to World War II, including Airline Charter Service, General Air Transport, and Northwest Air Activities.

Rozawick left St. Paul to work for the Martin Company, then joined TWA, and later, Pan-Am. He was loaned from Pan-Am to the military as test-pilot at the Ford Willow Run B-24 bomber plant. He became Director of Operations for the North Atlantic Division of the Military Air Transport Command.

Rosbach, John 1902 -
John Rosbach was born in Germany. He came to the U. S. with experience in aircraft sheet metal and began working for the Hamilton Company in Milwaukee under Professor John Akerman. When Akerman moved to the Mohawk Company in Minneapolis, he asked John to come along. There, Rosbach worked in the experimental shop, fashioning metal portions of Mohawk's cabin plane and twin-engined ship. In 1930, when the company began to experience financial trouble, he moved to Northwest Airways. He worked there until his retirement in 1967, at which time became foreman of the Component Department, fitting cowlings, windshields, etc.

Rueschenberg, Huey B.
Rueschenberg joined Northwest Airways in 1931. He was pilot of the first Northwest survey flight to Seattle from Minneapolis, on which Amelia Earhart was a passenger. He accumulated thousands of hours in the air while with Northwest, retiring in 1961.

Runholt, Frances
First woman flyer in Lyon County in the 1920s.

Ryan, Matthew J. 1899 - 1953
Born in Springfield, Minnesota, Matthew Ryan soloed in 1919 at Marshall, Minnesota with Irwin Stellmacher as instructor. He started the flying field at Marshall in 1933, and taught in the WTS program from 1943 to 1945. He became Director of Secondary Airports for the Metropolitan Airports Commission.

Rydholm, Rueben G. "Rudy" 1902 - 1989
Born in Renville County, Minnesota. Rydholm earned his pilot's license in 1928. He barnstormed and owned several aircraft during the 1930s, losing one in a windstorm in Iowa. He started his own airport at Milnor, North Dakota, and ran it from 1932 to 1935, then came to the Twin Cities and flew out of Cedar, Nicollet and Robbinsdale Airports during the later 1930s. He joined Northwest Airlines in 1940 as a mechanic and was a Production Job Instructor there during World war II.

Salisbury, Lt. K. B.
Commanding Officer of the Naval Reserve Squadron at Wold-Chamberlain, 1940.

Salut, Harold 1915 -
Born in Fargo, North Dakota, Salut learned to fly in the early 1930s, did some parachute jumping and barnstorming, and joined the Navy in 1935, serving as a carrier pilot. During World War II, he flew anti-sub and convoy patrol and was involved in air-sea rescue. He was a model builder and worked for the CAA in the office of flight standards as High-Altitude (jet) Facility Inspector. In the late 1940s, he flew air cargo for Flamingo Air Service out of Teterboro, NJ. He wrote a book about barnstorming in the 1930s based on his own experiences.

Sampson, Arthur M. 1900 - 1962
Born in Belview, Minnesota. Sampson got his first air ride in 1919, but worked as a farmer while taking flying lessons. In 1924, he teamed up with James Rodebaugh, William Yunker, and Noel Wien in Alaska, where he flew charter flights for about a year. He left Alaska to return to Minnesota where he continued barnstorming. He received his Transport and Mechanics licenses in 1928 and was hired by the Wahpeton School of Science in North Dakota, where he headed the aviation school. He taught aviation mechanics, and with his students, overhauled engines and rebuilt aircraft for individuals across the region. He retired from the school in 1953.

Saunders, Charles
Saunders was a well-known flyer during the 1930s. He opened a restaurant called Charlie's Cafe Exceptionale in downtown Minneapolis which became the favorite fine-dining spot for flyers from the area. Charlie sponsored the Quiet Birdmen's Twin Cities hangar for many years. He flew in the "Peace Armada" in 1939, dropping leaflets across the state that extolled the virtues of staying out of a European war.

Schaeffer, Dorothy L. 1914 -
A native of Iowa, Schaeffer came to Minnesota as a teenager, going to school in Braham, Minnesota, near where her family owned a cabin. She came to the Twin Cities to attend college at the University of Minnesota, but took a job with the Park Board as secretary to Larry Hammond soon after he became airport manager at Wold-Chamberlain. She was the acknowledged expert on airport systems and business. Her work experience, dating from 1937, never stopped. She is, at this writing, still involved with airport activity.

Schauss, Frederick A. "Al" 1904 -
One of Minnesota's most popular homebuilders and an acknowledged propeller carving expert. Schauss was a North Dakota native. He came to the Twin Cities to work in a radiator shop as a teenager. He was inventive, often devising unique machines and techniques to make jobs easier. He taught himself the art of welding and built his own airplane. Once built, he had to learn to fly it and took lessons from Wally Neuman at Oxboro Airport. When his first airplane burned, he built another, finishing it in 1932. In 1935, he built a third plane with a Ford V-8 motor. His building continued after the war, and included construction of a Vollmer amphibian. He continued his hobby of making propellers for homebuilders.

Schlapkol, Captain Charles J.
Commanding Officer of the Marine Air Reserve Training unit at Wold-Chamberlain from 1932 to 1940. Schlapkohl was hired as a pilot by Northwest Airways in 1934 but resigned a year later.

Schlesselman, Harold R. 1905 - 1951
FBO at Mankato during most of the pre-war and wartime CPT and WTS programs.

Schroeder, Lester - 1989
Appointed to the new Minnesota Aeronautics Commission in 1941 by Governor Harold Stassen, Schroeder took over as head in 1943. Under his command, the Commission carried out its duty to license, inspect, regulate, plan, and operate all aviation in Minnesota.

Sell, Elmer L. 1901 - 1962

Sell graduated from North High School in Minneapolis, attended Dunwoody Institute, and joined the 109th Observation Squadron. He taught aviation and auto mechanics in Buffalo, and Jordan, raced cars, and took up flying. He opened the first airport in Carver County in the 1930s, turning an old log cabin into a hangar and doing weekend barnstorming and sight-seeing flights. He sold airplanes, cars and appliances from a store in Mayer, Minnesota, during the same period. The airport was closed during the first years of World War II, but reopened afterward and operated until 1960. During the postwar years, Sell continued to instruct auto mechanics at Tracy, and later at Minneapolis Roosevelt High school.

Sellman, Charles 1897 - 1988

One of the State's most active flying farmers, Sellman, from Mabel, Minnesota, started flying in 1934, learning from Max Conrad. He built an airstrip on his farm in Hesper Township and leased it to other flyers and crop-sprayers. He later bought another farm in Mabel and built a strip there. At the time of his death, in 1988, he was one of the oldest active pilots in Minnesota, still flying at age 91.

Sevdy, Howard H. 1913 - 1991

Sevdy, a native of Iowa, took his first plane ride in 1918. He learned to fly and barnstormed with Gus Imm, Jimmy Zarth, Ob Seim, and Pete LaFrance. He bought an American Eagle airplane in 1938, and flew many others, performing at local airshows. He gave exhibitions of stunt flying until World War II, when he was sent to 29 Palms Air Academy in California as a glider tow pilot in the training program there. After the war, he and Eldon Sorenson ran the Worthington Airport where Howard built up several Pitts aircraft and continued his aerobatic airshow performances.

Shaffer, Harold 1901 - 1961

Shaffer was half owner of Interstate Finance Company at Wold-Chamberlain Field during the 1930s. Officing out of Shorty De Ponti's hangars, Shaffer's finance company enabled many of the budding aviators of the area to purchase their own airplanes during a period when money was scarce. Shaffer and his partner, Harvey Cook, changed the name of the Corporation to Interstate Air Credit after the war. The two businessmen were regular faces in the airport gang and their company is still fondly remembered for helping out in a pinch. Many a pilot remembers making an emergency call to the loan company to have funds wired to a far off town for the purchase of a new prop, or other necessities. Shaffer's wife, Vida, was one of the first 99's in the State, helping organize a local chapter in 1937.

Shank, Eugene S. 1905 - 1942

Born in Morgan, Minnesota, Shank began his career by taking up flying after high school. He attempted to build his own airplane at age fourteen. In 1926, he piloted an amphibian in the Ford Reliability Tour, and in 1928, set a looping record of 515 loops. That record was broken later by Speed Holman. Shank raced in local air races and attempted a record endurance flight, spending fourteen and a half hours in the air before landing. In 1929, he established Shank Flying Service at Robbinsdale Airport and attended the St. Paul College of Law.

Gene Shank became Chief Pilot for Hanford Airlines in 1932 and in 1937 joined Northwest Airlines, becoming a check pilot. He and his co-pilot were killed in a DC-3 crash at Miles City, Montana. No passengers were injured. At the time of his death, he had logged over two million air miles during his career.

Shaw, William H., Sr. 1905 - 1984

Shaw was born in South Dakota, but came to Wold-Chamberlain in the early 1930s. He did some barnstorming at weekend airshows there, while working for Shorty De Ponti. He started his own flight school in 1935, and became a well-known instructor. He joined Northwest Airlines in 1942 and flew the Northern Division through Alaska and Canada during the war. He was on loan to Pan American for a year, flying routes in Lima, Peru. He retired from Northwest in 1962.

Siehl, Clarence

Siehl started an airshow troupe in 1937 called the "Hell Divers." They performed around the country during the next couple of years. Members of his group were Babe Alsworth, Ob Seim, Ed Mammann, Archie Geiser, Ernie Wille, Paul Mlinar, and Tom Hennessy. Sylvan Hugelin with his autogiro was a member of the show at certain times, as was Jack Robinson, another stunt pilot.

Slack, Glen A. 1915 -

Slack took his first flying lessons from Bill Shaw at Wold-Chamberlain and later instructed for Shaw. Slack worked for Shorty Hall, who had a Funk airplane dealership, picking up and delivering airplanes. He worked odd jobs at Wold and then instructed at Stanton Airport in the WTS program prior to World War II. In 1944, Slack worked at the glider factory in South Minneapolis for Shorty De Ponti. He went to work for the Metropolitan Airports Commission after the war, eventually becoming Deputy Chief of Airport Security.

Smith, Chadwick B. 1905 - 1931

Chad Smith was born in Iowa, but moved to Minneapolis with his family when he was quite young. He spent 1923 and 1924 with the Army Air Service at Kelly Field, Texas. He returned and obtained a degree in Pharmacy at the University of Minnesota. He joined the 109th Observation Squadron, and set an altitude record of 22,017 feet in a military plane. In 1927, he was hired as a pilot for Northwest Airways, and set a speed record between La Crosse and Milwaukee. He later set another record in a Ford Trimotor between St. Paul and Chicago. In 1928, he flew over 1173 hours, (an average of 3.2 hours/day,) quite a feat in planes of that period. He gave flight instruction in Northwest Airways' Waco trainers as a sideline to his airmail flights.

Chad Smith was a brother to twins, Lee and Les Smith, also hired by the airline. His sister, Gladys Roy, was a parachute jumper and wing-walker. Chad became Operations Manager of Northwest Airways in 1931 when Speed Holman was killed in a stunting accident. Chad, himself, died less than four months later, while undergoing an appendix operation.

Smith, Robert L. "Lee" 1907 - 1989

Younger brother of Chad Smith and a twin to Les Smith, Lee graduated from Minneapolis' South High School in 1926. He enlisted in the 109th Observation Squadron as a mechanic, and learned to fly from his older brother, Chad. He ventured to Hibbing, where he took a job with an air taxi service, also doing barnstorming and instructing. After earning his Transport license, he was hired by Midwest Air Transport in Wisconsin as a general service pilot. In June of 1929 he was hired by Northwest Airways. Lee was the first Northwest pilot to fly on instruments, flying a mail plane between St. Paul and Chicago.

He became the Eastern Division Superintendent in 1943, Vice-President of that Region in 1944, and retired in 1967. Lee was one of the founders of ALPA, the Air Line Pilot's Association.

Smith, Charles L. "Les" 1907 -

Twin brother to Lee, and younger brother of Chad Smith. Les took his first plane ride with Walter Bullock in 1924. He followed his two brothers in the barnstorming business and was hired by Midwest Air Transport in Madison, Wisconsin when Lee went to work for Northwest Airways. Les followed him there in 1930, being the twelfth pilot hired by Northwest. He also was a member of the 109th Observation Squadron from 1933 to 1937, during which time, he was forced to bail out of an O-38 observation plane. In 1943, he was one of the pilots who flew in a mass transport armada across the mountains from China to India in C-46 aircraft. He retired from Northwest in 1963.

Snyder, Delmar

Snyder served in the Army Air Service during World War I, stationed at Post Field, Fort Sill, Oklahoma. After the war, he took a job with Clarence Hinck's Federated Fliers, and became one of the group's most active stunt flyers and barnstormers. In 1925, he left Hinck and established his own Flying Circus, he continued this occupation until 1928. He joined Air Transportation, Inc. at Wold-Chamberlain Field as Regional Supervisor of Distribution of Curtiss Robin aircraft. That company later merged with Universal Air Lines. Snyder was later associated with Northland Aviation School at the field.

Soden, Glen

Soden was one of the Federated Fliers Flying Circus regular pilots during the 1922 and 1923 seasons. He was well-known in his day and the Minneapolis Tribune acknowledged him as one of the State's best flyers in 1922.

Sohler, Lawrence J.

Sohler was from Eagle Lake, Minnesota. He had been a barnstormer in the 1920s, exhibiting, flying sight-seers, and giving flight instruction. One of his students was Gus Imm. Sohler became the FBO at Mankato during the 1930s, operating Sohler Flying Service.

Sorenson, Eldon H. 1913 -
Born in Janesville, Minnesota, Sorenson was inspired by the flight of Lindbergh and went into aviation. He built model airplanes and then learned to fly, purchasing a Waco 10 aircraft from Marcellus King. Sorenson barnstormed through the region on weekends. In the period from 1937 to the beginning of the war, Sorenson and his wife, Verda, made a living by flying over farms, photographing them from the air, and later selling copies of the photos to the farmers. During the war, Sorenson flew as a crop-duster in Florida and North Carolina. He returned to Minnesota, and with Howard Sevdy, ran the airport at Worthington. He began building his own aerial spray rigs, patenting several systems and distributing them worldwide.

Sorensen, Niels H. 1912 - 1993
Born in Minneapolis, Sorensen learned to fly at Oxboro-Heath Airport in 1936. He took lessons from Wally Neuman in a Curtiss Robin. In 1932, he joined the Naval Air Reserve at Wold-Chamberlain while instructing for Neuman at Cedar Airport. Niels bought a Buhl Pup aircraft for his own use, and went into business with Ben and Frank Christian, selling Porterfield aircraft. He instructed aerobatics in the CPT program for Mac McInnis and Elmer Hinck at Wold until 1941, when he was commissioned in the Navy and called to active duty. He served in a PV-1 patrol squadron through the war, flying missions out of Widby Island to the Bremerton Yard area and into the Aleutians. Following the war, he, his brother, Oliver, and Ed Sieber opened Lakeland Skyways at Wold-Chamberlain. They moved the business to Crystal Airport in 1952. Niels was a successful FBO, retiring in 1977. After his retirement, he spent his time rebuilding vintage aircraft.

Sparboe, Jerome H. - 1942
Hired in 1931 by Northwest Airways, Sparboe was one of the pilots of the Northwest Sikorsky S-38 flying boats that operated for a short time between St. Paul and the Duluth harbor. Sparboe took military leave with the outbreak of World War II and saw action with the Navy. He was lost on a mission in Alaska.

Stebbins, Gerry C. 1909 - 1976
Considered one of the best aviation mechanics plying his trade during the 1930s and 1940s. Stebbins worked for Hanford Airlines at Wold-Chamberlain, then for Shorty De Ponti through the CPT program, and went to Stanton Airport to work for Clarence Hinck during the WTS. He was a jack of all trades, fixing instruments, propellers, engines and airframes. He was also an excellent pilot and test flew the aircraft he repaired. He went to work for Braniff after the war, retiring in 1973 as the supervisor of engine and propeller shops.

Stein, Camille L. "Rosie" - 1954
Rosie Stein was the office manager to Northwest Airways head, Colonel Brittin. She had worked for Brittin during his days at the St. Paul Association of Commerce and went with him when he started Northwest Airways. It was her cheery greeting "everything's rosy," when asked how things were, that earned her the nickname of "Rosie." Her handling of the routine and unusual daily affairs of Northwest, from firing the wood stove, brewing the coffee, answering phones and selling tickets, earned her a wealth of respect. She later became a company board officer and Supervisor of Stewardesses. In 1991, Stein was inducted into the Minnesota Aviation Hall of Fame.

Stellmacher, Irwin A. "Happy" 1895 - 1988
Stellmacher, from Cottonwood, Minnesota, is one of those legendary flyers that populate our state's colorful aviation lore. An inventor and mechanical genius, he devised what we would consider to be a snowmobile in 1915, and a propeller-driven automobile which he drove around the streets of Marshall, Minnesota. He was an auto mechanic by trade. He bought a Jenny airplane and taught himself how to fly it in 1924. He gave sight-seeing rides and flight instruction for a number of years.

Stelzig, Ronald E. 1909 -
Stelzig was born in St. Paul. He yearned to get a job with the airlines, and applied at Northwest as early as 1930 for a position as a steward. Because there were no openings, he began lobbying Jim LaMont, Northwest's chief mechanic, for a job as a mechanic. He was hired by Northwest in 1930 and often flew as a steward/copilot in the early years, but transferred to flight dispatch. He went to Seattle as Chief Flight Superintendent of the Western Region. Following the war, he became the Director of Flight Dispatch. At his retirement in 1974, Ron was the U. S. airlines senior employee with forty-five-years of continuous service. Ron was also a long-time member of the Zurrah Shrine Flyers organization.

Stenseth, Martinus
Stenseth trained at Kelly Field for the U. S. Air Service and became an Ace during World War I. He was a member of the Minnesota Air Guard during the period between the wars, and during active duty in World War II, became base commander at Las Vegas Army Airfield (later Nellis Air Force Base). He became a Brigadier General.

Stieler, Robert J. 1905 - 1963
Born in Albert Lea, Minnesota, Stieler began his flying career in 1927, barnstorming the area between his home town and Mason City, Iowa in the 1930s. He entered a CPT program in California prior to the war, and became a glider pilot instructor. He was Commissioned an officer in the Naval Reserve and flew as a Naval Ferry Pilot during the war. He remained in the Naval Reserve at Wold-Chamberlain for many years after the war. Stieler took up residence in St. Cloud and flew regularly until suffering heart problems in his later years.

Stodolka, Cyril L. 1892 - 1987
Born in Benton County, Langola Township, Stodolka grew up on the farm. He went to work in a fix-it shop in Royalton, but his head was in the clouds. He fashioned a toy helicopter before any such device was heard of, and built a full-sized airplane, which he flew in 1914. The plane was later destroyed in a windstorm. He was drafted , but found his way to the Lafayette Flying Corps in France, where he was learning to fly as the war ended. Stodolka came back home and took some flying lessons with Walt Bullock at the Brown Farm Airfield. Stodolka barnstormed for several years, and had the distinction of giving Charles Lindbergh one of his first air rides.

Stout, William B. 1880 - 1956
Stout came to Minnesota at age ten. He graduated from St. Paul's Mechanic Arts High School. Bill Stout was very inventive and had great insight into how things worked. He designed gadgets in school and devised children's toys, then wrote and illustrated their manufacture in a column for the St. Paul Dispatch newspaper. After four years of engineering at the University of Minnesota, he took a trip to Europe and there, became interested in aviation. He returned and taught manual arts at St. Paul Central High School, while continuing to write. In 1910, he staged a model airplane event which coincided with the big State Fair Air Meet.
In 1912, he was invited to become the aviation editor of the Chicago Tribune. He was the founder and first editor of Aerial Age Magazine. During this time, designed a new type motorcycle. Stout was hired away from the Tribune by the Scripps-Booth Motor Company as an engineer. He next worked for the Packard Motor Company and was sent to Washington as a consultant. He theorized that a thick-winged monoplane would be more efficient than the thin-winged biplanes of his day. He worked to perfect the cantilever wing with no outside drag-producing struts. Stout went to work for the Hamilton Aircraft Manufacturing Company, designing the basic structure of that airliner with its cantilever wing. Henry Ford hired Stout to design the famous Ford Trimotor. In 1926, Stout was elected the first Secretary of Northwest Airways, who later would purchase both the Hamilton Metalplane and the Ford Trimotor.

Strong, Lyle H. - 1972
Lyle Strong and his brother, Willis, owned and operated a gasoline filling station on 34th Avenue close to the Wold-Chamberlain Field terminal. Lyle learned to fly, probably by association with the local flyers that patronized his station. He barnstormed and flew in air races around the state. He joined Northwest Airlines as a pilot in 1935. In April of 1943, he and his brother were two of the pilots who took part in a mass transport flight to India, bringing supplies from the States to China to help the Chinese in their struggle with Japan.

Strong, Willis H. - 1961
Co-owner of Strong's Service Station at Wold-Chamberlain in the 1930s and early 1940s. Like his brother, Willis learned how to fly by association with the Wold-Chamberlain flyers, and went on to acquire his Transport license, also being hired by Northwest in 1940. He, too, took part in the mass flight to China in 1943.

Swank, Theodore 1904 - 1977
Swank was a barnstormer during the 1930s. He received his Transport license in 1931, when there were but 700 issued in the entire country. A 1937 crackup during a coyote hunt caused him to have a leg amputated, and the CAA insisted he be tested again before he could use his pilot's license. After much persistance, he succeeded in passing the flight tests and continued to fly with a wooden leg.

Swanson, Alvin E.
Swanson started flying in 1927. His career found him as an instructor at States Flying Service at Robbinsdale Airport in the 1930s. During World War II, he was a CPT instructor and following the war, opened Crystal Skyways at Crystal Airport.

Swanson, Carl E. 1907 - 1985
Carl Swanson was an engineer who graduated from the University of Minnesota in 1927. He taught there from 1929 to 1939. In 1940, he designed an improved version of the shielded ignition harness, helping to provide the military with better in-flight radio communication and all-weather performance.

Swanson, Edor S. "Pie" 1907 - 1982
Born in Moose Lake, Minnesota, Pie Swanson learned to fly in 1928. He flew as co-pilot on Universal Air Lines Fokker Trimotor airplanes between Minneapolis and Chicago in 1929, then went to work for Colonial Air Transport of Boston in 1930. When Colonial was bought out by American Airways in 1934, he stayed on, finishing his career, retiring in 1967 and returning to Minnesota.

Swanson, Melvin 1900 - 1959
Though born in Ohio, Mel Swanson was one of the more visible members of the Wold-Chamberlain pilots in the 1930s. He piloted the Freeman Ford Trimotor on weekend barnstorming sessions and when it dropped parachutists over the airport and the State Fairgrounds. He went to work for Northwest Airlines in 1938, first as an inspector, then as a pilot. He crash-landed a Lockheed Model 14 at the end of one of Wold's runways in 1938 when his engines ran out of fuel on landing approach during a test flight. During World War II, he was supervisor of flying for Northwest's Air Transport Command contract on the CANOL project near the Arctic Circle. He then flew Northern Region flights.

Swenson, Donald 1902 - 1975
Swenson soloed in 1931 in Dallas, Texas, having had his very first air ride with Charles Lindbergh. He became the airport manager at Rochester, Minnesota in 1932, a job he held until retiring in 1967. He was a licensed A & P mechanic.

Sylling, James A. 1908 -
From Spring Grove Township in southeastern Minnesota. Sylling began his flying career in 1928 with flying lessons across the border at La Crosse, Wisconsin. He purchased Bernard Pietenpol's first Model A powered Aircamper airplane. Sylling was one of the first Minnesota Flying Farmers in Houston County.

Thro, Lyle
Thro was a well-known figure around the Twin Cities. He was a stunt pilot who started flying with Clarence Hinck as early as the 1920s. He often flew sight-seers from Wold-Chamberlain Field, or parachute jumpers and rope ladder acts at the State Fairgrounds for Hinck's Thrill Day shows. Thro worked briefly for Northwest Airways in 1934. He went to Mexico and then to Oklahoma, where he was with Bowen Airlines.

Timm, Otto W. 1893 - 1978
Timm was born in Lakefield, Minnesota. He attended Windom High School where he got a reputation as a mechanical wizard. He built and raced automobiles as a teenager. He moved to Milwaukee at age 17 and began building airplanes. A move to Chicago brought him into contact with Max Lillie, Katherine Stinson, DeLloyd Thompson, Lincoln Beachey, and other well-known flyers of that period. Timm built several planes there and then returned to Minnesota, where he barnstormed. In 1916, he went to California where he was a flight instructor with the military. After the war, he opened an aircraft manufacturing plant, building passenger and racing planes. In 1921, he moved to Nebraska and became head engineer at the Lincoln-Standard Aircraft Company, building planes of his own design. In 1922, he gave Charles Lindbergh his very first airplane ride. In 1928, he inaugurated the O. W. Timm Aircraft Company in California, manufacturing the "Collegiate" aircraft. The company succumbed to the Depression, but soon Timm reopened, patenting the first aircraft tricycle landing gear. Timm built trainers and gliders for the military and was a pioneer in static (ground-based) testing of new aircraft models. Brother Wally Timm also designed and built aircraft.

Tinquist, Theodore 1910 -
Tinquist moved to Minnesota at age 11, finding a home at Grand Rapids. He soloed in 1936, fledged out by Leon "Babe" Alsworth. Tinquist received his Commercial and Instructors ratings. In 1942, Tinquist Aviation received a CPT contract to train glider pilots and after the war, remained in the FBO business until he sold out to Gordy Newstrom in 1947.

Toll, Frank
Early Northwest Airways mechanic.

Tosch, Orval W.
Tosch was an aircraft mechanic. He started in St. Paul, working for Al Brandt during the late 1930s, went to work for the Morrison-Knudsen transportation company in Alaska at the beginning of World war II, and later worked for Northwest Airlines. At the time of this writing, Tosch is still active in aviation in Seattle.

Tresise, Dean
Dean was a Duluth native. He took flying lessons from Land-O-Lakes Airways, soloing at the early age of fifteen. When he earned his Limited Commercial and full Commercial licenses, he was the youngest pilot with these ratings in the U. S. He bought his own aircraft and gave lessons and sight-seeing flights. He later moved to St. Paul, offering flight instruction there and flying the Freeman Ford Trimotor occasionally from Wold-Chamberlain Field. With business being slow during the Depression, he sailed on a Great Lakes ore carrier, then joined the WTS program as an instructor during World War II. He started Zenith City Air Service at Duluth after the war.

Trehus, Melvin
One of the earliest flyers in Houston County, Trehus began his flying career in 1928. He was an auto and machinery dealer who bought and sold airplanes as well. He would fly into a farmer's field to sell tractors, cars, or farm machinery. He was instrumental in promoting aviation in the southeastern Minnesota area during the 1930s and 1940s.

Truesdell, Orville S. 1911 - 1989
Truesdell came to Pine City, Minnesota with his pilot's license. He barnstormed and started a Civil Air Patrol unit at Albert Lea in 1940. He joined the Navy and became a ferry pilot, stationed in New York. He delivered aircraft from New York to Navy bases all over the country, once flying formation with Charles Lindbergh in Corsair fighters to California. He helped get many Minnesota airports started after the war, working for the Mobil Oil Company.

Vandre, Bernard G. "Van" or "B. G." - 1975
Vandre was a pilot, mechanic, promoter, businessman and showman. He began his flying career in the 1920s, flying briefly as a barnstormer for H. A. Kantrud of Fergus Falls. He found his way to Wold-Chamberlain Field in Minneapolis where he was a flight instructor. He moved to St. Cloud in the late 1930s where Van's Air Service, Inc., was successful in obtaining a CPT contract to instruct St. Cloud Teacher's College students. His contracts included the WTS 10-hour program of cadet evaluations. Following the war, he went into business in Winona, and booked airshows across Minnesota for Clarence Hinck.

Van Dusen, G. B. 1914 -
G. B. Van Dusen is one of Minnesota's most successful aviation businessmen. He started his aircraft parts business in the basement of the Wold-Chamberlain terminal building in 1940, and soon expanded into a hangar next to the terminal. He derived the idea of sending flying salesmen to call on airport operators in the small towns across Minnesota, and later, the nation. Among his sales reps were Sig Gudmundson, Don Hanson, and Johan Larsen. During the war, he moved to downtown Minneapolis, and after the war, opened offices in New York, Boston, Pennsylvania, New Jersey, Virginia and Miami. He eventually had offices at 24 locations here and abroad, though his main offices remained in the Twin Cities. Besides parts, the company also engaged in flight training, fueling, and other ground services. In 1954, the company became publicly held, and was later involved in a "takeover" by Aviall. Van Dusen was inducted into the Minnesota Aviation Fall of Fame in 1992.

Vacanti, Victor
Vacanti worked 30 years as a mechanic, line-man and office manager for Shorty De Ponti.

Van Dyke, Jean Wahlberg
Jean Wahlberg was hired by Continental Airlines in 1941 as Chief Hostess, to set up a flight attendant training program and supervise it. She had graduated from the University of Minnesota School of Nursing. She developed a manual and the protocol to be used by future generations of Continental flight attendants.

Vasey, John W., Jr. 1912 -
Vasey came to Minnesota from Montana. He took flying lessons and earned his license in 1940. He enlisted in the Air Air Force and became an instructor. After the war, he began rebuilding aircraft, and with John Lafferty, rebuilt and modified a Stearman for

airshow work in nine days. He flew airshows for about five years, earning a reputation in the Midwest. He did crop-dusting, entered air races, and was a part-owner of the Austin Flying Service at Austin, Minnesota. Vasey rebuilt and modified the Taylorcraft airplane that exhibition pilot Duane Cole flew in airshows nationwide for many years. The plane is now in the EAA Museum.

Vierow, Connie
Vierow was a career flight instructor. He taught in the CPT and WTS programs prior to and during World War II, then joined Northwest Airlines after the war as a Link trainer instructor. He then went to the Minneapolis Vocational School and later to the Aviation Training Center at Wold-Chamberlain in the same capacity until retirement in 1984.

Voge, Donald O. 1911 - 1969
Voge is considered one of the more colorful of Minnesota's golden-age aviators. He lived on his parent's farm adjacent to Robbinsdale Airport and learned to fly there. He was interested in auto racing as well as flying and competed at tracks across Minnesota. Voge never cared for air regulations, or licensing, and made headlines as a "house-crasher" during the late 1930s, often flying an unlicensed and decrepit airplane through mockup houses at local fairgrounds. He built a dirt stock car racetrack on the family property in Crystal when his parents died, and moved racing to New Brighton when his Robbinsdale neighbors petitioned to have the track closed. Voge's last house-crash was at the Crystal racetrack in 1949.

Vogt, Earl L.
Vogt was a writer for the St. Paul Dispatch newspaper. His column, "The Sock," appeared regularly in the paper in the 1930s, portraying the state's aviation personalities and activities. It is one of the more important reference sources for aviation lore of that period.

Walatka, John
Walatka was from Fairmont, Minnesota and found his way to Alaska in 1937. He helped found and became President of Northern Consolidated Airlines there. A mountain in Alaska is named after him.

Waldron, L. D. "Baldy"
Waldron was an industrialist, in the machinery manufacturing business. He incorporated the Waldron Aircraft and Manufacturing Company in South Dakota, but headquartered it in Minneapolis in 1928. The main portion of his airplane manufacturing business involved Orville Hickman's aircraft designs. The aircraft were built at Robbinsdale Airport. The Starling aircraft was produced by the Waldron company, and though a viable design, did not go into quantity production, probably suffering from lack of a market during the depths of the Depression. After production of only two aircraft, Waldron withdrew his support.

Wall, Elmore
A well-known pilot at Wold-Chamberlain during the 1930s. Wall was a barnstormer and one of the Mohawk Company's test pilots.

Wash, Major Carlton H. 1889 -
Wash was born in Minneapolis. He joined the Army and was a Cavalry Captain with Pershing's force in the 1916 Mexican campaign. He joined the Air Service in 1917 and was trained as a pilot, and given command of Souther Field at Americus, Georgia during World War I. After the war, he became chief of the Experimental Flying Section at Rockwell Field, San Diego and later, McCook Field, Dayton, Ohio.

Webb, Harold K.
Webb was a flying businessman in the Tracy, Minnesota area. At one time, he owned a Pitcairn Autogiro and had it flown around the region, advertising his oil and fuel products.

Weihe, Raymond H. 1906 - 1991
Weihe made his reputation as a radio and communications expert. He worked for a manufacturing company until he was hired by Dr. George Young to work at radio station WDGY in 1935. Though he wanted to get into commercial radio, Weihe took a job with Northwest Airlines in 1936, supervising and installing various electronic communications systems, both between ground stations, and between the ground and air. He pioneered the use of C-W (Morse code) in Northwest's early reservations systems, then helped set up weather stations in the Northern Region. He went on to integrate the teletype reservations systems in the main offices, and installed the first radio-telephone systems aboard Northwest's airliners, working with the airline to push its routes across the Pacific to Honolulu.

Weld, Lt. Frank E. 1898 - 1969
Born in Minneapolis. Weld enlisted in the Naval Reserve and was Commander of the Reserve unit meeting at the Minneapolis Armory at Lake Calhoun from 1920 to 1922. He became the first Commander of Naval Reserve Air Base, Minneapolis, at Wold-Chamberlain in 1928, holding that position until 1931.

Westover, Joseph F. 1890 -
Westover began his aviation career as a parachute jumper in 1908. He learned to fly in 1912 and barnstormed the country. He took a job with the Curtiss Aeroplane Company at Hammondsport, New York, where he became a skilled mechanic. He and Jim LaMont accompanied the famous woman aviator, Ruth Law, on her cross-country exhibition tours. In 1919, Westover went to work for Bill Kidder at Curtiss-Northwest Airfield. In 1922, he associated himself with Clarence Hinck's Federated Fliers Flying Circus, providing maintenance for the group's aircraft and vehicles. In 1925, Westover was issued Minnesota pilot's license #1 by Ray Miller, Minnesota Aeronautics Chairman. In 1926, Westover organized his own traveling show, the Westover Exhibition Company. In 1928, he went to work for Universal Air Lines at Wold-Chamberlain as Equipment Maintenance Superintendent. He had joined the 109th Observation Squadron 1921, and was put in charge of the engineering section. He was discharged from the 109th in 1932.

Wheelock, Charles P. 1914 -
Born in Minneapolis, Wheelock got his pilot's license in 1932. He was one of the very active weekend barnstormers at Wold-Chamberlain Field, carrying sight-seers and selling aviation to the masses. He joined Northwest Airlines in 1937, and flew on Northwest's Air Transport Command contracts, ferrying materials throughout Alaska and bringing supplies over the "Hump" between India and China. Wheelock retired in 1974.

Whempner, Robert J.
Whempner worked as a test pilot for the NACA (National Advisory Council on Aeronautics). He flew with Max Conrad for the Honeywell Corporation on test programs after World War II. Bob tested the Honeywell C-1 autopilot in fighter aircraft and once performed an Immelman aerobatic maneuver while on autopilot in a P-38. He aided Max Conrad with preparations for Max's first trans-Atlantic lightplane flight.

Whempner, Russell H. 1912 -
Brother of Robert Whempner, Russell learned to fly in 1939 from Bill Shaw at Wold-Chamberlain Field. He also went to work for the Honeywell Corporation and became their Chief Pilot during the test period of the C-1 autopilot, early in World War II. He worked with Army Air Force crews, teaching them the fundamentals of autopilot operation.

White, General Thomas Dresser 1901 - 1965
White was born in Walker, Minnesota, graduated from West Point in 1920, and went with the infantry to the Canal Zone. In 1924, he entered flight training at Brooks Field, Texas, and was posted with the 99th Observation Squadron at Boling Field, Washington, D. C. Sent to Peking in 1927, he learned the Chinese language and was assigned to Headquarters, U. S. Army Air Corps. He became the military attache for air to Russia and later Italy. In 1940, he graduated from the Command and General Staff School at Fort Leavenworth and became the military attache to Brazil, then Chief of Staff of the Third Air Force in Florida. In January of 1944, he went to the South Pacific as Deputy Commander of the Thirteenth Air Force.

White next commanded the Fifth Air Force in Japan. In 1948, he was transferred to office of the Secretary of the Air Force in Washington, D.C. and was promoted in following years through Deputy Chief of Operations, Vice Chief of Staff, and became Air Force Chief of Staff on July 1957. He retired from active duty in 1961.

Whittemore, Fred 1898 - 1938
Born in Minneapolis, Whittemore graduated from North High School and undertook the study of medicine at the University of Minnesota. He was instructed in flying by Deke DeLong at Robbinsdale Airport and went barnstorming in 1925, touring the country with Walter Bullock and DeLong. In 1928, he joined Northwest Airways as an airmail pilot, where he cut a resplendent figure, keeping his personal airmail plane, a Waco Taperwing, spit-shined and very visible on the airport. He became Operations Manager in 1934. Whittemore was killed at Glendale, California, when his Lockheed Model 14, being ferried to Minneapolis, struck a canyon wall.

Whyte, Edna Gardner 1902 - 1992
An exemplary Minnesota woman pilot, born in Garden City, Minnesota. Whyte left Minnesota as a youngster, earning her wings in 1926 in Illinois, barnstorming, air racing, and instructing through the 1930s She became a Navy nurse prior to World War II, and worked as an Army nurse during the war. After the war, she continued her flight instruction, started Aero Enterprises Flight School at Meacham Field, Texas, an operation that lasted 24 years. In 1970, at age 68, she organized Happy Valley Aero at Aero Valley Field near Dallas, Texas, where she was still instructing until only months before her death.

Wien, Fritz 1901 -

Wien, Noel 1899 - 1977

Wien, Ralph 1897 - 1930

Wien, Sigurd 1903 -
The Wien brothers were from Cook, Minnesota. Noel learned to fly in 1921, barnstormed with the Federated Fliers Flying Circus, then turned his sights on Alaska. In 1924, he began work with James Rodebaugh at Fairbanks. A year later, he returned to the lower 48 states to purchase a new aircraft for the business and brought his brother, Ralph, back to Alaska with him. In 1927, Noel brought brother Fritz to Alaska. In 1930, Ralph was killed in a crash in Kotzebue, where the airport is named after him. Sig Wien came to Alaska in 1931 and earned a reputation equally as significant as his brother, Noel. Sig bought Alaska Airways from Noel and went on to become Chairman of the Board of Wien Consolidated Airlines in 1968. The Company remained under Sig's control until 1968, and continued in business until 1983. Noel Wien was inducted into the Minnesota Aviation Hall of Fame in 1989.

Wiese, Rudolph E. "Friday" 1902 -
One of the early flyers in Swift County. Wiese built a homemade airplane in 1928 and a glider in 1930.

Wilcox, Ralph D.
Wilcox was a member of a prominent industrialist family from Minneapolis. He and a partner, Ashley C. Bennett, attempted to fly a homemade aircraft patterned after the Wright design, in 1909. The pair tried to fly the airplane from the ice of Lake Minnetonka, but several attempts failed to get them airborne. It was the first time anyone had tried to fly an indigenous Minnesota airplane.

Williams, Captain Trevor G. 1893 -
Williams came to St. Paul as assistant city chemist in 1915. He then went to work for Minnesota Mining and Manufacturing as a chemist. In 1916, he joined the Minnesota National Guard and in 1917, the Marine Corps. He was assigned to the First Aeronautic Company and was later attached to the Northern Bombing Group at Oye, France, where he flew bombing missions against the Germans. When the new Minnesota Air Guard's 109th Observation Squadron was formed in 1921, Trevor Williams was one of the first members to sign up and became the first Operations Officer. He was discharged as a Captain in 1934. He also was General Manager for Universal Air Lines at Wold-Chamberlain Field and later flew for the Pure Oil Company.

Williamson, Harvey F. 1904 - 1928
Born in Duluth, Williamson went through high School there and attended Princeton University, where he graduated in 1927. While there, he became interested in aviation and took government flying courses. He was commissioned an Ensign in the Navy and took flight training at Great Lakes Naval Training Center near Chicago, and at Pensacola, Florida. He became associated with Mid Plane Sales & Service's Duluth branch in 1928 and helped establish the first airline between Duluth and the Twin Cities. He was killed while giving a sight-seeing flight over the Duluth harbor. The Duluth Airport was dedicated to his memory in 1930.

Winteringer, "Pop"
From Eyota, Minnesota, Pop Winteringer was a parachute jumper and jumping instructor as well as a parachute rigger (repacker). He also was a hot air balloon pilot and performed jumps from balloons at the Minnesota State Fair.

Wiplinger, Bernard A. "Ben" 1915 - 1992
Born in St. Paul, Wiplinger took his first air ride at Holman Field, built a Pietenpol airplane, and had Burt Nieman give him lessons in it. Wiplinger flew from the small airfields in St. Paul; Luxingers, and Onion Patch. He joined the 109th Observation Squadron while a student at the University of Minnesota. He worked for the Douglas Aircraft Company in California prior to World War II as

a tool and die maker. When drafted, he served as a mechanic. After the war, he and Joe LaMotte started a mechanics school in St. Paul. In his later career, Wiplinger designed a line of aircraft floats, the successors of which are still being manufactured.

Witt, John L. 1911 - 1985
Though born in Michigan, Witt moved to Minnesota when he took a job with Northwest Airlines during World War II. He became one of Minnesota's most loved "adopted" aviators. Witt learned to fly in a plane which he rebuilt in Chicago. He barnstormed in the early 1930s and went to work for Pennsylvania Central Airlines in the late 1930s. He worked for Braniff Airlines and flew in Ferry Command during World war II. He was hired by Northwest to fly the Northern Region during the war and helped pioneer the Far East routes after the war. Witt's interests included racing boats, antique airplanes, and aerobatic flying. Following his retirement in 1970, he built a Pitts aerobatic airplane and, with his son, William, stunted at local airshows.

Wittag, L. Millar - 1956
Wittag began flying in the later 1920s. He learned how to fly at Universal Air Lines flight school at Wold-Chamberlain. Wittag did some barnstorming, flying Ben Freeman's Ford Trimotor and Major Mulzer's autogiro, did some aerial photography, flew in local air races, and gave flight instruction. He established the Millar Wittag Flying Service at the Hibbing Airport and prior to World War II, received a government contract to train flyers in the CPT program. He also received another contract to train glider pilots at Crookston. Following the war, he opened Arrowhead Air Service at Hibbing. Wittag died in a plane crash.

Wofford, Kenneth O. 1922 -
Ken Wofford took Air Forces flight cadet training as one of the Tuskegee Airmen, training at Tuskegee Army Airfield in Alabama in 1942. He became both a fighter and bomber pilot, then a transport aircraft commander, and functioned as an instructor and flight evaluator during his career. In 32 years of active duty with the Air Force, Wofford accumulated 9,000 flight hours, and won the Distinguished Flying Cross and Air Medal with 5 Oak Leaf Clusters, the Legion of Merit, and Meritorious Service Medal. During that period, he served as Professor of Aerospace Studies and AFROTC Commandant for the East and North Central Regions.

He served as Commander of the Airborne Command and Control Squadron for the Far East Command, and Deputy Wing Commander for support services for the Tokyo area. During Vietnam, he commanded an Airborne electrical countermeasures squadron. Many varying commands had his stamp before retirement in 1974. He then served ten years as Operations Director for the Aeronautics Office of the Minnesota Department of Transportation.

Wold, Ernest Groves 1897 - 1918
Wold was from a family of wealthy Minneapolis bankers. He went to France as an aviator with the French Lafayette Flying Corps and flew as an observation pilot over enemy lines, photographing positions. He shot down at least one aircraft, according to reports, but was himself shot down in aerial combat. Wold-Chamberlain (now known as Minneapolis, St. Paul International) Airport is named after him. Wold is a member of the Minnesota Aviation Hall of Fame.

Wolf, John J. 1910 -
Born in Hungary, Wolf came to St. Paul as a youth and learned to fly in 1928. He worked many jobs as a mechanic and pilot, including periods with Great Northern Aviation Company and the U. S. Weather Bureau. In 1934, he went with Hanford Airlines at Minneapolis, but left for California to work for Douglas and Consolidated. He returned to Minneapolis, where he worked for Shorty De Ponti in 1938 and 1939, but was back in California again in 1940 and 1941. He joined the Navy and became an aircraft crew chief. He worked briefly for Northwest Airlines as a pilot, flying in the Northern Region in 1943, and finally settled with Honeywell as lead mechanic in 1948, a position he continued until his retirement in 1972.

Woodhead, John F.
Woodhead went to work for Northwest Airways in 1932 as a steward. He progressed to co-pilot, and finally pilot. In the late 1930s he was one of the Sikorsky seaplane pilots flying the route between St. Paul and the Duluth boat harbor. He resigned in 1951, but returned as a consultant to the President of Northwest in 1968. He owned a successful Ford auto dealership in St. Paul in later years.

Wright, Charles L. "Skelly" 1905 - 1985

Wright took his training at Universal Air Lines flight school and attained his Limited Commercial license by 1930. The Skelly Oil Company opened a filling station on 34th Avenue just a few hundred feet from the terminal building at Wold-Chamberlain Field, selling gasoline for both airplanes and autos. The company hired Wright to manage it, furnishing him with the nickname "Skelly." From 1932 to 1935, he barnstormed, and went to work in 1935 for Hanford Airlines. He was hired by Northwest Airlines later the same year and flew for Northwest's Air Transport Command contract in the Northern Region.

In July, 1943, he was selected as one of the pilots to fly the Honeywell flight tests of the Norden Bomb Sight, the automatic landing system, and the "jink stick" controller for the B-24 bomber. He spent four months flying "Squirtin' Gertie," a B-24 rigged with water spray bars to artificially ice the wings of the bomber. A jet engine in the bomb bay would then provide hot air for experimental de-icers on the wings. He spent some time with the static research test program, and retired in 1965.

Young, Dr. George - 1945

One of the more interesting characters in Twin Cities flying circles, Dr. Young started the first radio station in the cities in 1923 above his jewelry shop on West Broadway in Minneapolis. He later moved WDGY to the Nicollet Hotel and innovated the use of commercial advertising by selling time to local merchants. His station featured sports, news, commentary and music. Skilled in many trades, Dr. Young was a Doctor of Optometry, but also he dabbled in watchmaking, engraving, and flying. He invested in early television technology and actually set up the area's first television studio in 1934. For the 1935 Aquatennial parade, he and Ray Weihe installed a transmitter and loudspeaker in a trailer and pulled it behind his Rolls-Royce automobile through the streets, broadcasting his station's programming. He got his flying license in 1932 and owned several airplanes. He was noted for spectacular airplane mishaps which tarnished his image as a pilot. In fact, he used his airplanes for business and flew them uneventfully for hundreds of hours, despite this reputation.

Yunker, William B.

A Rochester, Minnesota native. In 1924, Yunker had a reputation as a highly qualified mechanic. He joined Jimmy Rodebaugh's Alaska Aerial Transportation Company, going to work in Fairbanks, Alaska at Curtiss Northwest Airfield and reccommended Noel Wien as a pilot. Yunker remained as Rodebaugh's mechanic for many years. He was an uncle of another flying Minnesotan, Irwin Stellmacher.

Zum Brunnen, Marcus 1908 -

Born in Hasty, Minnesota, Zum Brunnen learned to fly from instructor Millar Wittag at St. Cloud. He joined a flying club at St. Cloud and got his Private license in 1932. He did much barnstorming on weekends from the family farm at Hasty and other fields in the Wright County area. In the late 1930s Zum Brunnen went to work for the Wright County park system and was instrumental in organizing the Lake Maria State Park. Another roadside park in Hasty is named Zum Brunnen Park, after him.

BIBLIOGRAPHY

Allard, Noel E., *Speed, The Biography of Charles W. Holman*, Minneapolis, 1976.

Berget, Alphonse, *The Conquest of The Air*, G.P. Putnam & Sons, New York, 1909.

Bilstein, Roger E., *Flight in America, 1900-1983*, Johns Hopkins University Press, Baltimore, 1984.

Bjerkebek, Helmer, *Pilgrim In The Sky*, Adventure Publications, Staples, MN, 1984.

Blair, Charles, *Red Ball In The Sky*, Random House, New York, 1969.

Blegen, Theodore C., *Minnesota, A History of the State*, University of Minnesota Press, Minneapolis, 1963.

Bowers, Peter M., *Curtiss Aircraft, 1907-1947*, Putnam, London, 1979.

Brandley, Raymond, *Waco, Ask Any Pilot*, Ray Brandley publisher, 1979.

Brooklyn Historical Society, *History of the Earle Brown Farm*, Jane Hallberg, Leone Howe, and Mary Jane Gustafson, 1983.

Buegeleisen, Sally, *Into The Wind*, Random House, New York, 1973.

Cernick, Cliff, *Skystruck*, Alaska Northwest Books, 1989.

Corn, Joseph J., *The Winged Gospel*, Oxford University Press, New York, 1983.

Crouch, Tom D., *The Eagle Aloft*, Smithsonian Institution Press, Washington, D. C., 1983.

Davies, R. E. G., *Airlines of the United States Since 1914*, Smithsonian Institution Press, Washington, D. C., 1972.

Department of Military Affairs, *50th Anniversary, Minnesota Air National Guard*, State of Minnesota, 1971.

Department of Transportation, *The Putt-Putt Air Force*, Patrick Strickland, 1970.

Donahue, Arthur Gerald, *Tally-Ho!*, McMillan & Co., New York, 1941.

Francillon, Rene J., *McDonnell Douglas Aircraft Since 1920*, Putnam, London, 1979.

Francillon, Rene J., *The Air Guard*, Aerofax, Austin, Texas, 1983.

Galbraith, David, *Aircraft History of Northwest Airlines*, American Aviation Historical Society Journal, California, Volume 21, #4.

Gibbs-Smith, Charles H., *Aviation*, HMSO, 1970.

Grace, Richard, *Visibility Unlimited*, Longmans, Green & Co., 1950.

Gresham, William L., *Monster Midway*, Rinehart & Co., New York, 1948.

Hall, Darwin S. and R. I. Holcombe, *History of the Minnesota State Agricultural Society*, McGill Warner Company, St. Paul, Minnesota, 1910.

Harkey, Ira, *Pioneer Bush Pilot*, University of Washington Press, 1974.

Harris, Sherwood, *The First to Fly*, Simon and Schuster, New York, 1970.

Haugland, Vern, *The Eagle Squadrons*, Ziff-Davis, New York, 1979.

Helmericks, Harmon, *The Last of the Bush Pilots*, Alfred A. Knopf Publishers, New York, 1969.

Hill, Jim Dan, *A History of the National Guard*, The Stackpole Company, Harrisburg, PA, 1964.

Hollbrook, Franklin F. and Livia Appel, *Minnesota In The War With Germany*, 2 volumes. Minnesota Historical Society, 1928.

Holmes, Donald B., *Air Mail*, Clarkson N. Potter, Inc., New York, 1981.

Hopkins, George E., *Flying The Line*, ALPA International, Washington, DC, 1985

Kinneberg, Glenn A., *Flaps Up*, self-published, 1990.

Kunz, Virginia B., *St. Paul, Saga of an American City*, Windsor Publications, Woodland Hills, California, 1977.

Kvale, Clarence O., *Memoirs of The Thirties*, self-published, 1950.

Lane, David R., *Aircraft in Northwest Airlines History*, Minneapolis, MN, 1985.

Larsen, Bruce L., *Lindbergh of Minnesota*, Harcourt, Brace, Jovanovich, Inc. New York, 1973.

Leary, William M., *Aerial Pioneers*, Smithsonian Institution Press, Washington, D. C., 1985.

Lindbergh, Charles A., *We*, G. P. Putnam & Sons, New York, 1927.

Lindbergh, Charles A., *Boyhood on the Upper Mississippi*, Minnesota Historical Society, St. Paul, 1979.

Lougheed, Victor, *Vehicles of The Air*, Reilly & Britton Co., Chicago, IL, 1909.

McLaughlin, Helen E., *Walking On Air*, State of the Art, Ltd., Denver, CO, 1986.

Maurer, Maurer, *Aviation in the U. S. Army, 1919-1939*, Office of Air Force History, Washington, D. C., 1987.

Milbank, Jeremiah, Jr., *The First Century of Flight in America*, Princeton University Press, New Jersey, 1943.

Mills, Stephen, *More Than Meets The Sky*, Superior Publications, Seattle, 1972.

Mosely, Leonard, *Lindbergh, A Biography*, Doubleday & Co., Garden City, New York, 1976.

Newstrom, Gordon K., *Fly A Seaplane*, self-published, 1983.

Northwest Airways, *A Million Miles Without An Accident*, Minneapolis, MN, 1929.

Oakes, Claudia M., *United States Women In Aviation 1930-1939*, Smithsonian Press, Washington, DC, 1985.

Otis, Arthur R., *The Challenge of Sissebakwet*, self-published, 1976.

Pellegreno, Ann H., *Iowa Takes to the Air*, Aerodrome Press, Story City, Iowa, Volume One-1980, Volume Two-1986.

Potter, Jean, *The Flying North*, Curtis Publishing Co., 1945.

Rawlings, General Edwin, *Born to Fly*, Great Way Publishing, Minneapolis, 1987.

Ruble, Kenneth D., *Flight To The Top*, Northwest Airlines/Viking Press, 1987.

Salut, Harold, *Fragile Wings and Gentle Giants*, Blackbird Press, Dubuque, IA, 1985.

Scamehorn, Howard L., *Balloons to Jets*, Henry Regnery Company, Chicago, 1957.

Serling, Robert J., *Ceiling Unlimited*, Walsworth Publishing, Marceline, MO, 1973.

Stout, William B., *So Away I Went*, Bobbs-Merrill Co., Inc., 1951.

Time-Life Books, *Barnstormers and Speed Kings*, Time-Life, Inc., Alexandria, VA, 1981.

Underwood, John, *Madcaps, Millionaires and Mose*, Heritage Press, Glendale, CA, 1984.

Young, David and Neal Callahan, *Fill the Heavens With Commerce*, Chicago Review Press, 1981.

White, Dale & Larry Florek, *Tall Timber Pilots*, Viking Press, New York, 1953.

Worth, Theodore, *Minneapolis Park System, 1883-1944*, Minneapolis, MN 1944.

Wynne, Hugh H., *The Motion Picture Stunt Pilots*, Pictorial Histories Publishing Co., Missoula, MT, 1987.

280

Office of Aeronautics

(612) 296-8202
(612) 297-1600
Fax: (612) 297-5643
Fax: (612) 296-1828

Dear Reader:

As this commissioned book goes to press, the Minnesota Office of Aeronautics is celebrating its 50th Anniversary. We are certainly pleased to have participated in the publication of this aviation history book chronicling the early development of aviation in Minnesota and the significant role aviation has played in Minnesota history and development. The authors have done an admirable job.

Reports issued by the Department of Aeronautics between 1943 and 1947 show that there were 75 licensed flight instruction ground schools. The Department had established standards and curricula for private, commercial, instructor, instrument, multi-engine, seaplane, airline pilot and related ground school courses. The Department of Aeronautics and the League of Minnesota Municipalities also prepared a zoning ordinance to be used by municipalities in adopting airport zoning regulations for safety of the pilot, aircraft and people on the ground.

Today there are 146 public use airports in Minnesota, of which 138 are publicly-owned. One hundred-eight of these airports have paved runways. Minnesota's publicly-owned airport facilities are supported through grants by the State Office of Aeronautics and Federal Aviation Administration. Commercial air service is available at 14 Minnesota airports.

Today the Minnesota Office of Aeronautics maintains 14 Very High Frequency Omni-Directional Radio Range/Distance Measuring Equipment (VOR/DME), 7 Instrument Landing Systems (ILS), 30 Non-Directional Beacons (NDB), and 36 Automated Weather Observation Stations (AWOS III), which supplement the Federal Aviation Administration systems in Minnesota. Additional programs include the Minnesota Weather Access System (MnWAS), Channel 17 Weather Program and Home User Weather Program to assist pilots in flight planning.

The Office of Aeronautics is currently assisting Minnesota educational systems in developing and coordinating aviation education programs for Minnesota youth, educators and adults.

Aviation in Minnesota has experienced significant changes in the last 50 years and no doubt many more changes will occur as aviation adjusts to meet the changing needs of society. We invite you to be an active participant as we soar into the future.

In the future, the Office of Aeronautics will seek to contract an additional volume of Minnesota aviation history beyond 1945. Although the authors have done a superb job capturing much of the early Minnesota aviation history, they have not been able to document everything; and no doubt some important items were missed that you, the reader, deem important. If you have additional information of historic significance, please contact the Minnesota Office of Aeronautics or the authors.

Sincerely,

Raymond J Rought, Director
Office of Aeronautics
Minnesota Department of Transportation

50
1943 to 1993
Mn/DOT OFFICE OF AERONAUTICS
50 YEARS OF AVIATION PARTNERSHIP

222 East Plato Boulevard, St. Paul, Minnesota 55107-1618

286